Unfunding Terror

Unfunding Terror

The Legal Response to the Financing of Global Terrorism

Jimmy Gurulé

Notre Dame Law School, University of Notre Dame, USA

Edward Elgar

Cheltenham, UK • Northampton, MA, USA

Published by
Edward Elgar Publishing Limited
The Lypiatts
15 Lansdown Road
Cheltenham
Glos GL50 2JA
UK

Edward Elgar Publishing, Inc.
William Pratt House
9 Dewey Court
Northampton
Massachusetts 01060
USA

A catalogue record for this book
is available from the British Library

Library of Congress Control Number: 2008939735

PEFC
PEFC/16-33-111
CATG-PEFC-052
www.pefc.org

ISBN 978 1 84542 962 1

Printed and bound in Great Britain by MPG Books Ltd, Bodmin, Cornwall

Contents

Acknowledgments

I would like to take this opportunity to compliment a stellar group of Notre Dame law students and staff who contributed to this project. I am enormously grateful and thankful for their dedicated hard work. My sincere thanks to Elizabeth O'Connell (Class of 2008), Geoffrey Gasperini (Class of 2008), and Jay Ward (Class of 2009) for their valuable research assistance and suggestions. Ms O'Connell's efforts editing some of the chapters are greatly appreciated. However, special recognition is deserved for Chris O'Byrne, research librarian, Andy Mason, staff assistant, and Sheryn Alexander, principal student research assistant. Chris O'Byrne is a valuable member of the Notre Dame Law School library staff. Mr O'Byrne's professionalism, timely response to research requests, pleasant demeanor, and 'can do' attitude made him an absolute pleasure to work with throughout the entire project. Andy Mason, my highly competent and extremely professional staff assistant, made required changes and edits to early drafts of the book. Whatever I needed, Andy was always there to assist. Notre Dame Law School is fortunate to have hired Mr O'Byrne and Mr Mason. Finally, Sheryn Alexander (Class of 2009) provided invaluable research assistance, researching domestic and international cases, Congressional hearings, U.S. government and United Nations reports, reports by non-governmental organizations, international treaties, law journal articles, and other materials. She worked tirelessly editing and cite-checking endnotes, and proofreading early drafts of chapters, making important suggestions for improvement. There is no doubt that, upon graduation from law school, Ms Alexander will be an outstanding lawyer.

PART I

The legal framework

1. The evolution of the legal framework to deprive al Qaeda of funding

> [T]he number and seriousness of acts of international terrorism depend on the financing that terrorists may obtain. . . . [E]xisting multilateral legal instruments do not expressly address such financing.[1]
>
> International Convention for the Suppression of the Financing of Terrorism, December 9, 1999

THE LEGAL FRAMEWORK PRIOR TO SEPTEMBER 11, 2001

The September 11, 2001 terrorist attacks that took the lives of 2,973 innocent civilians required as much as $500,000 to stage.[2] Money was needed to pay for recruitment, flight training, transportation, communications, and other related expenses. The FBI estimates that in 2001 al Qaeda, the jihadi terrorist organization responsible for the mass killings, was operating on an annual budget between $30 and 50 million.[3] At the organizational level, al Qaeda needs money to bribe government officials and acquire a safe haven, to pay for training camps, weapons, travel, false identification documents, and the printing and distribution of propaganda materials, and also to finance the terrorist activities of like-minded jihadi terrorist groups. Simply stated, the attacks on the Twin Towers and the Pentagon could not have occurred without substantial funding. However, despite the obvious fact that terrorists need money to terrorize, prior to 9/11 preventing the financing of terrorism was not a priority for the United States or the international community.[4] A comprehensive legal framework to combat terrorist financing had not been developed. There were no serious financial interdiction efforts against al Qaeda, the Taliban and affiliated terrorist organizations. Criminal enforcement actions against deep-pocket donors and terrorist financial networks were virtually non-existent. The United States Department of Justice was engaged in counter-terrorism prosecutions, including prosecutions against the perpetrators of the 1993 World Trade Center bombing and attacks on the United States embassies in Kenya and Tanzania in 1998. However, those actions were directed at the persons responsible for plotting and carrying out the attacks, not the financial sponsors.[5] Before 9/11, the United States Department of Justice was not targeting the financial donors, facilitators, and sponsors of international acts of terrorism for criminal prosecution.

The Treasury Department also failed to appreciate the importance of aggressively pursuing terrorist assets. While President Clinton had signed Executive Order 12947, which ordered the freezing of the assets of individuals and entities responsible for disrupting the Middle East peace process, few names were actually designated for blocking actions under the Executive Order.[6] Furthermore, there was no executive order to freeze the assets of al Qaeda, the Taliban, and individuals and entities associated with them. Additionally, government regulations imposed on the banking industry under the Bank Secrecy Act (1970) (BSA) were focused on preventing money laundering, not terrorist financing. Banks and other financial institutions were not scrutinizing customer accounts and transactions for the risk of terrorist financing. While banks were required to report 'suspicious transactions' to the Financial Crimes Enforcement Network (FinCEN), an agency within the Department of the Treasury, bank employees were monitoring accounts and transactions for possible money laundering, not investigating whether such accounts and transactions were intended to finance terrorist activities.[7] In sum, prior to 9/11 the United States government failed to recognize the importance of cutting off the flow of funds to al Qaeda, the Taliban, and affiliated terrorist organizations.

The United States, however, was not alone in failing to appreciate the importance of pursuing terrorist assets. Prior to the 2001 terrorist attacks, the international community was not seriously engaged in preventing the financing of terrorism. There were no international standards on the prevention of terrorist financing. The Financial Action Task Force on Money Laundering (FATF), the inter-governmental organization responsible for developing international standards to combat money laundering, had adopted the 'Forty Recommendations on Money Laundering.'[8] However, the FATF standards were directed at preventing money laundering, not suppressing terrorist financing. Additionally, the international community had failed to adopt a treaty condemning the financing of terrorism. In December 1999, the International Convention for the Suppression of the Financing of Terrorism (Terrorist Financing Convention) was drafted and open for signature.[9] However, there was no sense of urgency for countries to ratify the Convention until after the 9/11 terrorist attacks. The Terrorist Financing Convention did not become effective and enter into force until April 10, 2002, and the United States did not ratify the treaty until June 2002.[10]

While the United Nations Security Council adopted Resolutions 1267 (1999) and 1333 (2000), which condemned international terrorism and required States to implement counter-terrorist financing measures, efforts to enforce these measures were half-hearted at best. In October 1999, the Security Council decided that the threat of terrorism posed by al Qaeda merited an international response. The Taliban had provided Osama bin Laden and al Qaeda a safe haven in Afghanistan, where the terror group planned, supervised and executed the terrorist bombings of the United States embassies in Kenya and Tanzania, in August 1998. Accustomed to dealing with States, the Security Council decided to confront al Qaeda by imposing sanctions on the Taliban, which represented the *de facto* government of Afghanistan. The Security Council adopted Resolution 1267, which demanded that the Taliban stop providing a sanctuary for bin Laden and members of al Qaeda.[11] The Resolution required countries to impose various economic measures against the Taliban, including the duty to freeze the assets of the Taliban and individuals and entities associated with it.[12] A U.N. Committee was created, comprised of the members of the Security Council, to monitor implementation of the measures imposed by Resolution 1267, known as the 'Al-Qaida and Taliban Sanctions Committee.'[13] However, countries were largely non-compliant with Resolution 1267 and it had no deterrent effect against the Taliban.

On October 12, 2000, a small boat laden with explosives was detonated against the USS Cole in Aden, Yemen. The blast killed 17 American sailors and wounded 30 others.[14] The terrorist attack on the USS Cole and other ongoing terrorist activities by al Qaeda prompted the Security Council to adopt Resolution 1333, in December 2000.[15] Resolution 1333 went beyond imposing economic sanctions on the Taliban, requiring countries to freeze the financial assets of bin Laden, al Qaeda, and individuals and entities associated with them.[16] The Resolution also created a list of the individuals and entities designated as being associated with Osama bin Laden and the al Qaeda organization, known as the U.N. 'Consolidated List.'[17] Unfortunately, compliance with Resolution 1333 was equally disappointing and no names were submitted to the Al-Qaida and Taliban Sanctions Committee for designation and asset freeze.[18] Prior to September 11, 2001, international efforts to deprive terrorists of funding were weak, ineffective, and a dismal failure.

THE LEGAL RESPONSE TO THE 9/11 TERRORIST ATTACKS

The development and implementation of a global legal framework to deprive al Qaeda and affiliated terrorist organizations of funding began in earnest following the September 11, 2001 terrorist attacks. Within a few days of the attacks two major legal initiatives to confront the financing of terrorism were adopted. On September 23, 2001, President Bush signed Executive Order 13224 and five days later the United Nations Security Council adopted Resolution 1373.[19] Both actions were directed at freezing the assets of terrorists, terrorist organizations, and individuals and entities associated with them. The following month, in October 2001, a third important legal action was undertaken. Congress enacted the USA PATRIOT Act, which included significant amendments to the Bank Secrecy Act, intended to strengthen the financial regulatory regime to prevent, detect, and suppress money laundering and terrorist financing.[20] Later the same month, the FATF adopted Eight Special Recommendations on Terrorist Financing, which developed international standards for preventing and suppressing terrorist financing.[21] Finally, a few months later, in April 2002, the International Convention for the Suppression of the Financing of Terrorism became effective, imposing various legal obligations on State signatories to curtail terrorist funding.[22] The foundation for the legal framework to combat terrorist financing had been laid. The legal framework that exists today has largely evolved from these five initiatives that occurred within seven months following the 9/11 terrorist attacks.

The legal response to terrorist financing has five principal components:

- freezing terrorist-related assets, domestically and internationally;
- implementing and enforcing regulatory measures to prevent terrorists from abusing the international financial system;
- implementing international standards on terrorist financing;
- prosecuting terrorist financiers and facilitators;
- litigating civil tort actions brought by the victims of terrorist attacks.

A brief description of each component of the legal framework to deprive al Qaeda of funding follows.

Freezing Terrorist Assets

On September 23, 2001, President George W. Bush invoked his authority under the International Emergency Economic Powers Act (IEEPA) and signed Executive Order 13224.[23] The IEEPA authorizes the President to declare a national emergency 'to deal with any unusual and extraordinary threat, which has its source in whole or substantial part outside the United States, to the national security, foreign policy, or economy of the United States.'[24] The President determined that the September 11 terrorist attacks and the threat of future attacks against the United States constituted such an extraordinary threat.[25] Upon declaration of a national emergency, the IEEPA authorizes the President to use a broad range of economic powers, including the authority to 'investigate, block during the pendency of an investigation, regulate . . . prevent or prohibit, any acquisition, holding, withholding, use, transfer, withdrawal . . . dealing in . . . any property in which any foreign country or national thereof has any interest . . . subject to the jurisdiction of the United States.'[26] Under the Executive Order, President Bush invoked the IEEPA to designate 12 individuals and 15 entities and ordered that their assets be frozen in the United States.[27] These 27 individuals and groups were labelled 'Specially Designated Global Terrorists' (SDGTs) and identified in the Annex to Executive Order 13224. The Annex included core members of al Qaeda, affiliated terrorist groups, Islamic charities suspected of funding al Qaeda, and related front organizations.[28] With respect to the 27 SDGTs, banks and other financial institutions were ordered to block or freeze their property and interests in property in the United States.[29] By the end of 2001, within less than four months of the 9/11 terrorist attacks, the Treasury Department had designated approximately 164 individuals and organizations and the United States and the international community had frozen over $60 million in terrorist-related assets.[30] Several major financial networks used by al Qaeda to raise and transfer funds were shut down, including al Barakaat and Al Taqwa/Nada Management Group.[31] Of particular significance were the designations of several Islamic charities with ties to terrorist groups. Numerous foreign charities affiliated with al Qaeda and other jihadist terrorist organizations were designated and their offices shut down.[32] By 2008, over 490 individuals and entities had been designated pursuant to Executive Order 13224.[33] However, the number of designations has dramatically declined over the last few years.

Executive Order 13224 is a major step towards isolating terrorists, terrorist organizations, and their financial facilitators from the United States financial system. It also imposes a legal duty on banks to freeze any funds held in the bank accounts of individuals and entities included on the Treasury list of SDGTs. As a result, financial institutions have been conscripted to participate in the global war on terror and forced to assume a major role in the United States government's efforts to combat the financing of terrorism.

A few days after President Bush signed Executive Order 13224, the U.N. Security Council adopted Resolution 1373, which imposes several important duties on countries to combat the threat of international terrorism.[34]

Resolution 1373 requires States to prevent the movement of terrorists by imposing border controls and restricting the issuance of travel documents (travel ban).[35] The Resolution further prohibits the supply of weapons to terrorists (weapons embargo), denies safe haven to those individuals who plan, support or commit terrorist acts (safe haven ban), and requires States to afford one another the greatest measure of cooperation and assistance in connection with terrorism investigations (mutual assistance). Finally, Resolution 1373 imposes certain obligations on States to prevent and suppress the financing of terrorism, including 'freez[ing] without delay funds and other financial assets or economic resources' of persons who commit terrorist acts, finance acts of terrorism, and associated persons and entities.[36] Resolution 1373 is much broader than its predecessors, Resolutions 1267 and 1333, which are limited to freezing the assets of Osama bin Laden, al Qaeda, the Taliban and their associates. Resolution 1373 covers all terrorists and terrorist organizations, requiring States to freeze the assets of persons and entities designated under the Security Council resolution. Equally important, adopting Resolution 1373 reinforced the importance placed by the international community on curtailing the flow of funds to terrorist organizations. Prior to 9/11, countries were largely non-compliant with Resolutions 1267 and 1333. Resolution 1373 reaffirmed the U.N. Security Council's commitment to going after the sources of terrorist funding. The Resolution further renewed and strengthened the Security Council's commitment to enforcing Resolutions 1267 and 1333, requiring countries to freeze the assets of Osama bin Laden, al Qaeda, and the Taliban. As the result, countries began to submit names to the Al-Qaida and Taliban Sanctions Committee for inclusion on the U.N. Consolidated List for designation and asset freeze. By the end of 2001, 285 names had been submitted to the U.N. Sanctions Committee and approximately $52 million in terrorist assets were ordered frozen worldwide.[37] In 2008, over 490 names have been placed on the Consolidated List and $85 million in terrorist-related assets frozen.[38] Today, the duty to freeze terrorist assets imposed on States by Resolutions 1267, 1333, 1373, and successor resolutions remains the centerpiece of the international legal framework to combat terrorist financing. However, the international economic sanctions program has experienced a downward trend with States being reluctant to submit names for designation and freezing terrorist-related assets.

Regulatory Measures to Prevent Terrorists from Abusing the Financial System

On October 26, 2001, Congress responded to the September 11 terrorist attacks by enacting the USA PATRIOT Act.[39] Title III of the Act, known as the International Money Laundering Abatement and Anti-Terrorist

Financing Act of 2001 (IMLAA), made a number of amendments to the Bank Secrecy Act to promote the prevention, detection, and prosecution of international money laundering and terrorist financing.[40] For example, the IMLAA expanded the definition of 'financial institutions' covered by the BSA, to require non-depository institutions such as money transmitting businesses and other alternative remittance systems, such as hawala, to establish a program to prevent money laundering and terrorist financing, and report suspicious transactions to the Treasury Department.[41] Such money transmitting businesses are also required to register with FinCEN.[42] The IMLAA requires financial institutions to apply due diligence and, in some cases, enhanced due diligence standards, with regard to 'private banking accounts' and 'correspondent accounts' involving foreign persons.[43] Also, the anti-money laundering and anti-terrorist financing provisions of the Act authorize the Secretary of the Treasury to impose a set of graduated 'special measures' against a foreign jurisdiction, foreign financial institution, type of account or international transaction designated a 'primary money laundering concern.'[44] Finally, the IMLAA enacted other important changes, such as criminalizing the cross-border transportation of currency to avoid BSA reporting requirements.[45]

The regulatory measures enacted pursuant to the Patriot Act have made it more difficult to transfer terrorist funds using banks and non-traditional financial institutions. However, these important regulations need to be more rigorously enforced by FinCEN and the federal financial regulators to prevent the financing of terrorism.

International Standards on Terrorist Financing

In the aftermath of the 9/11 terrorist attacks, the Financial Action Task Force on Money Laundering (FATF) held an extra-plenary session in Washington, D.C. to consider expanding its mandate to address terrorist financing.[46] Prior to this time, FATF's responsibilities had been limited to developing and promoting international standards against money laundering. At the conclusion of the special meeting, on October 31, 2001, the FATF issued Eight Special Recommendations on Terrorist Financing.[47] A ninth special recommendation on terrorist financing was adopted by FATF in 2004.[48] The Nine Special Recommendations, combined with the Forty Recommendations on Money Laundering, represent the international standards for preventing and suppressing the financing of terrorism. The Nine Special Recommendations require countries to:

- ratify the Terrorist Financing Convention; comply with measures contained in Security Council Resolutions 1267, 1333 and 1373;

- criminalize the financing of terrorism;
- freeze and confiscate terrorist assets;
- impose obligations on financial institutions to report suspicious transactions linked to terrorism;
- afford States the greatest measure of cooperation in terrorist financing investigations;
- apply anti-money laundering regulations to alternative remittance system;
- require financial institutions to include accurate originator information on funds transfers;
- protect non-profit organizations, such as charities, from being misused to finance terrorism;
- detect and prevent bulk cash smuggling.[49]

Remarkably, within seven weeks following the terrorist attacks on the World Trade Center and the Pentagon, the FATF developed a comprehensive set of international standards to prevent the financing of terrorism that previously had eluded the international community.

Al Qaeda's attacks against the United States also served as a catalyst for the international community to ratify the International Convention for the Suppression of the Financing of Terrorism. In April 2002, the Terrorist Financing Convention was ratified by the requisite number of States and entered into force.[50] The Terrorist Financing Convention requires signatory parties to adopt domestic legislation to criminalize and punish terrorist financing, license or register all money transmitting services, detect and control the physical cross-border transportation of currency and negotiable instruments, and develop and implement internal controls to prevent financial institutions from being used to transfer funds to terrorists.[51] Of particular importance, the Convention requires States Parties to freeze terrorist assets. Article 8 provides that each State Party '*shall* take appropriate measures . . . for the identification, detection and freezing or seizure of any funds used or allocated for the purpose' of committing acts of terrorism.[52] Thus, the duty to freeze terrorist assets is established by multiple legal authority, including Security Council resolutions, the FATF Nine Special Recommendations on Terrorist Financing, and the Terrorist Financing Convention.

Criminal Enforcement Actions

The material support statutes, 18 U.S.C. §2339A and §2339B, have been the principal criminal provisions used to prosecute terrorist donors, fundraisers, and financial facilitators.[53] Enacted as part of the Violent Crime Control and Law Enforcement Act of 1994, 18 U.S.C. §2339A makes it a crime to knowingly provide 'material support or resources' 'knowing or intending' that they be used in preparation for, or in carrying out, various enumerated terrorist-related crimes.[54] Two years later, Congress enacted §2339B as part of the Antiterrorism and Effective Death Penalty Act of 1996 (AEDPA), which is aimed at depriving foreign terrorist groups of funding and other resources.[55] Section 2339B punishes whoever knowingly provides 'material support or resources' to a 'foreign terrorist organization' knowing that the organization has been designated as such by the Secretary of State or knowing that the organization has engaged or engages in terrorist activity.[56] The Secretary of State has designated 44 'foreign terrorist organizations,' and providing 'material support or resources' to members of these groups is criminalized by section 2339B.[57] While '§2339A was limited to donors intending to further the commission of specific federal offenses, Congress passed §2339B to encompass donors who acted *without* the intent to further federal crimes.'[58] Both §§2339A and 2339B prohibit the provision of 'material support or resources,' which includes 'currency or monetary instruments or financial securities, [and] financial services,' as well as other forms of assistance to terrorists and terrorist organizations.[59]

In 2002, Congress enacted the Suppression of the Financing of Terrorism Convention Implementation Act (2002 Act), criminalizing certain financial transactions made in furtherance of enumerated terrorist crimes.[60] The 2002 Act implemented the International Convention for the Suppression of Terrorist Financing, which was ratified by the United States Senate in June 2002.[61] The Act created a new statute, 18 U.S.C. §2339C, which criminalizes whoever 'provides or collects' funds with the intention or knowledge that the funds are to be used to carry out an offense within the scope of various international counter-terrorism treaties specified in the statute.[62] Section 2339C also punishes financing any other act intended to cause death or serious bodily injury to a civilian, when the purpose of such act is to intimidate a population, or to compel a government or international organization to do or refrain from doing any act.[63] Unfortunately, prior to the 9/11 terrorist attacks, §§2339A and 2339B were seldom, if ever, used to prosecute the donors, fund-raisers, or financial facilitators of terrorist organizations such as al Qaeda and the Taliban. Moreover, since 9/11, §2339C has been sparingly used to prosecute terrorist financiers. Thus, while Department of Justice attorneys have the legal tools, they have been reluctant to use them to punish and deter terrorist funding.

Finally, after September 11, 2001, Congress enacted additional legislation to prosecute terrorist financiers and facilitators. Those statutes include 31 U.S.C. §5332, which punishes the smuggling of cash and negotiable instruments into or outside the United States with the intent to evade a currency reporting requirement, and 18 U.S.C. §1960, which prohibits money transmitting businesses, including hawala, from operating without a State license or without registering with the Treasury Department.[64] The Justice Department, however, has a mixed record of success in prosecuting terrorist financing cases. Several trials have ended in an embarrassing acquittal or a hung jury.[65]

Private Civil Causes of Action

There are several federal statutes that authorize a private cause of action for acts of terrorism. Victims of terrorist attacks may file suit pursuant to 18 U.S.C. §2333(a), enacted as part of the Antiterrorism Act of 1991 (ATA).[66] Section 2333(a) authorizes any national of the United States injured in his person, property, or business by reason of an act of international terrorism, or his estate, survivors, or heirs, to sue in federal district court, and, if successful, recover treble damages, court costs, and attorney's fees.[67] The ATA was intended 'to fill a gap in the law by establishing a civil counterpart to the existing criminal statutes.'[68] Section 2333(a) has been used against Islamic charitable organizations, terrorist front groups, and banks suspected of raising money for or providing financial services to terrorist organizations.[69]

The Alien Tort Claims Act, also referred to as the Alien Tort Statute (ATS), 28 U.S.C. §1350, affords *foreign* terrorism victims a civil cause of action.[70] Section 1350 authorizes a cause of action for injuries suffered as the result of a 'violation of the law of nations or a treaty of the United States.'[71] The federal tort statute was enacted by the nation's founders during the First Congress in 1789. In the terrorist financing context, the ATA has been used by foreign nationals to support a cause of action against Arab Bank, a Jordanian bank with a New York branch, for knowingly providing banking and administrative services to HAMAS and other Palestinian terrorist organizations that sponsored suicide attacks killing innocent civilians.[72]

Recent legislation enacted by Congress authorizes a private cause of action for nationals of the United States, employees of the United States, or individuals performing a private contract awarded by the United States against a foreign state sponsor of terrorism.[73] The new legislation, codified at 28 U.S.C. §1605A, eliminates sovereign immunity for foreign states designated as 'state sponsor of terrorism' (SST).[74] There are currently five states that have been designated by the Secretary of State as SSTs, Cuba, Iran, North Korea, Sudan, and Syria.[75] Pursuant to §1605A, which became effective January 28, 2008, these States lose their foreign sovereign immunity where plaintiffs are seeking money damages against a foreign state for personal injury or death that was caused by an 'act of torture, extrajudicial killing, aircraft sabotage, hostage-taking, or the provision of material support or resources' if the provision of material support was by 'an official, employee, or agent of such foreign state while acting within the scope of his . . . office, employment or agency.'[76] In essence, the statute holds foreign SSTs vicariously liable for the acts of their officials, employees, or agents.[77]

The importance of civil actions cannot be over emphasized. The Department of Justice has limited resources, restricting its ability to prosecute terrorism cases. Civil tort actions seeking substantial monetary damages complement federal prosecutions by deterring and holding terrorist financiers accountable. The civil tort claims are discussed *infra* at Chapter 11 – 'Private causes of action: using the civil justice system to hold terrorist financiers accountable'.

In sum, the legal landscape to prevent the financing of terrorism changed dramatically following the September 11, 2001 attacks on the World Trade Center and the Pentagon. A robust legal regime has evolved to combat terrorist financing that consists of multiple components: domestic and international asset freeze; regulatory measures on financial institutions to prevent terrorist financing; imposition of international counter-terrorist financing standards; criminal enforcement actions; and civil tort claims. However, the critical question is whether the anti-terrorist financing legal regime that evolved in the wake of September 11th has been effective in disrupting the terrorist financing network and depriving Osama bin Laden, al Qaeda and the Taliban of funding. If not, why not? What else should be done to cut off the flow of funds to international terrorists that have declared jihad against the West and maintain that killing civilians is justified in the name of Islam? The following chapters are intended to answer these important questions and propose recommendations to strengthen the legal framework to deprive al Qaeda and affiliated terrorist organizations of the money needed to wage a global jihad, acquire weapons of mass destruction, and kill thousands of innocent civilians.

NOTES

1. S. Treaty Doc. No. 106–49, 2178 U.N.T.S. 229.
2. The National Commission on Terrorist Attacks, The 9/11 Commission Report: Final Report of the National Commission on Terrorist Attacks Upon the United States 169 (W.W. Norton & Company 2004), *available at* http://www.9-11commission.gov/report/911Report.pdf [hereinafter 9/11 Commission Report].
3. *Id.* at 171; *see also* Rohan Gunaratna, Inside Al Qaeda: Global Network of Terror 61 (Columbia University Press 2002).
4. *See* Charge Sheet of the Military Commission (Feb. 11, 2008), alleging various criminal charges against Khalid Sheikh Mohammed, Walid Muhammad Salih Mubarek Bin

'Attash, Ramzi Binalshibh, Ali Abdul Aziz Ali, Mustafa Ahmed Adam al Hawsawi, and Mohamed al Kahtani in connection with the murder of 2,973 civilians on September 11, 2001, *available at* http://www.defenselink.mil/news/Feb2008/20080211chargesheet.pdf.

5. *See* United States v. Usama Bin Laden, et al., Indictment, No. S(6) 98 Cr. 1023 (LBS) (S.D.N.Y. 2000) (indictment charging Osama bin Laden and 14 other defendants with the bombings of the U.S. embassies in Kenya and Tanzania); *see also* United States v. Rahman, 189 F.3d 88 (2d Cir.), *cert. denied*, 528 U.S. 982, 120 S.Ct. 439, 145 L.Ed.2d 344 (1999) (Sheik Omar Abdel Rahman was convicted of conspiring to commit acts of terrorism against the United States); United States v. Rahman, 854 F. Supp. 254 (S.D.N.Y. 1994) (conspiracy to bomb the World Trade Center in 1993).
6. Executive Order 12,947: Prohibiting Transactions with Terrorists Who Threaten to Disrupt the Middle East Peace Process, 60 Fed.Reg. 5079 (Jan. 23, 1995).
7. *See* 31 U.S.C. §5318(g) (2000) (authorizing the Secretary of the Treasury to require financial institutions to report suspicious transactions); 31 C.F.R. §103.18 (requiring banks to file suspicious activity reports or SARs).
8. *See* Financial Action Task Force on Money Laundering, The Forty Recommendations, June 20, 2003, *available at* http://www.fatf-gafi.org/dataoecd/7/40/34849567.PDF. 'Blocking,' also called 'freezing,' is a form of controlling assets under U.S. jurisdiction. While title to blocked property remains with the designated individual or entity, the exercise of the powers and privileges normally associated with ownership is prohibited without authorization from OFAC. Blocking prohibits transfers or transactions of any kind with regard to the property.
9. International Convention for the Suppression of the Financing of Terrorism, 9 G.A. Res. 109, U.N. GAOR 54th Sess., 76th mtg., U.N. Doc. A/RES/54/109 (2000) (Dec. 9, 1999), *available at* http://untreaty.un.org/English/Terrorism/Conv12.pdf [hereinafter 'Terrorist Financing Convention'].
10. *Id.*
11. S.C. Res. 1267, ¶1, U.N. Doc. S/RES/1267 (1999).
12. *Id.* at ¶4(b).
13. *Id.* at ¶6.
14. *See* STEVE COLL, GHOST WARS: THE SECRET HISTORY OF THE CIA, AFGHANISTAN, AND BIN LADEN, FROM THE SOVIET INVASION TO SEPTEMBER 10, 2001 537 (Penguin Books 2004).
15. S.C. Res. 1333, U.N. Doc. S/RES/1333 (2000).
16. *Id.* at ¶8(c).
17. *Id.*
18. *See* U.N. SECURITY COUNCIL, ANALYTICAL SUPPORT AND SANCTIONS MONITORING TEAM, SEVENTH REPORT OF THE ANALYTICAL SUPPORT AND SANCTIONS MONITORING TEAM, ¶25 n.37, U.N. Doc. S/2007/677 (Nov. 29, 2007), *available at* http://www.un.org/sc/committees/1267/monitoringteam.shtml [hereinafter SEVENTH REPORT OF THE SANCTIONS MONITORING TEAM]; *see also* The Consolidated List of the U.N. Security Council's Al-Qaida and Taliban Sanctions Committee, *available at* http://www.un.org/sc/committees/1267/consolist.shtml [hereinafter the Consolidated List].
19. Blocking Property and Prohibiting Transactions with Persons Who Commit, Threaten to Commit, or Support Terrorism, Exec. Order No. 13,224, 3 C.F.R. 786–90 (2001), *reprinted as amended in* 50 U.S.C. §1701 note (Supp. IV 2004) [hereinafter E.O. 13224]. The IEEPA was enacted by Congress in 1977 and amended by Uniting and Strengthening America by Providing Appropriate Tools Required to Intercept and Obstruct Terrorism (USA PATRIOT) Act of 2001, Pub. L. No. 107–56, §314(a) 115 Stat. 272 (codified in scattered sections of the U.S.C.). IEEPA is codified at 50 U.S.C. §§1701–7 [hereinafter IEEPA]; *see also* S.C. Res. 1373, U.N. Doc. S/RES/1373 (2001).
20. USA PATRIOT Act of 2001, Pub. L. No. 107–56, 115 Stat. 272 (codified in scattered sections of the U.S.C.) [hereinafter PATRIOT Act].
21. A ninth special recommendation was adopted by FATF in 2004. *See* Financial Action Task Force, 9 Special Recommendations (SR) on Terrorist Financing (TF) (last visited Apr. 14, 2008), *available at* http://www.fatf-gafi.org/document/9/0,3343,en_32250379_

32236920_34032073_1_1_1_1,00.html [hereinafter Nine Special Recommendations on Terrorist Financing].

22. Terrorist Financing Convention, *supra* note 9.
23. E.O. 13224, *supra* note 19.
24. IEEPA, *supra* note 19, at §1701(a).
25. E.O. 13224, *supra* note 19.
26. IEEPA, *supra* note 19, at §1702(a)(1)(B).
27. E.O. 13224 and Annex, *supra* note 19.
28. *Id.*
29. *See* 31 C.F.R. §594.201(a) (2007).
30. *See* TERRORIST ASSETS REPORT, CALENDAR YEAR 2001, ANNUAL REPORT TO THE CONGRESS ON ASSETS IN THE UNITED STATES OF TERRORIST COUNTRIES AND INTERNATIONAL TERRORISM PROGRAM DESIGNEES, U.S. DEP'T OF TREASURY, at 4; *see also* Press Release, U.S. Dep't of Treasury, Terrorist Financing Fact Sheet (Dec. 20, 2001), *available at* http://www.treasury.gov/press/releases/po886.htm.; Press Release, U.S. Dep't of Treasury, Shutting Down the Terrorist Financial Network (Dec. 4, 2001), *available at* http://www.treasury.gov/press/releases/po841.htm.
31. *See* Press Release, U.S. Dep't of Treasury, Statement of John B. Taylor (Nov. 7, 2001), *available at* http://www.treasury.gov/press/releases/po771.htm.
32. *See* Protecting Charitable Organizations, Terrorism and Financial Intelligence, U.S. Dep't of Treasury, *available at* http://www.treas.gov/offices/enforcement/key-issues/protecting/fto.shtml.
33. *See* OFAC list of SDGTs, *available at* http://www.treas.gov/offices/enforcement/programs/terror/terror.pdf (last visited Apr. 21, 2008); *see also* SEVENTH REPORT OF THE SANCTIONS MONITORING TEAM, *supra* note 18.
34. S.C. Res. 1373, U.N. Doc. S/RES/1373 (Sept. 28, 2001).
35. *Id* at ¶2(a), (c), and (f). *See also* ALISTAIR MILLAR & ERIC ROSAND, ALLIED AGAINST TERRORISM 16 (Century Foundation Press 2006).
36. S.C. Res. 1373, at ¶1(c).
37. *See* SEVENTH REPORT OF THE SANCTIONS MONITORING TEAM, *supra* note 18, at Annex III.
38. *Id.*
39. Uniting and Strengthening America by Providing Appropriate Tools Required to Intercept and Obstruct Terrorism (USA PATRIOT) Act of 2001, Pub. L. No. 107–56, §314(a) 115 Stat. 272 (codified in scattered sections of the U.S.C.).
40. Title III of the USA PATRIOT Act amends the anti-money laundering provisions of the BSA, codified at 12 U.S.C. §1829b, 12 U.S.C. §§1951–9, and 31 U.S.C. §§5311–14, 5316–32. Regulations implementing the BSA appear at 31 C.F.R. Part 103.
41. Under 31 U.S.C. §5312(a)(2)(R), 'financial institution' means 'a licensed sender of money or any other person who engages as a business in the transmission of funds, including any person who engages as a business in an informal money transfer system or any network of people who engage as a business in facilitating the transfer of money domestically or internationally outside of the conventional financial institutions system.' *See also* 31 C.F.R. §103.20 (2006) (requiring all money services businesses, other than check cashiers and issuers, sellers, or redeemers of stored value, to file suspicious transaction reports).
42. 31 U.S.C. §5330(a)(1) (2000 & Supp. IV 2004).
43. *Id.* at §5318(i).
44. *Id.* at §5318A (2000 & Supp. IV 2004).
45. 31 U.S.C. §5332.
46. Created by the G7 countries in 1989, the FATF consists of 34 member countries, along with numerous observers, including the United Nations, the International Monetary Fund, and the World Bank. It further consists of several FATF-style regional bodies and numerous international organizations. *See* About the Financial Action Task Force on Money Laundering, *available at* http://www.fatf-gafi.org. Additionally, on September 11, 2001, I was serving as Under Secretary (Enforcement), U.S. Department of the Treasury. After the 9/11 terrorist attacks, I directed the head of the U.S. delegation to

FATF to organize a special meeting of FATF to consider developing international standards on terrorist financing.

47. Nine Special Recommendations on Terrorist Financing, *supra* note 21.
48. *Id.*
49. *Id.*
50. Terrorist Financing Convention, *supra* note 9.
51. *Id.* at arts. 4 and 18(1) and (2).
52. *Id.* at art. 8(1) (emphasis added).
53. 18 U.S.C.A §§2339A (West 2008) and 2339B (2000 & Supp. IV 2004).
54. Violent Crime Control and Law Enforcement Act of 1994, Pub. L. No. 103–322, 108 Stat. 1796, 2022–3 (1994) (codified at 18 U.S.C. §2339A).
55. Antiterrorism and Effective Death Penalty Act of 1996, Pub. L. No. 104–132, 110 Stat. 1214 (1996) (codified at 28 U.S.C. 1605(a)(7)) (codified at 18 U.S.C. §2339B).
56. 18 U.S.C. §2339B(a)(1).
57. Country Reports on Terrorism, U.S. Dep't of State, Office of the Coordinator for Counterterrorism (Apr. 30, 2007), *available at* http://www.state.gov/s/ct/rls/crt/2006/82738.htm. Harkat-ul-Jihad al Islami became the 43rd foreign terrorist organization designated by the Secretary of State. The group was designated on February 15, 2008. *See* Press Release, U.S. Dep't of State, Designation of HUJI-B as a Foreign Terrorist Organization (Feb. 15, 2008), *available at* http://www.state.gov/s/ct/rls/other/08/102877.htm; *see also U.S. Brands Bangladeshi Islamic Group 'Terrorist,'* REUTERS, Mar. 7, 2008, *available at* http://www.reuters.com/article/latestCrisis/idUSN07285929. The State Department designated the 44th FTO when it designated the military wing of al-Shabab, which means 'the Youth,' on February 29, 2008. *See U.S. Designates Somali Group Terrorists*, AP, Mar. 18, 2008, *available at* http://news.lp.findlaw.com/ap_stories/a/w/1152/03-18-2008/20080318153505_15.html.
58. Humanitarian Law Project v. Gonzales, 380 F. Supp. 2d 1134, 1146 (C.D. Cal. 2005) (emphasis added).
59. The term 'material support or resources' means 'currency or monetary instruments or financial securities, financial services, lodging, training, expert advice or assistance, safehouses, false documentation or identification, communications equipment, facilities, weapons, lethal substances, personnel (1 or more individuals who may be or include oneself) and transportation.' 18 U.S.C. §2339A(b)(1) (West 2008).
60. Suppression of the Financing of Terrorism Convention Implementation Act of 2002, Pub. L. No. 107–197, tit. II, 116 Stat. 724 (2002) (codified at 18 U.S.C.A. §2339C (2000 & Supp. IV 2004).
61. Terrorist Financing Convention, *supra* note 9.
62. 18 U.S.C.A §2339C(a)(1)(A) (West 2008).
63. *Id.* at §2339C(a)(1)(B).
64. 31 U.S.C. §5332 and 18 U.S.C. §1960.
65. *See* discussion *infra*, at Chapter 10 – 'The law enforcement response to terrorist financing'.
66. Antiterrorism Act of 1991, 18 U.S.C. §2333 (2000).
67. 18 U.S.C. §2333(a) (2000). Section 2331(1) defines 'international terrorism' as activities that

    (A) involve violent acts or acts dangerous to human life that are a violation of the criminal laws of the United States or of any State, or that would be a criminal violation if committed within the jurisdiction of the United States or any State;
    (B) appear to be intended –
    (i) to coerce a civilian population;
    (ii) to influence the policy of a government by intimidation or coercion; or
    (iii) to affect the conduct of a government by mass destruction, assassination or kidnapping; and
    (C) occur primarily outside the territorial jurisdiction of the United States, or transcend national boundaries in terms of the means by which they are accomplished, the

persons they appear intended to intimidate or coerce, or the locale in which their perpetrators operate or seek asylum.

68. Ungar ex rel. Strachman v. Palestinian Auth., 304 F. Supp. 2d 232, 238 (D.R.I. 2004).
69. *See* Boim v. Quranic Literacy Inst. & Holy Land Found., 291 F.3d 1000 (7th Cir. 2002), *aff'g* 127 F. Supp. 2d 1001; Boim v. Holy Land Found., 2007 WL 4553654 (7th Cir. 2007) (overturning verdict and $156 million judgment against the Holy Land Foundation); *see also* Linde v. Arab Bank, PLC, 384 F. Supp. 2d 571 (E.D.N.Y. 2005); Weiss v. Nat'l Westminster Bank, 453 F. Supp. 2d 609 (E.D.N.Y. 2006); Strauss v. Credit Lyonnais, Case No. CV-06–0702 (CPS), 2006 WL 2862704 (E.D.N.Y. 2006).
70. Alien Tort Claims Act, Pub. L. No. 102–256 (codified at 28 U.S.C. §1350).
71. *Id.*; *see also* Sosa v. Alvarez-Machain, 542 U.S. 692, 729 (2004).
72. *See* Almog v. Arab Bank, 471 F. Supp. 2d 257, 272 (E.D.N.Y. 2007).
73. H.R. 4986, Pub. L. No. 110–181, §1083, codified at 28 U.S.C. §1605A (effective Jan. 28, 2008).
74. 28 U.S.C.A §1605A(a)(2) (West 2008).
75. *See* State Sponsors of Terrorism, U.S. Dep't of State, http://www.state.gov/s/ct/c14151.htm (last visited Apr. 5, 2008). The term 'state sponsor of terrorism' is defined to mean a state which the Secretary of State has determined, for purposes of section 6(j) of the Export Administration Act of 1979 (50 U.S.C. App. 2405(j)), section 620A of the Foreign Assistance Act of 1961 (22 U.S.C. §2371), section 40 of the Arms Export Control Act (22 U.S.C. §2780), or any other provision of law, is a government that has repeatedly provided support for acts of international terrorism. 28 U.S.C. §1605A(h)(6) (West 2008).
76. 28 U.S.C. §1605A(a)(1) (West 2008).
77. *Id.* at §1605A(c).

PART II

Why go after the money?

2. Terrorists need money to terrorize

> Terrorists seldom kill for money, but they always need money to kill.
> Terry Davis,
> Secretary General of the Council of Europe,
> Plenary of MONEYVAL and Financial
> Action Task Force,
> February 21, 2007

> It is a duty for the Umma with all its categories, men, women and youths, to give . . . their money, experiences and all types of material support. . . . Jihad today is an imperative for every Muslim. The Umma will commit sin if it did not provide adequate material support for jihad.
>
> Osama bin Laden,
> April 23, 2006

Money is the 'lifeblood' of al Qaeda (Arabic for 'the base') and other like-minded terrorist groups.[1] Al Qaeda and its global network of affiliated terrorist organizations cannot successfully implement their deadly agenda without financial resources. Shutting off the flow of funds to the global jihadists can disrupt their short-term operations while undermining their long-term capabilities.[2] 'Disrupting and dismantling terrorist financing networks is essential to combat terrorism. Terrorist organisations' diverse requirement for financing creates a strong logic for seeking to disrupt terrorism by choking off funding flows to all terrorist-linked activities.'[3] Money is critical to financing al Qaeda's terrorist operations (operational costs) as well as sustaining its organizational infrastructure (organizational costs).[4] Al Qaeda cannot pursue sophisticated operations like the 9/11 terror attacks without adequate funding. However, the Islamist militants also need money to finance their organizational activities, including paying operatives, recruiting and training new members, bribing government officials, forging ties with other jihadist organizations, paying travel and communications expenses, and acquiring military weapons, explosives and radiological materials to construct a nuclear device or 'dirty bomb.'[5]

Attacking the financial infrastructure of al Qaeda is fundamentally a preventive strategy. That is, starving the terrorists of funding worldwide is critical to preventing terrorist acts. The ultimate goal is to save lives by preventing the use of funds to fuel terrorist attacks. However, going after the money is important for other reasons as well. Investigating al Qaeda's financial network may 'expose terrorist financing "money trails" that may generate leads to previously unknown terrorist cells and financiers.'[6] Identifying and disrupting channels of funding may also force members of al Qaeda to use more costly and less efficient and reliable means to transfer money globally to finance terrorist activities.[7] Blocking the assets of front companies, arresting terrorist financiers, and shutting down corrupt Islamic charities may further deter wealthy donors from providing financial assistance to al Qaeda. Simply stated, depriving al Qaeda of funding is as important as targeting the operational terror cells themselves.[8]

Al Qaeda is pursuing a deadly agenda that threatens global peace and security. Osama bin Laden, the Islamist militant group's inspirational and ideological leader, has declared war against America and called upon all Muslims to join in waging jihad or holy war against the United States and its allies.[9] Bin Laden's global jihad sanctions the killing of innocent civilians. Sheikh Omar Abdel Rahman, the so-called 'Blind Sheikh' and bin Laden's spiritual adviser, [10] has directed Muslims everywhere to:

> Cut off all relations with [the Americans, Christians, and Jews], tear them to pieces, destroy their economies, burn their corporations, destroy their peace, sink their ships, shoot down their planes and kill them on air, sea, and land. And kill them wherever you may find them, ambush them, take them hostage . . . Kill these Infidels. . . . Fight them, and God will torture them through your hands, and he will disgrace them and make you victorious over them.[11]

Al Qaeda intends to dramatically alter U.S. and Western policies toward the Islamic world. Specifically, al Qaeda seeks to expel the U.S. from all Muslim lands; remove U.S. and Western military forces from Iraq and Afghanistan; destroy the State of Israel; and overthrow so-called secular, 'apostate' Muslim regimes in the Middle East and other Muslim lands.[12] Bin Laden and his Islamist militant followers further intend to unify and radicalize the ummah (Islamic nation) of approximately 1.3 billion Muslims worldwide under a caliphate, governed by strict Sharia law.[13]

One terrorism expert maintains that al Qaeda has a short-range, middle-range and long-range strategic plan.[14] The short-range strategic stage has three objectives: '(a) [c]leansing of the Arab-Muslim states from the secular and corrupt regimes . . . and [replacing] them with Islamic regimes under the rule of the Islamic law (Shari'ah)'; '(b) [f]ighting against the outside infidel powers that take hold in the Arab-Muslim states . . . that threaten the holy places of Islam, in Iraq and in Palestine'; and '(c) [l]iberating all other Arab-Muslim countries.'[15] The middle-range strategic stage has two objectives: '(a) [a]fter having liberated the *jahili* political regimes of the Arab and Muslim countries, the task is to work to unite all Arab-Muslim lands, by establishing the legacy of the old Islamic Community (*al-Ummah al-Islamiya*) according to the *Shari'ah*; [and] (b) [a]cting to bring back all the historical lands conquered by the Muslim dynasties, from the seventh century to the seventeenth century – from India to Spain.'[16] Finally, the long-range strategic period is 'to stage the inevitable war, to complete the classical demand of the Islamic religion as a world exclusive superior one, to subdue the entire lands under *dar al-harb* rule to *dar al-Islam*'s . . . and to bring about *Allah*'s supreme reign.'[17] In short, al Qaeda is pursuing a deadly, radically ambitious global agenda. However, the terror group's geopolitical goals and objectives cannot be realized without substantial financial resources.

OPERATIONAL COSTS

Major terrorist attacks require substantial funding to plan and execute. It has been estimated that the 9/11 attacks cost as much as $500,000 to stage.[18] While other al Qaeda-related bombings may have cost substantially less,[19] it would be a fundamental error to conclude that terrorists do not need much money to terrorize. Significant financial resources are required to fund multiple, smaller terrorist attacks as well. Since September 11, 2001, al Qaeda has been implicated, directly or indirectly, in a series of deadly terrorist bombings around the world. Hundreds of thousands of dollars have been spent on these terrorist bombings. For example, Jemaah Islamiya (JI), the largest Islamist terrorist group in Southeast Asia, with strong ties to al Qaeda, has been implicated in several post-9/11 terrorist bombings.[20] In October 2002, a minivan loaded with explosives was detonated in front of two nightclubs located on the Indonesian island of Bali, killing 202 people, including seven Americans, and injuring more than 300 civilians.[21] In August 2003, a bombing at the Marriott Hotel in Jakarta by JI terrorists killed 12 people and injured scores of others, including several American citizens. On September 9, 2004, approximately one year after the Marriott Hotel bombing, JI was linked to a car bombing outside the Australian Embassy in Jakarta that killed 11 and wounded more than 180 people. On October 1, 2005, three simultaneous bombs exploded in Bali killing 22 people and injuring more than 100 others. The cost of the October 2002 Bali bombing alone has been estimated at $50,000,[22] while the money required to finance the other three JI-related terrorist attacks in Bali and Jakarta likely totaled tens, if not, hundreds of thousands of dollars more.

Since the 9/11 terrorist attacks, al Qaeda has been implicated in terrorist activities in other parts of the world, including the following bombings:

- Djerba, Tunisia (April 11, 2002) (killing 14 tourists and wounding seven others);[23]

- Karachi, Pakistan (March 2002) (killing 15 and wounding more than 40);[24]
- Riyadh, Saudi Arabia (May 12, 2003) (34 killed and 200 wounded);[25]
- Casablanca, Morocco (May 16, 2003) (45 dead and 100 injured);[26]
- Mumbai, India (August 23, 2003) (killing 53 and wounding more than 190);[27]
- Istanbul, Turkey (November 15 and 20, 2003) (58 killed and 750 wounded);[28]
- Madrid, Spain (March 11, 2004) (killing 191 and wounding 2,000 others);[29]
- London, England (July 7, 2005) (56 killed and over 700 wounded);[30]
- Amman, Jordan (November 9, 2005) (57 killed and nearly 100 more injured);[31]
- Mumbai, India (July 11, 2006) (200 killed and hundreds more wounded);[32]
- Algiers, Algeria (April 11, 2007) (24 people killed and 222 wounded);[33]
- Batna, Algeria (September 6, 2007) (20 people killed and 107 wounded);[34]
- Dellys, Algeria (September 8, 2007) (37 people killed);[35]
- Algiers, Algeria (December 11, 2007) (at least 37 people killed).[36]

Approximately 1,000 innocent civilians were murdered in these terrorist incidents and thousands more were seriously injured.[37]

When considered collectively the operational costs associated with the planning and execution of these bombings was substantial. The 2003 Istanbul suicide bombings alone cost as much as $170,000.[38] To focus on the money needed to finance a single, small terrorist operation is therefore misleading and does not accurately reflect the money needed to terrorize. At the same time, the actual terrorist operations represent a relatively small cost of al Qaeda's annual operating budget.[39] The true cost involves 'organizational' expenses that are needed to sustain the infrastructure of the terrorist network.

ORGANIZATIONAL COSTS

At the super-structure or organizational level, al Qaeda needs money to pay for salaries, recruitment, training camps, a safe haven, vehicles, weapons, ammunition, explosives and precursor chemicals for bombs, communications, travel, false identification documents, safe houses, bribing government officials, buying the support of other terrorist groups, and printing and distributing propaganda materials, including producing audio and video recordings and developing terrorist training manuals.[40] Prior to the terrorist attacks of 9/11, al Qaeda's annual operating budget was estimated at between $30 and $50 million.[41] The estimated annual operating budget of other terror groups such as HAMAS and Hizballah is even higher. HAMAS's annual operating budget has been estimated to range from $30 million to $90 million. The U.S. government believes that HAMAS's annual budget is at least $50 million.[42] Hizballah's operating budget may be as high as $200 million per year.[43] Collectively, hundreds of millions of dollars are required annually to sustain these terrorist groups. The money is needed to finance the following:

Al Qaeda's Propaganda Campaign

Al Qaeda has developed an elaborate global propaganda campaign that manipulates Islamic religious teachings to justify the murder of innocent civilians, including women and children.[44] In a letter to Abu Musab al-Zarqawi, the former leader of al Qaeda in Iraq, al-Zawahiri stated, 'I say to you: that we are in a battle, and that more than half of this battle is taking place in the battlefield of the media. And that we are in a media battle in a race for the hearts and minds of our Umma.'[45] The Internet 'provides terrorist groups a new means to spread its propaganda and increase publicity.'[46] As-Sahab, the media branch of al Qaeda, regularly releases Internet videos showing purported insurgent attacks against U.S. forces in Afghanistan and Iraq to recruit foreign fighters. The propaganda videos include graphic films of beheadings, deadly car bombings and other terrorist attacks. Al Qaeda and its sister organizations have also built expansive Internet libraries of sophisticated texts, pamphlets, and video and audio recordings advocating violence against the United States and moderate Muslim governments.[47] Terrorist websites deliver a wide range of products and services, including e-books by the leading ideologues of the jihad or holy war, terrorist training manuals, and other materials that encourage the growth of home-grown militant cells around the world.[48] 'Al Qaeda's ideology, long-term strategy, training materials and justification of jihad are freely available on the Internet, enabling any independent cell or group to operate within its framework.'[49] Video and audio recordings have been produced, aimed at disenfranchised Muslim youth, imploring them to join the jihad against America and the infidels. Funding is absolutely essential to developing and sustaining al Qaeda's worldwide propaganda campaign.

Recruiting New Members

Funding for recruitment is critical to providing a steady flow of terrorist fighters and suicide volunteers willing to commit mass murder of civilians. According to one terrorism expert, '[e]ngaged in a conflict as asymmetric as their battle with America, the only way al Qaeda considers it can make any military impact is with an endless supply of mujahedin prepared to die for their cause.'[50] Financial inducements are used to recruit suicide bombers. Terrorist recruits are often promised that, if they join the jihad and sacrifice their life in a suicide attack, their families will receive a monthly financial stipend to compensate them for their loss. Those payments may involve a one-time grant of approximately $5,000 and monthly payments thereafter.[51] Payments of up to $5,000 may represent more than a year's pay for some Muslim families and therefore serve as an important incentive for Palestinian and Islamist terrorists.[52] Terrorist organizations such as HAMAS and Hizballah distribute millions of dollars in monthly annuities to the surviving family members of suicide bombers.[53]

Funding Madrasas

Tens of millions of dollars are raised annually to fund madrasas or Islamic schools that promote Islamic extremism and are a recruiting ground for terrorism.[54] Some of these so-called religious schools preach that Muslims have a religious duty and obligation to join the jihad and kill the infidels. According to one terrorism expert, '[t]he biggest expense to propagate the growth of radical Islam is . . . the madrassas that churn out rabid young Islamic fundamentalists primed for jihad.'[55] The radical madrasas are important to the future of the global jihadist movement, indoctrinating and grooming the next wave and generation of Islamist terrorists.[56]

Training Camps

Terrorists also need money to finance training camps. Between 1996 and 2000, as many as 20,000 al Qaeda fighters were trained in a dozen or more-training camps in Afghanistan that were operated and financed by Osama bin Laden.[57] 'Al-Qaeda's Afghan training camps have also attracted a rainbow coalition of Jordanians, Turks, Palestinians, Iraqis, Saudis, Sudanese, Moroccans, Omanis, Tunisians, Tanzanians, Malaysians, Bangladeshis, Indians, Filipinos, Chechens, Uzbeks, Tajiks, Chinese, Uighurs, Burmese, Germans, Swedes, French, Britons, Arab-Americans, and African-Americans.'[58] At the training camps, terrorists are instructed on how to construct deadly roadside bombs and execute suicide attacks to maximize civilian deaths and casualties. Terrorists are trained in the use of automatic weapons, grenade launchers, shoulder-fired missiles, and other military weaponry. Al Qaeda operates training facilities in Afghanistan, Pakistan, the Maghreb region in North Africa, and other parts of the world. Substantial funding is needed to sustain these camps and train new jihadists.

Terrorist Safe Havens

Money is also used to bribe government officials to pay for protection and asylum and to secure a safe haven for terrorists to plan future attacks.[59] Between 1991 and 2001, bin Laden directed tens of millions of dollars to Sudanese government officials and members of the Taliban to secure safe havens in Sudan and Afghanistan. The *9/11 Commission Report* found that 'Bin Laden provided approximately $10–$20 million per year to the Taliban in return for safe haven.'[60] Additionally, terrorist groups such as al Qaeda distribute money to like-minded terrorist organizations to leverage their support and purchase their loyalty.[61]

Weapons of Mass Destruction

Finally, funds are needed to purchase firearms, ammunition, explosives, and also weapons of mass destruction, including nuclear, chemical and biological weapons.[62] It is no secret that Osama bin Laden is intent on acquiring weapons of mass destruction (WMD).[63] When asked by a journalist whether he had been seeking WMD, bin Laden responded that 'it was an Islamic duty to possess them in the defense of Islam and that it would be a sin not to attempt to possess such weapons to deter the infidels (that is, the United States, the West, and Israel) from using them on Muslims.'[64] During a later media interview, bin Laden stated that he already possessed weapons of mass destruction and asserted that 'al-Qa'ida will continue to try to acquire and employ chemical, biological, radiological, or nuclear material in attacks and would not hesitate to use them if it develops what it deems is sufficient capability.'[65] Considerable funding is obviously needed to acquire such weapons.

MONEY AND THE EVOLUTION OF AL QAEDA

Money has been critical to the growth and evolution of al Qaeda from the beginning. Many of the donors and financiers who currently fund al Qaeda first became acquainted with Osama bin Laden when he was a mujahedeen

(Islamic warrior) fighting in the Soviet–Afghanistan war; the money from those donors would go to support a services bureau that recruited mujahedeen from around the world to fight in the decade-long Soviet–Afghanistan conflict (1979–89). Money would again play an important role in the development of al Qaeda when bin Laden was exiled from his native Saudi Arabia and sought refuge in Sudan and Afghanistan. In Sudan and later with the Taliban in Afghanistan, bin Laden paid vast sums of money to both governments to secure a terrorist sanctuary within their respective countries. Sudan and Afghanistan provided a safe haven for bin Laden to raise money, build his terror network, recruit and train jihadists, and plan terrorist attacks, including the slaying of about 3,000 civilians on September 11, 2001. Sudan also protected him from law enforcement and intelligence agents looking to capture or kill him.

The Soviet–Afghanistan War (1979–89)

The al Qaeda terrorist organization, under the inspirational leadership of Osama bin Laden, has its origins in the Soviet–Afghanistan war.[66] After gaining power in 1978, the Communist-led government in Afghanistan was unable to maintain control. At the end of 1979, the Soviet government sent in military forces to reinforce the Communist regime and ensure that it remained securely under Moscow's influence. The response was an Afghan national resistance movement which ultimately defeated the Soviets. In April 1988, after a bloody armed conflict that spanned almost ten years, Moscow declared that it would remove its military forces from Afghanistan. Withdrawal of Soviet military troops was completed nine months later in 1989. Osama bin Laden played a prominent role in defeating the Soviets in Afghanistan. More importantly, his activities in the Soviet–Afghanistan conflict laid the foundation, including the financial infrastructure, for the global terrorist network that would become known as al Qaeda or 'The Base.'

In 1980, bin Laden, then a 23-year-old graduate of King Abdul Aziz University in Jeddah, departed Saudi Arabia to join the mujahedeen fighting against the Soviets in Afghanistan.[67] Bin Laden appears to have adopted his militant Islamic views at King Abdul Aziz University, where he studied Islamic culture under Muhammed Qutb, an eminent Islamic scholar and political philosopher. Muhammed Qutb was the brother of Sayyid Qutb, an Egyptian Islamic radical and leading figure in the Muslim Brotherhood, who is regarded by some analysts as 'the spiritual father of Islamic radical groups.'[68] In 1966, Sayyid Qutb was executed in Egypt for treason and for his political activities in opposition to the government of Egyptian President Gamal Abd al-Nasser.[69]

While attending King Abdul Aziz University, bin Laden was also introduced to the teachings of Dr Abdullah Yusuf Azzam, an early contributor to the development of political Islam and a key figure in the Jordanian branch of the Muslim Brotherhood.[70] In 1975, Azzam accepted a teaching position at King Abdul Aziz University, where he met the student bin Laden.[71] Azzam has been identified by some experts as 'the Godfather of *Jihad*,'[72] as well as the intellectual architect of the anti-Soviet jihad movement, and ultimately of al Qaeda itself.[73] Azzam became bin Laden's first mentor and deeply influenced his view of the Muslim world, planting the seeds of radical, fundamentalist Islam.[74]

After the Soviet Union invaded Afghanistan in 1979, Azzam resigned his teaching post and emigrated to Pakistan to assist in the anti-Soviet jihad.[75] Ultimately, he was put in charge of organizing and operating a paramilitary infrastructure for recruiting and training Arab fighters in Afghanistan.[76] Azzam instructed the mujahedeen in the extremist views of radical Islamic scholars, such as Ibn Taymiyah, Ibn Abd al-Wahhab, and Sayyid Qutb.[77] After joining Azzam in Afghanistan, bin Laden was involved in organizing the flow of funds from wealthy Saudi donors and recruiting Arab fighters for the anti-Soviet conflict.[78] He was a key fundraiser, raising tens of millions of dollars for arms and equipment for the mujahedeen, and encouraging thousands of Saudis to either join or donate money to the jihad.[79] Bin Laden paid for the transportation of new recruits to Afghanistan, and set up paramilitary training camps to train them. Bin Laden was further instrumental in transporting heavy construction equipment, diggers and bulldozers to Afghanistan from his family's construction firm in Saudi Arabia.[80] The equipment was used for border infrastructure projects, including building blacktopped roads to facilitate the delivery of military arms and needed supplies across the mountainous Afghanistan–Pakistan border.[81] Bin Laden's access to money and heavy equipment was the key factor that elevated his profile among the mujahedeen fighting in Afghanistan.

In 1984, bin Laden and Abdullah Azzam established a network of recruiting and fund-raising offices in the Middle East, Europe, and the United States called Maktab al Khidamat (the MAK), meaning the 'Bureau of Services.'[82] The MAK, considered the 'organizational front-runner of [a]l Qaeda,' channeled recruits into Afghanistan from across the Arab world.[83] This organization also included a financial support network known as the 'Golden Chain,' which consisted of wealthy financiers from Saudi Arabia and other Gulf countries.[84] Also, bin Laden's familial contacts with the Saudi royal family and other wealthy Saudis allowed him access to substantial financial resources. Through his efforts money flowed from deep-pocket donors, Saudi-based charities and non-governmental organizations, which bin Laden and his agents used to purchase arms and supplies for the mujahedeen fighters.[85] Bin Laden served as the paymaster for the Arab fighters, 'pay[ing] the expenses – about $300 per month – of any Arab who wanted to fight on Afghanistan's battlefields.'[86] The MAK dispersed around $2 billion in donations through its network of offices around the world to finance the Soviet–Afghanistan war.[87]

In 1986, bin Laden expanded his efforts and opened his first training camp known as al Masada (the Lions' Den) to teach young Arab jihadists how to use assault weapons, explosives and detonators.[88] While in Afghanistan, bin Laden met Ayman al-Zawahiri, a young doctor from a wealthy Egyptian family, long active in the militant Islamist movement.[89] Al-Zawahiri has been described as the intellectual, ideological and operational force of al Qaeda and the 'real leader behind the scenes.'[90] Al-Zawahiri was the founder and leader of the Egyptian Islamic Jihad and a prominent member of the Muslim Brotherhood.[91] In the early 1980s, al-Zawahiri was tried and imprisoned on conspiracy charges for his involvement in the plot to assassinate Egyptian President Anwar Sadat.[92] Meeting for the first time in 1987, bin Laden and al-Zawahiri agreed on 'the need for a global jihad against not only the Soviet Union but the corrupt secular governments of the Middle East, the United States and Israel.'[93] Ultimately, al-Zawahiri would become one of bin Laden's closest confidants and the deputy head of al Qaeda.[94]

In 1988, as the Soviet–Afghanistan conflict was coming to an end, bin Laden, Azzam, al-Zawahiri and other jihad leaders debated what to do next. While they agreed that the MAK, the recruitment and funding organization successfully created for Afghanistan, should not be dissolved, there were internal differences on how to utilize the volunteer network.[95] Bin Laden had global aspirations for what he called 'al Qaeda.' He viewed al Qaeda as an organization for waging global jihad.[96] He aimed to train Muslim fighters to continue the jihad outside Afghanistan to advance the cause of radical Islam.[97] Bin Laden sought to dispatch al Qaeda operatives to attempt to topple secular, pro-Western Arab leaders. Egyptian President Hosni Mubarak, Pakistan President Benazir Bhutto, and King Hussein of Jordan were denounced as false Muslims or 'kufr,' meaning apostates and non-believers, and bin Laden argued that they should be violently overthrown.[98] Bin Laden was not alone in his view. His vision for al Qaeda was strongly supported by the Egyptians in his inner circle, including al-Zawahiri and Sheikh Abdel al Rahman, the 'Blind Sheikh,' who, among other things, wanted to use al Qaeda to overthrow the Egyptian government and replace the secular regime with a radical, fundamentalist Islamic state.[99]

Azzam, bin Laden's partner in the MAK, disagreed with bin Laden's prescribed goals for al Qaeda. He believed that Afghanistan should be the focus for the Arab volunteers, not other countries across the Middle East.[100] He adamantly opposed the undertaking of a global jihad before the creation of an Islamic state in Afghanistan that would serve as a 'world Islamic revolutionary center . . . a place of refuge from which the mujahidin fighters would be able to emulate Muhammad's hijrah to Medina before embarking on a world scale jihad.'[101] Azzam rejected bin Laden's call for a wider war against impious Muslim governments, such as those in Egypt and Saudi Arabia, and 'favored continuing to fight in Afghanistan until it had a true Islamic government.'[102] Azzam advocated a traditional fundamentalist interpretation of jihad but wanted no part in conflicts between Muslims. Instead, he sought to reclaim once-Muslim lands from non-Muslim rule in places such as Palestine, the former Soviet Union, and even southern Spain, which had been under Muslim rule five centuries earlier.[103] For Azzam, Israel was the top priority for the next stage of the jihad.

While Azzam sought to build gradually toward the ideal of Islamic government, one convert at a time, he was not totally averse to accomplishing change by violent means.[104] His 'main slogan was "jihad and the rifle alone: no negotiations, no conferences, and no dialogues." '[105] He often referred to al Qaeda as a 'vanguard,' meaning a small band of militants sent by Allah to restore the Muslim people to the 'path of truth.'[106] For Azzam, killing and martyrdom were legitimate means to accomplish the social changes and reforms he sought to achieve. Azzam declared:

> When the *umma* goes astray . . . God sends an individual or small group of people who will rescue it from perdition and restore it to the path of truth. This small elite are the ones who carry conviction and ambitions. And an even smaller group from this band are those who flee from the worldly life in order to spread and act upon those ambitions. And an even smaller group from this elite . . . are those who sacrifice their souls and their blood in order to bring victory to these ambitions and principles.[107]

The dispute about the future of al Qaeda and the jihad movement was resolved on November 24, 1989, when Azzam and both of his sons were killed by a remotely-controlled car bomb.[108] While the murders were never solved, some terrorism experts suggest that bin Laden was responsible for Azzam's assassination.[109] Others believe that al-Zawahiri was responsible for his death.[110] Ultimately, Azzam's death left bin Laden in complete control of the MAK's funds and operational mechanisms, which were folded into the evolving al Qaeda organization. For bin Laden, the time had come to wage global jihad against America, the West and secular Muslim rulers.

Bin Laden's Triumphant Return to Saudi Arabia (1989–91)

After the Soviets completed their withdrawal from Afghanistan in early 1989, bin Laden returned to his homeland of Saudi Arabia, where he was greeted as a hero.[111] Bin Laden's reputation and stature in the militant Muslim community were enormously enhanced by his activities in Afghanistan. He gained the respect and admiration of the mujahedeen for leaving his safe, comfortable lifestyle in Saudi Arabia for a harsh, rugged and dangerous existence in Afghanistan. He was further admired for his effective fund-raising for the Afghan Arabs, obtaining large donations from wealthy donors in Saudi Arabia and other Gulf states.

Shortly after bin Laden's return to Saudi Arabia in August 1989, Iraqi President Saddam Hussein invaded Kuwait. Bin Laden reacted by lobbying the Saudi government to permit him to raise a mujahedeen army to protect the Kingdom and wage a guerilla war against Iraq.[112] He boasted that he could muster an army of 100,000 battle-tested Afghan war veterans at his command to protect the Saudi Kingdom from Iraq and oust its army from Kuwait.[113] However, bin Laden's plan was never taken seriously by the Saudi government and was summarily rejected.[114] Instead, the Saudis agreed to join the U.S.-led coalition against Iraq and permit 500,000 U.S. troops to be based in the Kingdom.[115] Bin Laden angrily protested the Saudi royal family's decision and the subsequent occupation of U.S. troops in Saudi Arabia. Joined by a number of conservative Islamic clerics, bin Laden began to publically denounce the arrangement and criticize the Saudi royal family. In informal lectures delivered at Jeddah mosques, bin Laden characterized the U.S. forces as 'occupiers' of sacred Islamic ground and the Saudi royal family as the facilitators of that 'occupation.'[116]

The Saudi government responded by arresting scores of dissenters and placing conservative clerics under house arrest. Saudi leaders further exerted efforts to silence bin Laden and persuade him to stop protesting the Saudi royal family by, among other things, seizing his passport.[117] In April 1991, bin Laden left Saudi Arabia under the pretext of attending an Islamic conference in Pakistan and fled to Sudan, where he remained until 1996.[118] By 1994, the Saudi government had frozen bin Laden's assets and revoked his citizenship.[119] Bin Laden was no longer welcome in Saudi Arabia. He was a man without a country.

Bin Laden's Flight to Sudan (1991–96)

In December 1991, bin Laden sought refuge in Sudan, where al Qaeda was headquartered until 1996.[120] While living in Sudan money was instrumental in facilitating bin Laden's plans to establish a true global terrorist network. Bin Laden spent millions of dollars to purchase the protection of Sudanese government officials and acquire a safe haven.[121] He spent funds to provide weapons, training and money to like-minded terrorist groups to cultivate their support, loyalty, and to expand al Qaeda's global jihad.[122]

Exiled from Saudi Arabia, bin Laden was warmly welcomed to Sudan by Hassan al-Turabi, the *de facto* leader of Sudan who headed the National Islamic Front, a coalition that had recently seized power in the country.[123] Al-Turabi and bin Laden entered into an agreement whereby bin Laden was to help fund al-Turabi's ongoing conflict against African-Christian separatists in southern Sudan, as well as subsidize major development projects in Sudan. In return, al-Turabi agreed to provide bin Laden a safe haven to conduct his worldwide business operations and expand his global terrorist network.[124]

The Sudanese government was eager for the financial assistance of this wealthy Saudi benefactor. Bin Laden did not disappoint it, spending massive amounts of money to cement his relationship with al-Turabi. The leader of al Qaeda spent tens of millions of dollars funding large-scale construction projects such as building a 1,200-kilometer-long highway linking Khartoum to Port Sudan and constructing the new airport at Port Sudan.[125] Bin Laden also devoted much of his time in Sudan to developing and operating various business ventures. He reportedly bought a farm in Khartoum for $250,000 and a salt farm near Port Sudan for $180,000.[126] Bin Laden owned Al Thimar al Mubaraka, an agricultural business that exported corn, sunflowers and other agricultural products.[127] The agricultural company employed 10,000 workers.[128] Bin Laden further invested as much as $50 million in a Sudanese bank and was linked to other business ventures, including a tannery and bakery.[129] Bin Laden's personal investments in Sudan reportedly amounted to about $200 million.[130]

On the terrorism front, bin Laden remained quite active as well. He funded jihad operations in the Balkans, Chechnya, Egypt, Yemen, Kashmir, and the Philippines.[131] Bin Laden purchased weapons, military equipment and paid for training for several terrorist organizations, including the Moro Islamic Liberation Front and the Abu Sayyaf Brigade in the Philippines, and Jemaah Islamiya, the largest terror group in Indonesia with cells in Malaysia, Singapore, and the Philippines.[132] He also funded military and basic explosives training for al Qaeda operatives in Afghanistan, and training on how to create cell structures for terrorist operations abroad.[133] Bin Laden provided financial assistance to Lashkar-e-Tayyiba, a Pakistani group engaged in insurgent attacks in Kashmir, and a band of Tajikistan Islamists involved in ethnic conflicts in Central Asia.[134] According to one report, the Jamaat-e-Jihad of Eritrea and the Abu Ali group operating in Jordan were given $100,000 grants to fund terror operations.[135]

Bin Laden established a terrorist cell in Nairobi and used it to transport arms and recruit fighters to assist warlords battling U.S. forces in Somalia.[136] Al Qaeda members provided military training and assistance to Somali militants opposed to the United Nations' intervention in Somalia.[137] The Islamist terror group claimed responsibility for arming Somali militants who shot down two U.S. Black Hawk helicopters and killed 18 U.S. Army Rangers in Mogadishu in October 1993.[138] The attack on the U.S. military helicopters was directed by al Qaeda's military commander, Abu Ubaydah al-Banshiri, who drowned in a 1996 ferry accident.[139]

While residing in Sudan, bin Laden established an 'Islamic Army Shura' that served as the coordinating body for a confederation of terrorist groups committed to global jihad.[140] The Shura was directed by bin Laden and Ayman al-Zawahiri. It was composed of representatives from al Qaeda and the leaders of other Islamist extremist groups. In building his 'Islamic Army,' bin Laden 'enlisted groups from Saudi Arabia, Egypt, Jordan, Lebanon, Iraq, Oman, Algeria, Libya, Tunisia, Morocco, Somalia, and Eritrea.'[141] Al Qaeda established less formal relations with other radical Islamists from the African states of Chad, Mali, Niger, Nigeria, and Uganda, and from the Southeast Asian countries of Burma, Thailand, Malaysia, and Indonesia.[142] Representatives came from other militant Islamic organizations such as the Palestine Liberation Organization, HAMAS, and Hizballah.[143] Many of these affiliated terrorist organizations were covertly financed by bin Laden, who often funneled money through Islamic charities such as the Benevolence International Foundation in Sarajevo, which supported the Bosnian Muslims engaged in the ethnic conflict with Serbia and Croatia, as well as the International Islamic Relief Organization and the Muslim World League, two Saudi-sponsored charities.[144] One terrorism expert described bin Laden in Sudan as the 'Ford Foundation of Sunni Islamic terrorism, a grant-giving source of cash for violent operations.'[145]

In 1996, the Sudanese government began to rethink its support of bin Laden.[146] The attempted assassination in June 1995 of Egyptian President Hosni Mubarak in Ethiopia was the 'tipping point.'[147] The would-be assassins, who were members of the Egyptian Islamic Jihad, had been sheltered in Sudan and aided by bin Laden.[148] When the Sudanese government refused to surrender three co-conspirators involved in the assassination plot against the Egyptian leader, the U.N. Security Council adopted a resolution criticizing and eventually sanctioning Sudan.[149] The United States, Saudi Arabia, and other Middle East governments began to exert diplomatic pressure on Sudan to stop providing a haven for al Qaeda and expel bin Laden from Sudan.[150] At one point, the US threatened to close its embassy in Khartoum because of the terror threats to American personnel.

Concerned that closure of the US embassy and bin Laden's continued presence in Khartoum would have negative economic repercussions for Sudan by driving away foreign investments, Sudanese officials ordered bin Laden to leave the country.[151] However, because the Saudi government had previously revoked bin Laden's citizenship, he could not be expelled to Saudi Arabia.[152] Bin Laden reached out to contacts he had developed during the Soviet–Afghanistan conflict, who invited him to return to Afghanistan.[153]

Return to Afghanistan – the Taliban Connection (1996–2001)

Bin Laden departed Sudan in May 1996.[154] Sudan's government arranged for a commercial Afghan jet to transport bin Laden, his family, bodyguards and close associates from Khartoum, Sudan, to Jalalabad, Afghanistan, where he was warmly welcomed.[155] When bin Laden arrived in Jalalabad, the Taliban (meaning 'students of Islam'),[156] a reformist group, was rising to power and controlled much of Afghanistan.[157] The Taliban had first surfaced in 1994 as a small militia force carrying out attacks against criminal warlords near Kandahar city. Its goal was to establish a new Islamic order for Afghanistan based on strict Sharia law.[158] The Taliban preached that Muslims were obliged to live as the earliest followers of the Prophet Mohammed had done and drew up a list of rules designed to eliminate all modern influences that detracted from a pious Muslim life. The Taliban's list of banned items and activities included television, videos, dancing, listening to music, singing, cards, kite-flying, most sports, cigarettes, American-style haircuts, and reading American magazines.[159] Additionally, the filming and photography of living objects was strictly prohibited. 'The First Amendment did not appear to be a feature of *sharia* law' under the Taliban.[160] The government was convinced that once Sharia law was properly implemented, 'Afghans would become virtuous and the perfect society would be created.'[161]

Muslim women were treated particularly harshly under Taliban rule. The Taliban decreed that women should neither work nor be educated.[162] Laws were enacted prohibiting women from working in government offices and pursuing a college education.[163] In addition, 8,000 female undergraduate students were expelled from Kabul University and a similar number of female school teachers lost their jobs.[164] Women were ordered to cover their faces and wear a burqa whenever in public. Taxi drivers were prohibited from stopping for any woman who did not wear a full Iranian-style burqa.[165] As a Taliban governor stated: 'We have given women their rights that God and his Messenger have instructed, that is to stay in their homes and to gain religious instruction in *hejab* [seclusion].'[166]

The list of Taliban regulations was enforced and offenders were severely punished by the religious police, poetically named the 'Ministry for the Promotion of Virtue and the Prevention of Vice.'[167] For example, a tailor could be sentenced to prison for taking female body measurements or displaying fashion magazines.[168] A man was allegedly beaten and sentenced to two and a half months in prison for drinking.[169] Summary execution by hanging was ordered for persons suspected of more serious crimes such as rape.[170]

The Taliban was led by Mullah Mohammed Omar, who was anointed in the spring of 1996 by a group of more than one thousand religious scholars as the Amir-ul-Momineen, or 'Commander of the Faithful,' in charge of the Taliban.[171] In September 1996, the Taliban secured its control of Afghanistan by successfully seizing Kabul, the country's capital.[172] To strengthen his ties with Mullah Omar and the Taliban, bin Laden provided about $3 million to aid the conquest of Kabul,[173] and colluded with the Taliban to train foreign volunteers to fight in the military campaign.[174] By 1999, as many as 400 Arabs under bin Laden's direction were fighting with the Taliban.[175]

While he was in Afghanistan, money flowed from bin Laden to finance expensive civil construction projects, including an elaborate mosque in Kandahar located near the Governor's House and a grand new Eid Mosque to celebrate the end of Ramadan.[176] To further ingratiate himself with Mullah Omar, bin Laden constructed the Taliban leader's extravagant suburban estate located outside Kandahar, which consisted of an 'ornate main palace, a house for servants, a lavish guest house, and a blue mosque.'[177] In addition, bin Laden spent approximately $10 to $20 million per year in return for Taliban protection and a sanctuary to train and indoctrinate terrorist fighters, import weapons, forge ties with other terror groups and leaders, and plot and staff terrorist attacks.[178] 'The Taliban provided al Qaeda with a safe haven and sheltered the training camps that would mass-produce mujahedin for the coming global jihad against what they regarded as the Muslim world's new enemy, the US.'[179] It is estimated that, between 1996 and 2001, between 10,000 and 20,000 jihadists were trained in bin Laden's camps in Afghanistan.[180]

During his stay in Afghanistan, bin Laden strengthened the global reach of the al Qaeda network, collaborating closely with terrorist groups in Egypt, Algeria, Yemen, Lebanon, Morocco, Tunisia and Somalia, as well as the Balkans, the Caucasus, Indonesia, Iraq, Malaysia, the Philippines and Kashmir.[181] By late 1999, the CIA estimated that al Qaeda operated in more than 60 countries worldwide, evolving into a loose-knit confederation of radical Islamist organizations with bin Laden serving as its inspirational leader.[182] In 2000 and 2001, members of Ansar al-Islam (AI) visited bin

Laden in Afghanistan to receive his 'blessing.'[183] AI later received between $300,000 and $600,000 in 'seed money' from bin Laden to support its terrorist operations.[184] AI also received training and logistical assistance from al Qaeda.[185] In a relatively short period, al Qaeda had become the 'general headquarters for international terrorism.'[186]

One counter-terrorism expert has noted that 'under the patronage of the Taliban, bin Laden launched his holy war in earnest against the United States.'[187] No longer constrained by the Sudanese government, bin Laden initiated a global media propaganda campaign, publishing his appeals for a global jihad. While the Taliban was making plans for the final assault on the Afghan capital of Kabul, bin Laden issued a declaration of war against the United States on August 23, 1996, calling for a jihad against the United States for its continued military presence in Saudi Arabia and purported oppression of Muslims around the world.[188] Bin Laden described the presence of U.S. troops in the Arabian Peninsula as the 'most serious aggression since the death of the Prophet [Muhammad].'[189] Bin Laden called on the youth of Islam to raise the banner of jihad up high against the Judeo-American alliance that has occupied the holy places of Islam.[190] More specifically, he called on all Muslims to join the jihad and to sacrifice their lives as martyrs for the cause. Quoting from selective Islamic religious texts, bin Laden stated:

> [A]nd so for those who are slain in the way of God, He will by no means allow their deeds to perish. He will guide them and improve their condition and cause them to enter the Garden Paradise which He has made known to them. . . . [A] martyr's privileges are guaranteed by God; forgiveness with the first gush of his blood, he will be shown his seat in Paradise, he will be decorated with the jewels of *Iman* [belief], married off to the beautiful ones, protected from the test in the grave, assured security in the Day of Judgment, crowned with the crown of dignity, a ruby of which is better than this whole *Duniah* [world] and it's [sic] entire content, wedded to seventy-two of the pure houris [beautiful young women of Paradise] and his intercession on the behalf of seventy of his relatives will be accepted.[191]

Bin Laden's 1996 declaration of war was faxed to London newspapers for publication and global dissemination.[192]

On February 23, 1998, bin Laden continued his global propaganda campaign by announcing the formation of a new coalition called the 'World Islamic Front for Jihad Against the Jews and Crusaders.'[193] The new jihadist enterprise was announced in a so-called fatwa (rulings on Islamic law) signed by bin Laden; Ayman al-Zawahiri, the leader of the Egyptian Islamic Jihad; Abu Yasir Rifa'i Ahmad Taha, leader of the Egyptian Islamic Group; Sheikh mil Harnzah, secretary general of the Jamiat-e-Ulema of Pakistan; and Maulana Fazlur Rahman, leader of the Jihad

Movement in Bangladesh.[194] The manifesto declared that Americans had been occupying the most sacred lands of Islam, stealing Muslim resources, dictating to its leaders, humiliating its people and terrorizing its neighbors, and 'had declared war on Allah, His Prophet, and Muslims.'[195] According to bin Laden and his terrorist associates, Muslims were therefore justified in taking up arms in a 'defensive jihad'[196] against the United States and Israel.[197]

The 1998 declaration was significant for two other reasons. The manifesto by the World Islamic Front eliminated the distinction between military and civilian personnel as legitimate targets of jihad. The declaration also represented an escalation of bin Laden's global jihad, justifying the killing not only of Americans but also of their allies, including civilians. Bin Laden and his confederates declared:

> By the ruling, it is an individual duty for every Muslim who can do it to kill Americans and their allies – civilian and military – in any country where it is possible . . . With God's Help, we call upon every Muslim who believes in God and wishes to be rewarded to comply with God's Order to kill the Americans and plunder their money wherever and whenever they find it.[198]

For bin Laden, American civilians were legitimate targets of terror and every Muslim had a religious duty to kill them in any country where they might be living. CIA analysts reported that these statements were 'the first from these groups that explicitly justify attacks on American civilians anywhere in the world. . . . the first religious ruling sanctifying such attacks.'[199]

Equally significant was the 1998 manifesto's expansion of the terrorism battlefront. The threat of terrorist attacks was no longer limited to U.S. targets, domestic and abroad, but extended to America's allies anywhere in the world. According to bin Laden, any country that supported the U.S. was an enemy of al Qaeda. The manifesto states: 'We also call on the Muslim *Ulema* [Islamic scholars], leaders, youth, and soldiers to launch raids on Satan's American troops and Satan's supporters allying with them in order to displace their leaders so that they may learn a lesson.'[200] In short, America's allies were put on notice: aid the U.S. and you will pay the price of jihad.

Al Qaeda's role with respect to terrorist operations fundamentally changed after bin Laden relocated to Afghanistan. Prior to the summer of 1998, al Qaeda concentrated on providing funds, training and weapons for attacks carried out by members of allied terror affiliates.[201] After bin Laden moved to Afghanistan, al Qaeda became involved in planning, supervising, and executing terrorist operations. Bin Laden was no longer merely a financier, funding and encouraging Islamist violence around the world: he had made the transition from providing material support to terrorists to planning and initiating terrorist attacks.

Reports indicate that when bin Laden published the February 1998 *Declaration by the World Islamic Front for Jihad Against the Jews and Crusaders*, the decision to launch terrorist attacks against the U.S. embassies in Nairobi, Kenya, and Dar es Salaam, Tanzania, had already been made.[202] Over the next several months, bin Laden finalized the plans for the terrorist bombings. On August 7, 1998, two teams of homicide bombers drove bomb-laden trucks into the two U.S. embassies.[203] The terrorist attacks were meticulously coordinated, occurring roughly five minutes apart.[204] In Nairobi, the impact of the truck-bomb sheared off the U.S. embassy's rear facade, killing 213 people, including 12 Americans.[205] The remaining murder victims were almost all Kenyans. Additionally, approximately 5,000 civilians were injured.[206] The terrorist attack in Dar es Salaam killed 11 people and injured 85 others.[207] The Africa embassy bombings represented the most devastating terrorist attacks against American targets since the suicide bombings of a Marine barracks in Lebanon by Shiite Islamic radicals in 1983.[208] When confronted on whether he indeed had masterminded the East Africa embassy bombings, bin Laden did not deny responsibility.[209] Recalling the February 1998 manifesto, bin Laden sought to justify the killing of innocent civilians. He declared that if murdering Jews and Americans to expel them from the holy places 'is considered a crime . . . let history be a witness that I am a criminal.'[210]

Al Qaeda's new role of planning and directing terrorist attacks was further manifested on October 12, 2000, when a small boat laden with explosives was detonated against a U.S. Navy destroyer, the USS Cole, docked at Aden, Yemen. The blast blew a 40-foot wide hole in the hull of the vessel, killing 17 American crew members and wounding at least 40 others.[211] According to the Report of the 9/11 Commission, the terrorist attack on the USS Cole was 'a full-fledged al Qaeda operation, supervised directly by Bin Laden. He chose the target and location of the attack, selected the suicide operatives, and provided the money needed to purchase explosives and equipment.'[212] Attacking the USS Cole was a bold and brazen act, exhibiting extensive planning and coordination by al Qaeda. Bin Laden selected the USS Cole to convey the message that al Qaeda could attack the U.S. whenever and wherever it wanted. CIA analysts concluded that with slightly more skilled execution, the suicide bombers would have killed more than 300 crew members and completely sunken the U.S. naval vessel.[213]

The terrorist bombings against the U.S. embassies in Africa and the USS Cole in Yemen demonstrated that al Qaeda was growing in strength, sophistication and confidence. Its safe haven in Afghanistan allowed bin

Laden to plan and execute ever more ambitious and deadly terror operations.[214] The terrorist attacks on the World Trade Center and the Pentagon and the hijacking of a commercial airliner that crashed in a field in Pennsylvania, which together killed approximately 3,000 innocent civilians, would follow within less than a year.

The terrorist attacks on the U.S. embassies in Kenya and Nairobi cost about $50,000.[215] The operational costs associated with the USS Cole bombing have been estimated at even less, approximately $10,000.[216] In reality, however, these terrorist operations cost much more. At the time, bin Laden had acquired a terrorist sanctuary in Afghanistan, where he plotted and successfully executed the terrorist attacks against the African embassies and the USS Cole. The terrorist base of operations cost bin Laden approximately $10 to $20 million per year in protection money funneled to Mullah Omar and the Taliban.[217] Substantial financial resources were therefore essential for bin Laden to carry out these deadly terror attacks against U.S. targets in Africa.

A brief review of the history of al Qaeda clearly establishes that money has played a crucial role at every major stage in the development of the al Qaeda network. Funding was needed to support the activities of Maktab al-Khidamat (MAK), a network established by bin Laden and Abdullah Azzam to recruit Arabs to fight in the Afghan–Soviet war. Bin Laden used the MAK to raise hundreds of millions of dollars to purchase arms and equipment for the mujahedeen in Afghanistan. Money was essential to bin Laden's plans in Sudan and Afghanistan, where he laid the organizational foundation for his global jihadist network. Bin Laden spent tens of millions of dollars to purchase the protection of the Sudanese government and millions of dollars more to secure the support of the Taliban in Afghanistan. Bin Laden's leadership and reputation were further greatly enhanced by his ability to provide funds to other militant Islamic groups. Finally, upwards of $500,000 was required to finance the September 11, 2001 attacks, the most destructive and deadly terrorist plot ever implemented against the United States.

Unfortunately, the threat of international terrorism from al Qaeda did not end on September 11, 2001. Bin Laden has declared war against America and its allies and called upon all Muslims to join al Qaeda's global jihad and kill American civilians anywhere in the world.[218] However, bin Laden's so-called 'holy war' against America and the West cannot be successfully waged without substantial funding.[219] This realization leads to one inescapable conclusion: al Qaeda and the global jihadist movement it has inspired need vast sums of money to achieve their geopolitical goals and objectives. More simply stated, terrorists need money to terrorize.

NOTES

1. NATIONAL STRATEGY FOR COMBATING TERRORISM 17 (2003), *available at* http://www.whitehouse.gov/news/releases/2003/02/counter_terrorism/counter_terrorism_strategy.pdf.
2. *See* NATIONAL COMMISSION ON TERRORIST ATTACKS, THE 9/11 COMMISSION REPORT: FINAL REPORT OF THE NATIONAL COMMISSION ON TERRORIST ATTACKS UPON THE UNITED STATES 382 (W.W. Norton & Company 2004), *available at* http://www.9-11commission.gov/report/911Report.pdf [hereinafter THE 9/11 COMMISSION REPORT] ('The government has recognized that information about terrorist money helps us to understand their networks, search them out, and disrupt their operations.').
3. Financial Action Task Force, Terrorist Financing (Feb. 29, 2008), *available at* http://www.fatf-gafi.org/dataoecd/28/43/40285899.pdf [hereinafter FATF Terrorist Financing].
4. *See* JEAN-CHARLES BRISARD, TERRORISM FINANCING: ROOTS AND TRENDS OF SAUDI TERRORISM FINANCING, REPORT PREPARED FOR THE PRESIDENT OF THE SECURITY COUNCIL, UNITED NATIONS 6–7 (Dec. 19, 2002), *available at* http://www.apgml.org/frameworks/docs/7/TF-Saudi%20financing%20Nov2002%20-%20UN%20Security%20Council.pdf.
5. Al Qaeda 'remains interested in using a radiological dispersal device or "dirty bomb," a conventional explosive designed to spread radioactive material.' THE NATIONAL COMMISSION ON TERRORIST ATTACKS UPON THE UNITED STATES, TWELFTH PUBLIC HEARING 12 (June 16, 2004), *available at* http://govinfo.library.unt.edu/911/staff_statements/staff_statement_15.pdf; *see also* THE 9/11 COMMISSION REPORT, *supra* note 2, at 381 ('Our report shows that al Qaeda has tried to acquire or make weapons of mass destruction for at least ten years.').
6. U.S. DEP'T OF TREASURY, NATIONAL MONEY LAUNDERING STRATEGY 7 (2003), *available at* http://www.treasury.gov/offices/enforcement/publications/ml2003.pdf.
7. *See* THE 9/11 COMMISSION REPORT, *supra* note 2, at 382 (going after terror funds 'has decreased the amount of money available to al Qaeda and has increased the costs and difficulty in raising and moving that money').
8. Tracking terrorist revenues may have an even greater impact on the terrorist organization than arresting its leaders. 'The trouble is that every time a seemingly "essential" al Qaeda leader has been arrested, he has been replaced with no effect at all on the organization.' MICHAEL SCHEUER, IMPERIAL HUBRIS: WHY THE WEST IS LOSING THE WAR ON TERROR 69 (Potomac Books 2004) [hereinafter IMPERIAL HUBRIS] (quoting Sanjoy Anand, *Osama Bides His Time*, THE SPECTATOR, June 21, 2003, at 16).
9. *See* Osama bin Laden, 'Declaration of War Against the Americans Occupying the Land of the Two Holy Places,' Aug. 23, 1996. The word 'jihad' literally means 'struggle' in the way of God. 'The "great jihad," an internal (personal) moral and spiritual struggle, is distinguished from the "lesser jihad," holy war for the defence or expansion of Islam.' MARIAM ABOU ZAHN & OLIVER ROY, ISLAMIST NETWORKS: THE AFGHAN–PAKISTAN CONNECTION, at vii (Columbia University Press 2004) [hereinafter ISLAMIST NETWORKS). The doctrine of jihad is divided into two categories: offensive and defensive jihad. An offensive or expansionist jihad means to conquer new lands for Islam and convert new peoples to the faith. IMPERIAL HUBRIS, *supra* note 8, at 7. 'The threat facing America is the defensive jihad, an Islamic military reaction triggered by an attack by non-Muslims on the Islamic faith, on Muslims, on Muslim territory, or on all three.' *Id.*
10. Sheikh Omar Abdel Rahman has been convicted of conspiring to commit acts of terrorism against the United States, including the 1993 World Trade Center bombing and a plot to destroy other New York City landmarks. *See* United States v. Rahman, 189 F.3d 88 (2d Cir. 1999), *cert. denied*, 534 U.S. 967 (1999).
11. *See* PETER L. BERGEN, THE OSAMA BIN LADEN I KNOW 204–5 (New York: Free Press 2006) [hereinafter THE OSAMA BIN LADEN I KNOW].

12. *See* IMPERIAL HUBRIS, *supra* note 8, at xviii; THE OSAMA BIN LADEN I KNOW, *supra* note 11, at 182; *see also* Osama bin Laden, 'Statement to America,' Oct. 26, 2002 ('[W]e advise you to stop supporting Israel, and to end your support of the Indians in Kashmir, the Russians against the Chechens and to also cease supporting the Manila Government against the Muslims in Southern Philippines.'); Osama bin Laden, 'Message to the Islamic World,' Dec. 16, 2004, *reprinted in* MESSAGES TO THE WORLD: THE STATEMENTS OF OSAMA BIN LADEN 245–75 (Bruce Lawrence ed., James Howarth trans., Verso 2005) [hereinafter STATEMENTS OF OSAMA BIN LADEN] (declaring that the leaders of Saudi Arabia and Jordan are 'apostates' or 'kufr' (non-believers) and should be overthrown).
13. *See* REPORT OF THE HOUSE PERMANENT SELECT COMMITTEE ON INTELLIGENCE, AL-QAEDA: THE MANY FACES OF AN ISLAMIST EXTREMIST THREAT, at 6 (June 2006). The *Quran* and the *Sunnah*. which consists of the words, acts, and deeds of the Prophet Muhammad, form the basis of the system of Islamic jurisprudence known as the *Sharia*. *See* OSAMA BIN LADEN: AMERICA'S ENEMY IN HIS OWN WORDS, at lix (Randall B. Hamud ed., Nadeem Pub. 2005) [hereinafter BIN LADEN'S OWN WORDS]; ISLAMIST NETWORKS, *supra* note 9, at viii; IMPERIAL HUBRIS, *supra* note 8, at 2 ('For Muslims, God's word – as He revealed it in the Koran – and the Prophet's sayings and traditions (the Sunnah) are meant to guide all aspects of life: personal, familial, societal, political, and international.').
14. *See* DAVID BUKAY, FROM MUHAMMAD TO BIN LADEN 246–7 (Transaction 2007) [hereinafter FROM MUHAMMAD TO BIN LADEN].
15. *Id.* at 246.
16. *Id.* at 247.
17. *Id.*
18. THE 9/11 COMMISSION REPORT, *supra* note 2, at 169.
19. For example, the 2002 bombings in Bali, Indonesia, that killed over 200 tourists and injured hundreds of other innocent civilians are estimated to have cost $50,000. The 1998 African embassy bombings cost approximately $50,000. The Jakarta J.W. Marriot Hotel bombing in 2003 is believed to have cost $30,000. *See* FATF Terrorist Financing, *supra* note 3, at 7.
20. Al Qaeda has allegedly provided funding, training and other material resources to JI. *See* STEVEN EMERSON, JIHAD INCORPORATED 150–53 (2006) [hereinafter JIHAD INCORPORATED]; THE 9/11 COMMISSION REPORT, *supra* note 2, at 58 ('Al Qaeda helped Jemaah Islamiya (JI), a nascent organization headed by Indonesian Islamists with cells scattered across Malaysia, Singapore, Indonesia, and the Philippines.'). JI's principal goal is to establish a Southeast Asian caliphate or Islamic state, governed by strict Sharia or Islamic law. The caliphate would include Indonesia, Malaysia, Singapore, Brunei, and the south Philippines. *See* JIHAD INCORPORATED, at 150.
21. Eleven days after the Bali terrorist attack, the U.S. Treasury Department designated JI a foreign terrorist organization. *See* Press Release, U.S. Department of Treasury, Statement by Secretary Paul O'Neill on Designation of Jemaah Islamiya (Oct. 23, 2002), *available at* http://www.ustreas.gov/press/releases/po3569.htm. A few days later, the United Nations added JI to its terror list. *See* Press Release, Security Council, 1267 Committee Adds Name of an Entity to Its List, U.N. Doc. SC/7548 (Oct. 25, 2002), *available at* http://www.un.org/News/Press/docs/2002/SC7548.doc.htm.
22. *See* FATF Terrorist Financing, *supra* note 3, at 7.
23. It has been estimated that the Djerba synagogue truck bombing cost approximately $20,000. *See* BRISARD, *supra* note 4, at 6.
24. Lashkar i Jhangvi (LJ), meaning 'army of Jhang,' is responsible for a March 2002 bus bombing that killed 15, including 11 French technicians. LJ has strong ties to al Qaeda and the Taliban, receiving sanctuary from the Taliban, fighting alongside Taliban fighters and allegedly receiving training from al Qaeda. The Pakistani Interior Minister, speaking of LJ members, stated, 'They have been sleeping and eating together, receiving training together, and fighting against the Northern Alliance together in Afghanistan.' Press Release, U.S. Dep't of Treasury, Treasury Department Statement Regarding the

Designation of Lashkar i Jhangvi (Jan. 30, 2003), *available at* http://www.treas.gov/press/releases/kd3814.htm; *see also* 2005 Country Reports on Terrorism, U.S. Dep't of State, Office of the Coordinator for Counterterrorism (Apr. 30, 2006), at 208–9, *available at* http://www.state.gov/documents/organization/65479.pdf [hereinafter 2005 Country Reports] (detailing terrorist attacks, including the abduction and murder of U.S. journalist Daniel Pearl, linked to LJ).

25. IMPERIAL HUBRIS, *supra* note 8, at 97. On May 6, 2003, Saudi security officials raided an al Qaeda safe house in Riyadh and recovered more than 800 pounds of explosives, 55 hand grenades, dozens of assault rifles, 2,500 rounds of ammunition, and $80,000 in cash. *See id.* at 89.
26. *See* Craig S. Smith, *8 Sentenced in Morocco for Plotting Terror Attacks*, N.Y. TIMES, March 2, 2007, *available at* http://www.nytimes.com/2007/03/03/world/africa/03morocco.html?_r=1&oref=slogin; Olivier Guitta, *The Islamization of Morocco*, WEEKLY STANDARD, Oct. 2, 2006, *available at* http://www.weeklystandard.com/Content/Public/Articles/000/000/012/740boykt.asp. Local Islamist terror groups reportedly received $50,000 from al Qaeda to fund the operations. *See* IMPERIAL HUBRIS, *supra* note 8, at 97.
27. Lashkar-e-Tayyiba (LT) is suspected in the attack. LT is one of the three largest and best-trained groups fighting in Kashmir against India. The terror group has been implicated in numerous attacks in India, including the December 2001 attack on the Indian Parliament building. Al Qaeda is believed to be providing funding and training to LT members. Senior al Qaeda lieutenant Abu Zabayadah was captured at an LT safe house in Faisalabad in March 2002, providing evidence of LT links to al Qaeda. *See* 2005 Country Reports on Terrorism, *supra* note 24, at 207–8; *see also* Associated Press, *Chronology of Major Attacks in India*, WASH. POST, Feb. 19, 2007, *available at* http://www.washingtonpost.com/wp-dyn/content/article/2006/07/11/AR2006071100694.html.
28. *See* Karl Vick, *Al-Qaeda's Hand in Istanbul Plot*, WASH. POST, Feb. 13, 2007, *available at* http://www.washingtonpost.com/wp-dyn/content/article/2007/02/12/AR2007021201715.html (reporting that an al Qaeda operative delivered conspirators $100,000 to finance the truck bombings). A Turkish court sentenced seven suspected al Qaeda operatives to life in prison for the deadly 2003 suicide bombings in Istanbul. *See* Sebnem Arsu, *7 Get Life Sentences in Bombings of Istanbul Synagogue and Office*, N.Y. TIMES, Feb. 17, 2007, *available at* http://www.nytimes.com/2007/02/17/world/europe/17turkey.html (one of the defendants was accused of giving Islamist militants $170,000 to carry out the attacks); Benjamin Harvey, *Death Toll in Turkey Bombings Rises to 10*, WASH. POST, Sept. 13, 2006, *available at* http://www.washingtonpost.com/wp-dyn/content/article/2006/09/13/AR2006091300270.html.
29. *See Train Bomb Trial Starts in Madrid*, BBC NEWS, Feb. 15, 2007, *available at* http://news.bbc.co.uk/1/hi/world/europe/6363149.stm (29 people have been charged by a Spanish court with involvement in the Madrid train bombings, the deadliest al Qaeda-related terrorist attack in Europe).
30. On July 7, 2005, four al Qaeda-inspired terrorists detonated bombs on three subway trains and a double-decker bus in London. All four of the suicide bombers were British. One of the four militant Islamists appeared on a martyrdom videotape distributed on the Internet accusing the British government of declaring war on Islam and oppressing Muslims in Palestine, Afghanistan, Iraq, and Chechnya. He claimed that the London attack was only the beginning of a series of attacks that would continue until Britain pulled their soldiers from Afghanistan and Iraq. *See London Bomber Outlines Motives in Video*, N.Y. TIMES. July 7, 2006.
31. *See* 2005 Country Reports, *supra* note 24, at 218–20; *see also Iraqi Woman's Death Sentence Upheld*, WASH. POST, Jan. 27, 2007, *available at* http://www.washingtonpost.com/wp-dyn/content/article/2007/01/27/AR2007012700463.html.
32. On July 11, 2006, seven bombs were detonated on railway cars and train platforms in Mumbai, India, the country's financial hub, killing at least 135 people and injuring approximately 200 others. Lashkar-e-Tayyiba (LT), one of the principal terrorist groups fighting in Kashmir against India, is believed to be responsible for the attacks. Al Qaeda

is suspected of providing training and financing to LT. *See* Attacks in India: Lashkar-e-Taiba and the al Qaeda Playbook (July 11, 2006), *available at* http://www.stratfor.com/products/premium/read_article.php?id=268903. Bin Laden has voiced his support for the conflict in Kashmir to create a separate Muslim state. *See* BIN LADEN'S OWN WORDS, *supra* note 13, at 70–72.

33. *See* Craig Whitlock, *Al-Qaeda Branch Claims Algeria Blasts*, WASH. POST, Apr. 12, 2007, *available at* http://www.washingtonpost.com/wp-dyn/content/article/2007/04/11/AR2007041100371.html.
34. *See Militant Attacks in North Africa*, N.Y. TIMES, Dec. 11, 2007.
35. *See* Whitlock, *supra* note 33.
36. *See Algeria Violence Death Toll Jumps in December*. REUTERS, Jan. 3, 2008, *available at* http://africa.reuters.com/world/news/usnAHM258436.html. The terrorist group al Qaeda in the Islamic Maghreb, the North African wing of al Qaeda, claimed responsibility for the attacks, which involved twin car bombs near United Nations offices and Algeria's Constitutional Council. The group also claimed responsibility for the attacks in Batna and Dellys as well. *See* Katrin Bennhold & Craig S. Smith, *Twin Bombs Kill Dozens in Algiers*, N.Y. TIMES, Dec. 12, 2007, *available at* http://www.nytimes.com/2007/12/12/world/africa/12algiers.html.
37. *See* IMPERIAL HUBRIS, *supra* note 8, at 97–100 (detailing post-9/11 al Qaeda-linked terrorist attacks); REPORT OF THE HOUSE PERMANENT SELECT COMMITTEE ON INTELLIGENCE, AL-QAEDA: THE MANY FACES OF AN ISLAMIST EXTREMIST THREAT, at 16–23 (JUNE 2006); *Italy Convicts Egyptian Linked to Madrid Bombings*, N.Y. TIMES. Nov. 6, 2006; Don Van Natta, et. al., *Details Emerge in British Terror Case*, N.Y. TIMES, Aug. 27, 2006. Al Qaeda has also been linked to the June 1996 bombing of the American military base at Khobar Towers in Dharan, Saudi Arabia, where 19 U.S. soldiers were killed and 500 people injured. *See* ABDEL BARI ATWAN, THE SECRET HISTORY OF AL QAEDA 36 (University of California Press 2006) [hereinafter THE SECRET HISTORY OF AL QAEDA].
38. *See Turkish Court Sentences 7 for Istanbul Bombings*, N.Y. TIMES. Feb. 16, 2007.
39. THE 9/11 COMMISSION REPORT, *supra* note 2, at 171.
40. *See* FATF Terrorist Financing, *supra* note 3, at 4.
41. *See* THE 9/11 COMMISSION REPORT, *supra* note 2, at 171; ROHAN GUNARATNA, INSIDE AL QAEDA: GLOBAL NETWORK OF TERROR 61 (Columbia University Press 2002).
42. *See* MATTHEW LEVITT, HAMAS, POLITICS, CHARITY AND TERRORISM IN THE SERVICE OF JIHAD 54 (New Haven: Yale University Press 2006) [hereinafter HAMAS].
43. Matthew Levitt, *Hezbollah: Financing Terror Through Criminal Enterprise*, Testimony before the Senate Committee on Homeland Security and Governmental Affairs (May 25, 2005).
44. In an interview with an Al-Jazeera correspondent, aired in February 2002, Osama bin Laden attempted to justify the killing of innocent civilians: 'We kill the kings of the infidels, kings of the crusaders, and civilian infidels in exchange for those of our children they kill. This is permissible in law and intellectually. . . . If they kill our women and our innocent people, we will kill their women and innocent people.' Osama bin Laden, Interview with Tayseer Alouni, *Al-Jazeera*, October 2001 (translation from Arabic).
45. THE SECRET HISTORY OF AL QAEDA, *supra* note 37, at 85; *see also* Letter from Ayman al-Zawahiri to Abu Musab al-Zarqawi (July 9, 2005) (discussing al Qaeda's propaganda campaign).
46. REPORT OF THE HOUSE PERMANENT SELECT COMMITTEE ON INTELLIGENCE, AL-QAEDA: THE MANY FACES OF AN ISLAMIST EXTREMIST THREAT, at 26 (June 2006).
47. *See* PETER L. BERGEN, HOLY WAR, INC.: INSIDE THE SECRET WORLD OF OSAMA BIN LADEN 40 (New York: Simon & Schuster 2002) [hereinafter HOLY WAR, INC.].
48. One of the most popular is a 1,600 page treatise entitled 'Call to Global Islamic Resistance,' a comprehensive guide to militant life by senior al Qaeda operative Abu Musab al-Suri, who was captured in Pakistan. *See U.S. Seen Balking at Challenge by Islamist Web*, N.Y. TIMES, Oct. 28, 2006. Between 1990 and 1993, members of al Qaeda drafted the *Encyclopedia of the Afghan Jihad*. The terrorist encyclopedia is thousands of pages long and details everything learned by the Afghan Arabs in the jihad against the

Soviets. The *Encyclopedia* contains hundreds of pages on how to use military weapons, including American Stinger missiles, and 250 pages on how to mount terrorist attacks. A CD-ROM version was produced and made available online. *See* HOLY WAR, INC., *supra* note 47, at 87.

49. THE SECRET HISTORY OF AL QAEDA, *supra* note 37, at 88.
50. *Id.* at 85.
51. Almog v. Arab Bank, 471 F. Supp. 2d 257, 262 (E.D.N.Y. 2007).
52. *See id.*; HAMAS, *supra* note 42, at 59.
53. HAMAS reportedly distributes $2–3 million in monthly payments to the families of suicide bombers. *See* HAMAS, *supra* note 42, at 59; *see also* Almog v. Arab Bank, 471 F. Supp. 2d 257, 262 (E.D.N.Y. 2007).
54. *See* Husain Haqqani, *Islam's Medieval Outposts*, FOREIGN POLICY no. 133, Nov/Dec.2002; Anna Kuchment et al., *School by the Book*, NEWSWEEK, Mar. 11, 2002.
55. Joel Mowbray, *Saudis Behaving Badly*, NAT'L REVIEW ONLINE, Dec. 20, 2002.
56. *See* HOLY WAR, INC., *supra* note 47, at 152 (madrasas in Pakistan supplied tens of thousands of recruits to the Taliban in 1997).
57. *See* HOLY WAR, INC., *supra* note 47, at 167–8; THE 9/11 COMMISSION REPORT, *supra* note 2, at 67; FROM MUHAMMAD TO BIN LADEN, *supra* note 14, at 262 (estimating the number of Arabs trained in Afghanistan at 10,000). Zacarias Moussaoui, the so-called '20th hijacker' linked to the 9/11 World Trade Center attack, allegedly trained at the al Qaeda-affiliated Khalden camp in Afghanistan in April 1998. *See* United States v. Zacarias Moussaoui, Superseding Indictment, Cr. No. 01–455-A (E.D. Va. 2002).
58. *See* HOLY WAR, INC., *supra* note 47, at 32.
59. While residing in Sudan and Afghanistan prior to 9/11, Osama bin Laden paid the governments of those countries millions of dollars annually to secure a terrorist safe haven. *See* HOLY WAR, INC., *supra* note 47, at 82, 165 (Bin Laden gave the Taliban $3 million to finance the military assault on Kabul).
60. *See* THE 9/11 COMMISSION REPORT, *supra* note 2, at 171.
61. *Id.* (noting that bin Laden may have used money to create alliances with other Islamic militant groups).
62. Bin Laden has made clear his desire to acquire weapons of mass destruction: 'We don't consider it a crime if we tried to have nuclear, chemical, biological weapons . . . We have the right to defend ourselves.' Jamal Ismail, *I Am Not Afraid of Death*, Interview with Osama bin Laden, NEWSWEEK, Jan. 11, 1999, at 37.
63. Press Release, U.S. Dep't of Treasury, Statement of Under Secretary Stuart Levy, Netherlands' Terrorist Financing Conference (Mar. 16, 2006), *available at* http://www.treas.gov/press/releases/js4119.htm.
64. BIN LADEN'S OWN WORDS, *supra* note 13, at xlvii–xlviii.
65. *Id.* at xlviii. Abu Musa'ab al-Zarqawi's network established a poisons and explosives training camp in Northwest Iraq. *See* Press Release, U.S. Dep't of Treasury, Treasury Designates Six Al-Qaida Terrorists (Sept. 24, 2003), *available at* http://www.ustreas.gov/press/releases/js757.htm; *see also* THE 9/11 COMMISSION REPORT, *supra* note 2, at 381 ('Our report shows that al Qaeda has tried to acquire or make weapons of mass destruction for at least ten years.'); OFFICE OF THE DIRECTOR OF NATIONAL INTELLIGENCE, THE TERRORIST THREAT TO THE U.S. HOMELAND, NATIONAL INTELLIGENCE ESTIMATE (July 2007).
66. Osama bin Laden was born in Riyadh, Saudi Arabia, in July 1957, the 17 of 55 or 57 children born to the elder bin Laden and his multiple wives. *See* BIN LADEN'S OWN WORDS, *supra* note 13, at xxxvi–xxxvii; THE SECRET HISTORY OF AL QAEDA, *supra* note 37, at 40–41; THE 9/11 COMMISSION REPORT, *supra* note 2, at 55. His father, Muhammad Awad bin Laden, was a self-made construction magnate, who came to the Kingdom of Saudi Arabia from Yemen. *See* KENNETH KATZMAN, AL QAEDA: PROFILE AND THREAT ASSESSMENT, CRS REPORT FOR CONGRESS, at 1 (Aug. 17, 2005) [hereinafter AL QAEDA: PROFILE AND THREAT ASSESSMENT]. Muhammad bin Laden became a trusted

confidante of the al-Saud royal family, securing numerous lucrative government-funded building contracts. *See* THE SECRET HISTORY OF AL QAEDA, *supra* note 37, at 41. Bin Laden's father died in a plane crash in 1968, leaving a fortune of $11 billion to his children. Osama bin Laden was ten years old when his father died. *Id.* Estimates of his inheritance have ranged between $80 and $300 million. *See* BIN LADEN'S OWN WORDS, *supra* note 13, at xxxvii.

67. Bin Laden studied economics and business administration at King Abdul-Aziz University in Jeddah, where he received his BA degree. *See* THE SECRET HISTORY OF AL QAEDA, *supra* note 37, at 42; *see also* BIN LADEN'S OWN WORDS, *supra* note 13, at xxxvii (other sources say that bin Laden received a degree in civil engineering from the University in 1979 and a degree in public administration in 1981).
68. *See* THE SECRET HISTORY OF AL QAEDA, *supra* note 37, at 43; AL QAEDA: PROFILE AND THREAT ASSESSMENT, *supra* note 66, at 1; FROM MUHAMMAD TO BIN LADEN, *supra* note 14, at 214–15 ('Sayyid Qutb (1906–1966) was one of the most important figures in the development of contemporary *jihadi* ideology and played a key role in the emergence of the *sahwa* (awakening) Islamic movement.'). The Muslim Brotherhood, a major Sunni Islamic fundamentalist movement, was founded in 1928 in Egypt. AL QAEDA: PROFILE AND THREAT ASSESSMENT, *supra* note 66, at 1, n.2.
69. *See* BIN LADEN'S OWN WORDS, *supra* note 13, at xxxviii.
70. *See* THE SECRET HISTORY OF AL QAEDA, *supra* note 37, at 43; BIN LADEN'S OWN WORDS, *supra* note 13, at xxxviii.
71. *See* FROM MUHAMMAD TO BIN LADEN, *supra* note 14, at 256.
72. *Id.* at 255.
73. *Id.*
74. *See* THE OSAMA BIN LADEN I KNOW, *supra* note 11, at 24; FROM MUHAMMAD TO BIN LADEN, *supra* note 14, at 256–8.
75. *See* FROM MUHAMMAD TO BIN LADEN, *supra* note 14, at 256.
76. *Id.* at 257.
77. *Id.* at 256.
78. *See* THE SECRET HISTORY OF AL QAEDA, *supra* note 37, at 43–4; AL QAEDA: PROFILE AND THREAT ASSESSMENT, *supra* note 66, at 1.
79. *See* THE OSAMA BIN LADEN I KNOW, *supra* note 11, at 63; FROM MUHAMMAD TO BIN LADEN, *supra* note 14, at 262.
80. *See* THE SECRET HISTORY OF AL QAEDA, *supra* note 37, at 43.
81. *See* STEVE COLL, GHOST WARS: THE SECRET HISTORY OF THE CIA, AFGHANISTAN, AND BIN LADEN, FROM THE SOVIET INVASION TO SEPTEMBER 10, 2001, at 156–7 (Penguin Books 2004) [hereinafter GHOST WARS].
82. *See* THE 9/11 COMMISSION REPORT, *supra* note 2, at 56; *see also* GHOST WARS, *supra* note 81, at 164; AL QAEDA: PROFILE AND THREAT ASSESSMENT, *supra* note 66, at 2.
83. AL QAEDA: PROFILE AND THREAT ASSESSMENT, *supra* note 66, at 2.
84. *See* THE 9/11 COMMISSION REPORT, *supra* note 2, at 55.
85. *Id.* at 55–6; FROM MUHAMMAD TO BIN LADEN, *supra* note 14, at 260–61. Bin Laden also reportedly used some of his personal funds to finance the Afghan mujahedeen. From approximately 1970 through 1994, when his citizenship was revoked by the Saudi government, bin Laden received about $1 million per year through a personal inheritance. THE 9/11 COMMISSION REPORT, *supra* note 2, at 170; FROM MUHAMMAD TO BIN LADEN, *supra* note 14, at 260.
86. GHOST WARS, *supra* note 81, at 155.
87. *See* STATEMENTS OF OSAMA BIN LADEN, *supra* note 12, at 76–7.
88. *See* THE SECRET HISTORY OF AL QAEDA, *supra* note 37, at 44; GHOST WARS, *supra* note 81, at 157; THE OSAMA BIN LADEN I KNOW, *supra* note 11, at 49–51.
89. *See* THE OSAMA BIN LADEN I KNOW, *supra* note 11, at 66–7; FROM MUHAMMAD TO BIN LADEN, *supra* note 14, at 282 (Ayman al-Zawahiri graduated from Cairo University with a degree in medicine in 1974, and earned a Master's degree in surgery from Cairo University in 1978).
90. FROM MUHAMMAD TO BIN LADEN, *supra* note 14, at 282.

91. *See* AL QAEDA: PROFILE AND THREAT ASSESSMENT, *supra* note 66, at 2.
92. *See* GHOST WARS, *supra* note 81, at 154; THE OSAMA BIN LADEN I KNOW, *supra* note 11, at 66–7; FROM MUHAMMAD TO BIN LADEN, *supra* note 14, at 283.
93. *See* GHOST WARS, *supra* note 81, at 163.
94. In the early 1990s, al-Zawahiri reportedly made two visits to the United States to raise funds for the Egyptian Islamic Jihad. *See* United States v. Ali Mohamed, Transcript of Guilty Plea, S(7) 98 Cr. 1023 (LBS) (Oct. 20, 2000) (transcript of entry to guilty plea to various terrorism-related charges).
95. *See* AL QAEDA: PROFILE AND THREAT ASSESSMENT, *supra* note 66, at 2 (estimating that the size of the network was between 10,000 and 20,000 volunteers).
96. *Id.; see also* THE 9/11 COMMISSION REPORT, *supra* note 2, at 56–8.
97. JASON BURKE, AL-QAEDA: CASTING A SHADOW OF TERROR 79 (London & New York: I.B. Tauris 2003) [hereinafter CASTING A SHADOW OF TERROR].
98. *See* GHOST WARS, *supra* note 81, at 203; THE OSAMA BIN LADEN I KNOW, *supra* note 11, at 74.
99. *See* GHOST WARS, *supra* note 81, at 203; THE OSAMA BIN LADEN I KNOW, *supra* note 11, at 74.
100. *See* GHOST WARS, *supra* note 81, at 203.
101. FROM MUHAMMAD TO BIN LADEN, *supra* note 14, at 257 (emphasis omitted).
102. THE 9/11 COMMISSION REPORT, *supra* note 2, at 56.
103. *See* THE OSAMA BIN LADEN I KNOW, *supra* note 11, at 74.
104. THE 9/11 COMMISSION REPORT, *supra* note 2, at 56.
105. FROM MUHAMMAD TO BIN LADEN, *supra* note 14, at 257.
106. CASTING A SHADOW OF TERROR, *supra* note 97, at 36.
107. *Id.*; *see also* FROM MUHAMMAD TO BIN LADEN, *supra* note 14, at 258. Bin Laden often references al Qaeda as a 'vanguard.' On October 7, 2001, he specifically referred to the September 11th hijackers as 'vanguards of Islam' 'rendered successful' by Islam. Osama bin Laden, *Bin Laden's Warning*, full text, BBC ONLINE, Oct. 7, 2001.
108. THE 9/11 COMMISSION REPORT, *supra* note 2, at 56; THE OSAMA BIN LADEN I KNOW, *supra* note 11, at 95–6.
109. *See* AL QAEDA: PROFILE AND THREAT ASSESSMENT, *supra* note 66, at 3; GHOST WARS, *supra* note 81, at 204.
110. *See* FROM MUHAMMAD TO BIN LADEN, *supra* note 14, at 258.
111. *See* BIN LADEN'S OWN WORDS, *supra* note 13, at xli.
112. *See* AL QAEDA: PROFILE AND THREAT ASSESSMENT, *supra* note 66, at 3; GHOST WARS, *supra* note 81, at 222.
113. *See* GHOST WARS, *supra* note 81, at 222; THE SECRET HISTORY OF AL QAEDA, *supra* note 37, at 45; BIN LADEN'S OWN WORDS, *supra* note 13, at xli; THE OSAMA BIN LADEN I KNOW, *supra* note 11, at 112–13.
114. *See* GHOST WARS, *supra* note 81, at 222.
115. *Id.*; *see also* THE 9/11 COMMISSION REPORT, *supra* note 2, at 57.
116. *See* GHOST WARS, *supra* note 81, at 229.
117. *See* THE 9/11 COMMISSION REPORT, *supra* note 2, at 57.
118. *Id.* at 57, 63.
119. *See id. at* 57; BIN LADEN'S OWN WORDS, *supra* note 13, at xlv. From 1970 to 1994, bin Laden reportedly received $1 million per year from his inheritance, which was cut off when his assets were frozen by the Saudi government. Consequently, bin Laden's personal assets are not believed to be a source of funding for al Qaeda. *See* THE 9/11 COMMISSION REPORT, *supra* note 2, at 169–70; *see also* GHOST WARS, *supra* note 81, at 270. The Saudis froze approximately $200 million in bin Laden's bank account. *See* THE OSAMA BIN LADEN I KNOW, *supra* note 11, at 151.
120. *See* THE SECRET HISTORY OF AL QAEDA, *supra* note 37, at 47–51; BIN LADEN'S OWN WORDS, *supra* note 13, at xliv; THE 9/11 COMMISSION REPORT, *supra* note 2, at 57, 63.
121. *See* THE SECRET HISTORY OF AL QAEDA, *supra* note 37, at 47.
122. *See* THE 9/11 COMMISSION REPORT, *supra* note 2, at 58.

123. *Id.* at 57; THE SECRET HISTORY OF AL QAEDA, *supra* note 37, at 48; BIN LADEN'S OWN WORDS, *supra* note 13, at xlii; THE OSAMA BIN LADEN I KNOW, *supra* note 11, at 122.
124. *See* THE 9/11 COMMISSION REPORT, *supra* note 2, at 57; THE SECRET HISTORY OF AL QAEDA, *supra* note 37, at 47.
125. *See* THE 9/11 COMMISSION REPORT, *supra* note 2, at 57; THE SECRET HISTORY OF AL QAEDA, *supra* note 37, at 47; BIN LADEN'S OWN WORDS, *supra* note 13, at xliii; FROM MUHAMMAD TO BIN LADEN, *supra* note 14, at 264.
126. *See* GHOST WARS, *supra* note 81, at 268; THE OSAMA BIN LADEN I KNOW, *supra* note 11, at 121.
127. *See* THE SECRET HISTORY OF AL QAEDA, *supra* note 37, at 47; THE OSAMA BIN LADEN I KNOW, *supra* note 11, at 126–7.
128. *See* THE OSAMA BIN LADEN I KNOW, *supra* note 11, at 126–7.
129. *See* GHOST WARS, *supra* note 81, at 269; *see also* CASTING A SHADOW OF TERROR, *supra* note 97, at 132–3; BIN LADEN'S OWN WORDS, *supra* note 13, at xliii (Bin Laden 'established legitimate businesses, including a tannery, two large farms, and a major road construction company'); FROM MUHAMMAD TO BIN LADEN, *supra* note 14, at 264 (bin Laden invested $50 million in the al-Shamal Islamic Bank in Khartoum).
130. *See* THE SECRET HISTORY OF AL QAEDA, *supra* note 37, at 47.
131. *See* AL QAEDA: PROFILE AND THREAT ASSESSMENT, *supra* note 66, at 3; FROM MUHAMMAD TO BIN LADEN, *supra* note 14, at 264.
132. *See* AL QAEDA: PROFILE AND THREAT ASSESSMENT, *supra* note 66, at 3; HOLY WAR, INC., *supra* note 47, at 221.
133. *See* United States v. Ali Mohamed, S(7) 98 Cr. 1023 (LBS) (S.D.N.Y., Oct. 20, 2000) (transcript of entry of guilty plea to various terrorism-related charges).
134. *See* AL QAEDA: PROFILE AND THREAT ASSESSMENT, *supra* note 66, at 3; CASTING A SHADOW OF TERROR, *supra* note 97, at 133.
135. *See* CASTING A SHADOW OF TERROR, *supra* note 97, at 133.
136. *See* THE 9/11 COMMISSION REPORT, *supra* note 2, at 60.
137. *See* United States v. Usama Bin Laden, et al., Indictment, S(2) 98 Cr. 1023 (LBS) (S.D.N.Y. Nov. 4, 1998).
138. *See* THE SECRET HISTORY OF AL QAEDA, *supra* note 37, at 48–9; BIN LADEN'S OWN WORDS, *supra* note 13, at xliv; THE OSAMA BIN LADEN I KNOW, *supra* note 11, at 138 ('Al Qaeda viewed the entry of the Americans into Somalia not as a move that is meant to save the Somalis from [famine], but to control Somalia and then spread U.S. hegemony over the region.'); *see also* United States v. Usama Bin Laden, et al., Indictment, S(2) 98 Cr. 1023 (LBS) (Nov. 4, 1998) (criminal indictment alleging that persons trained by al Qaeda participated in an attack on U.S. military personnel serving in Somalia as part of Operation Restore Hope, which resulted in the killing of 18 U.S. Army soldiers).
139. *See* THE SECRET HISTORY OF AL QAEDA, *supra* note 37, at 48–9.
140. *See* THE 9/11 COMMISSION REPORT, *supra* note 2, at 58.
141. *Id.*
142. *Id.*
143. *Id.* at 61; *see also* THE SECRET HISTORY OF AL QAEDA, *supra* note 37, at 48.
144. GHOST WARS, *supra* note 81, at 278–9.
145. *Id.* at 272.
146. The U.S. had apparently been concerned about Sudan's support of terrorism for some time. In 1993, Sudan had been placed on the U.S. State Department's list of countries supporting terrorism. RAPHAEL F. PERLE, TERRORISM, THE FUTURE, AND U.S. FOREIGN POLICY, CRS REPORT FOR CONGRESS (Sept. 13, 2001).
147. THE 9/11 COMMISSION REPORT, *supra* note 2, at 62; *see also* GHOST WARS, *supra* note 81, at 276; THE OSAMA BIN LADEN I KNOW, *supra* note 11, at 128; FROM MUHAMMAD TO BIN LADEN, *supra* note 14, at 265.
148. *See* FROM MUHAMMAD TO BIN LADEN, *supra* note 14, at 265.
149. *See* THE 9/11 COMMISSION REPORT, *supra* note 2, at 62.
150. *See* GHOST WARS, *supra* note 81, at 322–5.
151. *Id.* at 325.

152. *See* THE 9/11 COMMISSION REPORT, *supra* note 2, at 63.
153. *See* THE SECRET HISTORY OF AL QAEDA, *supra* note 37, at 50–51.
154. *Id.* at 81; *see also* BIN LADEN'S OWN WORDS, *supra* note 13, at xlv.
155. *See* GHOST WARS, *supra* note 81, at 325; THE SECRET HISTORY OF AL QAEDA, *supra* note 37, at 81; THE 9/11 COMMISSION REPORT, *supra* note 2, at 63. Bin Laden's warm reception was payment in part for his efforts and support of the Afghan warriors during the anti-Soviet jihad. *See* THE OSAMA BIN LADEN I KNOW, *supra* note 11, at 159.
156. GHOST WARS, *supra* note 81, at 283; THE SECRET HISTORY OF AL QAEDA, *supra* note 37, at 81; AHMED RASHID, TALIBAN: MILITANT ISLAM, OIL AND FUNDAMENTALISM IN CENTRAL ASIA 22 (Yale NB 2001) (a *talib* is an Islamic student) [hereinafter TALIBAN].
157. *See* GHOST WARS, *supra* note 81, at 328.
158. *See id.* at 349; THE SECRET HISTORY OF AL QAEDA, *supra* note 37, at 81; TALIBAN, *supra* note 156, at 22.
159. *See* GHOST WARS, *supra* note 81, at 334; HOLY WAR, INC., *supra* note 47, at 158; TALIBAN, *supra* note 156, at 2.
160. HOLY WAR, INC., *supra* note 47, at 155.
161. *Id.* at 159.
162. *See* THE OSAMA BIN LADEN I KNOW, *supra* note 11, at 163.
163. *See* TALIBAN, *supra* note 156, at 2.
164. *See* GHOST WARS, *supra* note 81, at 334.
165. *Id.*; *see also* HOLY WAR, INC., *supra* note 47, at 158.
166. HOLY WAR, INC., *supra* note 47, at 159.
167. *See id.* at 158.
168. *See* GHOST WARS, *supra* note 81, at 334.
169. *See* HOLY WAR, INC., *supra* note 47, at 163.
170. *See* GHOST WARS, *supra* note 81, at 283.
171. *Id.* at 328.
172. *See* THE SECRET HISTORY OF AL QAEDA, *supra* note 37, at 81.
173. *Id.* at 332; *see* HOLY WAR, INC., *supra* note 47, at 165; AL QAEDA: PROFILE AND THREAT ASSESSMENT, *supra* note 66, at 3.
174. *See* GHOST WARS, *supra* note 81, at 343, 407; HOLY WAR, INC., *supra* note 47, at 165; THE OSAMA BIN LADEN I KNOW, *supra* note 11, at 161.
175. *See* HOLY WAR, INC., *supra* note 47, at 165.
176. *See* GHOST WARS, *supra* note 81, at 342.
177. *Id.* at 554.
178. *See* THE 9/11 COMMISSION REPORT, *supra* note 2, at 171.
179. THE SECRET HISTORY OF AL QAEDA, *supra* note 37, at 80; *see also* THE OSAMA BIN LADEN I KNOW, *supra* note 11, at 161.
180. *See* THE 9/11 COMMISSION REPORT, *supra* note 2, at 67.
181. *Id.* at 67.
182. *See* GHOST WARS, *supra* note 81, at 474.
183. Press Release, U.S. Dep't of Treasury, Treasury Department Statement Regarding the Designation of Ansar al-Islam (Feb. 20, 2003), *available at* http://www.ustreas.gov/press/releases/js 48.htm.
184. *Id.*
185. *Id.*
186. THE 9/11 COMMISSION REPORT, *supra* note 2, at 67.
187. THE OSAMA BIN LADEN I KNOW, *supra* note 11, at 161.
188. *See* Osama bin Laden, 'A Declaration of War Against the Americans Occupying the Land of the Two Holy Places,' *reprinted in full in* BIN LADEN'S OWN WORDS, *supra* note 13, at 32–59. The 'Two Holy Places' refers to the holy mosques in Mecca and Medina.
189. *Id.* at 33.
190. *Id.* at 55.

191. *Id.* at 50–51.
192. *See* GHOST WARS, *supra* note 81, at 332; DANIEL BENJAMIN & STEVEN SIMON, THE AGE OF SACRED TERROR 134 (Random House 2002) [hereinafter BENJAMIN & SIMON].
193. *See* BIN LADEN'S OWN WORDS, *supra* note 13, at 60–63, reprinted in full.
194. *Id.* at 60. Ayman al-Zawahiri did not initially join bin Laden when he returned to Afghanistan. Instead, al-Zawahiri traveled to Chechnya to start his independent branch of the Egyptian Islamic Jihad. The manifesto al-Zawahiri jointly published with bin Laden on February 23, 1998, 'marked the public rebirth of their partnership.' GHOST WARS, *supra* note 81, at 382.
195. BIN LADEN'S OWN WORDS, *supra* note 13, at 61–2.
196. Bin Laden elaborated on the theme of waging a 'defensive jihad' in a media interview. He declared: '[D]efensive *jihad* against the US does not stop with its withdrawal from the Arabian peninsula; rather, it must desist from aggressive intervention against Muslims throughout the whole world.' STATEMENTS OF OSAMA BIN LADEN, *supra* note 12, at 48. He went on to say in a subsequent interview that 'America won't be able to leave this ordeal unless it pulls out of the Arabian peninsula, and it ceases its meddling in Palestine and throughout the Islamic world.' *Id.* at 127.
197. *See* BIN LADEN'S OWN WORDS, *supra* note 13, at 61–2.
198. *Id.* at 62.
199. GHOST WARS, *supra* note 81, at 383; *see also* THE OSAMA BIN LADEN I KNOW, *supra* note 11, at 208 (discussing Sheikh Omar Abdel Rahman's fatwa which provided the religious legal authority to kill civilians).
200. BIN LADEN'S OWN WORDS, *supra* note 13, at 62.
201. *See* THE 9/11 COMMISSION REPORT, *supra* note 2, at 67.
202. *Id.* at 69; *see also* FROM MUHAMMAD TO BIN LADEN, *supra* note 14, at 265 (discussing bin Laden's role in the American embassy attacks).
203. THE 9/11 COMMISSION REPORT, *supra* note 2, at 70; *see also* GHOST WARS, *supra* note 81, at 403.
204. THE 9/11 COMMISSION REPORT, *supra* note 2, at 70; *see also* United States v. Usama bin Laden, et al., Indictment, S(2) 98 Ct. 1023 (LBS) (S.D.N.Y. Nov. 4, 1998) (federal indictment charging bin Laden with U.S. embassy bombings in Africa).
205. *See* THE 9/11 COMMISSION REPORT, *supra* note 2, at 70.
206. *Id.*
207. *See* GHOST WARS, *supra* note 81, at 404; THE 9/11 COMMISSION REPORT, *supra* note 2, at 70.
208. GHOST WARS, *supra* note 81, at 404.
209. On November 4, 1998, Osama bin Laden, Muhammad Atef, Wadih el Hage, Fazul Abdullah Mohammed, Mohamed Sadeek Odeh, and Mohamed Rashed Daoud al-'Owhali were charged in a 238-count indictment filed in the U.S. District Court for the Southern District of New York for the August 7, 1998, bombings of the U.S. embassies in Nairobi, Kenya, and Dar es Salaam, Tanzania. *See* United States v. Usama Bin Laden, et al., S(2) 93 Cr. 1023 (LBS) (S.D.N.Y.). Mohamed al-'Owhali and Mohamed Sadiq Odeh were prosecuted and convicted in federal district court for their involvement in the U.S. embassy bombings in Africa. Both men were subsequently sentenced to life in prison without possibility of parole. *See* THE OSAMA BIN LADEN I KNOW, *supra* note 11, at 220–21. Ali Mohamed was subsequently indicted for his involvement in the African embassy bombings. On October 20, 2000, Ali Mohamed entered a guilty plea to five counts charging conspiracy to kill nationals of the United States, in violation of 18 U.S.C. §2332(b); conspiracy to murder, kidnap and maim in places outside the United States, in violation of 18 U.S.C. §§956(a)(1) and 956(a)(2); conspiracy to murder, in violation of 18 U.S.C. §1117; conspiracy to destroy buildings and property of the United States, in violation of 18 U.S.C. §844(n); and conspiracy to destroy national-defense utilities of the United States, in violation of 18 U.S.C. §2155, related to the African bombings. *See* United States v. Ali Mohamed, Transcript of Guilty Plea, S(7) 98 Cr. 1023 (LBS) (S.D.N.Y.) (Oct. 20, 2000).
210. Osama bin Laden, Interview with Rahimullah Yusufzai, ABC News (1999).

211. *See* THE 9/11 COMMISSION REPORT, *supra* note 2, at 190; *see also* GHOST WARS, *supra* note 81, at 537.
212. THE 9/11 COMMISSION REPORT, *supra* note 2, at 190; *see also* GHOST WARS, *supra* note 81, at 537.
213. *See* GHOST WARS, *supra* note 81, at 537.
214. *Id.* at 538.
215. FATF Terrorist Financing, *supra* note 3, at 7.
216. *Id.*
217. *See* THE 9/11 COMMISSION REPORT, *supra* note 2, at 171.
218. *See* Osama bin Laden, 'Statement to America,' Oct. 26, 2002 ('And we have the right to kill the civilians of whoever has killed our civilians.').
219. On the fifth anniversary of the September 11 attacks, Osama bin Laden's deputy, Ayman al-Zawahiri, warned that Persian Gulf countries and Israel would be al Qaeda's next targets. He also advocated expelling American troops from the Arabian peninsula, including Iraq. *See Al-Zawahiri: Gulf, Israel Next Targets*, N.Y. TIMES. Sept. 11, 2006; *see also* Letter from al-Zawahiri to Abu Musab al-Zarqawi (July 9, 2005) (setting forth al Qaeda's goals and objectives).

3. Al Qaeda's call to jihad

> [J]ihad is an individual duty when an enemy attacks Muslim countries . . . To kill the Americans and their allies – civilians and military – is an individual duty incumbent upon every Muslim in all countries . . . so that their armies leave all the territory of Islam, defeated, broken, and unable to threaten any Muslim.
>
> Osama bin Laden[1]

The global fight against al Qaeda has been characterized as 'the defining conflict of the early 21st century.'[2] Some observers describe al Qaeda's 'holy war' against America and its allies as representing an 'existential struggle' against non-Islamic societies and values;[3] others, including Osama bin Laden himself, have said it reflects a 'clash of civilizations.'[4] Whatever description is most appropriate, it is clear that al Qaeda is waging a global campaign of terror unfettered by nationality, ethnicity, age, race, or gender. Its operations have targeted thousands of people, military and civilian, in deadly attacks around the world. 'Killing and dying for Allah are viewed as the highest form of sacrifice.'[5] All targets are considered legitimate if seen to be in opposition to al Qaeda's fundamentalist interpretation of Islam. This ideology further rejects compromise, embraces martyrdom and demands complete victory.[6] Effectively, bin Laden's message is this: you are either a believer or a non-believer, a righteous Muslim or an infidel.[7] With this message, bin Laden has inspired a movement that is intent on targeting the 'non-believing' world in the name of Islam.[8]

Al Qaeda is not simply a politically motivated terrorist organization with operational cells scattered throughout worldwide Muslim populations.[9] At its core, it is the standard bearer of a movement designed to ignite a global Islamic uprising. '[B]in Laden is promoting (and at times directing) a "worldwide, religiously inspired, and professionally guided Islamist insurgency." '[10] The network advancing this global insurgency has the will, financial resources, history of violence and access to lethal weapons that causes it to be a serious threat not only to the United States, but the international community. According to one source,

> [w]hat makes [bin Laden] and the Apocalyptic Global Jihad Groups a lethal threat to the Free World's national security is the combination of wealth; fanatical motivational religious ideology; and the command over radical Islamic

> highly ambitious militants, bound up with deep belief in the cause and hideous hatred of the West, of modernity and of all democratic liberal values.[11]

Understanding the motivation and ultimate objectives of this radical Islamist movement is essential to developing and implementing an effective strategy to defeat it, including a comprehensive plan to dismantle its financial infrastructure.

AL QAEDA'S IDEOLOGY: THE RISE OF MODERN JIHADIST-SALAFISM

The ideology of al Qaeda has been described as jihadist-salafism, a movement based on 'a profound "respect for the sacred texts in their most literal form [combined with] an absolute commitment to jihad." '[12] Salafists believe in using violence as a means of establishing a global Islamic state under the control of Muslims and governed by the teachings of the Prophet Muhammad.[13] Osama bin Laden has been the chief spokesperson for the ideology that drives al Qaeda and its network of terror. Al Qaeda's version of jihadist-salafism demands strict adherence to a literal interpretation of the Qur'an and rejects reliance on any other sources for guidance on religious, social, and political issues.[14] This ideology also demands complete dedication to warfare against its enemies, with only victory or martyrdom as acceptable results. Al Qaeda preaches that '[j]ihad is every Muslim's obligation.'[15] For those jihadists inspired by the al Qaeda ideology, any means necessary for accomplishing its ends in the name of Islam are justified. Thus, suicide bombings, torture, beheadings, and the killing of civilians and fellow Muslims are acceptable methods of defending the Islamic faith.[16] And although al Qaeda is a relatively new entity to militant Islamism, its ideology reflects strains of Islamic religious, social and political thought that have been espoused by extreme elements of the Muslim community for centuries.

Taqi al-Din ibn Taymiyya (1262–1328)

The most important theoretical predecessor of the contemporary Islamism that informs al Qaeda's ideology is Taqi al-Din ibn Taymiyya, whom bin Laden frequently references and quotes in his public statements and media interviews.[17] Ibn Taymiyya, the spiritual father of modern radical, revolutionary Islam, was based mainly in Damascus.[18] He lived and wrote during the period of the Mongol invasions and European–Crusader presence in the late 13th and early 14th centuries.[19] The arrival of the Mongols ended the unifying influence of the caliph in Baghdad and ushered in a period of change in the Muslim world.[20] Ibn Taymiyya believed that the 'weakness that had allowed the defeat was a result of the failure of the Muslim community, or *umma*, to properly follow the injunctions of the early Holy texts.'[21] The Mongols, though converts to Islam, terrorized much of the region and practiced a form of Islam heavily influenced by traditional Mongol customs and religious practices. These practices disgusted ibn Taymiyya, who practiced a rigorous form of Muslim devotion that favored a strictly literal interpretation of the Qur'an.[22] His ideology did not separate religious practice from political and social life. Rather, 'church and state were inextricably linked in ibn Taymiyya's world view, with religion dominating and guiding the state through force and authority to the glory of God and the betterment of the individual believer.'[23]

Ibn Taymiyya had no tolerance for Arab leaders and clerics who he believed had abandoned the true practice of the faith. By forsaking strict adherence to the Qur'an and hadith, Arab regimes lacked the ability to defend the Islamic ummah[24] and restore it to its past glory under a unified caliphate.[25] Instead, their deviation from Islamic religious law, known as Sharia, made them apostates.[26] Ibn Taymiyya maintained that a professing Muslim who did not live by a strict interpretation of the Qur'an and hadith was a *kufr* or non-believer opposed to God and the ummah. He believed that it was the responsibility of all Muslims to resist invaders and also apostate rulers by violent means in the name of jihad or 'holy war.'[27] For him, '[an] apostate has to be killed in all circumstances.'[28] By portraying unorthodox Muslims as apostates, ibn Taymiyya was able to skirt the Sharia prohibition against internal warfare among Muslims in order to justify his call for jihad.[29]

For ibn Taymiyya, jihad was as important to the devotion of each believer as the five pillars of Islam.[30] Traditionally, Islamic jurists understood jihad as an obligation of the community rather than the individual. In the event that Muslim rule was under physical attack, Islamic law required that the ummah wage 'defensive' jihad. This requirement concerned the community and the individual Muslim did not have to fight as long as others carried the banner of jihad.[31] Ibn Taymiyya, however, considered jihad an individual duty; failure to participate was a sin that indicated failure to live by the faith. 'Jihad against the unbelievers (*kufr*) is compulsory, since they are the enemies of Allah and his messenger.'[32] Failure to wage jihad forfeited the ruler's right to govern and demanded he be overthrown by the ummah.[33]

Some commentators maintain that by asserting that '*jihad* against apostates within the realm of Islam is justified, by turning jihad inward . . ., [ibn Taymiyya] plant[ed] the seed of revolutionary violence in the heart of

Islamic thought.'[34] It is certainly true that ibn Taymiyya's teachings heavily influence al Qaeda's ideology. Bin Laden frequently draws upon ibn Taymiyya in his calls for jihad, as he did in his 1996 manifesto *Declaration of War Against the Americans Occupying the Land of the Two Holy Places.* There, bin Laden quoted ibn Taymiyya in support of his call to all Muslims to conduct jihad against the West and 'corrupt' Middle Eastern governments:

> As Ibn Taymiya stated, fighting in defense of Belief is a collective duty; and there is no duty after Belief other than fighting the enemy who is corrupting life and The Religion. . . . Ibn Taymiya then stated that the ultimate aim is to please God, raise His Word, institute His Religion, obey His Messenger and fight the enemy in every respect.[35]

The message advanced by ibn Taymiyya and echoed today by bin Laden is one motivated by religious belief. Essentially, it is the sacred duty of all Muslims to wage war against their secular leaders and non-Muslim enemies around the world.[36]

Muhammad ibn Abd al-Wahhab (1703–92)

Muhammad ibn Abd al-Wahhab, a militant Islamic preacher and founder of Wahhabism, revived ibn Taymiyya's teachings. Al-Wahhab embraced a radical, fundamentalist interpretation of Islam. He believed that Allah's message as transmitted to Muhammad had become obscured over time and called for a strict interpretation of Islam that returned to its sources.[37] He preached that 'all Muslims must rigorously observe all the laws of Islam if a true and just Islamic society was to become a reality.'[38] Al-Wahhab was particularly incensed by intercessionary practices such as the use of shrines and prayer addressed to God by means of the Prophet or saints, which he believed constituted shirk, or polytheism.[39] Al-Wahhab denounced the traditional praise and celebration of the Prophet Muhammad, comparing it to the Christian worship of Jesus. Christian belief in the divinity of Jesus, rejected by Muslims, was viewed by al-Wahhab as denying monotheism and returning to the belief in many gods.[40] Al-Wahhab also condemned dancing, wearing jewelry and playing music, because such practices distracted from religious prayer and worship.[41] He burned many books, arguing that the Qur'an was the ultimate source of knowledge and salvation. Muslims unwilling to accept his views were branded idolaters and apostates, who had fallen into unbelief, and if they did not change their ways they should be killed.[42] Shi'as and Sufis that al-Wahhab judged unorthodox were to be exterminated and their property confiscated, and all other faiths were to be destroyed.[43] Like ibn Taymiyya, al-Wahhab emphasized the importance of jihad in Islam. He 'extolled the need for armed jihad against all infidels and classified not only Jews and Christians as infidels, but also those Muslims who did not subscribe to Wahhabi beliefs.'[44] He believed that fighting in God's cause should be elevated to a sixth pillar of Islam.[45] Al-Wahhab preached that jihad was the duty of every Muslim, and any Muslim who evaded this duty was a hypocrite and should be killed.[46] To the Wahhabis, death in the cause of jihad would gain them entry to heaven as martyrs.[47]

Al-Wahhab's campaign to reform Islam evoked strong opposition in his birthplace of Najd. In 1744, al-Wahhab took refuge in the village of Dariyah, in a district ruled by Muhammad ibn Saud, leader of the al-Saud clan.[48] In 1747, al-Wahhab and al-Saud formed an alliance based on a power-sharing agreement with the former serving as religious leader and the latter as political ruler.[49] They contracted marriage to cement their alliance and agreed that power should be inherited exclusively by their descendants.[50] The Wahhab–Saud alliance extended its influence into other parts of the Middle East, launching raids into Syria, Iraq, and Kuwait. By 1788, the Wahhabis had managed to control much of the Saudi Arabian Peninsula.[51] However, their domination of the Middle East was short-lived. In 1818, the Ottoman army invaded and destroyed the Wahhabi capital of Dariyah, defeating the Wahhabis.[52] Over the next century, the Wahhabis made repeated attempts to regain control of the Arabian Peninsula, but were repelled by the Ottomans.[53]

When the House of Saud assumed the leadership of Arabia in 1926, Wahhabism was declared to be the dominant creed of the renamed Kingdom of Saudi Arabia.[54] To this day, a *quid pro quo* exists between Wahhabis and the House of Saud in Saudi Arabia: '[T]he Sauds take care of the politics and the Wahhabi clerics take care of the religion.'[55]

The Muslim Brotherhood

Hassan al-Banna (1906–49)

Ibn Taymiyya's and Abd al-Wahhab's ideas were an important component of the jihadist resurgence that began in the early 20th century, as Ottoman hegemony in the Middle East faded and Western influence increased. Out of this resurgence of revolutionary sentiment and jihadist ideology came the Muslim Brotherhood, a radical social and religious reform organization founded by Hassan al-Banna in Egypt in 1928.[56] The Muslim Brotherhood grew in influence at the same time that secular nationalist and socialist movements began to call for reform in Egypt. These reformers all shared a dislike for British colonial rule and were angered by the poverty and stagnant growth that plagued the country. However, unlike the other reform-minded groups, the Brotherhood proposed a religious solution to the social and economic malaise confronting the country. Their credo reflected the organization's religious focus: 'The Prophet is our leader; *Qur'an* is our law; *jihad* is our way; dying in the way of Allah is our highest hope.'[57] According to al-Banna, the inequity and social injustice faced by the Muslim community were the result of the failure of Muslims to follow the 'straight path' of Islam.[58]

Al-Banna's political and ideological objectives can be summarized as follows:

> (a) to oppose the ascendancy of secular and Western ideas in the Middle East in general and Egypt in particular; . . . (b) the rejection of Western influences means the return to pure Islam (*salaf*), to the precepts revealed by Muhammad during his life and deeds at Mecca and Medina, as the only solution to all the ills that had befallen Muslim societies; (c) rejection of extreme Islamic mysticism (*Sufism*), and all other tendencies and traditions that exist in the Muslim's daily life and are against Islamic teaching and tenets; (d) the moral reform of the individual as a precondition to the Islamization of society, by establishing a government that ruled on the basis of Muslim values and norms.[59]

Al-Banna hoped that the Muslim Brotherhood would inspire a political movement among the Muslim community that would culminate in a newly formed state true to orthodox Islam.

By 1948, the Muslim Brotherhood had dramatically grown in size in Egypt and had branches in 70 countries throughout the Middle East and beyond.[60] At the same time, the organization had become increasingly more violent, establishing a military wing. The Brotherhood began attacking British and Jewish businesses in an effort to accelerate Britain's withdrawal from Egypt and to protest Jewish settlement in Palestine. The group also targeted the Egyptian government, assassinating several government officials, including Egyptian Prime Minister Mahmud Fahmi Nukrashi on December 28, 1948.[61] In 1949, the Egyptian secret police responded to the Brotherhood's violent tactics through a tough crackdown that culminated in the assassination of al-Banna when he was only 43 years old.[62]

Sayyid Qutb (1906–66)

Though the suppression of the Muslim Brotherhood and the death of al-Banna frustrated some of the plans of the organization, the spirit and ideology of the movement had already become entrenched among some Muslim intellectual circles. One of the most important and influential scholars to adopt and advance the Brotherhood's cause was Sayyid Qutb. Qutb is regarded as 'the religious father of the Apocalyptic Global Jihad

Groups, the figure who has most influenced al-Qa'idah leadership's ideology, and the homicide bombings.'[63] While al-Banna was a 'political Islamist' who looked to appropriate the apparatus of the state to implement his political and social goals, Qutb, a radical Sunni Islamist, preferred a more violent and radical course. After having spent three years studying in America, Qutb joined the Muslim Brotherhood in 1951.[64] He returned from the United States convinced that Western society was decadent, sexually depraved and materialistic.[65] Qutb was appalled by what he considered a society infused with immorality and excessive materialism. He called American life 'primitive' and believed its values represented the antithesis of the moral code of virtue available through adherence to Islam.[66]

In 1954, the Muslim Brotherhood was banned in Egypt and Qutb, who had become one of the group's most outspoken members, was imprisoned for his anti-government activities.[67] While incarcerated, he authored his most influential work, *Milestones*, which has been characterized as 'political Islam's Communist Manifesto.'[68] Qutb believed that the Muslim world had become plagued by the problems of poverty, tyranny, immorality, and ignorance, a condition he called *jahiliyya*, the religious term for the period of ignorance prior to the revelations given to the Prophet Mohammed.[69] In *Milestones*, he wrote:

> [T]he Muslim community must be restored to its original form . . . [It is] buried under the debris of the man-made traditions of several generations, and . . . is crushed under the weight of those false laws and customs that are not . . . related to Islamic teachings.[70]

According to Qutb, the reason for Islam's decline was corruption of the Qur'an by the secular governments in the Middle East. His writings advanced certain core principles concerning governance: that 'the oneness and sovereignty of God preclude human rule, which should be violently overturned if necessary; [and] that the only legitimate form of government over Muslims is an Islamic state headed by a caliph.'[71] Much like ibn Taymiyya before him, Qutb maintained that Muslim political leaders who did not strive to live according to the teachings of Islam were *kufr*, unbelievers and hypocrites, and should be deposed. Arab governments, whether democratic, monarchical, or socialist, were based on man-made law and thus incompatible with and contrary to Islam. Because of their apostasy, such governments were the legitimate targets of jihad. Assassination of political leaders was justified as 'one stage in the destruction of the political regimes,' and he declared that 'a society whose legislation does not rest on divine law (Shari'at Allah) is not Muslim.'[72] Qutb called for a 'full revolt against human rulership in all its shapes and forms, systems and arrangements.'[73] There was no middle ground in what Qutb conceived as a struggle between God and Satan.

This was a sweeping call for all Muslims to take up arms in the fight. The righteous purpose of all true Muslims was to destroy the kingdom of man and establish one ruled by Allah. Any Muslim who failed to heed the call to jihad was just one more non-believer worthy of destruction.[74]

In 1954, the Muslim Brotherhood was banned and Qutb was arrested for an attempt to assassinate President Gamal Abdul Nasser.[75] He was released from prison in 1964, and re-arrested in 1965 for plotting to overthrow the government and assassinate public figures.[76] The trial of Qutb and 42 of his followers lasted approximately three months.[77] Qutb was subsequently found guilty of attempting to overthrow the Egyptian government and sentenced to death. He was hanged on August 29, 1966.[78]

Bin Laden's Jihadist Ideology

The Muslim Brotherhood has been extremely influential on bin Laden and the development of al Qaeda's ideology. Prior to joining the anti-Soviet jihad in Afghanistan, bin Laden attended the Management and Economics School at King Abdul Aziz University in Jeddah. He took courses in Islamic studies taught by conservative Islamic scholars Abdullah Azzam and Muhhamed Qutb, the brother of Sayyid Qutb, which deeply influenced bin Laden's religious thinking and political views.[79] These views were further reinforced by his interaction with jihadists in Afghanistan. It was there that bin Laden solidified his dangerous ideology and created the network through which that ideology could be put into action.

It is important to recognize that bin Laden's world-view is set within a theological framework. God comes before all things, and men are called to order their lives according to God's law. This law demands strict adherence to a literalist interpretation of the Qur'an and the hadith. God reveals his truth through Sharia law, and any deviation from it makes the offender an enemy of God and the ummah. According to bin Laden, Sharia must control all aspects of life, including government and politics. Faithful Muslims must not tolerate governments, including democratic regimes, that deviate from Sharia law. Instead, righteous Muslims must overthrow moderate Arab governments in favor of protecting the ummah from the corruption, immorality and ignorance that comes with apostasy. These apostate governments are nothing less than enemies of Islam whose duplicity has fostered a decline in the greatness of Islam. For bin Laden, both the problem and solution are clear:

> [T]he rulers are incapable and treacherous, and . . . they have not followed the right path of Islam but followed their wishes and lusts – this is the reason for the setbacks in the [Islamic] nation's march during the past decades. Therefore, it is

> clear to us that the solution . . . lies in adhering to the religion of God, by which God granted us pride in the past centuries, and installing a strong and faithful leadership that applies the Qur'an among us and raises the true banner of *jihad*.[80]

Bin Laden's jihadist movement sees itself as the defender of the true Islamic faith and way of life. All aspects of life must conform to the jihadist view of Sharia. Compromise between Sharia and human systems such as democracy and socialism (and the laws and rights they create) is forbidden, for that would be compromising God's absolute truth. Instead, all Muslims must follow Sharia, and non-Muslims must not impede the dominance of Sharia law wherever Islam exists or spreads. Likewise, because the jihadist cause is the cause of God's truth, the righteousness of their cause justifies whatever actions jihadists take to advance God's law and defeat their enemies.

For bin Laden, there is an enemy even greater than the apostate Muslim governments. That enemy is the United States and the 'Zionist–Crusader' alliance it leads.[81] In bin Laden's view, the United States seeks the destruction of Islam and is responsible for all warfare involving Muslims around the world. Even in conflicts to which the United States is not an active party, such as those between Israel and Palestine, Russia and Chechen rebels, and India and Kashmiri Muslims, bin Laden accuses America of instigating the bloodshed as part of its campaign to destroy the Muslim ummah.[82] He further points to Kosovo and Bosnia-Herzegovina, where he claims that thousands of Muslims were murdered before the U.S. and Western powers intervened to stop the killing.[83] Bin Laden further condemns the United States for supporting Arab apostate governments that are derided by bin Laden as its agents.[84] To combat the Zionist–Crusader attack on the faith, bin Laden calls for a global defensive jihad against America and its allies.[85]

Bin Laden believes that only by eliminating the influences of American infidels throughout the Muslim world can a true Islamic state be established, restoring the greatness of Islam's golden age. Thus, all Muslims have a sacred duty to wage jihad against the United States by killing Americans, including civilians, anywhere in the world.[86] Moreover, the killing of American civilians may be perpetrated by any means, including by the use of weapons of mass destruction. In fact, bin Laden has declared: 'There is a duty on Muslims to acquire [weapons of mass destruction], and America knows today that Muslims are in possession of such a weapon, by the grace of God Almighty.'[87]

Despite bin Laden's rhetoric against the United States, al Qaeda's fight is not with specific countries or political systems. The United States is merely a figurehead of what bin Laden defines as a global conflict between the righteous Islamic community (which subscribes to his form of jihadist-salafism) and the world's unbelievers and apostates:

> The conflict is partly regional, but it is also a greater struggle between two camps: one camp is America, representing the global *Kufr* [non-believers] and accompanied by all of the apostates. The other camp is the *Ummah* [Islamic nation], headed by its *Mujahideen* [Islamic warriors] brigades.[88]

Any who oppose al Qaeda's interpretation of Islam and support the unbelievers are themselves apostates and enemies of God. In their minds, bin Laden and his followers are ultimately waging a war of religion that can only end with the triumph of the true faith.

AL QAEDA'S STRATEGIC OBJECTIVES

Al Qaeda represents a deadly threat not only to the United States but to the entire international community. In 1998, when asked about the objectives to which bin Laden and al Qaeda aspire, he provided the following response: 'This is our goal, to liberate the lands of Islam from unbelief and to apply the law of God Almighty in it until we meet Him and He is pleased with us.'[89] For bin Laden, the 'lands of Islam' are not confined to the Middle East. The leader of al Qaeda seeks 'to bring back all the historical lands conquered by Muslim dynasties, from the seventh century to the seventeenth century – from India to Spain.'[90] After having liberated all Arab-Muslim lands from the infidels and apostate rulers, bin Laden would impose strict Sharia law to bring about Allah's supreme reign.[91] Bin Laden's mission statement succinctly captures the jihadist-salafism ideology and suggests the 'strategic view of terror' held by the al Qaeda leader and his associates.[92] The tactical measures to achieve al Qaeda's strategic objectives include the infliction of 'inhuman terrorism against the Free World, headed by the United States and Israel, so as to move its public opinion and to bring the retreat of their military forces and civil presence from the Arab-Muslim lands'[93] Through the use of violence and extreme rhetoric, bin Laden provokes aggressive responses from his enemies that can then be used to ignite passions throughout the restive Muslim world in support of an extremist Islamist insurgency.[94] This insurgency will provide the power to 'liberate' Muslims from global unbelief and establish an Islamic state that will properly apply the law of God (as bin Laden interprets it) and restore the faith to its proper place of superiority.

Creating a Strict Islamic State

Al Qaeda's ultimate goal is to unify the world's 1.3 billion Muslims under a theocratic state governed by strict Sharia law.[95] Many jihadists regard the period of the ancient caliphates as the golden age of Islam, and they seek to restore the Muslim world to its former greatness by installing a new caliphate. Such a system would also ensure orthodox practice of the faith. In bin Laden's view, secular governments are incompatible with and even contrary to Islamic faith because they empower man-made legal systems rather than the 'law of God.'[96] Democracies are equally unacceptable to al Qaeda and considered an assault on God's right to rule. In January 2005, in an apparent effort to intimidate voters from participating in a nationwide election, terrorist leader Abu Musab al-Zarqawi released an audio-recorded statement declaring war on democracy in Iraq. He stated: 'We have declared a bitter war against the principle of democracy and all those who seek to enact it . . . . Those who vote . . . are infidels. And with God as my witness, I have informed them [of our intentions].'[97] Bin Laden has specifically characterized democracy as a rival 'religion' to Islam, and democratic principles such as freedom of speech and freedom of religion have been criticized as 'un-Islamic and tantamount to apostasy punishable by death.'[98]

Al Qaeda intends to establish a strict Islamic state in the 'heart of the Islamic world,' which, according to bin Laden's deputy Ayman al-Zawahiri, is located in Egypt, Iraq, Syria, and Palestine.[99] Al-Zawahiri has stated:

> It has always been my belief that the victory of Islam will never take place until a Muslim state is established in the manner of the Prophet in the heart of the Islamic world, specifically in the Levant, Egypt and the neighboring states of the Peninsula and Iraq; however, the center would be in the Levant and Egypt . . . . It is like a bird whose wings are Egypt and Syria and whose heart is Palestine.[100]

While the exact political contours of this type of strict Islamic government have not been well defined by bin Laden or other senior al Qaeda leaders, they have provided some clues. The only developed example of this type of system in modern times with which al Qaeda has been directly associated was the Taliban regime in Afghanistan from 1996 to 2001.[101] Like Afghanistan under the Taliban, al Qaeda's Islamic state would be motivated by the clear banner of Islam. This Islamic state would be governed by a shura council, or Sharia-based judiciary comprised of religious clerics that would be responsible for ensuring obedience to Sharia law.[102] Only laws and edicts consistent with Islamic law would be enforced, and conduct considered inconsistent with Islamic principles would be prohibited and punished.

Under the Taliban, Afghanistan welcomed jihadists from around the world and provided them sanctuary, training and support as the militants prepared to pursue their objectives elsewhere. A caliphate state envisioned by the likes of al Qaeda would provide similar support for jihad waged beyond its borders. As noted in the *9/11 Commission Report*, according to bin Laden, unless the United States and all other non-Muslim nations abandon the Middle East, convert to Islam, and end the immorality and godlessness of their society and culture, they will find themselves at war with the Islamic nation.[103] Enemies of non-Muslim governments would find an ally in the new caliphate. In essence, bin Laden's Islamist state would be the ultimate state sponsor of terrorism.

This type of Islamic state may be on the rise in Somalia. In June 2006, Islamic forces, unified under the title of the Islamic Courts Union, took power in Mogadishu and quickly established a strict system based on Sharia law.[104] International observers are concerned that under the leadership of the Islamists, who now call themselves the Conservative Council of Islamic Courts, Somalia will become a breeding ground for jihadi terrorists.[105] These fears were intensified when, within weeks of seizing Mogadishu, the Council of Islamic Courts appointed known terrorist supporter Hassan Dahir Aweys as its new leader.[106] Although the Islamic Courts claim that there is no al Qaeda presence in Somalia, the world community remains on guard for the proliferation of al Qaeda-inspired terrorist activity there. As one Islamist militia commander in Somalia declared, 'Al Qaeda's concept is right and one day they will rule.'[107]

Expelling the American 'Crusaders' from the Lands of Islam

The first step in al Qaeda's plan of achieving a united caliphate state is to expel Americans and their 'Zionist–Crusader alliance' from the lands of Islam. This goal was first articulated by bin Laden in his manifesto published in August 1996, entitled *A Declaration of Jihad Against the Americans Occupying the Land of the Two Holy Places.* At that time, bin Laden's focus was on expelling U.S. military forces stationed in Saudi Arabia following Iraq's invasion of Kuwait. Bin Laden believed that the occupation of Saudi Arabia by American forces was 'the greatest disaster to befall Muslims since the death of the Prophet Mohammed.'[108] In his view, the presence of the 'American Crusaders' desecrated the holy lands and brought shame to an Islamic nation that could not defend itself from the secular regime of Saddam Hussein.

Bin Laden has since revised and expanded this goal, mandating the expulsion of American influence not from Saudi Arabia alone but from the entire Islamic world.[109] Bin Laden has stated, '[I]n our religion it is our duty to make *jihad* . . . so that we drive the Americans away from *all* Muslim countries.'[110] He further vows that 'neither America nor anyone who lives there will enjoy safety until . . . all the infidel armies leave the land of Muhammad.'[111] Bin Laden's broad vision of the 'land of Muhammad' includes Saudi Arabia and every other Middle East country, as well as states conquered by Muslim dynasties located in Central Asia, the

Caucasus, the Balkans, Southeast Asia, South Asia, Africa, and Europe.[112] In October 2003, bin Laden released a videotaped message urging Iraqis to wage holy war against the American Crusaders to expel them from Iraq.[113]

Al Qaeda's goal is not limited to removing America's military presence, but extends to the elimination of all American *influence* from Muslim lands. Bin Laden could be said to seek America's unconditional surrender through its withdrawal of all economic, political and cultural influence from the Muslim world.[114] He has threatened America with future terrorist attacks 'unless it pulls out of the Arabian peninsula and it ceases its meddling . . . throughout the Islamic world.'[115] In a letter posted on the Internet in October 2002, bin Laden repeated his threat, saying: 'Do not interfere in our politics and method of education. Leave us alone, or else expect us in New York and Washington.'[116] Given that the feat of eliminating American ties with the Muslim world – in light of modern day globalization – would be nearly impossible, it would be a mistake to assume that al Qaeda's jihad against the U.S. and the West would stop with the withdrawal of its remaining military forces in Saudi Arabia, Iraq, and Afghanistan. Rather, 'concessions regarding Israel, troops in the Arabian peninsula, and so on would simply be milestones on al-Qaeda's path to victory.'[117]

The long list of terrorist attacks credited to al Qaeda demonstrates the global threat it poses. The most deadly and spectacular, of course, was conducted against the United States on September 11, 2001. The 9/11 terror attacks demonstrated the extent to which innocent civilians are particularly at risk from al Qaeda-inspired jihad. Bin Laden has repeatedly stressed that every Muslim has a religious obligation to kill American civilians.[118] According to bin Laden's reasoning, Americans bear responsibility for atrocities against Muslims because they elect members of Congress, who endorse and formulate U.S. government policy. Bin Laden has stated that the American people 'are not exonerated from responsibility, because they chose this government and voted for it despite their knowledge of its crimes in Palestine, Lebanon, Iraq, and in other places.'[119] Every American is the enemy of al Qaeda, 'whether he fights directly or whether he pays taxes.'[120]

Al Qaeda is equally prepared to kill non-American civilians, including Muslims, to strike U.S. targets anywhere in the world. In fact, according to one commentator, 'bin Laden has killed more Muslims than non-Muslims, more Afghans than Americans.'[121] When questioned about the killing of over 200 innocent civilians, mostly Africans, during the U.S. embassy bombings in Kenya and Tanzania, bin Laden made no apologies. Evincing a callous disregard for the loss of innocent human life, he stated: '[W]hen it becomes apparent that it would be impossible to repel these Americans without assaulting them, even if this involved the killing of Muslims, this is permissible under Islam.'[122] Al Qaeda exhibited a similar callousness in its approach to combating U.S.-led coalition forces in Iraq, where Iraqi civilians are targeted with even greater frequency in the name of repelling the infidel invaders. Abu Musab al-Zarqawi, the former leader of al Qaeda in Iraq, justified the killing of innocent Iraqis, stating that '[t]he shedding of Muslim blood . . . is allowed in order to avoid the greater evil of disrupting *jihad*.'[123]

Overthrowing Secular Muslim Governments

Al Qaeda has embraced a third major goal. The terror group advocates extending the anti-American jihad to secular Muslim governments around the world and has called for all Muslims to resist and overthrow rulers who violate Islamic laws and principles.[124] Bin Laden believes that Muslims must liberate themselves from their enslavement to apostate ruling regimes that are supported by the United States. The failure of these regimes to adhere strictly to the Qur'an makes them apostates, so they must be converted or overthrown. Bin Laden accuses most of these governments of being weak puppets of America and facilitators of its campaign against Islam.

Bin Laden has been particularly critical of Muslim governments that have supported or aided, directly or indirectly, the U.S.-led occupation of Iraq. In April 2003, bin Laden posted an audio-tape recording on the Internet urging Muslims to take up arms and join a jihad against the apostate Muslim governments supporting the U.S. invasion of Iraq – namely Pakistan, Afghanistan, Bahrain, Kuwait and Saudi Arabia.[125] With respect to Arab nations, bin Laden has stated that '[e]veryone that supports [the United States] with one word, even without offering help and aid . . . is nothing but a traitor.'[126] This attitude allows the jihadists to justify the fact that the victims of attacks on apostate Muslim governments are more often innocent civilians rather than government agents.

Saudi Arabia has been a major target of deadly *jihadi* terror attacks for its perceived appeasement of American hostility to the Muslim world. Prior to 2003, the Saudi government was criticized by the United States for weak and inattentive efforts in combating terrorism, including preventing the financing of terrorism, despite the fact that the country was the most important source of such funding.[127] Saudi efforts intensified after May 2003, when suicide bombers targeted foreign residential compounds in Riyadh, killing 35 people and wounding 200 others.[128] Al Qaeda launched numerous other strikes in the Kingdom, including attacks in Riyadh in November 2003 and April 2004, and an assault on an oil company facility in Khobar in May 2004. Though al Qaeda claimed to be targeting foreign interests in hopes of toppling the Saudi royal regime, the attacks mostly claimed the lives of innocent Saudi Muslims.

Civilians in Amman, Jordan, were the victims of terrorist suicide bombings in 2005. On November 9, 2005, terrorists detonated bombs at three American hotels in Amman, killing 57 people and injuring over 100 more.[129] Al Qaeda in Iraq, the group formerly headed by Abu Musab al-Zarqawi, claimed responsibility for the bombings. As in Saudi Arabia, al Qaeda claimed to target Jordan because of its complicity with American foreign policy, including the U.S.-led conflict in Iraq. Almost all of the victims, however, were Jordanian Muslims – a significant number of whom were attending a wedding at the time of the blasts. The disproportionate number of innocent Muslim casualties caused by an attack supposedly conducted in the name of Islam has led to an increased awareness among the population of the true threat posed by al Qaeda and its affiliates.

According to bin Laden, '[t]he countries most in need of liberation [from unrighteous governments] are Egypt, Jordan, Morocco, Nigeria, Pakistan, . . . Saudi Arabia, and Yemen.'[130] However, al Qaeda's jihad extends to all apostate Muslim states, including Afghanistan, Iraq, Kuwait, the Philippines, Indonesia, and Chechnya.[131] Following the expulsion of the American Crusaders, overthrowing the governments of these secular Muslim states would clear the way for the mujahedeen to unify the ummah under a caliphate and return Islam to its historical place of dominance in the world.

More than an organization composed of regional terror cells, al Qaeda's danger lies in its global mission of establishing a strict Islamic state. Bin Laden and his group are the newest followers of a centuries-long strain of radical jihadist-salafism thinking. Fundamentalists ranging from Taqi al-Din ibn Taymiyya in the 13th century to Hassan al-Banna of the Muslim Brotherhood and Sayyid Qutb in the 20th century have advocated the necessity of returning to the pure Islam revealed by Muhammad through the Qur'an and hadith. Contending that the decline of Islam is the result of straying from the path of pure Islam, they affirmed that it is the sacred duty of all Muslims to wage war, under the banner of jihad, against their enemies around the world. Al Qaeda's ideology reflects many of the teachings espoused by these extreme elements of the Muslim community.

In order to develop a strategy to defeat an organization such as al Qaeda, it is important to recognize that its motives are not short-term or confined to certain areas of the world. Rather, its mission is to create a worldwide, unified Islamic state based on a literalist interpretation of the Qur'an and hadith. Muslims must destroy any governments that deviate from the true path of Islam. The targets of this jihad include Muslim apostate governments, and the United States and its allies; in short, those who stand in the way of a true Islamic state. The United States simply represents the larger group of unbelievers who are at war with the Muslims who hold the true faith. Thus, al Qaeda poses a threat not only to the United States but to the entire global community.

Some mistakenly argue that this threat can be removed if the United States withdraws from Afghanistan and Iraq. This argument ignores al Qaeda's overarching goals. If the United States withdraws from the Middle East, al Qaeda could become a greater threat if, for example, a radical regime takes over and provides the organization a safe haven. Al Qaeda's mission will not end until it establishes a strict Islamic global state. As long as the United States and others oppose such a mission, al Qaeda's threat will not vanish.

NOTES

1. On February 23, 1998, Osama bin Laden issued a fatwa on behalf of the 'World Islamic Front,' announcing a jihad against the Jews and Crusaders and condemning U.S. foreign policy in the Middle East. *See* MESSAGES TO THE WORLD: THE STATEMENTS OF OSAMA BIN LADEN 61 (Bruce Lawrence ed., James Howarth trans., Verso 2005) [hereinafter STATEMENTS OF OSAMA BIN LADEN].
2. ROHAN GUNARATNA, INSIDE AL QAEDA: GLOBAL NETWORK OF TERROR 221 (Columbia University Press 2002) [hereinafter INSIDE AL QAEDA].
3. Daniel L. Byman, *Al-Qaeda as an Adversary: Do We Understand Our Enemy?*, 56 WORLD POLITICS, at 139, 143 (2003) [hereinafter *Al-Qaeda as an Adversary*].
4. Bernard Lewis originally used this term in his essay *The Roots of Muslim Rage*, ATLANTIC MONTHLY 266 (Sept. 1990), though Samuel P. Huntington made the term internationally known in his work, THE CLASH OF CIVILIZATIONS AND THE REMAKING OF THE WORLD ORDER (1996). Bin Laden refers to a 'greater struggle' between two camps: one camp is America, representing the global *Kufr* [non-believers] and accompanied by the apostate Arab rulers, and the other camp is represented by the Ummah [Islamic community], headed by its mujahedeen [Islamic warriors]. *See* OSAMA BIN LADEN, AMERICA'S ENEMY IN HIS OWN WORDS 173 (Randall B. Hamud ed., Nadeem Pub. 2005) [hereinafter BIN LADEN'S OWN WORDS].
5. INSIDE AL QAEDA, *supra* note 2, at 91.
6. *See* BIN LADEN'S OWN WORDS, *supra* note 4, at 151 ('[T]here can be no dialogue with occupiers except through arms.'); INSIDE AL QAEDA, *supra* note 2, at 230 ('Al Qaeda was founded on the premise that it will not compromise, however long it takes, however hard the fight and whatever the losses it suffers.').
7. For bin Laden, any Muslim rulers that have allied themselves with *Kufr* [non-believers], represented by America, have become apostates. *See* Osama bin Laden, 'Second Statement To Iraqis' (Oct. 12, 2003), *reprinted in* BIN LADEN'S OWN WORDS, *supra* note 4, at 143 ('Whatever their official titles, those who assist the United States and the coalition forces are renegades and infidels.').
8. *See* James Phillips, *The Evolving Al-Qaeda Threat*, HERITAGE FOUND., Mar. 17, 2006, *available at* http://www.heritage.org/Research/HomelandSecurity/hl928.cfm ('Al-Qaeda has developed elaborate ideological constructs that manipulate Islamic religious teachings to justify the mass murder of innocent people, which is prohibited by the Koran and rejected by mainstream Muslim religious leaders.').
9. Al Qaeda has established terror cells in as many as 60 countries around the world. *See* MICHAEL SCHEUER, IMPERIAL HUBRIS: WHY THE WEST IS LOSING THE WAR ON TERROR 71 (Potomac Books 2004) [hereinafter IMPERIAL HUBRIS].

10 *Al-Qaeda as an Adversary*, *supra* note 3, at 150 (quoting ANONYMOUS, THROUGH OUR ENEMIES' EYES: OSAMA BIN LADEN, RADICAL ISLAM, AND THE FUTURE OF AMERICA, xviii (Brassey's 2002)); *see also* CHRISTOPHER M. BLANCHARD, AL QAEDA: STATEMENTS AND EVOLVING IDEOLOGY, CRS REPORT FOR CONGRESS, at 17 (July 9, 2007) (Bin Laden's professed 'goal is to "move, incite, and mobilize the [Islamic] nation" until it reaches a revolutionary "ignition point" ') (*quoting Bin Laden Interviewed on Jihad Against U.S.*, AL QUDS AL ARABI, Nov. 27, 1996).

11 DAVID BUKAY, FROM MUHAMMAD TO BIN LADEN 260 (Transaction 2007) [hereinafter FROM MUHAMMAD TO BIN LADEN].

12 WILLIAM ROSENAU, WAGING THE 'WAR OF IDEAS' (RAND Corp. 2006) (quoting GILLES KEPEL, JIHAD: THE TRAIL OF POLITICAL ISLAM 220 (Harvard University Press 2002)), *in* THE MCGRAW-HILL HOMELAND SECURITY HANDBOOK 1131–48 (2006). The term 'salafism' comes from the Arabic word 'salaf,' which is a term used to describe the early, supposedly uncorrupted Muslims during and immediately after the life of the Prophet Muhammad. 'Salafism is rooted in the belief that the Koran and the teachings of the Prophet Mohammed and his companions are the most legitimate sources of religious conduct and reasoning, and as such should be emulated and put into practice in contemporary Islamic communities.' REPORT OF THE HOUSE PERMANENT SELECT COMMITTEE ON INTELLIGENCE, AL-QAEDA: THE MANY FACES OF AN ISLAMIST EXTREMIST THREAT, at 6 (June 2006) [hereinafter AL-QAEDA: AN ISLAMIST EXTREMIST THREAT].

13 AL-QAEDA: AN ISLAMIST EXTREMIST THREAT, *supra* note 12, at 6.

14 Islam's holy book is the Qur'an, which has 114 chapters (*suras*). Muslims consider the Qur'an to be the word of Allah as divinely revealed to His Prophet Muhammad. *See* BIN LADEN'S OWN WORDS, *supra* note 4, at lviii.

15 BIN LADEN'S OWN WORDS, *supra* note 4, at 133 (quoting Osama bin Laden, *Comments on Jihad* (July 2003)).

16 *See* AL-QAEDA: AN ISLAMIST EXTREMIST THREAT, *supra* note 12, at 6.

17 *See* Douglass E. Streusand, *What Does Jihad Mean?*, MIDDLE EAST Q., Sept. 1997; DANIEL BENJAMIN & STEVEN SIMON, THE AGE OF SACRED TERROR 43 (Random House 2002) [hereinafter BENJAMIN & SIMON] ('To grasp the worldview of al-Qaeda and its leader, Usama bin Laden, it is essential to start with ibn Taymiyya.'); David A. Funk, *Traditional Islamic Jurisprudence: Justifying Islamic Law and Government*, 20 S.U.L. REV. 213, 264 (1993) [hereinafter *Traditional Islamic Jurisprudence*]; Osama Bin Laden, 'Declaration of War Against the Americans Occupying the Land of the Two Holy Places' (Aug. 1996) (quoting Ibn Taymiyya), Osama bin Laden, 'Message to the Islamic World' (Dec. 16, 2004) (same), Osama bin Laden, 'Sermon for the Feast of the Sacrifice' (Feb. 16, 2003) (same).

18 *See* ABDEL BARI ATWAN, THE SECRET HISTORY OF AL QAEDA 71 (University of California Press 2006) [hereinafter THE SECRET HISTORY OF AL QAEDA].

19 *Id.*

20 *See* JASON BURKE, AL-QAEDA: CASTING A SHADOW OF TERROR 29 (London & New York: I.B. Tauris 2003) [hereinafter CASTING A SHADOW OF TERROR].

21 *Id.* at 29; *see also* FROM MUHAMMAD TO BIN LADEN, *supra* note 11, at 195 (advocating the need to return to the Qur'an and Sunnah as the only means for Islamic revival).

22 *See* FROM MUHAMMAD TO BIN LADEN, *supra* note 11, at 195.

23 *See Traditional Islamic Jurisprudence*, *supra* note 17, at 264.

24 Ummah is the Arabic term referring to the community of Muslim believers throughout the world. All Muslims are part of the ummah regardless of ethnicity or nationality.

25 *See* BENJAMIN & SIMON, *supra* note 17, at 48. After the Prophet Muhammad's death in 632 A.D., Islamic scholars attempted to document the actual words and deeds of the Prophet from his companions and followers. These 'traditions' were compiled into books known as the hadith. *See* BIN LADEN'S OWN WORDS, *supra* note 4, at lviii; THE SECRET HISTORY OF AL QAEDA, *supra* note 18, at 68. The hadith are important because they explain and complement the Qur'an. *See* THE SECRET HISTORY OF AL QAEDA, *supra* note 18, at 68.

26 Benjamin & Simon, *supra* note 17, at 51.
27 *See* From Muhammad to Bin Laden, *supra* note 11, at 200. Islam distinguishes between a defensive and an offensive jihad. *See* Imperial Hubris, *supra* note 9, at 6–7. According to the Qur'an, Allah gave all Muslims permission for jihad to defend themselves and deter their enemies from attacking them. This is referred to as a defensive jihad. An offensive jihad is waged to conquer new lands for Islam and convert new people to the faith. *Id.* at 7. However, an offensive jihad can only be called for by a caliph or head of the ummah. *Id.*
28 From Muhammad to Bin Laden, *supra* note 11, at 200.
29 *See* Stephen Schwartz, The Two Faces of Islam: The House of Sa'ud From Tradition to Terror 55 (Doubleday 2002) [hereinafter The Two Faces of Islam].
30 From Muhammad to Bin Laden, *supra* note 11, at 200. Muslims express their faith through five essential affirmations or 'pillars.' The five pillars include: 'declaration of belief in One God, daily prayer at five set times, the giving of charity, fasting in the month of Ramadan, and the hajj pilgrimage to the Ka'bah.' *See* The Two Faces of Islam, *supra* note 29, at 27.
31 Streusand, *supra* note 17, at 2.
32 From Muhammad to Bin Laden, *supra* note 11, at 200.
33 Streusand, *supra* note 17, at 2.
34 Stefan M. Aubrey, The New Dimension of International Terrorism 111 (2004).
35 Osama bin Laden, 'Declaration of War Against the Americans Occupying the Land of the Two Holy Places' (August 1996), *reprinted in* Bin Laden's Own Words, *supra* note 4, at 39–40.
36 *See* From Muhammad to Bin Laden, *supra* note 11, at 200 ('Ibn-Taymiyah's main interest was the legitimacy of waging *jihad* against Muslims who revolt against the Islamic authorities or refuse to abide by the rules of the *Shari'ah*, and against the unbelievers who threaten the march of Islam.').
37 *See* Casting a Shadow of Terror, *supra* note 20, at 41; From Muhammad to Bin Laden, *supra* note 11, at 203.
38 Casting a Shadow of Terror, *supra* note 20, at 41.
39 *Id.*; *see also* The Two Faces of Islam, *supra* note 29, at 69; From Muhammad to Bin Laden, *supra* note 11, at 203.
40 *See* The Two Faces of Islam, *supra* note 29, at 70.
41 *See* Casting a Shadow of Terror, *supra* note 20, at 41; *see also* The Two Faces of Islam, *supra* note 29, at 71.
42 *See* The Two Faces of Islam, *supra* note 29, at 71.
43 *Id.*
44 From Muhammad to Bin Laden, *supra* note 11, at 205.
45 Bin Laden's Own Words, *supra* note 4, at lxiii.
46 *See id.* at lxiv.
47 *See* Casting a Shadow of Terror, *supra* note 20, at 41.
48 *See id.* at 42; The Two Faces of Islam, *supra* note 29, at 73.
49 *See* The Two Faces of Islam, *supra* note 29, at 74.
50 *Id.*
51 *Id.* at 75. In 1765, Muhammad ibn Saud died and was succeeded by his son Abd al-Azziz ibn Saud. In 1792, Ibn Abd al-Wahhab died and Abd al-Azziz took over the leadership of the Wahhab Saud alliance. *Id.*
52 *See* The Two Faces of Islam, *supra* note 29, at 80–81.
53 For a more comprehensive discussion of the early Wahhabi movement and the conquest of Arabia, see *id.* at 66–120.
54 *See* From Muhammad to Bin Laden, *supra* note 11, at 204.
55 *See* Bin Laden's Own Words, *supra* note 4, at lxii; Casting a Shadow of Terror, *supra* note 20, at 42. Since 1979, Saudi Arabia has sought to spread Wahhabism throughout the Muslim world by funding the building of thousands of madrasas or religious schools. *See* Bin Laden's Own Words, *supra* note 4, at lxiv.

56 *See* FROM MUHAMMAD TO BIN LADEN, *supra* note 11, at 208; *see also* BENJAMIN & SIMON, *supra* note 17, at 57.
57 FROM MUHAMMAD TO BIN LADEN, *supra* note 11, at 208; *see also* BENJAMIN & SIMON, *supra* note 17, at 57.
58 BENJAMIN & SIMON, *supra* note 17, at 57; *see also* FROM MUHAMMAD TO BIN LADEN, *supra* note 11, at 207.
59 FROM MUHAMMAD TO BIN LADEN, *supra* note 11, at 207–8.
60 *See* THE SECRET HISTORY OF AL QAEDA, *supra* note 18, at 73; FROM MUHAMMAD TO BIN LADEN, *supra* note 11, at 206.
61 *See* CASTING A SHADOW OF TERROR, *supra* note 20, at 47; FROM MUHAMMAD TO BIN LADEN, *supra* note 11, at 207.
62 *See* CASTING A SHADOW OF TERROR, *supra* note 20, at 47; FROM MUHAMMAD TO BIN LADEN, *supra* note 11, at 207.
63 FROM MUHAMMAD TO BIN LADEN, *supra* note 11, at 215.
64 *Id.*
65 *See* CASTING A SHADOW OF TERROR, *supra* note 20, at 50; FROM MUHAMMAD TO BIN LADEN, *supra* note 11, at 215.
66 John Calvert, *The World is an Undutiful Boy!: Sayyid Qutb's American Experience,* 11 ISLAM AND CHRISTIAN–MUSLIM RELATIONS, 2000, at 87, 99.
67 *See* FROM MUHAMMAD TO BIN LADEN, *supra* note 11, at 207; CASTING A SHADOW OF TERROR, *supra* note 20, at 50; THE SECRET HISTORY OF AL QAEDA, *supra* note 18, at 73.
68 CASTING A SHADOW OF TERROR, *supra* note 20, at 52; *see also* FROM MUHAMMAD TO BIN LADEN, *supra* note 11, at 215.
69 *See* THE NATIONAL COMMISSION ON TERRORIST ATTACKS, THE 9/11 COMMISSION REPORT: FINAL REPORT OF THE NATIONAL COMMISSION ON TERRORIST ATTACKS UPON THE UNITED STATES (2004), at 382, *available at* http://www.9-11commission.gov/report/911Report.pdf [hereinafter THE 9/11 COMMISSION REPORT]; THE SECRET HISTORY OF AL QAEDA, *supra* note 18, at 73.
70 SAYYID QUTB, MILESTONES 3, *available at* http://majalla.org/books/2005/qutb-milestone.pdf.
71 THE SECRET HISTORY OF AL QAEDA, *supra* note 18, at 73.
72 FROM MUHAMMAD TO BIN LADEN, *supra* note 11, at 215.
73 BENJAMIN & SIMON, *supra* note 17, at 65.
74 *See* THE 9/11 COMMISSION REPORT, *supra* note 69, at 51.
75 *See* CASTING A SHADOW OF TERROR, *supra* note 20, at 50; THE SECRET HISTORY OF AL QAEDA, *supra* note 18, at 73.
76 See LAWRENCE WRIGHT, THE LOOMING TOWER: AL-QAEDA AND THE ROAD TO 9/11, at 30 (Knopf 2006).
77 *Id.* at 31.
78 *Id.*; *see also* FROM MUHAMMAD TO BIN LADEN, *supra* note 11, at 215. The Muslim Brotherhood has since become involved in mainstream politics, sponsoring its candidates as independents for political elections in Egypt. In 2006, members of the Muslim Brotherhood held 88 of 454 seats in the lower house of parliament. *See* Daniel Williams, *Egypt's Muslim Brotherhood May Be Model for Islam's Political Adaptation*, WASH. POST, Feb. 3, 2006.
79 *See* CASTING A SHADOW OF TERROR, *supra* note 20, at 50; THE SECRET HISTORY OF AL QAEDA, *supra* note 18, at 73.
80 STATEMENTS OF OSAMA BIN LADEN, *supra* note 1, at 229 (Audiotape message, Jan. 2, 2004).
81 For a concise list outlining offenses al Qaeda accuses the United States of perpetrating, such as a blasphemous military presence or a bias toward Israel, see *Al Qaeda as an Adversary*, *supra* note 3, at 144; *see also* Osama bin Laden, 'Declaration of War Against the Americans Occupying the Land of the Two Holy Places' (Aug. 1996) (noting that Muslims are the main targets of the 'Zionist–Crusader alliance['s]' aggression).
82 *See* IMPERIAL HUBRIS, *supra* note 9, at 12.
83 *See* BIN LADEN'S OWN WORDS, *supra* note 4, at 216.

84 Osama bin Laden, 'Declaration of War Against the Americans Occupying the Land of the Two Holy Places' (Aug. 1996); *see also* BIN LADEN'S OWN WORDS, *supra* note 4, at 214.

85 As evidence of the so-called Crusader war against Islam, bin Laden points to six U.S. policies that he denounces: '1) support for Israel; 2) support for the autocratic regimes of the Middle East; 3) support for non-Muslim countries outside the Middle East who are either repressing Muslims or battling Muslim insurgencies; 4) stationing of military forces in Saudi Arabia and the Gulf States; 5) invasions of Afghanistan and Iraq; and 6) exploitation of Middle East oil resources.' BIN LADEN'S OWN WORDS, *supra* note 4, at 196.

86 Osama bin Laden, Interview with al-Jazeera (Dec. 1998) ('Every American is our enemy, whether he fights directly or whether he pays taxes.').

87 STATEMENTS OF OSAMA BIN LADEN, *supra* note 1, at 72.

88 Osama bin Laden, 'Message to the Islamic World' (Dec. 16, 2004), *reprinted in* BIN LADEN'S OWN WORDS, *supra* note 4, at 173.

89 Osama bin Laden, Interview with al-Jazeera (Dec. 1998), *reprinted in* STATEMENTS OF OSAMA BIN LADEN, *supra* note 1, at 90–91.

90 FROM MUHAMMAD TO BIN LADEN, *supra* note 11, at 247.

91 *Id.*

92 *Al-Qaeda as an Adversary*, *supra* note 3, at 149.

93 FROM MUHAMMAD TO BIN LADEN, *supra* note 11, at 247.

94 *Al-Qaeda as an Adversary*, *supra* note 3, at 149, 153.

95 *See* THE SECRET HISTORY OF AL QAEDA, *supra* note 18, at 220.

96 BLANCHARD, *supra* note 10, at 10.

97 *See 'Zarqawi' vows war on Iraq poll,* BBC NEWS, Jan. 23, 2005, *available at* http://news.bbc.co.uk/1/hi/world/middle_east/4199363.stm.

98 BLANCHARD, *supra* note 10, at 10. Bin Laden harshly denounced and criticized HAMAS leaders for participating in Palestinian elections in 2006. *See* Michael Slackman, *Bin Laden Says West is Waging War Against Islam,* N.Y. TIMES, Apr. 23, 2006, *available at* http://www.nytimes.com/2006/04/24/world/middleeast/24binladen.html. Al Zarqawi has condemned Iraqis for participating in the 2005 constitutional referenda and parliamentary elections, and dismissed Afghan and Egyptian elections as being inconsistent with Islamic principles. *See* BLANCHARD, *supra* note 10, at 11.

99 *See* THE SECRET HISTORY OF AL QAEDA, *supra* note 18, at 224.

100 *See* Letter from al-Zawahiri to al-Zarqawi (July 9, 2005).

101 Saudi Arabia was among the first foreign nations to recognize the Taliban as the legitimate government of Afghanistan. Saudi Arabia gave its official recognition in May 1997, despite the fact that it was known that the Taliban was providing refuge to several international terrorists, including Osama bin Laden. *See* STEVE COLL, GHOST WARS: THE SECRET HISTORY OF THE CIA, AFGHANISTAN, AND BIN LADEN, FROM THE SOVIET INVASION TO SEPTEMBER 10, 2001, at 349 (Penguin Books 2004).

102 BLANCHARD, *supra* note 10, at 12.

103 THE 9/11 COMMISSION REPORT, *supra* note 69, at 51–2 (citing Bin Laden's 'Letter to America,' OBSERVER WORLDVIEW, Nov. 24, 2002).

104 One Mogadishu sheikh who runs a sharia court declared, 'He who does not perform prayer will be considered as [an] infidel and our sharia law orders that person to be killed.' *Pray or Die, Somali Sheikh Tells Muslims*, REUTERS, July 7, 2006.

105 American officials know that three terrorists involved in the 1998 U.S. embassy bombings in Tanzania and Kenya have found safe haven in Somalia. *See* Jendayi E. Frazer, Assistant Secretary for African Affairs, *Somalia: U.S. Government Policy and Challenges*, Testimony before Senate Committee on Foreign Relations Subcommittee on African Affairs, Washington, DC (July 11, 2006), *available at* http://www.state.gov/p/af/rls/rm/2006/68869.htm.

106 Aweys appears on U.S. and U.N. lists of people suspected of having ties to terrorism and is known to have founded the group al-Ittihad al-Islami (AIAI) that had links to bin Laden and al Qaeda in the early 1990s. *See* Salad Duhul, *Somali Militia Head Tied to*

Bin Laden, WASH. POST, June 25, 2006, at A19; *see also* Fredrick Nzwili, *Leadership Profile: Somalia's Islamic Courts Union*, 3 TERRORISM FOCUS, Issue 23, June 13, 2006, *available at* http://www.jamestown.org/terrorism/news/article.php?articleid=2370028.

107 Marc Lacey, *In Somalia, Islamic Militias are Fighting Culture Wars*, N.Y. TIMES, June 19, 2006, at A11, *available at* http://www.nytimes.com/2006/06/19/world/africa/19somalia.html?pagewanted=2&n=Top/Reference/Times%20Topics/Organizations/A/Al%20Qaeda.

108 Osama bin Laden, 'A Declaration of Jihad Against the Americans Occupying the Land of the Two Holy Places' (Aug. 23, 1996).

109 Letter from Ayman al-Zawahiri to Abu Musab al-Zarqawi (July 9, 2005) (exhorting al-Zarqawi to '[e]xpel the Americans from Iraq').

110 STATEMENTS OF OSAMA BIN LADEN, *supra* note 1, at 47 (interview with CNN, March 1997) (emphasis added).

111 *Id.* at 105 (video message, October 7, 2001).

112 *Al-Qaeda as an Adversary*, *supra* note 3, at 145.

113 *See* THE SECRET HISTORY OF AL QAEDA, *supra* note 18, at 203.

114 *See* STATEMENTS OF OSAMA BIN LADEN, *supra* note 1, at 147, 155.

115 *Id. at* 127 (al-Jazeera interview, Jan. 31, 2002). Apparently, the 'Muslim World' includes any country with a large Muslim population. For example, Indonesia, the Philippines, Bangladesh, India, Pakistan, Nigeria, Mauritania, Bosnia, Chechnya and Tajikistan are part of the Muslim world, according to bin Laden. *See id.* at 134.

116 *Id.* at 171 (Internet statement, October 6, 2002).

117 *Al-Qaeda as an Adversary*, *supra* note 3, at 147.

118 STATEMENTS OF OSAMA BIN LADEN, *supra* note 1, at 117 (interview with al-Jazeera, Oct. 20, 2001).

119 *Id.* at 47 (interview with CNN, March 1997).

120 *Id.* at 70 (interview, December 1998). 'The American people are the ones who pay taxes which fund the planes that bomb us in Afghanistan.' *Id.* at 165.

121 Phillips, *supra* note 8.

122 THE 9/11 COMMISSION REPORT, *supra* note 69, at 70.

123 THE SECRET HISTORY OF AL QAEDA, *supra* note 18, at 224 (audio recording of al-Zarqawi, May 18, 2005).

124 *See* Osama bin Laden, 'Message to the Islamic World' (Dec. 16, 2004), *reprinted in* BIN LADEN'S OWN WORDS, *supra* note 4, at 172 ('[I]f the ruler deviates from God's Path and becomes an apostate, the people are obliged to disobey him and remove him from power.').

125 *See* THE SECRET HISTORY OF AL QAEDA, *supra* note 18, at 200.

126 STATEMENTS OF OSAMA BIN LADEN, *supra* note 1, at 128 (interview with al-Jazeera, Oct. 20, 2001).

127 *See generally* COUNCIL ON FOREIGN RELATIONS, TERRORIST FINANCING: REPORT OF AN INDEPENDENT TASK FORCE SPONSORED BY THE COUNCIL ON FOREIGN RELATIONS (Oct. 2002), *available at* http://www.cfr.org/pdf/Terrorist_Financing_TF.pdf; ALFRED B. PRADOS & CHRISTOPHER M. BLANCHARD, SAUDI ARABIA: TERRORIST FINANCING ISSUES, CRS REPORT FOR CONGRESS (Sept. 15, 2007).

128 *See Saudi Arabia Says 42 Islamist Militants Arrested*, N.Y. TIMES, June 24, 2006; Phillips, *supra* note 8 ('[A]fter al-Qaeda's May 2003 bombings inside Saudi Arabia, the Saudis cracked down on al-Qaeda supporters and undertook limited reforms in religious charities that had been funding bin Laden.').

129 *See* Hassan M. Fattah & Michael Slackman, *3 Hotels Bombed in Jordan; At Least 57 Die*, N.Y. TIMES, Nov. 10, 2005, *available at* http://www.nytimes.com/2005/11/10/international/middleeast/10jordan.html.

130 *See* BIN LADEN'S OWN WORDS, *supra* note 4, at 111; *see also Al-Qaeda as an Adversary*, *supra* note 3, at 183.

131 Bin Laden has stated that 'this jihad is very dear to us in Palestine, Chechnya, Afghanistan, Kashmir, Indonesia, the Philippines, and other lands of Islam.' BIN LADEN'S OWN WORDS, *supra* note 4, at 203.

4. Al Qaeda's global presence

> [The ummah] has a duty to maintain the *jihad* that exists today and to help it with all its might, for this *jihad* is very dear to us in Palestine, Chechnya, Afghanistan, Kashmir, Indonesia, the Philippines, and other lands of Islam.
>
> Osama bin Laden[1]

Since its inception in 1988, al Qaeda has evolved from a single entity into a global network of like-minded terrorist organizations. Al Qaeda is ' "larger, more ethnically diverse, more geographically dispersed, younger, richer, better educated, better led, and more military trained and combat experienced" than other terrorist groups in history.'[2] The group's terror network is comprised of a core group, affiliates, sympathizers and willing partners working in concert for common goals.[3] Its ultimate goal is to unite the world's Muslim population in an Islamic caliphate governed by a radical version of Islamic law.[4] Al Qaeda's global jihad is being fought on multiple fronts by al Qaeda surrogate groups around the world. Al Qaeda's brigades occupy a realm much larger than the Arabian Peninsula. Bin Laden proudly notes that their terror operations extend 'from the easternmost point in the Islamic world to its westernmost point, from Indonesia, the Philippines, Bangladesh, India, and Pakistan to the Arab world and finally to Nigeria and Mauritania.'[5] Al Qaeda's affiliated entities are principally located in five regions around the world: the Middle East, Europe, Africa, Southeast Asia, and South Asia.[6]

Money has been central to the growth and development of al Qaeda's terror network. Al Qaeda has used its substantial financial resources to establish links, leverage support and maintain the loyalty of more than 20 militant jihadist groups globally.[7] Al Qaeda has provided financial assistance to these terrorist surrogates to underwrite specific jihadi operations, purchase weapons, and train thousands of their members at al Qaeda-run camps in Afghanistan, Pakistan, Somalia, North Africa and elsewhere.[8] The ability to raise and transfer funds to these terrorist organizations is essential to sustaining terrorist operations in these regions of the world. Money is critical to sustaining al Qaeda's global presence and successfully waging its global jihad.

MIDDLE EAST

On March 19, 2003, the U.S. invaded Iraq, dispatching 150,000 U.S. troops to the Arab country to overthrow the regime of Iraqi President Saddam Hussein.[9] Since then Iraq has become a central front in the global conflict against al Qadea.[10] According to one terrorism expert, '[Iraq] has become a rallying point, a major propaganda issue, a staging area, and a potentially fertile recruiting ground for al Qaeda.'[11] In April 2003, bin Laden issued a tape recording imploring his followers to take up arms and join a jihad against the Muslim governments which supported the U.S. invasion of Iraq, namely Pakistan, Afghanistan and Saudi Arabia.[12] In October 2003, bin Laden posted a videotaped message on the Internet urging Iraqis to 'wage a holy war against the American Crusaders in Iraq.'[13] Abu Musab al-Zarqawi, a formidable leader of his own terror group in Iraq, al-Tawhid wal-Jihad ('Monotheism and Jihad'), responded to bin Laden's call.[14] After meeting with senior al Qaeda leaders, al-Zarqawi assumed responsibility for providing coordination and logistical support to al Qaeda terrorists and Arab fighters joining the anti-American jihad in Iraq.[15] In October 2004, al-Zarqawi strengthened his ties with al Qaeda by changing the name of al-Tawhid wal-Jihad to 'al Qaeda in the Land of the Two Rivers,' more commonly known as 'al Qaeda in Iraq' (AQI). In December 2004, al-Zarqawi and al Qaeda announced their formal alliance.[16] Bin Laden gave al-Zarqawi his blessing as emir and leader of the al Qaeda insurgency in Iraq.[17] In return, al-Zarqawi swore his allegiance or *bayat* to bin Laden.

Al Qaeda has devised an ambitious agenda for Iraq. In a letter from Ayman al-Zawahiri, al Qaeda's second in command, to al-Zarqawi, the leader of AQI, dated July 9, 2005, al-Zawahiri set forth a four-part plan for the jihad in Iraq.[18] The first stage is to expel the Americans from Iraq.[19] In the second stage, al Qaeda intends to establish an Islamic authority or emirate in Iraq.[20] The third stage involves '[e]xtend[ing] the *jihad* wave to the secular countries neighboring Iraq.'[21] Fourth and finally, al Qaeda intends the destruction of the State of Israel.[22]

AQI has claimed responsibility for a series of grisly killings, hostage beheadings, and hundreds of suicide and car bombings in Iraq.[23] In August 2003, a suicide bomber drove a truck laden with 10,600 pounds of military explosives into the U.N. Headquarters in Baghdad, killing 23 people, including the U.N. Secretary General's Special Representative for Iraq, Sergio Vieira de Mello.[24] Al-Zarqawi is believed to be responsible for the bloody attack.[25] That same month AQI conducted a suicide bombing against Shi'a worshippers at the Imam Ali Mosque in al Najaf, killing 85 people, including the leader of the Supreme Council for the Islamic Revolution in Iraq.[26] Al-Zarqawi is also suspected of complicity in the massacre of 185 Shi'ite pilgrims who were killed by terrorist attacks in Karbala and Baghdad during Ashura.[27] The terror group is further credited with the videotaped beheadings of Americans Nicholas Berg (May 8, 2004), Jack Armstrong (September 20, 2004), and Jack Hensley (September 21, 2004).[28] AQI has further targeted Iraqi and Coalition forces, and relief agencies such as the Red Cross. During a three-month period in 2005, AQI carried out as many as 1,700 attacks on Coalition and Iraqi security forces in Mosul.[29] Al Qaeda is believed to finance, at least in part, AQI's terrorist operations.[30]

At the same time, AQI's terrorist bombings have not been limited to targets in Iraq. In 2005, AQI claimed credit for suicide bombings against hotels in Amman, Jordan, a rocket attack against U.S. Navy ships in the port of Aqaba, and firing several rockets into Israel from Lebanon.[31] The terrorist bombings in Amman, Jordan were directed at three American hotels, killing 60 people and wounding more than 100 others.[32] One of the suicide bombers entered a hotel ballroom and detonated his explosives belt, ripping through a wedding party in the room. The terrorist attack was the worst in Jordan's history.

In June 2006, Abu Musab al-Zarqawi was killed when U.S. warplanes dropped two 500-pound bombs on a house where he was meeting with other Iraqi insurgent leaders.[33] However, al-Zarqawi's death has not halted the bloodshed in Iraq. Al-Zarqawi's successor, Abu Hamza al-Muhajir, also known as Abu Ayyub al-Masri, and other AQI leaders have continued deadly terrorist attacks against Iraqi and Coalition forces, and Iraqi civilians, predominately Shi'ites.[34]

Another al Qaeda-affiliated terrorist group operating in Iraq is Ansar al-Islam (AI), also known as Ansar al-Sunnah. AI emerged in December 2001 with a stronghold near Iraq's northeastern border with Iran. With as many as 1,000 members, AI is closely allied with al Qaeda. Like al Qaeda, AI is a Salafist-Sunni group that advocates jihad.[35] AI's goals include expelling the U.S.-led Coalition forces from Iraq and establishing a radical Islamic state. Senior members of AI are responsible for coordinating recruitment efforts to send suicide bombers, anti-coalition fighters, and funds for anti-coalition fighters in Iraq.[36] AI is responsible for numerous kidnappings, executions and assassinations in Iraq. AI members have directed attacks against U.S.-led Coalition forces, Iraqi government officials and security forces, and Kurdish and Shi'ite leaders. In February 2004, AI conducted simultaneous suicide bombings of the Patriotic Union of Kurdistan (formerly led by Jalal Talabani, President of Iraq) and the Kurdistan Democratic Party (formerly led by Masud Barzani, President of the Kurdish Assembly) offices in Irbil.[37] AI was also reportedly responsible for bombing the U.S. military dining facility in Mosul in December 2004.[38]

In February 2003, AI was designated by the U.S. Treasury Department as a foreign terrorist group affiliated with al Qaeda.[39] The Treasury Department claims that AI has provided safe haven to al Qaeda terrorists in Iraq. AI has received training and logistical assistance from al Qaeda and financial support from bin Laden. Bin Laden reportedly provided AI with an estimated $300–600,000 in seed money.[40] Some of its members have trained in al Qaeda training camps in Afghanistan. AI has also developed close links to AQI, and its former leader al-Zarqawi.[41]

Al Qaeda's presence in the Middle East extends well beyond Iraq. The Islamist terror group has displayed an active presence in Saudi Arabia, unleashing a wave of terrorist attacks in 2003 and 2004. Al Qaeda's primary goal is to overthrow the House of Saud, whom bin Laden and his followers believe are apostates and unfit to rule.[42] In May 2003, three near-simultaneous car bombs were detonated at residential compounds in Riyadh, Saudi Arabia, killing nearly 100 people, including 10 Americans, and wounding scores more.[43] The three compounds housed American and expatriate workers. Saudi officials linked the bombings to a group of 19 suspected al Qaeda sympathizers. Furthermore, there were striking similarities between the Riyadh explosions and the coordinated bombings of the U.S. embassies in Kenya and Tanzania in 1998.[44] In November 2003, militants bombed another residential compound in Riyadh that killed 17 people and wounded more than 100 others.[45] Of those persons killed, 12 were Arab nationals from other countries.[46] On April 21, 2004, an al Qaeda node staged a suicide car bomb attack against the Saudi government's General Security Services headquarters. A group calling itself the 'al-Haramain Brigades' claimed credit for the massive car bombing, praising Sheikh bin Laden as the inspiration for the attack.[47] A few weeks later, on May 1, 2004, there was a terror attack in Yanbu, and on May 29, 2004, a residential compound in Khobar was struck.[48]

The most grisly, barbaric attack occurred in June 2004, when Lockheed Martin employee Paul Johnson was kidnapped and beheaded on video.[49] The video of the beheading was distributed over the Internet. That same day, the al Qaeda Organization in the Arabian Peninsula released a signed statement on the al-Islah website claiming responsibility for the gruesome murder.[50] Terrorist attacks continued in Saudi Arabia when al Qaeda launched an armed assault against the U.S. Consulate in Jeddah. However, the attackers were unable to gain entry to the consulate or kill any Americans and the plot failed. This incident was followed on December 29, 2004, by suicide car bomb attacks at the Saudi Interior Ministry and the Special Emergency Force Training Center. In February 2006, al Qaeda militants carried out a car bomb attack against an oil processing center in Abqaiq, attempting to strike at the heart of the Saudi oil infrastructure.[51]

This latter attack appeared to be in response to Ayman al-Zawahiri's call in December 2005 to 'concentrate . . . attacks on Muslims' stolen oil, from which most of the revenues go to the enemies of Islam, while most of what they leave is seized by the thieves who rule our countries.'[52] The Saudi branch of al Qaeda has vowed to continue strikes at energy-related targets that provide 'the Crusaders with oil.'[53]

Al Qaeda also has strong connections to Egypt. The Egyptian Islamic Jihad (EIJ), also known as Al-Jihad, formally merged with bin Laden's al Qaeda organization in 2001. Bin Laden's deputy, Ayman al-Zawahiri, is the former head of the EIJ. Al-Zawahiri first announced that his group had aligned itself with al Qaeda in 1998, when he and other leaders of Islamic terrorist groups signed bin Laden's Khost fatwa confirming their participation in the World Islamic Front for Jihad Against the Jews and Crusaders.[54] Active since the 1970s, the EIJ's primary goal has been to overthrow the Egyptian government and establish an Islamic state governed by strict Sharia law. The EIJ was responsible for the 1981 assassination of Egyptian President Anwar Sadat. The group was also allegedly responsible for the 1993 attempted assassinations of Interior Minister Hassan al-Alfi and Prime Minister Atef. According to the U.S. State Department, since 1998 EIJ has received most of its funding from al Qaeda.[55] Several members of EIJ have been designated by the U.S. Treasury Department as Specially Designated Global Terrorists (SDGTs) for providing training and material support to al Qaeda.[56] The designations were pursuant to U.N. Security Council Resolution 1617, which requires member states to financially isolate individuals and entities added to the U.N. 1267 Committee's consolidated list of terrorists tied to the Taliban, al Qaeda, and Osama bin Laden.[57]

EUROPE

Al Qaeda considers Europe a central arena for the promotion of global jihad and the realization of its vision of an Islamic caliphate. Following the attacks on September 11, 2001, Europe has been the target of widespread terrorist activity designed to cause instability, spread fear, and ignite the spark of Islamic revolution throughout the continent. The existence of large Muslim communities in various European countries affords al Qaeda a target population for recruitment into the ranks of the Islamic jihad. Al Qaeda has inspired multiple deadly terror attacks by local extremist groups and homegrown jihadists. This was made clear through the transit bombings in Madrid on May 11, 2004, and in London on July 7, 2005. In Madrid, remote-detonated bombs killed 191 people and injured 1,400, while in London suicide bombers killed 52 people and injured more than 700.[58] Both bombings are believed to have been in direct response to the Spanish and British governments' military support for the U.S. in Iraq.[59] One of the London suicide bombers appeared on an Internet video accusing his country of declaring war on Islam and oppressing Muslims in Palestine, Afghanistan, Iraq and Chechnya.[60] The London criminal investigation further revealed that the terror cell's ringleader, Mohammed Siddique Khan, and a fellow suicide bomber, Shahzad Tanweer, both visited Pakistani training camps between November 2004 and February 2005, where they were trained by al Qaeda operatives.[61]

The Madrid and London transit bombings highlight the threat faced by Europe generally. The nature of the attacks reflects the shifting trend of terrorism in which local Islamic extremist groups that have indirect or even tenuous ties to al Qaeda carry out attacks without direct coordination of al Qaeda leaders. The London terrorist attacks are particularly alarming because the perpetrators were not formally affiliated with al Qaeda. According to one counter-terrorism analyst, the 'Muslims involved in *jihadist* activities in Spain leading up to the Madrid bombing were not necessarily members of al Qaeda. Instead, they were religious activists that, either individually or in groups or cells, decided to act locally in support of al Qaeda's global jihad ideology.'[62] Even if al Qaeda is not directly involved, its ideology is a potent and dangerous weapon for like-minded jihadists.[63] As one commentator argues, 'Osama bin Laden's greatest threat may be that simply by claiming to act in his name, regional groups are better able to recruit and coordinate operations.'[64]

London has become a magnet for Islamic militants inspired by al Qaeda. In February 2006, Abu Hamza al-Masri, a radical Islamic cleric and imam at the infamous Finsbury Park mosque in North London, was convicted of 11 charges of soliciting murder and sentenced to seven years in prison for using his sermons to encourage followers to kill non-Muslims.[65] During the trial, the jury heard video recordings of al-Masri's sermons exhorting his followers to kill Americans and Jews. In one sermon he declared: 'Killing a Kaffir [non-believer] for any reason, you can say it is O.K. – even if there is no reason for it.'[66] The Egyptian-born al-Masri is not a recent convert to al Qaeda's jihad. Al-Masri fought in Afghanistan during the anti-Soviet jihad, where he lost one eye and both hands.[67] While fighting in Afghanistan, al-Masri became acquainted with Abdullah Azzam, Osama bin Laden and senior al Qaeda leaders.

The North London Central Mosque has attracted other Islamic extremists and jihadists including Richard Reid, the so-called 'shoe bomber,'[68] and Zacarias Moussaoui, the only person to have been convicted in the United States in connection with the September 11 terrorist attacks.[69] In January

2003, the Finsbury Park Mosque was raided by British police, who found nuclear, biological and chemical protective suits, blank-firing weapons and other 'terrorist paraphernalia' believed to have been used in terror training camps in Britain.[70]

Al Qaeda has inspired other terror plots in the U.K. In November 2006, an al Qaeda operative pleaded guilty in a British court to conspiring to commit mass murder and was sentenced to life in prison.[71] Dhiren Barot, a Hindu who converted to Islam, planned to pack three limousines with gas cylinders and explosives and detonate them in underground parking garages at landmark London hotels, identified as the Ritz and the Savoy, and railway stations, including London's Waterloo, Paddington and King's Cross stations as possible targets.[72] Barot trained at terror training camps affiliated with al Qaeda where he gained extensive training in the use of weapons, explosives, chemicals and constructing car bombs. According to British prosecutors, Barot intended to kill hundreds if not thousands of innocent people without warning and create a state of panic and chaos in London.[73]

More recently, in December 2006, British and American authorities thwarted an al Qaeda plot to detonate bombs on board as many as 12 commercial airliners flying direct routes between the U.K. and the United States.[74] The terrorists planned to smuggle the peroxide-based liquid explosive TATP and detonators on board the aircrafts and blow them up in mid-air. Intelligence officials estimate that if the terrorist scheme had succeeded about 2,700 people would have perished.[75] The terror plot had the hallmarks of an al Qaeda operation, resembling the infamous Bojinka plan devised by 9/11 mastermind, Khalid Sheikh Mohammed, to destroy 11 airliners over the Pacific in 1995.[76] In January 2007, British police arrested nine suspected terrorists for planning to kidnap, torture and behead a British Muslim soldier and broadcast the killing on the Internet.[77] The intent was to mimic an 'Iraqi-style execution' and broadcast it on the Internet.[78] Finally, in July 2007, British authorities arrested three doctors in connection with botched car-bomb attacks in London and Glasgow, Scotland.[79]

Al Qaeda has been extremely active in Italy and Germany. In August 2002, the United States and Italy designated 25 individuals for providing financial support to al Qaeda.[80] Of the 25 designations, 11 individuals were related to the Salafist Group for Call and Combat (GSPC). In November 2003, the U.S. Treasury Department and the Italian government designated 15 other individuals as al Qaeda-related terrorists under U.N. Security Council resolutions requiring member states to freeze their assets.[81] The individuals were designated for their involvement in al Qaeda terrorist cells in Milan, Cremona, and Parma. According to Italian authorities, some of the persons listed had provided financial and material support for terrorist activities and recruited volunteers for military camps in Iraq organized by Ansar al-Islam, an al Qaeda-affiliated terrorist group.[82]

In March 2004, at the request of the Italian authorities, the U.S. Treasury Department designated ten al Qaeda terrorists operating a terror cell in Italy.[83] All ten of these individuals had been convicted by the Tribunale di Napoli for criminal activities tied to al Qaeda, in particular through a relationship with the Armed Islamic Group (GIA) and the GSPC.[84] Italian officials maintain that these individuals provided the GIA with material and financial means for committing terrorist activities in Algeria and abroad. More recently, in August 2005, the U.S. Treasury Department designated three individuals for operating an al Qaeda-linked terror cell in Italy.[85] The individuals were designated for providing financial support to the Moroccan Islamic Combat Group, a terror group tied to al Qaeda, and Ansar al-Islam cells operating in Italy and abroad.[86]

Germany has served as the base of operations for some of the most deadly terrorists associated with al Qaeda. Mohamed Atta, the leader of the September 11 terror group, who piloted American Airlines Flight 11, Marwan al Shehhi, the pilot on United Airlines Flight 75, Ziad Jarrah, the pilot on United Airlines Flight 93, and Ramzi Binalshibh, one of the other 9/11 conspirators, all resided in Hamburg, Germany, where they formed a terror cell and plotted the 9/11 terrorist attacks.[87] Mamoun Derkanzali had close ties to the members of the Hamburg cell and helped to fund their activities. Between 1994 and 1998, $600,000 was transferred through his accounts to fund al Qaeda-related activities in Germany.[88]

Before assuming the leadership of al Qaeda in Iraq, Abu Musab al-Zarqawi was the operational leader of al-Tawhid wal-Jihad, a terrorist organization with strong connections to al Qaeda. According to German government officials, Al Tawhid formed an independent terror cell in Germany in September 2001. The group was involved in raising donations, recruiting terrorist fighters, forging passports, and planning attacks in Germany.[89] In addition to al-Zarqawi, the German government has submitted several al-Tawhid members to be added to the U.N. Security Council Resolution 1267 list of terrorists and terrorist supporters.[90] Further, in September 2007, German police arrested three Islamic militants suspected of planning large-scale terrorist attacks against sites frequented by Americans, including discos, bars, airports and military facilities.[91]

Finally, while al Qaeda has attacked American allies in the war in Iraq and the broader global conflict against the Islamic jihadists, lacking an alliance with the United States does not protect nations from the jihadist threat. The unrest of French Muslim minorities, the murder of film-maker Theo Van Gogh, and the Danish cartoon demonstrations revealed underlying tension between radical Islamic groups and European nations not allied with America's conflict in Iraq.[92]

NORTH AND EAST AFRICA

In a video released on September 11, 2006, coinciding with the fifth anniversary of the 9/11 terrorist attacks, Ayman al-Zawahiri formally announced that the Salafist Group for Preaching and Combat, known by its French acronym GSPC, had joined forces with al Qaeda in a union he hoped would be 'a thorn in the neck of the American and French Crusaders and their allies, and an arrow in the heart of the French traitors and apostates.'[93] The new organization is called 'Al Qaeda in Islamic Maghreb' (AQIM), a reference to African lands north of the Sahara.[94] This new group is led by the GSPC and seeks to unite hard-core militant Islamist groups in North Africa, including the Morocco Islamic Combatant Group (MICG), Libya's Islamic Fighting Group (LIFG) and the Tunisian Combatant Group. The objective of the merger is to organize extremist groups across North Africa with the remnants of al Qaeda into a new international force for jihad, and to coordinate and expand their terrorist activities into Europe.[95] A united Islamist terrorist front in North Africa poses a significant threat to the international community. An enhanced al Qaeda presence in the region through its affiliation with AQIM will likely result in increased attacks against oil-related targets, more strikes against soft targets such as restaurants and hotels, like those seen in Bali, Indonesia and Amman, Jordan, and more North African militants receiving training at al Qaeda-run camps.[96]

The GSPC is an Algerian-based terror group that operates in France, Germany, Italy, Spain and Switzerland.[97] A separatist faction of the Armed Islamic Group (GIA) created in 1998, the GSPC is currently the most effective and largest armed terror group in Algeria.[98] The number of active GSPC fighters is estimated at several hundred.[99] The network operates training camps in the Sahara and Sahel that attract foreign fighters from countries bordering Algeria, but also recruits from Europe. The terrorists are instructed on bomb-making and guerrilla tactics.[100] In its early stages, the GSPC's principal aim was to overthrow the Algerian government and replace it with a fundamentalist Islamic state.[101] However, the Algerian terror network has recently transformed itself into a regional threat targeting the United States and other so-called enemies of Islam. In 2006, Deputy al Qaeda leader Ayman al-Zawahiri released a videotape recording urging the militant Algerian Islamist group to attack the United States and the 'Crusader nation' France.[102] On September 24, 2001, the GSPC and the

GIA were designated SDGTs by the U.S. Treasury Department, and on October 8, 2002, the United Nations placed them both on the list of terrorist entities linked to al Qaeda.[103]

The AQIM/GSPC is responsible for a long string of deadly attacks in Algeria. In December 2007, two bombs exploded in close succession in Algiers, killing at least 45 people. Thirty were killed in a blast near the Constitutional Court building, while another 15 were killed in a second blast near United Nations offices.[104] In September 2007, 60 people were killed in multiple bomb attacks in Algeria, which included an assassination attempt on President Abdelaziz Bouteflika.[105] Al Qaeda's new affiliate in North Africa asserted responsibility for attacks in Algeria's capital, which killed 33 people and wounded 57, in April 2007.[106] In February 2007, the AQIM/GSPC claimed responsibility for a series of seven deadly bombings in a district east of Algiers that mainly targeted police stations, killing six people and injuring 30 others.[107] In a telephone call to the al-Jazeera network, an unidentified spokesman declared the group's intentions to expand its targets to focus on American interests. 'Wherever we can find a U.S. presence, we will, God willing, pursue it and its agents,' he stated.[108] French authorities thwarted a GSPC terror plot in Paris that targeted the Paris Metro, the city's Orly Airport, and the headquarters of the Direction de la Surveillance du Territoire, France's domestic intelligence agency.[109] One counter-terrorism expert noted that the 'G.S.P.C.'s mission is now to recruit people in Morocco and Tunisia, train them and send them back to their countries of origin or Europe to mount attacks.'[110]

In December 2006, a few months after the formal merger with al Qaeda, the AQIM/GSPC launched a deadly attack near Algiers on a bus carrying employees of an affiliate of the U.S. company Halliburton, killing the Algerian bus driver and wounding nine people, including four Britons, one Canadian, and an American.[111] The assailants hurled a bomb and opened fire at two vehicles transporting the foreign workers. In a statement posted on the Internet, the GSPC leader Abu Mus'ab al-Woud identified Halliburton as the target of the operation.[112] He stated that the attack was 'a gift to all Muslims who are suffering from the new Crusader campaign targeting Islam and its holy places,' and warned of future attacks.[113] In 2005, about 150 of the group's fighters attacked a Mauritanian military outpost, killing 15 soldiers, and signaling a shift in strategy to a broader global conflict beyond Algerian borders.[114] In 2003, a GSPC cell kidnapped 32 European tourists.[115] The GSPC reportedly received a $5 million ransom from the German government for the release of the German hostages.[116]

Al Qaeda has jihadist sympathizers in Morocco as well. The Moroccan Islamic Combatant Group, also known as the Groupe Islamique Combattant Marocain (GICM), is committed to establishing an Islamic state in Morocco and supporting al Qaeda's jihad against the West.[117] The al Qaeda-affiliated group is comprised of Moroccan recruits who trained in Afghanistan, Bosnia, and Chechnya, including some who fought in the Soviet–Afghanistan war. The group has cells in Belgium, France, Spain and elsewhere.[118] The GICM is one of the groups believed to have been involved in the May 2003 Casablanca suicide attacks on Western and Jewish targets that left 45 people dead and hundreds injured.[119] Eight Moroccans accused of belonging to the GICM were convicted and sentenced for their participation in the Casablanca attacks.[120] The group is further suspected of involvement in the March 2004 Madrid train bombings that killed 191 people and wounded about 2,000 others.[121] Twenty of the individuals charged with the Madrid attacks are Moroccan.[122] The al Qaeda-linked terror group has further been accused of recruiting and funneling Moroccan fighters to Iraq.[123]

In November 2002, the U.S. Treasury Department designated the GICM as an SDGT, authorizing a freeze of its assets.[124] The group was further designated a Foreign Terrorist Organization (FTO) by the U.S. State Department in October 2005. The GICM is believed to have joined AQIM.

Al Qaeda has another ideological ally operating in North Africa. The Libyan Islamic Fighting Group (LIFG) is committed to overthrowing the secular government of Libyan leader Muammar Qadhafi and replacing his regime with a rigid Islamic state.[125] A senior Treasury Department official has stated: 'The Libyan Islamic Fighting Group threatens global safety and stability through the use of violence and its ideological alliance with al Qaida and other brutal terrorist organizations.'[126] The LIFG is responsible for several operations inside Libya, including a 1996 attempt to assassinate President Qadhafi.[127] The LIFG is aligned with Osama bin Laden and al Qaeda and its members are believed to have planned the Casablanca suicide bombings in May 2003.[128] The U.S. designated the group as an SDGT on September 23, 2001.[129] In October 2001, the U.N. Security Council added the LIFG to its consolidated list of terrorist entities associated with al Qaeda.[130] The recently formed umbrella group of terrorist organizations in North Africa, AQIM, is believed to include the LIFG.[131]

Al Qaeda has established terror cells in other parts of Africa, including the Horn of Africa. Al Qaeda operatives, including persons involved in the 1998 bombings of the U.S. embassies in Kenya and Tanzania, who sought refuge in Somalia, comprise the core of the East Africa cell. In June 2006, Somali Islamic fundamentalists under the control of an al Qaeda cell in East Africa attacked and temporarily seized the Somali capital of Mogadishu and took control of much of southern Somalia.[132] After seizing control of the capital, a radical Islamist group known as the 'Council of Islamic Courts' attempted to establish a Taliban-like regime governed by strict Islamic law.[133] However, the Islamist militants were forced to flee the country by Ethiopian military forces supported by the United States.

SOUTHEAST ASIA

Indonesia and the Philippines have been victimized by *jihadi* terrorism for their perceived opposition to Islamic interests. Jemaah Islamiyah (JI) has emerged as the most dangerous jihadist group in the region.[134] JI is an al Qaeda-linked military group that has conducted several major terrorist attacks in Indonesia.[135] The group has been described as a 'terrorist franchise of al Qaida,' receiving significant training, financing and direction from bin Laden's organization.[136] JI has been designated as a Specially Designated Global Terrorist (SGDT) entity by the U.S. Treasury Department and added to the United Nations 1267 Committee's list of terrorist organizations tied to al Qaeda, requiring member States to freeze their assets.[137] Notably, 36 countries supported the U.N. listing of JI, including Australia, Indonesia, the Philippines, Singapore and other Southeast Asian and European countries.[138]

JI has conducted a violent campaign of terror in hopes of establishing a pan-Islamic state in Southeast Asia spanning Indonesia, Malaysia, southern Thailand, Singapore, Brunei, and the southern Philippines.[139] The terror group's most devastating attack occurred on October 12, 2002, when a minivan loaded with explosives and two smaller bombs were detonated in front of the American consulate and two nightclubs in Bali, Indonesia, killing 202 people, including more than 80 Australians.[140] The nightclubs were targeted because the patrons were foreigners, primarily from Western nations, though dozens of Indonesian nationals were also killed.[141] Other deadly attacks attributable to JI include bombings outside a J.W. Marriott Hotel in Jakarta, killing 12 people and injuring 150 others, in August 2003.[142] In September 2004, at least nine people were killed and 100 more injured when a suicide bomber detonated a car bomb near the Australian Embassy in Jakarta.[143] In May 2005, two bombs ripped through a busy market in a Christian town in eastern Indonesia, killing as many as 21 people. In October 2005, three simultaneous bombs exploded outside the Four Seasons hotel and a shopping center in Bali, killing at least 25 people and seriously injuring 101 others.[144] Australians, Japanese, South Koreans and Indonesians were reportedly among the dead.[145]

The campaign of terror will no doubt continue. In 2005, JI's supreme leader, Abu Bakar Bashir, reiterated his call for the destruction of the United States, England, Australia, Singapore, Thailand and the Philippines through violent jihad.[146] At the same time, international counter-terrorism efforts continue to meet with tempered success. In August 2003, Nurjaman Riduan Isamuddin (aka Hambali), a senior JI leader with close ties to al Qaeda and a long history of involvement in terrorist activity, was captured in Thailand, and he is in American custody.[147] In June 2007, Zarkasih, the group's overall leader, and Abu Dujana, JI's military chief, were captured by Indonesia's anti-terror police.[148] However, the threat existing in and proceeding from Southeast Asia remains high in a region that has served as an important financial hub for the international jihadist network.

JI is not the only al Qaeda-affiliated terror group in Southeast Asia. The Abu Sayyaf Group (ASG) is a violent Muslim terrorist organization operating in the southern Philippines.[149] According to the U.S. Treasury Department, '[t]he Abu Sayyaf Group instills terror throughout Southeast Asia through kidnappings, bombings and brutal killings.'[150] In the early 1990s, the group split from the much larger Moro National Liberation Front. The ASG's membership has been estimated at between 400 and 500 members.[151] The terror group's primary goal is to establish an independent Islamic state in western Mindanao and the Sulu Archipelago, areas in the southern Philippines heavily populated by Muslims.[152] The ASG is responsible for a series of brutal murders, kidnappings, acts of piracy and terrorist bombings, including the Philippines' worst terror attack – the February 2004 ferry bombing that killed more than 100 people.[153] In May 2001, ASG members kidnapped 17 Philippine nationals and three American tourists (a missionary couple, Martin and Gracia Burnham, and Guillermo Sobero) from a tourist resort in Palawan, the Philippines.[154] In June 2001, Sobero and two of the Philippine hostages were beheaded by the militants.[155] Martin Burnham and his wife Gracia were held hostage for another year before Gracia was rescued on June 7, 2002. Martin Burnham and one of the Philippine hostages were both killed during an encounter between the ASG and Philippine military forces.[156]

In October 2002 in Zamboanga, the Philippines, ASG members conducted bombings at shopping centers and near a restaurant, killing 11 Filipino civilians and an American soldier and wounding more than 200 others.[157] In March 2004, the Philippine authorities thwarted an ASG terrorist plot whose bombing targets included the U.S. Embassy in Manila. Finally, in February 2005, the Muslim extremist group claimed responsibility for a series of deadly bombs, all detonated within an hour, in Manila and two other cities, killing at least 11 people and wounding dozens of others.[158]

The ASG has multiple connections to al Qaeda. The International Islamic Relief Organization (IIRO), a Saudi-based charity with a long history of facilitating fundraising for al Qaeda and affiliated terrorist organizations, has been a source of funding for the ASG. Abd al Hamid

Sulaiman Al-Mujil (Al-Mujil), a high-ranking IIRO official, is a close associate of bin Laden and senior al Qaeda operational planner Khalid Sheik Muhammad.[159] Al-Mujil has been identified as a major fundraiser for both the ASG and JI.[160] The ASG has also received funding from the Philippine branch offices of the IIRO (IIRO-PHL). The founder and former director of the IIRO-PHL is Muhammad Jamal Khalifah, Osama bin Laden's brother-in-law, who has been identified as a senior member of al Qaeda.[161] As the result of its terrorist activities, the ASG has been named an FTO and SDGT by the U.S. Government.[162]

SOUTH ASIA

There are seven main groups of jihadists operating in Pakistan and Kashmir: al-Badr; Lashkar-e-Tayyiba; Jaish-e-Muhhamad; Harakat-ul-Mujahedeen; Harakat-ul-Jihad-Islam; Jamaat-ul-Mujahedeen; and the Jammu and Kashmir Islamic Front.[163] Of these seven groups, three, Lashkar-e-Tayyiba, Jaish-e-Muhhamad, and Harakat-ul-Mujahedeen, have been linked to al Qaeda.[164] These militant groups share the goal of expelling India from the majority-Muslim region of Jammu and Kashmir and establishing an Islamic state.[165] Osama Bin Laden has embraced the Kashmir conflict in his public statements calling for all Muslims to join his global jihad.[166] In an interview conducted with al-Jazeera which aired in January 2002, bin Laden declared that it is mandatory for all Muslims to engage in *jihad* to free the Muslim lands from the polytheists, including expelling the infidel from the disputed territory of Jammu and Kashmir.[167] In June 2007, al Qaeda hardened its position on Kashmir when it distributed a DVD to media organizations in Srinigar declaring war on India.[168]

There is a growing nexus between al Qaeda and Kashmiri Islamist militant groups operating in India. Lashkar-e-Tayyiba (LT) (meaning 'Army of the Pure') is one of the extremist groups linked to al Qaeda.[169] LT is reputed to be one of the largest and most brutal terrorist groups fighting in Kashmir against India. It was established in 1993 as the military wing of the Pakistan-based religious organization, the Markaz-ud-Dawa-wal-Irshad madrasa.[170] LT's leader is Hafiz Mohammed Sayeed.[171] With approximately 1,500 fighters in Kashmir, the group operates in the Srinigar Valley from its bases in Gujranwala. LT's goals are to institute a fundamentalist theocratic state in Pakistan and to exploit tensions in Kashmir to spur a movement across all of India.[172] LT has conducted a number of operations against Indian troops and civilian targets in Jammu and Kashmir since 1993, resulting in hundreds of fatalities and injuries.[173] The Indian government publicly implicated LT, along with Jaish-e-Muhhamad, for the attack in December 2001 on the Indian parliament building, although LT's complicity has not been firmly established. Senior al Qaeda leader Abu Zubaydah was captured at an LT safe house in Faisalabad in March 2002, further establishing links between LT and al Qaeda.[174] In July 2006, seven bombs ripped through railway cars and platforms during the rush hour in Mumbai, India, killing approximately 135 civilians and injuring 200 others.[175] LT is suspected of responsibility for these terrorist bombings.

In 2001, the U.S. State Department designated LT as an FTO and the Treasury Department designated the group as an SDGT.[176] As a result, all transactions with members of LT and any U.S. person are prohibited and any assets belonging to the militant extremist group are required to be frozen. The following year, Pakistan's President Pervez Musharraf banned LT.

Jaish-e-Muhhamad (JEM) (literally the 'Soldiers of Muhammad') and Harakat-ul-Mujahedeen (HUM) (literally the 'Movement of Holy Warriors') have also been directly linked to bin Laden's network. JEM is an Islamic extremist group based in Pakistan that was created by Masood Azhar, a former senior leader in HUM.[177] According to the State Department, '[t]he group's aim is to unite Kashmir with Pakistan, and it has openly declared war against the United States.'[178] JEM has several hundred armed supporters.[179] It has claimed responsibility for several suicide car bombings in Kashmir, including a suicide attack on the Jammu and Kashmir legislative assembly building in October 2001 that killed more than 30 people.[180] The Pakistan government has implicated elements of JEM in two assassination attempts against President Musharraf in December 2003.[181] In July 2004, Pakistani police arrested a JEM member in connection with the 2002 abduction and murder of U.S. journalist Daniel Pearl.[182] In February 2007, four members of JEM were arrested for plotting bomb blasts in crowded market areas of India's capital, New Delhi.[183] JEM was designated an SDGT by the Treasury Department in October 2001.[184] Pakistan outlawed the group in 2002.[185] In addition to its increasingly wider aims against the United States, bin Laden is suspected of providing funding to JEM.[186]

HUM was formed in 1985 as fighters in the Soviet–Afghanistan campaign.[187] Since approximately January 2005, the group has been led by Dr Badr Munir.[188] The organization has approximately 300 members.[189] HUM advocates a strong pan-Islamic ideology, calling for the secession of Jammu and Kashmir as the first step in a war against India.[190] The former leader of the group, Maulana Fazlur Rehman, has been linked to bin Laden, and his signature was found on bin Laden's 1998 Khost fatwa issued on behalf of the World Islamic Front.[191]

HUM has conducted a number of terrorist operations against Indian troops and civilian targets in Kashmir. HUM is alleged to have hijacked an

Indian Airlines flight in 1999 with the support of the Taliban.[192] The hijacking resulted in the release of Masood Azhar, an important leader in the former Harakat-ul-Ansar, who founded JEM after his release.[193] In November 2006, HUM gunmen shot and killed a former Special Police Officer in Baramulla.[194] As a result of its terrorist activities, HUM was designated an SDGT by the Treasury Department in September 2001.[195] The Pakistani government banned the group in 2002.[196]

The first sign of ties to al Qaeda occurred in August 1998 after the U.S. struck Afghanistan with cruise missiles in retaliation for the attacks against the American embassies in Kenya and Tanzania.[197] Twenty-one of the militants that were killed in al Qaeda camps were found to be affiliated with both HUM and LT.[198] A considerable number of LT militants have been killed or captured in militant centers run by al Qaeda.[199] Some Pakistani sources suggest that financial flows exist between al-Qaeda and these groups.[200]

A 2006 RAND report stated that, although there is no conclusive evidence to verify concerted ties between al Qaeda and Kashmiri groups, the internationalist and anti-Western ideology of these groups has increased markedly.[201] For instance, LT is alleged to have been key in 'recruiting jihadists to fight coalition forces in Iraq' and some of those involved in the July 2005 London bombings may have sought militant training in LT's camps in Pakistan.[202] Also, there have been signs of greater cooperation between these different Kashmiri groups through the creation of umbrella organizations.[203] The RAND report noted that '[w]ith Pakistan coming under increased pressure to curtail all overt physical support for militant extremism on its soil, it is conceivable that LT, HUM, and JEM could move to consolidate links with outside jihadists, including those associated with al-Qaeda.'[204] Finally, in March 2008, the U.S. State Department designated Harakat ul-Jihad-I-Islami/Bangladesh (HUJI-B) as a specially designed global terrorist. HUJI-B is linked to al Qaeda and advocates a system of Islamic rule across Bangladesh.[205]

Al Qaeda and the Taliban have exerted a formidable and deadly presence in Afghanistan. The Taliban are resurgent and dominate large areas in southern Afghanistan. Tehrik-e-Taliban Pakistan, also known as the Taliban Movement of Pakistan, has emerged as a new terrorist threat. The Taliban Movement of Pakistan, headed by Baitullah Mehsud, operates in the Waziristan region, along the Pakistan border with Afghanistan, where Western intelligence sources maintain that al Qaeda is regrouping.[206] There are currently estimated to be about 3,000 active and as many as 7,000 occasional Taliban fighters in Afghanistan, and the Taliban Movement of Pakistan is estimated to control a fighting force of 40,000.[207] Al Qaeda and the Taliban continue to have a close relationship. In September 2007,

Ayman al-Zawahiri, al Qaeda's second-in-command, delivered a video message referring to Mullah Omar, the head of the Taliban, as the supreme leader.

CONCLUSION

Once the scope of al Qaeda's global reach is fully understood, it becomes eminently clear that the Islamist militant group needs vast sums of money to sustain and support its global terrorist ties. Al Qaeda requires tens of millions of dollars annually to support its global terror network. Money is needed to provide logistical support to al Qaeda's surrogate groups operating around the globe, including in the Middle East, Europe, Africa, Southeast Asia, and South Asia. More money is needed to sustain al Qaeda's propaganda campaign intended to inspire homegrown jihadists and enlist new members. Finally, millions of dollars more are needed to secure a terrorist safe haven for bin Laden and al Qaeda's core leadership in Waziristan, Pakistan. In short, bin Laden's *dar el Harb* ('house of war') cannot be successfully waged on the cheap. Money is the key to al Qaeda's success.

Since the September 11, 2001 terrorist attacks, al Qaeda has emerged as the head of a global Islamist terror movement, comprised of dozens of deadly jihadist groups. Several members of the al Qaeda terror movement have been designated as FTOs by the U.S. Secretary of State.[208] FTOs are designated pursuant to section 219 of the Immigration and Nationality Act, which requires a finding by the Secretary of State that the organization is (1) a foreign organization (2) that engages in terrorist activity, and (3) threatens the security of U.S. nationals or the national security (defense, foreign relations, or economic interests) of the United States.[209] It is unlawful for a person in the United States to knowingly provide 'material support or resources' to such an organization.[210] According to the State Department, approximately 19 FTOs are affiliated with al Qaeda:

Abu Sayyaf Group;
Al-Shabaab;
Ansar al-Sunna;
Armed Islamic Group;
Asbat a-Ansar;
Gama'a al-Islamiyya (Islamic Group);
Harkat-ul-Jihad al Islami;
Harakat ul-Mujahedin;
Islamic Jihad Group;
Islamic Movement of Uzbekistan;
Jaish-e-Mohammed;
Jemaah Islamiya;
Al-Jihad (merged with al Qaeda);
Lashkar-e-Tayyiba;
Lashkar i Jhangvi;
Libyan Islamic Fighting Group;
Moroccan Islamic Combat Group;
Al Qaeda in Iraq; and
Al Qaeda in the Islamic Maghreb.[211]

These terrorist organizations operate throughout the world, underscoring al Qaeda's global presence and influence. These groups are inspired by Osama bin Laden's message of waging a global insurgency, overthrowing apostate Muslim governments, forcing American forces from Iraq, seeking the destruction of Israel, and establishing a theocratic state governed by strict Islamic law.[212] Some jihadist groups also receive funding, training, equipment and other material support from al Qaeda. Bin Laden also supports Palestinian terrorist groups that seek to expel Israel from the Middle East and establish a Palestinian state. Many of these organizations have also been designated as FTOs, such as the Al Aqsa Martyrs Brigade, Islamic Resistance Movement (HAMAS), Hizballah, Palestine Liberation Front, Palestine Islamic Jihad, Popular Front for the Liberation of Palestine, and Popular Front for the Liberation of Palestine-General Command.[213] Clearly, al Qaeda and its allies pose a serious threat not only to the United States but to the peace and security of the international community. The terrorist movement inspired by bin Laden transcends national boundaries. It cannot be defeated by any one country acting alone. Instead, a sustained, coordinated international response is required.

NOTES

1. MESSAGES TO THE WORLD: THE STATEMENTS OF OSAMA BIN LADEN (Bruce Lawrence ed., James Howarth trans., Verso 2005) [hereinafter STATEMENTS OF OSAMA BIN LADEN].
2. Daniel Byman, *Al-Qaeda as an Adversary: Do We Understand Our Enemy?*, 56 WORLD POLITICS 139, 154 (2003) (quoting ANONYMOUS, THROUGH OUR ENEMIES' EYES: OSAMA BIN LADEN, RADICAL ISLAM, AND THE FUTURE OF AMERICA 18 (Brassey's 2002)) [hereinafter *Al-Qaeda as an Adversary*].
3. *Id.* For a discussion on the different components of al Qaeda membership, see Bruce Hoffman, *Challenges for the U.S. Special Operations Command Posed by the Global Terrorist Threat: Al Qaeda on the Run or on the March*?, Written Testimony before the House Armed Services Subcomm. on Terrorism, Unconventional Threats & Capabilities, (Feb. 14, 2007), *available at* http://www.investigativeproject.org/documents/testimony/267.pdf [hereinafter *Bruce Hoffman Testimony: Al Qaeda on the Run or on the March*].
4. *See* Letter from Ayman al-Zawahiri to Abu Musab al-Zarqawi (July 9, 2005) (stating that al Qaeda's primary goal is the establishment of a caliphate in the manner of the Prophet), *available at* http://weeklystandard.com/Content/Public/Articles/000/000/006/203gpuul.asp.
5. *Al-Qaeda as an Adversary*, *supra* note 2, at 134.
6. *See generally* ANGEL RABASA, ET AL., BEYOND AL QAEDA: THE GLOBAL JIHADIST MOVEMENT (RAND 2006) [hereinafter BEYOND AL QAEDA]. The Islamists have also actively sought to create an Islamic state in the Caucasus and Central Asia. *Id.* at 105–12. However, the militant activity has slowed since the Chechen terrorists seized a public school in Beslan in 2004, resulting in the deaths of more than 300 civilians, which undermined support among Westerners for the separatists. *See* C.J. Chivers, *Success of Amnesty Program for Chechen Rebels is Contested*, N.Y. TIMES, Jan. 16, 2007, *available at* http://query.nytimes.com/gst/fullpage.html?res=9407E3D91030F935A25752C0A9

619C8B63&scp=157&sq=c.j.+chivers&st=nyt. The separatist movement has also been undermined by the deaths of former Chechen leaders, including Shamil Basayev, the Chechen terrorist leader, and two former senior aides, Aslan Maskhadov and Abdul Khalim Saidullayev. *Id.*

7. *See* 2006 Country Reports on Terrorism, U.S. Dep't of State, Office of the Coordinator for Counterterrorism (Apr. 30, 2007), *available at* http://www.state.gov/s/ct/rls/crt/2006/82738.htm [hereinafter 2006 Country Reports on Terrorism].
8. Bin Laden boasts that more than 15,000 Arab fighters were trained in jihad training camps in Afghanistan. *See* STATEMENTS OF OSAMA BIN LADEN, *supra* note 1, at 76.
9. *See* ABDEL BARI ATWAN, THE SECRET HISTORY OF AL QAEDA 179 (University of California Press, 2006) [hereinafter THE SECRET HISTORY OF AL QAEDA] ('The arrival of 150,000 US troops in Iraq in March 2003 created exactly the turning point in al Qaeda's history that bin Laden dreamed of.').
10. *See* Bruce Riedel, *Al Qaeda Strikes Back*, FOREIGN AFFAIRS, May/June 2007, *available at* http://www.foreignaffairs.org/20070501faessay86304/bruce-riedel/al-qaeda-strikes-back.html. According to one source, Iraq has the second-largest potential oil reserves in the world after Saudi Arabia, in excess of 300 billion barrels. *See* THE SECRET HISTORY OF AL QAEDA, *supra* note 9, at 184.
11. James Phillips, *The Evolving Al-Qaeda Threat*, HERITAGE FOUND., Mar. 17, 2006, *available at* http://www.heritage.org/Research/NationalSecurity/hl928.cfm [hereinafter *The Evolving Al-Qaeda Threat*].
12. THE SECRET HISTORY OF AL QAEDA, *supra* note 9, at 200.
13. *Id.* at 203.
14. Al-Zarqawi's connections to al Qaeda preceded his efforts to assist the terror group in Iraq. In 2000, he reportedly visited al Qaeda training camps in Afghanistan. *See id.* at 196.
15. *See id.* at 198.
16. *Id.* at 205.
17. *See The Evolving Al-Qaeda Threat*, *supra* note 11 (in audiotape released on Dec. 27, 2004, bin Laden named al-Zarqawi as his deputy in charge of al Qaeda operations in Iraq).
18. *See* Letter from Ayman al-Zawahiri to Abu Musab al-Zarqawi, *supra* note 4.
19. *Id.*
20. *Id.*
21. *Id.*
22. *Id.*
23. According to one commentator, al-Zarqawi's strategy in Iraq appears to have four goals: (1) isolating America from its allies and supporters; (2) preventing Iraqis from cooperating with the U.S.-led Coalition; (3) obstructing the efforts involved in the reconstruction of Iraq; and (4) fomenting secular conflict by targeting the Shiites. *See* THE SECRET HISTORY OF AL QAEDA, *supra* note 9, at 203–4.
24. *See id.* at 202.
25. *Id.* An organization called the Abu Hafez al Masri Brigade claimed responsibility for the attack on the U.N. headquarters in Baghdad, claiming that U.N. soldiers in Bosnia stood by when Serbs massacred Muslim women and children in 1992 and 1995. The group is believed to be a cover for al Qaeda. *See* SHAUL SHAY, ISLAMIC TERROR AND THE BALKANS 169 (Transaction Publ. 2006).
26. Al-Zarqawi has declared that killing civilian Muslims is justified under Islam as long as they are infidels. 'Islam does not differentiate between civilians and military, but rather distinguishes between Muslims and infidels.' *Zarqawi Justifies Killing of Civilians*, WASH. TIMES, Oct. 8, 2005; *see also* THE SECRET HISTORY OF AL QAEDA, *supra* note 9, at 205; *The Evolving Al-Qaeda Threat, supra* note 11 (al-Zarqawi has deployed truck bombs against Shiite mosques and religious ceremonies in Iraq to provoke a civil war).
27. THE SECRET HISTORY OF AL QAEDA, *supra* note 9, at 204.
28. *See* 2006 Country Reports on Terrorism, *supra* note 7, at 218–20.
29. *See* The Investigative Project on Terrorism, Al Qaeda in Iraq, *available at* http://www.investigativeproject.org/profile/124.

30. On June 7, 2006, al-Zarqawi was killed by a U.S. military airstrike north of Baghdad. *See Insurgent Leader Al-Zarqawi Killed in Iraq*, WASH. POST, June 8, 2006 *available at* http://www.washingtonpost.com/wp-dyn/content/article/2006/06/08/AR2006060800114.html.
31. *Id.*
32. *See Iraqi Woman's Death Sentence Upheld*, WASH. POST, Jan. 27, 2007, *available at* http://www.washingtonpost.com/wp-dyn/content/article/2007/01/27/AR2007012700463.html.
33. In a video aired on the Qatari-based Al-Jazeera television network following al-Zarqawi's death, Ayman al-Zawahiri, al Qaeda's second-in-command, paid tribute to the slain al Qaeda leader in Iraq, extolling him as 'a soldier, a hero, an imam (Islamic cleric) and the prince of martyrs.' *Al-Qaida Leader Praises al-Zarqawi*, NEWSDAY, June 24, 2006.
34. *See US Denies Qaeda Leader Dead, Baghdad Push Unoppose* [sic], REUTERS, Feb. 16, 2007 (the U.S. has placed a $5 million bounty for information resulting in the capture or death of al-Masri) *available at* http://www.alertnet.org/thenews/newsdesk/L16903919.htm.
35. THE SECRET HISTORY OF AL QAEDA, *supra* note 9, at 188.
36. *See* Press Release, U.S. Dep't of Treasury, Treasury Designations Target Terrorist Facilitators (Dec. 7, 2006), *available at* http://www.treas.gov/press/releases/hp191.htm.
37. *See* 2006 Country Reports on Terrorism, *supra* note 7.
38. *Id.*
39. *See* Press Release, U.S. Dep't of Treasury, Treasury Department Statement Regarding the Designation of Ansar al-Islam (Feb. 20, 2003), *available at* http://www.treas.gov/press/releases/js48.htm.
40. *Id.*
41. *See id.*
42. *See* STATEMENTS OF OSAMA BIN LADEN, *supra* note 1, at 45 ('By being loyal to the U.S. regime, the Saudi regime has committed an act against Islam.')
43. *See Riyadh: Car Bombings Signal New Phase in Saudi War*, STRATFOR, May 13, 2003, *available at* http://www.stratfor.com/products/premium; *see also The Evolving Al-Qaeda Threat*, *supra* note 11.
44. *Riyadh: Car Bombings Signal New Phase in Saudi War*, STRATFOR, May 13, 2003, *available at* http://www.stratfor.com/products/premium.
45. *See Riyadh Bombing Likely To Backfire on Militants*, STRATFOR, Nov. 10, 2003, *available at* http://www.stratfor.com/products/premium/print.php?storyId=224506.
46. *Id.*
47. *See* BEYOND AL-QAEDA, *supra* note 6, at 77.
48. *See Saudis Blame al Qaeda for Attack*, CNN.COM, *available at* http://www.cnn.com/2004/WORLD/meast/05/30/saudi.shooting/index.html.
49. *See Saudi Arabia Beheading: What Comes Next?*, STRATFOR, June 18, 2004, *available at* http://www.stratfor.com/products/premium.
50. *Id.*
51. *See Saudi Arabia: The Attack Near Tabuk*, STRATFOR, Feb. 26, 2007, *available at* http://www.stratfor.com/products/premium/print.php?storyId=284855 (discussing numerous al-Qaeda related attacks committed in Saudi Arabia since 2004).
52. *Sawt Al Jihad: Signs of a Saudi al Qaeda Resurgence?*, STRATFOR, Jan. 31, 2007, *available at* http://www.stratfor.com/sawt_al_jihad_signs_saudi_al_qaeda_resurgence.
53. *See Saudi Arabia: The Reappearance of al Qaeda's Online Magazine*, STRATFOR, Feb. 10, 2007, *available at* http://www.stratfor.com/saudi_arabia_reappearance_al_qaedas_online_magazine.
54. *See* OSAMA BIN LADEN, AMERICA'S ENEMY IN HIS OWN WORDS 60–63 (Randall B. Hamud ed., Nadeem Pub. 2005). In addition to bin Laden and Ayman al-Zawahiri, the 1998 fatwa was signed by Abu-Yasir Rifa'i Ahmad Taha, leader of the Egyptian Islamic Group, Sheikh Mil-Harnzah, Secretary of Jamiat-ul-Ulema-e-Pakistan, and Fazlur Rahman, leader of the Jihad Movement in Bangladesh. *Id.* at 60.
55. *See* 2006 Country Reports on Terrorism, *supra* note 7, at 204.

56. *See* Press Release, U.S. Dep't of Treasury, Treasury Designates Seven al Qaida Associates (Oct. 3, 2005), *available at* http://www.treas.gov/press/releases/js 2960.htm.
57. *Id.*
58. Mary Jordan & Kevin Sullivan, *Britain Arrests 9 in Anti-Terror Raids*, WASH. POST, Feb. 1, 2007 *available at* http://www.washingtonpost.com/wp-dyn/content/article/2007/01/31/AR2007013100290.html (discussing multiple terrorist plots in the U.K.); Elisabetta Povoledo & Ian Fisher, *Egyptian is Focus of Attention as Madrid Bomb Trial Opens*, N.Y. TIMES, Feb. 15, 2007, *available at* http://www.nytimes.com/2007/02/15/world/europe/15trial.html?scp=1&sq=madrid&st=nyt. While there has been much speculation about the involvement of al Qaeda, if any, the British government has concluded that it played some role. One of the terrorist bombers sought out and received training from al Qaeda operatives during a visit to Pakistan in 2003. Additionally, al-Zawahiri stated that al Qaeda was responsible for launching the attacks. *Id.*
59. *See* Elisabetta Povoledo & Ian Fisher, *Egyptian is Focus of Attention as Madrid Bomb Trial Opens*, N.Y. TIMES, Feb. 15, 2007, *available at* http://www.nytimes.com/2007/02/15/world/europe/15trial.html?scp=1&sq=madrid&st=nyt. *See also* Alan Cowell, *One Year Later, Video Shows Warning by London Bomber*, N.Y. TIMES, July 7, 2006, *available at* http://www.nytimes.com/2006/07/07/world/europe/07britain.html.
60. *See id.*
61. *See Bruce Hoffman Testimony: Al Qaeda on the Run or the March, supra* note 3.
62. Kathryn Haahr, *Assessing Spain's al-Qaeda Network*, 3 TERRORISM MONITOR 1 (July 1, 2005).
63. *Al-Qaeda as an Adversary*, *supra* note 2, at 157.
64. Scott Atran, *A Leaner, Meaner Jihad*, N.Y. TIMES, Mar. 16, 2004, *available at* http://query.nytimes.com/gst/fullpage.html?res=9C0DE7D91631F935A25750C0A9629C8B63&scp=11&sq=scott+atran&st=nyt.
65. *See British Jury Finds Muslim Cleric Guilty of Inciting Murder*, N.Y. TIMES, Feb. 7, 2006, *available at* http://www.nytimes.com/2006/02/07/international/europe/07cnd-cleric.html.
66. *Id.*
67. *Id.*
68. On December 22, 2001, Richard Reid attempted to detonate a bomb on board American Airlines passenger flight 63, which was traveling from Paris to Miami. His shoes were loaded with explosives that he attempted to ignite, in order to destroy the aircraft and kill its 196 passengers and crew members. Thanks to the alertness of a flight attendant, aided by other passengers on board, Reid's terror plot was foiled. *See* SHAY, *supra* note 25, at 162.
69. *See* United States v. Moussaoui, Statement of Facts, Crim. No. 01–455-A (E.D. Va. 2005).
70. *See British Jury Finds Muslim Cleric Guilty of Inciting Murder*, N.Y. TIMES, Feb. 7, 2006, *supra* note 65
71. Alan Cowell, *British Court Hears of Qaeda Plans for 'Black Day'*, N.Y. TIMES, Nov. 7, 2006 *available at* http://www.nytimes.com/2006/11/07/world/europe/07london.html?scp=1&sq=&st=nyt.
72. *Id.*
73. *Id.*
74. *See Thwarting the Airline Plot: Inside the Investigation*, TIME, Aug. 10, 2006, *available at* http://www.time.com/time/nation/article/0,8599,1225453,00.html. Two of the suspects allegedly involved in the terror plot had contact with a Pakistani suspected of being an al Qaeda operative. *See Terror Plot Leaves Britain on Highest Alert*, CNN, Aug. 11, 2006, *available at* http://www.cnn.com/2006/WORLD/europe/08/11/terror.plot/index.html.
75. *Id.*
76. *See Foiled Transatlantic Bomb Plot 'Was Ready to Go in Days'*, TIMES (LONDON), Aug. 10, 2006, *available at* http://www.timesonline.co.uk/tol/news/uk/crime/article605120.ece.

77. *See* Mary Jordan & Kevin Sullivan, *supra* note 58.
78. *Id.*
79. *See* Karla Adam, *2 More Doctors Charged in Botched British Bombings*, WASH. POST, July 15, 2007, *available at* http://www.washingtonpost.com/wp-dyn/content/article/2007/07/14/AR2007071400534.html.
80. *See* Press Release, U.S. Dep't of Treasury, The United States and Italy Designate Twenty-Five New Financiers of Terror, (Aug. 29, 2002), *available at* http://www.treas.gov/press/releases/po3380.htm.
81. *See* Press Release, U.S. Dep't of Treasury, U.S. Designates 15 Members of Italian Al-Qaida Cell–Designation Comes in Response to the Submission by Italy of these Individuals to the UN (Nov. 12, 2003), *available at* http://www.treas.gov/press/releases/js 993.htm.
82. *Id.*
83. *See* Press Release, U.S. Dep't of Treasury, Treasury Designates Ten Al Qaida Members Operating Italy-Based Terror Cell (Mar. 18, 2004), *available at* http://www.treas.gov/press/releases/js 1243.htm.
84. *Id.*
85. *See* Press Release, U.S. Dep't of Treasury, Treasury Designates Three Individuals Linked to Al Qaida Terror Cell in Italy (Aug. 1, 2005), *available at* http://www.treasury.gov/press/releases/js 2668.htm.
86. *Id.*
87. *See* THE NATIONAL COMMISSION ON TERRORIST ATTACKS, THE 9/11 COMMISSION REPORT: FINAL REPORT OF THE NATIONAL COMMISSION ON TERRORIST ATTACKS UPON THE UNITED STATES 160–68 (W.W. Norton & Company 2004), *available at* http://www.9-11commission.gov/report/911Report.pdf. Binalshibh was unable to obtain a U.S. visa to travel to the United States, which doomed his chances of participating firsthand in the 9/11 attacks. *Id.* at 168; *see also* Military Commission 9/11 Charge Sheet (Feb. 11, 2008), *available at* http://www.defenselink.mil/news/Feb2008/d20080211chargesheet.pdf.
88. *See* SHAY, *supra* note 25, at 147.
89. *See* Press Release, U.S. Dep't of Treasury, Treasury Designates Six Al-Qaida Terrorists (Sept. 24, 2003), *available at* http://www.treas.gov/press/releases/js 757.htm.
90. *Id.*
91. *See* Mark Landler, *German Police Arrest 3 in Terrorist Plot*, N.Y. TIMES, Sept. 6, 2007, *available at* http://www.nytimes.com/2007/09/06/world/europe/06germany.html?scp=2&sq=&st=nyt.
92. *See* Nicholas Kulish, *New Terrorism Case Confirms That Denmark is a Target*, N.Y. TIMES, Sept. 17, 2007, *available at* http://www.nytimes.com/2007/09/17/world/europe/17denmark.html?scp=2&sq=&st=nyt; Maggie Michael, *Al-Qaida: Bounty on Swedish Cartoonist*, ABC NEWS, Sept. 15, 2007, *available at* http://abcnews.go.com/International/wireStory?id=3606944; *see also Al-Qaeda 'Issues France Threat'*, BBC, Sept. 14, 2006, *available at* http://news.bbc.co.uk/2/hi/europe/5345202.stm; Bruce Reidel, *Al Qaeda Targets France*, L.A. TIMES, June 14, 2007, *available at* http://www.brookings.edu/views/op-ed/riedel/20070614.htm.
93. Fred Burton, *Al Qaeda's Pan-Maghreb Gambit*, STRATFOR, Nov. 11, 2006, *available at* http://www.stratfor.com/al_qaedas_pan_maghreb_gambit.
94. *Id.*
95. *Id.*; *see also* Andrew Black, *The Reconstructed Al-Qaeda Threat in the Maghreb*, 5 TERRORISM MONITOR 7 (Feb. 1, 2007), *available at* http://www.jamestown.org/terrorism/news/article.php?articleid=2370242.
96. Burton, *supra* note 93.
97. *See* Craig Whitlock, *Al-Qaeda's Far-Reaching New Partner*, WASH. POST, Oct. 5, 2006, *available at* http://www.washingtonpost.com/wp-dyn/content/article/2006/10/04/AR2006100402006_pf.html. The GSPC is also known as Le Groupe Salafist pour la Predication et le Combat. Algeria's insurgency began when the army canceled the country's first national multiparty elections in 1992, which a Muslim fundamentalist

party was expected to win. The group is led by Abu Musab Abd al-Wadoud. *See* Burton, *supra* note 93.
98. The GIA subscribed to *takfir*, an Islamic fundamentalist belief that any Muslim who does not embrace a strict, fundamentalist Islamic code of conduct is an apostate deserving of death. Adhering to this view, GIA killed thousands of so-called Muslim nonbelievers. Objecting to the killing of Muslims, the GSPC separated from the GIA and formed a separate group in 1998. *See* Whitlock, *supra* note 97.
99. *See* 2006 Country Reports on Terrorism, *supra* note 7, at 226.
100. According to a study released by the Saudi National Security Assessment Project, veterans of the GSPC training camps are fighting in Iraq. North Africans comprise approximately 30 percent of foreign fighters in Iraq, with 22 percent from Algeria alone. *See* Whitlock, *supra* note 97.
101. *See Al-Qaeda 'Issues France Threat'*, BBC, Sept. 14, 2006, *available at* http://news.bbc.co.uk/2/hi/europe/5345202.stm. Along with other Islamist militant groups, the GSPC fought a brutal decade-long civil war after the Algerian military canceled elections in 1992 because an Islamist party was expected to win. *Id.*
102. *Latest Al-Qaeda Tape Made France a Target*, N.Y. TIMES, Sept. 14, 2006; *see also* Bruce Riedel, *Al Qaeda Targets France*, L.A. TIMES, June 14, 2007, *available at* http://www.brookings.edu/views/op-ed/riedel/20070614.htm.
103. *See* Press Release, U.S. Dep't of Treasury, Statement of U.S. Treasury Under Secretary for Enforcement Jimmy Gurulé in Support of Today's New Terrorist Financing Designations (Aug. 29, 2002), *available at* http://www.treas.gov/press/releases/po3379.htm.
104. *See* Katrin Bennhold & Craig S. Smith, *Twin Bombs Kill Dozens in Algiers*, N.Y. TIMES, Dec. 12, 2007, *available at* http://www.nytimes.com/2007/12/12/world/africa/12algiers.html.
105. *See Maghreb al Qaeda Deputy Killed in Algeria*, REUTERS, Oct. 9, 2007, *available at* http://www.alertnet.org/thenews/newsdesk/L09732371.htm.
106. *See* Craig Smith, *Qaeda Affiliate in Algeria Kills 6 as Bombs Strike Police Stations*, N.Y. TIMES, Feb. 14, 2007, *available at* http://www.nytimes.com/2007/02/14/world/africa/14algeria.htm.
107. John Thorne, *Bombings May Signal New Algeria Violence*, WASH. POST, Feb. 15, 2007, *available at* http://www.washingtonpost.com/wp-dyn/content/article/2007/02/15/AR2007021500213.html.
108. Craig Whitlock, *Terrorist Networks Lure Young Moroccans to War in Far-Off Iraq*, WASH. POST, Feb. 20, 2007, *available at* http://www.washingtonpost.com/wp-dyn/content/article/2007/02/19/AR2007021901168.html.
109. Craig Smith, *North Africa Feared as Staging Ground for Terror*, N.Y. TIMES, Feb. 20, 2007, *available at* http://www.nytimes.com/2007/02/20/world/africa/20tunisia.html.
110. *Id.* (quoting French counter-terrorism magistrate, etc.)
111. *See* Craig Whitlock, *Al-Qaeda Branch Claims Algeria Blasts*, WASH. POST, Apr. 12, 2007, *available at* http://www.washingtonpost.com/wp-dyn/content/article/2007/04/11/AR2007041100371.html.
112. *See* Black, *supra* note 95, at 9.
113. *Group Takes Blame for Algeria Attack*, AP, Dec. 11, 2006, *available at* http://www.thefreelibrary.com/Group+takes+blame+for+Algeria+attack-a01610663858.
114. On the second anniversary of the September 11 attacks, a leader of the GSPC posted a statement on the Internet pledging the group's allegiance to al Qaeda, saying: 'We strongly and fully support Osama bin Laden's jihad against the heretic America.' *See* Whitlock, *supra* note 97. In March 2005, a similar statement praising bin Laden was posted by the GSPC. *Id.*
115. *See* Press Release, U.S Dep't of Treasury, U.S. Designates Individual Tied to Attacks on European Tourists (Dec. 5, 2003), *available at* http://www.treas.gov/press/releases/js1043.htm; *see also* Press Release, U.S. Dep't of Treasury, Terrorist Kidnappers Designated by Treasury – Captors Boast Ties to al Qaeda (Apr. 30, 2004), *available at* http://www.treas.gov/press/releases/js1500.htm. Sixteen Germans, ten Austrians, four Swiss, one Dutch, and one Swede were held hostage by the group.

116. *See* Whitlock, *supra* note 97.
117. *See* 2006 Country Reports on Terrorism, *supra* note 7, at 211.
118. *See id.* at 211.
119. *Death Sentences for Morocco Bombings*, BBC NEWS, Aug. 19, 2003, *available at* http://news.bbc.co.uk/1/hi/world/africa/3162285.stm; *see also* Olivier Guitta, *The Islamization of Morocco*, WEEKLY STANDARD, Oct. 2, 2006, *available at* http://www.weeklystandard.com/Content/Public/Articles/000/000/012/740boykt.asp.
120. *Death Sentences for Morocco Bombings, supra* note 119.
121. *See Morocco Arrests Islamist Suspected of Bombings*, REUTERS, Mar. 9, 2007, *available at* http://www.reuters.com/article/worldnews/idUSL0923094220070309.
122. BLAKE D. WARD, OSAMA'S WAKE: THE SECOND GENERATION OF AL QAEDA, USAF COUNTERPROLIFERATION CENTER (Aug. 2005), *available at* http://www.au.af.mil/au/awc/awcgate/cpc-pubs/ward2.pdf.
123. Whitlock, *supra* note 108.
124. *See* Office of Foreign Assets Control, U.S. Dep't of Treasury, Specially Designated Nationals and Blocked Persons List, *available at* http://www.treas.gov/offices/enforcement/ofac/programs/terror/terror.pdf (last visited Mar. 8, 2008) [hereinafter *OFAC SDGT List*].
125. *See* Press Release, U.S. Dep't of Treasury, Treasury Designates UK-Based Individuals, Entities Financing Al Qaida-Affiliated LIFG (Feb. 8, 2006), *available at* http://www.treas.gov/press/releases/js4016.htm.
126. *Id.*
127. *Id.*
128. *See* 2006 Country Reports on Terrorism, *supra* note 7, at 210.
129. *See* Press Release, U.S. Dep't of Treasury, *supra* note 125; *see also OFAC SDGT List, supra* note 124.
130. *Id.*
131. *See* 2006 Country Reports on Terrorism, *supra* note 7.
132. *See* Anthony Mitchell, *Somalia PM Says Government Surrounded*, WASH. POST, Dec. 12, 2006, *available at* www.washingtonpost.com/wp-dyn/content/article/2006/12/12/AR2006121200373.html.
133. *Id.*
134. *See* Press Release, U.S. Dep't of Treasury, Treasury Designates Four Leaders of Terrorist Group 'Jemaah Islamiyah' (April 13, 2006), *available at* http://www.treas.gov/press/releases/js4179.htm.
135. *See id.* JI was led by Abu Bakar Bashir, a prominent and influential Indonesian cleric, who has close ties to bin Laden. Bashir was succeeded by Zarkasih, who was captured by Indonesian authorities in June 2007. *See* Robin McDowell, *2 Terror Leaders Arrested in Indonesia*, WASH. POST, June 15, 2007, *available at* http://www.washingtonpost.com/wp-dyn/content/article/2007/06/15/AR2007061500395.html.
136. *See* Press Release, U.S. Dep't of Treasury, Treasury Designates Jemaah Islamiyah's Emir, Top Bomb Maker and Military Commander (May 12, 2005), *available at* http://www.treas.gov/press/releases/js2441.htm; *see also* Press Release, U.S. Dep't of Treasury, *supra* note 134. 'Members of JI have been trained, funded and directed by al Qaida to pursue a like-minded terrorist agenda, including executing some of the deadliest terrorist attacks against innocents since the war on terror began.'
137. *See* Press Release, U.S. Dep't of Treasury, Statement by Secretary Paul O'Neill on Designation of Jemaah Islamiya (Oct. 23, 2002), *available at* http://www.treas.gov/press/ releases/po3569.htm. In January 2003, two senior JI leaders, Nurjaman Riduan Isamuddin (aka Hambali) and Mohamad Iqbal Abdurrahman (aka Abu Jibril) were also designated SDGTs. Press Release, U.S. Dep't of Treasury, Statement by the Treasury Department Regarding Today's Designation of Two Leaders of Jemaah Islamiyah (Jan. 24, 2003), *available at* http://www.ustreas.gov/press/releases/kd3796.htm.
138. Press Release, U.S. Dep't of Treasury, Statement by Secretary Paul O'Neill, *supra* note 137. JI was subsequently added to the consolidated list of terrorist-related entities and

individuals pursuant to U.N. Security Council Resolutions 1267 and 1390. The U.N. listing requires all Member States to block the assets of this organization.

139. *See* 2006 Country Reports on Terrorism, *supra* note 7.
140. *See* Press Release, U.S. Dep't of Treasury, *supra* note 134.
141. The 2002 Bali attack began when a suicide bomber set off his explosive vest outside a nightclub, which drove panicked patrons out into the street, where another bomb was waiting. That bomb was hidden in a van parked outside the night-club and was set off by a second man a few seconds later, ripping through the crowd of patrons. *See Bali Bombings Kill at Least 25 in Tourist Spots*, N.Y TIMES, Oct. 2, 2005.
142. *See A Recent History of Major Explosions in Indonesia*, N.Y. TIMES, Oct. 2, 2005.
143. *See* Press Release, U.S Dep't of Treasury, *supra* note 134.
144. *See* Travel Warning – Indonesia, U.S. Department of State (Nov. 18, 2005), *available* at http://travel.state.gov/travel/cis_pa_tw/tw/tw_918.html.
145. *See* Raymond Bomer and Jane Perlez, *Bali Bombings Kill at Least 25 in Tourist Spots*, N.Y. TIMES, Oct. 2, 2005, *available at* http://www.nytimes.com/2005/10/02/international/asia/02bali.html?scp=1&sq=bali&st=nyt. Among the wounded were 49 Indonesians, 17 Australians, 6 Koreans, 3 Japanese and 2 Americans.
146. *See* Press Release, U.S. Dep't of Treasury, *supra* note 134.
147. *See* Press Release, U.S. Dep't of Treasury, Snow Announces Designation of 10 Jemaah Islamiyah (JI) Terrorists, (Sept. 5, 2003), *available at* http://www.treas.gov/press/releases/js700.htm. *See also* Press Release, U.S Dep't of Treasury, Statement by the Treasury Department Regarding Today's Designation of Two Leaders of Jemaah Islamiyah (Jan. 24, 2003), *available at* http://www.treas.gov/press/releases/kd3796.htm?IMAGE.X=24/&IMAGE.Y=15 (announcing designation of Hambali as SDGT).
148. *See* Robin McDowell, *2 Terror Leaders Arrested in Indonesia*, WASH. POST, June 15, 2007, available at http://www.washingtonpost.com/wp-dyn/content/article/2007/06/15/AR2007061500395.html.
149. *See* Press Release, U.S. Dep't of Treasury, Abu Sayyaf Senior Leaders Designated, (Nov. 30, 2005), *available at* http://www.treas.gov/press/releases/js3027.htm (stating that the U.S. and Australia were submitting the names of three ASG leaders to the United Nations 1267 Committee, which will consider adding them to its Consolidated List because of the ASG's association with al Qaeda and Osama bin Laden).
150. *See* Press Release, U.S. Dep't of Treasury, Abu Sayyaf Senior Leaders Designated (Nov. 30, 2005), *available at* http://www.treas.gov/press/releases/js3027.htm.
151. *See* 2006 Country Reports on Terrorism, *supra* note 7.
152. *Id.*
153. Six ASG members were arrested in connection with the ferry bombing, including one person who reportedly confessed to planting the bomb. *See World Brief – Asia: The Philippines: Bomb Caused Ferry Fire*, N.Y. TIMES, Oct. 12. 2004, *available at* http://query.nytimes.com/gst/fullpage.html?res=9C00E1D9113BF931a25753c1a9629c8b63&scp=2&sq=philippines&st=nyt.
154. In September 2007, Khadaffy Janjalani, the leader of the ASG, was killed during a clash with Philippine troops. Janjalani assumed the leadership of the ASG from his elder brother and group founder, Abdurajak Abubakar Janjalani, who was killed in 1995. *See DNA Test Confirms Death of Philippine Separatist Leader*, N.Y. TIMES, Jan. 21, 2007. In January 2007, the Philippine authorities claimed another major victory against the ASG. Jainal Antel Sali, aka Abu Sulaiman, one of the top five leaders of the ASG, was killed in a gun battle with the Philippine troops. Sulaiman is wanted by the United States for the kidnapping of three Americans from a tourist resort on Palawan Island in May 2001 and beheading one of the American hostages. *See* Manny Magato, *Abu Sayyaf Chief Dead – Philippine Military*, REUTERS, Jan. 20, 2007, *available at* http://www.reuters.com/article/latestcrisis/idusman162504. Sulaiman was also designated pursuant to E.O. 13224 by the U.S. Department of the Treasury for his senior leadership role in the ASG. *See* Press Release, U.S Dep't of Treasury, *supra* note 150.

155. *See* Press Release, U.S. Dep't of Treasury, Janjalani Designated for Leadership Position in the Abu Sayyaf Group (Dec. 17, 2004), *available at* http://www.treas.gov/press/releases/js2157.htm.
156. *Id.*
157. *See* Press Release, U.S. Dep't of Treasury, *supra* note 150.
158. *See* Carlos Conde, *World Briefing – Asia: The Philippines: Bombs in 3 Cities Kill 11*, N.Y. TIMES, Feb. 15, 2005, *available at* http://query.nytimes.com/gst/fullpage.html?res=9F02E5DB123AF936A25751C0A9639C8B63&fta=y.
159. *See* Press Release, U.S. Dep't of Treasury, Treasury Designates Director, Branches of Charity Bankrolling Al Qaeda Network (Aug. 3, 2006), *available at* http://www.treas.gov/press/releases/hp45.htm.
160. *Id.*
161. *Id.* In January 2007, Osama bin Laden's brother-in-law, Jamal Khalifa, was reportedly killed at his home in Madagascar. *See Saudi Relative of Bin Laden Killed*, REUTERS, Jan. 31, 2007, *available at* http://www.alertnet.org/thenews/newsdesk/L31640277.htm.
162. *See* Press Release, U.S. Dep't of Treasury, *supra* note 155. The Philippine military has realized some successes in pursuing Abu Sayyaf leaders. *See* Manny Mogato, *supra* note 154 (reporting the killing of Khaddafy Janalani, the leader of the ASG)
163. BEYOND AL-QAEDA, *supra* note 6, at 81.
164. *Id.*
165. Sovereignty over the Indian state of Jammu and Kashmir (J&K) has been disputed since August 1947, when India and Pakistan both gained their independence from British rule. Since 1947, Pakistan and India have fought three wars over the disputed territory. *See* ANGEL RABASA, LESLEY ANNE WARNER, ET AL, MONEY IN THE BANK: LESSONS LEARNED FROM PAST COUNTERINSURGENCY (Rand Corp. 2007), at 49 [hereinafter MONEY IN THE BANK]. India currently hold approximately two-thirds of the disputed territory, which it calls Jammu and Kashmir. Pakistan controls about one-third, which it calls Azad (meaning 'free') Kashmir. *See* Kashmir Militant Extremists, Council on Foreign Relations, (July 12, 2006), *available at* http://www.cfr.org/publication/9135/. Beginning in the late 1980s, a movement for independence within J&K began to grow. After the Soviet–Afghanistan conflict, a number of mujahedeen shifted to J&K with support from the Pakistani government. These mujahedeen 'began to view J&K through a religious lens as a *jihad*.' MONEY IN THE BANK, at 49. *See also* WALID PHARES, FUTURE JIHAD, 271–4 (Palgrave Macmillan 2005) (discussing al Qaeda's strategy in South Asia).
166. *See, e.g.*, STATEMENTS OF OSAMA BIN LADEN, at 140 ('The United States and their allies are killing us in Palestine, Chechnya, Kashmir, and Iraq.').
167. *Id.* at 115.
168. *See Al Qaeda's 'War' on India*, STRATFOR, June 8, 2007, *available at* http://www.stratfor.com/products/premium/print.php?storyId=289951.
169. *See* 2006 Country Reports on Terrorism, *supra* note 7, at 207. According to STRATFOR, LT has been succeeded by Jamaat-ud-Dawah, the largest radical Wahhabi group in Pakistan. *See Pakistan: Using the Media to Lay the Path Toward Negotiations*, STRATFOR, May 9, 2007, *available at* http://www.stratfor.com/products/premium/print.php?storyId=285466.
170. *See* BEYOND AL QAEDA, *supra* note 6, at 81–2. *See also* Press Release, U.S. Dep't of Treasury, Terrorist Financing Fact Sheet (Dec. 20, 2001), *available at* http://www.treas.gov/press/releases/po886.htm.
171. Press Release, U.S Dep't of Treasury, *supra* note 170.
172. *See* BEYOND AL QAEDA, *supra* note 6 at 83.
173. *See* 2006 Country Reports on Terrorism, *supra* note 7, at 207–8; Lashkar-e-Taiba, START Global Terrorism Database, *available at* http://209.232.239.37/gtd2.
174. *See* 2006 Country Reports on Terrorism, *supra* note 7, at 208.
175. *See Attacks in India: Lashkar-e-Taiba and the al Qaeda Playbook*, STRATFOR, July 11, 2006, *available at* http://www.stratfor.com/products/premium/print.php?storyId=268903.

176. *See* 2006 Country Reports on Terrorism, *supra* note 7, at 207. *See also* Press Release, U.S. Dep't of Treasury, *supra* note 170.
177. *See* 2006 Country Reports on Terrorism, *supra* note 7, at 201.
178. *Id.*
179. *Id.*
180. *Id.*
181. *Id.*
182. *Id.*
183. *See Indian Police Arrest 4 for Planning Blasts in Delhi*, REUTERS, Feb. 5, 2007, *available at* http://www.reuters.com/article/worldnews/idussp17065320070205.
184. *See* Press Release, U.S. Dep't of Treasury, Treasury Department Releases List of 39 Additional Specially Designated Global Terrorists (Oct. 12, 2001), *available at* http://www.treas.gov/press/releases/po689.htm.
185. *See* 2006 Country Reports on Terrorism, *supra* note 7, at 201.
186. *Id.* at 202.
187. *See* BEYOND AL QAEDA, *supra* note 6, at 83.
188. *See* 2006 Country Reports on Terrorism, *supra* note 7, at 196.
189. *See* Harakat ul-Mujahideen, START Global Terrorism Database, *available at* http://209.232.239.37/gtd2.
190. *See* BEYOND AL QAEDA, *supra* note 6, at 83.
191. Fazlur Rahman was one of the signatories to the 1998 fatwa, along with bin Laden; his deputy, Ayman al-Zawahiri; Abu-Yasir Rif'ai Ahmad Taha, Egyptian Islamic Group; and Sheikh Mir Mahzah, secretary of the Jamiat-ul-Ulema-e-Pakistan. *See* The World Islamic Front (Feb. 23, 1998), discussed in STATEMENTS OF OSAMA BIN LADEN, *supra* note 1, at 59.
192. *See* MONEY IN THE BANK, *supra* note 165, at 52.
193. *See* 2006 Country Reports on Terrorism, *supra* note 7, at 196.
194. *See* Harakat ul-Mujahideen, *supra* note 189.
195. HuM was one of the original 27 individuals and entities designated as SDGTs and included in an appendix to Executive Order (E.O.) 13224. *See* Recent OFAC Actions, U.S. Dep't of Treasury (Sept. 24, 2001), *available at* http://www.treas.gov/offices/enforcement/ofac/actions/20010924.shtml.
196. *See* BEYOND AL QAEDA, *supra* note 6, at 81.
197. *See id.* at 85.
198. *See id.*
199. *See id.*
200. *See id.* at 86.
201. *See id.* at 87.
202. *See id.* at 88.
203. *See id.* at 89.
204. *See id.* at 90.
205. *See* Designation of HUJI-B as a Specially Designated Global Terrorist, 73 Fed. Reg. 44 (March 5, 2008). *See also* BEYOND AL-QAEDA, *supra* note 6, at 98.
206. *See* Kathy Gannon, *New Taliban Chief Entering Limelight*, USA TODAY, Jan. 26, 2008, *available at* http://www.usatoday.com/news/world/2008-01-26-78451253_x.htm.
207. *Id. See* U.N. SECURITY COUNCIL, ANALYTICAL SUPPORT AND SANCTIONS MONITORING TEAM, SEVENTH REPORT OF THE ANALYTICAL SUPPORT AND SANCTIONS MONITORING TEAM, at 9, U.N. Doc. S/2007/677 (Nov. 29, 2007), *available at* http://www.un.org/sc/committees/1267/monitoringteam.shtml.
208. *See* 2006 Country Reports on Terrorism, *supra* note 7. On March 7, 2008, the Secretary of State designated a Bangladeshi Islamist Group, Harkat-ul-Jihad al Islami, as an FTO, subject to U.S. economic sanctions. *See U.S. Brands Bangladeshi Islamist Group 'Terrorist,'* REUTERS, March 7, 2008, *available at* http://www.reuters.com/article/topnews/idusn0728592920080307?feedType=RSS&feedname=topnews.
209. *See* Foreign Terrorist Organizations Fact Sheet, Office of Counterterrorism, U.S. Dep't of State (2005), *available at* http://www.state.gov/s/ct/rls/fs/37191.htm.

210. *Id.*
211. *See* 2006 Country Reports on Terrorism, *supra* note 7. *See also*, Fact Sheet, Office of the Coordinator for Counterterrorism, U.S. Dep't of State (April 8, 2008).
212. *See* Bruce Riedel & Bilal Y. Saab, *Al Qaeda's Third Front: Saudi Arabia*, WASH. Q. 33 (Spring 2008).
213. See 2006 Country Reports on Terrorism, *supra* note 7.

PART III

Financing the global jihad

5. State sponsors of terrorism, drug trafficking, and deep-pocket donors

> Without state sponsors, terrorist groups would have much more difficulty obtaining the funds, weapons, materials, and secure areas they require to plan and conduct operations.[1]
>
> Office of the Coordinator for Counterterrorism,
> U.S. Department of State,
> April 28, 2006

> The Taliban and other insurgent groups operating in poppy-growing regions gain . . . financial support as a result of their ties to local opium traffickers. Drug money is an important source of income, especially at the local level where some Taliban commanders accrue their own operational funding.[2]
>
> J. Michael McConnell, Director of National Intelligence,
> February 5, 2008

WHAT IS TERRORIST FINANCING?

The magnitude of the threats and acts of international terrorism depends on the financing received by terrorists. Recognizing the importance of stemming the flow of funds to terrorists, international law imposes a duty on States to implement measures to prevent and suppress the financing of terrorism.[3] Among other duties, each State is required to enact domestic legislation to make terrorist financing a criminal offense and authorize the freezing of any funds used or allocated for the purpose of committing terrorist acts.[4] U.S. domestic law is in accord, criminalizing terrorist financing and authorizing the freezing of terrorists assets.[5] However, terrorist financing has multiple dimensions and the implementation of sanctions is required at every stage in the process of funding terrorist activity, including the provision, collection and transfer of terror funds.

Under principles of international and U.S. domestic law, a person engages in terrorist financing if he, directly or indirectly, 'provides or collects' funds with the intention or knowledge that they will be used to carry out an act of terrorism.[6] 'Providing' is defined to include 'giving, donating and transmitting' terrorist funds.[7] 'Collecting' is construed to cover both 'raising and receiving' such funds.[8] The 'transmit' language further extends liability to persons who knowingly transfer money to terrorists and terrorist groups.[9] Thus, the provision of financial services and other administrative assistance to transfer money globally to fund terrorist activities is criminally actionable. In sum, the donors, fund raisers, and persons or entities responsible, directly or indirectly, for transmitting terror money may be held criminally liable for engaging in terrorist financing. Their assets are further subject to asset freeze under international and domestic law.[10]

Terrorist financing is similar in several respects to money laundering. Both offenses involve an element of concealment. Money laundering is the 'process by which one conceals the existence, illegal source, or illegal application of income, and then disguises that income to make it appear legitimate.'[11] The objective of money laundering is to disguise the source of the illicit proceeds to make it appear that the funds were derived from a legitimate source.[12] '[M]oney laundering . . . criminalizes behavior that masks the relationship between an individual and his illegally obtained proceeds . . . .'[13] This is accomplished through complex or unnecessary financial transactions intended to add extra 'degrees of separation' between the owner and the illegal source of the funds.[14]

Unlike money laundering, terrorist financing may involve funds derived from legal, as well as illegal, activity. A terrorist sympathizer may choose to support the activities of a terrorist organization using funds derived from legitimate business activity or some other legal source. Thus, terrorist financing may involve using legitimate income to finance illegal activity, which is money laundering in reverse. Regardless of the source of the funds, the terrorist financier must conceal the true *purpose* of the financial donation. The objective is to make it appear that the funds are being given, donated, or transmitted for a legitimate purpose, such as funding charitable or social activities. In the case of money laundering, the concealment element is directed backwards at concealing the illegal source of the funds. In terrorist financing, the concealment element looks forward, disguising the illegal purpose and intended beneficiary of the funds.

The terrorist purpose may be disguised by transferring the funds through a corrupt organization or fictional intermediary which claims to have charitable, social or cultural goals.[15] Terrorist financing may also involve complex or highly unusual financial transactions intended to disguise the relationship between the donor and the illegal purpose of the donation. In both money laundering and terrorist financing, the owner of the funds seeks to disguise the money trail, but for different purposes. While the money launderer seeks to conceal where the money came from, the terrorist financier attempts to disguise where the money is going. There are multiple sources of terrorist financing, including state sponsors of terrorism, drug trafficking and deep pocket donors. Chapter 6 will focus on the use of charities to finance terrorist acts.

SOURCES OF TERRORIST FINANCING

State Sponsors of Terrorism

The Islamic jihad is partially funded by countries such as Iran and Syria. Both countries have been designated by the U.S. Department of State as 'state sponsors of terrorism' (SSTs).[16] State sponsors of terrorism are determined by the Secretary of State to provide critical support to non-State terrorist groups, including financial assistance.[17] These States are designated pursuant to three laws: section 6(j) of the Export Administration Assistance Act (50 App. U.S.C.A. §2405), section 40 of the Arms Export Control Act (22 U.S.C.A. §2780), and section 620A of the Foreign Assistance Act (22 U.S.C.A. §2371).[18] Countries placed on the State Department terrorism list are subject to four main sets of U.S. government sanctions:

(1) A ban on arms-related exports and sales.
(2) Controls over exports of dual-use items, requiring 30-day Congressional notification for goods or services that could significantly enhance the terror-list country's military capability or ability to support terrorism.
(3) Prohibitions on economic assistance.
(4) Imposition of miscellaneous financial and other restrictions.[19]

Iran has remained the most active SST, 'encouraging anti-Israeli terrorist activity – rhetorically, operationally, and financially.'[20] Iran is a major funding source for Hizballah ('Party of God'), providing the terror group $100–200 million per year.[21] Hizballah has been designated as a 'foreign terrorist organization' by the U.S. State Department.[22] It has been described as 'an organization with capability and worldwide presence [that] is [al Qaeda's] equal, if not a far more capable organization.'[23] Iran provides extensive funding, training, and weapons to Lebanese Hizballah and Palestinian terrorist groups such as HAMAS, Palestinian Islamic Jihad (PIJ), the al-Aqsa Martyrs Brigade, and the Popular Front for the Liberation of Palestine–General Command (PFLP–GC).[24]

The State Department claims that Iran's Islamic Revolutionary Guard Corps (IRGC) and Ministry of Intelligence and Security (MOIS) have been involved in planning and supporting terrorist attacks.[25] In October 2007, the Treasury Department took unprecedented action designating the IRGC-Qods Force, a branch of the Islamic Revolutionary Guard Corps, as a 'specially designated global terrorist.'[26] The Treasury Department maintains that the IRGC-Qods Force provides material support, including financial assistance, to the Taliban, Lebanese Hizballah, HAMAS, PIJ and PFLP–GC.[27] For example, the Qods Force allegedly funded Hizballah with $100–200 million.[28] Authorized by E.O. 13224, the designation was aimed at freezing the assets of the Qods Force and its supporters, and isolating it from the U.S. financial system.[29] The designation further prohibits all transactions between the Qods Force and any U.S. person, and freezes any assets it may have under U.S. jurisdiction.[30] In support of the designation, Treasury Department officials stated:

> The Qods Force is the Iranian regime's primary instrument for providing lethal support to the Taliban. The Qods Force provides weapons and financial support to the Taliban to support anti-U.S. and anti-Coalition activity in Afghanistan. Since at least 2006, Iran has arranged frequent shipments of small arms and associated ammunition, rocket propelled grenades, mortar rounds, 107mm rockets, plastic explosives and probably man-portable defense systems to the Taliban.[31]

The U.S. government further maintains that the Qods Force operates training camps for Hizballah in Lebanon's Bekaa Valley and has trained more than 3,000 Hizballah fighters at IRGC training facilities in Iran.[32] The Qods Force also reportedly provides weapons, training, and funding to select groups of Iraqi Shi'a militants responsible for killing Coalition and Iraqi forces and innocent Iraqi civilians.[33]

Additionally, the Treasury Department has designated, pursuant to E.O. 13224, Iran's state-owned Bank Saderat as a terrorist financier, including its branches and subsidiaries. Bank Saderat allegedly transferred $50 million, between 2001 and 2006, from the Central Bank of Iran through the Bank's subsidiary in London to its branch in Beirut for the benefit of Hizballah.[34] The Treasury Department has described Iran as a 'central banker of terrorism,' deeply integrated into the international banking system and able to evade its controls.[35] For instance, one method Iranian banks allegedly use is to ask other financial institutions to remove their names when processing transactions, 'allowing Iran's banks to remain undetected as they move money through the international financial system to pay for the Iranian regime's illicit and terrorist-related activities.'[36] The Treasury Department has also found substantial deficiencies in Iran's anti-money laundering and combating the financing of terrorism (AML/CFT) regime, including the failure to criminalize terrorist financing and the lack of a financial intelligence unit.[37]

Moreover, elements of the IRGC and Iran's Ministry of Defense and Armed Forces Logistics (MODAFL) have been listed in the annexes to U.N. Security Council Resolutions 1737 and 1747.[38] These resolutions require governments worldwide 'to prevent the provision to Iran of any financial assistance, or the transfer of any financial resources or services, related to the supply, sale, transfer, manufacture, or use of prohibited items associated with Iran's nuclear and missile programs.'[39] Under Resolutions 1737 and 1747, States are required to freeze the assets of designated individuals and entities providing support for Iran's nuclear proliferation activities.[40] The U.S. government has taken similar action against Iran pursuant to E.O. 13382, which is aimed at freezing the assets of proliferators of weapons of mass destruction and their supporters.[41] The Treasury Department, for example, has designated several Iranian banks for providing financial support and services to Iran's nuclear proliferation programs, including Bank Sepah, Bank Saderat, Bank Melli, and Bank Mellat.[42]

Iran is not alone in providing material support to Islamist terrorist organizations. Syria is alleged to provide material and financial support to Hizballah and other Palestinian terror groups, including HAMAS, PIJ, and PFLP–GC.[43] While the Syrian government has condemned international terrorism, it has promoted what it considers to be 'legitimate armed resistance' by Palestinians in the Occupied Territories and Hizballah in Lebanon.[44] According to the Treasury Department, PIJ, a designated foreign terrorist organization, is based in Damascus, Syria, where its members are provided a safe haven to plan and organize terrorist attacks in the West Bank and Gaza.[45]

In May 2004, the U.S. government imposed financial sanctions against senior Syrian officials and their associates for supporting Lebanese terrorist groups Hizballah, HAMAS, Palestinian Islamic Jihad, the PFLP, and PFLP-GC. The economic sanctions banned all U.S. exports to Syria except for food and medicine, banned flights to and from the United States, and authorized the Treasury Department to freeze the assets of Syrian nationals and entities designated because of their involvement in terrorism.[46] The economic sanctions were also directed at individuals and entities responsible for undermining Lebanon's sovereignty and fomenting terrorism in Iraq.[47] The Syrian economic sanctions were expanded in 2006 and 2008 to include additional persons subject to sanctions.[48]

Finally, while Saudi Arabia has not been designated an SST, it has been criticized for funding radical Islamic charities that are believed to serve as a conduit for HAMAS and other radical Islamist groups.[49] On the one hand, notes a senior Treasury Department official, Saudi Arabia is serious about fighting al Qaeda in the Kingdom on the operational level.[50] For instance, Saudi Arabia has killed an estimated two dozen al Qaeda terrorists and arrested many others.[51] However, 'the seriousness of purpose with respect to the money going out of the Kingdom is not as high, and Saudi Arabia today remains the location from which more money is going to terror groups and the Taliban . . . than from any other place in the world.'[52] For instance, according to the Treasury Department, Saudi Arabia has a financial intelligence unit that has not met the criteria for admission to the Egmont Group, which is the international organization of financial intelligence units.[53] Furthermore, the Saudi government has not set up a charity oversight commission to track whether donations end up in the hands of extremists, despite repeated promises to do so.[54] The alleged lack of Saudi oversight of charitable donations, especially those flowing outside the Kingdom, has raised serious concerns for counter-terrorism officials.[55] For instance, Al-Haramain Islamic Foundation (AHIF), a major Saudi charity, operated in as many as 50 countries.[56] It was largely unregulated by Saudi Arabia until 2002, when the United States and Saudi Arabia jointly designated the Bosnian and Somalian branches of AHIF as financiers of terror.[57] However, questions were raised by critics as to whether Saudi Arabia actually closed the offshore branches of AHIF.[58] While the Saudi government has made some progress in this area, including the implementation of new laws and regulations governing charitable giving, much remains to be done to combat terrorist financing in the Kingdom.[59]

Drug Trafficking

The opium drug trade has emerged as a major funding source of the Taliban in Afghanistan. In a report released by the U.N. Office on Drugs and Crime (UNODC), the U.N. stated that profits from opium cultivation are fuelling the Taliban insurgency in Afghanistan.[60] Antonio Maria Costa, Executive Director of the UNODC, stated that 'Afghan opium poppy cultivation has reached a record high . . . generating billions of dollars to help finance the Taliban militants and corrupt officials.'[61] Costa's view was reinforced by Michael McConnell, Director of U.S. National Intelligence, who stated that '[d]rug money is an important source of income, especially at the local level where some Taliban commanders accrue their own operational funding.'[62] According to the U.N. report, in 2007 Afghanistan cultivated 193,000 hectares of opium poppies, a 17 percent increase over 2006.[63] '[T]he amount of Afghan land used for opium is now larger than the corresponding total of coca cultivation in Latin America (Columbia, Peru and Bolivia combined).'[64] Afghanistan is now the source of 93 percent of the world's opium supply, highlighting the failure of Afghan and international efforts to combat the problem.[65] The total export value of opium and heroin trafficked in Afghanistan in 2007 was $4 billion, an increase of 29 percent over 2006.[66] The opium drug trade now accounts for more than half (53 percent) of the country's GDP.[67]

In 2007, approximately 70 percent of the country's poppies were cultivated in five provinces along the Afghanistan–Pakistan border.[68] However, a staggering 50 percent of the total Afghan opium crop comes from the Hilmand province, territory controlled by the Taliban.[69] The UNODC report states: 'With just 2.5 million inhabitants, this relatively rich southern province [Hilmand] has become the world's biggest source of illicit drugs, surpassing the output of entire countries like Colombia (coca), Morocco (cannabis), and Myanmar (opium) – which have populations up to twenty times larger.'[70]

The Taliban has used the opium trade to benefit its interests. From 1996 to 2000, 15,000 tons of opium were produced and exported in areas controlled by the Taliban, providing the regime's sole source of foreign exchange.[71] In 2000, Taliban leader Mullah Omar banned opium cultivation, but not its export, arguing that opium use offended the teachings of Islam.[72] The Taliban has reversed its previous position and 'started to extract from the drug economy resources for arms, logistics and militia pay.'[73] The resurgence of the Taliban over the last two years appears to coincide with the rise in Afghanistan's opium production, which has reached a staggering new level, twice the amount produced just two years ago.[74]

The Taliban has become closely aligned with Afghan drug syndicates. The drug organizations provide financial support to the Taliban.[75] In exchange for financial assistance, the Taliban provides the Afghan drug lords protection for their opium crops, their heroin laboratories, their drug transportation routes, and their members.[76] An Afghan drug dealer purportedly told his co-conspirators that 'selling heroin in the United States was a "jihad" because they were taking the Americans' money and the heroin was killing them.'[77] Trafficking in opium and heroin in Afghanistan affords the Taliban a limitless source of funding and threatens the country's national security.[78]

The 2007 Afghan Opium Survey has generated calls for a new strategy to counter the flourishing opium trade in Afghanistan and the financial support it is providing the Taliban. Those proposals include: (1) appointing a high-level coordinator for Afghan narco-terrorism policy; (2) increasing extradition of major drug kingpins to the U.S. for prosecution; (3) expanding Colombia's National Police anti-narcotic unit's role in training Afghan police; (4) promoting Afghan trade to provide alternatives to poppy cultivation; (5) aerial spraying of the poppy crops with herbicides that do not harm the environment; and (6) having NATO take on a greater role in combating the flourishing opium trade in Afghanistan.[79] While these proposals have merit, and aggressive criminal prosecution of heroin king-pins is welcomed, holding persons criminally responsible for laundering Afghan drug proceeds should be emphasized as well. Interdicting drug money is as important as interdicting the drugs themselves.

Afghan opium and heroin are undoubtedly being shipped to markets in the United States, Europe and Asia for distribution. Once the illicit drugs are sold on the streets, the drug conspirators must arrange for millions of dollars in illegal drug proceeds to be transferred back to members of the drug enterprise in Pakistan and Afghanistan.[80] This involves an element of concealment to avoid detection and seizure by law enforcement agents. The process of concealing the true ownership and illegal source of the funds, and disguising that income to make it appear that it is legitimate, is known as money laundering.[81] Such a scheme involves taking raw proceeds of crime, held by the offender, manoeuvring the funds through financial transactions that conceal their source and confuse or break the money trail, and then returning them to the offender for further use.[82] An aggressive anti-money-laundering strategy can prevent or disrupt the flow of illicit drug proceeds to Pakistan and Afghanistan. Therefore, any new strategy to suppress the flourishing Afghan opium drug trade should include an emphasis on criminalizing money laundering under domestic criminal provisions such as the U.S. money laundering statutes,18 U.S.C. §§1956–7.[83]

Deep-pocket Donors

Islamist terrorist groups also receive funding from individuals and deep-pocket donors. Some of these individuals have been designated by the Treasury Department as SDGTs and placed on the Treasury List of terrorists and terrorist financiers. Their names have also been included on the U.N. Al-Qaida and Taliban Sanctions List or Consolidated List.[84] However, relatively few major terrorist financiers have been included on the U.S. and U.N. terror lists. For example, while the U.N. Consolidated List includes over 200 names of individuals associated with the al Qaeda organization, less than 15 of those designees could be described as major financial donors to the terrorist group.[85] The U.S. list is equally deficient, and few al Qaeda donors appear on the OFAC List.[86] The absence of designations of major donors demonstrates a serious problem in the present scheme to cut off terror funding.

One of the more prominent names on the terror lists is Abdel Abdul Jalil Batterjee, a former Executive Director of BIF and financial supporter of al Qaeda and Osama bin Laden.[87] Other designated individuals include: Ali Ahmed Nur Jim'ale (Chairman of Barakaat Bank); Wa'el Hamza Julaidan (head of Rabita Trust); Abdullah Hussein Kahie (communications manager of al Barakaat phone company); Youssef Mustapha Nada (associated with Bank al Taqwa); and Yasin Abdullah Qadi (former head of Saudi-based Muwafaq, an al Qaeda front organization).[88]

Some Hizballah fundraisers have been designated by the Treasury Department and their assets ordered frozen in the United States. Muhammad Yusif Abdallah and Muhammad Fayez Barakat were designated for hosting fund-raising events for Hizballah in the Tri-Border Area (TBA) of Argentina, Brazil and Paraguay.[89] Individual donors can raise significant amounts of money for terrorist groups. Ali Muhammad Kazan was designated for allegedly raising $500,000 for Hizballah from Lebanese businessmen in the TBA.[90]

Finally, various criminal schemes have enabled terrorist cell members to generate funding at the local level. These criminal activities include organized retail theft, theft of infant formula, vehicle theft, and interstate cigarette smuggling.[91] However, these criminal operations have not served as a major source of funding for al Qaeda, the Taliban and Palestinian terrorist groups.

CONCLUSION

This chapter has revealed that al Qaeda, the Taliban, and affiliated groups have ready access to multiple sources of funding, including: (1) state sponsors of terrorism, most notably Iran and Syria; (2) the opium and heroin trade in Afghanistan; and (3) sympathetic deep-pocket donors. Collectively, these sources provide terrorist organizations hundreds of millions of dollars per year to finance deadly terrorist attacks throughout the world. Chapter 6 will examine another major source of terrorist financing in the form of corrupt charities and those who wittingly and unwittingly donate to them. The implementation of sanctions and prevention measures must be able to match the variety of the sources of terrorist financing at every stage.

NOTES

1. *See* 2005 Country Reports on Terrorism, Office of the Coordinator for Counterterrorism, U.S. Dep't of State (Apr. 28, 2006), *available at* http://www.state.gov/s/ct/rls/crt/2005/64337.htm [hereinafter *Country Reports on Terrorism*].
2. Annual Threat Assessment of the Director of National Intelligence for the Senate Select Committee on Intelligence, at 18 (Feb. 5, 2008).
3. *See, e.g.*, U.N. Security Council Resolutions 1267, U.N. Doc. S/RES/1267 (1999), 1333 U.N. Doc. S/RES/1333 (2000), and 1390, U.N. Doc. S/RES/1267 (2001); *see also* International Convention for the Suppression of the Financing of Terrorism, Dec. 9, 1999, S. Treaty Doc. No. 106–49, 2178 U.N.T.S. 229, *available at* http://untreaty.

un.org/ENGLISH/bible/englishinternetbible/partI/chapterXVIII/treaty12.asp [hereinafter 'Terrorist Financing Convention']. The Terrorist Financing Convention has been ratified by over 130 countries, including the United States on June 25, 2002. The United States implemented the Convention by enacting the Suppression of the Financing of Terrorism Convention Implementation Act of 2002. *See* Pub. L. No. 107–197, 116 Stat. 721 (2002). Additionally, the Financial Action Task Force (FATF) on Money Laundering has adopted Nine Special Recommendations on Terrorist Financing, which represent the international standards to prevent and suppress terrorist financing. *See* Financial Action Task Force, 9 Special Recommendations (SR) on Terrorist Financing (TF) (last visited Apr. 14, 2008), *available at* http://www.fatf-gafi.org/document/ 9/0,3343,en_32250379_32236920_34032073_1_1_1_1,00.html [hereinafter 9 Special Recommendations].

4. Terrorist Financing Convention, *supra* note 3, at arts. 4, 8.
5. *See* 18 U.S.C.A §2339C (West 2008); *see also* Blocking Property and Prohibiting Transactions with Persons Who Commit, Threaten to Commit, or Support Terrorism, Exec. Order No. 13,224, 3 C.F.R. 786–90 (2001), *reprinted as amended in* 50 U.S.C. §1701 note (Supp. IV 2004) [hereinafter E.O. 13224].
6. Terrorist Financing Convention, *supra* note 3, at art. 2(1) (defining terrorist financing to include the provision or collection of funds with the intention that the funds be used to carry out a terrorist act); *accord* 18 U.S.C. §2339C. Article 2(1) defines the predicate acts for the commission of terrorist financing to include:

   > (a) An act which constitutes an offence within the scope of and as defined in one of the [12 counter-terrorism] treaties listed in the annex; or
   > (b) Any other act intended to cause death or serious bodily injury to a civilian, or to any other person not taking an active part in the hostilities in a situation of armed conflict, when the purpose of such act, by its nature or context, is to intimidate a population, or to compel a government or an international organization to do or abstain from doing any act.

7. 18 U.S.C.A §2339C(e)(4) (West 2008).
8. 18 U.S.C.A §2339C(e)(5) (West 2008).
9. *See* Linde v. Arab Bank, 384 F. Supp. 2d 571, 588 (E.D.N.Y. 2005); *see also* Strauss v. Credit Lyonnais, Case No. CV-06-0702 (CPS), 2006 WL 2862704, at *17 (E.D.N.Y. Oct. 5, 2006) (quoting *Linde*, 384 F. Supp. 2d at 588); *Strauss*, 2006 WL at *16.
10. *See* Articles 2 and 8 of the Terrorist Financing Convention, *supra* note 3; *see also* 18 U.S.C. §2339C and E.O. 13224, *supra* note 5.
11. PRESIDENT'S COMMISSION ON ORGANIZED CRIME, THE CASH CONNECTION: ORGANIZED CRIME, FINANCIAL INSTITUTIONS, AND MONEY LAUNDERING 7 (1984).
12. JIMMY GURULÉ, COMPLEX CRIMINAL LITIGATION: PROSECUTING DRUG ENTERPRISES AND ORGANIZED CRIME 120 (Lexis Law Publ. 2nd edn) (2000).
13. United States v. Adefehinti, 510 F.3d 319, 322 (D.C. Cir. 2007).
14. *See* United States v. Blankenship, 382 F.3d 1110, 1129 (11th Cir. 2004).
15. *See* Terrorist Financing Convention, *supra* note 3, at Preamble.
16. There are currently four countries designated by the U.S. State Department as SSTs: Cuba (designated March 1, 1982); Iran (designated January 19, 1984); Sudan (designated August 12, 1993); and Syria (designated December 29, 1979). *See* U.S. Dep't of State, State Sponsors of Terrorism, http://www.state.gov/s/ct/c14151.htm (last visited Apr. 5, 2008) [hereinafter *State Sponsors of Terrorism*].
17. *See Country Reports on Terrorism, supra* note 1.
18. *See State Sponsors of Terrorism, supra* note 16.
19. *Country Reports on Terrorism, supra* note 1. The financial restrictions include:

   - requiring the United States to oppose loans by the World Bank and other international financial institutions;
   - lifting diplomatic immunity to allow families of terrorist victims to file civil lawsuits in U.S. courts;

- denying companies and individuals tax credits for income earned in terrorist-listed countries;
- denial of duty-free treatment of goods exported to the United States;
- authority to prohibit any U.S. citizen from engaging in a financial transaction with a terror-list government without a Treasury Department license;
- prohibition of Defense Department contracts above $100,000 with companies controlled by terrorist-list countries. *Id.*

20. *Id.*
21. *See* Matthew Levitt, *Hezbollah: Financing Terror Through Criminal Enterprise*, Testimony before the U.S. Senate Committee on Homeland Security and Governmental Affairs, at 3–4 (May 25, 2005) [hereinafter *Hezbollah: Financing Terror Through Criminal Enterprise*]; *see also* Press Release, U.S. Dep't of Treasury, Fact Sheet: Designation of Iranian Entities and Individuals for Proliferation Activities and Support for Terrorism (Oct. 25, 2007), *available at* http://www.ustreas.gov/press/releases/hp 644.htm.
22. *See* U.S. Dep't of State, Patterns of Global Terrorism (2003), *available at* http://www.state.gov/s/ct/rls/crt/2003/c12108.htm.
23. George Tenet, Director of the CIA, *Threats to National Security*, Testimony before the Senate Armed Services Comm. (Feb. 12, 2003); *see also Hezbollah: Financing Terror Through Criminal Enterprise*, *supra* note 21, at 3.
24. *See Country Reports on Terrorism, supra* note 1.
25. *Id.*
26. *See* Press Release, U.S. Dep't of Treasury, Fact Sheet: Designation of Iranian Entities and Individuals for Proliferation Activities and Support for Terrorism (Oct. 25, 2007), *available at* http://www.ustreas.gov/press/releases/hp 644.htm; *see also* E.O. 13224, *supra* note 5, discussed *infra* at Chapter 7.
27. *See* Press Release, Fact Sheet: Designation of Iranian Entities, *supra* note 26.
28. *See* Daniel Glaser, Deputy Assistant Secretary for Terrorist Financing and Financial Crimes, Testimony before the House Foreign Affairs Subcomm. on the Middle East and South Asia and the Subcomm. on Terrorism, Nonproliferation and Trade (Apr. 17, 2008).
29. *Id.*
30. *Id.*
31. *Id.*
32. *Id.*
33. *Id.*; *see also* Glaser, *supra* note 28.
34. Press Release, Fact Sheet: Designation of Iranian Entities, *supra* note 26; *see also* Glaser, Testimony, *supra* note 28.
35. Glaser, Testimony, *supra* note 28.
36. *Id.*
37. *Id.*
38. *See* S.C. Res. 1737, Annex, U.N. Doc. S/RES/1737 (2006); S.C. Res. 1747, Annex I, U.N. Doc. S/RES/1747 (2007).
39. Daniel Glaser, Deputy Assistant Secretary for Terrorist Financing and Financial Crimes, & Adam J. Szubin, Director of the Office of Foreign Assets Control, U.S. Dep't of Treasury, *Isolating Proliferators and Sponsors of Terror: The Use of Sanctions and the International Financial System to Change Regime Behavior*, Joint Testimony before the House Foreign Affairs Subcomm. on Terrorism, Nonproliferation, and Trade, and the Financial Services Subcomm. on Domestic and International Monetary Policy, Trade, and Technology, at 5 (Apr. 18, 2007).
40. *See* S.C. Res. 1737, art. 12, U.N. Doc. S/RES/1737 (2006); *see also* S.C. Res. 1747, art. 4, U.N. Doc. S/RES/1747 (2007).
41. *See* Blocking Property of Weapons of Mass Destruction Proliferators and Their Supporters, Exec. Order No. 13,382, 3 C.F.R. 170 (2005).
42. *See* Press Release, U.S. Dep't of Treasury, Iran's Bank Sepah Designated by Treasury, Sepah Facilitating Iran's Weapons Program (Jan. 9, 2007), *available at* http://www.treasury.gov/press/releases/hp 219.htm; *see also* Press Release, Fact Sheet: Designation of

Iranian Entities, *supra* note 26 (designating the Islamic Revolutionary Guard Corps, Ministry of Defense and Armed Forces Logistics, Bank Saderat, Bank Melli, and Bank Mellat and related individuals and entities), *available at* http://www.treasury.gov/press/releases/hp 644.htm.
43. *Country Reports on Terrorism, supra* note 1.
44. *Id.* The preliminary findings of a U.N. investigation into the assassination of former Lebanese Prime Minister Rafik Hariri have indicated a strong likelihood of Syrian government involvement. *Id.*
45. *See* Press Release, U.S. Dep't of Treasury, Treasury Designates Charity Funneling Money to Palestinian Islamic Jihad – Action Marks 400th Designation of a Terrorist or Financier (May 4, 2005), *available at* http://www.treass.gov/press/releases/js 2426.htm; *see also* U.S. Dep't of State, Patterns of Global Terrorism (2003), *available at* http://www.state.gov/s/ct/rls/crt/2003/c12108.htm.
46. Executive Order: Blocking Property of Certain Persons and Prohibiting the Export of Certain Goods to Syria (May 11, 2004), *available at* http://www.whitehouse.gov/news/releases/2004/05/print/20040511-6.html.
47. *Id.*
48. *See* Executive Order Blocking Property of Additional Persons in Connection with the National Emergency with Respect to Syria (Apr. 25, 2006), *available at* http://www.whitehouse.gov/news/releases/2006/04/20060426-1.html; *see also* Executive Order Blocking Property of Additional Persons in Connection with the National Emergency with Respect to Syria (Feb. 13, 2008), *available at* http://www.whitehouse.gov/news/releases/2008/02/20080213-7.html.
49. *See* Steven Emerson, *Money Laundering and Terror Financing Issues in the Middle East*, Testimony before the U.S. Senate Committee on Banking, Housing, and Urban Affairs, 23–4 (July 13, 2005), *available at* http://www.investigativeproject.org/documents/testimony/19.pdf. [hereinafter *Money Laundering and Terror Financing*].
50. *See* Stuart A. Levey, Under Secretary, Office of Terrorism and Financial Intelligence, U.S. Department of Treasury, *Anti-Terrorism Financing: Progress Made and the Challenges Ahead*, Testimony before the Senate Finance Committee (Apr. 1, 2008) [hereinafter *Anti-Terrorism Financing*].
51. Steven Emerson, *Saudi Arabia: Friend or Foe in the War on Terror*, Testimony before the Senate Committee on the Judiciary, at 3 (Nov. 8, 2005) [hereinafter *Saudi Arabia in the War on Terror*], *available at* http://judiciary.senate.gov/testimony.cfm?id=1669&wit_id=4791.
52. *Anti-Terrorism Financing*, *supra* note 50.
53. *Id.*
54. *See id; see also* Josh Meyer, *Saudi Arabia is Prime Source of Terror Funds, U.S. Says*, L.A. TIMES, Apr. 2, 2008. For a more in-depth discussion of Saudi efforts to combat the use of charities in terrorist financing, see Chapter 6, *infra*.
55. *Id.*
56. *See* JOHN ROTH, ET AL., NATIONAL COMMISSION ON TERRORIST ATTACKS UPON THE UNITED STATES, MONOGRAPH ON TERRORIST FINANCING: STAFF REPORT TO THE COMMISSION 106 (Wash., D.C.: Gov't Printing Office 2004), *available at* http://govinfo.library.unt.edu/911/staff_statements/911_TerrFin_Monograph.pdf [hereinafter STAFF MONOGRAPH ON TERRORIST FINANCING].
57. *See* U.S. Dep't of Treasury, Office of Terrorism and Financial Intelligence, Designated Charities and Potential Fundraising Front Organizations for FTOs, *available at* http://www.treas.gov/offices/enforcement/key-issues/protecting/fto.shtml [hereinafter 'U.S. Designated Charities']; *see also* The Al-Qaida and Taliban Sanctions Committee, The Consolidated List of the United Nations Security Council's Al-Qaida and Taliban Sanctions Committee, *available at* http://www.un.org/sc/committees/1267/consolist.shtml (last visited Apr. 15, 2008) [hereinafter 'Consolidated List']. The U.S. Treasury Department recently designated the AHF as a specially designated global terrorist for having provided financial and material support to al Qaeda, including its headquarters in Saudi Arabia. *See* Press Release, U.S. Dep't of Treasury, Treasury Designates Al

Haramain Islamic Foundation (June 19, 2008), *available at* http://www.treasury.gov/press/releases/hp1043.htm. Previously, only select branch offices of AHF had been so designated.

58. *See* STAFF MONOGRAPH ON TERRORIST FINANCING, *supra* note 56, at 123, 125; *see also* Josh Lefkowitz & Jonathan Levin, *Kingdom Cover*, NAT'L REVIEW ONLINE, Feb. 11, 2004.
59. *See* STAFF MONOGRAPH ON TERRORIST FINANCING, *supra* note 56, at 122–30. For more information on al-Haramain Islamic Foundation, see Chapter 6, *infra*.
60. *See* Afghanistan Opium Survey 2007, U.N. Office on Drugs and Crime (Oct 2007), *available at* http://www.unodc.org/pdf/research/Afghanistan_Opium_Survey_2007.pdf [hereinafter *Afghan Opium Survey 2007*].
61. *See* Paul Ames, *UN Drugs Chief Urges Stronger NATO Role Against Flourishing Afghan Opium Trade*, ASSOC. PRESS, Sept. 5, 2007.
62. ANNUAL THREAT ASSESSMENT OF THE DIRECTOR OF NATIONAL INTELLIGENCE FOR THE SENATE SELECT COMMITTEE ON INTELLIGENCE, at 18 (Feb. 5, 2008).
63. *Id.* at Preface iii.
64. *Id.*
65. *Id.*; *see also Opium Windfall Fuels Afghan Insurgents: U.N.*, N.Y. TIMES, Nov. 16, 2007.
66. *See Afghan Opium Survey 2007, supra* note 60, Preface iii.
67. *Id.*
68. *Id.*
69. *Id.* The Taliban control seven out of 12 districts in the Hilmand province. *Id.*
70. *See id.*
71. *Id.* at Preface iv.
72. *Id.*
73. *Id.*
74. *Id.* at Preface iii; *see also* Colum Lynch & Griff Witte, *Afghan Opium Trade Hits New Peak*, WASH. POST, at A07, Aug. 28, 2007, *available at* http://www.washingtonpost.com/wp-dyn/content/article/2007/08/27/AR2007082701356.html.
75. *See* Press Release, U.S. Dep't of Justice, Heroin Kingpin – First Defendant Ever Extradited from Afghanistan – Sentenced in Manhattan Federal Court to Over 15 Years in Prison (Oct. 5, 2007) (announcing the sentencing of Afghan heroin kingpin Baz Mohammad, who pleaded guilty to conspiracy to import heroin into the United States).
76. *Id.*
77. *Id.*
78. Drug trafficking has also been a source of funding for Hizballah. *See Money Laundering and Terror Financing*, *supra* note 49, at 16; *see also Hezbollah: Financing Terror Through Criminal Enterprise*, *supra* note 21, at 10.
79. *See* Jim Abrams, *GOP Urges Change in Afghan Drug Policy*, ASSOC. PRESS, Feb. 7, 2007; *see also* Paul Ames, *U.N. Drugs Chief Urges Stronger NATO Role Against Flourishing Afghan Opium Trade*, ASSOC. PRESS, Sept. 5, 2007.
80. *See* Press Release, U.S. Dep't of Justice, First Heroin Kingpin Ever Extradited From Afghanistan Pleads Guilty to Smuggling Heroin Into the United States (July 11, 2006).
81. *See* PRESIDENT'S COMMISSION, CASH CONNECTION, *supra* note 11.
82. *See* WILLIAM C. GILMORE, DIRTY MONEY – THE EVOLUTION OF INTERNATIONAL MEASURES TO COUNTER MONEY LAUNDERING AND THE FINANCING OF TERRORISM 32, COUNCIL OF EUROPE PRESS (3rd edn, 2004); *see generally* GURULÉ, *supra* note 12, at 123–8 (discussing the federal money laundering statute).
83. The Money Laundering Control Act of 1986 makes it a crime to knowingly engage in a 'financial transaction' with the proceeds of some form of unlawful activity either with the intent to promote the carrying on of 'specified unlawful activity,' or knowing that the transaction is designed to conceal the nature, location, source, ownership, or control of the illicit proceeds. *See* 18 U.S.C. §1956(a)(i)(A)–(B)(i); *see also* the FATF 40 Recommendations on Money Laundering that require States to enact domestic legislation to criminalize money laundering.
84. *See* discussion of the process for freezing funds of persons and entities included on the

U.N. Consolidated List, *infra* at Chapter 7.
85. *See* Consolidated List, *supra* note 57.
86. For a comprehensive list of the individuals and entities designated as SDGTs on the OFAC website, see U.S. Dep't of Treasury Office of Foreign Assets Control, Terrorism: What You Need to Know About U.S. Sanctions (Updated 2007), *available at* http://www.treasury.gov/offices/enforcement/ofac/programs/terror/terror.pdf.
87. *See* Press Release, U.S. Dep't of Treasury, U.S. Treasury Designates Two Individuals with Ties to al Qaida, UBL: Former BIF Leader and al-Qaida Associate Named Under E.O. 13224 (Dec. 21, 2004), *available at* http://www.treasury.gov/press/releases/js2164.htm.
88. *See* Treasury Department List of Terrorist Financiers, *available at* http://www.treasury.gov; *see also* Consolidated List, *supra* note 57.
89. *See* Press Release, U.S. Dep't of Treasury, Treasury Targets Hizballah Fundraising Network in the Triple Frontier of Argentina, Brazil, and Paraguay (Dec. 6, 2006), *available at* http://www.treasury.gov/press/releases/hp190.htm. Treasury has also designated two Venezuela-based financial supporters of Hizballah, along with two related travel agencies. *See* Press Release, U.S. Dep't of Treasury, Treasury Designates Hizballah in Venezuela (June 18, 2008), *available at* http://www.treasury.gov/press/releases/hp1036.htm.
90. *Id.*
91. *See Money Laundering and Terror Financing*, *supra* note 49, at 13–20; *see also Hezbollah: Financing Terror Through Criminal Enterprise*, *supra* note 21, at 8–11; United States v. Hammoud, 381 F.3d 316 (4th Cir. 2004).

6. Corrupt Islamic charities

> [Islamic charities are involved in a] new type of jihad, financial jihad, through which financial support is guaranteed to the martyr's families, Palestinian prisoners and detainees, and every Palestinian whose property is damaged during conflict.[1]
>
> Dr Yusuf al-Qaradawi,
> Executive Director, Union of the Good

> God equated martyrdom through JIHAD with supplying funds for the JIHAD effort.[2]
>
> Global Relief Foundation (fund-raising pamphlet)

For years, Islamic charities have been one of the most important sources of funds for al Qaeda, HAMAS, and other related terrorist organizations.[3] It is estimated that it cost al Qaeda about $30 million per year to sustain its activities before 9/11.[4] A substantial portion of this was raised by 'diversions of money from Islamic charities and the use of well-placed financial facilitators who gathered money from both witting and unwitting donors, primarily in the Gulf region.'[5] The final report by the National Commission on Terrorist Attacks Upon the United States (9/11 Report) indicates that Saudi Arabia 'was a place where Al Qaeda raised money directly from individuals and through charities.'[6] However, charitable donations to terrorist groups are not limited to al Qaeda. It is estimated that one third of HAMAS' multi-million-dollar annual budget comes from charitable fund-raising activity in North America and Western Europe.[7] A portion of the HAMAS-related funds allegedly go to 'pay stipends to the families of Hamas terrorists 'killed in action' to encourage others to volunteer for suicide missions.'[8] By abusing the principle of zakat or almsgiving, radical Islamists raise tens of millions of dollars annually to finance their lethal activities.[9] Terrorists depend on foreign contributions solicited by corrupt Islamic charities around the world to sustain their operations.[10] Islamic charities act as an intermediary or conduit between sympathetic donors and terrorist organizations. Donations are given to these charities, creating the appearance that the funds are going to finance hospitals, orphanages, or other humanitarian activities. 'These organizations' purportedly humanitarian functions mask their mission of raising and funnelling money and other resources to [terrorist] operatives to support their terrorist campaigns.'[11] After a series of convoluted financial transactions intended to obstruct the money trail, the funds eventually reach their intended recipients, terrorist operatives.[12]

One terrorism expert notes that the use of Islamic charities to raise, launder, and transfer funds employed by terrorists offers a number of important advantages:

> [T]he humanitarian nature of most of these charities and service organizations places their offices and employees on the ground in conflict zones of particular interest to terrorist organizations without raising undue suspicion . . . . [C]harities provide an outlet not only for raising significant amounts of money, but, even more critically, are ideal vehicles for laundering and transferring those and other funds. [Finally], charities not only serve as the perfect cover for terrorist operatives they employ, by sending the funds through recipient service organizations they offer simple and extremely secure means of laundering funds and shielding the ultimate end-users from scrutiny.[13]

Additionally, while funds raised and wire-transferred abroad may be traced, for example, to a particular HAMAS-run charity in the Palestinian Territories, the actual funds disbursed by cash courier to HAMAS operatives are almost impossible to trace without extremely strong intelligence.

The U.S. Treasury Department has designated over 40 Islamic charities as 'Specially Designated Global Terrorists' (SDGT).[14] These charities were designated under Presidential Executive Order (E.O.) 13224 for providing financial assistance to terrorists, terrorist organizations or individuals and entities 'act[ing] for or on behalf of' or 'owned or controlled by' designated terrorists.[15] Pursuant to the authority granted the Treasury Department by E.O. 13224, these charities' property and property interests in the United States have been ordered to be frozen.[16] Moreover, these designated charities operate around the world, maintaining offices and branches in North America, Europe, the Middle East, Africa, Central Asia, South Asia, and Southeast Asia.[17] Thirty of these charities are suspected of raising money for al Qaeda.[18] Eight others are believed to be fund-raisers for HAMAS.[19] The remaining five charities designated by the U.S. Treasury Department have been linked to raising funds for Hizballah, the Palestinian Islamic Jihad, or the Liberation Tigers of Tamil Eelam, listed by the State Department as foreign terrorist organizations.[20] The 30 al Qaeda-related charities have also been included on the U.N. Consolidated List and their assets have been ordered to be frozen by the U.N. Security Council's Al-Qaida and Taliban Sanctions Committee.[21]

THE RELIGIOUS-BASED IDEOLOGY DRIVING THE FUNDING OF TERRORISM

Individuals who donate money to Islamic charities, knowing it will be used to carry out terrorist attacks against civilians, justify their conduct by perverting principles of Islam. Certain donors and fund-raisers contend that such donations are consistent with the religious obligation of zakat.[22] Distributing money for 'the cause of Allah' is one of the recognized purposes of zakat.[23] Fighting a holy war or 'jihad' is believed to be fighting for 'the cause of Allah.'[24] According to Osama bin Laden, Muslims have a religious duty to '[r]aise the banner of jihad up high against the Judeo-American alliance that has occupied the holy places of Islam.'[25] Some Islamic clerics, religious scholars and other extremists equate terrorism with jihad and maintain that zakat must be donated in support.[26] For instance, in 2006, a jury in London convicted Britain's most prominent radical Muslim cleric, Abu Hamza al-Masri, for inciting murder.[27] Al-Masri, the former imam at the London Finsbury Park mosque, preached that Muslims have a religious duty to kill anyone who does not follow the Islamic faith.[28] In his sermons, he exhorted his followers to 'bleed' the enemies of Islam and kill Jews.[29] Apparently, donations were collected at the Finsbury Park mosque for these criminal purposes.

Osama bin Laden and other radical Islamists have declared a jihad or holy war against the so-called infidels and enemies of Islam, the United States, Israel, and the West.[30] According to bin Laden, Muslims have a religious duty to join the jihad or, if they are unable to take up arms, to donate zakat to support the holy war. Bin Laden has instructed Muslims 'to give their money to the *jihad* and *jihadi* movements who apply themselves specifically to fighting Jews and Crusaders.'[31]

Zakat

Zakat or almsgiving is one of the five pillars of the Islamic faith.[32] This principle of Islam imposes a religious duty on Muslims to give 2.5 percent of their annual income for specified religious purposes.[33] 'Zakat' derives from the verb 'zakâ,' which means 'to purify.'[34] By giving a portion of their wealth, Muslims purify the portion that remains and purify themselves from greed.[35] The Qur'an states: 'Of their wealth, take alms so you may purify and sanctify them.'[36] 'Zakat' is referred to 32 times in the Qur'an and the command to give zakat is so often joined with the command to offer prayer (salat) that zakat has been termed the 'companion to prayer.'[37] Zakat is symbolic of the Islamic view that all wealth and property belong to God.[38] A person is a trustee of his wealth and property, and has the responsibility to spend and manage it well.[39] In that sense, 'the poor have a right to part of it.'[40] Muslims believe that, on the Day of Judgment, each person will be asked to account for his acts of charity.[41]

According to the Qur'an, there are eight specific purposes for which zakat may be given: for the poor (*al-fuqarâ*); for the indigent or needy (*al-masâkîn*); employees involved in the collection and administration of zakat (*amilun alayha*); converts to Islam whose support is in doubt; captives; debtors; travelers; and for the cause of Allah (*fi sabil Allah*).[42] The Qur'an states:

> Zakat is only for the poor, and the needy and those who collect for them, and to attract the hearts of those who have been inclined (towards Islam); and to free the captives and those in debt, and for *the cause of Allah*, and for the wayfarers; a duty imposed by Allah.[43]

However, zakat is more praiseworthy if given in secret, which has contributed to the problem of transparency.[44] Finally, a Muslim is obligated to donate zakat only if he has a specified amount of property (nisab).[45]

Vast amounts of money are generated every year by the practice of zakat. The Muslim community is comprised of over one billion Muslims, many of whom strictly adhere to the duty of zakat.[46] In Saudi Arabia, one expert has estimated that the annual collection of zakat is approximately $12 billion.[47] In the United States, the figure is close to $1 billion per year.[48] In addition to the usual zakat payment, there is an obligation on every Muslim to pay a zakat-al-fitr to the needy at the end of Ramadan, the Islamic holy month, and at the festival of Eid al-Fitr.[49] Zakat donations for these purposes are estimated at $35–40 million annually.[50]

The importance of zakat in the Muslim culture is difficult to overstate. 'It is broader and more pervasive than Western ideas of charity, in that it also functions as a form of income tax, educational assistance, foreign aid, and political influence.'[51] In many Muslim countries, Islamic charities supported by zakat do what Westerners typically conceive of State agencies or secular entities such as the Red Cross are doing. For example, when Egypt suffered floods in 1994, the chief entity responsible for the organization of relief was not the government but the Muslim Brothers and Islamic charities.[52] Islamic charities also fund schools and orphanages, and provide food for the needy and compensation for unemployment.[53] Further, 'a major goal of Saudi charities is to spread Wahhabi beliefs and culture throughout the world.'[54] Thus, Islamic charities fund mosques and madrasas or religious schools in other parts of the world, including Pakistan, Central Asia and Europe, which promote a strict interpretation of Islam. One charity in Jordan exists for the purpose of making it more financially feasible for young people to get married (early marriage is seen as a stabilizing factor in society in Islamic culture), even providing interest-free loans.[55] In Saudi

Arabia, zakat substitutes for income tax.[56] Zakat may even be seen as the world's first social security system.[57] Further, the practice of zakat has been touted by some as the possible basis for a wholly Islamic economy, free of interest (riba), which is forbidden by the Qur'an.[58]

Lax Saudi Government Regulation of Zakat and Islamic Charities

Zakat is an important source of financial support for the al Qaeda network because of the amount of money it generates every year and the lack of government oversight.[59] Islamist terrorist organizations are believed to receive tens of millions of dollars annually by diversions of money from Islamic charities.[60] The donors fall into two categories: those who are aware that their money is going to terrorist organizations (witting donors) and those who are not (unwitting donors).[61] The donors who are aware that their donations are going to support terrorist activity represent one of the most disturbing aspects of zakat: the fact that radical Islamic scholars have equated terrorism in one form or another with jihad, and contend that charitable donations must be used for this cause. However, that there are donors who contribute unwittingly to charitable organizations is no less troubling. Many people who have donated to Islamic charities intending and expecting that their zakat contribution would be used on humanitarian aid may have unwittingly supported a terrorist organization.

Zakat donations may be made in several different ways, making the practice difficult to regulate. A Muslim may donate zakat money directly to a particular charity or to a special zakat committee established by the government that determines the recipients and channels donations to these individuals.[62] The donation of zakat may be even more informal and anonymous, coming from collection boxes in mosques and shopping malls.[63] Furthermore, many Islamic scholars maintain that zakat must go where it is needed most. Thus, many of the zakat donations made in Saudi Arabia are distributed to the needy in other countries. Saudi charities send approximately 10 to 20 percent of the contributions they receive abroad.[64] It is estimated that about $100 million in Saudi charitable donations are disseminated abroad annually.[65]

Al Qaeda has been able to penetrate Islamic charities because of 'lax [government] oversight and the charities' own ineffective financial controls.'[66] For example, prior to 2003, Saudi Arabia lacked legislation criminalizing money laundering and terrorist financing. Moreover, government regulation and auditing of Saudi charities to ensure that they were not used for terrorist purposes was virtually non-existent.[67] In Saudi Arabia, zakat funds are under the control of the Department of Zakat and Income Tax (DZIT), whose primary duty is to ensure payment of zakat.[68] The DZIT is part of the Saudi Ministry of Finance and National Economy. Its mission is to administer and collect zakat on commercial goods from Saudi individuals and companies, as well as individuals and companies of Gulf Cooperation Council (GCC) States who conduct business in Saudi Arabia.[69] The Department examines, assesses and ensures payment of zakat, although private payment of zakat is still permitted.

In response to criticisms and allegations that Saudi charities are involved in terrorist financing, the Saudi government announced a series of steps to provide greater oversight and transparency to charitable giving in the Kingdom. Prior to 2002, the foreign operations of charities were not regulated by the Saudi government. In December 2002, Saudi Arabia announced the creation of the High Commission for Oversight of Charities to assist Saudi charities in reforming their operations and improving transparency.[70] However, by the spring of 2003, the U.S. government had not seen any documentation to support the creation of such a Commission.[71] Although Saudi officials declared that all Saudi charities had been audited, these audits were not made public.[72] While some progress was being made,[73] the Saudi government failed to carry out a number of actions promised, such as closing the branch offices of the al-Haramain Islamic Foundation. At its peak, al-Haramain had offices in as many as 50 countries, and a budget ranging from $30 to $80 million.[74]

Terrorist attacks have motivated the Saudi government to take measures to combat terrorist financing, including against corrupt charities. In May 12, 2003, al Qaeda operatives detonated three bombs in an expatriate community in Riyadh that killed Westerners and Saudi citizens.[75] The Saudi government responded, 'declar[ing] war on the internal Saudi terrorist infrastructure, killing some two dozen al Qaeda terrorists and arresting scores of others.'[76] Motivated by the threat of future al Qaeda attacks, on May 24, 2003, the Saudi government adopted a set of comprehensive banking regulations imposing restrictions on the financial activities of Saudi charities. These measures included

> [a requirement that] charitable accounts can be opened only in Saudi riyals; enhanced customer identification requirements for charitable accounts; a requirement that charities must consolidate all banking activity into one principal account, with subaccounts permitted for branches but for deposits only, with all withdrawals and transfers serviced through the main account; a prohibition on cash disbursements from charitable accounts, with payments allowed by check payable to the first beneficiary and deposited into a Saudi bank; a prohibition on the use of ATM and credit cards by charities; and a prohibition on transfers from charitable accounts outside of Saudi Arabia.[77]

However, the banking regulations that prohibit private charities from transferring funds abroad until it is shown that the money is not going to support terrorist activities did not apply to 'multilateral' charitable organizations based in Saudi Arabia, such as the Muslim World League (MWL), the International Islamic Relief Organization (IIRO), and the World Assembly of Muslim Youth (WAMY), three of the most prominent and radical Saudi NGOs.[78] In August 2006, the Philippine and Indonesian branches of the IIRO were designated by the U.S. Treasury Department as Specially Designated Global Terrorists and their names were added to the U.N. Consolidated List, requiring countries to freeze their assets.[79] Moreover, WAMY has allegedly funded HAMAS.[80]

In November 2003, al Qaeda struck again, perpetrating another deadly bombing in Riyadh.[81] The terrorist attack caused the Saudi government to take further action to combat terrorist financing in the Kingdom. In February 2004, a royal decree was issued establishing the Saudi National Commission on Relief and Charity Work Abroad.[82] The Saudi government claimed that the Commission would be 'the sole vehicle' through which all private Saudi donations marked for international distribution would flow.[83] The decree stated that the task of forming and administering this non-governmental Commission would be carried out by a select group of citizens working in the charity field. The order also charged the Commission with exclusive responsibility for all charity work and relief abroad.[84] Moreover, the Saudi government claimed that it had investigated bank accounts suspected of having links to al Qaeda terrorists and frozen more than 40 such accounts and regulated hawalas through a mandatory licensing requirement.[85] However, the Saudi government's commitment to combating terrorist financing and preventing charitable donations from falling into the hands of terrorists remains in doubt. In July 2007, a top counterterrorism official at the U.S. Treasury Department stated that the National Commission to oversee Saudi-based charities was not operational.[86] While the Saudi government has taken some positive steps to control the activities of Islamic charities and abuse of zakat overseas, it has failed to fully implement and enforce its laws.[87]

The lack of rigorous oversight of charitable giving is not restricted to Saudi Arabia. The problem is more pervasive. According to one terrorism expert:

> There is no serious effort to date, neither by any individual country nor any group or [sic] countries or international organizations, to regulate and account for the flow of funds from donors to charities, from charities to grassroots organizations and aid groups, and from these recipient organizations to the people and projects they claim to fund.[88]

Without transparency and regular audits, charitable giving will remain vulnerable to abuse by unscrupulous charities intent on funding terrorism.

Modern Jihad

The use of zakat to fund international terrorism is promoted by radical Muslim clerics, religious scholars and terrorist sympathizers who equate terrorism with legitimate jihad. The term 'jihad' comes from the root word 'jihd' ('effort' or 'striving') and means 'a state of permanent efforts' for the ummah, the State, and Allah.[89] There are four different ways that a Muslim can fulfil the duty of jihad: by the heart, tongue, hands and the sword. Jihad of the heart is the internal struggle against one's own sinful inclinations;[90] Jihad of the tongue calls upon Muslims to speak on behalf of the cause of righteousness and protest against evil;[91] Jihad of the hand involves using the pen against evil; and jihad of the sword calls for the defense of Islam and the propagation of the faith.[92] At the same time, a distinction is made between the greater jihad (against oneself) and lesser jihad (holy war).[93] When Muhammad returned from battle, he is reported to have said: 'We have all returned from *jihad asghar* [lesser jihad] to *jihad akhbar* [greater jihad],' denoting the jihad against desires as *jihad akhbar*.[94]

Lesser jihad as a state tool

The lesser jihad (holy war) is an obligation on the community rather than the individual, 'which made possible its use as an instrument of the state.'[95] One reason jihad is not one of the pillars of Islam is that it must be enforced by the state, while the five pillars are enforced by the individual.[96] Throughout all Muslim conquests from the seventh century to the collapse of the Ottoman Empire, jihad was in the control of the state. It was the responsibility of the caliph to summon jihad and the duty of able-bodied Muslims to respond.[97] The call for jihad was only within the power of the ruler (the Prophet Muhammad, his successors and the official representatives of the caliph).[98] Jihad could not be proclaimed or conducted for personal reasons and declaration of jihad was strictly regulated.[99] To declare a jihad required issuing a fatwa (religious edict).[100] With the end of World War I and the collapse of the Ottoman Empire, jihad was no longer under the control of the state for the first time since the seventh century.[101] Today, jihadists believe that they are heirs of the Islamic state. Bin Laden and other leaders have indicated that they have 'assumed responsibility of jihad after the fall of the authority that was entitled to wage it for centuries: the caliphate.'[102]

Jihad in the Qur'an

The verses dealing with jihad are not very numerous, with only ten clearly and unambiguously referring to war. However, those jihadic verses are problematic because they are seemingly contradictory. Because of these contradictions, several themes are not easy to reconcile. For instance, some verses call for a non-military manner of spreading the faith, while some permit fighting but only in self-defense.[103] Other verses permit offensive war within certain limits, while still others seem to command warring without reservation.[104] Moreover, some verses encourage patience and reconciliation with the 'People of the Book' (Jews and Christians), while others call for subduing them.[105]

To support his call for violent jihad against the West, Osama bin Laden has relied on selective verses of the Qur'an as well as the statements of the leaders of earlier radical Islamic movements, such as Taqi al-Din ibn Taymiyya (1262–1328). Ibn Taymiyya, the ideological father of modern radical, revolutionary Islam, advocated a return to a literal interpretation of the Qur'an, Sunnah and Sharia, and labelled those who deviated from the path as infidels.[106] Drawing a stark contrast between dar al-Islam (abode of territory of Islam) and dar-al-Harb (abode of territory of war), ibn Taymiyya issued a fatwa labeling the Mongols as unbelievers (kufirs), just as bin Laden later would issue a fatwa against the unbelievers in the West.[107] Bin Laden quotes ibn Taymiyya's fatwa: 'There is no greater duty after faith than unconditionally fighting the attacking enemy who corrupts religion and the world.'[108]

Bin Laden's declarations concerning jihad portray it as a defensive war against the aggressors, the 'Crusader-Jewish forces.'[109] According to bin Laden, America is the aggressor because it has attacked Muslims in Somalia and supported Russian atrocities in Chechnya, the Indian oppression in Kashmir, and Jewish aggression in Lebanon.[110] Bin Laden declares: 'It is commanded by our religion and intellect that the oppressed have a right to respond to aggression. Do not expect anything from us but *jihad*, resistance and revenge.'[111] He asks that the banner of Islam be 'raised once again over every stolen land, from Palestine to al-Andalus and other Islamic lands that were lost because of the betrayals of rulers and the feebleness of Muslims.'[112] Moreover, in waging a defensive jihad against the United States, the killing of civilians is justified. Bin Laden states:

> The American people are the ones who pay the taxes which fund the planes that bomb us in Afghanistan . . . Also, the American army is part of the American people. It is this very same people who are shamelessly helping the Jews fight against us. The American people are the ones who employ both their men and their women in the American forces which attack us. This is why the American people cannot be innocent of all the crimes committed by the Americans and Jews against us.[113]

Finally, in calling for jihad, bin Laden echoes earlier radical teachings, stating that the 'divine punishment afflicting the *umma* is due to the neglect of its religion and the abandonment of *jihad* for the sake of God Almighty.'[114]

Understanding the relationship between charitable giving (zakat) and jihad (holy war) in the practice of Islam is necessary to fully appreciate why some Islamic charities raise and distribute funds to support Islamist extremist causes. For these charitable organizations and their sympathetic donors, raising money for violent jihad against the United States and its allies is morally justified as a legitimate purpose of zakat.

THE INTERNATIONAL DIMENSIONS OF THE RELIGIOUS FUNDING OF TERRORISM

Despite attempts by the international community to prevent the flow of funds to terrorist organizations, charitable organizations remain a major source of revenue for these groups. The abuse of zakat is pervasive and not limited to a few unscrupulous Islamic charities. As previously noted, the United States has designated over 40 Islamic charities for directly or indirectly funding al Qaeda, HAMAS or Hizballah, and their assets have been ordered to be frozen in the United States.[115] Approximately 30 Islamic charities have been similarly designated by the U.N. Al-Qaida and Taliban Sanctions Committee.[116] These charitable organizations have not restricted their operations to Saudi Arabia or the Middle East, but fund-raise and distribute monies to jihadist groups around the world. More disturbing yet, many of these charities have operated in the United States. For example, the Islamic African Relief Agency (IARA), headquartered in Khartoum, Sudan, maintains over 40 offices globally, including one in the United States.[117] The IARA identified itself as a non-governmental organization (NGO) dedicated to raising funds for humanitarian relief programs. In October 2004, the IARA was designated by the U.S. Treasury Department for providing direct financial support to Osama bin Laden and serving as a conduit for HAMAS by moving funds to the Palestinian territories for use in terrorist activities.[118]

Al-Haramain Islamic Foundation (AHIF), one of the most prominent Saudi charities, operated in as many as 50 countries.[119] It has been described as the 'United Way' of Saudi Arabia.[120] AHIF represents itself as a private, charitable, and educational organization dedicated to promoting a conservative form of Islam throughout the world. At its peak, AHIF's total annual expenditures ranged from $30 to $80 million.[121] In 2002, the United States and Saudi Arabia jointly designated the Bosnian and Somalian branches of AHIF for providing financial aid to terrorists.[122] In 2004, the United States designated 11 other branches of AHIF, including the U.S. office located in Ashland, Oregon.[123] Fourteen AHIF branches have been included on the U.N. Al-Qaida and Taliban Consolidated List.[124] Most recently, the Treasury Department designated the entire entity, including AHIF's headquarters in

Saudi Arabia.[125] The designations were based on evidence that AHIF offices and representatives operating throughout Africa, Asia, and Europe provided financial and logistical support to al Qaeda and related jihadist groups such as the Egyptian Islamic Jihad, Jemaah Islamiyah, Al-Ittihad Al-Islamiya, Lashkar E-Taibah, and HAMAS, all of which have been designated foreign terrorist organizations by the U.S. State Department.[126]

Islamic charitable giving is not limited to al Qaeda. Certain charitable organizations and sympathetic donors are equally willing to fund HAMAS and Hizballah. For example, IARA has been linked to providing direct financial support to HAMAS, as well as al Qaeda.[127] Moreover, three other Islamic charities, known as the Islamic Resistance Support Organization (ISRO), the Martyrs Foundation, and the Goodwill Charitable Organization (GCO), are allegedly key fund-raisers for Hizballah.[128] According to the Treasury Department, the Martyrs Foundation is an Iranian-backed NGO that channels financial support from Iran to several terrorist organizations in the Levant, including Hizballah, HAMAS, and the Palestinian Islamic Jihad.[129] The GCO was established as the U.S. branch of the Martyrs Foundation, operating in Dearborn, Michigan.[130] Additionally, the solicitation materials distributed by the ISRO inform prospective donors that their contributions will be used to purchase weapons and conduct operations.[131] Thus, money raised by Islamic charities goes not only to provide indirect support to terrorist groups, such as death benefits to the families of suicide bombers, but to directly fund terrorist operations as well.[132] Announcing the designation of IRSO, a senior Treasury Department official stated:

> While some terrorist-supporting charities try to obscure their support for violence, IRSO makes no attempt to hide its true colors. IRSO's fundraising materials present donors with the option of sending funds to equip Hizballah fighters or to purchase rockets that Hizballah uses to target civilian populations.[133]

Thus, IRSO knowingly and wilfully raises money to support jihad in Lebanon and the Palestinian territories that targets Israeli citizens.[134]

AL QAEDA-RELATED CHARITABLE FUND-RAISING

Islamic charities have successfully raised funds in the United States to support terrorist activities abroad for years, both before and after 9/11. According to the Treasury Department, the U.S.-based Islamic charities include: Al Aqsa Foundation;[135] Al Haramain Islamic Foundation;[136] Benevolence International Foundation;[137] Global Relief Foundation;[138] Goodwill Charitable Organization;[139] Holy Land Foundation for Relief and Development;[140] Islamic African Relief Agency;[141] KindHearts;[142] and Maktab al-Kidmat/Al-Kifah Refugee Center (formerly U.S.-based).[143] Collectively, these charitable organizations have allegedly raised millions of dollars in the United States to fund jihad around the world.[144]

The Islamic American Relief Agency (IARA) (aka the Islamic African Relief Agency-USA) represents a relatively simple case study on how Islamic charities raise money in the United States and allegedly transfer it abroad to support terrorist-related activities.[145] In January 2008, a federal grand jury in Missouri returned a 42-count superseding indictment charging the IARA and several of its former officers and associates with making illegal transfers of approximately $1.4 million to Iraq.[146] The indictment alleges that IARA's former executive director, Mubarak Hamed, illegally transferred funds for the benefit of Gulbuddin Hekmatyar, an Afghan mujahedeen leader, who was designated by the U.S. Treasury Department in 2002 as a Specially Designated Global Terrorist.[147] According to the indictment, Hekmatyar participated in and supported terrorist acts by al Qaeda and the Taliban, and vowed to engage in a holy war against the United States and international troops in Afghanistan.[148] The funds were allegedly transferred to bank accounts in Peshawar, Pakistan, for Hekmatyar's benefit, in violation of the International Emergency Economic Powers Act.[149] The indictment further charges that funds were transferred from the United States to Iraq, using the charity's bank accounts in Amman, Jordan, in violation of Iraqi sanctions regulations.[150] The defendants were also charged with misusing IARA's tax-exempt charitable status to raise funds for unlawful purposes.[151]

In 1985, the IARA incorporated under Missouri law as a charitable organization.[152] On its application to the IRS to receive tax-exempt status, the organization stated:

> The primary purpose in forming the organization was to raise funds in the United States that could be donated abroad to assist in the famine crises in Africa, particularly in the Sudan region. The organization raises its funds in the United States primarily through personal contacts of the organization with other *foreigners* living in the U.S.[153]

On the IARA's website, it made the following representations regarding its purported charitable purpose: 'The Islamic American Relief Agency is an American non-profit organization . . . dedicated to the empowerment of disadvantaged people everywhere through relief and participatory development programs emphasizing human dignity, self-reliance, and social justice.'[154] The IARA used its website to solicit donations from the expatriate Muslim community living in the United States. The charity further promoted its federal tax exempt status to leverage donations.[155] According to the indictment, from 1998 to 2003, the IARA 'solicited donations through various means, including pamphlets, flyers, newsletters, and personal correspondence . . . improperly requesting contributions to pay for projects in Iraq.'[156] Hundreds of thousands of dollars allegedly raised by the IARA in the United States were deposited into the IARA's bank accounts in Missouri and later transferred to the Islamic Relief Agency's (ISRA) bank accounts in Amman, Jordan, and then to Iraq.[157] The ISRA is the international parent-holding company of the IARA, based in Khartoum, Sudan.[158] Finally, between February 2003 and August 2004, IARA sent approximately $130,000 to ISRA bank accounts in Peshawar, Pakistan, for the stated purpose of renovating buildings owned by Gulbuddin Hekmatyar, a SDGT.[159]

The IARA case illustrates how easily foreign charities can establish themselves as a legal entity in the United States, raise millions of dollars, and then transfer the proceeds abroad. The modus operandi involves several steps. The Islamic charity:

(1) incorporates itself under the laws of the relevant state;
(2) applies to the IRS for tax-exempt status as a charity or not-for-profit organization;
(3) creates a website for on-line fundraising;
(4) opens a domestic bank account to deposit the proceeds;
(5) begins fund-raising through personal correspondence, newsletters, and other means, focusing on the expatriate Muslim community residing in the U.S.;
(6) deposits the solicited funds into its domestic bank accounts; and
(7) transfers those funds to its overseas branches, and some of them are used to support jihadist activities.

Once transferred abroad, the funds are almost impossible to trace. While some of the charitable donations are used to provide humanitarian assistance, other funds are disbursed to jihadist groups.

The modus operandi for raising money for jihad in the U.S. has been repeated by the Global Relief Foundation (GRF) and the Benevolence International Foundation (BIF), two notorious Islamic charitable organizations based in the U.S. Both GRF and BIF have been accused of providing financial support to al Qaeda and international terrorism, and their assets ordered to be frozen by the U.S. Treasury Department and the U.N. Al-Qaida and Taliban Sanctions Committee.[160] In 1992, GRF was incorporated in Illinois.[161] The group's founders have been linked to Mektab al Khidmat (MAK), co-founded by Abdullah Azzam and Osama bin Laden in the 1980s to recruit and finance the mujahedeen to fight in the Soviet–Afghan conflict.[162] The MAK has been characterized as the 'precursor organization to al Qaida.'[163] A branch of the MAK in the United States, the Al Khifa Refugee Center in Brooklyn, allegedly facilitated the movement of jihadist fighters in Afghanistan.[164] According to the U.S. government, a number of individuals convicted in the first World Trade Center bombing were associated with the Al Khifa Refugee Center.[165] In addition to its historical links to bin Laden and the MAK, GRF is believed 'to support jihadists around the world, including in Europe, Bangladesh, India, and Pakistan.'[166]

In the United States, GRF described itself as a charitable organization that provided humanitarian relief to aid Muslims through its overseas offices located in Afghanistan, Bosnia, Chechnya, Kashmir, and Lebanon.[167] To facilitate its fund-raising efforts it received a tax-exempt status from the IRS. By 2000, GRF had become a proficient fund-raiser, reporting more than $5 million in annual contributions.[168] According to IRS reports, between 1994 and 2000, GRF transferred 90 percent of its donations overseas, using its network of foreign branch offices.[169] In 1999, GRF sent $3.2 million abroad, and it transferred $3.7 million to foreign locations in 2000.[170] While the FBI was unable to trace the millions of dollars GRF sent overseas to any specific terrorist organization, evidence uncovered by law enforcement officials revealed that GRF's interests were not restricted to humanitarian causes; it was raising money for jihad. GRF published several Arabic newsletters and pamphlets that 'advocated armed action through jihad against groups perceived to be un-Islamic.'[171] A GRF newsletter requested donations 'for equipping the raiders, for the purchase of ammunition and food, and for [the mujahedeen's] transportation so that they can raise God the Almighty's word[;] . . . it is likely the most important . . . disbursement of Zakat in our times is on the jihad for God's cause[.]'[172] A GRF pamphlet from 1995 stated, 'God equated martyrdom through JIHAD with supplying funds for the JIHAD effort. All contributions should be mailed to: GRF.'[173]

BIF followed a similar pattern. In 1992, BIF was incorporated in Illinois as a not-for-profit organization whose stated purpose was to fund humanitarian relief projects around the world.[174] It was afforded tax-exempt status from the IRS in 1993.[175] Like the IARA and GRF, BIF maintained a network of foreign branch offices. According to IRS filings, BIF collected more than $15 million in donations between 1995 and 2000.[176] However, the FBI estimated that BIF's cumulative fund raising was even higher. The FBI believed that BIF was receiving 'approximately forty to sixty thousand dollars a week, and that between 1997 and 1998, BIF sent more than $2.5 million to its overseas offices in Bosnia, Azerbaijan, Pakistan, and Tajikistan.'[177]

In 1993, Enaam Arnaout became BIF's executive director.[178] The government contends that Arnaout was a jihadist supporter with personal ties to

Osama bin Laden.[179] An article in an Arab newspaper in 1988, reporting bin Laden's activities at a mujahedeen training camp in Afghanistan, included a photograph of Arnaout and bin Laden together.[180] Further, in March 2002, a search of BIF's offices in Bosnia by criminal investigators revealed a treasure-trove of evidence linking Arnaout to bin Laden and al Qaeda.[181] Among other things, the evidence included letters between Arnaout and bin Laden.[182] In one letter, bin Laden authorized Arnaout to sign documents on bin Laden's behalf.[183] Further, one government source stated that BIF engaged in financial transactions for al Qaeda in the early 1990s and described how the terror group would receive cash from charitable NGOs.[184]

In December 2001, BIF's accounts were blocked pending investigation by the Treasury Department, and the charity was fully designated in November 2002.[185] In January 2003, Arnaout was charged in a criminal indictment with racketeering conspiracy, conspiracy to provide material support to terrorists, providing material support to terrorists, conspiracy to launder money, and wire and mail fraud.[186] Ultimately, Arnaout entered a guilty plea to criminal racketeering conspiracy, admitting that he fraudulently diverted charitable donations totalling over $315,000 to pay for boots, uniforms and other supplies for jihadists fighting in Chechnya and Bosnia-Herzegovina.[187] He was sentenced to more than 11 years in federal prison.[188]

The U.S. Department of Justice prosecutions are being recalibrated to focus on charging the leaders of unscrupulous charities with federal tax fraud for abusing their tax-exempt status. In several previous cases, federal prosecutors had unsuccessfully sought to convict the leaders of charitable organizations on charges of providing material support to a foreign terrorist organization, a violation of 18 U.S.C. §2339B. Several of those cases resulted in embarrassing acquittals or a hung jury on the material support charges.[189] Federal prosecutors appear to have changed their strategy, filing tax fraud charges instead. In January 2008, three former leaders of the defunct Care International Inc., a group that described itself as a charity for Muslim refugees, widows, and orphans, were convicted on federal tax fraud charges for using tax exemptions to conceal their support for religious militants and jihadists overseas.[190]

HAMAS-RELATED CHARITABLE FUND-RAISING

Saudi Committees

HAMAS receives most of its financial support from a complex network of Islamic charitable organizations allegedly supported by the Saudi government.[191] According to one counter-terrorism expert, 'Saudi Arabia has funneled money to Palestinian terrorist groups through terror-linked charities and committees for a number of years.'[192] In September 2000, following the collapse of peace negotiations between Israel and the Palestinian Authority, Palestinian terrorist groups launched what became known as the Al Aqsa Intifada or Intifada Al Quds – the 'Second Intifada.'[193] The Second Intifada was marked by numerous acts of violence by Palestinian terrorist groups that targeted Israeli civilians. Suicide bombings became the preferred method of carrying out such attacks. The objectives of the Second Intifada were to intimidate and coerce the civilian population of Israel and to influence the policy of the Israeli government to withdraw from the Occupied Territories.[194]

In October 2000, the Saudi government established two committees to solicit money for the Palestinian cause: the Saudi Popular Committee for Assisting the Palestinian Mujahideen (Saudi Popular Committee) and the Saudi Committee for the Support of the Al Quds Intifada, now known as the Saudi Committee for the Relief of the Palestinian People.[195] The Saudi Popular Committee gave money to the Palestinian Liberation Organization (PLO), while the Saudi Committee for the Support of the Al Quds Intifada distributed funds to the Palestinian Authority.[196] The Popular Committee was reportedly established and directed by Prince Salman bin Abd Al Aziz, the governor of Riyadh Province.[197] It raised approximately $8.8 million for the PLO from October 2000 to April 2003.[198]

The Saudi Committee for Support of the Al Quds Intifada allegedly has served as the main conduit for providing financial assistance to the Palestinian territories since its establishment by Royal Decree in October 2000.[199] According to a report issued by the Saudi Embassy in Washington, D.C., in 2003, the Committee has provided approximately $140 million to support 31 relief programs.[200] The Committee also distributed donations to charitable organizations in the West Bank and Gaza Strip and gave direct assistance to thousands of Palestinian individuals.[201]

While providing humanitarian aid to the needy is indeed a noble cause, not all of the funds raised by the Saudi Committee were used to provide humanitarian relief. In April 2002, the Al Quds Intifada Committee organized a telethon, sponsored by King Fahd, which raised more than $110 million for families of Palestinians killed or injured in the uprising.[202] Saudi officials reported that the proceeds of the telethon were funneled through Islamic charitable organizations to provide humanitarian support to needy Palestinian families.[203] However, because there was no effective Saudi government oversight to monitor or account for the disbursement of funds, the actual recipients cannot be verified. There are claims that monies raised during the telethon and by the Saudi Committee for Support of the Al Quds Intifada were distributed to the families of suicide bombers in the form of a 'comprehensive insurance death benefit' or 'universal death and dismemberment plan.'[204]

HAMAS-related Fund-raising in Europe

In 2002, more than 370 persons, including 10 Americans, were killed in Israel, the West Bank and the Gaza Strip by terrorist attacks.[205] HAMAS was responsible for carrying out more than 50 such attacks, including shootings, suicide bombings and rocket attacks against civilians.[206] To support its terrorist activities, 'HAMAS raises tens of millions of dollars per year throughout the world using charitable fundraising as cover.'[207] HAMAS allegedly conducts its affairs through a network of front organizations that have religious or charitable purposes and raise and distribute money on its behalf.[208] This network of HAMAS-related charitable and social institutions is commonly referred to by HAMAS as the 'Dawa.'[209] It is allegedly comprised of dozens of Islamic charities, including, but not limited to: 'the Orphan Care Society of Bethlehem ("Orphan Care Society"), Al-Islah Charitable Society in Ramallah-Al-Bireh ("Al-Islah"), the Ramallah Al-Bireh Charitable Society ("Ramallah Society"), the Jenin Charitable Committee ("Jenin Committee"), the Hebron Islamic Association ("Hebron Association"), Talkarem Charity Committee ("Tulkarem Committee"), Al-Mujama al-Islami, the Islamic Charitable Society in the Gaza Strip ("Islamic Charitable Society") and the Muslim Youth Association of Hebron ("Muslim Youth Association").'[210] Other HAMAS-related charities and not-for-profit groups allegedly have raised money for HAMAS in the United States, such as the Holy Land Foundation for Relief and Development (HLF).[211]

The collection and disbursement of finances to HAMAS has been coordinated by the Union of the Good. This was established by the Muslim Brotherhood in October 2000, and is comprised of more than 50 Islamic charitable foundations worldwide, including the Palestinian Relief and Development Fund (Interpal) and the Al-Aqsa Charitable Foundation (Al-Aqsa).[212] Interpal, headquartered in the United Kingdom, allegedly operated as the primary clearing house for the flow of funds raised by charitable organizations in Europe and the Middle East to HAMAS.[213] Al Aqsa, formerly headquartered in Germany, has been described as a 'critical part of HAMAS' terrorist support infrastructure.'[214] In 2003, the U.S. government designated both Interpal and the Al Aqsa Foundation as SDGTs.[215] In 2005, Sheik Mohammed Ali Hasan al-Moayad, the head of Al-Aqsa's Yemen branch, was convicted in the United States for conspiring to provide material support to al Qaeda and attempting to provide material support to HAMAS, in violation of 18 U.S.C. §2339B.[216]

The Union of the Good is headed by Dr Yusuf al-Qaradawi, a recognized Muslim scholar.[217] In 1999, Dr al-Qaradawi was placed on the U.S. Watch List and prohibited from travelling to the United States.[218] In 2001, the Al Taqwa Bank, of which he is allegedly a leading shareholder and principal, was designated by the Treasury Department as an SDGT.[219] The Treasury Department claimed that Al Taqwa Bank was a 'financier[] of terror' and 'acted as financial adviser[] to al Qaeda.'[220] In 2001, Dr al-Qaradawi described the activities of the Islamic charitable organizations he coordinated as a 'new type of jihad, financial jihad, through which financial support is guaranteed to the martyr's families [sic], Palestinian prisoners and detainees, and every Palestinian whose property is damaged during conflict.'[221] In 2002, he publicly extolled 'jihad and martyrdom' against Israeli citizens.[222]

Interpal allegedly served as the hub for the receipt and distribution of funds raised in Europe. According to allegations in a civil cause of action against National Westminster Bank (NatWest), a financial institution with its principal place of business in London, donations solicited by Islamic charities affiliated with the Union of the Good would be deposited into Interpal's bank accounts at NatWest and transferred to various HAMAS front organizations.[223] The civil complaint alleges that NatWest accepted deposits on behalf of Interpal from alleged terrorist groups on the following occasions:

(1) In April 2000 NatWest accepted a deposit of $66,000.00 for Interpal from HLF.
(2) In January 2001 NatWest accepted deposits totaling $70,000.00 on behalf of Interpal from the Al-Aqsa organization in Yemen.
(3) On March 27, 2003, NatWest deposited at least two payments to Interpal totaling 295,000 Euros from the Dutch branch of the Al-Aqsa Foundation.[224]

Further, NatWest allegedly transferred funds from Interpal's accounts to various HAMAS front organizations:

(1) On February 19, 2003, NatWest transferred £21,404 to the Tulkarem Committee.
(2) On July 30, 2003 NatWest transferred £73,757 to the Jenin Committee, debiting Interpal's Sterling account . . . This transaction is said to have been financed by WAMY.
(3) On November 5, 2003, NatWest transferred £32,329 to the Jenin Committee also from Interpal's Sterling account.[225]

A similar fund-raising scheme has been alleged involving the Comité de Bienfaisance et de Secours aux Palestiniens (CBSP), headquartered in France.[226] CBSP is a member of the Union of the Good and a primary fund-raiser for HAMAS in France.[227] CBSP opened accounts with Crédit Lyonnais, a retail bank with its principal place of business in Paris, France.[228] Between 2000 and 2003, Crédit Lyonnais allegedly transferred funds from CBSP to institutions within HAMAS' control, including: 'the Orphan Care Society, Al-Islah, the Ramallah Al-Bireh Charitable Society, the Jenin Charity Committee, the Hebron Islamic Association, the Tulkarem Charity Committee, Al-Mujama al-Islami, the Islamic Charitable Society in the Gaza Strip, the Al-Salah Society and the Muslim Youth Association of Hebron (collectively, "HAMAS controlled organizations").'[229]

The NatWest Bank and Crédit Lyonnais cases are instructive and reveal a modus operandi for HAMAS fund-raising in Europe. Islamic charities operating under the direction of Dr Yusuf al-Qaradawi, Director of the Union of the Good, would solicit funds from witting and unwitting donors for HAMAS. Those funds would be deposited into Interpal's accounts at NatWest and CBSP's accounts at Crédit Lyonnais. The pooled funds would then be redirected and transferred to front organizations for the benefit of HAMAS. According to one source:

> The final step in the process is for Hamas operatives in the West Bank and Gaza to use the money wired from the United States [and elsewhere] to buy weapons and carry out terrorist attacks . . . to finance training, weaponry, lodging, false documentation/identification, communications equipment, facilities, lethal substances, explosives, personnel, transportation, and other material support . . . [and] to pay stipends to the families of Hamas terrorists 'killed in action' to encourage others to volunteer for suicide missions.[230]

Using dozens of charitable organizations as fronts for HAMAS, the Union of the Good has developed an elaborate fund-raising scheme that allegedly has raised millions of dollars for HAMAS. These funds have supported, directly or indirectly, HAMAS' social and military wings, including targeting Israeli civilians for terrorist attacks.

HAMAS-related Charities in the U.S.

The U.S. government has designated eight HAMAS-related charities as SDGTs.[231] However, the Holy Land Foundation for Relief and Development (HLF) has been the most controversial. The HLF, originally known as the Occupied Land Fund, was founded in California in 1989 as a tax-exempt charity.[232] In 1992, HLF relocated to Richardson, Texas.[233]

The aim of the organization was to assist Palestinians affected by the Palestinian Intifada.[234] It had offices in California, New Jersey and Illinois, and representatives in the West Bank and Gaza.[235] In 2000, the HLF raised over $13 million.[236] In December 2001, HLF was designated by the Treasury Department as an SDGT and its assets were frozen in the United States.[237] The government maintained that HLF was the principal fund-raiser for HAMAS in the United States. The funds were transferred to Islamic charity committees (zakat committees) and other charitable organizations that are part of HAMAS or controlled by HAMAS members.[238] The government alleged that HLF's funds were used to support schools that encouraged children to become suicide bombers and to recruit suicide bombers by offering financial support to their families.[239]

In July 2004, HLF and several of its directors were indicted on criminal charges.[240] The indictment involved a total of 197 counts, including providing material support to a foreign terrorist organization.[241] However, after a lengthy federal trial, and 19 days of deliberation, the jury deadlocked and failed to convict any leaders of the Muslim charity who were charged with providing material support to terrorists, and the court declared a mistrial.[242] While the criminal action does not affect HLF's designation and its funds remain frozen, this is a major setback for the government.

In sum, although significant actions have been taken by the United States and the international community through the U.N. Security Council to prevent the funding of terrorism by Islamic charitable groups, charitable giving or zakat remains a principal source of funding for jihadists throughout the world. As long as terrorism is equated with religious jihad, unscrupulous Muslim charities will continue to funnel tens of millions of dollars annually to support suicide bombings and other terrorist activities. Because of the lack of transparency and auditing of charities, and the lack of effective government oversight of charitable donations collected in one country and transferred to the charity's foreign branches for disbursement abroad, foreign terrorist organizations will retain the financial ability to continue waging global jihad.

So long as al Qaeda and affiliated terrorist groups have the financial resources to wage jihad or holy war – whether through charities, state sponsors, drug trafficking or deep-pocket donors – the fight against international terrorism will continue unabated and with no end in sight. The United States and the international community must confront this reality and work collectively to deprive terrorists of funding. Interdicting terrorist finances must be a priority in the struggle against al Qaeda and undertaken with a sense of urgency. The next several chapters will provide a critical examination of the central components of the domestic and international legal regime developed to prevent and suppress the financing of terrorism, and whether this legal framework has proven effective.

NOTES

1. Weiss v. Nat'l Westminster Bank, 453 F. Supp. 2d 609, 617 (E.D.N.Y. 2006).
2. John Roth, et al., National Commission on Terrorist Attacks Upon the United States, Monograph on Terrorist Financing: Staff Report to the Commission 106 (Washington, D.C.: Gov't Printing Office 2004), *available at* http://govinfo.library.unt.edu/911/staff_statements/911_TerrFin_Monograph.pdf [hereinafter Staff Monograph on Terrorist Financing]; *see also* Press Release, U.S. Dep't of Justice, Treasury Department Statement Regarding the Designation of the Global Relief Foundation (Oct. 18, 2002), *available at* http://www.treas.gov/press/releases/po3553.htm.
3. *See* Staff Monograph on Terrorist Financing, *supra* note 2, at 19, 21; Report of an Independent Task Force Sponsored by the Council on Foreign Relations, Terrorist Financing, at 1 (Oct. 2002) ('For years, individuals and charities based in Saudi Arabia have been the most important source of funds for al-Qaeda.'), *available at* http://www.cfr.org/pdf/Terrorist_Financing_TF.pdf; Steven Emerson, *Saudi Arabia: Friend or Foe in the War on Terror*, Testimony before the Senate Committee on the Judiciary, at 3 (Nov. 8, 2005) ('The paper trail of Saudi money, funneled through a vast network of charities and religious organizations, has led to some of the most violent terrorist groups in the world, including Al-Qaeda and Hamas.'), *available at* http://judiciary.senate.gov/testimony.cfm?id=1669&wit_id=4791 [hereinafter *Saudi Arabia in the War on Terror*]; *see also* Boim v. Quranic Literacy Inst., 127 F. Supp. 2d 1002, 1005 (N.D. Ill. 2001); Almog v. Arab Bank, 471 F. Supp. 2d 257, 261–3 (E.D.N.Y. 2007); Linde v. Arab Bank, 384 F. Supp. 2d 571, 576–9 (E.D.N.Y. 2005); Weiss v. Nat'l Westminster Bank, 453 F. Supp. 2d 609, 617–19 (E.D.N.Y. 2006); Strauss v. Credit Lyonnais, Case No. CV-06–0702 (CPS), 2006 WL 2862704, *4–*6 (E.D.N.Y. Oct. 05, 2006).
4. Staff Monograph on Terrorist Financing, *supra* note 2, at 4, 27, 144; *see also* Alfred B. Prados & Christopher M. Blanchard, Saudi Arabia: Terrorist Financing Issues, Congressional Research Service Report for Congress 2 (2005) (stating that al Qaeda raised money through charities with significant Saudi government sponsorship).
5. Staff Monograph on Terrorist Financing, *supra* note 2, at 4.
6. Prados & Blanchard, *supra* note 4, at 2 (quoting the National Commission on Terrorist Attacks Upon the United States).
7. *Boim,* 127 F. Supp. 2d at 1005.
8. *Id.* at 1009–10; *see also* Prados & Blanchard, *supra* note 4, at 14–15 (payments of $5,300 were transmitted to the families of terrorist suicide bombers); *see also Almog*, 471 F. Supp. 2d at 261–3; *Linde*, 384 F. Supp. 2d at 576–9 (E.D.N.Y. 2005); *Weiss*, 453 F. Supp. 2d at 617–19, 623; *Strauss*, 2006 WL 2862704, *4–*6.
9. *See* Staff Monograph on Terrorist Financing, *supra* note 2, at 4; *see also* Stuart Levey, Under Secretary, Office of Terrorism and Financial Intelligence, U.S. Dep't of Treasury, *Combating Terrorist Financing in the Middle East*, Testimony before the House Financial Services Subcommittee on Oversight and Investigations and House International Relations Subcommittee on International Terrorism and Nonproliferation (May 4, 2005) (expressing concerns that charitable giving (zakat) is being used to fund terrorist activities); *Saudi Arabia in the War on Terror, supra* note 3, at 4 ('[I]n many cases, the Saudi-generated funding and direction for Islamic "humanitarian" or "religious" activities abroad was given in the noble Islamic tradition of Zakat or charity.').
10. *See Boim*, 127 F. Supp. 2d at 1005.

11. *Id.*; *see also Saudi Arabia in the War on Terror, supra* note 3, at 3 ('[I]t is the very external legitimacy of these groups that provides the perfect cover to siphon off, divert or launder financial support or provide cover to terrorist cells.').
12. *See* STAFF MONOGRAPH ON TERRORIST FINANCING, *supra* note 2, at 7; *see also Boim*, 127 F. Supp. 2d at 1005–9 (discussing how Islamic charities raise money to fund terrorist activities).
13. Matthew Levitt, *Charitable Organizations and Terrorist Financing: A War on Terror Status-Check,* The Washington Institute for Near East Policy (Mar. 19, 2004), *available at* http://www.washingtoninstitute.org/print.php?template=C07&CID=104.
14. *See* Blocking Property and Prohibiting Transactions with Persons Who Commit, Threaten to Commit, or Support Terrorism, Exec. Order No. 13,224, 3 C.F.R. 786–90 (2001), *reprinted as amended in* 50 U.S.C. §1701 note (Supp. IV 2004) [hereinafter E.O. 13224]. To assist charities in preventing terrorist abuse, the U.S. Department of the Treasury has published a set of best practices for U.S.-based charities. *See* U.S. Dep't of Treasury, Anti-Terrorist Financing Guidelines: Voluntary Best Practices for U.S.-Based Charities (revised Dec. 2005), *available at* http://www.treas.gov/offices/enforcement/key-issues/protecting/charities-intro.shtml. An international set of best practices for non-profit organizations has been published by the Financial Action Task Force on Money Laundering. *See* Financial Action Task Force on Money Laundering, Combating the Abuse of Non-Profit Organisations – International Best Practices (Oct. 11, 2002), *available at* http://www.oecd.org/dataoecd/39/19/34033761.pdf.
15. *See* E.O. 13224, *supra* note 14, at §1 (c),(d)(i)–(ii). For a comprehensive discussion of U.S. domestic blocking orders under E.O. 13224, see generally *infra* Chapter 7 on freezing terrorist assets.
16. *See* E.O. 13224, *supra* note 14, at §1 (c),(d)(i)–(ii); *see also* the International Emergency Economic Powers Act (IEEPA), 50 U.S.C. §§1701–7, enacted by Congress in 1977 and amended by the USA PATRIOT Act, Pub. L. No. 107–56, Title I, § 106, 115 Stat. 272 (Oct. 26, 2001).
17. *See* U.S. Dep't of Treasury, Office of Terrorism and Financial Intelligence, Designated Charities and Potential Fundraising Front Organizations for FTOs, *available at* http://www.treas.gov/offices/enforcement/key-issues/protecting/fto.shtml [hereinafter U.S. Designated Charities].
18. The names, dates of designation, and primary jurisdictions of known operations of the al Qaeda-related charities are as follows: Maktab al-Khidamat/Al Kifah (9/23/01) (formerly U.S.-based and Pakistan); Al Rashid Trust (9/23/01) (Pakistan); WAFA Humanitarian Organization (9/24/01) (Pakistan, Saudi Arabia, Kuwait, and United Arab Emirates); Rabita Trust (10/12/01) (Pakistan); Ummah Tameer E-Nau (12/20/01) (Pakistan); Revival of Islamic Heritage Society (01/09/02) (Kuwait, Pakistan, Afghanistan); Afghan Support Committee (01/09/02) (Afghanistan, Pakistan); Al Haramain Foundation (01/22/04) (Indonesia); Al Haramain Foundation (01/22/04) (Kenya, Pakistan, Tanzania); Al Haramain Foundation (03/11/02) (Bosnia, Somalia); Al Haramain Foundation (06/02/04) (Bangladesh, Afghanistan, Albania, Ethiopia, Netherlands); Al Haramain Foundation (09/09/04) (Comoros Islands, United States); Aid Organization of the Ulema (04/19/02) (Pakistan); Global Relief Foundation (10/18/02) (United States); Benevolence International Foundation (11/19/02) (United States, Canada); Bosanska Idealna Futura (11/19/02) (Bosnia); Stichting Benevolence International Nederland (01/21/03) (Netherlands); Lajnat al Daawa al Islamiyya (01/09/03) (Kuwait, Pakistan, Afghanistan); Al Akhtar Trust (10/14/03) (Pakistan); Taibah International (05/06/04) (Bosnia); Al Haramain and Al Masjed Al Aqsa Charity Foundation (05/06/04) (Bosnia); Al Furqan (05/06/04) (Bosnia); Islamic African Relief Agency (IARA)/Islamic Relief Agency (ISRA) (10/13/04) (Sudan, United States and 40 other branches globally); and International Islamic Relief Organization (08/03/06) (Philippines and Indonesia). *See* U.S. Designated Charities, *supra* note 17. Finally, in June 2008, the Treasury Department designated Al Haramain Islamic Foundation, not merely select branches, including its headquarters in Saudi Arabia *see* Press Release, U.S.

Dep't of Treasury, Treasury Designated Al Haramain Islamic Foundation (June 19, 2008), *available at* http://www.treasury.gov/press/releases/hp1043.htm.

19. The names, dates of designation, and primary jurisdictions of known operations of the HAMAS-related charities are as follows: The Holy Land Foundation for Relief and Development (12/04/01) (United States); Al Aqsa Foundation (05/29/03) (United States, Europe, Pakistan, Yemen, South Africa); Comité de Bienfaisance et de Secours aux Palestiniens (08/23/03) (France); Association de Secours Palestinien (08/23/03) (Switzerland); Interpal (Palestinian Relief and Development Fund) (08/23/03) (United Kingdom); Palestinian Association in Austria (08/23/03) (Austria); Sanibil Association for Relief and Development (08/23/03) (Lebanon); and Al Salah Society (08/07/07) (Palestinian territories). *Id.*
20. The names, dates of designation, and primary jurisdictions of known operations of the Hizballah-related and Palestinian Islamic Jihad-related charities are as follows: Islamic Resistance Support Organization (08/29/06) (Lebanon); Martyrs Foundation (07/24/07) (Iran, Lebanon); Goodwill Charitable Organization (07/24/07) (United States); and Elehssan Society (05/05/06) (Palestinian Territories). One charity has been designated for funding the Liberation Tigers of Tamil Eelam (LTTE): Tamils Rehabilitation Organisation (TRO) (11/15/07) (Sri Lanka). *Id.* Hizballah, the Palestinian Islamic Jihad and Liberation Tigers of Tamil Eelam have been included on the State Department list of foreign terrorist organizations. *See* 2006 Country Reports on Terrorism, U.S. Dep't of State, Office of the Coordinator for Counterterrorism (Apr. 30, 2007), *available at* http://www.state.gov/s/ct/rls/crt/2006/82738.htm.
21. *See* The Al-Qaida and Taliban Sanctions Committee, The Consolidated List of the United Nations Security Council's Al-Qaida and Taliban Sanctions Committee, *available at* http://www.un.org/sc/committees/1267/consolist.shtml (last visited Apr. 15, 2008) [hereinafter 'Consolidated List'].
22. *See* Staff Monograph on Terrorist Financing, *supra* note 2, at 17 ('[A]l Qaeda financial facilitators raise money from witting and unwitting donors, mosques and sympathetic imams, and nongovernmental organizations such as charities.').
23. *See* Starving Terrorists of Money: The Role of Middle Eastern Financial Institutions, Hearing Before the Subcommittee on Oversight and Investigations and the Subcommittee on International Terrorism and Nonproliferation of the House Committee on Financial Services, 109th Cong. 31, at 54 (statement of Zahid H. Bukhari, Director of American Muslim Studies Program, Fellow, School of For. Serv., Georgetown Univ.) [hereinafter *Cong. Hearing on Starving Terrorists of Money*].
24. *See* Osama bin Laden, Declaration of Jihad Against the Americans Occupying the Land of the Two Holy Places (1996) (Ladenese Epistle), *quoted in* Osama bin Laden, Messages to the World: The Statements of Osama bin Laden 29 (Bruce Lawrence ed., James Howarth trans., Verso 2005) [hereinafter 'Statements of Osama bin Laden']; *see also Saudi Arabia in the War on Terrorism, supra* note 3, at 23 (quoting from various jihadist websites declaring that 'jihad is Allah's cause,' and imploring Muslims to wage jihad against the Jews and Christians).
25. *See* Osama bin Laden, Declaration of Jihad Against the Americans Occupying the Land of the Two Holy Places (1996) (Ladenese Epistle), *supra* note 24, at 29.
26. *See Saudi Arabia in the War on Terrorism, supra* note 3, at 20 (discussing a program aired in Saudi Arabia calling on Muslims to support jihad and donate money to the Palestinian cause).
27. *See* Don Van Natta, *British Jury Finds Muslim Cleric Guilty of Inciting Murder*, N.Y. Times, Feb. 7, 2006, *available at* http://www.nytimes.com/2006/02/07/international/europe/07cnd-cleric.html.
28. *Id.*
29. *Id.*
30. *See* Statements of Osama bin Laden, *supra* note 24, at 58–62 (reproducing bin Laden's declaration 'The World Islamic Front,' dated Feb. 23, 1998).
31. *See* 'A Muslim Bomb' (Dec. 1998), *quoted in* Statements of Osama bin Laden, *supra* note 24, at 79; *see also* Osama bin Laden's 'Message to the United States' (Oct. 18, 2003)

('Those who can contribute effort, opinions, assistance, energy or money, this is the right time for giving. In such circumstances, people will be judged to sort the honest from the lying and the altruists from the selfish.').

32. Muslims express their faith through five essential affirmations or 'pillars.' The five pillars of Islam include 'declaration of belief in One God, daily prayer at five set times, the giving of charity [almsgiving], fasting in the month of Ramadan, and the hajj pilgrimage to the Ka'bah.' STEPHEN SCHWARTZ, THE TWO FACES OF ISLAM: THE HOUSE OF SA'UD FROM TRADITION TO TERROR 27 (Doubleday 2002).
33. *See Cong. Hearing on Starving Terrorists of Money*, *supra* note 23, at 29.
34. Jonathan Benthall, *Financial Worship: The Quranic Injunction to Almsgiving*, J. ROYAL ANTHROPOLOGICAL INST. 27, 29 (1999) [hereinafter The Quranic Injunction to Almsgiving].
35. *Id.*
36. Qur'an 9:103.
37. Thomas H. Weir & Aaron Zysow, *Zakat*, ENCYCLOPAEDIA OF ISLAM (CD ROM) (Leiden, 1999).
38. *See Cong. Hearing on Starving Terrorists of Money*, *supra* note 23, at 29.
39. *Id.*
40. *Id.; see also* Benthall, *supra* note 34, at 28–30.
41. *See Cong. Hearing on Starving Terrorists of Money*, *supra* note 23, at 53; *see also* Hartley Dean & Zafar Khan, *Muslim Perspectives on Welfare*, 26 J. SOC. POL'Y 193, 199 (1997).
42. *See* Benthall, *supra* note 34, at 30–31; *see also Cong. Hearing on Starving Terrorists of Money*, *supra* note 23, at 31.
43. Qur'an 9:60 (emphasis added).
44. *See Cong. Hearing on Starving Terrorists of Money*, *supra* note 23, at 29.
45. *See* Weir & Zysow, *supra* note 37.
46. *See* M.M. Metwally, *Economic Consequences of Applying Islamic Principles in Muslim Societies,* 24 INT'L J. SOC. ECON. 941, 943 (1997).
47. *See* LORETTA NAPOLEONI, MODERN JIHAD: TRACING THE DOLLARS BEHIND THE TERROR NETWORKS 120 (Pluto Press 2003) (claiming that zakat contributions from the Saudi Royal Family alone are $12 billion annually); *see also* STAFF MONOGRAPH ON TERRORIST FINANCING, *supra* note 2, at 17.
48. *See Cong. Hearing on Starving Terrorists of Money*, *supra* note 23, at 30.
49. *Id.* at 30.
50. *Id.*
51. STAFF MONOGRAPH ON TERRORIST FINANCING, *supra* note 2, at 21.
52. *See* Benthall, *supra* note 34, at 28.
53. *Id.* at 32–4.
54. STAFF MONOGRAPH ON TERRORIST FINANCING, *supra* note 2, at 21.
55. Quintan Wiktorowicz and Suha Taji Farouki, *Islamic NGOs and Muslim Politics: a Case from Jordan,* 21 THIRD WORLD QUARTERLY 685, 695 (2000).
56. *See* Benthall, *supra* note 34, at 39 n. 15.
57. *Id.* at 36.
58. *See generally* Saima Akbar Ahmed, *Global Need for a New Economic Concept: Islamic Economics,* 1 INT'L J. ISLAMIC FIN. SERV. (2000).
59. *See* STAFF MONOGRAPH ON TERRORIST FINANCING, *supra* note 2, at 17–19.
60. *See id.* at 4; PRADOS & BLANCHARD, *supra* note 4, at 2.
61. *See Cong. Hearing on Starving Terrorists of Money*, *supra* note 23, at 72 (statement of Stuart Levey, Under Secretary of Office of Terrorism and Financial Intelligence, U.S. Dep't of Treasury) (May 4, 2005).
62. *See* PRADOS & BLANCHARD, *supra* note 4, at 10–14.
63. *See* STAFF MONOGRAPH ON TERRORIST FINANCING, *supra* note 2, at 124.
64. *See* PRADOS & BLANCHARD, *supra* note 4, at 16.
65. *Id.*
66. STAFF MONOGRAPH ON TERRORIST FINANCING, *supra* note 2, at 21.
67. *See* PRADOS & BLANCHARD, *supra* note 4, at 17–18.

68. *See* Zakat Duty: Persons Subject to Zakat, Dept. of Zakat and Income Tax, *available at* http://www.dzit.gov.sa/en/GeneralInfo/generalinfo1.shtml.
69. *See* John D.G. Waszak, *The Obstacles to Suppressing Radical Islamic Terrorist Financing,* 36 CASE W. RES. J. INT'L L. 673, 697–8 (2004); Zakat Duty, *supra* note 68.
70. *See* STAFF MONOGRAPH ON TERRORIST FINANCING, *supra* note 2, at 122.
71. *Id.*
72. *See* PRADOS & BLANCHARD, *supra* note 4, at 17.
73. *See* STAFF MONOGRAPH ON TERRORIST FINANCING, *supra* note 2, at 123.
74. *Id.* at 114–15.
75. *Id.* at 124.
76. *Saudi Arabia in the War on Terror, supra* note 3, at 4.
77. *See* STAFF MONOGRAPH ON TERRORIST FINANCING, *supra* note 2, at 124–5.
78. *Id.*; *see also Saudi Arabia in the War on Terror, supra* note 3, at 5.
79. *See* U.S. Designated Charities, *supra* note 17; *see also* Consolidated List, *supra* note 21.
80. *See Saudi Arabia in the War on Terror, supra* note 3, at 14; *see also* Stuart Levey, Under Secretary of Office of Terrorism and Financial Intelligence, U.S. Dep't of Treasury, Testimony before the Senate Committee on Banking, Housing, and Urban Affairs (July 13, 2005), *available at* http://www.treas.gov/press/releases/js2629.htm.
81. *See* STAFF MONOGRAPH ON TERRORIST FINANCING, *supra* note 2, at 126.
82. *See* PRADOS & BLANCHARD, *supra* note 4, at 18.
83. *Id.*
84. Press Release, Royal Embassy of Saudi Arabia, Formation of New Charity Oversight Commission (Feb, 28, 2004), *available at* http://www.saudiembassy.net/2004News/News/TerDetail.asp?cIndex=1690.
85. *See* STAFF MONOGRAPH ON TERRORIST FINANCING, *supra* note 2, at 126–7.
86. *See* Glenn R. Simpson, *Terror Finance: U.S. Tracks Saudi Bank Favored by Extremists*, WALL STREET JOURNAL ONLINE, July 28, 2007, *available at* http://online.wsj.com/article/SB118530038250476405.html; *see also* PRADOS & BLANCHARD, *supra* note 4, at 18 (CRS report stating that as of March 2005, the National Commission was not operational); Josh Meyer, *Saudi Arabia is Prime Source of Terror Funds, U.S. Says*, L.A. TIMES, Apr. 2, 2008.
87. *See Saudi Arabia in the War on Terror, supra* note 3, at 4 ('Saudi Arabia has failed to carry out some of the publicly-proclaimed reforms, while in other cases, there is not enough independent evidence to determine whether Saudi Arabia has followed up on its pledges.'); Waszak, *supra* note 69, at 692 (noting that Saudi Arabia's laws are effective only on paper). In other countries, such as Jordan, where the zakat system is not institutionalized as a tax system but is wholly controlled by individuals and non-governmental organizations, there is even less government oversight. *See* Benthall, *supra* note 34, at 37.
88. Levitt, *Charitable Organizations*, *supra* note 13.
89. *See* WALID PHARES, FUTURE JIHAD: TERRORIST STRATEGIES AGAINST AMERICA 20–22 (Palgrave Macmillan/St Martin's Press 2005) [hereinafter FUTURE JIHAD].
90. *See* REUVEN FIRESTONE, JIHAD: THE ORIGIN OF HOLY WAR IN ISLAM 17 (Oxford University Press 1999) [hereinafter THE ORIGIN OF HOLY WAR IN ISLAM].
91. *Id.*
92. *Id.*
93. *See* Clinton Bennett & Geros Kunkel, *The Concept of Violence, War and Jihad in Islam,* 18 DIALOGUE & ALLIANCE 31, 40 (2004).
94. *Id.*
95. MAJID KHADDURI, WAR AND PEACE IN THE LAW OF ISLAM 61 (Johns Hopkins Press 1955).
96. *Id.* at 60.
97. *See* Bennett & Kunkel, *supra* note 93, at 41.
98. *See* FUTURE JIHAD, *supra* note 89, at 44.
99. *Id.*
100. *Id.*
101. *Id.* at 48.

102. *Id.* at 69.
103. THE ORIGIN OF HOLY WAR IN ISLAM, *supra* note 90, at 48. For example, Qur'an 41:34 encourages a peaceful response to threats of evil: 'Nor can goodness and evil be equal. Repel evil with what is better and those who were your enemy will be as your friends.' *See also* Qur'an 2:190, justifying a defensive jihad: 'Fight in the way of Allah those who do fight you, but do not provoke hostility – God does not love aggressors.'
104. *See* THE ORIGIN OF HOLY WAR IN ISLAM, *supra* note 90, at 48; *see also* Qur'an 9:5, promoting a perpetual war against unbelievers: 'And when the sacred months are passed, slay the unbelievers wherever you find them . . . beleaguer them, and lay in wait for them, and lay in wait for them in every stratagem of war.' Additionally, Qur'an 9:29 states: 'Fight those who do not believe in God or the last Day, and who do not forbid what has been forbidden by God and His Messenger, nor acknowledge the religion of truth from among the People of the Book, until they pay the poll tax out the hand, having been brought low.'
105. *See* KAREN ARMSTRONG, HOLY WAR 25 (Macmillan, 1988).
106. *See* DAVID BUKAY, FROM MUHAMMAD TO BIN LADEN 195 (Transaction 2007).
107. *See* JOHN ESPOSITO, UNHOLY WAR 46 (Oxford Univ. Press 2002); *see also* FROM MUHAMMAD TO BIN LADEN, *supra* note 106, at 200. This action of defining someone as an infidel was known as *takfir*, and was only to be done by the ulema or caliph. *See* FUTURE JIHAD, *supra* note 89, at 54.
108. *See* 'The Betrayal of Palestine' (Dec. 29, 1994), *quoted in* STATEMENTS OF OSAMA BIN LADEN, *supra* note 24, at 9.
109. *Id.*
110. *See* 'To the Americans' (Oct. 6, 2002), *quoted in* STATEMENTS OF OSAMA BIN LADEN, *supra* note 24, at 163.
111. *Id.* at 164.
112. 'The Betrayal of Palestine' (Dec. 29, 1994), *quoted in* STATEMENTS OF OSAMA BIN LADEN, *supra* note 24, at 14.
113. *See* 'To the Americans' (Oct. 6, 2002), *quoted in* STATEMENTS OF OSAMA BIN LADEN, *supra* note 24, at 165.
114. 'The Invasion of Arabia' (c. 1995/1996), *quoted in* STATEMENTS OF OSAMA BIN LADEN, *supra* note 24, at 18.
115. *See* U.S. Designated Charities, *supra* note 17.
116. *See* Consolidated List, *supra* note 21.
117. *See* Press Release, U.S. Dep't of Treasury, Treasury Designates Global Network, Senior Officials of IARA for Supporting bin Laden, Others (Oct. 13, 2004), *available at* http://www.treas.gov/press/releases/js 2025.htm.
118. *Id.*
119. *See* STAFF MONOGRAPH ON TERRORIST FINANCING, *supra* note 2, at 11, 114.
120. *Id.* at 114.
121. *Id.* at 11.
122. *See* U.S. Designated Charities, *supra* note 17; *see also* Consolidated List, *supra* note 21.
123. *See* Press Release, U.S. Dep't of Treasury, U.S-Based Branch of Al Haramain Foundation Linked to Terror – Treasury Designates U.S. Branch, Director (Sept. 9, 2004), *available at* http://www.treasury.gov/press/releases/js 1895.htm.
124. *See* Consolidated List, *supra* note 21.
125. *See* Press Release, U.S. Dep't of Treasury, Treasury Designates Al Haramain Islamic Foundation (June 19, 2008), *available at* http://www.treasury.gov/press/releases/hp 1043.htm.
126. For additional information on the designation of AHIF, see Press Release, U.S. Dep't of Treasury, Additional Al-Haramain Branches, Former Leader Designated by Treasury as Al Qaida Supporters – Treasury Marks Latest Action in Joint Designation with Saudi Arabia (June 2, 2004), *available at* http://www.treas.gov/press/releases/js 1703.htm.
127. *See* Press Release, U.S. Dep't of Treasury, Treasury Designates Global Network, Senior Officials of IARA for Supporting bin Laden, Others (Oct. 13, 2004), *available at* http://www.treas.gov/press/releases/js 2025.htm.

128. *See* Press Release, U.S. Dep't of Treasury, Twin Treasury Actions Take Aim at Hizballah's Support Network (July 24, 2007) (designating Martyrs Foundation and Goodwill Charitable Organization), *available at* http://www.treasury.gov/press/releases/hp503.htm [hereinafter *Twin Treasury Actions Take Aim at Hizballah's Support Network*]; *see also* Press Release, U.S. Dep't of Treasury, Treasury Designates Key Hizballah Fundraising Organization (Aug. 29, 2006) (designating the Islamic Resistance Support Organization), *available at* http://www.treasury.gov/press/releases/hp73.htm.
129. *See Twin Treasury Actions Take Aim at Hizballah's Support Network*, *supra* note 127.
130. *Id.*
131. Press Release, U.S. Dep't of Treasury, Treasury Designates Key Hizballah Fundraising Organization, *supra* note 127.
132. *See* Almog v. Arab Bank, 471 F. Supp. 2d 257, 262–5 (E.D.N.Y. 2007) (alleging that Islamic charities provided death benefit payments of $5,316.00 to designated families of Palestinian 'martyrs').
133. Press Release, U.S. Dep't of Treasury, Treasury Designates Key Hizballah Fundraising Organization, *supra* note 127.
134. *Id.*
135. *See* Press Release, U.S. Dep't of Treasury, Treasury Designates Al-Aqsa International Foundation as Financier of Terror Charity Linked to Funding of Hamas Terrorist Organization (May 29, 2003) ('Al Aqsa is a critical part of Hamas' terrorist support infrastructure.'), *available at* http://www.treas.gov/press/releases/js439.htm; *see also* U.S. Designated Charities, *supra* note 17 (suggesting that Al-Aqsa Foundation operates in the U.S.).
136. *See* Press Release, U.S. Dep't of Treasury, U.S.-Based Branch of Al Haramain Foundation Linked to Terror, *supra* note 123 ('The investigation shows direct links between the U.S. branch and Usama bin Laden.').
137. *See* Press Release, U.S. Dep't of Treasury, Treasury Designates Benevolence International Foundation and Related Entities as Financiers of Terrorism (Nov. 19, 2002), *available at* http://www.treas.gov/press/releases/po3632.htm (linked to fund-raising for Osama bin Laden).
138. *See* Press Release, U.S. Dep't of Treasury, Treasury Department Statement Regarding the Designation of the Global Relief Foundation (Oct. 18, 2002), *available at* http://www.treas.gov/press/releases/po3553.htm ('The Global Relief Foundation (GRF) has connections to, has provided support for, and has provided assistance to Usama bin Laden, the al Qaida Network, and other known terrorist organizations.').
139. *See Twin Treasury Actions Take Aim at Hizballah's Support Network*, *supra* note 127 (designating Martyrs Foundation and Goodwill Charitable Organization, both Hizballah fund-raising organizations).
140. *See* Press Release, U.S. Dep't of Treasury, Statement of Secretary Paul O'Neill on the Blocking of Hamas Financiers' Assets (Dec. 4, 2001), *available at* http://www.treas.gov/press/releases/po837.htm ('The Holy Land Foundation masquerades as a charity, while its primary purpose is to fund Hamas.').
141. *See* Press Release, U.S. Dep't of Treasury, Treasury Designates Global Network, Senior Officials of IARA for Supporting bin Laden, Others (Oct. 13, 2004) (provides direct financial support to Osama bin Laden), *available at* http://www.treas.gov/press/releases/js2025.htm.
142. *See* Press Release, U.S. Dep't of Treasury, Treasury Freezes Assets of Organization Tied to Hamas (Feb. 19, 2006), *available at* http://www.treas.gov/press/releases/js4058.htm (provides hundreds of thousands of dollars to HAMAS in Lebanon).
143. *See* Blocking Property and Prohibiting Transactions with Persons Who Commit, Threaten to Commit, or Support Terrorism, Exec. Order No. 13,224, Annex, 3 C.F.R. 786–90 (2001), *reprinted as amended in* 50 U.S.C. §1701 note (Supp. IV 2004) (listing 27 individuals and entities for asset freeze). MAK is the 'precursor organization to al Qaeda.' The Al Khifa Refugee Center in Brooklyn was an offshoot of the MAK and facilitated the movement of jihadist fighters into Afghanistan. A number of the individuals convicted in the first World Trade Center bombing were associated with the

Al Khifa Refugee Center. *See* STAFF MONOGRAPH ON TERRORIST FINANCING, *supra* note 2, at 88.

144. *See* STAFF MONOGRAPH ON TERRORIST FINANCING, *supra* note 2, at 87 (Global Relief Foundation and Benevolence International Foundation have raised millions of dollars in the U.S. and devoted a significant percentage of those funds to support Islamic extremist causes).
145. The IARA, formerly known as the Islamic African Relief Agency–USA, was closed in 2004, when it was identified by the Treasury Department as a Specially Designated Global Terrorist. *See* Press Release, U.S. Dep't of Treasury, Treasury Designates Global Network, *supra* note 140.
146. *See* Press Release, U.S. Dep't of Justice, Islamic Charity Charged with Terrorist Financing; Former U.S. Congressman Indicted for Money Laundering (Jan. 16, 2008), *available at* http://www.usdoj.gov/opa/pr/2008/January/08_nsd_029.html [hereinafter IARA Press Release]; *see also* United States v. Islamic American Relief Agency, et al., Indictment, Case No. 07-00087-01/07-CRT-W-NKL (W.D. Mo. 2008) [hereinafter *IARA Superseding Indictment*].
147. *See* IARA Press Release, *supra* note 145.
148. *Id.*
149. *Id.*
150. *IARA Superseding Indictment*, *supra* note 145, at 10; *see also* IARA Press Release, *supra* note 145.
151. *Id.* at 23; *see also* IARA Press Release, *supra* note 145. Finally, the indictment charges a former U.S. Congressman with money laundering, conspiracy and obstruction of justice for allegedly receiving about $50,000 in stolen funds from the charity. The former Congressman had been hired to advocate for the removal of the IARA from a U.S. Senate Finance Committee list of non-profit organizations suspected of being involved in supporting terrorism. However, when questioned by federal law enforcement officers, he allegedly made material false statements regarding his work for the IARA.
152. *IARA Superseding Indictment*, *supra* note 145, at 4.
153. *Id.* (emphasis added).
154. *Id.* at 4–5.
155. *See id.* at 10.
156. *Id.* at 24.
157. *Id.* at 11.
158. *Id.* at 6.
159. IARA Press Release, *supra* note 145. The alleged purpose of the donations was to renovate buildings located at a refugee camp owned by Hekmatyar. *Id.*
160. *See* U.S. Designated Charities, *supra* note 17; *see also* Consolidated List, *supra* note 21.
161. *See id.*
162. *Id.* Rabih Haddad, a senior GRF official who co-founded GRF and served as its president in the 1990s, allegedly worked for the MAK. *See* Press Release, U.S. Dep't of Treasury, Treasury Department Statement Regarding the Designation of the Global Relief Foundation, *available at* http://www.treas.gov/press/releases/po3553.htm (describing other GRF connections to al Qaeda).
163. *See* U.S. Designated Charities, *supra* note 17; *see also* Consolidated List, *supra* note 21.
164. *See* STAFF MONOGRAPH ON TERRORIST FINANCING, *supra* note 2, at 88.
165. *Id.*
166. *Id.* at 91.
167. *Id.* at 89.
168. *Id.*
169. *Id.*
170. *Id.* at 53.
171. U.S. Dep't of Treasury, Additional Background Information on Charities Designated Under Executive Order 13224, *available at* http://www.treas.gov/offices/enforcement/key-issues/protecting/charities_execorder_13224-a.shtml [hereinafter *Additional Background on Designated Charities*].

172. OFAC GRF Statement of the Case, *quoted in* STAFF MONOGRAPH ON TERRORIST FINANCING, *supra* note 2, at 106; *see also Additional Background on Designated Charities, supra* note 170.
173. STAFF MONOGRAPH ON TERRORIST FINANCING, *supra* note 2, at 106.
174. *See id.* at 94. GRF publicly described itself as an 'organization devoted to relieving the suffering of Muslims around the world.' *Id.* at 95; *see also Additional Background on Designated Charities, supra* note 170.
175. *See* STAFF MONOGRAPH ON TERRORIST FINANCING, *supra* note 2, at 94; *see also Additional Background on Designated Charities, supra* note 170.
176. *See* STAFF MONOGRAPH ON TERRORIST FINANCING, *supra* note 2, at 95.
177. *Id.* at 96.
178. *Id.* at 94. Adel Abdul Jalil Batterjee was the founder and original Director of BIF. A senior Treasury official described Batterjee as 'one of the world's foremost terrorist financiers, who employed his private wealth and a network of charitable fronts to bankroll the murderous agenda of al Qaida.' Press Release, U.S. Dep't of Treasury, U.S. Treasury Designates Two Individuals with Ties to al Qaida, UBL, Former BIF Leader and al-Qaida Associate Named Under E.O. 13224 (Dec. 21, 2004), *available at* http://www.treas.gov/press/releases/js2164.htm. In December 2004, Batterjee was designated by the U.S. Treasury Department as a terrorist financier. *Id.*
179. *Id.*
180. *See Additional Background on Designated Charities, supra* note 170.
181. *Id.*; *see also* STAFF MONOGRAPH ON TERRORIST FINANCING, *supra* note 2, at 98.
182. *See Additional Background on Designated Charities, supra* note 170.
183. *Id.*
184. *See* STAFF MONOGRAPH ON TERRORIST FINANCING, *supra* note 2, at 98.
185. *See* Press Release, U.S. Dep't of Treasury, Treasury Designates Benevolence International Foundation, *supra* note 136.
186. *See* STAFF MONOGRAPH ON TERRORIST FINANCING, *supra* note 2, at 103.
187. *See* Press Release, U.S. Dep't of Justice, Benevolence Director Pleads Guilty to Racketeering Conspiracy and Agrees to Cooperate with the Government (Feb. 10, 2003), *available at* http://www.usdoj.gov/usao/iln/pr/chicago/2003/pr021003_01.pdf; *see also* STAFF MONOGRAPH ON TERRORIST FINANCING, *supra* note 2, at 108.
188. *See* STAFF MONOGRAPH ON TERRORIST FINANCING, *supra* note 2, at 108.
189. See discussion of the unsuccessful prosecutions in the Sami al-Arian, Muhammad Salah, and Holy Land Foundation for Relief and Development cases, *infra* at Chapter 10.
190. *See* Dan Eggen, *Ex-Leaders of Islamic Charity Are Convicted*, WASH. POST, A02, Jan. 12, 2008, *available at* http://www.washingtonpost.com/wp-dyn/content/article/2008/01/11/AR2008011103409.html.
191. HAMAS was 'founded in the Israeli Occupied Territories in 1987 at the beginning of the Intifada, the Palestinian-led campaign to resist Israeli political dominion over the occupied territories.' Ungar Ex Rel. Strachman v. Palestinian Auth., 304 F. Supp. 2d 232, 250 (D.R.I. 2004). HAMAS' objective is the establishment of a Palestinian homeland. *Id.* HAMAS operates through a political and military wing. The political branch promotes political awareness and administers and funds humanitarian programs. The military branch engages in terrorist acts against Israel and has claimed responsibility for violent attacks against Israeli and other civilians. *Id.* Finally, it is now 'nearly universally recognized' as a terrorist organization. *Id.* (quoting United States v. Yousef, 327 F.3d 56, 108 (2d Cir. 2003)). HAMAS has been designated by the Treasury Department as a specially designated global terrorist and as a foreign terrorist organization by the State Department. *See* U.S. Dep't of State, Patterns of Global Terrorism (2003), *available at* http://www.state.gov/s/ct/rls/crt/2003/c12108.htm.
192. *Saudi Arabia in the War on Terror, supra* note 3, at 17.
193. *See* Linde v. Arab Bank, 384 F. Supp. 2d 571, 575–76 (E.D.N.Y. 2005).
194. *Linde*, 384 F. Supp. 2d at 576.
195. *See* PRADOS & BLANCHARD, *supra* note 4, at 9–10; *see also Linde*, 384 F. Supp. 2d at 575–6.

196. *See Saudi Arabia in the War on Terror, supra* note 3, at 17.
197. *See* PRADOS & BLANCHARD, *supra* note 4, at 10.
198. *Id.*
199. *Id.* at 10.
200. *Id.*
201. *Id.*
202. *Id.* at 11; *see also* Royal Embassy of the Kingdom of Saudi Arabia, *Telethon for Palestinian Victims Highly Successful*, Apr. 14, 2002, *available at* http://www.saudiembassy.net/2002News/News/ForDetail.asp?cIndex=1132.
203. *See* PRADOS & BLANCHARD, *supra* note 4, at 11.
204. *See* Linde v. Arab Bank, 384 F. Supp. 2d 571, 577 (E.D.N.Y. 2005).
205. *See* Press Release, U.S. Dep't of Treasury, U.S. Designates Five Charities Funding Hamas and Six Senior Hamas Leaders as Terrorist Entities (Aug. 22, 2003), *available at* http://www.ots.treas.gov/docs/4/48937.html (discussing terrorist activities attributable to HAMAS).
206. *Id.*
207. *Id.*
208. *See, e.g.*, Almog v. Arab Bank, 471 F. Supp. 2d 257, 261 (E.D.N.Y. 2007); Weiss v. Nat'l Westminster Bank, 453 F. Supp. 2d 609, 615–19 (E.D.N.Y. 2006); Strauss v. Credit Lyonnais, Case No. No. CV-06-0702 (CPS), 2006 WL 2862704, *4–*6 (E.D.N.Y. Oct. 05, 2006); Linde v. Arab Bank, 384 F. Supp. 2d 571, 576 (E.D.N.Y. 2005); Boim v. Holy Land Found., 291 F.3d 1000, 1003 (7th Cir. 2007); and Boim v. Quranic Literacy Inst., 127 F. Supp. 2d 1002, 1005–10 (N.D. Ill. 2001).
209. *See Weiss*, 453 F. Supp. 2d at 615.
210. *Id.*
211. *See Boim*, 127 F. Supp. 2d at 1007. In December 2001, the HLF was designated under E.O. 13224 and its assets were ordered to be frozen in the U.S. *See* Press Release, U.S. Dep't of Treasury, Shutting Down the Terrorist Financial Network (Dec. 4, 2001), *available at* http://www.treas.gov/press/releases/po841.htm.
212. *See Weiss*, 453 F. Supp. 2d at 615.
213. *Id.* at 616; *see also* Press Release, U.S. Dep't of Treasury, U.S. Designates Five Charities, *supra* note 204.
214. Press Release, U.S. Dep't of Treasury, Treasury Designates Al-Aqsa International Foundation, *supra* note 134.
215. Press Release, U.S. Dep't of Treasury, U.S. Designates Five Charities, *supra* note 204; http://www.ots.treas.gov/docs/4/48937.html; *see also* Press Release, U.S. Dep't of Treasury, Treasury Designates Al-Aqsa International Foundation, *supra* note 134. In 2003, the British Charity Commission cleared Interpal of any wrongdoing. *See Weiss*, 453 F. Supp. 2d at 617. However, Interpal is again being investigated by the Charity Commission for funding religious schools that promote religious hatred. *See* Ian Fisher, *Airplane Terrorism Case Prompts Questions About the Work of Islamic Charities in Britain*, N.Y. TIMES, Aug. 24, 2006, *available at* http://www.nytimes.com/2006/08/24/world/europe/24charity.html?emc=eta1.
216. *See* United States v. Mohammed Ali Hassan Al-Moayad, Judgment, 03-CR-1322 (SJ), (Mar. 10, 2004); *see also* Daniel Meron, Principal Deputy Assistant Attorney General, Civil Division, and Barry Sabin, Chief, Counterterrorism Section, Criminal Division, U.S. Dep't of Justice, Concerning the Federal Material Support Statutes, Testimony before the Senate Judiciary Subcommittee on Terrorism, Technology and Homeland Security (Apr. 20, 2005), *available at* http://www.lifeandliberty.gov/subs/testimony/042005-civ-meroncrm-sabin.pdf.
217. *Weiss*, 453 F. Supp. 2d at 617.
218. *Id.*
219. *See* Press Release, U.S. Dep't of Treasury, Statement by Treasury Secretary Paul O'Neill (Nov. 7, 2001) (announcing the designation of Bank al Taqwa), *available at* http://www.treasury.gov/press/releases/po770.htm.
220. *Id.*

221. *Weiss*, 453 F. Supp. 2d at 617.
222. *Id.* at 617–18.
223. *Id.* at 615, 618–19.
224. *Id.* at 618. The published court decision, *Weiss*, 453 F. Supp. 2d at 618, states that plaintiffs alleged that NatWest accepted deposits totaling $70 million on behalf of Interpal from the Al-Aqsa organization in Yemen. However, the plaintiffs' complaint states that the amount was $70,000. *See* Weiss v. Nat'l Westminster Bank, Second Amended Complaint Jury Trial Demanded, No. 05-CV-4622 (CPS)(KAM) (E.D.N.Y. Oct. 27, 2006).
225. *Weiss*, 453 F. Supp. 2d at 618–19.
226. *See* Strauss v. Credit Lyonnais, Case No. CV-06-0702 (CPS), 2006 WL 2862704, *4 (E.D.N.Y. Oct. 05, 2006).
227. *Id.* at *4.
228. *Id.* at *3, *6.
229. *Id.* at *6.
230. Boim v. Quranic Literacy Inst., 127 F. Supp. 2d 1002, 1009–10 (N.D. Ill. 2001).
231. *See Additional Background on Designated Charities, supra* note 170.
232. *See* Press Release, U.S. Dep't of Treasury, Shutting Down the Terrorist Financial Network, *supra* note 210; *see also Additional Background on Designated Charities, supra* note 170.
233. *See Additional Background on Designated Charities, supra* note 170.
234. *See The Holy Land Story: A Timeline*, THE DALLAS MORNING NEWS, Sept. 26, 2007, *available at* http://www.dallasnews.com/sharedcontent/dws/news/longterm/stories/092707dnmethlftimeline.1125ab6c1.html.
235. *See* Press Release, U.S. Dep't of Treasury, Shutting Down the Terrorist Financial Network, *supra* note 210.
236. *Id.*
237. *Id.*
238. *Id.*
239. *Id.*
240. *See Additional Background on Designated Charities, supra* note 170.
241. *See* discussion *infra* in Chapter 10 – 'the law enforcement response to terrorist financing.'
242. *See* Leslie Eaton, *No Convictions in Trial Against Muslim Charity*, N.Y. TIMES, Oct. 22, 2007, *available at* http://nytimes.com/2007/10/22/us/22cnd-holyland.html?ei=507. Three defendants were acquitted on almost all counts. *Id.*

PART IV

Developing a global legal framework to combat terrorist financing

7. Engaging the financial sector to prevent the financing of terrorism

> By requiring financial institutions to concentrate enhanced due diligence and suspicious activity monitoring on terrorist financing and money laundering schemes . . . [anti-money laundering/terrorist financing provisions] enable financial institutions to provide a much more effective first line of defense against money laundering, terrorist financing, and other financial crime.[1]
>
> U.S. Department of the Treasury,
> 2003 National Money Laundering Strategy

USE OF THE TRADITIONAL BANKING SYSTEM TO TRANSFER TERRORIST FUNDS

Terrorist financiers use various methods to collect and transfer funds to support jihadist activities throughout the world. The major methods used to move terror money include the traditional banking system, alternative remittance systems such as hawala, and bulk cash couriers.[2] Contrary to popular belief, terrorists use banks and other financial institutions to transfer funds. Deposit-taking institutions are particularly attractive because they provide an extensive range of financial services. For example, wire transfers offer terrorists many advantages: 'Speed, distance, minimal audit trail, and increased anonymity amid the enormous daily volume of electronic fund transfers are all major benefits.'[3] Additionally, monetary wire transfers are much safer than attempting to smuggle bulk cash across international borders. Physically transporting large quantities of cash by courier runs the risk of border and customs officials confiscating the funds, or having the money stolen by criminals. Also, banks provide wide geographic availability either through their foreign branch offices or through correspondent accounts with foreign banks.[4] Finally, large sums of money can be transferred instantaneously from a bank located in the United States, through bank accounts in the Middle East, to an offshore account in some other foreign country with the push of a button.

Following the 9/11 terror attacks, an investigation by the Federal Bureau of Investigation revealed that many of the al Qaeda hijackers had opened bank accounts at four United States banks.[5] The terrorists were able to open these accounts even though they lacked social security numbers, used addresses that frequently changed, and had minimal ties to the United States.[6] Money to finance the terrorist plot was transferred from bank accounts in Dubai, United Arab Emirates (U.A.E.) to accounts maintained at Sun Trust Bank, in Venice, Florida. Between July and September 2000, over $100,000 was transferred from terrorist operatives in Dubai, U.A.E to the joint bank account of 9/11 hijackers Mohamed Atta and Marwan al Shehhi at SunTrust Bank.[7] Mohamed Atta was the 'emir' of the terrorist group and flew a commercial aircraft (American Airlines Flight no.11) into the North Tower of the World Trade Center, while al Shehhi piloted the aircraft (United Airlines Flight no.175) that crashed into the adjacent South Tower.[8] According to the FBI, one transaction involved a funds transfer of $70,000 from Ali Abdul Aziz Ali in Dubai, U.A.E., to Atta and al Shehhi, which apparently did not raise any suspicions with bank officials at Sun Trust Bank.[9] Aziz Ali is being held at the detention facility at the U.S. Naval Base at Guantanamo Bay, Cuba, and has been charged by the U.S. Military Commission with complicity in the 9/11 terrorist attacks.[10]

The use of the traditional banking system by the 9/11 hijackers to move terrorist funds is not unique. Corrupt Islamic charitable organizations use the formal banking system to transfer funds to their network of foreign offices located around the world for disbursement to terrorist associates. Some of these charities maintain branch offices in as many as 40 countries globally.[11] A federal indictment filed against the Islamic American Relief Agency (IARA) and several of its former officers and associates revealed that approximately $1,375,000 was transferred from IARA's bank account in the Western District of Missouri to accounts belonging to the Islamic Relief Agency (ISRA) in Amman, Jordan, and Peshawar, Pakistan.[12] The funds transfers to Pakistan were intended for the benefit of a Specially Designated Global Terrorist (SDGT), Gulbuddin Hekmatyar, an Afghan mujahedeen leader, who allegedly participated in and supported terrorist acts by al Qaeda and the Taliban.[13] The funds transferred to the charity's accounts in Amman, Jordan, were then transferred to accounts in Iraq, in violation of economic sanctions imposed against Iraq.[14]

Other Islamic charitable organizations such as the Benevolence International Foundation (BIF) and the Global Relief Foundation (GRF) have used the formal banking system to transfer funds solicited in the United States to their foreign branch offices to support jihadist-related activities.[15] In 2003, Enaam Arnaout, the executive director of BIF, pleaded guilty to racketeering conspiracy, admitting that he fraudulently obtained charitable donations and diverted some of the funds to support fighters in Chechnya and Bosnia-Herzegovina.[16] Another example involves Bank al Taqwa, which was designated an SDGT for providing financial services to members of al Qaeda.[17] According to the U.S. government, al Taqwa is 'an association of offshore banks and financial management firms that have helped al-Qaeda shift money around the world.'[18] Further, the U.S. government has declared the Commercial Bank of Syria (CBS) a 'primary money laundering concern.' prohibiting financial institutions from establishing, maintaining, or administering correspondent accounts in the United States for the CBS.[19] The CBS was declared a primary money laundering concern because it was used to facilitate and promote money laundering and terrorist financing by terrorists and persons associated with terrorist organizations.[20]

Finally, at least three foreign banks, Arab Bank, National Westminster Bank (NatWest) and Credit Lyonnais, have been sued in private civil actions for knowingly providing financial services to front organizations controlled by HAMAS.[21] In 2004, American and Israeli victims of terrorism filed an $875 million lawsuit in federal court in the Eastern District of New York accusing Arab Bank–New York of providing material support to terrorists by transferring millions of dollars from a government-backed Saudi committee to HAMAS and other Palestinian terrorist groups.[22] Similar civil causes of action have been brought against NatWest Bank of Great Britain and Crédit Lyonnais of France on behalf of American victims of HAMAS attacks.[23] The lawsuits allege that the banks provided financial services to two European non-governmental organizations outlawed by Israel and designated by the Treasury Department as Specially Designated Global Terrorists' (SDGTs).[24]

Arab Bank was assessed a $24 million civil penalty by the Financial Crimes Enforcement Network (FinCEN), an agency of the U.S. Department of the Treasury, for violating the anti-money laundering (AML) and counter-terrorist financing (CTF) program requirements of the Bank Secrecy Act (BSA).[25] Action taken by the FinCEN was motivated by concerns that Arab Bank was used by HAMAS front entities to facilitate terrorist financing. According to FinCEN, Arab Bank's failure to implement an adequate system of internal controls to comply with BSA regulations 'posed heightened risks of money laundering and terrorist financing.'[26]

REGULATORY MEASURES TO PREVENT TERRORISTS FROM ABUSING THE INTERNATIONAL FINANCIAL SYSTEM

International Convention for the Suppression of the Financing of Terrorism (1999)

The international community has adopted various measures to prevent the abuse of the international financial system by terrorists and their front entities. The International Convention for the Suppression of the Financing of Terrorism (1999) (Terrorist Financing Convention) constitutes recognition by the international community that financial institutions play a critical role in preventing the financing of terrorism.[27] Over 130 States have ratified the Convention, including the United States.[28] The Terrorist Financing Convention imposes important legal obligations on signatory States to prevent banks and other financial institutions from being used to finance terrorism. These international legal duties include adopting domestic measures to criminalize and punish terrorist financing, license or register all money transmitting businesses, detect and control the physical cross-border transportation of currency and bearer negotiable instruments, and develop and implement internal controls to prevent financial institutions from being used to transfer funds to terrorists.[29] For example, article 18(1) imposes a legal duty on State Parties to adopt domestic measures requiring financial institutions to 'know your customer.'[30] Financial institutions are required to develop and utilize efficient measures to identify their customers, as well as 'customers in whose interest accounts are opened.'[31] In other words, banks have a duty to know their customers, as well as the beneficial or real owners of accounts they maintain. For this purpose, article 18(1)(b)(i) of the Convention provides that States Parties shall consider:

> (i) Adopting regulations prohibiting the opening of accounts the holders or beneficiaries of which are unidentified or unidentifiable, and measures to ensure that such institutions verify the identity of the real owners of such transactions.[32]

A similar obligation extends to States Parties to enact domestic legislation requiring financial institutions to verify the legal existence of corporations and other legal entities.[33] The objective of the 'know your customer' principle is to ensure that banks are not doing business with criminals, terrorists, and front or fictitious entities controlled by such individuals.

The Terrorist Financing Convention also imposes a duty on States Parties to enact domestic legislation requiring financial institutions to report to the competent authorities 'suspicious transactions' suspected of being involved in criminal activity, including terrorist financing. Under article 18(1)(b)(iii), States Parties shall consider

> Adopting regulations imposing on financial institutions the obligation to report promptly to the competent authorities all complex, unusual large transactions and unusual patterns of transactions, which have no apparent economic or obviously lawful purpose.[34]

Subsection (iii) imposes an obligation on States to require financial institutions to monitor transactions handled by the bank and report all complex, unusual large transactions and those that lack an apparent legitimate purpose. This requirement is intended to prevent banks from being used as a conduit to launder criminal proceeds and facilitate terrorist financing activity. Collectively, these provisions recognize that banks are the first line of defense against money laundering and terrorist financing. The duties imposed by the Terrorist Financing Convention are obligatory, not discretionary. Therefore, States Parties are mandated to enact domestic legislation to require banks to enhance their internal operating policies and procedures to protect the financial services sector from abuse by terrorists and other criminals.

FATF Nine Special Recommendations on Terrorist Financing

In response to the 9/11 terrorist attacks, the Financial Action Task Force (FATF) on Money Laundering, an inter-governmental organization responsible for development and promotion of international standards to detect, prevent, and suppress money laundering, held an extra-plenary session in Washington, D.C. to consider expanding its mandate to address terrorist financing.[35] On October 31, 2001, the FATF issued the Eight Special Recommendations on Terrorist Financing.[36] A ninth special recommendation on terrorist financing was adopted by FATF in 2004.[37] The Nine Special Recommendations on Terrorist Financing, combined with the Forty Recommendations on Money Laundering, represent the international standard for preventing and suppressing the financing of terrorism.[38]

Implementation of the Nine Special Recommendations is essential to establishing an effective counter-terrorist financing regime. The Terrorist Financing Recommendations impose an obligation on countries to:

I. Ratify the UN International Convention for the Suppression of the Financing of Terrorism and implement relevant UN Resolutions against terrorist financing.
II. Criminalize the financing of terrorism.
III. Freeze and confiscate terrorist assets.
IV. Require financial institutions to report suspicious transactions linked to terrorism.
V. Provide the widest possible assistance to other countries' law enforcement and regulatory authorities for terrorist financing investigations.
VI. Extend anti-money laundering requirements to alternative remittance systems.
VII. Require financial institutions to include accurate and meaningful originator information in money transfers.

VIII. Ensure that non-profit organizations cannot be misused to finance terrorism.
IX. Take measures to detect and prevent bulk cash smuggling.[39]

Two of the special recommendations have particular relevance to financial institutions. Special Recommendation IV requires financial institutions to report to the competent authorities transactions suspected of being linked to terrorists or terrorist activities.[40] Additionally, Special Recommendation VII requires financial institutions to include accurate originator information on funds transfers and ensure that financial institutions conduct enhanced scrutiny of suspicious activity for funds transfers that do not contain complete originator information.[41]

Bank Secrecy Act and USA PATRIOT Act

On October 26, 2001, 45 days after the tragic events of September 11, Congress enacted the Uniting and Strengthening America by Providing Appropriate Tools Required to Intercept and Obstruct Terrorism Act, known as the USA PATRIOT Act (Patriot Act).[42] The International Money Laundering Abatement and Anti-Terrorist Financing Act of 2001 (IMLAA) is contained within Title III of the broader anti-terrorism legislation.[43] Title III makes a number of amendments to the anti-money laundering provisions of the Bank Secrecy Act (BSA) intended to promote the prevention, detection, and prosecution of international money laundering and terrorist financing.[44] The IMLAA represents the most significant anti-money laundering legislation for financial institutions since the enactment of the BSA of 1970.

The drafters of the IMLAA were guided by several important principles: (1) enhancing transparency in financial institutions, (2) protecting the international gateways to the U.S. financial system, and (3) 'leveling the playing field' by increasing the vigilance of all financial institutions that serve as the gatekeepers of the financial system.[45] Congress further adopted a risk-based approach, requiring financial institutions to structure internal controls to address high-risk jurisdictions, financial institutions, transactions, and accounts vulnerable to money laundering and terrorist financing.[46]

Anti-money laundering/counter-terrorist financing program

The anti-money laundering (AML) and counter-terrorist financing (CTF) provisions of the USA PATRIOT Act are applicable to all 'financial institutions,' a legal term of art under the BSA. The definition of 'financial institution' found in 31 U.S.C. §§5312(a)(2) and (c)(1), as amended by the Act, is extremely broad. It includes traditional financial institutions such as banks, savings associations, credit unions, registered broker-dealers, and futures commission merchants.[47] Moreover, a foreign bank qualifies as a 'financial institution' and the duties imposed by the BSA, as amended by the Act, extend to foreign banks with branches or offices in the United States.[48] The definition further extends to non-traditional 'financial institutions,' such as insurance companies, travel agencies, persons engaged in real estate closings and settlements, sellers of vehicles, including automobiles, planes, and boats, and dealers in precious metals, stones or jewels.[49]

The centerpiece of the federal regulatory regime established by the BSA, and amended by the Patriot Act, is the requirement that financial institutions establish, implement, and maintain a program to prevent money laundering and terrorist financing. The BSA requires all financial institutions to establish an AML/CTF program designed to (1) enable compliance with the BSA requirements and (2) prevent financial institutions from being used for money laundering and terrorist financing.[50] Every financial institution is required to establish an AML/CTF program that includes the following minimum requirements: '(A) the development of internal policies, procedures and internal controls, (B) the designation of a compliance officer, (C) an ongoing employee training program, and (D) an independent audit function to test programs.'[51]

Internal policies, procedures and controls The internal policies and procedures should be based upon an assessment of money laundering and terrorist financing risks associated with services offered and customers and geographic areas served.[52] For example, the AML/CTF program should analyze the extent to which the bank customer conducts financial transactions in jurisdictions that have been identified as vulnerable to terrorism or money laundering. The risk-based program should also consider whether certain customers and accounts, such as correspondent accounts, pose a heightened risk of money laundering and terrorist financing. The plan should further establish written procedures to comply with the BSA requirements of filing currency transaction reports (CTRs) and suspicious activity reports (SARs). The BSA requires banks to monitor all accounts for possible money laundering and terrorist financing, and file reports if a customer engages in currency transactions totalling more than $10,000 (CTR), or if a transaction is suspected of being involved in criminal activity (SAR).[53] The SAR filing requirements impose an obligation on financial institutions to report transactions that the institution 'knows, suspects, or has reason to suspect' are connected to criminal activity.[54] A transaction is suspicious if it

(i) involves funds derived from illegal activities or is conducted to disguise funds derived from illegal activities;

(ii) is designed to evade the reporting or record-keeping requirements of the BSA (e.g., structuring transactions to avoid currency transaction reporting); or
(iii) has no business or apparent lawful purpose or is not the sort in which the particular customer would normally be expected to engage, and the bank knows of no reasonable explanation for the transaction after examining the available facts, including the background and possible purpose of the transaction.[55]

Some financial institutions are further required to file a SAR if there is reason to suspect that the transaction was intended to facilitate criminal activity, including acts of terrorism.[56] Banks must file SARs involving or aggregating at least $5,000.[57]

A bank must file a SAR no later than 30 calendar days after the date of the initial detection of facts that may constitute a basis for filing a SAR.[58] If no suspect is identified on the date of the detection of the incident requiring the filing, a bank may delay filing a SAR for an additional 30 days to identify a suspect. However, under no circumstances is reporting to be delayed more than 60 calendar days after the date of initial detection of a reportable transaction. When submitting a SAR, bank employees must provide a detailed description of why the transaction was unusual, irregular or suspicious in the narrative section of the form filed with FinCEN.[59]

The AML/CTF plan should include written procedures for filing suspicious activity reports with FinCEN. For example, if an employee identifies indicators that a transaction may involve money laundering or terrorist financing, procedures should outline what steps should be taken to attempt to verify the suspicions. If concerns remain, written procedures should detail what action should be taken by the bank employee, including refusing to enter into or complete a transaction that appears designed to further illegal activity.

The SAR filing requirement is particularly relevant to preventing banks and other financial institutions from being used to facilitate terrorist financing. The Bank Secrecy Act Anti-Money Laundering Examination Manual has identified several 'red flags' of potentially suspicious activity that may indicate terrorist financing.[60] For example, regarding charitable organizations, financial transactions for which there is no logical economic purpose, or no link between the stated activity of the charity and the other parties in the transaction, may indicate terrorist financing.[61] Likewise, funds sent to or received via international transfers involving high-risk countries for terrorism, as well as funds transfers in amounts indicating an intention to avoid triggering BSA reporting requirements, may constitute evidence of terrorist financing activity.[62] Financial transactions that are consistent with 'red flags' of terrorist financing should be closely monitored by bank employees, and SARs should be filed with FinCEN as well. In 2007, depository institutions filed approximately 325,000 SARs with FinCEN.[63]

Essential to any effective AML/CTF program is the principle of 'know your customer' (KYC), which 'has been the backbone of anti-money laundering and counter terrorist financing measures' by financial services providers.[64] Under the BSA, financial institutions, including foreign banks with U.S. branches, are required to implement reasonable procedures for identification and verification of customers opening an account. At a minimum, financial institutions are required to implement procedures for

> (A) verifying the identity of any person seeking to open an account to the extent reasonable and practicable; (B) maintaining records of information used to verify a person's identity, including name, address, and other identifying information; and (C) consulting lists of known or suspected terrorists or terrorist organizations provided to the financial institution by any government agency to determine whether a person seeking to open an account appears on any such list.[65]

Section 5318(l)(2) imposes the minimum requirements for identification and verification of customers opening an account. However, with respect to high-risk customers and accounts, the KYC policy and the requirement to file SARs impose an obligation on financial institutions to have an understanding of the customer's business and normal bank account patterns. More specifically, financial institutions should have knowledge of the volume and amount of transactions expected to flow through the customer's account during a specific time period. Once a baseline of financial transaction activity is determined, bank officials can better decide whether transactions inconsistent with that pattern are suspicious and should be reported to FinCEN. For example, if an Islamic charity opens a bank account representing itself as a charitable organization for Muslim refugees in Africa, but funds are being dispersed to accounts in Pakistan, such transactions would be inconsistent with the charity's stated purpose. Moreover, Pakistan is a high-risk country for terrorism and both al Qaeda and the Taliban operate along the Pakistan–Afghanistan border. Because the purpose of the charity is to provide humanitarian relief to refugees in Africa, funds transfers to Pakistan, a high-risk country for terrorism, would be suspicious and should be reported to FinCEN. However, in the absence of adequate KYC policies and procedures, these transactions would never be identified and reported to FinCEN as possibly indicating terrorist financing activity. Effective monitoring of suspicious transactions is dependent on effective KYC policies and procedures.

Designation of a BSA compliance officer Financial institutions are required to designate an individual responsible for coordinating and monitoring daily compliance with the BSA. The compliance officer is responsible for ensuring that (1) the program is being implemented effectively, (2) the program is updated as necessary to reflect the changes in the risk assessment, as well as further guidance by the Treasury Department, and (3) appropriate personnel are trained in accordance with the BSA regulations and requirements.[66] These responsibilities are substantial and appointing someone to the position on a part-time basis or assigning such individual other significant duties unrelated to BSA compliance could violate the BSA requirement.[67]

Education and training The AML/CTF program must ensure that employees are trained in the BSA requirements, including KYC and recognizing 'red flags' of money laundering and terrorist financing. Employees should be trained to detect these and other types of suspicious transactions. Bank employees should also receive periodic training updates and refresher training on money laundering and terrorist financing patterns and trends. Employees should be adequately trained on steps to be taken if a suspicious transaction is detected, including who should be contacted and whether the transaction should be temporarily blocked pending further examination.

Independent audit function A financial institution is required to conduct periodic independent testing of its AML/CTF program to ensure that it is functioning effectively. According to FinCEN, the testing may be accomplished by employees or the financial institution or unaffiliated service providers so long as those same individuals are not involved in the operation or oversight of the program.[68] Finally, the AML/CTF program is required to be approved by senior bank management.

Due diligence and enhanced due diligence for U.S. 'private banking accounts' and 'correspondent accounts' involving foreign persons

Title III of the USA PATRIOT Act requires all covered financial institutions to apply *due diligence* standards, and, in some cases, *enhanced due diligence* standards, with regard to 'private banking accounts' and 'correspondent accounts,' established, maintained, administered, or managed in the United States for foreign persons, to detect and report money laundering and terrorist financing through those accounts.[69] The term 'private banking account' means an account that (i) requires a minimum aggregate deposits of funds or other assets of not less than $1million; (ii) is established on behalf of one or more individuals who have a direct or beneficial ownership interest in the account; and (iii) is assigned to, administered or managed by, an officer, employee, or agent of a financial institution acting as a liaison between the financial institution and the direct or beneficial owner of the account.[70]

If a private banking account is maintained for a non-U.S. person, the financial institution is required to take reasonable steps 'to ascertain the identity of the nominal and beneficial owners of, and the source of funds deposited into, such account' and to report any suspicious transactions to FinCEN.[71] If the private banking account is requested or maintained by, or on behalf of 'a senior foreign political figure, or any immediate family member or close associate of a senior foreign political figure,' the financial institution must conduct *enhanced* due diligence reasonably designed to detect and report suspicious transactions that may involve the proceeds of foreign corruption.[72]

Financial institutions must conduct 'enhanced due diligence' on correspondent accounts requested or maintained by, or on behalf of, a foreign bank designated a 'high risk' under the statute.[73] High-risk banks include those (i) operating under an offshore banking license,[74] (ii) licensed in a jurisdiction found to be non-cooperative with international anti-money laundering standards by an inter-governmental organization of which the United States is a member, such as the FATF, and with which the United States concurs, or (iii) licensed in a jurisdiction designated by the Secretary of the Treasury as a 'primary money laundering concern,' pursuant to 31 U.S.C. §5318A.[75]

The *enhanced due diligence* policies, procedures and controls, at a minimum, require that financial institutions in the United States take reasonable steps

> (i) to ascertain for any such foreign bank, the shares of which are not publicly traded, the identity of each of the owners of the foreign bank, and the nature and extent of the ownership interest of each such owner;
> (ii) to conduct enhanced scrutiny of such account to guard against money laundering and report any suspicious transactions . . . ; and
> (iii) to ascertain whether such foreign bank provides correspondent accounts to other foreign banks and, if so, the identity of those foreign banks and related due diligence information.[76]

The last requirement imposes a duty on financial institutions not only to 'know your customer,' but also to know your customer's customer. In other words, financial institutions are required to ascertain whether their foreign bank customers provide correspondent accounts to other foreign banks and whether those banks are shell banks or otherwise high-risk banks.[77]

Title III of the Act also prohibits 'covered financial institutions' from establishing, maintaining, administering, or managing a correspondent account in the United States for a foreign 'shell bank.'[78] A shell bank is 'a foreign bank that does not have a physical presence in any country.'[79] The lack of transparency makes shell banks ideal vehicles for money laundering, terrorist financing, and other illicit financial activity.[80] The financial institutions prohibited from maintaining a correspondent account with a foreign shell bank include: an insured bank; a commercial bank or trust company; private banker; an agency or branch of a foreign bank in the United States; any credit union; a thrift institution; and broker or dealer registered with the Securities and Exchange Commission under the Securities Exchange Act of 1934.[81] A covered financial institution is also prohibited from providing *indirect* services to foreign shell banks. Such institutions are required to take reasonable steps to verify that any correspondent account they maintain for a foreign bank is not being used by that foreign bank to provide banking services to a foreign shell bank.[82]

Foreign bank records

Section 319(b) of the Patriot Act, codified at 31 U.S.C. §5318(k)(3), permits federal law enforcement authorities access to foreign bank records that may show whether the foreign bank is being used to transfer money overseas to facilitate terrorist activities.[83] Section 5318(k)(3)(A)(i) authorizes the Secretary of the Treasury and the Attorney General to issue a summons or subpoena to any foreign bank that maintains a correspondent account in the United States, and to request records related to such correspondent account, including records maintained *outside* of the United States relating to funds deposited into the foreign bank.[84] The financial institution that maintains a correspondent account for a foreign bank is required to maintain records identifying the owners of such foreign bank and the names and addresses of a person who resides in the United States who is authorized to accept service of legal process for records regarding the correspondent account.[85] Additionally, foreign banks must designate a registered agent in the U.S. to accept service of such subpoenas.[86]

Failure to comply with a summons or subpoena for foreign bank records could result in termination of the correspondent relationship. Under the statute, a covered financial institution is required to terminate any correspondent relationship with a foreign bank not later than ten business days after receipt of written notice from the Secretary of the Treasury or the Attorney General that the foreign bank has failed either to comply with the written request for documents or to initiate federal court proceedings to contest the summons or subpoena.[87] Finally, failure to terminate a correspondent relationship could result in the financial institution being held liable for a civil penalty of up to $10,000 per day until such banking relationship is terminated.[88]

Prior to the enactment of the Patriot Act, obtaining foreign bank records was a difficult task. Foreign banks would resist subpoenas for foreign bank records, claiming they were maintained abroad and the U.S. subpoena did not have extraterritorial application. Pursuant to section 319(b), foreign banks are now required to produce the requested records or suffer termination of the correspondent relationship with the U.S. bank.

Information sharing requirements

Enhanced coordination and information sharing between federal law enforcement and financial institutions are essential to successfully combating terrorist financing. The USA Patriot Act provides authority to enhance the flow of information relevant to money laundering and terrorist financing between the Federal government and financial institutions, and among financial institutions themselves.[89] Section 314 of the Act requires the Treasury Secretary to adopt regulations encouraging financial institutions to share information with law enforcement officials regarding individuals, entities, and organizations 'reasonably suspected . . . of engaging in terrorist acts or money laundering activities.'[90] According to FinCEN, section 314(a) 'enable[s] federal law enforcement agencies, through FinCEN, to reach out to more than 45,000 points of contact at more than 27,000 financial institutions to locate accounts and transactions of persons that may be involved in terrorism or money laundering.'[91] The statute also permits financial institutions, upon notice to the Treasury Department, to voluntarily share information with each other about individuals and organizations reasonably suspected of terrorist activity or money laundering.[92]

In September 2002, FinCEN adopted a final rule specifying the procedures for sharing information under section 314(a). Upon a request from federal law enforcement, FinCEN sends requests to designated contacts within financial institutions across the country. Upon receiving such a request, the financial institutions must query their records for data matches, including 'accounts maintained by the named subject during the preceding 12 months and transactions conducted within the last 6 months.'[93] Financial institutions have two weeks from the date of the section 314(a) request to respond.[94] However, it should be noted that section 314(a) provides lead information only and is not a substitute for a subpoena or other legal process. To obtain documents from a financial institution that has reported a match, the law enforcement agency must comply with relevant legal standards.[95]

Finally, while established prior to the enactment of the Patriot Act, information sharing is further facilitated by the Egmont Group, a global network of financial intelligence units (FIUs).[96] There are currently 101 countries whose FIUs comprise the Egmont Group.[97] The common purpose of every

FIU is to combat money laundering and terrorist financing. This purpose is reflected in the Egmont Group's definition of an FIU as:

> A central, national agency responsible for receiving, (and as permitted, requesting), analyzing and disseminating to the competent authorities, disclosures of financial information: I. concerning suspected proceeds of crime and potential financing of terrorism, or II. required by national legislation or regulation, in order to combat money laundering and terrorist financing.[98]

The United States' FIU is administered by FinCEN.[99]

Enforcement of the BSA

Authority for civil enforcement of the BSA reporting and record-keeping requirements resides with FinCEN.[100] Failure to comply with the BSA anti-money laundering and terrorist financing provisions could result in the imposition of a severe civil monetary penalty. For example, FinCEN has imposed multi-million-dollar civil sanctions against American Express Bank International ($25 million);[101] ABN AMRO Bank ($30 million); Riggs Bank ($25 million); Israel Discount Bank of New York ($12 million); and AmSouth Bank ($10 million).[102] However, only one FinCEN enforcement action involved concerns of terrorist financing. The other cases involved the heightened risk of financial institutions being used to launder criminal proceeds.

In 2005, FinCEN imposed a $24 million civil penalty against the New York branch of Arab Bank.[103] Arab Bank, with headquarters in Amman, Jordan, has approximately 400 branches, offices and subsidiaries – members of the Arab Bank Group, in 30 countries throughout the world.[104] The Bank has been characterized as 'a pillar of the Middle East economy' and the 'de facto treasurer for the Palestinian Authority.'[105] In December 2004, the Arab Bank Group had consolidated assets of $27 billion. The New York branch served as a clearing institution for a substantial volume of funds transfers in United States dollars for originators and beneficiaries in jurisdictions that posed a high risk for money laundering and terrorist financing.[106]

In February 2005, Arab Bank was ordered to cease its traditional banking activities in New York, including wire transfers and the opening of accounts. In August 2005, FinCEN announced the imposition of a $24 million civil penalty for failure to implement an AML program 'reasonably designed to assure and monitor compliance' with the reporting and record keeping requirements of the BSA.[107] The BSA reporting requirements include the duty to file suspicious transaction reports, which Arab Bank failed to do.[108] The Bank also failed to implement an AML program that satisfied the statutory minimum requirements, specifically 'a system of internal controls; (2) independent testing for compliance; (3) the designation of an individual, or individuals, to coordinate and monitor day-to-day compliance; and (4) training of appropriate personnel.'[109] As a result, Arab Bank's New York branch allegedly handled wire transfers of more than $20 million to or from 45 suspected Palestinian terrorists or terrorist groups.[110]

The Bank's system of internal controls failed to manage the risks of terrorist financing for senders and recipients of wire funds transfers.[111] While Arab Bank maintained correspondent accounts that operated in the Palestinian Territories, jurisdictions that posed heightened risks of terrorism and terrorist financing, the Bank only monitored the accounts of individuals and entities that it considered direct customers of Arab Bank.[112] It failed to monitor the financial transactions of originators and beneficiaries of funds transfers that did not maintain accounts at Arab Bank.[113] FinCEN stated that '[t]he requirement to report suspicious transactions applies to transactions 'conducted or attempted by, at, or through' Arab Bank–New York, regardless of whether the transactions involve direct customers of Arab Bank–New York.'[114] The Bank further failed to implement procedures for obtaining and utilizing publicly available information to monitor and identify suspicious funds transfers. According to FinCEN, names similar to those of originators and beneficiaries in funds transfers cleared by Arab Bank appeared in Congressional testimony, indictments in the United States, and research and media reports linked to terrorist activities.[115] In fact, some persons conducting financial transactions through Arab Bank appeared in subpoenas and other legal process that Arab Bank's New York branch received from U.S. law enforcement.[116] Some of these individuals were later designated by the Treasury Department's Office of Foreign Asset Control or the Department of State as 'specially designated terrorists,' 'specially designated global terrorists,' or 'foreign terrorist organizations.'[117] With respect to these individuals and entities, FinCEN stated:

> Once a designation occurred, Arab Bank–New York failed to review recent activity, occurring prior to the designation and associated with the designated entities, to identify potentially suspicious activity . . . Arab Bank–New York failed to review information in its possession that would have shown it was clearing funds transfers for individuals and entities dealing with subsequently designated terrorists and terrorist organizations, failed to analyze this information, and failed to file suspicious activity reports.[118]

Equally egregious, financial regulatory officials in the Palestinian Territories issued circulars containing the names of suspected terrorists and ordered institutions holding accounts in the names of those individuals to either freeze their accounts or place them on a terror watch list.[119] However, Arab Bank lacked procedures for cross-checking the names of these suspected terrorists against the originators and beneficiaries of transactions cleared by the Bank.[120] Thus, the accounts of individuals linked to terrorism were not frozen as requested. Furthermore, account monitoring by Arab Bank involved *manual* review of spreadsheets containing information on funds transfers. Given the volume of funds transfers, which approximated $500,000 per year, manual review could not adequately detect suspicious transactions.[121] Further, FinCEN found that the Bank failed to implement adequate procedures for independent testing and auditing of its AML/CTF program.[122] In short, FinCEN's findings demonstrate that Arab Bank failed to seriously undertake its legal obligations under the BSA to implement adequate internal controls for identifying suspicious transactions and preventing terrorist financing.

FinCEN's enforcement action against Arab Bank illustrates the importance placed on filing SARs by FinCEN. The $24 million civil fine was justified in large part by the Bank's failure to file SARs. However, the action by FinCEN is not unprecedented. Virtually every other civil enforcement action by FinCEN has been based on a finding that the depository institution failed to adequately file SARs.[123] Thus, to avoid being targeted by FinCEN, banks need to implement an effective system of internal controls to monitor suspicious transactions. The Arab Bank case is important for one other reason. It outlines some basic requirements of an effective AML/CTF program. For future guidance, an adequate system of internal procedures and controls to prevent terrorist financing should, among other things, (1) address any heightened risks associated with customers conducting financial transactions in high-risk countries for terrorism; (2) permit automated access to public source information, including Congressional testimony, criminal indictments, and domestic and international terror lists; (3) provide the ability to cross-reference the information against the banks' customer accounts; and (4) identify originators and beneficiaries of funds transfers that are not direct bank customers to assist in identifying suspicious transactions.[124]

FinCEN enforcement actions are an important tool to hold financial institutions accountable for compliance with the BSA, and ensure that they are not being used as conduits to facilitate terrorist activity. However, such enforcement actions need to be conducted in a timely fashion. Banks should not be permitted to blatantly violate their legal obligations under the BSA over long periods of time before FinCEN and the federal financial regulators intervene to stop such practices. Apparently, the audit of Arab Bank by the Office of the Comptroller of the Currency (OCC) was triggered by a civil lawsuit filed in July 2004 by victims of HAMAS-related terrorist attacks.[125] However, according to FinCEN, Arab Bank had been violating its duty to file SARs since at least as early as 2000.[126] During the interim four-year period, Arab Bank processed hundreds of funds transfers totalling more than $20 million for or on behalf of 45 suspected Palestinian terrorists or terrorist organizations.[127] Twenty million dollars is a substantial sum of money to finance terrorist activities. The OCC's failure to detect the flow of millions of dollars to suspected Palestinian terrorists is a matter of grave concern. The federal regulators need to explain why it took such a long time to detect these serious BSA violations. Additionally, despite compelling evidence that Islamic charitable organizations have raised tens of millions of dollars in the U.S. and used financial institutions to transfer those funds abroad to finance jihadist activities, FinCEN has imposed financial sanctions against only Arab Bank for breaching its duty to file SARs related to terrorist activity.[128] It is difficult to understand why more depository institutions have not been penalized for providing financial services to terrorist front organizations, including corrupt charities, and failing to detect and report suspicious transactions indicating terrorist financing. FinCEN and the federal regulatory agencies need to be held accountable for failure to adequately enforce the BSA requirements to prevent terrorist financing.

Section 311 – primary money laundering concern

The flagship provision of the IMLAA is section 311, codified at 31 U.S.C. §5318A, which authorizes the Secretary of the Treasury to require financial institutions to impose a graduated set of five 'special measures' if the Secretary determines that a foreign jurisdiction, foreign financial institution, or a type of international transaction or foreign account constitutes a 'primary money laundering concern' (PMLC).[129] The 'special measures' range from increased reporting requirements to prohibiting financial institutions from opening or maintaining certain correspondent or payable-through accounts with the designated PMLC.[130] The primary motivation for the rule was to give the Treasury Secretary the authority to impose a range of sanctions less than a freezing or blocking action by the Office of Foreign Assets Control (OFAC) against the assets of a particular individual or entity. Prior to the enactment of section 311, individuals and entities had their assets blocked and transactions with such designees were prohibited or no action was taken.[131] Congress recognized that there might be instances in which, for example, insufficient evidence exists to justify blocking the assets of a foreign financial institution, but some action might be desirable to prevent and detect money laundering or terrorist financing. In such an instance, an entity could be designated as a PMLC and one of the special measures authorized by section 311 could then be applied. '[S]ection 311 provides the [Treasury] Secretary with a range of options that can be adapted to target specific money laundering and terrorist financing concerns most effectively.'[132] Furthermore, section 311 serves as a 'useful tool for bringing pressure on countries and institutions to meet international standards' to combat money laundering and terrorist financing.[133]

Designation as a 'primary money laundering concern' The application of section 311 involves a two-part process – designation as a PMLC and application of special measures. The initial determination is based on the fairly permissive standard of whether 'reasonable grounds' exist to believe that the proposed entity is a PMLC.[134] This low threshold of proof is substantially less than the criminal standard of proof beyond a reasonable doubt, and even lower than the civil standard of preponderance of the evidence. In making a finding that reasonable grounds exist for concluding that a foreign jurisdiction, financial institution, type of international transaction, or type of account constitutes a PMLC, the Treasury Secretary is required to consult with the Secretary of State and the Attorney General.[135]

In making a PMLC finding, the statute delineates several factors that *shall* be taken into consideration. The statute further distinguishes between jurisdictional and institutional factors. In other words, if the subject is a foreign jurisdiction, the statute lists certain factors that shall be considered in reaching a decision that the jurisdiction is a PMLC.[136] However, if the target is a financial institution, transaction or account, within or involving a particular foreign jurisdiction, the statute identifies other factors that shall be considered.[137] In determining whether there are reasonable grounds for concluding that a foreign jurisdiction should be designated a PMLC, the Secretary shall consider all relevant information, including the following seven jurisdictional factors:

(i) evidence that organized criminal groups or international terrorists have transacted business in that jurisdiction;
(ii) the extent to which that jurisdiction or financial institutions operating in that jurisdiction offer bank secrecy or special regulatory advantages to nonresidents or nondomiciliaries of that jurisdiction;
(iii) the substance and quality of administration of the bank supervisory and counter-money laundering laws of that jurisdiction;
(iv) the relationship between the volume of financial transactions occurring in that jurisdiction and the size of the economy of the jurisdiction;
(v) the extent to which that jurisdiction is characterized as an offshore banking or secrecy haven by credible international organizations or multilateral expert groups;
(vi) whether the United States has a mutual legal assistance treaty with that jurisdiction, and the experience of United States law enforcement officials and regulatory officials in obtaining information about transactions originating in or routed through or to such jurisdiction; and
(vii) the extent to which that jurisdiction is characterized by high levels of official or institutional corruption.[138]

However, a PMLC designation does not require proof of all seven factors. Instead, a designation can be justified on a finding of the existence of one or more jurisdictional factors.

Determining whether a financial institution, a transaction or type of account should be designated a PMLC requires consideration of the following three factors:

> (i) the extent to which such financial institutions, transactions, or types of accounts are used to facilitate or promote money laundering in or through the jurisdiction;
> (ii) the extent to which such institutions, transactions, or types of accounts are used for legitimate business purposes in the jurisdiction; and
> (iii) the extent to which such action is sufficient to ensure that the purposes of this subchapter continue to be fulfilled, and to guard against international money laundering and other financial crimes.[139]

Once again, the Treasury is not required to find that all three factors support designation as a PMLC. A designation can be justified on the basis of a strong showing of one or more institutional factors.

Application of special measures If the Secretary of the Treasury, after consultation with the Secretary of State and the Attorney General, determines that a foreign jurisdiction, foreign financial institution, or type of transaction or account constitutes a PMLC, the second step in the process is to decide on the 'special measures' to be imposed. The five special measures are enumerated in 31 U.S.C. §5318A(b)(1)–(5), and require financial institutions to do the following: (1) keep records and file reports on particular transactions, including identities of the participants in the transaction and the beneficial owners of the funds involved; (2) obtain information on the beneficial ownership on any account opened or maintained in the U.S. by a foreign person or a foreign person's representative; (3) identify and obtain information about customers permitted to use or whose transactions are routed through, a foreign bank's 'payable-through' account;[140] (4) identify and obtain information about customers permitted to use, or whose transactions are routed through, a foreign bank's 'correspondent' account; or (5) prohibit, or impose conditions upon, the opening or maintaining in the United States of a correspondent account or payable-through account.[141]

In selecting which special measure to impose under section 5318A, the Secretary of the Treasury is required to consult with the Chairman of the Federal Reserve, any other federal banking agency, the Secretary of State, the Securities and Exchange Commission, the Commodity Futures Trading Commission, the National Credit Union Administration Board, and any other agencies and interested parties as the Secretary may find to be appropriate.[142] Imposition of the special measure described in subparagraph (b)(5) requires the Treasury Secretary to consult with the Secretary of State, the Attorney General, and the Chairman of the Board of Governors of the Federal Reserve System, as well as those persons previously specified.[143]

In deciding on the special measures to be imposed, the Secretary of the Treasury is required to consider several factors, including:

(1) whether other nations or multilateral groups have imposed similar measures or sanctions;[144]
(2) the economic implications and administrative burden on domestic financial institutions associated with compliance;
(3) any adverse systematic impact on the international payment, clearance, and settlement system;
(4) the adverse impact on legitimate business activities;
(5) the effect of the action on United States national security and foreign policy.[145]

It should be noted that the special measures described in subparagraphs (1) through (4), 31 U.S.C. §5318A(b), may be imposed by regulation, order, or otherwise as permitted by law.[146] However, the special measure authorized by subsection (b)(5), prohibiting or conditioning the opening or maintaining of certain correspondent or payable-through accounts, may be imposed only by regulation.[147] Thus, prior to imposition of special measure (b)(5), the Treasury Department must publish notice of its intention and afford an opportunity for public comment on the propriety of imposing such sanction against the previously designated PMLC.

Enforcement of section 311 – Commercial Bank of Syria Since the USA PATRIOT Act was signed into law in October 2001, three foreign jurisdictions have been designated as PMLCs (Ukraine, Nauru, and Burma).[148] In addition to foreign jurisdiction designations, the Treasury Department has designated several foreign financial institutions as being PMLCs. Examples include: Myanmar Mayflower Bank and Asia Wealth Bank (November 2003); First Merchant Bank of the 'Turkish Republic of Northern Cyprus' and Infobank of Belarus (August 2004); Multibanka and VEF Banka of Latvia (April 2005); and Banco Delta Asia SARL (September 2005). However, only one foreign financial institution has been designated under section 311 for facilitating terrorist financing.

In May 2004, Treasury designated the Commercial Bank of Syria (CBS) as a PMLC and published a notice of its intention to impose the special measure authorized by 31 U.S.C. §5318A(b)(5), prohibiting the opening or maintaining of correspondent accounts with CBS.[149] After consultation with the Secretary of State and the Attorney General, and consideration of the three institutional factors enumerated in 31 U.S.C. §5318A(c)(2)(B), the Treasury Secretary determined that reasonable grounds existed for finding that CBS is a financial institution of primary money laundering concern. Considering the first institutional factor, FinCEN found there was reason to believe that CBS was used to facilitate or promote money laundering and terrorist financing.[150] FinCEN stated that '[b]ecause the crime of money laundering includes the use of financial institutions to promote the carrying on of terrorist activity, the use of CBS by terrorists demonstrates that it is being used to promote money laundering.'[151] Focusing on the second institutional factor, FinCEN concluded that any legitimate use of CBS was significantly outweighed by the use of CBS to promote or facilitate terrorist financing and money laundering.[152] Finally, FinCEN found that imposition of special measures was necessary 'to ensure that CBS is not able to access the U.S. financial system to facilitate terrorist financing or money laundering, or to engage in any other criminal purpose.'[153]

After consultation with the Federal financial regulators, the Departments of Justice and State, and consideration of the enumerated factors for determining which special measure to select, FinCEN determined that reasonable grounds existed for imposition of the most serious sanction authorized under section 311.[154] As a result, domestic financial institutions are prohibited from opening or maintaining correspondent accounts for CBS. By virtue of the action taken by FinCEN, the Syrian bank has been effectively isolated from access to the U.S. financial system. Additionally, FinCEN advised that, pursuant to 31 U.S.C. §5318(i)(2)(B)(iii), covered financial institutions were required to apply enhanced due diligence to their correspondent accounts to guard against their indirect use by CBS.[155]

Section 311 is an important tool to ensure that financial institutions are not used as a conduit to fund terrorist activities. However, the Treasury Department has been reluctant to use the special measures authorized by section 311 against banks suspected of providing financial services to terrorists. Since being enacted in October 2001, section 311 has been used against a foreign financial institution on only one occasion related to terrorist financing, the Commercial Bank of Syria. However, there are other likely candidates. For example, American victims of terrorist attacks have filed lawsuits against Credit Lyonnais and NatWest Bank for providing financial services to HAMAS and front organizations. Both Credit Lyonnais and NatWest Bank have offices in the United States.[156] In 2006, a U.S. District Court judge denied the defendant banks' motions to dismiss the suits, and both cases are proceeding to trial.[157] Despite the apparent merits of the civil cases, neither bank has been targeted for the imposition of special measures under section 311. Thus, the under-utilization of section 311 against foreign financial institutions in the counter-terrorist financing context remains a matter of serious concern.

Use of on-line financial services to transfer terrorist funds

The Internet is used to raise funds and transfer monies to terrorists and terrorist organizations throughout the world because it has many attractive features that make it an effective tool for terrorist financing.[158] The Internet is (1) global, (2) inexpensive, (3) largely unregulated, and (4) may be used anonymously.[159] Corrupt charities use their websites to solicit donations, promoting their humanitarian mission. However, in many instances these charities serve as a financial conduit for the Taliban, al Qaeda, and Palestinian terrorist groups.[160] For example, Al-Rashid Trust, a Pakistan-based charity, described itself as a welfare organization whose comprehensive, charitable services are benefiting Muslims all over the world.[161] However, al-Rashid Trust was suspected of using its former website to raise money for Taliban supporters in Great Britain and the United States.[162] In fact, just days after September 11, 2001, the charity was designated by the Treasury Department as a 'specially designated global terrorist' for providing financial assistance to the Taliban and al Qaeda.[163] The Internet has been used to raise funds for other terrorist entities, including the Global Jihad Fund, Lashkar-e-Taiba, and HAMAS.[164]

Once the donations are collected, terrorist front groups may use online banking and other financial services to transfer the funds to support jihadist activities abroad. While the convenience and speed of online financial services are tremendous assets to customers and to the global economy, these same features make online banking an attractive vehicle for terrorists and terrorist organizations seeking to move funds overseas.[165] Banks can reduce the risk inherent in online banking by identifying a customer as he opens an account and verifying his identity.[166] Under the BSA, a financial institution has a duty to identify and verify the identity of each customer. At a minimum, financial institutions should

(1) identify customers as they open accounts by obtaining certain required information such as the customer's name, address, date of birth, and taxpayer identification number;
(2) exercise reasonable efforts to verify the customer's identity;
(3) maintain records of information obtained during the identification and verification process;
(4) consult lists identified by the Department of the Treasury of individuals and organizations whose assets have been blocked or frozen.[167]

However, a financial institution's responsibility to prevent abuse of the banking system by terrorist front organizations does not end once an account is opened. Financial institutions have a legal duty to monitor account transactions, including online transactions, and report any transaction exceeding $5,000 to FinCEN, if the financial institution has reason to believe that the funds were derived from criminal activity or serve no legitimate business purpose.[168] Ultimately, 'much of the burden of securing online financial services against abuse by terrorist organizations must be borne by financial institutions.'[169]

COMBATING THE ABUSE OF HAWALA AND ALTERNATIVE REMITTANCE SYSTEMS

What is Hawala?

Alternative remittance systems, such as hawala, are used by terrorists to transfer funds globally to finance terrorist activities.[170] According to various government reports, prior to 9/11 al Qaeda moved much of its money by hawala.[171] Apparently, '[t]he very features which make hawala attractive to legitimate customers (mainly expatriates remitting money to relatives in their home country) – efficiency, anonymity, and lack of a paper trail – also make the system attractive for the transfer of illicit funds.'[172] Hawala dealers can provide the same remittance service as banks with little documentation and at rates lower than those charged by the traditional banking sector. The absence of a paper trail makes hawala particularly attractive to terrorists and other criminals.

The hawala system allows individuals to transfer value from one location to another without actually moving funds.[173] An individual in one country gives funds to a hawala broker or hawaladar, who notifies a counterpart in another country to transfer an equivalent amount of money to a recipient in that country. For example:

> [A] U.S. resident who wants to send money to a friend in another jurisdiction (Country B) would give it to a U.S. hawaladar, who typically gives the sender a code or identification mechanism. The U.S. hawaladar then contacts a local hawaladar in Country B by telephone, fax, or e-mail, and the sender contacts the intended recipient to convey the code. The local hawaladar in Country B then delivers the specified funds to the recipient upon presentation of the code.[174]

The hawaladar charges a flat fee or commission for the transaction. When accounts need to be balanced between hawaladars, a number of methods are used including through compensatory payment, conventional wire transfers, physical movement of money by a courier, or invoice manipulation, such as over-and under-invoicing.[175] Settling accounts by under-invoicing is demonstrated by the following example:

> Hawaladar A contacts hawaladar B and asks him to deliver $50,000 to an associate. Hawaladar B transfers the funds, creating an outstanding debt; hawaladar A owes hawaladar B $50,000. Next, hawaladar B orders $200,000 in computer hardware from hawaladar A. However, hawaladar A sends an invoice to hawaladar B for $150,000 for the computer equipment valued at $200,000. Hawaladar B sends hawaladar A $150,000 for the computer hardware, which balances A's debt of $50,000 to B.[176]

The hawala system is prevalent throughout the world, including South Asia, the Middle East, Europe and the United States. While in some countries the practice is illegal, in other countries the practice is considered a part of the 'gray' economy.[177] While it is difficult to accurately estimate the total amount of money transferred through hawala, rough estimates place the figure in the tens of billions of dollars annually.[178] Officials in Pakistan estimate that more than $7 billion flows into the nation through the hawala system each year.[179]

International Response to Hawala and Other Alternative Remittance Systems

The Nine Special Recommendations (SR) on Terrorist Financing adopted by the Financial Action Task Force on Money Laundering (FATF) address the use of alternative remittance systems to transfer funds to terrorists.[180] SR VI (Alternative Remittance) calls on countries to 'take measures to ensure that persons or legal entities, including agents, that provide a service for the transmission of money or value, including transmission through an informal money or value transfer system or network [are] licensed or registered and subject to all the FATF Recommendations that apply to banks and non-bank financial institutions.'[181] To comply with SR VI, States are required to license or register persons and legal entities that provide money or value transfer services.[182] According to FATF, '[t]he key difference between the two is that licensing implies that the regulatory body has inspected and sanctioned the particular operator to conduct such a business whereas registration means that the operator has been entered into the regulator's list of operators.'[183] The objective of the licensing and registration requirement is to ensure that the regulatory body is aware of the existence of the alternative remittance business.[184]

SR VI also subjects money or value transfer services to the FATF Forty Recommendations on Money Laundering that apply to banks and non-depository financial institutions. Those Recommendations include the principle of 'know your customer' (KYC), the record-keeping requirement, and the duty to file suspicious transactions.[185] Application of FATF Recommendation 5 requires financial institutions to 'identify[ ] the customer and verify[ ] that customer's identity using reliable, independent source documents, data or information.'[186] The documents commonly accepted for identification purposes are driver's license, passport or social security card. The FATF record-keeping requirement also extends to alternative remittance systems. The FATF Recommendation 10 imposes a duty on financial institutions to maintain, for at least five years, all necessary records on transactions, both domestic and international, to comply with information requests by regulatory and law enforcement officials.[187] Additionally, FATF Recommendation 13 requires financial institutions to report suspicious transactions to the financial intelligence unit (FIU), if they suspect or have reasonable grounds to suspect that the funds represent the proceeds of crime or are related to terrorist financing.[188] Finally, FATF Recommendation 15 requires financial institutions to develop anti-money laundering/terrorist financing programs.[189] Under SR VI, these FATF Recommendations apply to money transmitting businesses as well.

One other central component of SR VI involves the imposition of sanctions against corrupt alternative remittance businesses. SR VI provides that '[e]ach country should ensure that persons or legal entities that carry out this service illegally are subject to administrative, civil or criminal sanctions.'[190] To comply with this provision, States are required to enact legislation to authorize the imposition of sanctions for money or value transfer service operators found to be non-compliant with registration, licensing, and anti-money laundering program requirements.[191] Finally, it should be noted that the FATF has drafted a set of international best practices on combating the abuse of alternative remittance systems that encourages States to closely monitor the money and value transfer services sector to identify illegal operators and prevent the use of these facilities by criminals and terrorist groups.[192] Consistent with the monitoring requirement, States should establish a process for identifying and classifying operators that are considered to be of 'high risk' for facilitating money laundering or terrorist financing.[193]

U.S. Regulation of Hawala and Money Services Businesses

The United States has developed a comprehensive regulatory regime to prevent the abuse of hawala and money services businesses (MSBs) to carry out the financing of terrorism. Within weeks of the attacks on the World Trade Center, Congress enacted the USA PATRIOT Act. Section 359(a) of the Act amended the definition of 'money transmitter' to encompass 'any person who engages as a business in an informal money transfer system or any network of people who engage as a business in facilitating the transfer of money domestically or internationally outside of the conventional financial institution system.'[194] Money transmitters constitute one of a number of non-bank financial institutions grouped within the category of MSBs.[195] Furthermore, because MSBs are included within the definition of 'financial institutions,' money transmitters and alternative remittance systems are subject to the BSA.[196] Under the BSA, as of December 31, 2001, all MSB principals have been required to register with FinCEN.[197] MSBs are required not only to provide contact information in the registration form, but also to identify their owners, controlling persons, directors, officers, and persons who participate in the conduct of the affairs of the business.[198] MSBs are also required to identify the primary depository institution where they maintain a transaction account.[199] Although agents of MSBs are not required to register separately with FinCEN, BSA regulations require all MSB principals to maintain a list of their agents and make the list available to FinCEN or any appropriate law enforcement agency upon request.[200] As a result of the BSA regulations, approximately 40,000 MSBs have registered with FinCEN.[201]

Failure to register with FinCEN, or submitting false or incomplete information in the registration statement, could result in a civil penalty of $5,000 per day while the violation continues.[202] Moreover, 18 U.S.C. §1960 makes it a crime to operate an MSB in violation of FinCEN's registration requirements.[203] Section 1960 also makes it a crime to operate an MSB in the absence of compliance with relevant state licensing requirements.[204] Any person who knowingly engages in a money transmitting business and has failed to comply with BSA registration requirements may be prosecuted and imprisoned for up to five years.[205] Finally, the Patriot Act makes it a crime for an MSB owner or operator to transfer funds that he knows are either the proceeds of a crime or intended to be used for criminal activity, including terrorism.[206]

Under current BSA regulations, MSBs are required to establish and maintain an anti-money laundering compliance program.[207] The program must be reasonably designed to prevent the MSB from being used to facilitate money laundering and terrorist financing. Additionally, the program must be commensurate with the risk posed by the nature, location, size and volume of the transactions handled by the money transmitting business.[208] All MSBs must obtain and verify the identity of the sender or receiver for funds transfers of more than $3,000, regardless of whether the transaction appears suspicious or not.[209] Money services businesses are also required to file currency transaction reports (CTRs) of transactions in currency of more than $10,000.[210] Further, multiple currency transactions occurring at an MSB must be aggregated if the financial institution has knowledge that the transactions are on behalf of the same person and total more than $10,000 in cash during one business day.[211] Transactions in currency of more than $10,000 are also subject to record-keeping requirements to support the filing of CTRs.[212] Finally, MSBs are subject to the SAR requirement.[213] An MSB is required to file a SAR with respect to any transaction of $2,000 or more if the MSB 'knows, suspects, or has reason to suspect' that it involves funds derived from illegal activity designed to conceal their origin, is designed to evade BSA obligations, or has no apparent business or law purpose or involves the use of the MSB to facilitate criminal activity, such as terrorism.[214] According to the Treasury Department, this new authority has been used to disrupt the operations of several illegal money transmitters allegedly involved in terrorist financing.[215]

FinCEN has been delegated the authority by the Treasury Secretary to determine whether a financial institution has violated the BSA. However, few MSBs have been sanctioned by FinCEN. As of April 2008, FinCEN had imposed an assessment of civil money penalty against only five MSBs: Western Union Financial Services, Inc., Sigue Corporation and Sigue LLC, Deprez's Quality Jewelry and Loans, Frost Food Mart, and El Noa Noa.[216] However, none of those cases involved allegations related to terrorist financing.[217] To date, no MSB has been assessed a civil penalty by FinCEN for violating BSA requirements where the MSB was suspected of being used to transfer money to terrorists. Further, there have been relatively few criminal prosecutions of corrupt hawaladars or other individuals for knowingly using MSBs to transfer funds to terrorists. Thus, the regulatory regime established in the aftermath of the 9/11 terrorist attacks to prevent MSBs from being used to assist the financing of terrorism is suffering from lack of enforcement.

OTHER ALTERNATIVE MEANS TO TRANSFER TERRORIST-RELATED FUNDS

Bulk Cash Smuggling

Because it has become more difficult to transfer money using the traditional banking system, terrorist financiers have resorted to alternative means of transferring money to terrorists. According to government and NGO reports and counter-terrorism experts, the use of cash couriers is a major method to move terror funds globally.[218] Cash couriers use a variety of methods to transport cash across international borders, including land border crossing, where the money is concealed in the courier's vehicle, and by use of the mail.[219] However, the preferred method is the use of commercial airlines. This method of smuggling currency is attractive to terrorists because '(1) the passenger (courier) can stay close to this money during transport, (2) many foreign destinations can be quickly reached, and (3) little pre-planning is required.'[220]

The International Convention for the Suppression of the Financing of Terrorism addresses the problem of currency smuggling, but in general terms. The Terrorist Financing Convention directs States to adopt '[f]easible measures to detect or monitor the physical cross-border transportation of cash.'[221] In 2004, FATF adopted Special Recommendation (SR) IX (Cash Couriers) with the objective of preventing terrorists and other criminals from physically transporting currency to finance their criminal activities.[222] SR IX requires countries to adopt the following measures:

(1) to detect the physical cross-border transportation of currency and bearer negotiable instruments;
(2) to stop or restrain currency and bearer negotiable instruments that are suspected to be related to terrorist financing or money laundering;
(3) to stop or restrain currency or bearer negotiable instruments that are falsely declared or disclosed;
(4) to apply appropriate sanctions for making a false declaration or disclosure;
(5) to enable confiscation of currency or bearer negotiable instruments that are related to terrorist financing or money laundering.[223]

The United States is in full compliance with the international standards articulated in SR IX. To detect the physical cross-border transportation of currency and bearer negotiable instruments, the BSA requires persons who transport monetary instruments of more than $10,000 into or outside of the United States to file a currency and monetary instrument report (CMIR) with the Treasury Department.[224] Pursuant to 31 U.S.C. §5316, persons engaged in cross-border transportation of funds are required to disclose the origin, destination, and route of the monetary instruments, the amount and kind of monetary instruments being transported, and some additional information.[225] Funds involved in a violation of section 5316 may be confiscated.[226] Further, a person not filing a report, or filing a report containing a material misstatement or omission, may be subject to a civil penalty. However, the civil penalty may not exceed the amount of the monetary instrument for which the report was required.[227] A person wilfully violating section 5316 shall be fined not more than $250,000, or imprisoned for not more than five years, or both.[228]

U.S. domestic law also criminalizes bulk cash smuggling and authorizes confiscation of funds involved in such an offense, as required by SR IX. Pursuant to 31 U.S.C. §5332, enacted as part of the Patriot Act, whoever, with the intent to evade a currency-reporting requirement, knowingly conceals more than $10,000 in currency or other monetary instruments on the person of such individual or in any conveyance, article of luggage, merchandise, or other container, and transports or attempts to transport it into or outside of the United States is guilty of currency smuggling.[229] A person convicted of currency smuggling may be imprisoned for a maximum term of five years.[230] In addition, the court, in imposing the sentence, *shall* order that the defendant forfeit to the United States any property involved in the offense, and property traceable to such property.[231] Finally, the statute also authorizes civil forfeiture of such property.[232] However, despite its enactment in 2001, 31 U.S.C. §5332 seldom has been used by federal prosecutors bulk cash smugglers. As of March 2008, there were no reported court decisions of convictions under the bulk cash smuggling statute.

Trade-based Terrorist Financing

International terrorists and their agents move money globally by using methods such as the false documentation and declaration of traded goods and services.[233] The process of disguising the proceeds of crime through the use of trade transactions is known as trade-based money laundering.[234] However, manipulating and falsifying trade invoices can also be used to conceal the transfer of funds to terrorists and terrorist organizations. Trade-based terrorist financing can be achieved through 'the misrepresentation of price, quantity or quality of imports or exports.'[235] The basic techniques of trade-based money laundering and terrorist financing include:

- over- and under-invoicing of goods and services;
- multiple invoicing of goods and services;
- over- and under-shipment of goods and services;
- falsely describing goods and services.[236]

Under-invoicing is one of the most common trade-based techniques to disguise the movement of funds. Under-invoicing occurs when the goods or services are invoiced below the 'fair market price'. The importer purchases goods and eventually sells them at fair market value. However, the buyer is invoiced at a lower price. The difference between the fair market price paid for the goods and the invoiced amount can be used to finance terrorist activity. The following example illustrates how value is transferred by under-invoicing. Company A (seller) ships goods valued at $2 million to Company B (buyer). However, Company B is under-invoiced and charged only $1 million for the goods. Company B eventually sells the products at fair market value ($2 million).[237] In this scenario, Company B made an extra $1 million (the difference between the invoiced price and actual sales price).[238] Alternatively, over-invoicing occurs when the goods are invoiced at a price above the fair market value. The exporter receives value from the importer because the payment for the goods is higher than the value the importer will receive when they are sold on the open market.

Another trade-based money laundering/terrorist financing technique is multiple invoicing, which involves issuing more than one invoice for the same commercial transaction. According to FATF, '[b]y invoicing the same good or service more than once, a money launderer or terrorist financier is able to justify multiple payments for the same shipment of goods or delivery of services.'[239] Again, the transfer to funds is disguised as a payment for goods or services. However, unlike under- and over-invoicing, multiple invoicing avoids the need to misrepresent the price of the good or service on the invoice. Additionally, individuals seeking to disguise the transfer of funds can do so by overstating or understating the quantity of goods being shipped. In the extreme case, 'an exporter may not ship any goods at all but simply collude with an importer to ensure that all shipping and customs documents associated with th[e] . . . "phantom shipment" are routinely processed.'[240] Finally, a money launderer or terrorist financier can transfer value by misrepresenting or falsely describing the quality or type of good or service. This occurs, for example, when an exporter ships a relatively inexpensive good but falsely invoices for a more expensive item.[241]

These trade-based money laundering and terrorist financing techniques expose a wide range of vulnerabilities in the international trade system that can be exploited by criminals and terrorist financiers. While there is no magic bullet to prevent funds from being transferred to terrorist organizations using these trade-based methods, the risk of abuse can be reduced by making use of red flag indicators and other forms of risk analysis to detect possible trade-based money laundering and terrorist financing. Moreover, sharing import and export information with foreign law enforcement and customs authorities is critical to detecting anomalies in the trade data. However, sharing trade data with foreign customs and law enforcement officials will require the execution of bilateral mutual assistance agreements.[242]

THE FUTURE ROLE OF FINANCIAL INSTITUTIONS IN THE GLOBAL WAR ON TERROR

Al Qaeda, the Taliban, and Palestinian terrorist groups, such as HAMAS and Hizballah, use conventional banks to transfer money to underwrite their global terrorist activities. Depository institutions are attractive to international terrorists and their financial sponsors because they offer a broad range of financial services, rapid transaction speed, security, and wide geographic availability. The risk of abuse of the financial services system by terrorists has international dimensions, threatening not only U.S. banks but the international banking system as well.

The international community has responded to the threats posed to international financial institutions by ratifying the International Convention for the Suppression of the Financing of Terrorism and adopting the FATF Nine Special Recommendations on Terrorist Financing.[243] The Terrorist Financing Convention and the FATF Special Recommendations recognize that financial institutions represent the first line of defense to prevent funds being used by terrorists and their front organizations to facilitate terrorist money transfers. Domestic laws and regulations have been adopted by States to comply with the legal obligations imposed by the Terrorist Financing Convention and international anti-terrorist financing standards. These new measures have forced financial institutions to assume quasi-law enforcement responsibilities to prevent terrorist financing, including monitoring high-risk accounts, reporting suspicious transactions, and sharing information with regulatory and law enforcement authorities.[244] Financial institutions that fail to comply with these legal obligations are vulnerable to being assessed a multi-million dollar civil penalty by FinCEN, being designated a 'primary money laundering concern' by the Secretary of the Treasury, pursuant to section 311, and, in the most egregious cases, having the matter referred to the U.S. Department of Justice for criminal prosecution.[245] Further, financial institutions targeted for sanctions are likely to have their professional reputation severely damaged as well. In short, financial institutions may pay a heavy price for non-compliance with federal banking laws and regulations intended to prevent money laundering and terrorist financing.

Almost seven years after the September 11, 2001 terrorist attacks, al Qaeda, the Taliban, and their terrorist affiliates continue to pose a serious threat to international peace and security.[246] Moreover, the risk of abuse of the international banking system by corrupt charities and NGOs and state sponsors of terrorism remains real and substantial. As long as the threat of terrorism persists, the quasi-law enforcement role financial institutions have been forced to play since 9/11 is likely to continue. In fact, in the event of a major terrorist attack, those preventative duties and responsibilities are likely to increase significantly to further restrict terrorist access to the international banking system. Financial institutions should therefore be prepared to continue to play an important role and assume even greater responsibilities in the global effort to combat the financing of terrorism.

To the extent that compliance with international standards and new banking laws and regulations make it more difficult for terrorists to access the financial services system, terrorists are likely to resort to greater use of hawala or other alternative remittance systems, as well as bulk cash smuggling. It is therefore imperative that States comply with their obligations under the Terrorist Financing Convention and FATF Special Recommendations VI and IX.[247] States must enact domestic legislation to regulate hawala and money transmitting businesses and criminally punish the use of such financial services for terrorist purposes. States must also criminalize the physical cross-border transportation of terrorist funds. Finally, while implementation of the legal framework outlined in the Terrorist Financing Convention and FATF Special Recommendations on Terrorist Financing is an important first step in preventing and suppressing the financing of terrorism, States must also rigorously enforce these new measures for them to be effective.

NOTES

1. U.S. Dep't of Treasury, 2003 National Money Laundering Strategy [hereinafter *2003 National Money Laundering Strategy*].
2. *See* Steven Emerson, *Fund-Raising Methods and Procedures for International Terrorist Organizations*, Testimony before the House Financial Services Subcomm. on Oversight and Investigations, at 18 (Feb. 12, 2002) ('[T]errorism fund-raising has also incorporated the use of banking and other financial institutions in addition to individual courier arrangements and the concept of hawala.'), *available at* http://www.investigativeproject.org/documents/testimony/14.pdf [hereinafter *Fund-Raising Methods and Procedures for International Terrorist Organizations*]; John Roth, et al., National Commission on Terrorist Attacks Upon the United States, Monograph on Terrorist Financing: Staff Report to the Commission 17 (Washington, D. C. Gov't Printing Office 2004), *available at* http://govinfo.library.unt.edu/911/staff_statements/911_TerrFin_Monograph.pdf (Al Qaeda moves 'money through its organization by a variety of conduits, including hawaladars . . . couriers, and financial institutions.') [hereinafter Staff Monograph on Terrorist Financing]; Financial Action Task Force, Combating the Abuse of Alternative Remittance Systems: International Best Practices, at 2 (June 20, 2003), *available at* http://www.fatf-gafi.org/dataoecd/32/15/34255005.pdf (unregulated money or value transfer services are 'increasingly vulnerable to abuse by money launderers and the financiers of terrorism') [hereinafter *FATF Alternative Remittance Systems: International Best Practices*]; Financial Action Task Force, Detecting and Preventing the Cross-Border Transportation of Cash by Terrorists and Other Criminals, International Best Practices (Feb. 12, 2005) ('The use of cash couriers is now recognised as a major method for terrorists to move funds.'), *available at* http://www.fatf-gafi.org/dataoecd/50/63/34424128.pdf [hereinafter *FATF Cash*

Couriers: International Best Practices]; and *2003 National Money Laundering Strategy*, Appendix H: Terrorist Financing Online, *supra* note 1 at 58–9.

3. William C. Gilmore, Dirty Money: The Evolution of Money Laundering Counter-Measures 42 (Council of Europe Press 1995) (quoting Savona, E.U., and De Feo, M.A., 'Money Trails: International Money Laundering Trends and Prevention/Control Policies,' paper presented at 1994 Money Laundering Conference, at 21).
4. For purposes of the Bank Secrecy Act, 31 U.S.C. §§5311 et seq. and 31 C.F.R. Part 103, a 'correspondent account' includes 'a formal banking or business relationship' 'established to make payments or other disbursements on behalf of [a] foreign bank, or to handle other financial transactions related to such foreign bank.' 31 C.F.R. §103.175(d).
5. *See* The National Commission on Terrorist Attacks, The 9/11 Commission Report: Final Report of the National Commission on Terrorist Attacks Upon the United States 169 (W.W. Norton & Company 2004), *available at* http://www.9-11commission.gov/report/911Report.pdf; *see also* Military Commission 9/11 Charge Sheet (Feb. 11, 2008), *available at* http://www.defenselink.mil/news/Feb2008/d20080211chargesheet.pdf [hereinafter *Military Commission Charge Sheet*].
6. *See* Ilias Bantekas, *The International Law of Terrorist Financing*, 97 Am. J. Intl L. 315, 321 (Apr. 2003) (discussing the use of the U.S. financial system by 9/11 hijackers); *see also Military Commission Charge Sheet, supra* note 5.
7. *See Military Commission Charge Sheet, supra* note 5, at ¶¶46, 47, 50, 53, 56.
8. *Id.* at ¶¶59, 161–2.
9. *Id.* at ¶56.
10. *See generally, Military Commission Charge Sheet, supra* note 5.
11. *See* Press Release, U.S. Dep't of Treasury, Treasury Designates Global Network, Senior Officials of IARA for Supporting bin Laden, Others (Oct. 13, 2004), *available at* http://www.treas.gov/press/releases/js2025.htm (IARA maintained over 40 offices worldwide).
12. *See* United States v. Islamic Am. Relief Agency, et al., Case No. 07–000–87–01/07-CR-W-NKL (W.D. Missouri).
13. *See* Press Release, U.S. Dep't of Justice, Islamic Charity Charged with Terrorist Financing; Former U.S. Congressman Indicted for Money Laundering (Jan. 16, 2008), *available at* http://www.usdoj.gov/opa/pr/2008/January/08_nsd_029.html.
14. *Id.*
15. *See* discussion *supra* at Chapter 6.
16. *See* Press Release, U.S. Dep't of Justice, Benevolence Director Pleads Guilty to Racketeering Conspiracy and Agrees to Cooperate with the Government (Feb. 10, 2003), *available at* http://usdoj.gov/usao/iln/pr/chicago/2003/pr021003_01.pdf.
17. *See* Press Release, U.S. Dep't of Treasury, Statement of Treasury Secretary Paul O'Neill (Nov. 7, 2001) (announcing the designation of Bank al Taqwa), *available at* http://www.treasury.gov/press/releases/po770.htm.
18. Press Release, White House, President Announces Crackdown on Terrorist Financial Network (Nov. 2001), *available at* http://www.whitehouse.gov/news/releases/2001/11/20011107-4.html.
19. Financial Crimes Enforcement Network, Amendment to the Bank Secrecy Act Regulations: Imposition of Special Measure Against Commercial Bank of Syria, Including Its Subsidiary, Syrian Lebanese Commercial Bank, as a Financial Institution of Primary Money Laundering Concern, Notice of Final Rule, 31 C.F.R. Part 103 (Mar. 15, 2006) [hereinafter *Imposition of Special Measures Against CBS (Final Rule)*]. *See* discussion, *infra*, of 31 U.S.C. §5318A, Special Measures for Jurisdictions, Financial Institutions, International Transactions, or Types of Accounts of Primary Money Laundering Concern.
20. *See Imposition of Special Measures Against CBS (Final Rule)*, *supra* note 19.
21. *See* Almog v. Arab Bank, 471 F. Supp. 2d 257 (E.D.N.Y. 2007); Weiss v. Nat'l Westminster Bank, 453 F. Supp. 2d 609 (E.D.N.Y. 2006); Strauss v. Credit Lyonnais, Case No. CV-06-0702 (CPS), 2006 WL 2862704 (E.D.N.Y. 2006).

22. *See* Marc Perelman, *Hamas's Banking Handmaidens*, NAT'L J., March 18, 2006; Glenn R. Simpson, *Arab Bank's Link to Terrorism Poses Dilemma for U.S. Policy*, WALL STREET JOURNAL, (April 20, 2005); *see also Almog*, 471 F. Supp. 2d at 262; Linde v. Arab Bank, 384 F. Supp. 2d 571 (E.D.N.Y. 2005).
23. *See Weiss*, 453 F. Supp. 2d at 612; *Strauss v. Credit Lyonnais*, 2006 WL 2862703, at *1.
24. *Id.*
25. *See* Assessment of Civil Money Penalty, In the Matter of the Federal Branch of Arab Bank PLC, New York, New York, No. 2005–2, U.S. Dep't of Treasury, Financial Crimes Enforcement Network (Aug. 17, 2005).
26. *Id.* at 3.
27. *See* International Convention for the Suppression of the Financing of Terrorism, Dec. 9, 1999, S. Treaty Doc. No. 106–49, 2178 U.N.T.S. 229, *available at* http://untreaty.un.org/ENGLISH/bible/englishinternetbible/partI/chapterXVIII/treaty12.asp. [hereinafter *Terrorist Financing Convention*].
28. *Id.*; *see also* Terrorist Bombings Convention Implementation Act of 2002, Pub. L. No. 107–197, 116 Stat. 721 (2002).
29. *Terrorist Financing Convention*, *supra* note 27, at arts. 4, 18(1)–(2).
30. *Id.* at art. 18(1)(b).
31. *Id.*
32. *Id.* at art. 18(1)(b)(i).
33. *Id.* at art. 18(1)(b)(ii).
34. *Id.* at art. 18(1)(b)(iii). This provision encourages State Parties to enact domestic legislation providing for a 'safe harbor' to protect financial institutions from criminal or civil liability for breach of any restriction on disclosure of such information. *Id.*
35. Created by the G7 countries in 1989, the FATF has since grown to 34 member countries, along with numerous observers, including the United Nations, the International Monetary Fund, and the World Bank. It further consists of several FATF-style regional bodies and numerous other international organizations. *See* Financial Action Task Force on Money Laundering, About the FATF, *available at* http://www.fatf-gafi.org/pages/0,3417,en_32250379_32236836_1_1_1_1_1,00.html. In the early 1990s, FATF adopted the Forty Recommendations on Money Laundering that represent the international standards for combating money laundering. In 2003, the Forty Recommendations were updated and revised. *See* Financial Action Task Force on Money Laundering, The Forty Recommendations, June 20, 2003, *available at* http://www.fatf-gafi.org/dataoecd/7/40/34849567.PDF [hereinafter *FATF Forty Recommendations*].
36. *2003 National Money Laundering Strategy, supra* note 1, at 8.
37. *See* Financial Action Task Force, 9 Special Recommendations (SR) on Terrorist Financing (TF) (last visited April 14, 2008), *available* at http://www.fatf-gafi.org/document/9/0,3343,en_32250379_32236920_34032073_1_1_1_1,00.html [hereinafter *Nine Special Recommendations on Terrorist Financing*]. Interpretive notes have been issued on the Nine Special Recommendations. *See infra* note 38.
38. *See* Financial Action Task Force on Money Laundering, The Interpretative Notes to the Special Recommendations (SR) on Terrorist Financing (TF), *available at* http://www.fatf-gafi.org/document/53/0,3343,en_32250379_32236947_34261877_1_1_1_1,00.html.
39. *2003 National Money Laundering Strategy*, *supra* note 1, at 9; *see also Nine Special Recommendations on Terrorist Financing, supra* note 37.
40. *See Nine Special Recommendations on Terrorist Financing*, Special Recommendation IV, *supra* note 37.
41. *Id.* Special Recommendation VII.
42. Uniting and Strengthening America by Providing Appropriate Tools Required to Intercept and Obstruct Terrorism (USA PATRIOT) Act of 2001, Pub. L. No. 107–56, 115 Stat. 272 (codified in scattered sections of the U.S.C.).
43. The International Money Laundering Abatement and Anti-Terrorism Financing Act of 2001, Pub. L. No. 107–56, tit. III, Oct. 26, 2001, 115 Stat. 296.

44. Title III of the USA PATRIOT Act amends the anti-money laundering provisions of the Bank Secrecy Act, codified at 12 U.S.C. §1829b, 12 U.S.C. §§1951–9, and 31 U.S.C. §§5311–14, 5316–32. Regulations implementing the BSA appear at 31 C.F.R. Part 103.
45. *See 2003 National Money Laundering Strategy*, *supra* note 1, at 26–7.
46. *See, e.g.*, 31 U.S.C.A §5318A (West 2008) (authorizing the Secretary of the Treasury to impose graduated counter-measures against a foreign jurisdiction, foreign financial institution, or a type of international transaction or account designated by the Secretary a 'primary money laundering concern').
47. 31 U.S.C. §5312(a)(2), (c)(1) and 31 C.F.R. §103.11.
48. *See* 31 U.S.C. §5312(a)(2)(D) and 31 C.F.R. §103.11. The Board of Governors of the Federal Reserve supervises and has the statutory authority to take formal enforcement actions against branches and offices of foreign banks operating in the United States. *See* Board of Governors of the Federal Reserve System, Bank Secrecy Act Anti-Money Laundering Examination Manual, §903.0 (1997), *available at* http://www.federalreserve.gov/boarddocs/supmanual/bsa/7-00bsaman.pdf.
49. *See* 31 U.S.C. §5312(a)(2) (2000 & Supp. IV 2004) and 31 C.F.R. §103.11.
50. 31 U.S.C. §5318(h)(1) (2000 & Supp. IV 2004).
51. *Id.*; *see also* 12 C.F.R. §326.8(c). The Financial Action Task Force on Money Laundering, Forty Recommendations, also requires financial institutions to implement a program to prevent money laundering and terrorist financing (Recommendation 15). *FATF Forty Recommendations*, *supra* note 35.
52. *See* Bank Secrecy Act Anti-Money Laundering Examination Manual, *supra* note 48.
53. *See* 31 C.F.R. §103.22 (requiring banks to file CTRs); *see also* 31 U.S.C. §5318(g) (2000 & Supp. IV 2004) (authorizing the Secretary of the Treasury to require financial institutions to file SARs); 31 C.F.R. §103.18 (requiring banks to file SARs).
54. 31 C.F.R. §103.18(a)(2); *see also* 31 U.S.C. §5318(g) (2000 & Supp. IV 2004).
55. 31 C.F.R. §103.18(a)(2)(i)–(iii).
56. *See* 31 C.F.R. §103.17(a)(2)(iv) (futures commission merchants and introducing brokers in commodities); 31 C.F.R. §103.19(a)(2)(iv) (brokers or dealers in securities); 31 C.F.R. §103.20(a)(2)(iv) (money services businesses); and 31 C.F.R. §103.21(a)(2)(iv) (casinos).
57. The $5,000 threshold for filing SARs also applies to futures commission merchants and introducing brokers in commodities, brokers or dealers in securities, and casinos. *See* 31 C.F.R. §§103.17(a)(2), 103.19(a)(2), and 103.21(a)(2). However, the monetary threshold for filing SARs for money services businesses is $2,000. *See* 31 C.F.R. §103.20(a)(2). The BSA regulation requiring money services businesses to file SARs became effective on January 1, 2002.
58. 31 C.F.R. §103.18(b)(3).
59. *Id.*
60. *See* Bank Secrecy Act Anti-Money Laundering Examination Manual, Appendix F: Money Laundering and Terrorist Financing 'Red Flags,' *available at* http://www.ffiec.gov/bsa_aml_infobase/pages_manual/OLM_106.htm. The Anti-Money Laundering Examination Manual is published by the Federal Financial Institutions Examination Council. *Id.*
61. *Id.*
62. *Id.*
63. *See* FinCEN, U.S. Dep't of Treasury, The SAR Activity Review – By the Numbers, Issue 9 (Jan. 2008), *available at* http://www.fincen.gov/sars/sar_by_numb_09.pdf. The SARs report represents the combined number of filings from four types of SAR forms: depository institutions; certain money services businesses; casinos and card clubs; and certain segments of the securities and futures industries. *Id.* at n. 5.
64. *FATF Alternative Remittance Systems: International Best Practices*, *supra* note 2, at 7.
65. 31 U.S.C. §5318(l)(2) (2000 & Supp. IV 2004). The importance of KYC policies and procedures precedes passage of the USA PATRIOT Act and is highlighted as a requirement in the Bank Secrecy Act Anti-Money Laundering Examination Manual (1997). Section 601.0 of the Manual states that, in order to develop and maintain a practical

and useful policy, financial institutions should incorporate the following principles into their business practices:

- Financial institutions should make a reasonable effort to determine the true identity of all customers requesting the bank's services;
- Financial institutions should take particular care to identify the ownership of all accounts and of those using safe-custody facilities;
- Identification should be obtained from all new customers;
- Evidence of identity should be obtained from customers seeking to conduct significant business transactions; and
- Financial institutions should be aware of any unusual transaction activity or activity that is disproportionate to the customer's known business.

See Bank Secrecy Act Anti-Money Laundering Examination Manual, *supra* note 48, at §601.0.

66. 12 CFR §21.21.
67. *See* Assessment of Civil Money Penalty, In the Matter of the New York Branch of ABN AMRO Bank, New York, New York, No. 2005–5, U.S. Dep't of the Treasury, (FinCEN Dec. 19, 2005) (ABN AMRO breached its duty to adequately staff the compliance function).
68. *See* U.S. Dep't of Treasury, Financial Crimes Enforcement Network, Frequently Asked Questions, Conducting Independent Reviews of Money Services Business Anti-Money Laundering Programs, at 2 (Sept. 22, 2006), *available at* http://www.fincen.gov/Guidance_MSB_Independent_Audits 9–21.pdf.
69. 31 U.S.C. §5318(i)(1) (2000 & Supp. IV 2004).
70. *Id.* §5318(i)(4)(B).
71. *Id.* §5318(i)(3)(a).
72. *Id.* §5318(i)(3)(B).
73. The term 'correspondent account' means 'an account established to receive deposits from, make payments on behalf of a foreign financial institution, or handle other financial transactions related to such institution.' 31 U.S.C.A. §5318A(e)(1)(B) (West 2008).
74. The term 'offshore banking license' means 'a license to conduct banking activities which, as a condition of the license, prohibits the licensed entity from conducting banking activities with the citizens of, or with the local currency of, the country which issued the license.' 31 U.S.C. §5318(i)(4)(A).
75. 31 U.S.C. §5318(i)(2(A).
76. *Id.* §5318(i)(2)(B)(i)–(iii).
77. *Id.* §5318(j)(2) (prohibiting covered financial institutions from providing indirect services to foreign shell banks).
78. *Id.* §5318(j)(1).
79. *Id.*
80. Shell companies are also used to facilitate money laundering and terrorist financing. *See* The Role of Domestic Shell Companies in Financial Crime and Money Laundering, Financial Crimes Enforcement Network (Nov. 2006), *available at* http://www.fincen.gov/LLCAssessment_FINAL.pdf.
81. *See* 31 U.S.C. §5312(a)(2)(A)–(G) (2000 & Supp. IV. 2004).
82. 31 U.S.C. § 5318(j)(2) (2000 & Supp. IV 2004).
83. *Id.* §5318(k)(3)(a)(i).
84. *Id.*
85. *Id.* §5318(k)(3)(B)(i).
86. *Id.* §5318(k)(3)(A)(ii).
87. *Id.* §5318(k)(3)(C)(i).
88. *Id.* §5318(k)(3)(C)(iii).
89. *2003 National Money Laundering Strategy, supra* note 1, at 2.
90. Uniting and Strengthening America by Providing Appropriate Tools Required to Intercept and Obstruct Terrorism (USA PATRIOT) Act of 2001, Pub. L. No. 107–56,

§314(a) 115 Stat. 272 (codified in scattered sections of the U.S.C.). Section 314 is reprinted in the Historical and Statutory Notes to 31 U.S.C. §5311. FinCEN issued a proposed rule on March 5, 2002, and the final rule on September 26, 2002 (67 Fed. Reg. 60,579). Section 314(a) requirements are now published in 31 C.F.R. Part 103.100.

91. U.S. Dep't of Treasury, FinCEN, FinCEN's 314(a) Fact Sheet (Dec. 4, 2007), *available at* http://www.fincen.gov/314afactsheet.pdf [hereinafter *FinCEN's 314(a) Fact Sheet*].
92. Uniting and Strengthening America by Providing Appropriate Tools Required to Intercept and Obstruct Terrorism (USA PATRIOT) Act of 2001, Pub. L. No. 107–56, §314(a) 115 Stat. 272 (codified in scattered sections of the U.S.C.).
93. *FinCEN's 314(a) Fact Sheet, supra* note 91; *see also* 31 C.F.R. §103.100(b)(2).
94. *Id.*
95. *Id.*
96. See TREASURY'S ROLES AND RESPONSIBILITIES RELATING TO SELECTED PROVISIONS OF THE USA PATRIOT ACT, AT 54, U.S. GOVERNMENT ACCOUNTABILITY OFFICE, REPORT TO THE CHAIRMAN, HOUSE JUDICIARY COMMITTEE (May 2006) [hereinafter TREASURY'S ROLES AND RESPONSIBILITIES RELATING TO SELECTED PROVISIONS OF THE USA PATRIOT ACT].
97. *Id.*
98. *Id.*; *see also* Egmont Group, Statement of Purpose of the Egmont Group of Financial Intelligence Units, *available at* http://www.egmontgroup.org.
99. TREASURY'S ROLES AND RESPONSIBILITIES RELATING TO SELECTED PROVISIONS OF THE USA PATRIOT ACT, *supra* note 96, at 12.
100. 31 U.S.C. §5321 (2000 & Supp. IV 2004) and 31 C.F.R. §103.57. For example, civil money penalties may be assessed for record-keeping violations (31 C.F.R. §103.29), for failure to file a currency transaction report (31 C.F.R. §103.22), and failure to file a suspicious activity report (31 C.F.R. § 103.21). At the same time, FinCEN has delegated BSA examination authority to various federal regulatory agencies. *See* 31 C.F.R. 103.56(b). Based on examinations by these agencies, findings may be referred to FinCEN for consideration of civil money penalties. Under Title 12, certain federal supervisory agencies, including the Office of Comptroller of the Currency, the Board of Governors of the Federal Reserve Supervision, the Federal Deposit Insurance Corporation, the Office of Thrift Supervision, and the National Credit Union Administration may also impose civil money penalties for failure to comply with Title 12 suspicious activity reporting and BSA compliance program requirements. *See 2003 National Money Laundering Strategy, supra* note 1, at 30 n. 22.
101. A civil penalty totalling $85 million was assessed against American Express Bank International. The FinCEN penalty of $25 million was issued concurrently with a deferred prosecution agreement and accompanying $55 million forfeiture by the Department of Justice, and a $20 million civil penalty by the Federal Reserve. However, the FinCEN $25 million penalty was satisfied by a single $10 million payment to the Department of the Treasury. The remaining $15 million of FinCEN's penalty was satisfied by a portion of the $55 million forfeiture to the Department of Justice. *See* Assessment of Civil Money Penalty, In the Matter of American Express Bank International, et al., No. 2007–1, FinCEN, U.S. Dep't of the Treasury [hereinafter *In the Matter of American Express Bank International*].
102. *See In the Matter of American Express Bank International, supra* note 101; Assessment of Civil Money Penalty, In the Matter of the New York Branch of ABN AMRO, No. 2005–5, FinCEN, U.S. Dep't of the Treasury; Assessment of Civil Money Penalty, In the Matter of Riggs Bank, No. 2004–01, FinCEN, U.S. Dep't of the Treasury; Assessment of Civil Money Penalty, In the Matter of Israel Discount Bank of New York, No. 2006–7, FinCEN, U.S. Dep't of the Treasury; and Assessment of Civil Money Penalty, In the Matter of AmSouth Bank, No. 2004–2, FinCEN, U.S. Dep't of the Treasury.
103. Assessment of Civil Money Penalty, In the Matter of the Federal Branch of Arab Bank PLC, New York, New York, No. 2005–2, FinCEN, U.S. Dep't of the Treasury, at 8, *available at* http://www.fincen.gov/arab081705.pdf [hereinafter *Assessment of Civil Money*

Penalty Against Arab Bank]. The New York branch of Arab Bank constitutes a 'financial institution' and a 'bank' with the BSA. *See* 31 U.S.C. §5312(a)(2) and 31 C.F.R. §103.11.
104. *Assessment of Civil Money Penalty Against Arab Bank*, *supra* note 103, at 1.
105. Glenn R. Simpson, *Arab Bank's Link to Terrorism Poses Dilemma for U.S. Policy*, WALL STREET JOURNAL (April 20, 2005) [hereinafter *Arab Bank's Link to Terrorism*].
106. *Assessment of Civil Money Penalty Against Arab Bank*, *supra* note 103, at 4. According to the claims made in a civil lawsuit, the Saudi Committee for the Support of the Al Quds (Jerusalem) Intifada sent hundreds of millions of dollars to the Palestinians through Saudi banks that transferred the money to the Arab Bank of Jordan, which directed the West Bank and Gaza. The Arab Bank's New York branch involvement was to convert Saudi riyals into dollars. *See* Linde v. Arab Bank, 384 F. Supp. 2d 571, 578 (E.D.N.Y. 2005).
107. *See Assessment of Civil Money Penalty Against Arab Bank*, *supra* note 103, at 4; *see also* 31 U.S.C. §5318(h).
108. *See Assessment of Civil Money Penalty Against Arab Bank*, *supra* note 103, at 3–4.
109. *Id.* at 4.
110. *See Arab Bank's Link to Terrorism*, *supra* note 105.
111. *See Assessment of Civil Money Penalty Against Arab Bank*, *supra* note 103, at 3.
112. *Id.* at 4.
113. *Id.*
114. *Id.*
115. *Id.* at 5; *see also* Almog v. Arab Bank, 471 F. Supp. 2d 257, 259, 265 (E.D.N.Y. 2007) (plaintiffs alleged that Arab Bank knowingly provided financial services to Palestinian terrorist organizations); Linde v. Arab Bank, 384 F. Supp. 2d 571, 575–9 (E.D.N.Y. 2005) (same).
116. *See Assessment of Civil Money Penalty Against Arab Bank*, *supra* note 103, at 7.
117. *Id.*
118. *Id.*
119. *Id.* at 5.
120. *Id.*
121. *Id.* at 3–4.
122. *Id.* at 6.
123. *See, e.g*, FinCEN assessment of civil money penalties against American Express Bank (Aug. 6, 2007); Israeli Discount Bank of New York (Oct. 31, 2006); New York Branch of ABN AMRO (Dec. 19, 2005); and AmSouth Bank (Oct 12, 2004).
124. *See Assessment of Civil Money Penalty Against Arab Bank*, *supra* note 103, at 4.
125. *See* Marc Perelman, *Hamas's Banking Handmaidens*, NAT'L J. (Mar. 18, 2006).
126. *See Assessment of Civil Money Penalty Against Arab Bank*, *supra* note 103, at 5.
127. *See Arab Bank's Link to Terrorism*, *supra* note 105.
128. The use of charities to raise money for terrorist activities is discussed *supra* at Chapter 6 – 'Corrupt Islamic charities.'
129. 31 U.S.C.A §5318A (West 2008).
130. *Id.* §5318A(b) (listing the special measures available to the Secretary of the Treasury).
131. *See* Blocking Property and Prohibiting Transactions with Persons Who Commit, Threaten to Commit, or Support Terrorism, Exec. Order No. 13,224, 3 C.F.R. 786–90 (2001), *reprinted as amended in* 50 U.S.C. §1701 note (Supp. IV 2004) (authorizing freezing actions against the assets of suspected terrorists).
132. *Imposition of Special Measures Against CBS (Final Rule)*, *supra* note 19.
133. TREASURY'S ROLES AND RESPONSIBILITIES RELATING TO SELECTED PROVISIONS OF THE USA PATRIOT ACT, *supra* note 96, at 12.
134. 31 U.S.C.A. §5318A(c)(1) (West 2008).
135. *Id.*
136. *Id.* §5318A(c)(2)(A).
137. *Id.* §5318A(c)(2)(B).
138. *Id.* §5318A(c)(2)(A).
139. *Id.* §5318A(c)(2)(B).

140. The term 'payable-through account' means an account 'opened at a depository institution by a foreign financial institution by means of which the foreign financial institution permits its customers to engage, either directly or through a subaccount, in banking activities usual in connection with the business of banking in the United States.' 31 U.S.C.A. §5318A(e)(1)(C) (West 2008).
141. *Id.* §5318A(b)(1)–(5); *see also* Ross Q. Panko, *Banking on the USA PATRIOT Act: An Endorsement of the Act's Use of Banks to Combat Terrorist Financing and a Response to Critics*, 122 BANKING L. J. 99, 115 (2005).
142. 31 U.S.C.A. §5318A(a)(4)(A) (West 2008).
143. 31 U.S.C. §5318(b)(5) (2000 & Supp. IV 2004).
144. For example, in deciding to impose special measures, it would be highly relevant if the Financial Action Task Force (FATF) had designated the particular jurisdiction as a 'non-cooperative country and territory,' meaning that it was non-compliant with the FATF 40 Recommendations on money laundering.
145. 31 U.S.C.A. §5318A(a)(4)(B)(i)–(iv) (West 2008).
146. *Id.* §5318A(a)(2)(B).
147. *Id.* §5318A(a)(2)(C).
148. *See* U.S. Dep't of Treasury, FinCEN, Section 311 – Special Measures, *available at* http://www.fincen.gov/reg_section311.html (listing imposition of special measures against foreign jurisdictions and financial institutions in chronological order) (last visited April 12, 2008). The designation of Ukraine as a PMLC was revoked on April 17, 2003. *Id.*
149. Imposition of a Special Measure Against Commercial Bank of Syria, Including Its Subsidiary, Syrian Lebanese Commercial Bank, as a Financial Institution of Primary Money Laundering Concern, 69 Fed. Reg. 28098 (Proposed Rule) (May 18, 2004) [hereinafter *Imposition of Special Measures Against CBS (Proposed Rule)*]. In March 2006, a final rule was issued imposing a special measure against CBS as a PMLC. *See Imposition of Special Measures Against CBS (Final Rule)*, *supra* note 19.
150. *Imposition of Special Measures Against CBS (Proposed Rule)*, *supra* note 149.
151. *Id.*
152. *Id.*
153. *Id.*
154. *Imposition of Special Measures Against CBS (Final Rule), supra* note 19.
155. 31 U.S.C. §5318(i)(2)(B)(iii).
156. Crédit Lyonnais maintains an office in Miami, Florida, and NatWest Bank operates a branch office in New York. *See* Strauss v. Credit Lyonnais, Case No. CV-06-0702 (CPS), 2006 WL 2862704, at *3 (E.D.N.Y. 2006); Weiss v. Nat'l Westminster Bank, 453 F. Supp. 2d 609, 615 (E.D.N.Y. 2006).
157. Strauss v. Credit Lyonnais, 2006 WL 2862704 at *19; *Weiss*, 453 F. Supp. 2d at 633. (E.D.N.Y. 2006).
158. *Fund-Raising Methods and Procedures for International Terrorist Organizations*, supra note 2, at 23; *see also 2003 National Money Laundering Strategy, supra* note 1, at Appendix H, 56–7.
159. *2003 National Money Laundering Strategy, supra* note 1, at Appendix H, 60.
160. *Id.* at 63; *see also Fund-Raising Methods and Procedures for International Terrorist Organizations*, *supra* note 2, at 23–5.
161. *2003 National Money Laundering Strategy, supra* note 1, at Appendix H, 63; *see also Fund-Raising Methods and Procedures for International Terrorist Organizations, supra* note 2, at 23.
162. *Id.*
163. *2003 National Money Laundering Strategy, supra* note 1, Appendix H, at 63; *see also* Press Release, U.S. Dep't of Treasury, Designation of 10 Terrorist Financiers Fact Sheet (Apr. 19, 2002), *available at* http://www.treas.gov/press/releases/po3014.htm.
164. *See Fund-Raising Methods and Procedures for International Terrorist Organizations*, *supra* note 2, at 23–5; *2003 National Money Laundering Strategy*, *supra* note 1, at Appendix H, 64.

165. *2003 National Money Laundering Strategy*, *supra* note 1, at Appendix H, 71.
166. According to the Treasury Department, '[r]egulation of the financial services industry is the primary tool for preventing terrorists from moving funds through the United States banking system,' including through the use of online financial services. *Id.*
167. *Id.* at 72.
168. *Id.*; *see also* 31 CFR §§103.18 and 103.19.
169. *2003 National Money Laundering Strategy, supra* note 1, at Appendix H, 72.
170. *Id.* at 14.
171. *See* STAFF MONOGRAPH ON TERRORIST FINANCING, *supra* note 2, at 25; *see also 2003 National Money Laundering Strategy*, *supra* note 1, at 14.
172. U.S. Dep't of Treasury, Hawala & Alternative Remittance Systems, Terrorism and Financial Intelligence, *available at* http://www.treasury.gov/offices/enforcement/key-issues/hawala [hereinafter *Hawala & Alternative Remittance Systems*].
173. *See* International Narcotics Control Strategy Report, Bureau for International Narcotics and Law Enforcement Affairs (Mar. 2006), *available at* http://www.state.gov/p/inl/rls/nrcrpt/2006/vol2/html/62144.htm (discussing use of hawala in India).
174. U.S. Dep't of Treasury, Report to Congress in Accordance with Section 359 of the Uniting and Strengthening America by Providing Appropriate Tools Required to Intercept and Obstruct Terrorism Act of 2001, at 5 (Nov. 2002), *available at* http://www.fincen.gov/hawalarptfinal11222002.pdf [hereinafter *Congressional Report on Section 359*].
175. *Id.*
176. *Id.* at 23–4.
177. *Id.* at 5.
178. *Id.*
179. *Hawala and Alternative Remittance Systems*, *supra* note 172.
180. *See* discussion of the FATF Nine Special Recommendations on Terrorist Financing, *supra* notes 35–41 and accompanying text.
181. *See Nine Special Recommendations on Terrorist Financing, supra* note 37; *see also Hawala & Alternative Remittance Systems, supra* note 172.
182. *See Nine Special Recommendations on Terrorist Financing, supra* note 37; *see also FATF Alternative Remittance Systems: International Best Practices*, *supra* note 2, at 3.
183. *FATF Alternative Remittance Systems: International Best Practices, supra* note 2, at 3. The International Convention on the Suppression of the Financing of Terrorism also encourages States to require licensing of all money transmission businesses. *See Terrorist Financing Convention, supra* note 27, at art. 18(2)(a), which provides:

    States Parties shall further cooperate in the prevention of [terrorist financing] offences . . . by considering:
    (a) Measures for the supervision, including, for example, the licensing, of all money-transmission agencies.

184. *See FATF Alternative Remittance Systems: International Best Practices, supra* note 2, at 3.
185. *Id.* at 7–8.
186. *Id.* at 7.
187. *Id.* at 8; *see also FATF Forty Recommendations, supra* note 35, Recommendation 10 (record-keeping requirement).
188. *FATF Alternative Remittance Systems: International Best Practices, supra* note 2, at 7; *see also FATF Forty Recommendations, supra* note 35, Recommendation 13 (reporting suspicious transactions).
189. *FATF Alternative Remittance Systems: International Best Practices, supra* note 2, at 7; *see also FATF Forty Recommendations, supra* note 35, Recommendation 15 (setting forth the minimum requirements for an effective anti-money laundering/terrorist financing program).
190. *Nine Recommendations on Terrorist Financing*, Recommendation VI, *supra* note 37.
191. *See FATF Alternative Remittance Systems: International Best Practices, supra* note 2, at 9.

192. *See id. generally*.
193. *Id.* at 9.
194. Uniting and Strengthening America by Providing Appropriate Tools Required to Intercept and Obstruct Terrorism (USA PATRIOT) Act of 2001, Pub. L. No. 107–56, 115 Stat. 272 (codified in scattered sections of the U.S.C.); *see also* 31 U.S.C. §5330(d)(1) (2000 & Supp. IV 2004) (defining a 'money transmitting business').
195. Under the BSA, MSBs include five distinct types of financial services providers and the U.S. Postal Service: (1) currency dealers or exchangers; (2) check cashers; (3) issuers of traveler's checks, money orders, or stored value; (4) sellers or redeemers of traveler's checks, money orders, or stored value; and (5) money transmitters. 31 C.F.R. §103.11(uu).
196. Under 31 U.S.C. §5312(a)(2)(R) (2000 & Supp. IV 2004), 'financial institution' means 'a licensed sender of money or any other person who engages as a business in the transmission of funds, including any person who engages as a business in an informal money transfer system or any network of people who engage as a business in facilitating the transfer of money domestically or internationally outside of the conventional financial institutions system.'
197. 31 U.S.C. §5330(a)(1) (2000 & Supp. IV 2004).
198. *Id.* §5330(b).
199. *Id.*
200. *See* 31 C.F.R. §103.41.
201. *See* U.S. Dep't of Treasury, FinCEN, MSB Registration List, *available at* http://www.msb.gov/pdf/msb_registration_list.pdf. Since December 31, 2001, MSBs have been required to register with FinCEN. *See 2003 National Money Laundering Strategy, supra* note 1, at 14.
202. 31 U.S.C. §5330(e) (2000 & Supp. IV 2004).
203. 18 U.S.C.A. §1960 (West 2008).
204. *Id.*
205. *Id.*
206. *Id.*
207. 31 C.F.R. §103.125; *see also* Financial Crimes Enforcement Network, Interpretive Release 2004–1, Anti-Money Laundering Program Requirements for Money Services Businesses with Respect to Foreign Agents or Foreign Counterparts, 69 Fed. Reg. 74,439 (Dec.14, 2004) [hereinafter *Anti-Money Laundering Program for MSBs*].
208. *See Anti-Money Laundering Program for MSBs*, *supra* note 207.
209. 31 C.F.R. §103.33(f).
210. 31 U.S.C. §5312 and 31 C.F.R. §103.22.
211. 31 C.F.R. §103.22(c)(2) (the 'Aggregation Rule').
212. 31 C.F.R. §103.28.
213. 31 C.F.R. §103.20 (requirement for MSBs, other than check cashiers and issuers, sellers, or redeemers of stored value, to file SARs).
214. *Id.*; *see also Report to Congress on Section 359, supra* note 174, at 8; U.S. Dep't of Treasury, Office of Terrorist Financing and Financial Crimes, U.S. Money Laundering Threat Assessment (Dec. 2005), at 10, *available at* http://www.treasury.gov/offices/enforcement/pdf/mlta.pdf.
215. *See 2003 National Money Laundering Strategy, supra* note 1, at 15; *see also* United States v. Elfgeeh, et al., Superseding Indictment, Cr. No. 03–133 (S-2)(CPS) (E.D.N.Y.) (charging violations of 18 U.S.C. § 1960); United States v Rehman, et al., Indictment, Cr. No. MJG-07–0418 (D. MD) (same); United States v. Ranjha, et al., Indictment, Cr. No. MJG-0239 (D. MD) (same).
216. *See* U.S. Dep't of Treasury, Financial Crimes Enforcement Network, In the Matter of Western Union Financial Services, Inc., No. 2003–02 (March 6, 2003), *available at* http://www.fincen.gov/western_union_assessment.pdf [hereinafter *In the Matter of Western Union Financial Services, Inc.*]; U.S. Dep't of Treasury, Financial Crimes Enforcement Network, In the Matter of Sigue Corporation and Sigue, LLC, No. 2008–1 (Jan. 24, 2008), *available at* http://www.sigue_assessment_final.pdf [hereinafter *In the*

Matter of Sigue Corporation]; U.S. Dep't of Treasury, Financial Crimes Enforcement Network, In the Matter of Deprez's Quality Jewelry and Loans, Inc., No. 2006–06 (July 2006), *available at* http://www.fincen.gov/deprez_assessment_07202006.pdf; U.S. Dep't of Treasury, Financial Crimes Enforcement Network, In the Matter of Frosty Food Mart, No. 2006–04 (May 2006), *available at* http://www.fincen.gov/frosty_cmp_consent.pdf; and U.S. Dep't of Treasury, Financial Crimes Enforcement Network, In the Matter of El Noa Noa Corporation (April 14, 2008), *available at* http://www.fincen.gov/ElNoaNoa.pdf.

217. Western Union Financial Services, Inc. was fined $3 million for 'not aggregating multiple currency transactions totaling more than $10,000 that occurred during one day through multiple agents.' *In the Matter of Western Union Financial Services, Inc., supra* note 216, at 2. Sigue Corporation, on the other hand, was assessed a $12 million civil penalty for violations of the requirement to implement an anti-money laundering program and the requirement to report SARs. The U.S. Department of Justice also entered into a deferred prosecution agreement that required Sigue to forfeit $15 million to the U.S. government. The evidence suggested that the Sigue MSBs were being used to launder illicit drug proceeds. *See* Press Release, Financial Crimes Enforcement Network, Sigue Corp. and Sigue, LLC of California to Pay $15 million to U.S. Government for Anti-Money Laundering Program Deficiencies (Jan. 28, 2008), *available at* http://www.fincen.gov/20080128.html.
218. *See FATF Cash Couriers: International Best Practices, supra* note 2, at 2; *see also 2003 National Money Laundering Strategy, supra* note 1, at 15; *Fund-Raising Methods and Procedures for International Terrorist Organizations, supra* note 2, at 22.
219. *FATF Cash Couriers: International Best Practices, supra* note 2, at 2.
220. *Id.*
221. *Terrorist Financing Convention, supra* note 27, at art. 18(2)(b).
222. *See Interpretative Notes to the Special Recommendations on Terrorist Financing, supra* note 38.
223. *Id.*
224. 31 U.S.C. §5316(a) (2000).
225. *Id.* §5316(b).
226. *Id.* §5317(c)(1)–(2) (2000 & Supp. IV 2004) (authorizing both criminal and civil forfeiture).
227. *Id.* §5321(a)(2).
228. *Id.* §5322(a).
229. Pub. L. No. 107–56, Title III, §371(c), Oct. 26, 2001, 115 Stat. 337, and amended Pub. L. No. 108–458, Title VI, §6203(h), Dec. 17, 2004, 118 Stat. 3747, codified at 31 U.S.C. §5332 (2000 & Supp. IV 2004).
230. 31 U.S.C. §5332(b)(1) (2000 & Supp. IV 2004).
231. *Id.* §5332(b)(2).
232. *Id.* §5332(c).
233. *See* Financial Action Task Force, Trade Based Money Laundering (June 23, 2006), *available at* http://www.faft-gafi.org/doc [hereinafter Trade Based Money Laundering].
234. *Id.*
235. *Id.*
236. *Id.*
237. *Id.*
238. Trade Based Money Laundering, *supra* note 233.
239. *Id.*
240. *Id.*
241. *Id.*
242. *Id.*
243. *Terrorist Financing Convention, supra* note 27; *see also Nine Special Recommendations on Terrorist Financing, supra* note 37.
244. *See* 31 C.F.R. §103.22 (requiring banks to file CTRs); 31 C.F.R. §103.18 (requiring banks to file SARs); and 31 C.F.R. §103.100 (information sharing provision).

245. *See e.g., Assessment of Civil Money Penalty Against Arab Bank, supra* note 103; *see also* 31 U.S.C. §5318A (primary money laundering concern provision).
246. *See* J. Michael McConnell, Director of National Intelligence, Annual Threat Assessment of the Director of National Intelligence for the Senate Select Committee on Intelligence, 5–8 (Feb. 5, 2008).
247. *Nine Special Recommendations on Terrorist Financing, supra* note 37.

8. Domestic asset freeze

> Today, we have launched a strike on the financial foundation of the global terror network. . . . We will direct every resource at our command to win the war against terrorists, every means of diplomacy, every tool of intelligence, every instrument of law enforcement, every financial influence. We will starve the terrorists of funding.
>
> President George W. Bush,
> September 24, 2001,
> announcing Executive Order 13224

EXECUTIVE ORDER 13224

Overview

The centerpiece of the U.S. Government's strategy to deprive al Qaeda and its global network of the funding needed to plan and launch deadly terrorist strikes is to freeze the assets of terrorists, terrorist-related entities, and also their financial supporters and sympathizers. The domestic authority to block terrorist funds derives from Executive Order (E.O.) 13224 issued by President George W. Bush on September 23, 2001.[1] A few days after al Qaeda terrorists hijacked four American commercial jetliners and used three of them as missiles against the World Trade Center twin towers and the Pentagon,[2] President Bush invoked his authority under the International Emergency Economic Powers Act (IEEPA).[3] The IEEPA authorizes the President to declare a national emergency 'to deal with any unusual and extraordinary threat, which has its source in whole or substantial part outside the United States, to the national security, foreign policy, or economy of the United States'[4] The President determined that the grave acts of terrorism and threats of terrorism committed by foreign terrorists, including the terrorist attacks in New York, Washington, D.C., and Pennsylvania on September 11, 2001, and the continuing threat of attacks against U.S. nationals constituted 'an unusual and extraordinary threat to the national security, foreign policy, and economy of the United States.'[5] The presidential E.O. specifically noted that 'because of the pervasiveness and expansiveness of the financial foundation of foreign terrorists, financial sanctions may be appropriate for those foreign persons that support or otherwise associate with these foreign terrorists.'[6]

The IEEPA grants the President broad economic powers. Upon declaration of a national emergency, the IEEPA authorizes the President to

> investigate, block during the pendency of an investigation, regulate . . . prevent or prohibit, any acquisition, holding, withholding, use, transfer, withdrawal . . . dealing in, or exercising any right, power, or privilege with respect to, or transactions involving, any property in which any foreign country or a national thereof has any interest by any person, or with respect to any property, subject to the jurisdiction of the United States[7]

Under the E.O., the President invoked the IEEPA to designate 12 individuals and 15 entities and freeze their assets in the United States.[8] These 27 individuals and groups were labeled 'Specially Designated Global Terrorists' (SDGTs) and identified in the Annex to E.O. 13224. They included core members of al Qaeda, affiliated terrorist groups, Islamic charities suspected of funding al Qaeda, and other businesses believed to be a front for al Qaeda.[9] With respect to the 27 SDGTs, their property and interests in property in the United States were ordered to be blocked.[10]

The Order also authorized the Secretary of the Treasury, in consultation with the Secretary of State and the Attorney General, to designate and block the property or property interests of future individuals and entities who 'act for or on behalf of' or are 'owned or controlled by' designated terrorists[11] or 'assist in, sponsor, or provide financial, material, or technological support for' or are 'otherwise associated with' them.[12] Finally, the E.O. authorized the Secretary of State, in consultation with the Secretary of the Treasury and the Attorney General, to designate persons determined 'to have committed, or to pose a significant risk of committing, acts of terrorism that threaten the security of U.S. nationals or the national security, foreign policy, or economy of the United States.'[13]

E.O. 13224 'expands the Treasury Department's power to target the support structure of terrorist organizations, freeze the assets subject to U.S. jurisdiction and block the transactions of terrorists and those that support them, and deny them access to U.S. markets.'[14] The impact of E.O. 13224 is to isolate from the U.S. financial system all designated terrorists and their financial supporters and control assets that could be used by terrorists to threaten the United States' national security. While E.O. 13224 was certainly directed at members of al Qaeda, it is much broader in coverage, authorizing blocking all property and interests in property of all individuals and entities linked to global terrorism.

A blocking action under the Order has several important legal consequences. First, all property and interests in property of designated individuals and entities in the United States or that come within the United States, or that come within the possession or control of U.S. persons, are blocked.[15] Second, any transaction or dealing by U.S. persons in property or interests in property blocked pursuant to the Order is prohibited.[16] Specifically, §2(a) prohibits any U.S. person from 'making or receiving . . . any contribution of funds, goods, or services to or for the benefit of' persons determined to be subject to E.O. 13224.[17] Third, any transaction by any U.S. person that evades or avoids, or has the purpose of evading or avoiding, or attempts to violate, any of the prohibitions of the Order is prohibited.[18] Finally, severe civil and criminal penalties may be assessed for violations of any license, order, or regulation issued pursuant to E.O. 13224.[19]

The use of economic sanctions by the President against foreign countries and their nationals is not unprecedented. In 1917, Congress enacted the Trading with the Enemy Act (TWEA) authorizing the President to control financial transactions or impose economic sanctions against foreign persons and entities regardless of the state of foreign affairs (peace or war time).[20] The TWEA conferred on the President the authority to deprive enemies, actual or potential, of the opportunity to perpetrate wrongs against the U.S. and its citizens through use of assets in this country. Specifically, the TWEA granted the President authority to 'investigate, regulate, . . . prevent or prohibit . . . transactions' in times of war or national emergency.[21] In 1977, Congress amended the TWEA and enacted the IEEPA to delineate the Executive Branch's exercise of emergency economic powers in response to wartime and peacetime crises. 'The IEEPA limited the TWEA's application to periods of declared wars and to certain existing TWEA programs, while the IEEPA was applicable during other times of declared national emergencies.'[22]

Bases for Designation

In addition to the 27 individuals and entities designated by the President and listed in the Annex to the E.O., the Order provides authority for the designation and blocking of assets of other individuals and entities.[23] E.O. 13224 authorizes the Secretary of the Treasury, in consultation with the Secretary of State and the Attorney General, to designate individuals and entities as SDGTs that are determined:

> (a) To be owned or controlled by, or act for or on behalf of, an individual or entity listed in the Annex to the Order or by or for persons determined to be subject to . . . [the] Order;
> (b) To assist in, sponsor, or provide financial, material, or technological support for, or financial or other services to or in support of, acts of terrorism or individuals or entities designated in or under the Order; or

(c) To be otherwise associated with certain individuals or entities designated in or under the Order.[24]

As previously noted, E.O. 13224 permits the Secretary of State, in consultation with the Secretary of the Treasury and the Attorney General, to designate as subject to the provisions of the Order any 'foreign individuals or entities that he determines have committed, or pose a significant risk of committing, acts of terrorism that threaten the security of U.S. nationals or the national security, foreign policy, or economy of the U.S.'[25] Thus, the Secretary of State as well as the Treasury Secretary may initiate designation and asset freeze under the executive order. Property and interests in property of persons designated under E.O. 13224 are blocked and may 'not be transferred, paid, exported, withdrawn or otherwise dealt in.'[26]

Designation Process

The preliminary decision regarding whether to designate a particular person or entity under E.O. 13224 is made by an inter-agency working group consisting of representatives from several U.S. agencies. The principal federal agencies participating in the working group include the Departments of Treasury, State, Justice, and Homeland Security, as well as the FBI and the intelligence community. Representatives from each of these federal agencies meet on a regular basis and review a broad range of evidence, including open-source information such as news reports, court documents, property and bank records, and hearsay declarations, as well as information generated from criminal investigations and classified intelligence reports, about persons and entities who commit, threaten to commit or support terrorism.[27] In certain instances, the designations are based on foreign governments' intelligence reports.[28]

The decision to designate an individual or group as an SDGT is an administrative, rather than a criminal action. Designation does not require that the party be prosecuted and convicted or even charged with committing criminal acts of terrorism or providing material support to terrorists or a foreign terrorist organization. Because the designations and blocking orders are administrative in nature, the Government is not required to satisfy the criminal standard of proof beyond a reasonable doubt. A lower standard of proof is applied. An individual or entity may be designated as an SDGT if there is a reasonable basis to believe that he is 'owned or controlled by,' 'act[s] for or on behalf of,' 'assist[s] in . . . or provide[s] financial, material, or technological support for, or financial or other services to' or is 'otherwise associated with' SDGTs.[29] A person may further be designated under the Order if there is a reasonable basis to believe that he has 'committed, or . . . pose[s] a significant risk of committing, acts of terrorism that threaten . . . the national security, foreign policy, or economy of the United States.'[30]

While the primary focus of the inter-agency working group is to determine whether the potential designee is directly or indirectly financing terrorism or poses a significant risk of committing acts of terrorism, the decision to recommend designating the individual or entity as an SDGT often involves resolving agency conflicts of interests. For example, despite compelling evidence of the proposed designee's role in providing financial support to terrorist groups, public designation might compromise an ongoing criminal investigation or jeopardize a covert intelligence operation. Placing the suspected terrorist financier's name on the Treasury list might disclose intelligence agency methods and operations, or jeopardize sensitive State Department negotiations or relations between the U.S. and some other foreign country. In such a case, the members of the working group would weigh and scrutinize the costs and benefits of public designation against important and competing agency interests. In an effort to resolve the inter-agency conflict, a decision to designate an individual might be postponed temporarily and reconsidered at a later date. In other cases, countervailing agency considerations might altogether trump the decision to publicly designate an individual. In this regard, members of the working group wield enormous discretion whether or not to designate someone, analogous to that of a criminal prosecutor.[31]

A subset of the inter-agency working group is responsible for developing a background file or 'statement of the case' which is reviewed by the larger group. These files are reviewed by Department of Justice attorneys for legal sufficiency under E.O. 13224. The final determination on the designation is then forwarded for decision to the National Security Council, which convenes a meeting of deputy agency heads. Upon their recommendation, the Secretary of the Treasury or the Secretary of the Department of State designates an individual or entity.

Pursuant to a delegation of authority from the Secretary of the Treasury, the Office of Foreign Assets Control (OFAC), an agency within the U.S. Department of the Treasury, takes appropriate action to block the assets of the individual or entity in the United States.[32] OFAC issues notification of the blocking order to U.S. financial institutions, directing them to block the assets of the designated parties. Notice of the designations is published in the Federal Register. OFAC also adds the individual or entity to its list of SDGTs, and posts a notice of these additions on the OFAC website. Once the designation is made public, U.S. financial institutions are required to check the names on the Treasury list to determine whether the financial services provider is administering accounts for any of the designated individuals or entities. If so, the financial institution is required to freeze any funds held in those accounts.[33] Furthermore, all transactions involving property in which any of the listed individuals and entities has any interest are prohibited without specific authorization from OFAC. Simply stated, persons in the United States are forbidden from doing any business with the SDGTs, isolating them from the U.S. financial system.

The Secretary of the Treasury also may block the property and interests in property of persons or entities during the pendency of an investigation. The USA PATRIOT Act amended IEEPA, 50 U.S.C. §1702, to explicitly authorize blocking actions 'during the pendency of an investigation.'[34] Finally, rules and regulations governing the blocking actions have been promulgated by OFAC.[35]

Licensing

Not all transactions with an SDGT are banned or are criminal. E.O. 13224 §7 confers on the Secretary of the Treasury the authority to promulgate rules and regulations to carry out the purposes of the Order.[36] However, the Secretary may re-delegate this authority to other officers and agencies of the U.S. government.[37] Pursuant to a delegation of authority from the Secretary of the Treasury, OFAC has promulgated general regulations governing the global terrorism sanctions program. These regulations authorize OFAC to issue both 'general' and 'specific' licenses permitting certain types of transactions otherwise subject to the prohibitions contained in E.O. 13224.[38] The purpose of issuing a license is to ameliorate the harsh effects of OFAC blocking actions, which freeze funds and prohibit transactions with designated persons.

OFAC has issued several general licenses authorizing transactions in property in which HAMAS has an interest.[39] In October 2001, HAMAS was designated an SDGT, resulting in the blocking of any property and interests in property of HAMAS. These restrictions prohibit U.S. persons from engaging in any transactions in property or interests in property of HAMAS. After parliamentary elections in the West Bank and Gaza, HAMAS members formed the majority party within the Palestinian Legislative Council. As a result of these elections, OFAC determined that HAMAS has a property interest in the transactions of the Palestinian Authority. Accordingly, pursuant to E.O. 13324 and relevant regulations, U.S. persons are prohibited from engaging in transactions with the Palestinian Authority unless authorized by OFAC. Consistent with U.S. foreign policy, OFAC issued seven general licenses authorizing U.S. persons to engage in certain transactions in which the Palestinian Authority may have an interest. One of those general licenses authorized in-kind donations of medicine by U.S. non-governmental organizations to the Palestinian Authority Ministry of Health, provided that such donations were strictly for distribution in the West Bank or Gaza and not intended for resale. OFAC expanded this license to all U.S. non-governmental organizations to make donations to the Ministry of Health of medical services and medical devices, which include medical supplies.[40] OFAC has also issued general licenses for the provision of legal services,[41] non-scheduled emergency medical services,[42] transactions related to telecommunications,[43] and transactions incident to the receipt or transmission of mail between U.S. persons and persons whose property or interests in property are blocked.[44]

OFAC regulations also permit a designated or blocked individual or entity to seek a 'specific license' to engage in any transaction involving blocked property.[45] A person seeking a specific license to engage in transactions otherwise prohibited by the Order must file an application for a license with the OFAC authorizing such transaction.[46] Granting an application for a specific license is discretionary with OFAC. In one reported case, OFAC exercised its discretion quite liberally, granting the Global Relief Foundation, Inc., a U.S.-based Islamic charity, licenses to access blocked funds to pay for legal fees, establishment of a legal defense fund, salaries, payroll taxes, health insurance, rent, utilities, and payment of other continuing expenses.[47] At the same time, the denial of a license is not final and a party may refile an application with OFAC at a later date.

De-Listing Process

Pursuant to a delegation of authority by the Secretary of the Treasury, OFAC has promulgated regulations to allow a person to seek 'administrative reconsideration' of a designation or blocking action.[48] A person may seek a review of his designation or blocking on two grounds. First, a blocked person may submit evidence establishing that an insufficient basis exists for the designation.[49] Second, a person may seek to have his designation rescinded, asserting that the circumstances resulting in the designation no longer apply.[50] In determining whether to remove the petitioner's name from the OFAC list on these latter grounds, the basic consideration is whether the petitioner has made a demonstrable break with the designated entity. To that end, the designated person might offer proof of his resignation from any position with the designated firm or organization or from any agency relationship with the listed entity, which would negate the basis for the designation.[51] For example, if a person was designated an SDGT because he served on the board of directors of an Islamic charity suspected of funneling money to terrorists, the designee might petition for de-listing claiming that he lacked knowledge that charitable donations were being used to finance terrorist activities and, upon learning of such activity, he resigned his position on the board of directors and severed all ties with the designated charity.

After receiving a removal petition, OFAC may seek clarifying, corroborating, or additional information from the petitioner and engage in other research and investigation to establish, or refute, petitioner's claim. Removals have nearly always been cases where the petitioner claimed that he was no longer engaged in the activity that qualified him for designation under the E.O.[52] An exchange of correspondence, additional fact-finding, and meetings usually occur before OFAC decides whether there is a basis for removal. Finally, after conducting its review of the request for reconsideration, regulations require OFAC to submit a written decision to the blocked person.[53]

One problem that banks face in following blocking orders is that many times those designated have common names that belong to multiple account holders. To resolve this problem, E.O. 13224 allows a party to challenge blocked funds on the basis of mistaken identity. When funds at a financial institution are blocked pursuant to E.O. 13224 and a party to the transaction believes the funds have been blocked due to mistaken identity, that party may request the release of the funds.[54] The party must submit a written request to OFAC to release the funds.[55] After a review of all applicable submissions, the Director of OFAC determines whether to release the funds.[56]

LEGAL CHALLENGES

Persons designated as SDGTs under E.O. 13224 have challenged their designations in federal court, seeking to 'unfreeze' any blocked assets, by alleging violations of the First, Fourth and Fifth Amendments of the Constitution, the Religious Freedom Restoration Act (RFRA), and the Administrative Procedure Act (APA). However, the courts have been extremely deferential to the U.S. Government, rejecting the legal arguments advanced by the plaintiffs and upholding the OFAC designations in almost every case. In short, the courts have not erected any serious legal hurdles to the designations and blocking orders issued pursuant to E.O. 13224.

The APA 'Arbitrary and Capricious' Standard

A person designated an SDGT bears a heavy burden to overturn his designation on the grounds of insufficient evidence. Under the APA, an agency's actions may be set aside only if deemed 'arbitrary, capricious, an abuse of discretion, or otherwise not in accordance with law.'[57] The court does not undertake its own fact-finding. Instead, the court must review the administrative record as assembled by the agency to determine whether the agency's decision was supported by a rational basis.[58] The review is highly deferential to the agency. Therefore, if OFAC's blocking actions were not arbitrary and capricious and were supported by a rational basis, the designations must be affirmed.[59]

In *Holy Land Foundation for Relief and Development v. Ashcroft*, the D.C. Circuit Court of Appeals affirmed the district court's ruling that OFAC's determination that the Holy Land Foundation for Relief and Development (HLF), a purported Islamic charity which acts for or on behalf of HAMAS, was supported by substantial evidence in the administrative record and was not arbitrary and capricious.[60] In December 2001, OFAC designated HLF as a specially designated terrorist (SDT)[61] and SDGT and blocked all of its assets pursuant to E.O. 12947, E.O. 13224 and the IEEPA.[62] The Treasury Department contended that HLF, a non-profit corporation organized in 1989, with headquarters in Richardson, Texas, was the principal fund-raiser for HAMAS in the United States.[63] Specifically, the government alleged that between 1992 and 1999 HLF contributed approximately $1.4 million to eight HAMAS-controlled charity committees, and between 1992 and 2001 HLF gave approximately $5 million to seven other HAMAS-controlled charitable organizations.[64] Further, Treasury maintained that HLF funds were used by HAMAS to support schools that encourage children to become suicide bombers and to recruit suicide bombers by offering financial support to their surviving family members.[65] HLF denied the allegations and argued that the blocking order violates the APA, as well as the First, Fourth and Fifth Amendments of the Constitution, and the RFRA.[66]

The district court found that the administrative record contained evidence that

> (1) HLF has had financial connections to Hamas since its creation in 1989; (2) HLF leaders have been actively involved in various meetings with Hamas leaders; (3) HLF funds Hamas-controlled charitable organizations; (4) HLF provides financial support to the orphans and families of Hamas martyrs and prisoners; (5) HLF's Jerusalem office acted on behalf of Hamas; and (6) FBI informants reliably reported that HLF funds Hamas.[67]

The D.C. Circuit Court of Appeals affirmed, stating that the 'Treasury's decision to designate HLF as an SDGT was based on ample evidence in a massive administrative record.'[68]

In *Islamic American Relief Agency v. Unidentified FBI Agents*, the U.S. District Court for the District of Columbia rejected a similar legal challenge.[69] The Islamic American Relief Agency (IARA) challenged OFAC's designation of it as an SDGT and the blocking of its accounts, funds and assets in the United States. OFAC maintained that IARA was formerly affiliated with the precursor to al Qaeda, Maktab Al-Khidamat (MAK), which was co-founded and financed by Osama bin Laden.[70] Information available to Treasury revealed that the overseas branches of IARA provided hundreds of thousands of dollars to bin Laden in 1999.[71] Finally, as early as 2003, information to the U.S. showed that IARA was responsible for moving funds to the Palestinian territories for use in terrorist attacks by HAMAS.[72]

IARA claimed that the administrative record lacked any evidence demonstrating that it had funded terrorist activities or that it knowingly interacted with known terrorists or terrorist organizations prior to its designation as an SDGT.[73] The court observed that the arbitrary and capricious standard is highly deferential to the agency. 'If the agency's reasons and policy choices . . . conform to "certain minimal standards of rationality" . . . the [decision] is reasonable and must be upheld.'[74] While recognizing that the plaintiff was disadvantaged because it was unable to review and analyze the entire administrative record, but rather was limited to those portions that are not classified, the court held that upon careful review of the entire record, OFAC's decision to block IARA's assets was not arbitrary and capricious but was supported by substantial evidence in the record.[75] Such a deferential standard makes it difficult for plaintiffs to challenge designations.

Fifth Amendment Due Process Concerns

Pre-deprivation procedures

The Executive Order specifically provides for designation and blocking of assets in the absence of prior notice and a hearing. The Order states:

> [B]ecause of the ability to transfer funds or assets instantaneously, prior notice to such persons of measures to be taken pursuant to this order would render these measures ineffectual . . . [F]or these measures to be effective in addressing the national emergency declared in this order, there need be no prior notice of a listing or determination made pursuant to this order.[76]

OFAC blocking orders have been challenged on the grounds that, in the absence of pre-designation notice and a hearing, the blocking actions violate due process. However, the courts have uniformly rejected plaintiffs' due process claims.

The Due Process Clause of the Fifth Amendment guarantees that '[n]o person shall . . . be deprived of life, liberty, or property, without due process of law.'[77] The due process clause generally requires the government to afford notice and a meaningful opportunity to be heard before depriving a person of his property.[78] The requirement of notice and a hearing is not meant to protect persons from deprivation, but from the mistaken or unjustified deprivation of life, liberty, or property.[79] The U.S. Supreme Court has noted: 'The purpose of this requirement is not only to ensure abstract fair play to the individual. Its purpose, more particularly, is to protect his use and possession of property from arbitrary encroachment– to minimize substantively unfair or mistaken deprivations of property.'[80] However, when exigent circumstances are present and the government demonstrates a 'pressing need for prompt action,' postponement of notice and a hearing until after the seizure does not deny due process.[81] In *Calero-Toledo v. Pearson Yacht Leasing Co.*, the Supreme Court outlined a three-part test for determining whether pre-deprivation notice and a hearing are required.[82] Immediate seizure is appropriate if (1) 'the seizure has been directly necessary to secure an important governmental or general public interest;' (2) 'there has been a special need for very prompt action;' and (3) 'the State has kept strict control over its monopoly of legitimate force: the person initiating the seizure has been a government official responsible for determining, under the standards of a narrowly drawn statute, that it was necessary and justified in the particular instance.'[83]

In *Holy Land Foundation for Relief and Development v. Ashcroft,* HLF argued that its designation as an SDT and SDGT, resulting in the blocking of its assets, violated its procedural due process rights.[84] The court dismissed plaintiff's due process challenge, finding that the *Calero-Toledo* standard had been satisfied. First, the court found that the OFAC designation and blocking order advanced an important government interest by combating terrorism and cutting off its funding.[85] Second, prompt action by the Government was necessary to prevent transfer of the funds subject to the blocking order. The court properly observed that '[m]oney is fungible, and any delay or pre-blocking notice would afford a designated entity the opportunity to transfer, spend, or conceal its assets, thereby making the IEEPA sanctions program virtually meaningless.'[86] Third and finally, the court posited that 'government officials, and not private parties, initiated the blocking action. . . [p]ursuant to the IEEPA and two Executive Orders that specifically authorized such action in limited circumstances.'[87]

In *Islamic American Relief Agency v. Unidentified FBI Agents,* the court once again rejected the argument that due process entitled plaintiff notice and a hearing prior to OFAC issuing a blocking order by applying the three-part test enunciated in *Calero-Toledo.* [88] The court further dismissed IARA's reliance on *National Council of Resistance of Iran (NCRI) v. Department of State,*[89] where the District of Columbia Circuit Court held that notice and a hearing must be afforded prior to designating an entity as a 'foreign terrorist organization' under the Anti-Terrorism and Effective Death Penalty Act (AEDPA). The *IARA* court distinguished *NCRI*, finding that it does not control cases where the designation was pursuant to IEEPA and action under the statute flows from a Presidentially declared national emergency.[90] The court reasoned that *NCRI* did 'not foreclose the possibility [that the government], in an appropriate case, [could] demonstrat[e] the necessity of withholding all notice and all opportunity to present evidence until the designation [was] already made.'[91] Ultimately, the *IARA* court found that protecting the public from a terrorist attack and preventing the transfer of assets subject to the blocking order constituted extraordinary circumstances, implicating important national security and foreign policy goals, and justifying immediate blocking of plaintiff's property.[92]

In *Global Relief Foundation, Inc. v. O'Neill*, the court reached the same result, dismissing plaintiff's due process challenge.[93] The Global Relief Foundation (GRF) began operating in 1992 as a non-profit corporation chartered and headquartered in Illinois. According to the Treasury Department, GRF is the largest U.S.-based Islamic charitable organization, raising over $3 million annually.[94] OFAC maintained that GRF acted 'for or on behalf of' terrorist organizations, including al Qaeda. In rejecting GRF's constitutional challenge, the court reasoned that, due to the exigencies of national security and foreign policy considerations, the Executive Branch historically has not provided pre-deprivation notice under the IEEPA sanctions programs.[95] 'Because of the Executive's need for speed in these matters, and the need to prevent the flight of assets and destruction of records, the President and his designees cannot provide pre-deprivation notice under these circumstances.'[96] According to the court, pre-deprivation notice would afford GRF an opportunity to remove assets out of the United States, which would be antithetical to the objectives of the IEEPA sanctions programs.[97]

Denial of access to classified information

The IEEPA expressly authorizes *ex parte* and *in camera* review of classified information in 'any judicial review of a determination made under this section [that] . . . was based on classified information.'[98] Plaintiffs have challenged OFAC designations and blocking orders claiming that disclosure of classified information only to the court *ex parte* and *in camera* violates due process. The courts have been uniformly unsympathetic to plaintiffs' plight, dismissing their due process claims. In *Holy Land Foundation for Relief and Development v. Ashcroft*, the D.C. Circuit held that denying HLF access to classified evidence did not violate due process.[99] A designation, the court stated, may be based on a broad range of evidence, including classified information to which the plaintiff has not had access.[100]

In support of its holding, the D.C. Circuit relied on its earlier ruling in *People's Mojahedin Organization of Iran v. Department of State*, where the court rejected a claim that use of classified information disclosed only to the court *ex parte* and *in camera* in the designation of a foreign terrorist organization under AEDPA offended due process.[101] The court justified withholding from plaintiffs classified information used in the designation of a foreign terrorist organization, emphasizing the primacy of the Executive in controlling and exercising responsibility over access to classified information and the Executive's 'compelling interest' in withholding national security information from suspected terrorists and other enemy aliens.[102] The *HLF* court found the reasoning in *People's Mojahedin Organization of Iran* equally applicable to a designation under E.O. 13224. According to the court, '[t]hat the designation comes under an Executive Order issued under a different statutory scheme makes no difference.'[103]

In *Global Relief Foundation, Inc. v. O'Neill*, the court reached the same conclusion, finding that GRF's due process rights were not violated because the designation was based on classified information.[104] The district court applied a balancing test, balancing the nature of the government's interest against the plaintiff's interest in challenging an erroneous deprivation of property. Deciding in favor of the government, the court stated that '[a]lthough Global Relief does have a substantial interest in being able to study and respond to the evidence against it, . . . the defendants ha[d] demonstrated a compelling state interest in national security which outweigh[ed] Global Relief's interest in this case.'[105]

The district court further rejected a related argument advanced by GRF. The court held that the Confrontation Clause of the Sixth Amendment, guaranteeing a defendant in a criminal prosecution the right to confront the witnesses against him, did not apply to IEEPA blocking actions. The Sixth Amendment is not applicable because GRF was not charged in a criminal prosecution or facing criminal sanctions.[106]

The Seventh Circuit affirmed the district court's rulings in GRF. The court observed that IEEPA authorizes the use of classified evidence that may be considered *ex parte* and *in camera* by the reviewing court. It further noted that *ex parte* and *in camera* review of classified information is not unprecedented and has been upheld by the courts. For example, *ex parte* consideration is common in criminal cases where the identity of the informant might otherwise be revealed,[107] and *ex parte* judicial review of classified information under the Foreign Intelligence Surveillance Act is constitutionally proper.[108] Finally, the court declared that '[t]he Constitution would indeed be a suicide pact if the only way to curtail enemies' access to assets were to reveal information that might cost lives.'[109]

Unconstitutional vagueness

Plaintiffs have realized limited success in challenging provisions of E.O. 13224 on constitutional vagueness grounds. A challenge to a statute on vagueness grounds requires the court to consider whether the statute is sufficiently clear so as not to cause persons of 'common intelligence . . . necessarily [to] guess at its meaning and [to] differ as to its application.'[110] A statute is unconstitutionally vague if it (1) fails to provide the kind of notice that will enable ordinary people to understand what conduct is prohibited; (2) authorizes and encourages arbitrary and discriminatory enforcement; or (3) has a chilling effect on activities protected by the First Amendment.[111]

In *Humanitarian Law Project v. United States Department of Treasury,* the plaintiffs raised numerous challenges to the E.O.[112] First, the Humanitarian Law Project (HLP) maintained that the E.O.'s ban on 'services' is unconstitutionally vague. HLP argued that the term 'services' was broadly defined under the Regulations, giving OFAC unfettered authority to designate a person or group as an SDGT.[113] The district court disagreed, finding that, while the Regulations' definition of 'services' may not be exact, it does not permit subjective standards of enforcement. The court stated that 'the word "services" is, by and large, a word of common understanding and one that could not be used for selective or subjective enforcement.'[114]

Second, HLP claimed that the E.O.'s ban on 'services' is unconstitutionally overbroad because it punishes a substantial amount of protected free speech.[115] The court found this argument unpersuasive as well. The E.O.'s ban on 'services,' the court stated, 'is content-neutral and serves the legitimate purpose of deterring groups and individuals from providing services to foreign terrorist organizations.'[116] Furthermore, the court found that the E.O.'s application to protected speech is not substantial relative to the scope of its plainly legitimate applications.[117]

Next, HLP challenged the term 'specially designated global terrorist,' as used in both the E.O. and the OFAC regulations.[118] HLP argued that neither the E.O. nor the Regulations define the term or set criteria for designating an individual or group as a 'specially designated global terrorist.'[119] The district court found HLP's challenge to the E.O.'s use of the term 'specially designated global terrorist' lacked merit.[120] The court stated that HLP's argument overlooked the limited circumstances under which the IEEPA affords the Executive the power to impose economic sanctions. Before the Executive may take any action under the IEEPA, he or she must first declare a national emergency. Furthermore, any action taken by the Executive must relate to that identified emergency.[121] The court stated that the E.O. provides adequate criteria for designating an individual or group as an SDGT.[122] For example, the Secretary of State, in consultation with the Secretary of the Treasury and the Attorney General, may designate a person as an SDGT if that person has committed, or poses a significant risk of committing, acts of terrorism that 'threaten the security of United States nationals or national security, foreign policy, or [the] economy of the United States.'[123] Additionally, the Secretary of the Treasury may designate a person as an SDGT if that person is 'owned or controlled by, or . . . act[s] for or on behalf of' other SDGTs.[124] Finally, a person may be designated as an SDGT if the Secretary of the Treasury determines that the person has assisted in, has sponsored, or 'has provided "financial, material, or technological support for, or financial or other services to or in support of," acts of terrorism or other SDGTs.'[125] The criteria set forth in the E.O. and Regulations ensures that the designating authorities are not afforded 'unfettered discretion' in designating individuals or groups as SDGTs.[126] Therefore, the court rejected HLP's constitutional challenge to the term 'specially designated global terrorist.'

HLP, however, was successful in challenging one other provision of the E.O. The E.O. authorizes the Secretary of the Treasury to designate an individual or group if the secretary finds the given person to be 'otherwise associated with' an SDGT.[127] HLP argued that this provision was unconstitutionally vague because it contains no identifiable criteria for designating individuals and groups for being 'otherwise associated with' an SDGT.[128] The court concurred, finding that the term 'otherwise associated with' is not susceptible to a clear meaning.[129] Moreover, the provision is not defined in the E.O. and contains no definable criteria for designating individuals and groups as SDGTs. The term is therefore vulnerable to subjective interpretation, giving the Government unfettered discretion in enforcing it. Thus, the court held the 'otherwise associated with' provision is unconstitutionally vague on its face.[130]

The court also found that the 'otherwise associated with' provision is unconstitutionally overbroad because it punishes mere association with an SDGT. The court posited: '[T]he First Amendment protects a citizen's right to associate with a political organization; even if that association includes ties with groups that advocate illegal conduct or engage in illegal acts, the power of the Government to penalize association is narrowly circumscribed.'[131] Guilt by association is an impermissible basis upon which to limit or deny a person's First Amendment rights. The court was particularly concerned by the absence of any language in the provision purporting to limit its application to those instances of association involving activity that furthers or advances an organization's illegal goals.[132] Thus, the court barred the Government from enforcing E.O. 13224, §1(d)(ii), against any person or entity by blocking its assets or subjecting it to designation as an SDGT for being 'otherwise associated with' a terrorist or terrorist organization.[133]

In response to the ruling in *Humanitarian Law Project,* OFAC amended the regulations implementing E.O. 13224. A new section 594.316 was added to subpart C, defining a person 'otherwise associated with.' Under the new provision, the term 'to be otherwise associated with' means:

> (a) To own or control; or
> (b) To attempt, or to conspire with one or more persons, to act for or on behalf of or to provide financial, material, or technological support, or financial or other services, to persons whose property and interests in property are blocked pursuant to section 594.201(a)(1), (a)(2) or (a)(4)(i).[134]

Whether the new regulation defining the term 'otherwise associated with' would withstand a constitutional challenge on void for vagueness grounds was quickly decided by the court.

In *Humanitarian Law Project v. U.S. Department of Treasury*, the district court granted the Government's motion for reconsideration, holding that the new regulation (31 C.F.R. §594.316) defining 'otherwise associated with' remedied the constitutional defects of E.O. §1(d)(ii).[135] The court stated that it had already found that the Secretary's authority to designate a person who is 'owned or controlled by, or . . . act[s] for or on behalf of' other SDGTs (E.O. §1(c)), or someone who has provided 'financial, material, or technological support for, or financial or other services to or in support of' acts of terrorism or other SDGTs (E.O. §1(d)(i)), was not vague and did not violate Fifth Amendment due process requirements.[136] Additionally, the meaning of the phrase 'to attempt, or to conspire,' the court stated, is 'sufficiently clear so as not to cause persons "of common intelligence . . . necessarily [to] guess at its meaning and [to] differ as to its application." '[137] Thus, 'to attempt, or to conspire' is not unconstitutionally vague.

The court also held that the phrase 'to attempt, or to conspire' is not unconstitutionally broad. The court reasoned that 'to attempt, or to conspire' does not punish mere association or a substantial amount of protected conduct.[138] Thus, the injunction issued against enforcement of E.O. 13224, §1(d)(ii), prohibiting OFAC from designating an individual or group under the 'otherwise associated with' provision, was no longer warranted and was lifted by the court.[139]

Fifth Amendment Takings Clause

Blocking orders issued pursuant to E.O. 13224 have been attacked as an uncompensated taking, in violation of the Takings Clause of the Fifth Amendment.[140] The courts have consistently rejected these claims, reasoning that the blocking actions under E.O. 13224 are temporary deprivations that do not vest the assets in the Government.[141] Therefore, the blocking of terrorist-related funds does not, as a matter of law, constitute takings within the meaning of the Fifth Amendment. However, at least one court left open the possibility of revisiting the matter on the basis of a long-term blocking order. In the *Holy Land Foundation for Relief and Development v. Ashcroft*, the court stated: 'Plaintiff may . . . some day have a credible argument that the long-term blocking order has ripened into a vesting of property in the United States.'[142] However, because HLF's assets had only been blocked for eight months, the court found it premature to determine that the temporary deprivation is equivalent to vesting.[143]

In *Islamic American Relief Agency v. Unidentified Agents,* the court also dismissed plaintiff's argument that the blocking of its assets violated the Takings Clause of the Fifth Amendment. The district court held that it lacked subject matter jurisdiction over the plaintiff's Fifth Amendment claim, stating that the matter should have been 'brought before the United States Court of Federal Claims pursuant to the Tucker Act, 28 U.S.C. §1491.'[144] Moreover, agreeing with the ruling in the *Holy Land Foundation for Relief and Development,* the court held that a blocking order under E.O. 13224 is not, as a matter of law, a takings within the meaning of the Fifth Amendment.[145]

First Amendment Claims

The federal courts have been unreceptive to plaintiffs' claims that OFAC designations and blocking orders violate their First Amendment rights to freedom of association and speech. The Supreme Court has recognized that the act of contributing money to an organization implicates the right of freedom of association.[146] The Court has also recognized that regulation of association is constitutional if it was closely drawn to further a sufficiently important government interest.[147] In *United States v. Al-Arian,* the district court upheld the constitutionality of the OFAC designation.[148] The court concluded that 'stopping the spread of terrorism is not just a sufficiently important governmental interest, but is a compelling governmental interest.'[149] The court further found that combating the spread of global terrorism by preventing the financing and support of foreign terrorist organizations is closely drawn to further this interest.[150]

In *Holy Land Foundation for Relief and Development v. Ashcroft,* HLF asserted that the Government violated its First Amendment right to freedom of speech by prohibiting it from making any humanitarian donations.[151] The court applied a heightened intermediate scrutiny standard to whether a prohibition on fund-raising and contribution is constitutional under the First Amendment. In denying HLF's free speech challenge to the E.O., the court applied a four-part test set forth by the United States

Supreme Court in *United States v. O'Brien* for determining whether the Government's restriction passes intermediate scrutiny.[152] Under the intermediate scrutiny standard, the government restriction is lawful if

> (1) it is within the constitutional power of the Government; (2) it furthers an important or substantial governmental interest; (3) the governmental interest is unrelated to the suppression of free expression; and (4) the incidental restriction on alleged First Amendment freedoms is no greater than is essential to the furtherance of that interest.[153]

The HLF court found that the E.O. and blocking order clearly meet these requirements. First, the President was authorized to issue the Executive Order pursuant to the IEEPA. Moreover, the IEEPA and the E.O. grant OFAC the authority to designate HLF and designate its assets.[154] Second, the E.O. and OFAC's actions promote an important and substantial government interest of preventing the financing of terrorism.[155] Third, the Government's interest in preventing terrorist attacks is unrelated to suppressing free speech. The court posited: '[T]he Government has merely restricted HLF's ability to provide financial support to Hamas. It has not restricted HLF's ability to express its viewpoints, even if these views include endorsement of Hamas.'[156] Fourth and finally, the incidental restriction is no greater than necessary to advance the Government's counter-terrorist financing interest. [157] 'Money is fungible, and the Government has no other, narrower, means of ensuring that even charitable contributions to a terrorist organization are actually used for legitimate purposes.'[158] Accordingly, the court held that the Government's restriction was 'narrowly enough tailored to only further its interest in stopping the flow of American dollars to Hamas.'[159]

The D.C. Circuit affirmed the district court's rulings, finding that neither HLF's First Amendment right of free speech or freedom of association had been violated. The court posited: '[T]here is no First Amendment right nor any other constitutional right to support terrorists.'[160] Other courts that have considered similar First Amendment challenges to OFAC designations and blocking orders have reached the same result.[161]

Fourth Amendment Claims

The courts have consistently rejected plaintiffs' argument that OFAC blocking actions constitute an unreasonable seizure under the Fourth Amendment. The Fourth Amendment provides:

> The right of the people to be secure in their persons, houses, papers, and effects, against unreasonable searches and seizures, shall not be violated, and no

> warrants shall issue, but upon probable cause, supported by oath or affirmation, and particularly describing the place to be searched, and the persons or things to be seized.[162]

In *Holy Land Foundation for Relief and Development v. Ashcroft,* the court held that OFAC's blocking of the Holy Land Foundation's assets does not constitute a seizure and therefore does not create a cognizable claim under the Fourth Amendment.[163] In *Islamic American Relief Agency v. Unidentified FBI Agents*, the court reached the same conclusion, dismissing the plaintiff's Fourth Amendment claim.[164]

Religious Freedom Restoration Act

Claims that OFAC designations and blocking orders substantially burden the exercise of religion in violation of the Religious Freedom and Restoration Act (RFRA) have been uniformly dismissed by the court.[165] RFRA prevents the Government from placing a 'substantial burden' on the exercise of religion 'even if the burden results from a rule of general applicability,' unless the Government demonstrates a 'compelling government interest' and that it has used the 'least restrictive means' of furthering that interest.[166] 'In passing RFRA, Congress expressed its purpose as being "to restore the compelling interest test . . . and to guarantee its application in all cases where free exercise of religion is substantially burdened." '[167]

In the *Holy Land Foundation for Relief and Development v. Ashcroft*, the D.C. Circuit held that HLF's activities do not fall within the RFRA.[168] The court reasoned that any OFAC designation and blocking order imposed a burden on HLF's ability to raise and distribute funds to finance HAMAS, a designated terrorist organization, not to practice its religion. The court stated:

> No one on behalf of Holy Land Foundation has forwarded the proposition that the fomenting and spread of terrorism is mandated by the religion of Islam. . . . Acting against the funding of terrorism does not violate the free exercise rights protected by RFRA and the First Amendment. There is no free exercise right to fund terrorists.[169]

The court therefore denied HLF's challenge to OFAC's designation and blocking order based on a violation of RFRA. [170]

Blocking Property in which any Foreign Country or National has 'Any Interest'

IEEPA authorizes blocking all property and interests in property in which any foreign person has an interest.[171] In *Global Relief Foundation v. O'Neill*,

GRF challenged OFAC's blocking order, arguing that the IEEPA does not apply to corporations that hold charters issued within the United States.[172] 'The argument is straightforward: a U.S. corporation is a U.S. citizen; the corporation owns all of its property (including its bank accounts); this property therefore cannot be "property in which any foreign country or a national thereof has any interest" for the purpose of §1702(a)(1)(B).'[173] Furthermore, GRF maintained that no foreign person or group, including any foreign terrorist organization, held any 'legal' interest in GRF's property.

The Seventh Circuit rejected GRF's interpretation of the statute, reasoning that '[t]he function of the IEEPA strongly suggests that beneficial rather than legal interests matter.'[174] The objective of the statute is to 'give the President the means to control assets that could be used by enemy aliens.'[175] The focus therefore must be on the nature of the property, how assets could be controlled and used, rather than on legal ownership. The court stated that 'the fact that GRF as a U.S. corporation owns all of its assets does not mean that the assets are free of any foreign national's interest.'[176] The court reasoned:

> Consider for a moment what would happen if Osama bin Laden put all of his assets into a trust, under Illinois law, administered by a national bank. If the trust instrument directed the trustee to make the funds available for purchases of weapons to be used by al Qaeda, then foreign enemies of the United States would have an 'interest' in these funds even though legal ownership would be vested in the bank. The situation is the same if al Qaeda incorporated a subsidiary in Delaware and transferred all of its funds to that corporation . . . What sense could it make to treat al Qaeda's funds as open to seizure if administered by a German bank but not if administered by a Delaware corporation under terrorist control?[177]

Ultimately, the Seventh Circuit held that because GRF conducts its operations outside the United States, 'the funds are applied for the benefit of non-citizens and thus are covered by §1702(a)(1)(B).'[178]

In *Holy Land Foundation for Relief and Development v. Ashcroft*, HLF claimed that OFAC exceeded its authority under the IEEPA.[179] HLF contended that the 'interest' referred to in 50 U.S.C. §1702(a)(1)(B) must constitute a 'legally enforceable interest.'[180] Accordingly, HLF reasoned that OFAC exceeded its statutory authority because it could not establish that HAMAS had any such interest in its property.[181] The district court disagreed, holding that OFAC need only determine that HAMAS has 'any interest' in HLF's property.[182]

The D.C. Circuit affirmed the district court's ruling, agreeing with the Seventh Circuit's holding in *Global Relief Foundation*. The D.C. Circuit observed:

> The plain text of the statute belies HLF's contention because it authorizes the blocking of property in which the designated foreign national or country has 'any interest.' 50 U.S.C. §1702(a)(1)(B). The language therefore imposes no limit on the scope of the interest, and OFAC has defined this statutory term . . . to mean, 'an interest of any nature whatsoever, direct or indirect.' 31 C.F.R. §500.311–12.[183]

Thus, the 'interest' need not be a legally enforceable one in order to fall within the scope of §1702. The court stated that OFAC need only determine that HAMAS had an interest (legal or beneficial) in HLF's property, and the record provided substantial evidence to support that conclusion.

PROGRESS IN THE WAR ON TERRORIST FINANCING

The Treasury Department has a mixed record on the utilization of its powers authorized by E.O. 13224 to prevent the financing of terrorism. While immediately following the issuance of the Order the Treasury Department acted with a heightened sense of urgency to designate suspected terrorists, terrorist groups and their supporters as SDGTs and block their assets, the number of blocking orders has since greatly diminished. In 2002, the Treasury Department submitted the *2001 Terrorist Assets Annual Report* to Congress on its efforts to cut off funding to al Qaeda and other global terrorist organizations. The report revealed that in a period of less than four months following the issuance of E.O. 13224 (September 23 to December 31, 2001) 164 individuals, entities and organizations were designated as SDGTs.[184] Continuing progress was reflected in the Treasury Department's *2002 Terrorist Assets Annual Report* to Congress. The 2002 Report indicated that an additional 87 individuals and entities had been designated as SDGTs, bringing the cumulative total to 251.[185] *The 2003 Terrorist Assets Report* highlighted sustained progress in shutting down the pipelines of terrorist funding. According to the Treasury Department, an additional 94 individuals and groups were designated in 2003, bringing the total number of SDGTs to 345.[186] The U.S. and its international partners had also seized or frozen nearly $200 million in terrorist-related assets.[187]

The SDGT designations included individuals ranging from organizational leaders, key lieutenants and terrorist operatives to financiers of al Qaeda.[188] The designees also included members of terrorist organizations not part of the al Qaeda network such as the Shining Path, the Real IRA, Liberation Tigers of Tamil Eelam (LTTE), HAMAS, Hizballah, and ETA, among others. All Foreign Terrorist Organizations (FTOs) previously designated as such by the U.S. Department of State, as well as 15 other terrorist organizations, were listed.[189] The designations further included over 100 companies, charitable organizations, and entities that supported and financed terrorism.[190] Pursuant to E.O. 13224, all assets of these terrorist sympathizers subject to U.S. jurisdiction were frozen and transactions by U.S. persons with the designees were prohibited. Further, approximately $200 million in terrorist assets were frozen worldwide in over 500 accounts. [191] Most importantly, however, the Treasury Department designations and freeze orders disrupted the ability of al Qaeda and affiliated terror groups to raise terror funds and transfer the money globally through the U.S. financial system.

Of particular significance were the designations of corrupt Islamic charities with ties to al Qaeda. Over a dozen foreign charities affiliated with al Qaeda and other jihadist terror groups were designated and two prominent U.S.-based charities with purported ties to Osama bin Laden and the Taliban were shut down.[192] Some of these charities were founded with the express purpose of financing terrorist activities. Others were infiltrated by terrorist operatives and supporters and corrupted from within. Three months after the September 11, 2001 attacks, the U.S. Government froze the assets of the Holy Land Foundation for Relief and Development (HLF). Based in Richardson, Texas, where it disguised itself as a charity, HLF provided millions of dollars of financial and logistical support to HAMAS, the militant Palestinian group officially designated as a foreign terrorist organization by the U.S. government.[193] HLF describes itself as 'the largest Muslim charity in the United States.'[194] In the year 2000, HLF raised over $13 million in the U.S. alone. Among other things, HLF was allegedly responsible for sending millions of dollars of HLF charitable donations to 'zakat' committees controlled by HAMAS to support madrasas, radical Islamist schools that encourage children to become suicide bombers, and provide financial assistance to the families of suicide bombers, thus rewarding past acts of terrorism and encouraging future suicide bombings and terrorist activities.[195]

The U.S. Department of Justice subsequently filed a multi-count criminal indictment in the Northern District of Texas against HLF and several of its officers.[196] The indictment charged HLF and its senior leadership with providing material support to a foreign terrorist organization (HAMAS), tax evasion, and money laundering. The indictment alleged that once the nation's largest Islamic charity, HLF, funneled at least $12 million to members of HAMAS.[197]

In December 2001, OFAC utilized its authority to block suspect assets 'during the pendency of an investigation'[198] of the Global Relief Foundation (GRF) and the Benevolence International Foundation (BIF), two Islamic charities with branches in the United States.[199] GRF began operating in 1992 as a domestic, non-profit corporation chartered and headquartered in the United States. It operated in approximately 25 foreign countries, including Afghanistan, Albania, Bosnia, Iraq, Kosovo, Lebanon, Pakistan, Palestine (West Bank and Gaza), Russia (Chechnya and Ingushetia), Somalia and Syria.[200] By 2000, GRF reported collecting nearly $3.7 million in charitable donations in the United States. Over 90 percent of its donations were sent overseas, where some of the funds allegedly provided financial support for and assistance to Osama bin Laden, al Qaeda, and other known terrorist groups.[201]

BIF, a Chicago-based charity, had branches in at least 20 foreign countries, including Afghanistan, Azerbaijan, Bangladesh, Bosnia and Herzegovina, Canada, Chechnya, Croatia, Georgia, the Netherlands, Pakistan, Russian Federation, Saudi Arabia, Sudan, Tajikistan, the United Kingdom and Yemen, as well as Daghestan, the Gaza Strip, and Ingushetia. In the late 1980s, Lajnat al-Bir al-Islamiah (LBI), the precursor to BIF, was founded in Saudi Arabia and Pakistan to provide financial and operational support to mujahedeen in Afghanistan.[202] LBI was affiliated with Maktab Al-Khidamat (MAK), the precursor organization to al Qaeda. In the early 1990s, LBI began operation under the name of BIF.[203] In 1993, BIF was incorporated in the United States, where it provided financial support to members of al Qaeda fighting in Afghanistan, Sudan, Bosnia-Herzegovina and Chechnya.[204] In 2003, Enaam Arnaout, BIF's Executive Director, pleaded guilty to federal criminal racketeering conspiracy, admitting that he concealed from donors that he fraudulently diverted more than $300,000 from the charity's humanitarian purposes to support Muslim fighters in Bosnia-Herzegovina and Chechnya.[205] Arnaout was sentenced to 136 months in prison.[206]

In January 2002, the Treasury Department designated the Afghan Support Committee (ASC), an Islamic charity linked to funding al Qaeda. Headquartered in Afghanistan, the ASC solicited donations from local charities in Arab countries. According to the Treasury Department, the ASC falsely claimed that the funds collected were for widows and orphans. In fact, the financial chief of the ASC served as a key fund-raiser for Osama bin Laden, who turned over funds collected by the ASC to al Qaeda operatives.[207] The Pakistani and Afghan branches of the Revival of Islamic Heritage Society (RIHS), a Kuwaiti-based charity, were designated as well.[208] The Treasury Department alleged that the Pakistan office defrauded RIHS donors to fund terrorism. In order to obtain additional funds from the Kuwait RIHS headquarters, the RIHS Pakistan office padded the number of orphans it claimed to care for by providing fictitious names or names of orphans who had died.[209] Funds sent for the purpose of caring for the non-existent orphans were illegally diverted to fund members of al Qaeda.

In March 2002, the United States and Saudi Arabia jointly designated the Bosnia-Herzegovina and Somalia branches of Al-Haramain Islamic Foundation (Al-Haramain). A Saudi-based charity with branch offices in as many as 49 countries around the world, Al-Haramain raised approximately \$30 million a year in donations. The Bosnia-Herzegovina and Somalia branches were directly implicated in providing financial support to al Qaeda and Al-Itihaad al-Islamiya (AIAI), an Islamist militant group in Somalia with ties to al Qaeda. AIAI had previously been designated an SDGT under E.O. 13224. The Al-Haramain Somalia branch allegedly funneled money to AIAI by disguising the funds as contributions for an orphanage project and Islamic school and mosque construction.[210] At the same time, the Bosnia office of Al-Haramain was linked to Jemaah Islamiyah (JI), an al Qaeda-affiliated terrorist group operating in Southeast Asia, and to Osama bin Laden himself. JI was designated an SDGT by the Treasury Department for its role in the October 2002 terrorist bombings of a holiday resort discotheque on the island of Bali, Indonesia, that killed over 190 innocent civilians and wounded hundreds of others.[211] Since the initial designation of the Bosnia-Herzegovina and Somalia branches of Al-Haramain in March 2002, the Treasury Department has designated Al-Haramain's branches in Afghanistan, Albania, Bangladesh, Comoros Islands, Ethiopia, Indonesia, Kenya, the Netherlands, Pakistan, and Tanzania, as well as the U.S. branch in Ashland, Oregon, and issued blocking orders against their assets.[212]

During the first two and a half years following the issuance of E.O. 13224, blocking orders were issued against several other corrupt charities, including the Al Aqsa Foundation, a major financier of the HAMAS terrorist organization, and Stichting Benevolence International Nederland, BIF's branch in the Netherlands.[213] Finally, several al Qaeda-affiliated terrorist organizations were added to the Treasury list during this period as well, including the Tunisian Combat Group, Moroccan Islamic Combatant Group (GICM), Lashkar i Jhangvi, Eastern Turkistan Islamic Movement and Ansar al-Islam (AI).[214]

Unfortunately, over approximately the last three and one-half years there has been a sharp drop in both the number of individuals and entities added to the Treasury list of SDGTs and assets frozen or blocked. The *2004 Terrorist Assets Report* indicated that only 51 names were added to the list of SDGTs.[215] That number represented a substantial decline from 2003, when 94 individuals and groups were designated as SDGTs. *The 2005 Terrorist Assets Report* continued the dramatic downward trend. In 2005, only 30 individuals and entities were designated as SDGTs.[216] An examination of the OFAC List revealed that 42 persons were designated SDGTs in 2006.[217] And worse yet, a similar review showed that during 2007 only 20

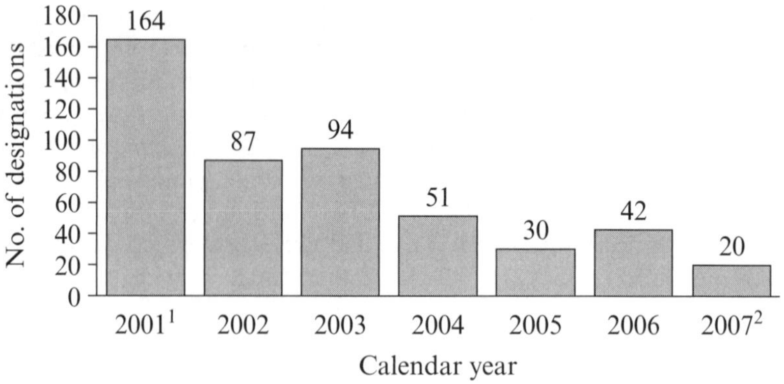

Notes:
1. September 23–December 31.
2. January 1–October 10.

Figure 8.1 Number of SDGT designations by year

persons were designated under E.O. 13224, for a cumulative total of 488 SDGTs.[218] Thus, during an approximate 27-month period, from September 23, 2001, to December 31, 2003, 345 persons were designated SDGTs. In contrast, over the past 46 months, from January 1, 2004, to December 31, 2007, only 143 names were added to OFAC's list of SDGTs. That number represents an average of approximately 39 designations per year over the last three years and ten months. Further analysis reveals that the Treasury Department designated more individuals (164) during the last three and a half months of 2001 (September 23 to December 31, 2001) than were designated during the past 46 months (January 1, 2004, to October 31, 2007), when only 143 individuals and entities were designated SDGTs (See figures 8.1 and 8.2.) Finally, the Treasury Department no longer publishes the amount of assets frozen pursuant to E.O. 13224, apparently because of the declining numbers.

The downward trend of SDGTs and frozen terrorist funds is particularly disturbing considering the universal recognition that al Qaeda has sufficient funds to launch another major terrorist attack on a scale even more deadly and destructive then what occurred on September 11, 2001. No credible person can suggest that the efforts to date to deprive al Qaeda of funding have in fact deprived the militant group of its ability to finance another major terrorist attack against the U.S. and its allies. In fact, just the opposite appears to be the case. In the 2007 National Intelligence Estimate (NIE) on 'The Terrorist Threat to the U.S. Homeland,' the National Intelligence Board, comprised of the heads of the 16 intelligence community agencies

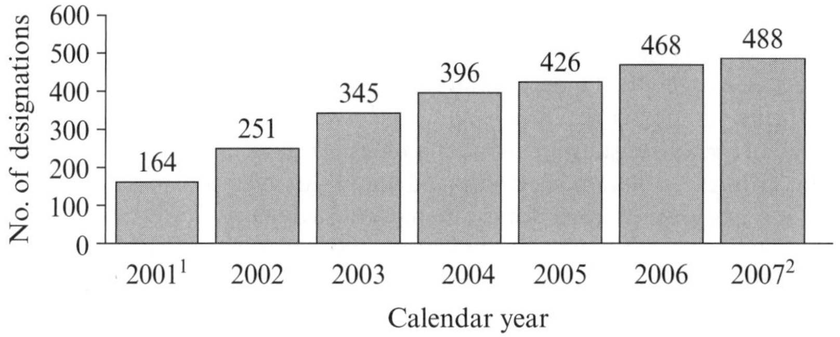

Notes:
1. September 23–December 31.
2. January 1–October 10.

Figure 8.2 Cumulative number of SDGT designations by year

and chaired by the Director of National Intelligence, concluded that the United States faces a persistent and evolving terrorist threat from Islamic terrorist groups and cells, especially al Qaeda.[219] More disturbing yet, the NIE found that al Qaeda has 'protected or regenerated key elements of its Homeland attack capability, including: a safe haven in the Pakistan Federally Administered Tribal Areas (FATA), operational lieutenants, and its top leadership.'[220] According to the NIE, al Qaeda continues to enhance its capabilities to attack the U.S. Homeland, focusing on prominent political, economic, and infrastructure targets with 'the goal of producing mass casualties, visually dramatic destruction, significant economic aftershocks, and/or fear among the U.S. population.'[221] Additionally, the NIE reported that al Qaeda continues to try to acquire and employ chemical, biological, radiological, or nuclear material and would not hesitate to use it against U.S. targets.[222] Thus, while the threat of an al Qaeda attack against the U.S. Homeland is growing, the number of designations and blocking orders to prevent the financing of such attacks has dramatically declined.

There is a direct nexus between al Qaeda's financial resources and its ability to reconstitute itself. According to the 9/11 Commission: 'The alliance with the Taliban provided al Qaeda a sanctuary in which to train and indoctrinate fighters and terrorists, import weapons, forge ties with other jihad groups and leaders, and plot and staff terrorist schemes.'[223] It has been estimated that between 10,000 and 20,000 terrorists underwent training in Bin Laden's training camps in Afghanistan prior to 9/11.[224] Similarly, al Qaeda's terrorist sanctuary in Wazeristan, Pakistan, has afforded the terror group a base of operations to recruit and train jihadists and plan and execute attacks on western targets. In fact, members of the terror cell responsible for the July 7, 2005 London bombings that killed over 52 commuters in the Underground and on a double-decker bus attended an al Qaeda training camp in Pakistan.[225] However, acquiring a terrorist safe haven requires substantial sums of money. Osama bin Laden reportedly paid Mullah Mohammed Omar and the Taliban approximately $10–20 million per year in return for a safe haven in Afghanistan,[226] and millions of dollars more to secure a safe haven in Sudan.[227] Bin Laden has likely paid tribal leaders millions of dollars for a secure base of operations in Wazeristan, Pakistan. Finally, the NIE report states that al Qaeda is committed to acquiring weapons of mass destruction (WMD) to employ against its enemies. Acquiring WMD also requires significant funding. Pre-9/11, bin Laden reportedly spent millions of dollars attempting to acquire highly enriched uranium to construct a WMD to use against the West.[228]

One terrorism expert has been critical of the United Nations designation process, questioning the will of the international community to make the economic sanctions regime against al Qaeda more than just a political statement.[229] It is maintained that the designation of individuals and entities has not kept pace with the rising tide of information about the al Qaeda terrorist network. Since 9/11 more than 4,000 people have been arrested or detained in more than 100 countries on the basis of their connections to al Qaeda.[230] However, only a few hundred individuals and even fewer entities associated with al Qaeda have been designated under either the U.N. or the Treasury Department list. In December 2003, the Saudi government published a list of its 26 most wanted 'terrorists' – most of whom have been subsequently killed– who were allegedly connected to a number of terrorist attacks inside the Kingdom, particularly the suicide bombings in May and November 2003. According to one source, at least 7 of the 26 terrorists trained in al Qaeda camps in Afghanistan.[231] However, none of the 26 terrorists was ever proposed for designation on either the U.N. or the Treasury list.[232] While directed at designations under various U.N. Security Council resolutions adopted post-9/11, those criticisms apply with equal force to designations under E.O. 13224.

The Treasury Department designated only 20 persons during 2007, while thousands of al Qaeda-affiliated terrorists are operating in over 60 countries around the world. During the summer of 2007 alone, dozens of individuals were arrested, charged, convicted or sentenced in connection with plotting major terrorist attacks in the United States, London, Glasgow, Copenhagen, Jakarta, Algiers, and other cities around the world. In July 2007, four men were found guilty of plotting to bomb London's public transport system in 2005, two weeks after a coordinated suicide bombing attack on the network killed 52 commuters.[233] In June 2007, three doctors were charged and three other persons detained in connection with failed car-bomb attacks in central London and Glasgow, Scotland.[234] That same month, Indonesian police arrested the most-wanted militant, Abu Dujana, who heads a military wing of the Southeast Asian terrorist group, Jemaah Islamiah, an al Qaeda-affiliated terrorist group, along with his military chief, Zarkasih.[235] In June 2007, a British court sentenced seven men to a total of 136 years in prison after they were convicted for being accomplices to an al Qaeda terrorist plot code-named 'Operation Rhyme,' targeting the New York Stock Exchange and the Citigroup headquarters along with the Washington, D.C. offices of the International Monetary Fund and the World Bank.[236] In May 2007, Algerian authorities arrested several individuals believed to be responsible for organizing a terrorist attack in Algiers, which killed 33 people and wounded 57. The defendants are members of a group called Al Qaeda in the Islamic Maghreb.[237]More recently, in early September 2007, Denmark's intelligence service arrested eight Islamic militants linked to leading al Qaeda figures for plotting an attack in Copenhagen involving explosives.[238] None of these individuals have been designated by the Treasury Department as SDGTs.

While it is difficult to explain the dramatic decrease in the number of designations of SDGTs when the threat of a terrorist attack by al Qaeda is persistent and evolving and the terror group appears to be flush with money, there are at least three possible explanations. First, perhaps stopping the flow of funding to al Qaeda and affiliated terror groups is no longer a priority for the U.S. Government, or has become less of a priority than it was after the 9/11 terrorist attacks. The anemic number of SDGT designations in 2007 would support that position. Second, perhaps OFAC lacks the resources needed to sustain a more robust effort to investigate, designate and block the assets of suspected terrorist financiers. OFAC is a relatively small Treasury agency with a staff of approximately 135 employees.[239] At the same time, it has responsibility for administering over 30 other economic sanctions programs.[240] OFAC simply may lack the funding and human resources to broaden its global terrorism sanctions program. If this is the reason for the declining designations, both Congress and the Administration should re-examine OFAC's budget to ensure it has the resources needed to fulfill its anti-terrorist financing mission. Finally, perhaps the Treasury Department has decided to pursue a more selective approach regarding implementation of E.O. 13224, designating only high-profile terrorists and terrorist entities. The Treasury Department may have decided not to designate every suspected terrorist, only those considered high-value targets. However, this does not explain why OFAC failed to designate Abu Dujana, the leader of the military wing of Jemaah Islamiya (JI), and Zarkasih, his military chief, after they were arrested by Indonesian authorities. Surely the top military leaders of JI, Southeast Asia's most feared Islamist terror group, are high-value targets. Whatever the explanation, the dramatic reduction of designations and blocking orders under E.O. 13224 has created the appearance that blocking the assets of suspected terrorists and their supporters is no longer a priority or a central component in the U.S. Government's counter-terrorism strategy.

NOTES

1. Blocking Property and Prohibiting Transactions with Persons Who Commit, Threaten to Commit, or Support Terrorism, Exec. Order No. 13,224, 3 C.F.R. 786–90 (2001), *reprinted as amended in* 50 U.S.C. §1701 note (Supp. IV 2004) [hereinafter E.O. 13224].
2. A fourth hijacked commercial jetliner, United Airlines (U.A.) Flight 93, was intended for the nation's capital, Washington, D.C. The al Qaeda terrorists were targeting either the White House or the Capitol building, but the terrorist plot was foiled by the alert and courageous passengers of U.A. Flight 93. *See* The National Commission on Terrorist Attacks, The 9/11 Commission Report: Final Report of the National Commission on Terrorist Attacks Upon the United States 10–14 (W.W. Norton & Company 2004), *available at* http://www.9-11commission.gov/report/911Report.pdf [hereinafter The 9/11 Commission Report].
3. 50 U.S.C. §§1701–7. The IEEPA was enacted by Congress in 1977 and amended by the Uniting and Strengthening America by Providing Appropriate Tools Required to Intercept and Obstruct Terrorism (USA PATRIOT) Act of 2001, Pub. L. No. 107–56, 115 Stat. 272 (codified in scattered sections of the U.S.C.).
4. 50 U.S.C. §1701(a) (2000).
5. E.O. 13224, *supra* note 1. The use of IEEPA against global terrorist groups is not unprecedented. On January 23, 1995, President Clinton issued E.O. 12,947, finding that 'grave acts of violence committed by foreign terrorists who threaten to disrupt the Middle East peace process' constituted an 'unusual and extraordinary threat to the national security, foreign policy, and economy of the United States.' Prohibiting Transactions with Terrorists Who Threaten to Disrupt the Middle East Peace Process, Exec. Order No. 12,947, 3 C.F.R. 319–20 (1995), *reprinted as amended in* 50 U.S.C. §1701 note (2000 & Supp. IV 2004). E.O. 12947 prohibits financial transactions with any Specially Designated Terrorist or 'SDT.'
6. E.O. 13224, *supra* note 1.
7. 50 U.S.C. §1702(a)(1)(B) (2000 & Supp. IV 2004). Section 1705(b), Title 50 of the United States Code, authorizes a civil penalty not to exceed $50,000 on any person who violates or attempts to violate any license, order, or regulation issued under IEEPA. Section 1705(c) further provides for a criminal penalty of imprisonment of not more than 20 years and a $50,000 fine for anyone who 'willfully' violates or attempts to violate any license, order, or regulation issued under IEEPA. 50 U.S.C.A. §1705(c) (West 2008).
8. Executive Order 13,268 amended the Annex to E.O 13224 by adding two names: the Taliban, and Mohammed Mullah Omar, the leader of the Taliban. *See* Exec. Order No. 13,268, 3 C.F.R. 240–41 (2002), *reprinted as amended in* 50 U.S.C. §1701 note (Supp. IV 2004).
9. The 27 names were Al Qaeda/Islamic Army, Abu Sayyaf Group, Armed Islamic Group, Haraket ul-Mujahidin (HUM), Al-Jihad (Egyptian Islamic Jihad), Islamic Movement of Uzbekistan (IMU), Asbet al-Ansar, Salafist Group for Call and Combat (GSPC), Libyan Islamic Fighting Group, Al-Ithihaad al-Islamiya (AIAI), Islamic Army of Aden, Osama bin Laden, Muhammad Atif (aka, Subhi Abu Sitta, Abu Hafs Al Masri), Sayf al-Adl, Shaykh Sai'id (aka, Mustafa Muhammad Ahmad), Abu Hafs the Maurianian (aka, Mahfouz Ould al-Walid, Khalid A-Shangiti), Ibn Al-Shaykh al-Libi, Abu Zubaydah (aka, Zayn al-Abidin Muhammed Husayn, Tariq),

Abd al-Hadi al-Iraqi (aka, Abu Abdallah), Ayman al-Zawahiri, Thirwat Salah Shihata, Tariq Anwar al-Sayyid Ahmad (aka, Fathi, Amr al-Faith), Muhammed Salah (aka, Nasr Fahmi Nasr Hasanayn), Makhtab Al-Khidamat/Al Kifah, Wafa Humanitarian Organization, Al Rashid Trust, Mamoun Darkazanli Import-Export Company.

10. *See* 31 C.F.R. §594.201(a) (2007). 'Blocking,' also called 'freezing' is a form of controlling assets under U.S. jurisdiction. While title to the blocked property remains with the designated person or entity, the exercise of powers normally associated with property ownership is prohibited without authorization from the Office of Foreign Assets Control. Blocking prohibits transfers and transactions of any kind involving property owned or controlled by the designated party.
11. E.O. 13224, *supra* note 1, at §1(c).
12. *Id.* §1(d)(i)–(ii).
13. *Id.* §1(b).
14. U.S. Dep't of Treasury, Contributions by the Department of the Treasury to the Financial War on Terrorism: Fact Sheet, at 7 (Sept. 2002), *available at* http://www.treasury.gov/press/releases/reports/2002910184556291211.pdf [hereinafter Contributions by the Department of Treasury]
15. E.O. 13224, *supra* note 1, at §1,
16. *Id.* §2(a).
17. *Id.*
18. *Id.* §2(b).
19. A civil penalty not to exceed $50,000 per violation may be imposed on any person who violates any license, order or regulation issued under E.O. 13224. 31 C.F.R. §594.701(a)(1) (2007). Whoever willfully violates any license, order or regulation issues under the Order shall, upon conviction, be fined not more than $50,000 and imprisoned for not more than 20 years, or both. 31 C.F.R. §594.701(a)(2) (2007).
20. *See* Trading with the Enemy Act of 1917, ch. 106, 40 Stat. 411 (codified as amended at 50 U.S.C. §§1–44 (2007).
21. Dames & Moore v. Regan, 453 U.S. 654, 669–70 (1981).
22. Islamic Am. Relief Agency v. Unidentified FBI Agents, 394 F. Supp. 2d 34, 41 (D.D.C. 2005); *see also* Regan v. Wald, 468 U.S. 222, 227–8 (1984).
23. The list of individuals and entities designated under E.O. 13224 has grown from the original 27 names to approximately 488 designations. For a comprehensive list of the individuals and entities designated as SDGTs on the OFAC website, see U.S. Dep't of Treasury Office of Foreign Assets Control, Terrorism: What You Need to Know About U.S. Sanctions (Updated 2007), *available at* http://www.treasury.gov/offices/enforcement/ofac/programs/terror/terror.pdf.
24. U.S. Dep't of State, Fact Sheet: Executive Order 13224 (Dec. 20, 2002), *available at* http://www.state.gov/s/ct/rls/fs/2002/16181.htm.
25. *Id.*
26. 31 C.F.R. §594.201(a) (2007).
27. *See* Nat'l Council of Resistance of Iran v. Dep't of State, 251 F.3d 192, 196 (D.C. Cir. 2001).
28. *See* Holy Land Found. for Relief & Dev. v. Ashcroft, 219 F. Supp. 2d 57, 71 (D.D.C. 2002) (it was reasonable for OFAC to rely on Israeli intelligence report in deciding to designate HLF).
29. E.O. 13224, *supra* note 1, at §1(c), (d)(i) (ii). *But see* Humanitarian Law Project v. U.S. Dep't of Treasury, 463 F. Supp. 2d 1049, 1070 (C.D. Cal. 2006) (holding that the 'otherwise associated with' provision is unconstitutionally vague). However, the provision was amended and upheld. *See* Humanitarian Law Project v. U.S. Dep't of Treasury, 484 F. Supp. 2d 1099, 1106–7 (C.D. Cal. 2007).
30. *Id.* § 1(b).
31. The author served as Under Secretary for Enforcement, U.S. Dep't of Treasury, 2001–3, and was present at some of these designation meetings; *see also* U.S. Dep't of Treasury, Blocking Process Fact Sheet (on file with author).

32. With a staff of only 135 employees, OFAC administers approximately 30 economic sanctions programs against international terrorists, proliferators of weapons of mass destruction, state sponsors of terrorism, narcotics traffickers, and other threats to national security. In addition to the Global Terrorism Sanctions Regulations, 31 C.F.R. part. 594, implementing E.O. 13224, OFAC administers the Terrorism Sanctions Regulations, 31 C.F.R. part. 595, implementing Executive Order 12947 (Jan. 23, 1995), in which the President declared a national emergency with respect to 'grave acts of violence committed by foreign terrorists that disrupt the Middle East peace process,' and the Foreign Terrorist Organizations Sanctions Regulations, 31 C.F.R. part 597 (FTOSR), implementing provisions of the Antiterrorism and Effective Death Penalty Act of 1996. *See* Press Release, U.S. Dep't of Treasury, Joint Testimony of Daniel Glaser, Deputy Assistant Secretary for Terrorist Financing and Financial Crimes, and Adam J. Szubin, Director of the Office of Foreign Assets Control, Before the Foreign Affairs Subcomm. on Terrorism, Nonproliferation, and Trade, and Financial Services Subcomm. on Domestic and International Monetary Policy, Trade, and Technology (April. 18, 2007), *available at* http://www.treas.gov/press/releases/hp361.htm.
33. Pursuant to OFAC regulations, all U.S. persons holding blocked funds are required to place them in a blocked interest-bearing account, located in the United States, earning interest at a 'commercially reasonable' rate. *See* 31 C.F.R. §594.203(b)(1)(i) (2007).
34. Section 106 of USA PATRIOT Act of 2001, Pub. L. 107–56, 115 Stat. 277 (Oct. 26, 2001).
35. *See* E.O. 13224, *supra* note 1, at §7.
36. *Id.*
37. *Id.*
38. *See* 31 C.F.R. §501.801(a), (b) (2007).
39. OFAC has issued the following seven general licenses dealing with the Palestinian Authority:

    (1) General License 1 – official activities of certain international organizations. 31 C.F.R. §594.510 (2007)
    (2) General License 2 – authorizing U.S. persons to engage in transactions with the Palestinian Authority that are 'ordinarily incident to their travel to and from, or employment, residence or personal maintenance within, the jurisdiction of the Palestinian Authority.' *Id.* §594.511.
    (3) General License 3 – authorizing U.S. persons to pay taxes and fees to, and purchase or receive permits or public utility services from, the Palestinian Authority. *Id.* §594.512.
    (4) General License 4 – authorizing U.S. persons to engage in transactions with certain Palestinian government agencies. *Id.* §594.513.
    (5) General License 5 – authorizing transactions and activities necessary to conclude ongoing contracts or programs with the Palestinian Authority. *Id.* §594.514.
    (6) General License 6 – authorizing U.S. persons to 'provide in-kind donations of medicine, medical devices, and medical services to the Palestinian Authority.' *Id.* at §594.515.
    (7) General License 7 – broad authorization for U.S. persons to engage in all transactions otherwise prohibited by the terrorism sanctions programs with the Palestinian Authority. *See* Office of Foreign Assets Control, U.S. Dep't of Treasury, General License No. 7, *available at* http://www.treas.gov/offices/enforcement/ofac/programs/terror/gls/gl7.pdf.

40. *See* 31 C.F.R. §594.515 (2007).
41. *Id.* §594.506.
42. *Id.* §594.507.
43. *Id.* §594.508.
44. *Id.* §594.509.
45. *Id.* §501.801(b).

46. *Id.* §501.801(b)(2).
47. *See* Global Relief Found., Inc. v. O'Neill, 207 F. Supp. 2d 779, at 786, 788, 805 (N.D. Ill. 2002).
48. *See* 31 C.F.R. §§501.806–7 (2007).
49. *Id.* §501.807(a).
50. *Id.*
51. *Id.*
52. For instance, OFAC removed two Somali Swedes from its list of designated entities. *See* John Roth, et al., National Commission on Terrorist Attacks Upon the United States, Monograph on Terrorist Financing: Staff Report to the Commission 86 (Washington., D.C.: Gov't Printing Office 2004), *available at* http:// govinfo.library.unt.edu/911/staff_statements/911_TerrFin_Monograph.pdf [hereinafter Staff Monograph on Terrorist Financing].
53. *See* 31 C.F.R. §501.807(d) (2007).
54. *Id.* §501.806.
55. A request for release of funds should include: '(1) [T]he name of the financial institution in which the funds are blocked; (2) the amount blocked; (3) the date of the blocking; (4) the identity of the original remitter of the funds and any intermediary financial institutions; (5) the intended beneficiary of the blocked transfer; (6) a description of the underlying transaction including copies of related documents (e.g., invoices, bills of lading, promissory notes, etc.); (7) the nature of the applicant's interest in the funds; and (8) a statement of the reasons why the applicant believes the funds were blocked due to mistaken identity.' *See* 31 C.F.R. §501.806(d) (2007).
56. *Id.* §501.806(f).
57. 5 U.S.C. §706(2)(A) (2000).
58. *See* Camp v. Pitts, 411 U.S. 138, 142 (1973); Holy Land Found. for Relief & Dev. v. Ashcroft, 333 F.3d 156, 162 (D.C. Cir. 2003).
59. *See Holy Land Found.*, 333 F.3d at 162 (D.C. Cir. 2003).
60. *Id.*
61. Executive Order 12947, issued by President Clinton on January 23, 1995, found 'grave acts of violence committed by foreign terrorists who threaten to disrupt the Middle East peace process' constitute an 'unusual and extraordinary threat to the national security, foreign policy, and economy of the United States.' E.O. 12947, *supra* note 5. The Executive Order blocks all property and interests in property of the persons and entities designated in the Order, known as 'Specially Designated Terrorists,' or SDTs. *Id.* §1. The Islamic Resistance Movement, commonly known as HAMAS, a Palestinian military and political organization, is one of the SDTs designated under the Order.
62. Press Release, U.S. Dep't of Treasury, Shutting Down the Terrorist Financial Network (Dec. 4, 2002), *available at* http://www.treas.gov/press/releases/po841.htm.
63. Holy Land Found. for Relief & Dev. v. Ashcroft, 219 F. Supp. 2d 57, 64 n.2 (D.D.C. 2002). HAMAS was designated as an SDT and SDGT by Treasury on January 23, 1995, and on October 31, 2001, respectively. *Id.*
64. Holy Land Found. For Relief & Dev. v. Ashcroft, 219 F. Supp. 2d at 70–71.
65. *Id.*
66. *Id.* at 62.
67. *Id.* at 69.
68. Holy Land Found. for Relief & Dev. v. Ashcroft, 333 F.3d 156, 162 (D.C. Cir. 2003).
69. Islamic Am. Relief Agency v. Unidentified FBI Agents, 394 F. Supp. 2d 34 (D.D.C. 2005).
70. Press Release, U.S. Dep't of Treasury, Treasury Designates Global Network, Senior Officials of IARA for Supporting bin Laden, Others (Oct. 13, 2004), *available at* http://www.treas.gov/press/releases/js 2025.htm.
71. *Id.*
72. *Id.*
73. *Islamic Am. Relief Agency*, 394 F. Supp. 2d at 45.
74. *Id.* (citations omitted).

75. *Id.* at 45–6.
76. E.O. 13224, *supra* note 1 at §10.
77. U.S. Const. amend. V.
78. *See* United States v. James Daniel Good Real Property, 510 U.S. 43, 62 (1993).
79. Carey v. Piphus, 435 U.S. 247, 259 (1978).
80. Fuentes v. Shevin, 407 U.S. 67, 80–81 (1972).
81. *James Daniel Good Real Property,* 510 U.S. at 56; Calero-Toledo v. Pearson Yacht Leasing Co., 416 U.S. 663, 679 (1974).
82. *Calero-Todedo*, 416 U.S. at 679.
83. *Id.* at 679 (citations omitted).
84. Holy Land Found. for Relief & Dev. v. Ashcroft, 219 F. Supp. 2d 57, 62 (D.D.C. 2002).
85. *Id.* at 76.
86. *Id.* at 77; *see also* Global Relief Found., Inc. v. O'Neill, 207 F. Supp. 2d 779, 804 (N.D. Ill. 2002) ('Pre-deprivation notice would, in fact, be antithetical to the objectives of [the IEEPA] sanctions program.').
87. *Holy Land Found.*, 219 F. Supp. 2d at 77.
88. Islamic Am. Relief Agency v. Unidentified Agents, 394 F. Supp. 2d 34, 49 (D.D.C. 2005).
89. Nat'l Council of Resistance of Iran (NCRI) v. Dep't of State, 251 F.3d 192, 205–8 (D.C. Cir. 2001).
90. *Islamic Am. Relief Agency*, 394 F. Supp. 2d at 49 (*quoting* Holy Land Found. for Relief & Dev. v. Ashcroft, 219 F. Supp. 2d 57, 76 (D.D.C. 2002).
91. *NCRI*, 251 F.3d at 208.
92. *Islamic Am. Relief Agency,* 394 F. Supp. 2d at 50–51.
93. Global Relief Found., Inc. v. O'Neill, 315 F.3d 748, 754 (7th Cir. 2002).
94. Global Relief Found., Inc. v. O'Neill, 207 F. Supp. 2d 779, 785 (N.D. Ill. 2002).
95. *Id.* at 803.
96. *Id.* at 803–4. The court further noted that, if the blocking action turned out to be invalid, GRF could obtain recompense under the Tucker Act, 28 U.S.C. §1491(a), which provides the parties with an adequate legal remedy: just compensation. *See* Global Relief Found., Inc. v. O'Neill, 315 F.3d 748, 754 (7th Cir. 2002).
97. *Id.* at 804. The courts have consistently held that orders issued without pre-blocking notice do not violate the Due Process Clause. *See* Milena Ship Mgmt. Co. v. Newcomb, 804 F. Supp. 846, 854 (OFAC had to act quickly because delay would have allowed the assets to leave the United States, thereby thwarting the purpose of the Executive Orders); IPT Co. v. U.S. Dep't of Treasury, Case No. 92 Civ. 5542, 1994 WL 613371, at *6 (S.D.N.Y. 1994) (pre-deprivation notice and hearing was not required in connection with OFAC blocking action).
98. 50 U.S.C. §1702(c) (2000 & Supp. IV 2004).
99. Holy Land Found. for Relief & Development v. Ashcroft, 333 F.3d 156, 164 (D.C. Cir. 2003).
100. *Id.*
101. People's Mojahedin Org. of Iran v. Dep't of State, 327 F.3d 1238, 1242 (D.C. Cir. 2003).
102. *Id.*
103. *Holy Land Found.*, 333 F.3d at 164.
104. Global Relief Found., Inc. v. O'Neill, 315 F.3d 748, 754 (7th Cir. 2002).
105. Global Relief Found., Inc. v. O'Neill, 207 F. Supp. 2d 779, 808 (N.D. Ill. 2002).
106. *Id* at 807–8.
107. *See* Roviaro v. United States, 353 U.S. 53, 60–62 (1957).
108. *See* United States v. Ott, 827 F.2d 473, 476 (9th Cir. 1987); United States v. Belfield, 692 F.2d 141, 147 (D.C. Cir. 1982).
109. *Global Relief Foundation*, 315 F.3d at 754 (citations omitted).
110. Connally v. Gen. Constr. Co., 269 U.S. 385, 391 (1926); *see also* Giaccio v. Pennsylvania, 382 U.S. 399, 402–3 (1966) ('It is established that a law fails to meet the requirements of the Due Process Clause if it is so vague and standardless that it leaves the public uncertain as to the conduct it prohibits.').

111. *See* Chicago v. Morales, 527 U.S. 41, 56 (1999); Grayned v. City of Rockford, 408 U.S. 104, 108–9 (1972).
112. Humanitarian Law Project v. U.S. Dep't of Treasury, 463 F. Supp. 2d 1049 (C.D. Cal. 2006).
113. 31 C.F.R. §594.406, defines 'provision of services' as follows:

> (a) Except as provided in §594.207, the prohibitions on transactions or dealings involving blocked property contained in §§594.201 and 594.204 apply to services performed in the United States or by U.S. persons, wherever located, including by an overseas branch of an entity located in the United States:
> (1) On behalf of or for the benefit of a person whose property or interests in property are blocked pursuant to §594.201(a); or
> (2) With respect to property interests subject to §§594.201 and 594.204.
> (b) Example: U.S. persons may not, except as authorized by or pursuant to this part, provide legal, accounting, financial, brokering, freight forwarding, transportation, public relations, educational, or other services to a person whose property or interests in property are blocked pursuant to §594.201(a).

114. *Humanitarian Law Project,* 463 F. Supp. 2d at 1063. The same court reached a different result in a case involving the 'material support statute,' 18 U.S.C. 2339(A)–(C). The court held that the undefined term 'services' contained in the definition of 'material support or resources' was impermissibly vague. Humanitarian Law Project v. Gonzales, 380 F. Supp. 2d 1134, 1151–2 (C.D. Cal. 2005).
115. Under the overbreadth doctrine, a 'showing that a law punishes a "substantial" amount of protected free speech, "judged in relation to the statute's plainly legitimate sweep, suffices to invalidate all enforcement of that law, until and unless a limiting construction or partial invalidation so narrows it as to remove the seeming threat or deterrence to constitutionally protected expression."' Virginia v. Hicks, 539 U.S. 113, 118–19 (2003).
116. *Humanitarian Law Project,* 463 F. Supp. 2d at 1064.
117. *Id.* at 1064–5.
118. *Id.* at 1065.
119. *Id.*
120. *Id.*
121. *Humanitarian Law Project,* 463 F. Supp. 2d at 1065.
122. *Id.*
123. *Id.* at 1065–6 (*quoting* E.O. 13224, *supra* note 1, at §1(b)).
124. *Id.* at 1066 (*quoting* E.O. 13224, *supra* note 1, at §1(c)).
125. *Id.* (*quoting* E.O. 13224, *supra* note 1, at §1(d)(i)).
126. *Id.* at 1065.
127. E.O. 13224, *supra* note 1, at §1(d)(ii), the 'otherwise associated with' provision states, in relevant part:

> [A]ll property and interests in property of the following persons that are in the United States or that hereafter come within the United States, or that hereafter come within the possession or control of United States persons are blocked: . . . persons determined by the Secretary of the Treasury . . . to be otherwise associated with [an SDGT].

128. *Humanitarian Law Project*, 463 F. Supp. 2d at 1067 (C.D. Cal. 2006).
129. *Id.* at 1070.
130. *Id.*
131. *Id.* at 1070–71.
132. *Id.* at 1071.
133. *Id.* The court also found the President's designation authority unconstitutionally vague. The President's authority was used to designate 27 individuals and entities as SDGTs. The court held that the Presidential designation authority was unconstitutional because there were no criteria limiting its use, rendering the authority subject only to the

President's unfettered discretion. *Id.* at 1067. However, in Humanitarian Law Project v. U.S. Dep't of Treasury, 484 F. Supp. 2d 1099 (C.D. Cal. 2007), the court reconsidered and reversed its prior ruling, finding that plaintiffs lacked standing to challenge the President's designation authority. *Id.* at 1108–9.

134. 31 C.F.R. §594.316 (Jan. 26, 2007).
135. Humanitarian Law Project v. U.S. Dep't of Treasury, 484 F. Supp. 2d 1099, 1106 (C.D. Cal. 2007).
136. *Id.* (*citing* Humanitarian Law Project v. U.S. Dept. of Treasury, 463 F. Supp. 2d 1049, 1065–6 (C.D. Cal. 2006)).
137. *Humanitarian Law Project,* 484 F. Supp. 2d at 1106 (citations omitted).
138. *Id.* at 1106–7.
139. *Id.* at 1107.
140. The Takings Clause forbids the Government from taking private property for public use without just compensation. U.S. Const. amend. V.
141. *See* Holy Land Found. for Relief & Dev. v. Ashcroft, 219 F. Supp. 2d 57, 78 (D.D.C. 2002); Global Relief Found., Inc. v. O'Neill, 207 F. Supp. 2d 779, 801–2 (N.D. Ill. 2002) (finding plaintiff unlikely to succeed on merits of takings claim because IEEPA blocking is temporary); *see also* Propper v. Clark, 337 U.S. 472 (1994) (blocking is not taking because it is a temporary action).
142. *Holy Land Found. for Relief & Dev.* 219 F. Supp. 2d at 78.
143. *Id.*
144. Islamic Am. Relief Agency v. Unidentified Agents, 394 F. Supp. 2d 34, 51 (D.D.C. 2005); *see also* Dames & Moore v. Regan, 453 U.S. 654, 688–9 (1981) (noting that the Court of Federal Claims is the proper forum for claims alleging an unconstitutional taking).
145. *Islamic Am. Relief Agency,* 394 F. Supp. 2d at 51.
146. *See, e.g.,* McConnell v. Fed. Election Comm'n, 540 U.S. 93, 135 (2003); Nixon v. Shrink Missouri Gov't PAC, 528 U.S. 377 (2000); Buckley v. Valeo, 424 U.S. 1 (1976).
147. *See McConnell*, 540 U.S. at 136; *Shrink Missouri Gov't PAC,* 528 U.S. at 387–8; *Buckley*, 424 U.S. at 30.
148. United States v. Al-Arian, 308 F. Supp. 2d 1322, 1342 (M.D. Fla. 2004).
149. *Id.* at 1343.
150. *Id.*
151. Holy Land Found. for Relief & Dev. v. Ashcroft, 219 F. Supp. 2d 57, 81 (D.D.C. 2002).
152. United States v. O'Brien, 391 U.S. 367 (1968).
153. *Holy Land Found.,* 219 F. Supp. 2d at 82 (*citing* United States v. O'Brien, 391 U.S. 367, 376–7 (1968)).
154. *Holy Land Found.,* 219 F. Supp. 2d at 82.
155. *Id.*
156. *Id.*
157. *Id.*
158. *Id.*
159. *Id.*
160. Holy Land Found. for Relief & Dev. v. Ashcroft, 333 F.3d 156, 166 (D.C. Cir. 2003).
161. *See* Islamic Am. Relief Agency v. Unidentified Agents, 394 F. Supp. 2d 34, 53 (D.D.C. 2005) ('The argument raised here is virtually identical to the argument raised and rejected by the Court in *Holy Land Found.,* and this Court sees no reason to depart from the very clear and persuasive logic in that case.'); Global Relief Found., Inc. v. O'Neill, 207 F. Supp. 2d 779, 806 (N.D. Ill. 2002) (holding that E.O. 13224 clearly meets the four-part test enunciated in U.S. v. O'Brien, 391 U.S. 367, 376–7 (1968) for determining whether regulations on protected speech violate the First Amendment).
162. U.S. Const. amend. IV.
163. Holy Land Found. for Relief & Dev. v. Ashcroft, 219 F. Supp. 2d 57, 78–9 (D.D.C. 2002) (citing Tran Qui Than v. Regan, 658 F.2d 1296, 1301 (9th Cir. 1981)); *see also* D.C. Precision Inc. v. United States, 73 F. Supp. 338, 343 n.1 (S.D.N.Y. 1999); Can v. United States, 820 F. Supp. 106, 109 (S.D.N.Y. 1993).

164. Islamic Am. Relief Agency v. Unidentified FBI Agents, 394 F. Supp. 2d 34, 48 (D.D.C. 2005).
165. 42 U.S.C. §2000bb-1 (2000).
166. 42 U.S.C. §2000bb-1(a), (b) (2000).
167. Holy Land Found. for Relief & Dev. v. Ashcroft, 333 F.3d 156, 167 (D.C. Cir. 2003) (citations omitted).
168. *Id.*
169. *Id.*
170. *Id.*
171. 50 U.S.C. 1702(a)(1)(b) (2000 & Supp. IV 2004).
172. Global Relief Found., Inc. v. O'Neill, 315 F.3d 748, 750 (7th Cir. 2002).
173. *Id.* at 752.
174. *Id.* at 753.
175. *Id.*
176. *Id.* at 753.
177. *Id.*
178. *Id.*
179. Holy Land Found. for Relief & Dev. v. Ashcroft, 219 F. Supp. 2d 57, 67 (D.D.C. 2002).
180. *Id.*
181. *Id.*
182. *Id.* at 67–8.
183. Holy Land Found. for Relief & Dev. v. Ashcroft, 333 F.3d 156, 162 (D.C. Cir. 2003).
184. *See* U.S. Dep't of Treasury, Terrorist Assets Report, Calendar Year 2001, Annual Report to the Congress on Assets in the United States of Terrorist Countries and International Terrorism Program Designees, at 4 (2001); *see also* Contributions by the Department of Treasury, *supra* note 14.
185. *See* U.S. Dep't of Treasury, Terrorist Assets Report, Calendar Year 2002, Annual Report to the Congress on Assets in the United States of Terrorist Countries and International Terrorism Program Designees, at 4 (2002), *available at* http://www.treas.gov/offices/enforcement/ofac/reports/tar 2002.pdf.
186. *See* U.S. Dep't of Treasury, Terrorist Assets Report, Calendar Year 2003, Twelfth Annual Report to the Congress on Assets in the United States of Terrorist Countries and International Terrorism Program Designees, at 4 (2003), *available at* http://www.treas.gov/offices/enforcement/ofac/reports/tar 2003.pdf.
187. *See* U.S. Dep't of Treasury, Progress in the War on Terrorist Financing, at 1 (Sept. 11, 2003), *available at* http://www.ustreas.gov/press/releases/reports/js 721.pdf.
188. *See* Contributions by the Department of Treasury, *supra* note 14.
189. *Id.*
190. *Id.*
191. *See* U.S. Dep't of Treasury, Progress in the War on Terrorist Financing, at 1 (Sept. 11, 2003), *available at* http://www.ustreas.gov/press/releases/reports/js 721.pdf.
192. The designated charities include: Wafa Humanitarian Organization and Al Rashid Trust (designated Sept. 23, 2001); Rabita Trust (designated Oct. 12, 2001); Asat Trust and Somali International Relief Organization (U.S.A.) (designated Nov. 7, 2001); Holy Land Foundation for Relief and Development (designated Dec. 4, 2001); Afghan Support Committee (ASC) and Revival of Islamic Heritage Society (RIHS) (designated Jan. 9, 2002); Al-Haramain Islamic Foundation (Bosnia-Herzegovina and Somalia branches) (designated March 11, 2002); and the Aid Organization of the Ulema (designated April 19, 2002). U.S. Dep't of Treasury Office of Foreign Assets Control, Terrorism: What You Need to Know About U.S. Sanctions (Updated 2007), *available at* http://www.treasury.gov/offices/enforcement/ofac/programs/terror/terror.pdf.
193. *See* Contributions by the Department of Treasury, *supra* note 14, at 14. Harakat-al-Muqawamah al-Islamiyya is Arabic for 'The Islamic Resistance Movement' and is known by the acronym HAMAS.
194. Holy Land Found. for Relief & Dev. v. Ashcroft, 333 F.3d 156, 160 (D.C. Cir. 2003).

195. *See* Press Release, U.S. Dep't of Treasury, Shutting Down the Terrorist Financial Network (Dec. 4, 2001), *available at* http://www.treas.gov/press/releases/po841.htm.
196. *See* United States v. Holy Land Found. for Relief & Dev., 493 F.3d 469, 472 (5th Cir. 2007).
197. United States v. Holy Land Found. for Relief & Dev., Superseding Indictment, No. 3:04-CR-240G (N.D. Tex., 2005).The trial ultimately ended in either an acquittal or a hung jury on all counts. The HLF criminal prosecution is discussed *infra* at Chapter 10, The Law Enforcement Response to Terrorist Financing.
198. In response to the September 11 terrorist attacks, Congress enacted the Uniting and Strengthening America by Providing Appropriate Tools Required to Intercept and Obstruct Terrorism Act of 2001, Pub. L. No. 107-56, 115 Stat. 272 (the 'USA PATRIOT Act'), which expanded the authority of the President and his designees under the IEEPA. Section 106 of the PATRIOT Act authorized the President to block assets 'during the pendency of an investigation.' 50 U.S.C. §1702(a)(i)(B) (2000 & Supp. IV 2004).
199. On October 18, 2002, the Treasury department designated GRF under the authority of E.O. 13224. *See* Press Release, U.S. Dep't of Treasury, Statement Regarding the Designation of the Global Relief Foundation (Oct. 18, 2002), *available at* http://www.treas.gov/press/releases/po3553.htm. On November 19, 2002, BIF was designated an SDGT. *See* Press Release, U.S. Dep't of Treasury, Treasury Designates Benevolence International Foundation and Related Entities as Financiers of Terror (Nov. 19, 2002), *available at* http://www.treas.gov/press/releases/po3632.htm.
200. *See* Global Relief Found. v. O'Neill, 315 F.3d 748, 750 (7th Cir. 2002) (challenging GRF's designation as an SDGT under E.O. 13224).
201. *See* Press Release, U.S. Dep't of Treasury, Statement Regarding the Designation of the Global Relief Foundation (Oct. 18, 2002), *available at* http://www.treas.gov/press/releases/po3553.htm.
202. *See* Press Release, U.S. Dep't of Treasury, U.S. Treasury Designates Two Individuals with Ties to al Qaida, UBL: Former BIF Leader and al Qaida Associate Named Under E.O. 13224 (Dec. 21, 2004), *available at* http://www.treas.gov/press/releases/js2164.htm.
203. *Id.*
204. *Id.*; *see also* Indictment, United States v. Arnaout, 282 F. Supp. 2d 838 (N.D. Ill. 2003) (No. 02 CR 892).
205. Plea agreement, at p. 5, United States v. Arnaout, 282 F. Supp. 2d 838 (N.D. Ill. 2003) (No. 02 CR 892).
206. *See United States* v. *Arnaout*, 431 F.3d 994, 1000 (7th Cir. 2005).
207. *See* Contributions by the Department of Treasury, *supra* note 14, at 13.
208. *Id.*
209. *Id.*
210. *Id.*
211. JI has been linked to other deadly terror attacks including the August 2003 bombing of the Marriott Hotel in Jakarta, Indonesia, killing 13 people and injuring 149 others.The al Haramain organization, not merely its branches, has recently been designated by the Treasury Department. *See* Press Release, U.S. Dep't of Treasury, Treasury Designates Al Haramain Islamic Foundation (June 19, 2008), *available at* http://www.treasury.gov/press/releases/hp1043.htm.
212. *See* Press Release, U.S. Dep't of Treasury, U.S.-Based Branch of Al-Haramain Foundation Linked to Terror, Treasury Designates U.S. Branch, Director (Sept. 9, 2004), *available at* http://www.treas.gov/press/releases/js1985.htm; *see also* U.S. Dep't of Treasury, Office of Terrorism and Financial Intelligence, Protecting Charitable Organizations, *available at* http://www.treas.gov/offices/enforcement/key-issues/protecting/.
213. The Al-Aqsa Foundation was designated on May 29, 2003. *See* OFAC list of SDGTs.
214. The following terrorist organizations have been designated SDGTs by OFAC: Tunisian Combat Group (designated October 10, 2002); Jemaah Islamiyah (designated October 23, 2002); Moroccan Islamic Combatant Group (designated November 22, 2002);

Lashkar i Jhangvi (designated January 30, 2003); and Ansar Al-Islam (designated February 20, 2003). U.S. Dep't of Treasury Office of Foreign Assets Control, Terrorism: What You Need to Know About U.S. Sanctions (updated 2007), *available at* http://www.treasury.gov/offices/enforcement/ofac/programs/terror/terror.pdf; 31 C.F.R. Ch. V. App. A (2006) (the OFAC SDN List as printed in the Code of Federal Regulations); 31 C.F.R. §500.306 (2006).

215. *See* U.S. Dep't of Treasury, Terrorist Assets Report, Calendar Year 2004, Thirteenth Annual Report to the Congress on Assets in the United States of Terrorist Countries and International Terrorism Program Designees (2004), at 4, *available at* http://www.treas.gov/offices/enforcement/ofac/reports/tar 2004.pdf.
216. *See* U.S. Dep't of Treasury, Terrorist Assets Report, Calendar Year 2005, Fourteenth Annual Report to the Congress on Assets in the United States of Terrorist Countries and International Terrorism Program Designees (2005), at 4, *available at* http://www.treas.gov/offices/enforcement/ofac/reports/tar 2005.pdf.
217. *See* OFAC list of SDGTs available at U.S. Dep't of Treasury Office of Foreign Assets Control, Terrorism: What You Need to Know About U.S. Sanctions (updated 2007), *available at* http://www.treasury.gov/offices/enforcement/ofac/programs/terror/terror.pdf.
218. *Id.*
219. *See* The Terrorist Threat to the U.S. Homeland, National Intelligence Estimate (July 2007), *available at* http://www.dni.gov/press_releases/20070717_release.pdf. 'National Intelligence Estimates (NIEs) are the Intelligence Community's (IC) most authoritative written judgments on national security issues and designed to help U.S. civilian and military leaders develop policies to protect U.S. national security interests.' *Id.*
220. *Id.*
221. *Id.*
222. *Id.*
223. The 9/11 Commission Report, *supra* note 2, at 66.
224. *Id.* at 67.
225. Alan Cowell, *Prosecutors Outline British Bomb Plot*, N.Y. Times, Jan. 15, 2007, *available at* http://www.nytimes.com/2007/01/15/world/europe/15cnd-london.html?ei=5090&en=c0f8418c05ab0b54&ex=1326517200&partner=rssuserland&emc=rss&pagewanted=all.
226. The 9/11 Commission Report, *supra* note 2, at 171.
227. *Id.* at 57–8.
228. Steve Coll, Ghost Wars: The Secret History of the CIA, Afghanistan, and Bin Laden, From the Soviet Invasion to September 10, 2001, at 367 (Penguin Books 2004).
229. *See* Michael Chandler & Rohan Gunaratna, Countering Terrorism 138 (Reaktion Books Ltd. 2007).
230. *Id.*
231. *Id.* at 140.
232. *Id.*
233. *See* Alan Cowell, *4 Guilty of Failed 2005 London Plot,* N.Y. Times, July 9, 2007, *available at* http://www.nytimes.com/2007/07/09/world/europe/09cnd-london.html.
234. *See* Karla Adam, *2 More Doctors Charged in Botched British Bombings,* Wash. Post, July 15, 2007, at A16, *available at* http://www.washingtonpost.com/wp-dyn/content/article/2007/07/14/AR2007071400534_pf.html.
235. *See* Robin McDowell, *2 Terror Leaders Arrested in Indonesia,* Wash. Post, June 15, 2007, *available at* http://www.washingtonpost.com/wp-dyn/content/article/2007/06/15/AR2007061500395.html.
236. *See* Alan Cowell, *Britain Sentence 7 in Terror Plot*, N.Y. Times, June 15, 2007, *available at* http://www.nytimes.com/2007/06/15/world/europe/15cnd-terror.html.
237. *See Report: Algerians Arrest Terror Suspects,* GMANews.TV, May 8, 2007, *available at* http://www.gmanews.tv/story/41486/Report-Algerians-arrest-terror-suspects; *see also 8 Sentenced in Morocco for Plotting Terror Attacks*, N.Y. Times, Mar. 3, 2007, *available at* http://www.nytimes.com/2007/03/03/world/africa/03morocco.html?_r=1&oref=slogin.

238. *See* Associated Press, *Denmark Arrests 8 over Alleged Terrorist Plot*, MSNBC, Sept. 4, 2007, *available at* http://www.msnbc.msn.com/id/20580246/.
239. *See* Press Release, U.S. Dep't of Treasury, Joint Testimony of Daniel Glaser, Deputy Assistant Secretary for Terrorist Financing and Financial Crimes, and Adam J. Szubin, Director of the Office of Foreign Assets Control, Before the Foreign Affairs Subcommittee on Terrorism, Nonproliferation, and Trade, and Financial Services Subcommittee on Domestic and International Monetary Policy, Trade, and Technology (April 18, 2007), *available at* http://www.treas.gov/press/releases/hp361.htm.
240. *Id.*

9. International asset freeze

> [T]he financing of terrorism is a matter of grave concern to the international community as a whole.[1]
>
> Convention for the Suppression of the Financing of Terrorism, December 9, 1999

THE INTERNATIONAL LEGAL DUTY TO FREEZE TERRORIST-RELATED ASSETS

In response to the September 11, 2001 terrorist attacks and the growing prevalence of terrorist activities around the world, the international community has devised and implemented a global legal framework to freeze the funds and other assets of individuals and groups who finance acts of terrorism. The U.N. Security Council has played a critical leadership role in developing, revising, strengthening and implementing the legal regime.[2] The Security Council has adopted numerous resolutions imposing important duties on Member States to prevent and suppress the financing of terrorism.[3] Among other things, these resolutions require countries to 'freeze without delay' the funds, financial assets and economic resources of Osama bin Laden, members of al Qaeda, the Taliban and persons and entities associated with them.[4] The international economic sanctions regime established by these resolutions is 'the sole vehicle for truly global action against the twin threats of Al-Qaida and the Taliban.'[5]

The 1999 International Convention for the Suppression of the Financing of Terrorism (Terrorist Financing Convention), also recognizing the need for the world community to work in concert to deprive terrorists of funding, complements the work of the Security Council.[6] The Terrorist Financing Convention is supported by 132 signatories, including the United States.[7] Among other important duties, it requires parties to the Convention to enact domestic legislation to criminalize and punish as perpetrators of a grave offense those persons who wilfully provide or collect funds with the intention or knowledge that they will be used to carry out acts of terrorism.[8] The Terrorist Financing Convention further requires States Parties to hold legal entities, such as banks, liable for providing financial services to terrorists by the imposition of criminal, civil, or administrative sanctions.[9] Most importantly, the Convention imposes a legal obligation on signatories to freeze any funds used or allocated for the purpose of committing a terrorist offense.[10] Article 8(1) provides that '[e]ach State Party shall take appropriate measures . . . for the identification, detection and freezing or seizure of any funds used or allocated for the purpose of committing [terrorist-related] offences.'[11]

The Financial Action Task Force on Money Laundering and Terrorist Financing (FATF), an inter-governmental body responsible for developing and promoting international standards to combat terrorist financing and money laundering, also acknowledges the importance of international action to freeze terrorist assets.[12] The FATF is comprised of 34 member countries, associate members, FATF-style regional bodies, and several international organizations.[13] In response to the 9/11 terrorist attacks, the FATF held an extra-plenary session in Washington, D.C., in October 2001, where it adopted Eight Special Recommendations on Terrorist Financing, including a provision on terrorist asset freezing.[14] Special Recommendation III: Freezing and Confiscating Terrorist Assets provides that '[e]ach country should implement measures to freeze without delay funds or other assets of terrorists, those who finance terrorism and terrorist organisations in accordance with the United Nations resolutions relating to the prevention and suppression of the financing of terrorist acts.'[15] Special Recommendation III is intended to implement the obligations imposed on States by Resolutions 1267 (1999) and 1373 (2001) to freeze terrorist-related assets.[16] The combination of these three authorities – the U.N. Security Council anti-terrorist financing resolutions, the Terrorist Financing Convention, and the FATF's Special Recommendation III: Freezing and Confiscating Terrorist Assets – makes a compelling case that every country has a legal duty to freeze the funds and curtail the flow of financial assets to terrorists and their financial supporters.

The successful implementation of an effective terrorist asset freezing regime is critical in combating the financing of terrorism. The U.N. working group of counter-terrorism experts established by the 2004 Security Council Resolution 1566 has stated that 'freezing of financial assets is an indispensable tool in curtailing terrorism.'[17] It is estimated that approximately $85 million in terrorist-related funds have been frozen under the international sanctions regime.[18] However, the asset freeze sanctions program serves several other valuable purposes. Asset freeze acts as a deterrent against those who otherwise might be willing to finance terrorist activity.[19] Persons designated under relevant Security Council resolutions are isolated from the international financial community. Their funds, financial assets and economic resources are subject to being frozen anywhere in the world. Thus, the fear of having their funds and other assets frozen may cause potential donors to reconsider funding terrorist activities. Asset freeze reduces the flow of money and other support to terrorists and makes the transfer of funds more difficult to effect.[20] The economic sanctions program 'terminates terrorist cash flows by shutting down the pipelines used to move terrorist-related assets.'[21] An effective financial ban may further expose terrorist financing 'money trails' that may generate leads to previously unknown terrorist cells and financiers.[22] Finally, asset freeze may restrict terrorists from operating extensive terrorist networks, training camps and social programs for funding the families of homicide bombers, especially across borders.[23] In short, there are compelling reasons for curtailing the flow of money to terrorists and terrorist organizations and blacklisting their financial sponsors.

The U.N. Security Council has been at the forefront of developing and monitoring the implementation of the anti-terrorism assets freeze program. In addition to adopting numerous resolutions that impose a legal duty on Member States to 'freeze without delay' terrorist-related assets, the Security Council has established various committees and expert working groups to monitor the action taken by States to comply with these resolutions.[24] The Council has created a list, known as the 'Consolidated List' or 'Sanctions List,' of individuals and entities associated with Osama bin Laden, al Qaeda, or the Taliban, whose assets are required to be frozen by Member States.[25] However, each year fewer and fewer names are being submitted by States for inclusion on the Consolidated List for asset freeze.[26] Most recently, in 2007, only eight names were added to the Sanctions List, the lowest annual rate ever, continuing a downward trend observable since 2001.[27] Equally disturbing, the amount of terrorist assets frozen over the last several years has stalled. There has been no increase in terrorist assets frozen since 2004.[28] In fact, the trend is going in the opposite direction. At the end of 2007, approximately $85 million remained frozen under the sanctions regime, down from a previous high of $91.4 million.[29]

While the number of U.N. designations is declining and Member States are reluctant to freeze terrorist-related funds, the threats from al Qaeda and the Taliban remain persistent. According to U.N. counter-terrorism experts:

> Al-Qaida has continued to show its determination to mount major attacks; it has extended its base of support; its leaders have consolidated their ability to communicate their message and their operational plans, and the Taliban have increased their influence not just in Afghanistan, but in North-Western Pakistan as well.[30]

While much has been written about al Qaeda's organizational disposition and strength, analysts agree that its global influence has not declined, nor has its intention or ability to attack.[31] In 2007, suspected members of al

Qaeda were reported to be arrested or killed in more than 40 countries around the world, suggesting a high volume of terrorist planning.[32] Al Qaeda videos released in 2007 demonstrate an increasing level of professionalism achieved by As-Sahab (meaning 'the clouds' in Arabic), al Qaeda's public affairs and media production unit.[33] Through these video and audio recordings, al Qaeda hopes to recruit new members and inspire terrorist attacks by home-grown terrorists. Moreover, in 2007, al Qaeda in the Islamic Maghreb, the North Africa wing of al Qaeda, claimed responsibility for killing hundreds of innocent civilians and wounding hundreds more in Algeria.[34] These attacks included a suicide bombing near the U.N. building in Algiers and another attack the same day against a government office building that killed a total of 41 people, including 17 U.N. employees.[35]

The Taliban remains a serious threat to international peace and security. The group is resurgent and dominates large areas in southern Afghanistan. Furthermore, Tehrik-e-Taliban Pakistan, also known as the Taliban Movement of Pakistan, has emerged as a new terrorist threat. The Taliban Movement of Pakistan, headed by Baitullah Mehsud, operates in the Waziristan region, along the Pakistan border with Afghanistan, where Western intelligence suggests al Qaeda is regrouping.[36] According to one U.N. report, the Taliban 'have enough money to hire foot soldiers and to buy weapons, including the components for sophisticated improvised explosive devices, and their ability to cross the long and porous border with Pakistan is largely unconstrained.'[37] There are currently estimated to be about 3,000 active and up to 7,000 occasional Taliban fighters in Afghanistan, and the Taliban Movement of Pakistan is estimated to control a fighting force of 40,000.[38] Moreover, al Qaeda and the Taliban appear to have a close relationship. In a September 2007 video message delivered by Ayman al-Zawahiri, al Qaeda's second-in-command, he once again referred to Mullah Omar, the head of the Taliban, as the supreme leader.[39] Further, the Taliban appears to have adopted some of al Qaeda's terrorist tactics. In January 2008, the Taliban claimed responsibility for a suicide bombing that killed seven people, including an American, at a luxury hotel in Kabul, Afghanistan, where the Norwegian foreign minister was staying.[40] Finally, Baitullah Mehsud, the leader of the Taliban Movement in Pakistan, is suspected of involvement in the tragic assassination of former Pakistani Prime Minister Benazir Bhutto in December 2007.[41]

The Security Council's international asset freeze program has reached a critical juncture. Senior counter-terrorism officials seem less enthusiastic about the economic sanctions regime than ever before and Member States are reluctant to submit names for inclusion on the Consolidated List.[42] Terrorist-related assets are no longer being frozen.[43] As a result, al Qaeda and the Taliban retain ample funding to sustain their operations and finance deadly terrorist attacks.[44] Based on every objective measurement, the international economic sanctions program appears to be failing. Unless significant measures are taken to hold Member States accountable for their failures to comply with their duties to freeze terrorist-related funds 'without delay,' the sanctions regime will cease to be relevant in the struggle against global terrorism.

U.N. Security Council Resolutions 1267 (1999) and 1333 (2000)

The international assets freeze program has its origins in three important U.N. Security Council Resolutions: 1267, 1333 and 1373. While the Security Council has adopted a number of successor resolutions intended to strengthen the mandate of these resolutions (at least 13 in total), these three resolutions constitute the foundation for the international legal framework to freeze terrorist-related assets.[45] In October 1999, the Security Council decided that the threat posed by al Qaeda merited an international response. The Taliban had provided al Qaeda a safe haven, where the terror group was able to plan, supervise, and execute terrorist attacks, including those against the U.S. embassies in Nairobi, Kenya and Dar es Salaam, Tanzania in August 1998. Accustomed to dealing with States, the Council decided to confront al Qaeda by imposing sanctions on the Taliban, who represented the *de facto* government in Afghanistan. The Security Council adopted Resolution 1267, which imposed various obligations on Member States, including the duty to freeze funds and other financial resources owned or controlled by the Taliban.[46] Paragraph 4(b) requires countries to '[f]reeze funds and other financial resources, including funds derived or generated from property owned or controlled, directly or indirectly by the Taliban, or by any undertaking owned or controlled by the Taliban.'[47] Resolution 1267 further created a committee, consisting of members of the Security Council, to monitor action taken by States to implement the measures imposed by the resolution ('Al-Qaida and Taliban Sanctions Committee' or '1267 Committee').[48]

The Taliban failed to comply with the Security Council's mandates, and terrorist attacks by al Qaeda continued. On October 12, 2000, a small boat laden with explosives was detonated near the USS Cole, docked in Aden, Yemen. The blast killed 17 American sailors and wounded at least 40 others. Members of al Qaeda continued to operate a network of terrorist training camps in Afghanistan, responsible for training as many as 10,000 terrorists. In response to the attack on the USS Cole and other terrorist activities by al Qaeda, in December 2000 the Security Council adopted Resolution 1333, calling on the Taliban to comply with the sanctions imposed by Resolution 1267.[49] However, the Resolution went beyond imposing sanctions on State actors such as the Taliban. Resolution 1333 imposed measures on individuals and non-State entities, mandating a freeze on the financial assets of Osama bin Laden, al Qaeda, and individuals and entities associated with them.[50] In essence, through Resolution 1333, the Security Council sought to isolate bin Laden, al Qaeda, and their associates from the international community, including sympathetic Muslim donors.

Paragraph 8(c) of Resolution 1333 requires the Sanctions Committee established pursuant to Resolution 1267 'to [establish and] maintain an updated list, based on information provided by States and regional organizations, of the individuals and entities designated as being associated with Osama bin Laden, including those in the Al-Qaida organization.'[51] Member States were encouraged to submit information to the members of the Al-Qaida and Taliban Sanctions Committee on individuals and entities associated with bin Laden and al Qaeda for designation and placement on the list by the Committee. After inclusion on the list, Member States would be obliged to 'freeze without delay' the 'funds and other financial assets' of those individuals and entities. The List includes persons and entities associated with the Taliban, as well as bin Laden and al Qaeda, and is referred to as the 'Consolidated List.'[52] Unfortunately, the Security Council sanctions aimed at al Qaeda and the Taliban achieved less than was expected. Few names were placed on the Consolidated List.[53] However, the Security Council's determination to deal with international terrorism was strengthened by the tragic events that occurred in 2001.

U.N. Security Council Resolution 1373 (2001)

In the aftermath of the September 11, 2001 terrorist attacks, the U.N. Security Council unanimously adopted Resolution 1373,[54] which imposes several important duties on Member States to combat the threat of global terrorism. As a result of this resolution, States are required to prevent the movement of terrorists by effective border controls and controls on the issuance of travel documents (travel ban), to prevent the supply of weapons to terrorists (arms embargo), to deny safe haven to those who plan, support or commit terrorist acts (safe haven ban), and to afford States the greatest measure of assistance in connection with criminal terrorism investigations (mutual assistance).[55] Resolution 1373 further imposes certain obligations on Member States to prevent and suppress the financing of terrorism. First, States are required to criminalize the wilful provision or collection of terrorist-related funds.[56] To comply with this provision, States must enact domestic legislation, if necessary, to make it a crime to collect or provide funds to terrorists.[57] Second, States must ensure that any person who participates in financing terrorists acts is prosecuted and brought to justice.[58] Third, States must prohibit persons and entities from making financial assets, economic resources and financial services available to persons who commit or facilitate the commission of terrorist acts.[59] Finally, Resolution 1373 authorizes states to 'freeze without delay funds and other financial assets or economic resources' of terrorists, those who finance terrorism, and terrorist organizations around the world.[60]

The assets freeze provision is particularly broad in scope and coverage. Paragraph 1(c) of Resolution 1373 requires all countries to 'freeze without delay' the funds and other financial assets, or economic resources of (1) persons who commit, or attempt to commit, participate in, or facilitate the commission of terrorist acts; (2) 'entities owned or controlled by such persons;' (3) 'persons and entities acting on behalf of, or at the direction of, such persons and entities, including funds derived or generated from property owned or controlled directly or indirectly by such persons;' and (4) associated persons and entities.[61]

Countries are required to freeze not only the 'funds and other financial assets' of terrorists and their associates, but also their 'economic resources.'[62] In addition to freezing the financial assets of designated persons and entities, paragraph 1(c) requires States to freeze their non-monetary assets, such as real estate, vehicles, aircraft, ships, equipment, precious stones, and other personal property.[63] More importantly, Resolution 1373 is not limited to freezing the funds and assets owned and controlled by al Qaeda, bin Laden, the Taliban and individuals and entities associated with them, but reaches the financial resources of any person or entity involved in the commission of terrorist acts. For example, Resolution 1373 authorizes States to freeze the assets of HAMAS,[64] Hizballah,[65] the Liberation Tigers of Tamil Elam (LTTE),[66] the Revolutionary Armed Forces of Colombia (FARC),[67] and other terrorist groups not controlled by al Qaeda, bin Laden, and the Taliban.

There are two other significant differences between Resolutions 1267 and 1333 and Resolution 1373. Resolution 1373 does not create a list of terrorist organizations, entities or individuals subject to asset freeze. While States are obliged to freeze the funds, financial assets and other economic resources of persons involved in the commission of terrorist acts, Resolution 1373 does not require that their names be placed on a U.N.-administered list.[68] The Consolidated List created by Resolutions 1267 and 1333, targeting al Qaeda, Osama bin Laden, the Taliban, and individuals and entities associated with them, is the only U.N-administered terrorist financing list. Additionally, the Counter-Terrorism Committee (CTC) created by Resolution 1373 is not a sanctions body. It is not responsible for freezing the assets of terrorists and their supporters. Under Resolution

1373, a decision to freeze assets takes place on two levels.[69] Initially, a competent *national* authority decides whether certain assets should be frozen because the person or entity falls within the mandate of paragraph 1(c) of the resolution ('freeze without delay').[70] Other States must then decide, in the exercise of their discretion, whether to adopt the sanction and impose an asset freeze on the party concerned. Freezing the assets of such persons and entities is not mandated by the CTC.

U.N. SECURITY COUNCIL COUNTER-TERRORISM COMMITTEES

1267 Committee

The Committee established by Resolution 1267 (Al-Qaida and Taliban Sanctions Committee) is responsible for overseeing States' implementation of the sanctions (assets freeze, travel ban and arms embargo) imposed by the Security Council to combat the terrorist threat posed by Osama bin Laden, al Qaeda, the Taliban, and persons and entities associated with them.[71] The Committee's mandate was originally limited to the Taliban, but was extended to include al Qaeda, Osama bin Laden, and their associates by Resolutions 1333 and 1390.[72] The Committee maintains a list of individuals and entities for this purpose (referred to as the 'Consolidated List'). To prevent and suppress the financing of terrorism, States are obliged to freeze the assets of individuals and entities on the Consolidated List.[73] The mandate of the Committee further includes regularly updating the List, examining reports submitted by Member States documenting their compliance with Resolutions 1267 and 1333 and other related resolutions, considering requests for de-listing or removal from the List, and submitting periodic reports to the Security Council.[74]

Analytical Support and Sanctions Monitoring Team

In 2004, to further strengthen the mandate of the 1267 Committee, the Security Council established an eight-person Analytical Support and Sanctions Monitoring Team (the 'Monitoring Team').[75] The Monitoring Team, which operates under the direction of the Committee, was initially mandated to monitor and make recommendations on implementation of the measures imposed by Resolution 1267. The Monitoring Team was further tasked with submitting three comprehensive, independent reports to the 1267 Committee on implementation by States of the measures imposed by Resolution 1267, including recommendations for improved implementation and possible new measures.[76] The mandate of the

Monitoring Team was extended by Resolutions 1617 (2005) and 1735 (2006). To date, the Monitoring Team has submitted a total of eight reports to the Al-Qaida and Taliban Sanctions Committee.[77] The Monitoring Team has been involved in other activities intended to enhance the effectiveness of the sanctions measures imposed by Resolution 1267, including visiting Member States, participating in national, sub-regional, regional, and international conferences, and meeting with intelligence and security services and representatives of financial institutions.[78]

1373 Counter-Terrorism Committee

To monitor implementation of the duties imposed on Member States by Resolution 1373, the Security Council established the Counter-Terrorism Committee (CTC), consisting of all 15 members of the Council, to be assisted by appropriate experts.[79] One of the CTC's most important functions is to help States get the technical assistance they need to implement the provisions of Resolution 1373.[80] The CTC coordinates and facilitates the delivery of training and technical assistance to States to prevent the financing of terrorism. The CTC's mandate also includes strengthening contacts and coordination both within the U.N. system of organizations and among international, regional and inter-governmental bodies, and identifying and promoting best practices in all key areas of Resolution 1373.[81] Over time the CTC's responsibilities have expanded to include reviewing hundreds of reports from Member States on action taken to implement Resolution 1373.[82] Finally, in 2005, pursuant to Resolution 1624, the CTC's mandate was extended to include working with States to implement measures to prohibit and prevent incitement to commit acts of terrorism.[83]

Counter-Terrorism Committee Executive Directorate

Initially, the CTC's work was performed by consultants hired by the U.N. Secretariat on short-term contracts. Realizing the need for a more permanent and professional staff, in March 2004 the Security Council adopted Resolution 1535, creating the Counter-Terrorism Committee Executive Directorate (CTED), comprised of 35 counter-terrorism experts and support staff.[84] The CTED consists of an Assessment and Technical Assistance Office (ATAO) and the Information and Administrative Office (IAO).[85] The ATAO is composed of 20 counter-terrorism experts and is responsible for evaluating the technical assistance needs of States to assist them in implementing all aspects of Resolution 1373.[86] The IAO is in charge of handling the administrative needs of the CTC, including overseeing personnel and financial matters.[87]

The CTED's mandate includes providing the CTC with expert advice on all areas covered by Resolution 1373, reviewing Member States' reports on their implementation of their obligations, visiting countries to verify their reports, facilitating technical assistance to countries to enhance their asset freeze regimes, and coordinating with other U.N. counter-terrorism agencies.[88] The CTED's mandate also includes monitoring Member States' implementation of Security Council Resolution 1624, condemning incitement to commit acts of terrorism.[89] The CTED works closely and coordinates its activities with the Monitoring Team created to enhance the work of the 1267 Committee.[90] With this larger group, the CTC is now able to send small teams of experts to different countries to assess their efforts to implement Resolution 1373.[91]

1566 Working Group

Following the terrorist incident involving the seizure of approximately 1,200 hostages and the deaths of hundreds of children at a school in Beslan, Russia, in October 2004, the U.N. Security Council adopted Resolution 1566.[92] The Council condemned acts of terrorism, especially the killing of innocent children, and called upon States to cooperate fully with the Counter-Terrorism Committee (CTC) established pursuant to Resolution 1373, including the recently established Counter-Terrorism Committee Executive Directorate (CTED), the Al-Qaida and Taliban Sanctions Committee established pursuant to Resolution 1267, and its Analytical Support and Sanctions Monitoring Team, and the WMD Committee established pursuant to Resolution 1540.[93] Most notably, Resolution 1566 established a working group consisting of 'all members of the Security Council to submit recommendations to the Council on practical measures to be imposed upon individuals, groups or entities involved in or associated with terrorist activities, other than those designated by the Al-Qaida/Taliban Sanctions Committee.'[94] The working group was further tasked to look into the possibility of establishing an international fund to compensate the victims of terrorist acts.[95] The CTC is now aided by two administrative bodies created by the Security Council, the CTED and the 1566 Working Group, in evaluating the implementation of Resolution 1373, facilitating technical assistance to Member States, and promoting close cooperation and coordination with international organizations.[96]

Finally, it should be noted that, in Resolution 1566, the Security Council agreed on a definition of 'terrorism.'[97] In Resolutions 1267, 1333, and 1373, the Council had imposed various measures on Member States to prevent and suppress acts of terrorism, including the financing of terrorism, without an international agreement on the definition of terrorism. Thus, States were left to apply their own definition of the term. Now, Member

States have a working definition of terrorism unanimously agreed to by the 15 members of the U.N. Security Council.[98]

Non-Proliferation Committee

In response to the disclosure in February 2004 that Pakistani scientist A.Q. Khan had provided nuclear technology on the black market, and concerned that such technology may have been provided to non-State actors for terrorist purposes, the Security Council adopted Resolution 1540 in April 2004.[99] The resolution imposes a duty on Member States to refrain from providing any form of support (including financial support) to non-State actors attempting to develop, acquire, transfer or use nuclear, chemical or biological weapons and their means of delivery.[100] Resolution 1540 further requires States to enact domestic legislation to prevent non-State actors from acquiring, developing, transferring or using weapons of mass destruction, and to implement effective measures for such weapons which encompass (a) accountability, (b) physical protection, (c) border controls and law enforcement efforts, and (d) national export and trans-shipment controls, including controls on providing funds and financial services.[101]

Resolution 1540 established a Committee ('1540 Committee') of the members of the Security Council to monitor action taken by States to implement the resolution.[102] The Committee's mandate further included reviewing reports required to be submitted by Member States on action taken to implement the resolution. A working group of eight experts to support the Committee's work was also created. Initially, the 1540 Committee was established for a period not to exceed two years.[103] However, Resolution 1673 (2006) extended the Committee's mandate for a period of two years, until April 27, 2008.[104]

LISTING PROCESS

The Consolidated List has been characterized as the 'cornerstone' of the Al-Qaida and Taliban sanctions regime.[105] Designation under Resolutions 1267 and 1333 involves a two-step process: (1) Member States submit the names of persons and entities for inclusion on the Consolidated List to the Al-Qaida and Taliban Sanctions Committee, and (2) the Committee reviews the submissions and makes a final determination on whether to add the names to the List. Initially, a competent national authority decides that the concerned party falls within the coverage of the relevant resolutions and therefore should be placed on the Consolidated List. The Sanctions Committee must then decide whether to include the person on the List, on the basis of the information and evidence submitted by the Member State to justify the proposed designation.[106]

By the end of 2007, approximately 480 names had been placed on the Consolidated List, the vast majority of which were submitted by the United States after the September 11 terrorist attacks.[107] The List consists of five sections: the first for individuals belonging to or associated with the Taliban (142 individuals); the second for entities belonging to or associated with the Taliban (none); the third for individuals belonging to or associated with the al Qaeda organization (225 individuals); the fourth for entities belonging to or associated with the al Qaeda organization (112 entities); and the fifth for individuals and entities that have been removed from the list pursuant to a decision by the Al-Qaida and Taliban Sanctions Committee (11 individuals and 24 entities).[108]

Submission by Member States

Cover sheet for Member State submissions to the Committee

Member States play a crucial role in the designation process. States identify and propose who should be placed on the List. All names on the Consolidated List have been submitted to the Committee by Member States.[109] Further, the accuracy of the List is dependent on the accuracy of the information included in the State submissions. Thus, States are responsible for both the accuracy and sufficiency of the information provided to the Committee. When proposing names to the Committee for inclusion on the Consolidated List, States are required to use the Cover Sheet for Member State Submission to the Committee, attached as an annex to the Guidelines of the Committee for the Conduct of Its Work (Committee Guidelines).[110] The cover sheet is intended to simplify the designation process and enhance the quality of the identifier information submitted with State proposals for designation. The cover sheet details the type of identifier information that should be included in the listing proposal. Specific identifier information is needed to enable the accurate identification of individuals and entities by the competent authorities that are required to implement the sanctions measures against such persons and entities. Use of the cover sheet ensures clarity, uniformity and consistency with regard to names submitted by Member States for inclusion on the List.

For individuals, States are required to identify: '[F]amily name/surname, given names, other relevant names, date of birth, place of birth, nationality/citizenship, gender, aliases, employment/occupation, residence, passport or travel document and national identification number, current and previous addresses, website addresses, and current location.'[111] States are encouraged to submit known aliases used by the individual proposed for designation, and whether the alias is considered a 'good quality' or 'low quality' alias.[112] For groups, the following identifier information should be provided: 'name, acronyms, address, headquarters, subsidiaries, affiliates, fronts, nature of business or activity, leadership, tax or other identification number and other names by which it is known or was formerly known' and website address.[113]

However, if submissions are found to be inadequate, the Committee retains discretion to request additional identifier information or refuse to approve the designation until additional information is provided. While less than perfect, the quality of the identifier information included in State submissions has generally improved over time through enhanced listing procedures adopted by the Committee.

Statement of the case

The Guidelines of the Committee for the Conduct of Its Work further requires States to provide a 'statement of the case' with their submission that establishes the justification for the listing in accordance with the relevant resolutions. The 'statement of the case' should provide as much detail as possible for listing, including:

> (1) specific findings demonstrating the association or activities alleged;
> (2) the nature of the supporting evidence (e.g., intelligence, law enforcement, judicial, media, admissions by subject, etc.); and
> (3) supporting evidence or documents that can be supplied. . . . [and]
> (4) the details of any connection with a currently listed individual or entity.[114]

Before a State proposes a name for addition to the Consolidated List, it is encouraged to contact the State of residence or citizenship of the individual or entity concerned to obtain additional information to support the designation.[115] States are also required to indicate to the Committee what portions of the statement of the case may be released to the public or other Member States.[116]

Standard of proof

A criminal charge or conviction is not required for an individual's inclusion on the Consolidated List. Asset freeze is a preventive measure intended to stop the flow of funds to terrorists, rather than punish the owner for the commission of a crime.[117] The legal standard for asset freeze is whether there are 'reasonable grounds' or a 'reasonable basis' to believe that such funds or other assets could be used to finance terrorist activity, not the criminal standard of proof beyond a reasonable doubt.[118] The European Court of First Instance (Second Chamber) has stated that 'freezing of funds is a precautionary measure which, unlike confiscation, does not affect the very substance of the right of the persons concerned to property in their financial assets but only the use thereof.'[119] This point was reiterated in the Third Report of 1526 Sanctions Monitoring Team, stating that

> Although many of those on the List have been convicted of terrorist offences, and others indicted or criminally charged, the List is not a criminal list. . . . [T]he sanctions do not impose a criminal punishment or procedure such as detention, arrest or extradition, but instead apply administrative measures such as freezing assets . . . .[120]

The Sixth Report of the Monitoring Team provides a criminal profile of the individuals on the List:

> [A]bout two thirds of the individuals on the Al-Qaida list have been charged with a criminal offence; about 40 per cent have been convicted and sentenced; the cases against about 20 per cent remain pending; and less than five per cent have been acquitted. More than half of the total were facing charges or had been convicted (even if in absentia) before they were put on the List. About half have been arrested at some point, two thirds of whom were arrested before their listing. No more than 25 per cent of the individuals on the Al-Qaida list can be presumed to be alive, not in custody and never arrested, charged or convicted of a criminal offence.[121]

Many of these individuals are senior leaders of al Qaeda and affiliated terrorist groups. Entities on the Consolidated List associated with the al Qaeda organization read like a 'Who's Who' of Islamist terrorist organizations. These extremist terror groups include: the Abu Sayyaf Group, Al-Itihaad Al-Islamiya, Al Qaeda in the Islamic Maghreb, Al-Jihad/Egyptian Islamic Movement, Ansar Al-Islam, Armed Islamic Group, Eastern Turkistan Islamic Movement, Islamic Army of Aden, Islamic International Brigade, Islamic Jihad Group, Islamic Movement of Uzbekistan, Jaish-i-Mohammed, Jama'at al-Tawhid Wa'al-Jihad, Jemaah Islamiyah, Lashkar-e-Tayyiba, Lashkar-i-Jhangvi, Libyan Islamic Fighting Group, Moroccan Islamic Combat Group, and the Tunisian Combatant Group.[122] Additionally, a number of Islamic charities responsible for funding al Qaeda have been placed on the List, including 14 foreign branches of Al-Haramain, a purported charity based in Saudi Arabia.[123]

Joint designations

In the months following the September 11, 2001 attacks, Member States often submitted joint designations to the Al-Qaida and Taliban Sanctions Committee. For example, in March 2002, the United States participated in its first joint designation of a terrorist supporter. The United States and Saudi Arabia jointly designated the Somalia and Bosnia-Herzegovina offices of Al-Haramain, a Saudi-based charity.[124] These charities are linked to al Qaeda and their names were forwarded to the Committee for inclusion on the Consolidated List. In September 2002, the United States and Saudi Arabia jointly referred to the Sanctions Committee Wa'el Hamza Julaidan, an associate of Osama bin Laden and a supporter of al Qaeda.[125] In April 2002, the United States and the other G7 members jointly designated nine individuals and one organization.[126] All of these groups were European-based al Qaeda organizers and terrorist financiers.[127] In August 2002, the United States and Italy jointly designated 11 individuals and 14 entities linked to the Salafist Group for Call and Combat, an al Qaeda-linked terrorist group operating in Algeria.[128] The group has since changed its name to Al Qaeda in the Islamic Maghreb, and strengthened its affiliation with al Qaeda. In October 2002, following the terrorist attack in Bali, Indonesia, where a mini-van loaded with explosives was detonated in front of two nightclubs, killing 202 people and injuring more than 300 civilians, the United States, Australia, Indonesia, the Philippines, Singapore and several other countries designated Jemaah Islamiya, an al Qaeda-affiliated group operating in Southeast Asia.[129] A few days later, the 1267 Committee added Jemaah Islamiya to its terror list.[130]

While Member States are encouraged to establish a national mechanism or procedure to identify and assess appropriate candidates to propose to the Committee for listing, serious concerns remain regarding the lack of due process involved in the listing procedures.[131] States should enact legislation, if necessary, to empower a competent authority or a court to issue, administer and enforce freezing and unfreezing actions. The competent authorities should ensure that persons and entities within their jurisdictions are prohibited from making any funds or other assets available to designated persons and groups. At the same time, adequate procedures must be put in place to protect the due process rights of the persons designated. The support of the Committee's work seems to be eroding as a result of these due process concerns.[132] These concerns will be discussed more fully in Chapter 12 – 'Accomplishments, failures, and recommendations for enhancing the Anti-Terrorist Financing Legal Regime.'

Review and Final Determination by the Committee

The Committee is required to expeditiously consider requests to update the Consolidated List. Once a submission is received, it is circulated to all 15 Committee members, who have five working days to raise any objection.[133] If no one objects, the listing is approved.[134] However, a Committee member may ask for additional time to consider the submission, in which case a decision is suspended until that member is ready to proceed. Such a 'hold' may occur when a member believes more information is needed to justify the listing, the submission lacks specific identifier information to accurately identify the subject, or more time is needed to evaluate the listing.[135] In practice, the Committee does not reach a decision on submissions within the five-day no-objection period. Since the beginning of 2005, more time has often been required. In fact, it has not been uncommon for a decision on a submission to take weeks.[136]

The decision to approve a submission is made by consensus of the Committee's members.[137] As previously noted, because inclusion on the List is not intended as punishment for a crime, the criminal standard of proof does not apply. Instead, the decision to list is measured against a lower standard of 'reasonable grounds' or 'reasonable basis' to believe that funds or other assets are terrorist-related.[138]

Checklist

Once a proposed designation is approved, the Committee issues an announcement on its website and updates the Consolidated List. All U.N. Member States are thereafter required to 'freeze without delay' any assets owned or controlled by the designated parties.[139] This requires Member States to notify appropriate authorities, agencies and private sector offices within their jurisdictions so that action can be taken to implement the freeze order 'without delay,' which ideally means within a few hours of a designation by the Al-Qaida and Taliban Sanctions Committee. Prompt action is necessary 'to prevent the flight or dissipation of terrorist-linked funds or other assets, and . . . to interdict and disrupt their flow swiftly.'[140] Any delay between a listing becoming public and measures being taken by Member States affords the listed party an opportunity to move assets out of the reach of the sanctions.[141] Additionally, the duty to freeze the assets of persons and groups on the List is an ongoing obligation. For example, when opening a new account, banks should check the name of the new customer against the names on the Consolidated List. The Committee is further responsible for updating the List.

A checklist was introduced by Security Council Resolution 1617 to remind Member States of the action that should be taken with regard to new listings.[142] 'The checklist was designed to minimize the time and resources needed by States to supply the Committee with essential information.'[143] States are required to answer 'yes' or 'no' on several questions, including whether the Member State has notified financial institutions of the designation and frozen any assets.[144] Member States are encouraged to submit any additional information on listed individuals and entities that would improve the existing information on the Consolidated List.[145]

Member States were further required by Resolution 1617 to submit a checklist by March 1, 2006, to the Committee on any individuals and entities on the Consolidated List.[146] However, many States have been unwilling, to submit a checklist to the Committee. In the Seventh Report of the Monitoring Team submitted to the Sanctions Committee in November 2007, the Team observed that submission of the checklist had been less frequent than hoped. The Report states:

> There are . . . 135 States which had not submitted a checklist 19 months after the reporting date (1 March 2006). [T]he checklists have only provided limited information from 57 States on the 24 names added to the List between 29 July 2005 and 31 January 2006, and nothing concerning the 443 names that were already there, or on the 23 names added since February 2006.[147]

The unwillingness of Member States to comply with measures taken by the Security Council to enhance implementation of Resolution 1267 seriously undermines the effectiveness of the financial embargo imposed by the Security Council on members of al Qaeda, the Taliban, and affiliated entities, intended to prevent the commission of terrorist attacks.

DE-LISTING PROCESS

A person whose name is added to the Consolidated List is afforded a process to present his case to the Sanctions Committee for review. The Committee's Guidelines authorize de-listing or removing names from the Consolidated List.[148] Individuals, groups or entities may submit a petition to consider their cases for de-listing through their States of residence or citizenship.[149] Alternatively, a petitioner can submit a request for de-listing through an administrative 'focal point' established within the Security Council Subsidiary Organs Branch to receive de-listing requests.[150] The focal point would forward the de-listing request for information and comment to the designating State and the petitioner's State of residence or citizenship regarding whether they support or oppose the petition for de-listing.[151] The views of the concerned States are then forwarded to the Sanctions Committee for review and a decision on the petition for de-listing. This process is outlined in paragraph 8 of the Committee's Guidelines.[152]

If the petitioner submits the de-listing petition to the State of residence or citizenship, the State should review all relevant information.[153] If the petitioned State wishes to pursue a de-listing request, it should then seek to persuade the designating State to submit jointly or separately a request for de-listing to the Committee.[154] However, the petitioned State may, without an accompanying request from the designating State, submit a request for de-listing to the Committee.[155] The Committee is required to reach a decision by consensus. However, if consensus cannot be reached, the matter may be submitted by the Chairman of the Committee to the Security Council for final resolution.[156]

A name may be removed from the Consolidated List for two reasons: (1) the individual or entity was placed on the List due to a mistake of identity, or (2) the individual or entity no longer meets the criteria set out in the relevant resolutions.[157] In deciding whether to approve the petition for de-listing, the Committee members may consider whether the individual or entity has severed ties with al Qaeda, Osama bin Laden, the Taliban, and their supporters.[158] While de-listing requests are not liberally granted, 11 individuals and 24 entities have been removed from the Consolidated List.[159]

HUMANITARIAN EXCEPTION

Resolution 1452 recognizes a humanitarian exception to assets frozen pursuant to Resolutions 1267 and 1390, creating an exception for assets necessary to cover basic living expenses such as food, rent, mortgage, medicines and medical treatment, taxes, public utilities, and insurance premiums, and for reasonable professional fees including legal fees.[160] In *Ayadi v. Council of the European Union*, the Court of First Instance interpreted the humanitarian exception to prohibit asset freeze of 'any kind of funds or economic resources . . . for the carrying on of employed or self-employed professional activities and the funds received or receivable in connection with such activity.'[161] More specifically, the Court found that granting the applicant a taxi-driver's license, permitting him to use his car for business purposes, and allowing him to keep the receipts produced by working as a taxi-driver could be the object of derogation from the freezing of applicant's funds and economic resources under Resolution 1452.[162]

The resolution also authorizes access to frozen assets necessary to pay 'extraordinary expenses.'[163] What constitutes an 'extraordinary expense' is not defined or explained in the resolution and therefore is subject to liberal interpretation by the concerned State. Under the Committee's Guidelines, Member States are required to notify the Committee of the intention to authorize access to frozen funds or assets needed to cover basic or extraordinary expenses. After receiving notice, the Committee has 48 hours to inform the submitting State of the Committee's position.[164] Once again, the Committee's decision is by consensus, although notifications pursuant to Resolution 1452 are regularly granted by the Committee.[165]

Finally, the creation of a humanitarian exception is consistent with the view that asset freeze is a preventative measure, rather than punishment for the commission of a crime. Assuming the process is not abused, the

Committee is not concerned with funds being used to cover basic living expenses.[166] The purpose of the terrorist financial embargo is to keep money and other financial resources out of the hands of terrorists to prevent the financing of terrorist activities.

LEGAL CHALLENGES TO INTERNATIONAL ACTIONS FREEZING TERRORIST ASSETS

Individuals and entities have challenged their placement on the Consolidated List on grounds that the listing process violates fundamental human rights and due process principles. The majority of these cases have been filed in the United States, the United Kingdom and the European Union.[167] However, in most of these cases the courts dismissed applicants' claims and upheld the sanctions imposed. For example, with respect to designations under Resolution 1267, the Court of First Instance of the European Communities has regularly rejected applicants' human rights and due process claims, upholding application of the sanctions.[168] The appeals in three cases brought in the United Kingdom were dismissed by the courts.[169] In another contested action, a Turkish court overturned a lower court decision that would have unfrozen the petitioner's assets, thereby ending the lawsuit.[170] Finally, the U.S. courts have regularly dismissed challenges to Treasury Department freeze orders, finding that the procedures comported with due process principles.[171]

Arbitrary Deprivation of Property

In *Yusuf and Barakaat International Foundation v. Council of the European Union, et al,* (*Yusuf*) the European Court of First Instance (Second Chamber) rejected applicants' claims that European Union (E.U.) Council of Minister sanctions that were imposed to implement Resolution 1267 constituted an arbitrary deprivation of property, in violation of article 17(2) of the Universal Declaration of Human Rights.[172] Article 17(2) specifies that '[n]o one shall be arbitrarily deprived of his property.'[173] In rejecting applicants' claim, the E.U. Court stressed the importance of the fight against international terrorism and the legitimate role played by the U.N. Security Council in combating threats to international peace and security caused by terrorist acts.[174] The freezing of funds is intended to cut off the flow of funds to terrorists, which the Court viewed as 'an objective of fundamental public interest for the international community.'[175]

The E.U. Court distinguished between the 'freezing' and 'confiscation' of assets. The freezing of assets, the Court stated 'does not affect the very substance of the right of the persons concerned to property in their financial assets but only the use thereof.'[176] Unlike confiscation of funds, where title vests in the government, the applicants continue to own the property. The asset freeze only affects their use of the property, a lesser infringement on their right to own property, the Court stated. The E.U. Court also found significant the exceptions to asset freeze authorized by the Security Council when it adopted Resolution 1452. The resolution exempts assets necessary to cover basic living expenses, such as food, rent, medicine and medical care, taxes and public utility charges.[177] In addition, funds necessary for any 'extraordinary expense' may be unfrozen under Resolution 1452.[178] Thus, any infringement on applicants' property interests is alleviated by the exemptions permitted by Resolution 1452.

The E.U. Court also noted that applicants could petition the Sanctions Committee for de-listing or removal from the Consolidated List.[179] With regard to the procedures for exceptions and de-listing, and the legitimate objective served by freezing the assets of persons and entities suspected of being linked to Osama bin Laden, al Qaeda, and the Taliban, the Court held that the action taken does not constitute an arbitrary interference with or deprivation of the fundamental right to property.[180]

Pre-Deprivation Notice and a Hearing

In *Yusuf*, the European Court of First Instance held that lack of notice and a hearing *before* the applicants' inclusion on the Consolidated List does not infringe fundamental rights guaranteed by Article 6 of the European Convention for the Protection of Human Rights and Fundamental Freedoms.[181] The Court divided the issue into two parts: (1) the right to be heard by the Sanctions Committee before inclusion on the Consolidated List, and (2) the right to be heard by E.U. institutions before the adoption of regulations implementing the relevant sanctions.[182] The E.U. Court rejected both claims. The Court stated that affording applicants notice and a hearing before the Sanctions Committee prior to being placed on the List would 'jeopardise the effectiveness of the sanctions and would have been incompatible with the public interest objective pursued.'[183] The Court further remarked: 'A measure freezing funds must, by its very nature, be able to take advantage of a surprise effect and to be applied with immediate effect. Such a measure cannot, therefore, be the subject-matter of notification before it is implemented.'[184]

The E.U. Court stated that the applicants' fair trial rights were adequately protected by the procedures adopted by the Sanctions Committee affording them a process for review and de-listing *after* their designation.[185] The Court further noted that two of the applicants were in fact heard by the Sanctions Committee through the Swedish government, and their names were removed from the List.[186] Thus, the Court held that lack of notice and a hearing before the Sanctions Committee prior to one's inclusion on the Consolidated List does not offend due process.[187] Applicants must therefore avail themselves of the de-listing procedures set forth in the Committee's Guidelines to challenge their designation and seek removal from the List.

The Court also rejected applicants' claim that they were entitled to notice and a hearing before the E.U. adopted regulations implementing the sanctions imposed by the Al-Qaida and Taliban Sanctions Committee. The Court reasoned that the E.U. had merely transposed into the E.U. legal order, as they were required, resolutions of the Security Council, and decisions of the Sanctions Committee that in no way authorized them to provide for any mechanism for the examination of individual situations, since these matters fell wholly within the competence of the Security Council and the Sanctions Committee.[188] As a result,

> [T]he Community institutions had no power of investigation, no opportunity to check the matters taken to be facts by the Security Council and the Sanctions Committee, no discretion with regard to those matters and no discretion either as to whether it was appropriate to adopt sanctions vis-à-vis the applicants.[189]

The Court held that the right to be heard cannot apply in such circumstances and therefore the E.U. institution was not required to hear the applicants before the contested regulation was adopted.[190] In other words, E.U. courts are not authorized to second-guess designations by the U.N. Sanctions Committee.

The Right to Notice and a Hearing in Freezing Actions Pursuant to Resolution 1373

The European Court of First Instance (Second Chamber) adopted a different approach on the right to notice and a hearing with respect to freezing actions imposed under Resolution 1373.[191] In *Jose Maria Sison v. Council of the European Union*,[192] the Court invalidated on due process grounds sanctions imposed on the applicant that are intended to implement Resolution 1373.[193] The E.U. Court distinguished between sanctions imposed under Resolutions 1267 and 1373.[194] Under Resolution 1373, the Security Council does not identify specific individuals and entities whose assets must be frozen nor does it promulgate specific procedures for freezing funds. Instead, Member States are permitted to exercise broad discretion regarding whose funds are to be frozen under procedures developed by each State.[195] The exercise of discretion, coupled with the lack of uniform procedures for determining whose assets should be frozen, mandates that any decision to freeze funds should be subject to more searching review by the court.[196] The involvement of the courts in the implementation of Resolution 1373 is further justified by the absence of a universally accepted definition of 'terrorism' and 'terrorist act' in international law.[197]

The Court explained that the procedure to impose a measure to freeze funds pursuant to Resolution 1373 takes place on two levels. Initially, a competent national authority must decide whether assets are subject to asset freeze under paragraph 1(c) of the Resolution. Secondly, the E.U. Council must decide whether the facts and evidence justify adding the person to the E.U. list.[198] While the right to notice and a hearing should be safeguarded in the national procedure, the responsibility lies with the national court, consistent with adopted national procedures. There is no right to be heard at the E.U. level. The Court declared:

> [I]t is not for the Council to decide whether the proceedings instigated against the party concerned and resulting in that decision, as provided for by the national law of the relevant Member State, were correctly conducted, or whether the fundamental rights of the party concerned were respected by the national authorities.[199]

That power, the Court stated, belongs exclusively to the national court or to the European Court of Human Rights.[200] The Council is obligated to defer as far as possible to the assessment conducted by the competent national authority.[201] In short, the Court is unwilling to second-guess the decision of the competent national authority.[202]

However, the Court stated that, if the European Council decides to include that person's name on the E.U. list and freeze any funds located within the E.U., the party concerned should be informed by the Council of the specific information and material in its possession which indicates that a decision was made by a competent authority of a Member State to impose measures pursuant to Resolution 1373.[203] Additionally, the Council must disclose why it decided to exercise its discretion to impose sanctions with respect to the party concerned.[204] The Court added that the party should be afforded an opportunity to make known its view on the disclosed information and material.[205] Finally, any subsequent decision to continue freezing funds must be preceded by the opportunity for a hearing and notification of the information relied upon to justify the decision, including, if applicable, any new incriminating evidence.[206] In other words, according to the Court, the concerned party must be afforded notice and an opportunity for a hearing *prior to* making a decision to *continue* the sanctions.

Nevertheless, with respect to the European Council's initial decision to adopt the sanctions imposed by a Member State, the Court agreed with the decision in *Yusuf* that pre-deprivation notice and a hearing 'would be liable to jeopardise the effectiveness of the sanctions and would thus be incompatible with the public-interest objective pursued . . . in accordance with Security Council Resolution 1373 (2001).'[207] Instead, the Court stated that such persons should be notified of the evidence against them either concomitantly with or as soon as possible *after* the adoption of the decision to freeze the funds.[208] Thus, a party is not entitled to pre-deprivation notice and a hearing by the European Council before it decides whether to place the person on the E.U. list.

At the same time, the right to disclosure of evidence relied upon by the Council in deciding to place the party on the E.U. list is not absolute. The Court stated:

> [E]xceptions to the general right to be heard in the course of an administrative procedure are permitted . . . on grounds of public interest, public policy or the maintenance of international relations, or when the purpose of the decision to be taken would or could be jeopardised if that right were observed.[209]

Thus, considerations involving the security of E.U. Member States, or the conduct of their international relations, may preclude disclosure to the parties concerned of certain evidence adduced against them.[210] The Court stated that the case law of the European Court of Human Rights and requirements of Article 6 of the European Convention on Human Rights provide that 'certain restrictions on the right to a fair hearing may be envisaged, especially concerning disclosure of evidence adduced or terms of access to the file.'[211] The Court suggested that restrictions on access may include the particular reasoning of the decision and even the identification of the Member State or third country, if disclosure would jeopardize public security.[212]

Finally, the Court observed that the European Council enjoys broad discretion regarding the matters to be taken into consideration in deciding whether to impose or continue economic sanctions under Resolution 1373.[213] Therefore, a court on review may not substitute its assessment of the evidence, facts and circumstances justifying the adoption of such measures for that of the Council.[214] Instead, the scope of judicial review is limited. The Court stated that review must be restricted to 'checking that the rules governing procedure and the statement of reasons have been complied with, that the facts are materially accurate, and that there has been no manifest error of assessment of the facts or misuse of power.'[215] In short, the Court adopted a restrictive 'manifest error' (not *de novo*) standard of judicial review of European Council decisions.

HOLDING STATES ACCOUNTABLE FOR BREACHING THEIR DUTY TO FREEZE TERRORIST ASSETS

The international legal framework established by the U.N. Security Council to freeze terrorist assets, and reinforced by the Terrorist Financing Convention and the FATF Special Recommendation III on Terrorist Financing, is failing. The economic sanctions regime suffers from two major problems. First, fewer and fewer names are being added to the Consolidated List each year. In 2007, the number of designations reached an all-time low when only eight names were added to the List.[216] The United States contributed to the decline by submitting only 11 names for inclusion on the List, a low mark for the United States.[217] The terrorist financing designations have been trending downward since 2001, when, following the terrorist attacks of September 11, 278 names were placed on the Sanctions List.[218] This downward trend is particularly disturbing considering improvements to the listing procedures, such as the use of a cover sheet to enhance the quality, accuracy and consistency of identifier information included in Member State submissions to the Al-Qaida and Taliban Sanctions Committee, and the creation of an administrative focal point to coordinate petitions for de-listing.[219] U.N. counter-terrorism experts maintain that '[t]he inconsistent relevance of the List to the current [terrorism] threat continues to undermine the effectiveness of the sanctions regime.'[220]

The sanctions regime suffers from a second problem: lack of implementation by Member States. After a name is placed on the Consolidated List, States are required to 'freeze without delay' the assets of such persons.[221] Failure to take swift action creates a risk that funds intended to finance terrorist activities will be transferred or dissipated to circumvent sanctions. However, there has been no significant increase in the amount of funds frozen under the sanctions regime since 2004.[222] (See Figure 9.1.) Terrorist-related assets are not being frozen by Member States obligated to do so by Security Council resolutions. Furthermore, the U.N. Sanctions Monitoring Team estimates that 95 percent of the total value of the assets frozen to date results from the freezing actions of only nine States.[223] The finding of the Monitoring Team suggests that few States are taking seriously their obligations to freeze al Qaeda- and Taliban-related assets. Even when names are added to the List, States are refusing to freeze the assets of those individuals and entities.

Several reasons have been proffered for the decline in the number of listing submissions to the Committee and the lack of enforcement by Member States, including: (1) lack of capacity by certain States to administer the economic sanctions program;[224] (2) lack of identifier information on the List;[225] and (3) due process and human rights concerns regarding the

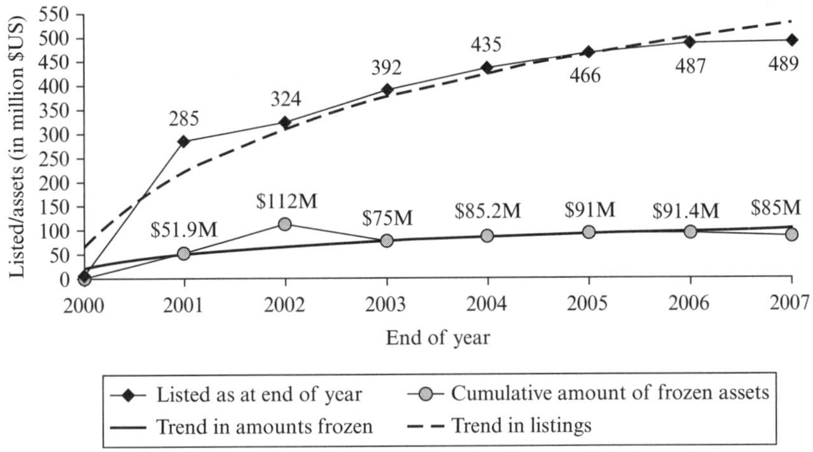

Source: Annex III – Impact of Listing on the Value of Frozen Assets, Seventh Report of the Analytical Support and Sanctions Monitoring Team, U.N. Doc. S/2007/677 (November 29, 2007), p. 45.

Figure 9.1 Impact of listings on the value of assets frozen

procedures employed for designation.[226] While these concerns may have some merit, and the Al-Qaida and Taliban Sanctions Committee has been responsive to them, these reasons fail to adequately explain the paucity of listing submissions and the lack of rigorous enforcement of sanctions by Member States. Inevitably, this leads to the conclusion that the more likely reason for State non-compliance is lack of political will.[227]

Lack of Administrative Capacity

While some States may lack the administrative capabilities and require training and technical assistance to implement the economic sanctions program, the 34 countries that comprise the FATF do not fall within that category.[228] These countries are fully or largely in compliance with major international standards to prevent money laundering and terrorist financing and are fully capable of compliance with relevant anti-terrorist financing resolutions.[229] Furthermore, countries granted 'observer status,' such as India and the Republic of Korea, which are striving for FATF membership, also have adequate laws, regulations, procedures and administrative systems in place to detect and prevent terrorist financing.[230] At a minimum, these 36 countries have the administrative capabilities to implement the mandates of Resolutions 1267 and 1333.[231] Therefore, the lack of administrative capacity argument does not explain why only nine countries are responsible for freezing 95 percent of the funds frozen under the international sanctions regime, or why no countries have frozen terrorist assets since 2004.

Lack of Accurate Identifier Information

The lack of accurate identifier information argument likewise does not explain the lack of new listings and the reluctance of Member States to freeze the assets of individuals and entities on the List. The Sixth Report of the Analytical Support and Sanctions Monitoring Team conservatively estimates that the number of Taliban fighters is 4,000 and 5,000 men.[232] The Taliban Movement of Pakistan is reported to have a force totalling as many as 40,000 fighters.[233] However, while the revival of the Taliban continues to accelerate, only one Taliban name has been added to the Consolidated List since February 2001. This includes the failure to add the names of new senior leaders of the Taliban.[234] For example, Baitullah Mehsud, the head of the Taliban Movement in Pakistan, and other senior Taliban leaders have been included on the Consolidated List.[235]

Since 9/11 more than 4,000 people have been arrested or detained in more than 100 countries on the basis of their connection to al Qaeda.[236] Several dozen members have been convicted for plotting terrorist attacks, and for providing financial assistance and other material assistance to al Qaeda.[237] However, only a few hundred individuals and even fewer entities associated with al Qaeda have been placed on the Consolidated List.[238] In some cases, well-known senior leaders of al Qaeda or affiliated terrorist organizations have been omitted from the List. Neither Abu Hamza al-Muhajir, the leader of Al Qaeda in Iraq, nor Abu Dujana, the head of the military wing of Jemaah Islamiya, a Southeast Asian terrorist group affiliated with al Qaeda, have been placed on the List. There is certainly sufficient identifier information regarding the senior leadership of al Qaeda, the Taliban, and affiliated terrorist groups to include them on the terror list. Abu Dujana was arrested by Indonesian authorities in the summer of 2007. His date of birth and other identifier information should be a matter of public record. This problem was highlighted in the Sixth Report of the Analytical Support and Sanctions Monitoring Team: 'The absence of certain well-known names from the List undermines States' belief that it is a current, relevant, dynamic and well-considered list of the key members of the Taliban, al Qaeda and associated groups.'[239] The paucity of State submissions for inclusion on the Consolidated List cannot be attributed to lack of identifier information.

Nor can the lack of action taken to *freeze* the assets of individuals and entities on the terror list be explained by lack of accurate identifier information. A review of the Consolidated List reveals that names added between

2006 and 2008 included the following identifier information: the individual's full name, date of birth, place of birth, high-quality aliases, and one or more additional identifiers, such as address, nationality, or passport number.[240] In short, there is ample identifier information included on the Consolidated List to reassure States that the assets of the right person are being frozen.

Due Process Concerns

As previously noted, while several legal actions have been filed challenging the freezing actions taken under Resolutions 1267 and 1333, claiming violations of due process and fundamental human rights, almost all of those claims have been rejected by the courts. The Court of First Instance of the European Communities has denied due process claims brought by Ali Ahmed Yusuf and the Barakaat International Foundation;[241] Yasin Abdullah Qadi;[242] Shafiq ben Mohamed ben Mohamed Al-Ayadi;[243] and Faraj Hussein Al-Sa'idi.[244] In upholding the sanctions against these individuals, the Court of First Instance found that the burden imposed by the asset freeze was diminished by possible derogations, allowing exceptions for basic living expenses permitted by procedures adopted by the Committee.[245] Such legal claims have been regularly denied by courts in the United States and the United Kingdom as well.[246] Thus, adverse court judgments have not posed a major obstacle to implementation of the sanctions imposed pursuant to Resolution 1267.

Lack of Political Will

A more reasonable explanation for the current decline of the international legal regime to freeze terrorist assets is the lack of political will by certain Member States.[247] The States that lack interest in compliance with Resolutions 1267 and 1333, whether because they question the relevance or the value of the sanctions, should be reminded that compliance is mandatory. Pursuant to Article 25 of the U.N. Charter, States are required to accept and carry out the decisions of the Security Council.[248] Thus, the duty to freeze the assets of persons included on the Consolidated List is obligatory, not discretionary. A State that fails to comply has violated Article 25 of the U.N. Charter. Additionally, with respect to parties to the Terrorist Financing Convention, failure to take appropriate measures to freeze terrorist assets constitutes a breach of Article 8(1) of the Convention.[249] Finally, such States are in violation of FATF Special Recommendation III, which requires jurisdictions to freeze terrorist-related assets 'without delay' in accordance with relevant United Nations resolutions.[250]

States that demonstrate a consistent lack of interest in compliance should themselves be subject to sanctions for violating their legal obligations under principles of international law. The members of the Sanctions Monitoring Team maintain that some type of sanction may be appropriate for non-compliant countries. The Fifth Report of the Analytical Support and Sanctions Monitoring Team, released in September 2006, states:

> Sometimes a State may need a quiet reminder of its obligations in order to tighten its procedures, but at other times, a more public encouragement might be necessary. . . . The Committee may need to decide what action to take in what circumstances. . . . It will want to exhaust every possible avenue before allowing the situation to become confrontational. The intermediate steps should involve a close and confidential dialogue between the Committee and the State concerned . . . to establish the facts and illuminate the underlying reasons for non-compliance.[251]

While the Security Council might consider imposing economic measures against non-compliant States pursuant to its Chapter VII powers, the veto authority possessed by the five permanent Members of the Security Council could make imposition of any such measures difficult, if not impossible.[252] Another option for holding non-compliant States accountable would be to revive the FATF list of Non-Cooperative Countries and Territories (NCCT), this time for those countries not in compliance with the Nine Special Recommendations on Terrorist Financing. Special Recommendation III substantially overlaps with Resolutions 1267 and 1333, encouraging States to freeze without delay the funds or other assets of terrorists in accordance with relevant U.N. resolutions.[253]

In 2000, the FATF established a procedure to evaluate countries and territories for compliance with accepted international standards for preventing money laundering.[254] A total of 47 countries or territories were examined by members of the FATF in 2000 and 2001, and 23 countries were placed on the FATF NCCT list.[255] 'The goal of the initiative [was] to secure the adoption by all financial centres of international standards to prevent, detect and punish money laundering, and thereby effectively cooperate internationally in the global fight against money laundering.'[256] Being placed on the NCCT list had a sobering yet positive effect. States realized that being identified by the FATF as an NCCT was harmful to their reputation.[257] Also, countries appreciated that adopting current anti-money laundering standards was important for the protection and soundness of their financial systems.[258] Most NCCT countries began immediately to improve their anti-money laundering regimes after being listed.[259] All 23 countries were eventually removed from the NCCT list for implementing effective measures to prevent money laundering and no additional jurisdictions are currently being reviewed under this process.[260]

A similar process could be employed to ensure State compliance with international standards on terrorist financing. The U.N. Sanctions Committee or Monitoring Team could propose States for evaluation by the FATF. The Monitoring Team would work closely with the FATF, sharing its expertise, experience and knowledge on lack of State compliance with Resolutions 1267 and 1333, and jointly they could prepare a report outlining areas of deficiency. The States concerned would be given an opportunity to comment on the report and provide a timeline for implementing needed changes to ensure compliance with the duty to freeze terrorist assets. Failure to implement needed changes could result in the States being placed on the terrorist financing NCCT list.[261] Being placed on the NCCT list for terrorist financing could have a deterrent effect and cause States to begin to improve their anti-terrorist financing regimes to avoid being placed on the new NCCT list.

Finally, the United States needs to assume a stronger leadership role in the implementation of Resolutions 1267 and 1333. Leadership must be demonstrated by example. The submission of 11 names for listing in 2007, when al Qaeda and the Taliban are amply funded and remain a serious threat to international peace and security, is unacceptable. There are over 20 al Qaeda-affiliated terrorist groups on the Consolidated List.[262] At the very least, the U.S. needs to submit the names of the senior leaders of these terrorist organizations for inclusion on the Consolidated List in order to ensure that individuals and entities are deterred from providing them funds, financial assistance, and economic resources of any kind.

The effectiveness of the international economic sanctions program to freeze terrorist assets can be revived. However, maintaining the status quo is not a viable option. States must be held accountable for lack of cooperation and breach of their legal duties imposed by relevant Security Council resolutions and the Terrorist Financing Convention. The failure to take action to hold such States accountable runs the risk of rendering the international sanctions regime irrelevant in the fight against terrorism.

NOTES

1. International Convention for the Suppression of the Financing of Terrorism, Dec. 9, 1999, S. Treaty Doc. No. 106–49, 2178 U.N.T.S. 229, *available at* http://untreaty.un.org/ENGLISH/bible/englishinternetbible/partI/chapterXVIII/treaty12.asp [hereinafter Terrorist Financing Convention].
2. Pursuant to Article 24(1) of the United Nations Charter, the members of the United Nations 'confer on the Security Council primary responsibility for the maintenance of international peace and security, and agree that in carrying out its duties under this responsibility the Security Council acts on their behalf.' U.N. Charter art. 24.

3. The major Security Council resolutions adopted to strengthen and enhance the measures imposed under Resolutions 1267 and 1333 (imposing a financial embargo on al Qaeda, Osama bin Laden, the Taliban, and their associates) include: S.C. Res 1363, U.N. Doc. S/RES/1363 (2001) (establishing a mechanism to monitor implementation of measures imposed by Resolutions 1267 and 1333); S.C. Res. 1390, U.N. Doc. S/RES/1390 (2002) (expanding the financial embargo); S.C. Res. 1452, U.N. Doc. S/RES/1452 (2002) (recognizing certain exceptions to the asset freeze); S.C. Res. 1455, U.N. Doc. S/RES/1455 (2003) (calling for updated reports from States on implementation of measures); S.C. Res. 1526, U.N. Doc. S/RES/1526 (2004) (creating Analytical Support and Sanctions Monitoring Team); S.C. Res. 1617, U.N. Doc. S/RES/1617 (2005) (providing definition of 'associated with' and calling for submission of checklist); S.C. Res. 1730, U.N. Doc. S/RES/1730 (2006) (establishing 'focal point' to receive de-listing requests); and S.C. Res. 1735, U.N. Doc. S/RES/1735 (2006) (providing for a cover sheet listing submissions and extending mandate of Monitoring Team). The Security Council resolutions relevant to Resolution 1373 (2001) (creating Counter-Terrorism Committee) include: S.C. Res. 1535, U.N. Doc. S/RES/1535 (2004) (creating Counter-Terrorism Committee Executive Directorate (CTED)); S.C. Res. 1566 (2004), U.N. Doc. S/RES/1566 (creating working group); S.C. Res. 1624, U.N. Doc. S/RES/1624 (2005) (prohibiting the incitement to commit terrorist acts); S.C. Res. 1631, U.N. Doc. S/RES/1631 (2005) (encouraging better cooperation between U.N. and regional and subregional organizations); and S.C. Res. 1787, U.N. Doc. S/RES/1787 (2007) (extending the mandate of CTED).
4. *See, e.g.*, S.C. Res. 1390, U.N. Doc. S/RES/1390 (2002), S.C. Res. 1333, U.N. Doc. S/RES/1333 (2000), and S.C. Res. 1267, U.N. Doc. S/RES/1267 (1999).
5. U.N. Security Council, Analytical Support and Sanctions Monitoring Team, Seventh Report of the Analytical Support and Sanctions Monitoring Team, ¶2, U.N. Doc. S/2007/677 (Nov. 29, 2007), *available at* http://www.un.org/sc/committees/1267/monitoringteam.shtml [hereinafter Seventh Report of the Sanctions Monitoring Team].
6. *See* Terrorist Financing Convention, *supra* note 1.
7. *See* Jean-François Thony, *Money Laundering and Terrorism Financing: An Overview*, at 12, *available at* http://www.imf.org/external/np/leg/sem/2002/cdmfl/eng/thony.pdf. The U.S. ratified the convention on June 25, 2002. *See* Terrorist Bombings Convention Implementation Act of 2002, Pub. L. No. 107–197, 116 Stat. 721 (2002).
8. Terrorist Financing Convention, *supra* note 1, at art. 4.
9. *Id.* at art. 5(3).
10. *Id.* at art. 8(1).
11. *Id.*
12. In response to growing concerns over money laundering and the threat posed to the banking system and financial institutions, the Financial Action Task Force on Money Laundering (FATF) was established by the G7 summit held in Paris in 1989. In April 1990, the FATF issued a report containing a set of Forty Recommendations, which set out a basic legal framework to detect, prevent and suppress money laundering. In October 2001, the FATF expanded its mission to include the prevention of terrorist financing. The FATF has adopted Nine Special Recommendations on Terrorist Financing. *See* Financial Action Task Force (FATF), 9 Special Recommendations (SR) on Terrorist Financing (TF) (last visited Apr. 14, 2008), *available at* http://www.fatf-gafi.org/pages/0,2987,en_32250379_32235720_1_1_1_1_1,00.html [hereinafter Nine Special Recommendations on Terrorist Financing]; Financial Action Task Force (FATF), The 40 Recommendations, June 20, 2003, *available at* http://www.fatf-gafi.org/document/28/0,3343,en_32250379_32236930_33658140_1_1_1_1,00.html [hereinafter Forty Recommendations].
13. The FATF is comprised of 34 member countries. India and the Republic of Korea are observer countries. The associate members include: the Asia/Pacific Group on Money Laundering (APG), the Grupo de Acción Financiera de Sudamérica (GAFISUD), Middle East and North Africa Financial Action Task Force (MENAFATF), and the

Council of Europe Select Committee of Experts on the Evaluation of Anti-Money Laundering Measures (MONEYVAL). The Caribbean Financial Action Task Force, Eurasian Group, Eastern and Southern Africa Anti-Money Laundering Group, and the Intergovernmental Action Group against Money Laundering in Africa are FATF-style regional bodies. *See* Financial Action Task Force (FATF), FATF Members and Observers, *available at* http://www.fatf-gafi.org/document/52/0,3343,en_32250379_32237295_34027188_1_1_1_1,00.html.

14. In 2004, a Ninth Special Recommendation on Terrorist Financing was adopted. *See* Nine Special Recommendations on Terrorist Financing, *supra* note 12. At the time, I served as Under Secretary (Enforcement), U.S. Department of the Treasury, and directed U.S. efforts to organize a special meeting of FATF member countries in Washington, D.C.
15. *Id.* Special Recommendation III further provides: 'Each country should also adopt and implement measures, including legislative ones, which would enable the competent authorities to seize and confiscate property that is the proceeds of, or used in, or intended or allocated for use in, the financing of terrorism, terrorist acts or terrorist organisations.' *Id.*
16. In Resolution 1617, the Security Council strongly urges all Member States to implement the comprehensive international standards set forth in the Financial Action Task Force's Forty Recommendations on Money Laundering and Nine Special Recommendations on Terrorist Financing. S.C. Res. 1617, U.N. Doc. S/RES/1617 (2005).
17. U.N. Sec. Council, Report of the Security Council Working Group Established Pursuant to Resolution 1566, ¶16, U.N. Doc. S/2005/789 (2004), *available at* http://seagrass.goatchurch.org.uk/~undemocracy/undata/pdf/S-2005-789.pdf. The mandate of the Working Group is to advise the Security Council on practical measures to be imposed on individuals and groups involved in terrorist activities, other than those designated by the Al-Qaida and Taliban Sanctions Committee. *See* S.C. Res. 1566, art. 9, U.N. Doc. S/RES/1566 (2004).
18. Seventh Report of the Sanctions Monitoring Team, *supra* note 5, ¶57. The Monitoring Team estimates that approximately $85 million remains frozen, down from the $91.4 million quoted in its last two reports. *Id.*
19. *See* U.N. Sec. Council, Analytical Support and Sanctions Monitoring Team, Sixth Report of the Analytical Support and Sanctions Monitoring Team (March 8, 2007), ¶53, U.N. Doc. S/2007/132, *available at* http://www.un.org/sc/committees/1267/monitoringteam.shtml [hereinafter Sixth Report of the Sanctions Monitoring Team].
20. *Id.*
21. Press Release, U.S. Dep't of Treasury, United States Designates bin Laden Loyalist (Feb. 24, 2004), *available at* http://www.ustreas.gov/press/releases/js1190.htm.
22. FATF, Freezing of Terrorist Assets: International Best Practices, at 2 (Oct. 3, 2003), *available at* http://www.oecd.org/dataoecd/30/43/34242709.pdf.
23. Sixth Report of the Sanctions Monitoring Team (Mar. 8, 2007), *supra* note 19, ¶54.
24. *See, e.g.*, S.C. Res. 1267, U.N. Doc. S/RES/1267 (1999) & S.C. Res. 1333, U.N. Doc. S/RES/1333 (2000).
25. *See* S.C. Res. 1333, ¶8(c).
26. *See* Seventh Report of the Sanctions Monitoring Team, *supra* note 5, ¶25.
27. *Id.* According to the Monitoring Team, in 2000 there were seven listings; 2001 – 278; 2002 – 54; 2003 – 77; 2004 – 44; 2005 – 32; 2006 – 24; and 2007 – 5. *Id.* at ¶25 & n. 37. However, the Consolidated List shows that eight, not five, names were added in 2007. The Al-Qaida and Taliban Sanctions Committee, The Consolidated List of the United Nations Security Council's Al-Qaida and Taliban Sanctions Committee, *available at* http://www.un.org/sc/committees/1267/consolist.shtml (last visited Jan. 17, 2008) [hereinafter 'Consolidated List'].
28. *See* Seventh Report of the Sanctions Monitoring Team, *supra* note 5, at Appendix III.

29. *Id.* at ¶57.
30. *Id.* at ¶1.
31. *Id.* at ¶11.
32. *Id.*
33. *Id.* at ¶15.
34. *See Algeria Violence Death Toll Jumps in December*, REUTERS, Jan. 3, 2008, *available at* http://www.reuters.com/article/latestCrisis/idUSAHM258436.
35. *Id.*; *see also U.S. Tells Embassy Staff to Raise Algiers Security*, REUTERS, Jan. 20, 2008, *available at* http://www.nytimes.com/reuters/washington/politics-algeria-usa.html?
36. *See* Kathy Gannon, *New Taliban Chief Entering Limelight*, ASSOC. PRESS, Jan. 26, 2008, *available at* http://ap.google.com/article/ALeqM5i38Cj7htJXGfd40DmfC37DGw778AD8UDNOQO1.
37. SEVENTH REPORT OF THE SANCTIONS MONITORING TEAM, *supra* note 5, ¶17.
38. *Id.*; Gannon, *supra* note 36.
39. SEVENTH REPORT OF THE SANCTIONS MONITORING TEAM, *supra* note 5, ¶19.
40. Hamid Shalizi, *Suicide Attack on Afghan Luxury Hotel Kills Seven*, REUTERS, Jan. 14, 2008, *available at* http://www.reuters.com/article/worldNews/idUSISL374622008 0115. Norway has about 500 soldiers in Afghanistan as part of a NATO-led international force deployed there after the U.S.-led opposition forces ousted the Taliban in 2001. *Id.*
41. *See* Gannon, *supra* note 36; *CIA Links al Qaeda, Allies to Bhutto Attack*, REUTERS, Jan. 18, 2008, *available at* http://www.reuters.com/article/topNews/idUSN1751121820080118?feedType=RSS&feedName=topNews.
42. *See* SEVENTH REPORT OF THE SANCTIONS MONITORING TEAM, *supra* note 5, ¶¶8, 25.
43. *Id.* at ¶¶57–8, and 58 n. 55; *see also* SIXTH REPORT OF THE SANCTIONS MONITORING TEAM, *supra* note 19, ¶3 ('[F]ew names have been added to the Consolidated List of individuals, groups and entities subject to the Al-Qaida/Taliban sanctions measures, and States have not reported much action against those who are already on it.') (footnotes omitted).
44. *See* SIXTH REPORT OF THE SANCTIONS MONITORING TEAM, *supra* note 19, ¶6 ('[I]t seems clear that the [Taliban] movement has no current shortage of money, either to hire fighters or to provide them with weapons.') (footnotes omitted); *see also id.* at ¶¶9–12.
45. *See supra* note 3 and accompanying text (noting that the sanctions regime established by Resolutions 1267 and 1333 has been modified and strengthened by subsequent resolutions, including Resolutions 1390 (2002), 1455 (2003), 1526 (2004), 1617 (2005) and 1735 (2006)).
46. S.C. 1267, U.N. Doc. S/RES/1267 (1999). Resolution 1267 also imposed a ban on air travel to and from territory owned or controlled by the Taliban, ordered the Taliban to cease providing al Qaeda a safe haven, and ordered that bin Laden be immediately turned over to appropriate authorities for prosecution in connection with the African embassy bombings. *Id.*
47. S.C. 1267, ¶4(b), U.N. Doc. S/RES/1267 (1999).
48. *Id.* at ¶6. The Al-Qaida and Taliban Sanctions Committee is responsible for overseeing implementation by States of the sanctions measures (assets freeze, travel ban and arms embargo) imposed by the Security Council on individuals and entities belonging to or associated with the Taliban, Osama bin Laden, and the Taliban. *See* Al-Qaida and Taliban Sanctions Committee, *available at* http://www.un.org/sc/committees/1267/index.shtml.
49. S.C. Res. 1333, ¶5(a) (weapons ban), ¶8(b) (requiring Member States to close all offices of Ariana Afghan Airlines in their territories), and ¶11 (air travel ban), U.N. Doc. S/RES/1333 (2000).
50. S.C. Res. 1333.
51. *Id.* at ¶8(c).
52. *See* Al-Qaida and Taliban Sanctions Committee, Fact Sheet on Listing, *available at* http://www.un.org/sc/committees/1267/fact_sheet_listing.shtml [hereinafter Fact Sheet on Listing]. Resolution 1390 (2002) expanded the sanctions imposed under Resolutions 1267 and 1333 beyond the Islamic Emirate of Afghanistan, the name given to the

country of Afghanistan under Taliban rule. The sanctions imposed by the Security Council are no longer confined to a country or a specific territory, but refer to terrorist groups and individuals generally. *See* Case T-306/01, Yusuf v. Council of the E.U., 2005 ECR II-3533, ¶128 ('[A]lthough [Resolution 1390] still expressly refers to the Taliban, the resolution is no longer aimed at their fallen regime, but rather directly at Usama bin Laden, the Al-Qaeda network and the persons and entities associated with them.').

53. *See* SEVENTH REPORT OF THE SANCTIONS MONITORING TEAM, *supra* note 5, ¶25 n. 37 (in 2000 there were only seven listings).
54. S.C. Res. 1373, U.N. Doc. S/RES/1373 (2001).
55. *See id.* at ¶2(a), (c), (f) & (g); *see also* ALISTAIR MILLAR & ERIC ROSAND, ALLIED AGAINST TERRORISM 16 (Century Foundation Press 2006).
56. S.C. Res. 1373, ¶1(b), U.N. Doc. S/RES/1373 (2001).
57. The duty to establish the financing of terrorism as a criminal offense under a State's domestic legislation is further imposed as a term of the International Convention for the Suppression of the Financing of Terrorism. *See* Terrorist Financing Convention, *supra* note 1, at art. 4. The U.S. is a signatory to the Terrorist Financing Convention, which was ratified by the U.S. Senate on June 25, 2002. *See* Terrorist Bombings Convention Implementation Act of 2002, Pub. L. No. 107–197, 116 Stat. 721 (2002).
58. S.C. Res. 1373, ¶2(e), U.N. Doc. S/RES/1373 (2001).
59. *Id.* at ¶1(d).
60. *Id.* at ¶1(c).
61. *Id.* Resolution 1617 (2005) defines the acts or activities indicating that an individual or entity is 'associated with' al Qaeda, Osama bin Laden, or the Taliban to include:

    - participating in the financing, planning, facilitating, preparing, or perpetrating of acts or activities by, in conjunction with, under the name of, on behalf of, or in support of;
    - supplying, selling or transferring arms and related materials to;
    - recruiting for; or
    - otherwise supporting acts or activities of;

    Al Qaida, Usama bin Laden or the Taliban, or any cell, affiliate, splinter group or derivative thereof. S.C. Res. 1617, ¶2, U.N. Doc. S/RES/1617 (2005).

62. S.C. Res. 1373, ¶1(c), U.N. Doc. S/RES/1373 (2001).
63. *See* SEVENTH REPORT OF THE SANCTIONS MONITORING TEAM, *supra* note 5, ¶¶82, 84.
64. In 1997, HAMAS was designated as a terrorist organization pursuant to Executive Order 12947. In November 2001, it was added to the list of terrorist organizations subject to asset freeze under Executive Order 13224. *See* Press Release, U.S. Dep't of Treasury, Shutting Down the Terrorist Financial Network (Dec. 4, 2001), *available at* http://www.treasury.gov/press/releases/po841.htm.
65. On January 25, 1995, Hizballah was listed as a Specially Designated Terrorist (SDT). The State Department designated the extremist group as a Foreign Terrorist Organization in 1997. Additionally, on October 31, 2001, Hizballah was designated by the Treasury Department as a Specially Designated Global Terrorist under Executive Order (E.O.) 13224. *See* Press Release, U.S. Dep't of Treasury, Treasury Designates Hizballah's Construction Arm (Feb. 20, 2007), *available at* http://www.treasury.gov/press/releases/hp271.htm.
66. On October 8, 1997, the State Department designated the LTTE an FTO. On November 2, 2001, the State Department named the LTTE an SDGT under E.O. 13224. The LTTE is also listed as a terrorist organization by the European Union and Canada. *See* Press Release, U.S. Dep't of Treasury, Treasury Targets Charity Covertly Supporting Violence in Sri Lanka (Nov. 15, 2007), *available at* http://www.treasury.gov/press/releases/hp683.htm.
67. The FARC was named as an FTO by the State Department in October 1997. In addition, in November 2001, the FARC was designated as an SDGT pursuant to E.O. 13224. *See* Press Release, U.S. Dep't of Treasury, Treasury Targets 15 Leaders of

Colombian Narco-Terrorist Group (Nov. 1, 2007), *available at* http://www.treasury.gov/press/releases/hp661.htm.

68. *See* S.C. Res. 1373, U.N. Doc. S/RES/1373 (2001).
69. *See* Case T-47/03, Sison v. Council of the E.U., 2007 ECR 00, ¶¶164–7 (discussing the process for asset freeze under Resolution 1373).
70. *Id.*
71. MILLAR & ROSAND, *supra* note 55, at 19.
72. S.C. Res. 1333, U.N. Doc. S/RES/1333 (2000) and S.C. Res. 1390, U.N. Doc. S/RES/1390 (2002).
73. *See* S.C. Res. 1333, ¶8(c).
74. For a more comprehensive list of the 1267 Committee's mandate see Al-Qaida and Taliban Sanctions Committee, Guidelines of the Committee for the Conduct of Its Work (adopted Nov. 7, 2002, as amended most recently on Feb. 12, 2007), *available at* http://www.un.org/sc/committees/1267/pdf/1267_guidelines.pdf [hereinafter Guidelines of the Committee].
75. *See* S.C. Res. 1526, ¶¶6, 7, U.N. Doc. S/RES/1526 (2004).
76. *Id.* at ¶8.
77. The last report of the Monitoring Committee was submitted on May 13, 2008. *See generally* EIGHTH REPORT OF THE SANCTIONS MONITORING TEAM, U.N. Doc.S/2008/324 (May 13, 2008).
78. *Id.* at ¶¶118–38. Between November 2006 and September 2007, the Monitoring Team visited 15 countries to assess the progress being made by these States to implement Resolution 1267. *Id.* at ¶118.
79. S.C. Res. 1373, ¶6, U.N. Doc. S/RES/1373 (2001).
80. *See* U.N. SEC. COUNCIL, COUNTER-TERRORISM COMMITTEE, REPORT OF THE COUNTER-TERRORISM COMMITTEE TO THE SECURITY COUNCIL, ¶¶12–14, U.N. Doc. S/2007/675 (Nov. 20, 2007).
81. *Id.* at ¶2.
82. *See* MILLAR & ROSAND, *supra* note 55, at 16–17; *see also* U.S. Gov't Accountability Office, *Better Strategic Planning Needed to Coordinate U.S. Efforts to Deliver Counter-Terrorism Financing Training and Technical Assistance Abroad*, at 40 (2005), *available at* http://www.gao.gov/new.items/d0619.pdf.
83. U.N. Security Council Resolution 1624 directs the CTC to report back on steps being taken by States to prohibit by law incitement to commit terrorist acts. *See* S.C. Res. 1624, ¶¶5–6, U.N. Doc. S/RES/1624 (2005).
84. *See* S.C. Res. 1535, ¶2, U.N. Doc. S/RES/1535 (2004). The CTED's mandate is set to expire on March 31, 2008. *See* S.C. Res. 1787, U.N. Doc. S/RES/1787 (2007); *see also* Mike Smith, Executive Director of the CTED, Security Council Counter-Terrorism Committee, Presentation to John Jay College of Criminal Justice (Dec. 13, 2007), *available at* http://www.un.org/sc/ctc/pdf/JohnJayCollegespeech.pdf.
85. *See* U.N. Sec. Council, Letter from the Chairman of the Security Council Committee established pursuant to Resolution 1373 (2001) concerning counter-terrorism addressed to the President of the Security Council, ¶8, U.N. Doc. S/2004/124 (Feb. 19, 2004), *available at* http://www.un.org/Docs/journal/asp/ws.asp?m=S/2004/124. The CTED has been fully staffed since September 2005 and was declared fully operational in December 2005. *See* MILLAR & ROSAND, *supra* note 55, at 17; *see also* CTED web page, *available at* http://www.un.org/sc/ctc/cted.shtml.
86. *See* U.N. Sec. Council, Organizational Plan for the Counter-Terrorism Committee Executive Directorate, ¶¶14–16, U.N. Doc. S/2004/642 (Aug. 12, 2004), *available at* http://www.un.org/sc/ctc/cted.shtml.
87. *Id.* at ¶¶17–18.
88. *See* Mike Smith, Executive Director of the CTED, Security Council Counter-Terrorism Committee, Presentation to John Jay College of Criminal Justice, (Dec. 13, 2007), *available at* http://www.un.org/sc/ctc/pdf/JohnJayCollegespeech.pdf.
89. *See* CTED web page, *available at* http://www.un.org/sc/ctc/cted.shtml.
90. *See* SEVENTH REPORT OF THE SANCTIONS MONITORING TEAM, *supra* note 5, at ¶¶118, 121.

91. *See* MILLAR & ROSAND, *supra* note 55, at 17.
92. Press Release, Security Council Acts Unanimously to Adopt Resolution Strongly Condemning Terrorism as One of Most Serious Threats to Peace (Aug. 10, 2004), U.N. Doc. SC/8214, *available at* http://www.un.org/News/Press/docs/2004/sc8214.doc.htm.
93. S.C. Res. 1566, U.N. Doc. S/RES/1566 (2004).
94. *Id.* at ¶9.
95. *Id.* at ¶10.
96. As of January 2008, the 1566 Working Group has only published one report proposing some general practical measures to prevent terrorist financing. *See* REPORT OF THE SECURITY COUNCIL WORKING GROUP ESTABLISHED PURSUANT TO RESOLUTION 1566 (Dec. 14, 2005).
97. The Security Council condemned criminal acts, including those

    [A]gainst civilians, committed with the intent to cause death or serious bodily injury, or taking of hostages, with the purpose to provoke a state of terror in the general public or in a group of persons or particular persons, intimidate a population or compel a government or an international organization to do or to abstain from doing any act, and all other acts which constitute offences within the scope of and as defined in the international conventions and protocols relating to terrorism, are under no circumstances justifiable by considerations of a political, philosophical, ideological, racial, ethnic, religious or other similar nature. S.C. Res. 1566, ¶3, U.N. Doc. S/RES/1566 (2004).

98. Whether the definition of 'terrorism' articulated by the U.N. Security Council rises to the level of customary law is unsettled at this time. However, the support of such a definition by the 15 members of the Security Council, including its five permanent members, is highly significant in elevating the definition to a principle of international law.
99. S.C. Res. 1540, U.N. Doc. S/RES/1540 (2004); *see also* MILLAR & ROSAND, *supra* note 55, at 18.
100. S.C. Res. 1540, ¶1.
101. *Id.* at ¶¶2–3; *see also* S.C. Res. 1673, ¶5, U.N. Doc. S/RES/1673 (2006).
102. *See* S.C. Res. 1540, ¶4.
103. *Id.* at ¶4
104. S.C. Res. 1673, ¶4.
105. U.N. SEC. COUNCIL, ANALYTICAL SUPPORT AND SANCTIONS MONITORING TEAM, FIFTH REPORT OF THE ANALYTICAL SUPPORT AND SANCTIONS MONITORING TEAM, ¶22, U.N. Doc. S/2006/750 (Sept. 20, 2006), *available at* http://www.un.org/Docs/sc/committees/1267/1267mg.htm.
106. The proposed designations are submitted to the Committee through their Permanent Mission to the United Nations in New York. See Guidelines of the Committee, *supra* note 74, ¶12(c).
107. *See* 1267 Committee web page, *available at* http://www.un.org/sc/committees/1267/ (last visited Feb. 16, 2008); *see* MILLAR & ROSAND, *supra* note 55, at 19–20.
108. Consolidated List, *supra* note 27.
109. In Resolution 1735, the Security Council has directed the Committee to encourage Member States to submit names for inclusion on the Consolidated List. *See* S.C. Res. 1735, ¶8, U.N. Doc. S/RES/1735 (2006).
110. The Cover Sheet for Member State Submission to the Committee was created by Resolution 1735 and attached as an annex to the Resolution. S.C. Res. 1735, ¶8, U.N. Doc. S/RES/1735 (2006).
111. Guidelines of the Committee, *supra* note 74, ¶6(e).
112. *See* Consolidated List, *supra* note 27.
113. Guidelines of the Committee, *supra* note 74, ¶6(e).
114. *Id.* at ¶6(d).
115. *See id.* at ¶6(c).

116. *See id.* at ¶6(d).
117. *See* Fact Sheet on Listing, *supra* note 52; *see also* FATF, The Interpretative Notes to the Special Recommendations (SR) on Terrorist Financing (TF), Interpretative Note to Special Recommendation III: Freezing and Confiscating Terrorist Assets, ¶2 (Oct. 3, 2003), *available at* http://www.fatf-gafi.org/dataoecd/53/32/34262136.pdf (the intent of freezing terrorist-related assets is preventative, not punitive). This view is further consistent with Resolution 1452, which exempts from asset freeze funds needed to cover basic living expenses. S.C. Res. 1452, ¶1, U.N. Doc. S/RES/1452 (2002).
118. FATF Interpretative Note to Special Recommendation III: Freezing and Confiscating Terrorist Assets, *supra* note 117, ¶¶2, 6.
119. Case T-306/01, Yusuf v. Council of the E.U., 2005 ECR II-3533, ¶299.
120. U.N. SEC. COUNCIL, ANALYTICAL SUPPORT AND SANCTIONS MONITORING TEAM, THIRD REPORT OF THE ANALYTICAL SUPPORT AND SANCTIONS MONITORING TEAM, ¶¶39–41, U.N. Doc. S/2005/572 (Sept. 9, 2005).
121. SIXTH REPORT OF THE SANCTIONS MONITORING TEAM, *supra* note 19, ¶33.
122. *See* Consolidated List, *supra* note 27. Most of these terrorist organizations have been designated by the Department of State as foreign terrorist organizations. *See* U.S. Dep't of State, 2005 Country Reports on Terrorism (Apr. 2006), *available at* http://www.state.gov/documents/organization/65462.pdf.
123. The Consolidated List includes the following branches of Al-Haramain: Al-Haramain and Al Masjed Al-Aqsa Charity Foundation; Al-Haramain Afghanistan Branch; Al-Haramain Albania Branch; Al-Haramain Bangladesh Branch; Al-Haramain Ethiopia Branch; Al-Haramain Foundation (Indonesia); Al-Haramain Foundation (Pakistan); Al-Haramain Foundation (Union of the Comoros); Al-Haramain Foundation (United States); Al-Haramain Islamic Foundation (two offices); Al-Haramain Netherlands Branch; Al-Haramayn Foundation (Kenya); and Al-Haramayn Foundation (Tanzania). *See* Consolidated List, *supra* note 27.
124. *See* Jimmy Gurulé, Testimony before the U.S. Senate Finance Committee (Oct. 9. 2002), *available at* http://www.treasury.gov/press/releases/po3518.htm.
125. *See id*; *see also* Press Release, U.S. Dep't of Treasury, Treasury Department Statement on the Designation of Wa'el Hamza Julidan (Sept. 9, 2002), *available at* http://www.treasury.gov/press/releases/po3397.htm.
126. *See* Jimmy Gurulé, Testimony before the U.S. Senate Finance Committee (Oct. 9. 2002), *available at* http://www.treasury.gov/press/releases/po3518.htm.
127. *Id.*
128. *Id.*
129. *See* Press Release, U.S. Dep't of Treasury, Statement by Secretary Paul O'Neill on Designation of Jemaah Islamiya (JI) (Oct. 23, 2002), *available at* http://ustreas.gov/press/releases/po3569.htm.
130. *See* Press Release, United Nations, 1267 Committee Adds Name of an Entity to Its List, U.N. Doc. SC/7548 (Oct. 25, 2002), *available at* http://www.un.org/News/Press/docs/2002/SC7548.doc.htm.
131. MILLAR & ROSAND, *supra* note 55, at 20.
132. *See* The 1267 (Al Qaida/Taliban) Committee and the 1540 (WMD) Sanctions Committee, Update Report No. 5 (Jan. 16, 2006), *available at* http://www.securitycouncilreport.org/site/c.glKWLeMTIsG/b.1355491/k.48B7/UPDATE_REPORT_NO_5BR The_1267_AlQaidaTaliban_Committee_and_The_1540_WMD_Sanctions_Committee BR16_JANUARY_2006.htm; *see also* Millar & Rosand, *supra* note 55, at 20.
133. *See* Guidelines of the Committee, *supra* note 74, ¶4(b).
134. *Id.*
135. *See* SIXTH REPORT OF THE SANCTIONS MONITORING TEAM, *supra* note 19, ¶43.
136. *Id.* at ¶44.
137. *See* Guidelines of the Committee, *supra* note 74, ¶4(a).
138. *See* FATF on Money Laundering, Freezing of Terrorist Assets: International Best Practices, at 3 (2003), *available at* http://www.fatf-gafi.org/dataoecd/39/15/34033495.pdf; FATF Interpretative Note to Special Recommendation III: Freezing and

Confiscating Terrorist Assets, *supra* note 117, ¶¶2, 6 (legal standard for freezing assets is whether there are 'reasonable grounds, or a reasonable basis, to suspect or believe that such funds or other assets could be used to finance terrorist activity').

139. The term 'freeze' means: 'to prohibit the transfer, conversion, disposition or movement of funds or other assets on the basis of, and for the duration of the validity of, an action initiated by a competent authority or a court under a freezing mechanism. The frozen funds or other assets remain the property of the person(s) or entity(ies) that held an interest in the specified funds or other assets at the time of the freezing and may continue to be administered by the financial institution or other arrangements designated by such person(s) or entity(ies) prior to the initiation of an action under a freezing mechanism.' FATF Interpretative Note to Special Recommendation III: Freezing and Confiscating Terrorist Assets, *supra* note 117, ¶7(a).
140. FATF Interpretative Note to Special Recommendation III: Freezing and Confiscating Terrorist Assets, *supra* note 117, ¶7(h)(i).
141. *See* Seventh Report of the Sanctions Monitoring Team, *supra* note 5, ¶62.
142. S.C. Res. 1617, ¶10, U.N. Doc. S/RES/1617 (2005). The checklist is available on the 1267 Committee's website at http://www.un.org/sc/committees/1267/pdf/checklist.pdf.
143. Sixth Report of the Sanctions Monitoring Team, *supra* note 19, ¶24.
144. *See* S.C. Res. 1617, Annex II, U.N. Doc. S/RES/1617 (2005).
145. *See* Guidelines of the Committee, *supra* note 74, ¶7.
146. *See* S.C. Res. 1617, ¶10, U.N. Doc. S/RES/1617 (2005).
147. Seventh Report of the Sanctions Monitoring Team, *supra* note 5, ¶143; *see also* Fifth Report of the Sanctions Monitoring Team, *supra* note 105, ¶34.
148. *See* Fact Sheet on De-Listing, *available at* http://www.un.org/sc/committees/1267/fact_sheet_delisting.shtml (last visited Feb. 18, 2008); *see also* FATF Interpretative Note to Special Recommendation III: Freezing and Confiscating Terrorist Assets, *supra* note 117, ¶8(d). The U.S. domestic legal regime for freezing terrorist-related assets provides a procedure for de-listing or removing names from the U.S. list. That process is discussed *supra*, at Chapter 8.
149. *See* Guidelines of the Committee, *supra* note 74, ¶8(a).
150. S.C. Res. 1730, U.N. Doc. S/RES/1730 (2006).
151. *Id.*
152. *See* Guidelines of the Committee, *supra* note 74, ¶8; *see also* S.C. Res. 1730, U.N. Doc. S/RES/1730 (2006).
153. *Id.* at ¶8(b).
154. *Id.* at ¶8(d).
155. *Id.*
156. *Id.* at ¶8(e).
157. *See* Fact Sheet on De-Listing, *supra* note 148.
158. *Id.*; *see also* S.C. Res. 1735, ¶14, U.N. Doc. S/RES/1735 (2006).
159. *See* Consolidated List, *supra* note 27.
160. S.C. Res. 1452, ¶1, U.N. Doc. S/RES/1452 (2002). Resolution 1452 exempts funds, financial assets and economic resources needed to pay

> basic expenses, including payments for foodstuffs, rent or mortgage, medicines and medical treatment, taxes, insurance premiums, and public utility charges, or exclusively for payment of reasonable professional fees and reimbursement of incurred expenses associated with the provision of legal services, or fees or service charges for routine holding or maintenance of frozen funds or other financial assets or economic resources . . . . S.C. Res. 1452, ¶1(a), U.N. Doc. S/RES/1452 (2002).

The U.S. domestic regime for freezing terrorist-related assets also recognizes an exception for basic living expenses.

161. Ayadi v. Council of the European Union, Case T-253/02, ¶130, 2006 ECR II-2139.
162. *Id.* at ¶131.
163. S.C. Res. 1452, ¶1(b), U.N. Doc. S/RES/1452 (2002).

164. Guidelines of the Committee, *supra* note 74, ¶9(a).
165. *See* Sixth Report of the Sanctions Monitoring Team, *supra* note 19, ¶47 ('Between August and October 2006, the Committee received seven notifications pursuant to resolution 1452 (2002) and approved them all.').
166. *See Ayadi,* ¶¶129–32.
167. *See* Seventh Report of the Sanctions Monitoring Team, *supra* note 5, Annex I, ¶¶1–10. The following cases have been filed before the European Court of First Instance: Case T-306/01, Yusuf v. Council of the E.U., 2005 ECR II-3533; Case T-315-01, Kadi v. Council & Comm'n, 2005 ECR 3649; Case T-253/02, Ayadi v. Council of the E.U., 2006 ECR II-2139; Case T-49/04, Hassan v. Council & Comm'n, 2006 ECR 52; Case T-318/01, Othman v. Council & Comm'n, OJ 2006 C165/30; Case T-135/06, Al-Faqih, v. Council, OJ 2006 C165/29; Case T-136-06, Sanabel Relief Agency Ltd. v. Council, OJ 2006 C165/30; Case T-137/06, Abdrabbah v. Council; Case T-138/06, Nasuf v. Council, OJ 2006 C165/30.
168. *See* Case T-253/02, Ayadi v. Council of the E.U., 2006 ECR II-2139; Case T-306/01, Yusuf v. Council of the E.U., 2005 ECR II-3533; Case T-315/01, Kadi v. Council of the E.U., 2005 ECR 3649.
169. Seventh Report of the Sanctions Monitoring Team, *supra* note 5, Annex I, ¶7.
170. *Id.* at ¶6.
171. *See* discussion *supra*, at Chapter 8.
172. Case T-306/01, Yusuf v. Council of the E.U., 2005 ECR II-3533. The applicants advanced three claims. The first two claims challenged the European Council's authority to impose sanctions on citizens of the European Union. These claims were rejected by the Court. *See id.* at ¶¶171, 189. The third claim raised challenges to the procedures afforded applicants and whether they were denied their fundamental rights under the ECHR. *See id.* at 190. After the manuscript for this book was submitted to the publisher, the European Court of Justice issued its opinion in Yassin Abdullah Kadi and Al Barakaat International Foundation v. Council and Commission, Cases C-402/05 P and C-415/05 P (Sept. 3, 2008), holding that the measures adopted by the Community to give effect to U.N. Security Council Resolutions to prevent the financing of terrorism violated petitioners' right to be heard, right to effective judicial review and right to property under Community law. At the time of this writing (Oct. 2008), the European Community has not yet implemented procedures to comply with the Court's ruling.
173. Universal Declaration of Human Rights, G.A. Res. 217A, U.N. GAOR, 3d Sess., 1st plen. mtg., art. 17(2), U.N. Doc. A/810 (Dec. 12, 1948).
174. *Yusuf*, ¶¶296–8.
175. *Id.* at ¶298.
176. *Id.* at ¶299.
177. *Id.* at ¶290.
178. *Id.*
179. *Id.* at ¶301.
180. *Id.* at ¶302.
181. *Id.* at ¶¶330–31.
182. *Id.* at ¶305.
183. *Id.* at ¶308.
184. *Id.*
185. *Id.* at ¶312. *See* Kadi and Al Barakaat v. Council and Commission, *supra* note 172.
186. *Id.* at ¶318.
187. The European Court of First Instance also dismissed the applicants' due process claims and upheld the sanction in *Ayadi v. Council of the European Union*. *See* Case T-253/02, Ayadi v. Council of the E.U., 2006 ECR II-2139, ¶¶126–32.
188. *Yusuf*, ¶328.
189. *Id.*
190. *Id.* at ¶329. Applicants also invited the court to review the appropriateness and proportionality of the measures imposed by the Security Council in Resolution 1267. The court refused, stating that such a review 'entails a political assessment and value judg-

ments which in principle fall within the exclusive competence of the authority to which the international community has entrusted primary responsibility for the maintenance of international peace and security.' *Id.* at ¶339. The court stated that it lacked the authority to review whether the Security Council's resolutions are compatible with fundamental rights. *Id.* at ¶338. The European Court of Justice took a different view. *See* Kadi and Al Barakaat, *supra* note 172.

191. To implement the obligations imposed by U.N. Security Council Resolution 1373 (2001), the E.U. developed a legal framework, which included the creation of an E.U. list of designated persons whose funds were to be frozen in accordance with the resolution. The Council of the European Union adopted Articles 15 EU and 34 EU, Common Position 2001/930 CFSP on combating terrorism (OJ 2001 L 344, p, 90) and Common Position 2001/931/CFSP on the application of specific measures to combat terrorism (OJ 2001, L 344, p. 93). 'Article 1(1) of Common Position 2001/931 provides that it applies "to persons, groups and entities involved in terrorist acts listed in the Annex." Article 1(2) and (3) of Common Position 2001/931 defines "persons, groups and entities involved in terrorist acts."' Article 1(4) provides that the 'list in the Annex is to be drawn up on the basis of precise information or material in the relevant file which indicates that a decision has been taken by a competent authority in respect of the persons, groups and entities concerned, irrespective of whether it concerns the instigation of investigations or prosecution for a terrorist act . . . based on serious and credible evidence or clues, or condemnation [sic] for such deeds. "Competent authority" means a judicial authority, or where judicial authorities have no competence in the area covered, an equivalent competent authority in that area. Article 1(6) . . . provides that the names of persons and entities on the list in the Annex are to be reviewed at regular intervals and at least once every six months to ensure that there are grounds for keeping them on the list. Articles 2 and 3 . . . provide that the European Community, acting within the limits of the powers conferred on it by the EC Treaty, is to order the freezing of the funds and other financial assets or economic resources of persons, groups and entities listed in the Annex, and is to ensure that funds, financial assets or economic resources or financial or other related services are not made available, directly or indirectly, for the benefit of those persons.' Finally, the original list of persons, groups and entities to which the E.U. regulations apply was set out in Council Decision 2001/927/EC, adopted on Dec. 27, 2001. *See* Case T-327/03, Stichting Al-Aqsa v. Council of the E.U., 2007 ECR 00, ¶¶1–10.

192. Case No. T-47/03, Sison v. Council of the E.U., 2007 ECR 00.
193. *Id.* at ¶227.
194. *Id.* at ¶¶147–50.
195. *Id.* at ¶151.
196. *Id.* at ¶167.
197. *Id.* at ¶152.
198. *Id.* at ¶164.
199. *Id.* at ¶168.
200. *Id.*
201. *Id.* at ¶171.
202. *Id.*
203. *Id.* at ¶173. *Accord* Case T-327/03, Stichting Al-Aqsa v. Council of the E.U., 2007 ECR 00, ¶54 ('[A]n initial decision to freeze funds . . . must at least make actual and specific reference to the reasons why the Council considers, having regard to the precise information or material in the relevant file available to it, that a decision satisfying the definition given in Article 1(4) has been taken by a competent authority of a Member State in respect of the person concerned.').
204. *Sison*, ¶198. *Accord Stichting*, ¶54 ('The statement of the reasons for . . . a decision must . . . indicate why the Council takes the view, in the exercise of its discretion, that the person concerned must be the subject of such a measure.').
205. *Sison*, ¶198.
206. *Id. Accord Stichting*, ¶54.

207. *Sison*, ¶175.
208. *Id.* at ¶176.
209. *Id.* at ¶181.
210. *Id.* at ¶180.
211. *Stichting*. at ¶182.
212. *Id.* at ¶183.
213. *Id.* at ¶206.
214. *Id.*
215. *Id.*
216. The eight individuals placed on the Consolidated List in 2007 include: Aly Soliman Massoud Abdul Sayed (QI.A.229.07); Said Youseef Ali Abu Aziza (QI.A.230.07); Salem Nor Eldin Amohamed Al-Dabski (QI.A.231.07); Abdelmalek Droukdel (QI.D.232.07); Fahd Muhammad 'Abd Al-'Aziz Al-Khashiban (Q.I.A.233.07); Abdul Rahim Al-Talhi (QI.A.234.07); Muhammad 'Abdallah Salih Sughayr (QI.S.235.07); and Sirajuddin Jallaloudine Haqqani (TI.H.144.07). *See* Consolidated List, *supra* note 27. The Seventh Report of the Monitoring Team states that only five names were added in 2007. *See* SEVENTH REPORT OF THE MONITORING TEAM, *supra* note 5, ¶25. However, the Report was prepared on November 29, 2007, and the three additional names that appear on the Consolidated List could have been added after the Report was prepared and submitted to the Committee.

    The Committee has assigned a permanent reference code to each name on the List. The reference code consists of three letters and two numbers. The Monitoring Team explained: 'The first letter, T or Q, indicates Taliban or Al-Qaida; the second letter, I or E, indicates individual or entity; the third letter represents the first letter of the last name. The first number represents the order in which the individual or entity was added to the Consolidated List, and the second number represents the year this was done.' FIFTH REPORT OF THE SANCTIONS MONITORING TEAM, *supra* note 105, ¶24.
217. In 2007, the U.S. Treasury Department designated ten individuals and one entity associated with al Qaeda. However, the two South African individuals and related entity were not placed on the Consolidated List, nor was Fawzi Mutlaq Al-Rawi, designated by U.S. authorities in December 2007. *See* Press Release, U.S. Dep't of Treasury, Treasury Targets Al-Qaida Facilitators in South Africa (Jan. 26, 2007), *available at* http://www.ustreas.gov/press/releases/hp230.htm (designating two South African individuals and a related company); Press Release, U.S. Dep't of Treasury, Treasury Designates Al Qaida, LIFG Operatives (June 15, 2007), *available at* http://www.ustreas.gov/press/releases/hp462.htm (designating Nur Al-Din Al-Dibiski, Sa'id Yusif Ali Abu Azizah, and 'Ali Sulayman Mas'ud 'Abd Al-Sayyid, three Libyans who are members of al Qaeda and Libyan Islamic Fighting Group); Press Release, U.S. Dep't of Treasury, Treasury Designates AQIM Emir (Dec. 4, 2007) *available at* http://www.treas.gov/press/releases/hp708.htm (designating Abdelmalek Droukdel, the leader or emir of Al Qaeda in the Islamic Mahgreb, the north Africa wing of al Qaeda); and Press Release, U.S. Dep't of Treasury, Treasury Designates Individuals with Ties to Al Qaida, Former Regime (Dec. 7, 2007), *available at* http://www.ustreas.gov/press/releases/hp720.htm (designating Fawzi Mutlaq Al-Rawi for providing financial and material support to Al-Qaeda in Iraq). Additionally, three individuals were designated by the Treasury Department on October 10, 2007 (Abdul Rahim Al-Talhi, Muhammad Abdallah Salih Sughayr, and Fahd Muhammad Abd Al-Aziz Al-Khashiban). *See* U.S. Dep't of Treasury Office of Foreign Assets Control, Terrorism: What You Need to Know About U.S. Sanctions (updated 2007), available at http://www.treasury.gov/offices/enforcement/ofac/programs/terror/terror.pdf. The two South African individuals and the entity designated on January 26, 2007, and the individual designated on December 7, 2007, were not placed on the Consolidated List by the Committee.
218. The number of designations under Resolution 1267 declined to 54 in 2002; 77 in 2003; 44 in 2004; 32 in 2005; and 24 in 2006. SEVENTH REPORT OF THE SANCTIONS MONITORING TEAM, *supra* note 5, ¶¶24–5 n. 37.
219. The cover sheet was introduced by Annex I of Resolution 1735. *See* S.C. Res. 1735, Annex I, U.N. Doc. S/RES1735 (2006). A focal point for submitting petitions for de-

listing was established by U.N. Security Council Resolution 1730. S.C. Res. 1730, U.N. Doc. S/RES/1730 (2006).

220. Seventh Report of the Sanctions Monitoring Team, *supra* note 5, ¶25.
221. S.C. Res. 1333, ¶8(c), U.N. Doc. S/RES/1333 (2000).
222. Seventh Report of the Sanctions Monitoring Team, *supra* note 5, Annex III: Impact of Listings on the Value of Assets Frozen.
223. *Id.* at ¶58.
224. *Id.* at ¶60 (some States have no legal basis to freeze assets and therefore do not circulate the Consolidated List to banks).
225. *Id.* at ¶29; *see also* U.N. Sec. Council, Analytical Support and Sanctions Monitoring Team, Fourth Report of the Analytical Support and Sanctions Monitoring Team, ¶29, U.N. Doc. S/2006/154 (Mar. 10, 2006), *available at* http://www.un.org/Docs/sc/committees/1267/1267mg.htm.
226. *See* Sixth Report of the Sanctions Monitoring Team, *supra* note 19, ¶16; *see also* Report of the Committee on Legal Affairs and Human Rights, Council of Europe, United Nations Security Council and European Union Blacklists ¶¶22–34 (Nov. 16, 2007), *available at* http://assembly.coe.int/Main.asp?link=/Documents/WorkingDocs/Doc07/EDOC11454.htm; Report prepared by the Watson Institute for International Studies, Strengthening Targeted Sanctions Through Fair and Clear Procedures (2006), *available at* http://www.watsoninstitute.org/pub/Strengthening_Targeted_Sanctions.pdf. The report prepared by the Watson Institute for International Studies outlined the following recommendations to enhance due process concerns related to the Al-Qaida/Taliban Sanctions regime:

> (1) detail the criteria for listing in resolutions; (2) establish general standards for statements of the case for listings; (3) extend the time period for review of listing proposals from five to 10 working days; (4) require that targets be notified, to the extent possible, of their listing, the sanctions and procedures for de-listing and exemptions, and receive a redacted statement of case and basis for listing; (5) designate a focal point within the United Nations Secretariat to handle de-listing and exemption requests and to notify targets of listing; (6) establish a biennial review of listings; (7) set time periods to respond to listing, de-listing and exemption requests and to establish clear standards for de-listing; and (8) improve websites, issue more frequent press statements and broadly circulate procedures of the committees.
> Cited in Fifth Report of the Sanctions Monitoring Team, *supra* note 105, ¶38.

227. *See* Sixth Report of the Sanctions Monitoring Team, *supra* note 19, ¶24 ('[W]hether through lack of capacity, lack of interest or lack of will, States are no longer as ready to devote time and energy to preparing written reports to the Council's counter-terrorism committees').
228. The 34 members of the FATF are: Argentina; Australia; Austria; Belgium; Brazil; Canada; China; Denmark; the European Commission; Finland; France; Germany; Greece; the Gulf Co-operation Council; Hong Kong; Iceland; Ireland; Italy; Japan; Luxembourg; Mexico; Kingdom of the Netherlands; New Zealand; Norway; Portugal; Russian Federation; Singapore; South Africa; Spain; Sweden; Switzerland; Turkey; the United Kingdom; and the United States. *See* FATF, FATF Members and Observers, *available at* http://www.fatf-gafi.org/document/52/0,3343,en_32250379_32237295_34027188_1_1_1_1,00.html (last visited Feb. 18, 2008).
229. To qualify for membership in FATF, a country must:

> (a) Be strategically important;
> (b) Be a full and active member of a relevant FATF-style Regional Body;
> (c) Provide a letter from an appropriate Minister or person of equivalent political level making a political commitment to implement the FATF Recommendations within a reasonable time frame and undergo the mutual evaluation process; and

(d) Effectively criminalise money laundering and terrorist financing; make it mandatory for financial institutions to identify their customers, to keep customer records and to report suspicious transactions; and establish an effective FIU, so that the country will be assessed fully or largely compliant with Recommendations 1, 5, 10, and 13, and Special Recommendations II and IV.

FATF, Member Countries and Organisations FAQ, *available at* http://www.fatf-gafi.org/document/5/0,3343,en_32250379_32236869_34310917_1_1_1_1,00.html (last visited Feb. 18, 2008).

230. Being afforded 'observer status' by FATF is the last step before full membership. The FATF members would not have afforded India and the Republic of Korea observer status unless these countries were viewed as being largely compliant, or soon to be compliant, with important international standards on money laundering and terrorist financing. *See id.*
231. *See* FATF, FATF Members and Observers, *available at* http://www.fatf-gafi.org/document/52/0,3343,en_32250379_32237295_34027188_1_1_1_1,00.html (last visited Feb. 18, 2008).
232. *See* SIXTH REPORT OF THE SANCTIONS MONITORING TEAM, *supra* note 19, ¶6.
233. *See* Gannon, *supra* note 36.
234. *See* SIXTH REPORT OF THE SANCTIONS MONITORING TEAM, *supra* note 19, ¶8.
235. Other Taliban leaders not included on the Consolidated List include Maulvi Fazlullah; Faqir Mohammed, Sadiq Noor, and Maulvi Gul Bahadar. *See Taliban Leaders in Pakistan*, ASSOC. PRESS, Jan. 26, 2008, *available at* http://www.boston.com/news/world/asia/articles/2008/01/26/taliban_leaders_in_pakistan; *see also* the Consolidated List, *supra* note 27.
236. *See* MICHAEL CHANDLER AND ROHAN GUNARATNA, COUNTERING TERRORISM 138 (Reaktion Books Ltd. 2007).
237. *See, e.g.*, *German Court Convicts Terror Suspect*, ASSOC. PRESS, Jan. 24, 2008, *available at* http://www.boston.com/news/world/europe/articles/2008/01/24/german_court_convicts_terror_suspect/.
238. CHANDLER & GUNARATNA, *supra* note 236, at 140. With respect to al Qaeda-related designations, 225 individuals and 112 entities have been added to the Consolidated List.
239. SIXTH REPORT OF THE SANCTIONS MONITORING TEAM, *supra* note 19, ¶18.
240. *See* Consolidated List, *supra* note 27.
241. Case T-306/01, Yusuf v. Council of the E.U., 2005 ECR II-3533. But *see* Kadi and Al Barakaat v. Council and Commission, *supra* note 172.
242. Case T-315–01, Kadi v. Council & Comm'n, 2005 ECR 3649. But *see* Kadi and Al Barakaat v. Council and Commission, *supra* note 172.
243. Case T-253/02, Ayadi v. Council of the E.U., 2006 ECR II-2139.
244. Case T-49/04, Hassan v. Council & Comm'n, 2006 ECR 52.
245. *Ayadi*, ¶¶126–32; *Yusuf*, ¶¶329–30, & *Kadi*, ¶259.
246. *See* SEVENTH REPORT OF THE SANCTIONS MONITORING TEAM, *supra* note 5, Annex I, ¶¶7–8.
247. *See* FIFTH REPORT OF THE SANCTIONS MONITORING TEAM, *supra* note 105, ¶¶30–31 (discussing issues of compliance, including lack of political will by certain States).
248. U.N. Charter art. 25.
249. Terrorist Financing Convention, *supra* note 1, art. 8(1).
250. *See* Nine Special Recommendations on Terrorist Financing (TF), *supra* note 12.
251. FIFTH REPORT OF THE SANCTIONS MONITORING TEAM, *supra* note 105, ¶¶30–31.
252. *See* U.N. Charter art. 41, which provides that the Security Council 'may decide what measures not involving the use of armed force are to be employed to give effect to its decisions. . . . These may include complete or partial interruption of economic relations and of rail, sea, air, postal, telegraphic, radio, and other means of communication, and the severance of diplomatic relations.'
253. *See* Nine Special Recommendations on Terrorist Financing (TF), *supra* note 12.

254. For an explanation of the NCCT review process, see Financial Action Task Force, About the Non-Cooperative Countries and Territories (NCCT) Initiative, *available at* http://www.fatf-gafi.org/pages/0,3417,en_32250379_32236992_1_1_1_1_1,00.html (last visited Feb. 18, 2008).
255. FATF, Annual Review of Non-Cooperative Countries and Territories 2006–2007: Eighth NCCT Review, ¶6 (Oct. 12, 2007), *available at* http://www.fatf-gafi.org/dataoecd/14/11/39552632.pdf.
256. *Id.* at ¶5.
257. *Id.* at ¶7.
258. *Id.*
259. *Id.*
260. As of October 13, 2006, there are no NCCTs. *See* FATF, Non-Cooperative Countries and Territories Timeline, *available at* http://www.fatf-gafi.org/document/54/0,3343,en_32250379_32236992_33919542_1_1_1_1,00.html (last visited Apr. 18, 2008).
261. The FATF could decide whether to evaluate States for compliance with all Nine Special Recommendations or only Special Recommendation III on freezing terrorist assets. The Nine Special Recommendations on Terrorist Financing, include:

    I. Ratification and Implementation of U.N. Instruments;
    II. Criminalising the Financing of Terrorism and Associated Money Laundering;
    III. Freezing and Confiscating Terrorist Assets;
    IV. Reporting Suspicious Transactions Related to Terrorism;
    V. International Co-operation;
    VI. Alternative Remittance;
    VII. Wire Transfers;
    VIII. Non-Profit Organisations; and
    IX. Cash Couriers.

    Nine Special Recommendations on Terrorist Financing (TF), *supra* note 12.; *see also* FATF, The Interpretative Notes to the Special Recommendations on Terrorist Financing, *available at* http://www.fatf-gafi.org/document/53/0,3343,en_32250379_32236947_34261877_1_1_1_1,00.html (last visited Feb. 18, 2008).
262. *See* Consolidated List, *supra* note 27.

10. The law enforcement response to terrorist financing

> A central element of our strategy is to identify, disrupt and destroy those organizations that supply the financing that make terrorism possible.[1]
>
> Attorney General John Ashcroft (2002), announcing indictment of Enaam Arnaout, Director, Benevolence International Foundation

> [F]oreign organizations that engage in terrorist activity are so tainted by their criminal conduct that any contribution to such an organization facilitates that conduct.[2]
>
> Anti-Terrorism Effective Death Penalty Act 1996)

ANTI-TERRORIST FINANCING STATUTES

Congress has enacted significant legislation aimed at cutting off financial aid, assistance, and services to terrorists and terrorist groups. The principal criminal provisions used by the U.S. Department of Justice to prosecute the financiers and financial facilitators of terror are the 'material support' statutes, 18 U.S.C. §§2339A and 2339B.[3] The material support statutes have been characterized as the 'antiterror weapon of choice'[4] and the 'cornerstone' of the Justice Department's counter-terrorist financing enforcement efforts.[5] Sections 2339A and 2339B enable federal prosecutors to punish those who provide 'material support or resources,' including money and other financial assistance, to terrorists and designated foreign terrorist organizations (FTOs).[6] Section 2339A makes it a crime to provide 'material support or resources' 'knowing or intending' that they be used to prepare for or carry out statutorily enumerated crimes.[7] That is, the statute prohibits knowingly providing material support or resources to facilitate a specified terrorism-related crime, such as a bombing plot.[8] By contrast, §2339B punishes whoever knowingly provides 'material support or resources' to an FTO, with knowledge that the organization has been designated an FTO, or has engaged in or engages in acts of terrorism.[9] Upon conviction, both §§2339A and 2339B provide that the defendant shall be fined, or imprisoned not more than 15 years, or both, and, if the death of any person results, imprisoned for any term of years or for life.[10]

In 2002, Congress enacted the Suppression of the Financing of Terrorism Convention Implementation Act ('Suppression of the Terrorist Financing Act' or '2002 Act'), criminalizing certain financial transactions made in furtherance of specified terrorist crimes.[11] The Suppression of Terrorist Financing Act implements the International Convention for the Suppression of Financing of Terrorism, which was adopted by the United Nations General Assembly on December 9, 1999.[12] The 2002 Act created a new statute, 18 U.S.C. §2339C, which criminalizes unlawfully and willfully 'provid[ing] or collect[ing]' funds with the intention or knowledge that the funds are to be used to carry out an offense within the scope of various counter-terrorism treaties specified in the statute. Section 2339C also punishes unlawfully or willfully financing any other act intended to cause death or serious bodily injury to a civilian, when the purpose of such act is to intimidate a population, or to compel a government or international organization to do or refrain from doing any act.[13] Anyone who violates the terrorist financing statute can be fined, imprisoned for not more than 20 years, or both.[14] Further, any property involved in a violation or attempted violation is subject to forfeiture, as is property that constitutes or is derived from proceeds traceable to a violation of §2339C.[15] Finally, there is extraterritorial jurisdiction for violations of §§2339B and 2339C.[16]

Regulations imposed by the Bank Secrecy Act, as amended by the USA PATRIOT Act of 2001 (PATRIOT Act), have made it more difficult for terrorists and their financial sponsors to transfer money through the U.S. banking system.[17] To avoid these regulations and possible detection by federal law enforcement, the jihadists often resort to physically smuggling currency into and out of the United States to fund their deadly operations.[18] In response, Congress enacted §371(c) of Title III of the PATRIOT Act, codified at 31 U.S.C. §5332, which punishes bulk cash smuggling into or out of the United States with the intent to evade a currency reporting requirement.[19] A person convicted of currency smuggling shall be imprisoned for not more than five years.[20]

Another important weapon in the prosecutor's armament is 18 U.S.C. §1960, which prohibits money transmitting businesses from operating without a license.[21] To avoid creating a financial paper trail and causing banks to file currency transaction reports with the Treasury Department, the financial supporters of terrorist groups often use such money transmitting businesses, known as hawalas, to transfer money abroad. As part of the PATRIOT Act, Congress enacted 18 U.S.C. §1960 in an attempt to regulate these alternative remittance systems, or hawalas.[22] Section 1960 makes it a crime to operate a money transmitting business without an appropriate license in a state where such operation is punishable as a misdemeanor or felony under state law, or where the operator fails to register the business with the Treasury Department as required under federal law.[23] Section 1960 also punishes the operators of such businesses involved in the transportation or transmission of funds known to have been derived from criminal activity or intended to be used to promote such activity, including acts of terrorism.[24]

The International Economic Emergency Powers Act (IEEPA), 50 U.S.C. §1705(b), affords prosecutors another important tool to stem the flow of terrorist funds. Section 1705 punishes whoever willfully engages in financial transactions with persons and organizations determined by the President to be a threat to the national security, foreign policy, or economy of the United States.[25] The names of individuals and entities designated under IEEPA are placed on two lists administered by the Treasury Department. The persons and groups on the lists are designated either Specially Designated Global Terrorists (SDGTs) or Specially Designated Terrorists (SDTs).[26] Pursuant to §1705, a person is subject to a fine and a term of imprisonment of not more than 20 years for engaging in a financial transaction with any individual or organization designated an SDGT or SDT.[27] Finally, a wide range of laws not directly related to terrorism are important to the Justice Department's counter-terrorism disruption efforts. Those statutes include: 18 U.S.C. §1956 (money laundering), 18 U.S.C. §§1961–3 (RICO), 31 U.S.C. §5324 (structuring transactions to evade reporting requirement), 18 U.S.C. §1341 (mail fraud), 18 U.S.C. §1343 (wire fraud), and 26 U.S.C. §1701 (tax evasion).

While Congress has afforded federal prosecutors a wide range of criminal statutes to prosecute and punish whoever raises, collects or transfers money to fund terrorist activities, several of these criminal provisions have been under-utilized by federal prosecutors. For example, there are no reported convictions under 18 U.S.C. §2339C, the terrorist financing statute, and very few prosecutions under 31 U.S.C §5332, the currency smuggling provision.[28] Further, there have been relatively few successful prosecutions targeting major terrorist donors and financial networks of al Qaeda and affiliated terror groups.[29] Instead, in many instances, the Justice Department has focused its enforcement efforts on low-level donors, which is unlikely to have a significant impact on stemming the flow of funds to al Qaeda and other Islamic militant groups. To make matters worse, Justice Department data suggest that there has been a dramatic decline in the number of terrorist financing cases over the past three to four years.[30] One study estimates that the number of terrorism-related financing prosecutions brought by the U.S. Department of Justice in 2007 is down 40.8 percent over the past fiscal year.[31] Finally, while there have been some successful terrorism financing prosecutions, the Justice Department has experienced some disappointing legal setbacks where the jury acquitted the defendants or could not reach a verdict on the main terrorism financing charges.[32] The Justice Department's limited progress on the terrorism financing front is particularly disturbing considering that al Qaeda has 'protected or regenerated key elements of its Homeland attack capability' and poses a 'persistent and evolving terrorist threat' to the United States, according to the 2007 National Intelligence Estimate.[33] Despite the Justice Department's prosecution efforts over the last six years, al Qaeda possesses the financial resources to sustain its global organizational infrastructure and launch major terrorist attacks against the United States.

MATERIAL SUPPORT STATUTES, 18 U.S.C. §§2339A AND 2339B

Many of the terrorist financing cases brought by the Department of Justice have been prosecuted under 18 U.S.C. §§2339A and 2339B, which make it a crime to provide 'material support or resources' to terrorists and foreign terrorist organizations.[34] By enacting the material support statutes, Congress recognized that eliminating material support and resources, including currency and other financial assistance, to terrorists and terrorist organizations is critical to preventing future terrorist attacks. Among other objectives, the material support statutes were intended to prevent terrorists from raising money within the United States, or using the United States as a conduit for the receipt of funds raised in other nations.[35] As part of the Violent Crime Control and Law Enforcement Act of 1994, Congress enacted 18 U.S.C. §2339A, making it a federal crime to knowingly provide material support or resources 'knowing or intending' that they be used in preparation for, or in carrying out, various violent federal crimes enumerated in the statute.[36] To convict under §2339A, the Government must prove four elements: (1) the defendant knowingly (2) provided 'material support or resources,' (3) knowing or intending that the provision of 'material support or resources' be used in preparation for, or in carrying out (4) one or more of the violent crimes specified in the statute.[37]

Congress enacted §2339B two years later as part of the 1996 AntiTerrorism and Effective Death Penalty Act (AEDPA).[38] Section 2339B was intended to close a loophole left by §2339A and to criminalize knowingly providing material support or resources to organizations designated by the Secretary of State as FTOs. This provision is primarily aimed at depriving terrorist groups of funding and other resources. In *Humanitarian Law Project v. Gonzales*, the court examined the legislative history of the statute, stating:

> Congress enacted §2339B in order to close a loophole left by §2339A. Congress, concerned that terrorist organizations would raise funds 'under the cloak of a humanitarian or charitable exercise,' sought to pass legislation that would 'severely restrict the ability of terrorist organizations to raise much needed funds for their terrorist acts within the United States' [citation omitted]. As §2339A was limited to donors intending to further the commission of specific federal offenses, Congress passed §2339B to encompass donors who acted without the intent to further federal crimes.[39]

The court further observed:

> [T]he AEDPA sought to prevent the United States from becoming a base for terrorist fundraising. Congress recognized that terrorist groups are often structured to include political or humanitarian components in addition to terrorist components. Such an organizational structure allows terrorist groups to raise funds under the guise of political or humanitarian causes. Those funds can then be diverted to terrorist activities.[40]

The AEDPA, as amended by the PATRIOT Act and the Intelligence Reform and Terrorism Prevention Act of 2004 (IRTPA),[41] defines 'material support and resources' to mean:

> any property, tangible or intangible, or service, including currency or monetary instruments or financial securities, financial services, lodging, training, expert advice or assistance, safehouses, false documentation or identification, communications equipment, facilities, weapons, lethal substances, explosives, personnel (1 or more individuals who may be or include oneself), and transportation, except medicine or religious materials.[42]

For purposes of §2339B, a 'foreign terrorist organization' is 'an organization designated as a terrorist organization under section 219 of the Immigration and Nationality Act.'[43] Section 219 of the Immigration and Nationality Act, codified at 8 U.S.C. §1189, authorizes the Secretary of State to designate a group as a 'foreign terrorist organization' if the group meets the following criteria:

> (A) the organization is a foreign organization;
> (B) the organization engages in terrorist activity (as defined in section 1182(a)(3)(B) of this title) or terrorism (as defined in section 2656f(d)(2) of Title 22), or retains the capability and intent to engage in terrorist activity or terrorism); and
> (C) the terrorist activity or terrorism of the organization threatens the security of United States nationals or the national security of the United States.[44]

Pursuant to 8 U.S.C. §1189, the Secretary of State has designated 44 groups as FTOs. Those groups include, but are not limited to: al Qaeda; al Qaeda in Iraq; al Qaeda in the Islamic Maghreb; HAMAS; Hizballah; Palestinian Islamic Jihad; Islamic Jihad Group; Jemaah Islamiya; Lashkar i Jhangvi; Libyan Islamic Fighting Group; Moroccan Islamic Combatant Group; and the Salafist Group for Call and Combat.[45] Pursuant to §2338B, it is illegal to provide virtually any type of asset or assistance to any of these designated FTOs.

Section 2339A requires proof of a heightened *mens rea* not required under §2339B. To convict for a violation of §2339A, the Government must prove that the defendant provided 'material support or resources' 'knowing or intending' that they are to be used to carry out certain terrorism-related crimes. Section 2339B is much easier to prove and does not require proof of a heightened *scienter* or specific intent. To prove a violation of §2339B, the defendant must have knowledge that the organization is a designated foreign terrorist organization or engages or has engaged in acts of terrorism.[46] The Government is not required to prove that the defendant intended to further the illegal aims of the FTO by the provision of material support or resources. Under §2339B, the donor is criminally liable even if he intended to fund the *humanitarian* activities of the organization, if he had knowledge that the group had been designated an FTO or engaged or engages in terrorist activities.[47] However, §2339B does not render §2339A totally obsolete. For instance, a prosecutor may file charges under §2339A rather than §2339B if the material support-type of activity was not undertaken on behalf of a particular designated FTO or where the provision of material support benefitted a terrorist group that has not been designated an FTO.[48]

CONSTITUTIONALITY OF THE MATERIAL SUPPORT STATUTES, 18 U.S.C. §§2339A AND 2339B

Prosecutions under 18 U.S.C. §§2339A and 2339B have been challenged on a number of constitutional grounds. Specifically, it has been argued that: (i) the statutory prohibitions against the provision of 'material support' to an organization designated as an FTO impermissibly punishes the exercise of the First Amendment right of freedom of association; (ii) the statutes are overbroad, sweeping a substantial amount of constitutionally protected activity within its definition of prohibited conduct; (iii) the statute is impermissibly vague in providing notice of what conduct constitutes unlawful 'material support' to an FTO; and (iv) in the absence of pre-deprivation notice and a hearing the process for designating an organization as an FTO violates the Due Process Clause of the Fifth Amendment. Further, defendants maintain that in the absence of proof of specific intent to further the terrorist organization's unlawful activities §2339B offends the Due Process Clause. Finally, they argue, the defendant's inability to challenge the validity of an organization's designation as an FTO deprives him of the Fifth and Sixth Amendment rights to a jury determination of guilt on each element of the charged offense. The courts have uniformly rejected claimants' First Amendment freedom of association and overbreadth challenges, as well as arguments that the inability to challenge the FTO designation at trial violates the Fifth and Sixth Amendments. However, the courts have been more sympathetic to defendants' due process notice and hearing, and void-for-vagueness claims. On the *scienter* issue, the courts remain divided on whether due process principles require proof of specific intent to further the criminal activities of the FTO.

Fifth Amendment Due Process – *Scienter*

Amending §2339B, the Intelligence Reform and Terrorism Prevention Act of 2004 (IRTPA)[49] added the *mens rea* requirement that 'a person must have knowledge that the organization is a designated terrorist organization . . . [or] that the organization has engaged in or engages in terrorist activity [or] . . . terrorism.'[50] Despite the additional requirement imposed by the IRTPA, some have argued that in the absence of proof of specific intent to further the terrorist activities of the foreign terrorist organization §2339B runs afoul of the Fifth Amendment Due Process Clause.[51] The proponents of this legal theory maintain that knowingly providing money and other financial support to a designated FTO violates the due process requirement of personal guilt unless the donor intended that the money or other support be used to further the criminal activities of the terrorist organization.

The Supreme Court has recognized a 'presumption in favor of a *scienter* requirement,' mandating a showing of *mens rea* as to 'each of the statutory elements that criminalize otherwise innocent conduct.'[52] Defendants contend that, in the absence of proof of specific intent to further the unlawful aims of the FTO, the statute would criminalize wholly innocent conduct, such as donating books and supplies to a school operated by an FTO.[53] This concern cannot be avoided in the absence of a statutory requirement that the defendant knowingly provided material support or resources to an FTO with the specific intent to further the organization's illegal activities.

However, all but one of various courts that have considered the nature and constitutional sufficiency of §2339B's *scienter* requirement have held that the statute satisfies due process.[54] These courts have advanced three reasons for upholding the constitutionality of §2339B. First, the Supreme Court's decision in *Scales v. United States*[55] is not controlling with respect to the AEDPA. In *Scales*, the Supreme Court addressed a Fifth Amendment challenge to a conviction under the Smith Act, which prohibited membership in the Communist Party, a group advocating the overthrow of the government by force and violence.[56] The defendant maintained that the Smith Act violated the Fifth Amendment because it unconstitutionally imputed guilt based on associational membership alone. In response to *Scales*' due process claim, the Supreme Court explained:

> In our jurisprudence guilt is personal, and when the imposition of punishment on a status or on conduct can only be justified by reference to the relationship of that status or conduct to other concededly criminal activity (here advocacy of violent overthrow), that relationship must be sufficiently substantial to satisfy the concept of personal guilt in order to withstand attack under the Due Process Clause of the Fifth Amendment.[57]

The Supreme Court ultimately upheld the conviction because the Government was required to prove more than the defendant's mere membership; it had to prove that the defendant 'knew that the organization engages in criminal advocacy, and that it was his purpose to further that criminal advocacy.'[58]

At the same time, while the *Scales* opinion is concerned with criminalizing associational membership in violation of the Fifth Amendment, it does not support a general rule that specific intent is always constitutionally required. 'In contrast, the AEDPA does not criminalize mere membership, association, or expressions of sympathy with foreign terrorist organizations.'[59] Rather, §2339B satisfies the personal guilt requirement because it prohibits the affirmative conduct of providing material support or resources to an FTO or organization engaged in terrorist activity and does not punish mere association in such a group.[60]

The second reason advanced by the courts for rejecting the due process *scienter* argument is that imposing an additional element of *mens rea* would contravene the clearly expressed intent of Congress. In *Humanitarian Law Project v. Gonzales*, the court reasoned that a separate statute, 18 U.S.C. §2339A, criminalizes the provision of 'material support or resources' with the knowledge or intent that they be used for various violent federal offenses.[61] However, the language of §2339B, enacted just two years after §2339A, lacked any such element of specific intent to further illegal activities. Because 'Congress knows how to include a specific intent requirement when it so desires, as evidenced by §2339A,' the court reasoned that 'Congress acted deliberately in excluding such an intent [from] §2339B.'[62]

In enacting §2339B, Congress made the legislative finding that 'foreign organizations that engage in terrorist activity are so tainted by their criminal conduct that any contribution to such an organization facilitates that conduct,' regardless of the donor's intent.[63] Congress's finding was reinforced by the Ninth Circuit in *Humanitarian Law Project I v. Reno*, where the court stated: '[M]oney is fungible; giving support intended to aid an organization's peaceful activities frees up resources that can be used for terrorist acts.'[64] Finally, Congress, through the enactment of IRTPA, once again had the opportunity to incorporate into §2339B a requirement of specific intent to further the FTO's unlawful conduct, but chose instead to 'clarif[y] that the only *mens rea* required under §2339B is that a donor know that the recipient is a foreign terrorist organization.'[65]

Third, the Government must prove beyond a reasonable doubt that the accused knew the organization was an FTO or knew of the unlawful activities that caused it to be so designated. Therefore, because the defendant must know that he is materially supporting an FTO, courts have held that §2339B satisfies the notion of personal guilt under the Due Process Clause.[66]

Fifth Amendment Due Process Right to Notice and a Hearing

Whether the Due Process Clause of the Fifth Amendment bars the Government from designating organizations as FTOs without first giving them notice and an opportunity to be heard has been the subject of extensive litigation.[67] As previously discussed, §1189(a)(1), Title 8, United States Code, empowers the Secretary of State to designate an organization as a 'foreign terrorist organization.' The statute, however, does not require that the entity be afforded notice of the impending designation and a hearing to challenge the Secretary's findings.[68]

In *National Council of Resistance of Iran v. Department of State*, [69] the National Council of Resistance of Iran (NCRI) and the People's Mojahedin of Iran (PMOI) argued that their designation as foreign terrorist organizations violated Due Process because they did not receive notice or a hearing.[70] The D.C. Circuit Court of Appeals agreed, holding that the Secretary of State must afford notice to putative 'foreign terrorist organizations' that designation is impending and a meaningful opportunity to be heard by the Secretary upon the relevant findings.[71]

As a general proposition, foreign entities receive constitutional protections only when 'they have come within the territory of the United States and developed substantial connections' with the country.[72] Thus, the threshold question is whether a foreign entity is present within the United States and has sufficient connections with the United States to bring it within its constitutional framework.[73] When a foreign entity does not have 'sufficient connections' with the U.S., it has no constitutional rights under the Due Process Clause, including the right to notice and hearing.[74] In *National Council of Resistance of Iran (NCRI)*, the court set a low bar for determining whether the two designated organizations had developed substantial connections with the United States. After examining the record, the court found that the designated organizations had 'an overt presence within the National Press Building in Washington, D.C. . . and . . . claim[ed] an interest in a small bank account,' which was sufficient to satisfy the 'substantial connections' test.[75] Apparently, maintaining an office in the National Press Building and possessing an interest in a small bank account were sufficient connections to entitle the foreign entities to the protections afforded by the Due Process Clause of the Fifth Amendment.

The court next proceeded to determine whether the Secretary's decision to designate the organizations as FTOs deprived them of life, liberty, or property. The court stated that foreign organizations that 'acquire[ ] or hold[ ] property in this country may invoke the protections of the Constitution when that property is placed in jeopardy by government intervention.'[76] The court found that at least one of the organizations had an interest in a bank account in the United States and the property interest in that account was impaired by the Secretary's designation. The Government's interference with that protected property right was adequate to entitle petitioners to due process.[77]

Having dispensed with the issue as to whether petitioners are entitled to due process, the court turned its attention to the remaining questions of what process is due and when. The court framed the inquiry as follows: '[T]o what procedural devices must the petitioners have access in order to protect their interests against the deprivations worked by the statute, and must that access be afforded before the Secretary's declaration, or is it sufficient under the circumstances that such access be available post-deprivation?'[78] Generally, before the Government can constitutionally deprive a person of the protected liberty or property interest, it must afford him notice and a hearing.[79] However, the Supreme Court has made clear that due process is not a technical concept. Instead, ' "due process is flexible and calls for such procedural protections as the particular situation demands." '[80] In determining whether notice and a hearing are required by the Due Process Clause pre-deprivation, the *NCRI* court applied the three-part test established by the Supreme Court in *Mathews v. Eldridge*, which examines: (1) the private interests that will be affected by the official action; (2) the risk of erroneous deprivation in the absence of notice and a hearing; and (3) the Government's interest, including the administrative burdens that the additional procedural requirements would entail.[81]

Applying the first *Mathews v. Eldridge* factor, the D.C. Circuit found that the NCRI's interest in a bank account was sufficiently important to warrant due process.[82] As to the second factor, the risk of erroneous deprivation, the court concluded that this factor weighed in favor of pre-deprivation notice and a hearing as well.[83] The court rejected the Government's argument that the risk of erroneous deprivation was substantially minimized by the fact that, under the statute, the Secretary of State must consult with the Attorney General and the Secretary of the Treasury before designating a foreign terrorist organization.[84] The court posited:

> The United States functions with a unitary executive, created in Article II of the Constitution and constrained by the Fifth Amendment from depriving anyone protected by that Amendment of life, liberty or property without due process of law. The involvement of more than one of the servants of that unitary executive in commencing a deprivation does not create an apparent substitute for the notice requirement inherent in the constitutional norm.[85]

As to the final factor, the court conceded that national security and foreign policy constitute compelling governmental interests.[86] However, the court stated that the Secretary of State failed to show how affording the organizations due process before their designations as foreign terrorist organizations would jeopardize national security or interfere with the Secretary's duty to carry out foreign policy.[87] Consequently, the D.C. Circuit held that the Secretary must afford limited due process to the putative foreign terrorist organizations prior to designating those entities as FTOs.[88] At the same time, the court left open the possibility of the Secretary, in an appropriate case, demonstrating the necessity of withholding all notice and opportunity to present evidence until after the designation.[89] However, the Secretary failed to make a showing of such particularized need in the present case.

On the question of what process is due, the court stated that the notice to the putative FTOs need not disclose classified information to be presented *in camera* and *ex parte* to the court under the statute.[90] However, the Government must give entities notice of the administrative record to be filed publicly at the time of the court's review. [91] The court posited that 'as soon as the Secretary has reached a tentative determination that the designation is impending, the Secretary must provide notice of those unclassified items upon which he proposes to rely to the entity to be designated.'[92] Further, while compliance with the hearing requirement does not mandate a hearing closely approximating a trial, the court stated that the Secretary must 'afford entities considered for imminent designation the opportunity to present, at least in written form, such evidence to rebut the administrative record or otherwise negate the proposition that they are [FTOs].'[93]

Void for Vagueness

The IRTPA of 2004 amended the definition of 'material support or resources,' to include 'any property, tangible or intangible, or service.'[94] As amended, §2339B criminalizes the provision of all 'services,' except for medicine and religious materials, to an FTO.[95] Further, Congress defined the terms 'training,' 'expert advice or assistance,'[96] and 'personnel,' included within the definition of 'material support or resources.' The IRTPA amendments also added a new section, §2339B(h), on the provision of personnel, which provides:

> No person may be prosecuted under this section in connection with the term 'personnel' unless that person has knowingly provided, attempted to provide, or conspired to provide a foreign terrorist organization with 1 or more individuals (who may be or include himself) to work under that terrorist organization's direction or control or to organize, manage, supervise, or otherwise direct the operation of that organization. Individuals who act entirely independently of the foreign terrorist organization to advance its goals or objectives shall not be considered to be working under the foreign terrorist organization's direction and control.[97]

The IRTPA further defined the term 'training' to mean 'instruction or teaching designed to impart a specific skill, as opposed to general knowledge.'[98] The term 'expert advice or assistance' was defined to mean 'advice or assistance derived from scientific, technical or other specialized knowledge.'[99] Finally, the IRTPA defined the term 'personnel' to include '1 or more individuals who may be or include oneself.'[100] These definitions were added to the material support statute in response to federal court decisions holding that those particular terms were unconstitutionally vague in violation of the Fifth Amendment Due Process Clause.[101]

In the *Humanitarian Law Project (HLP)* cases from the Ninth Circuit, individuals and organizations wishing to provide support to the legitimate humanitarian and political activities of entities designated as FTOs challenged the constitutionality of 18 U.S.C. §2339B on void-for-vagueness grounds. In *Humanitarian Law Project v. Reno (District Court–HLP I)*, the district court struck down the AEDPA's prohibition on providing 'training' and 'personnel' to foreign terrorist organizations.[102] In *Humanitarian Law Project v. Ashcroft (District Court–HLP II)*, the Government was enjoined from enforcing the 'expert advice or assistance' provision of the material support statute, because the term was impermissibly vague.[103] Both of those cases were decided prior to the enactment of the IRTPA.

'[T]he void-for-vagueness doctrine requires that a penal statute define the criminal offense with sufficient definiteness that ordinary people can understand what conduct is prohibited and in a manner that does not encourage arbitrary and discriminatory enforcement.'[104] This doctrine serves two goals. First, it ensures fair notice by requiring that a statute 'give the person of ordinary intelligence a reasonable opportunity to know what is prohibited, so that he may act accordingly.'[105] Second, the doctrine aims to provide standards for enforcement to discourage 'arbitrary and discriminatory enforcement.'[106] A challenge to a statute based on vagueness grounds requires the court to consider whether the statute is sufficiently clear so as not to cause persons of 'common intelligence . . necessarily [to] guess at its meaning and [to] differ as to its application.'[107] A party may raise a vagueness challenge by arguing either that a statute is vague as applied to the case at hand or that a statute is vague on its face. With respect to the vagueness as applied theory, where a party 'receive[s] fair warning of the criminality of his own conduct from the statute in question' he may not challenge the statute on grounds that 'the language would not give similar fair warning with respect to other conduct which might be within its broad and literal ambit. One to whose conduct a statute clearly applies may not successfully challenge it for vagueness.' [108] As to a facial vagueness attack, a court must strike down a statute 'only if the enactment is impermissibly vague in all of its applications.'[109] At the same time, courts may strike down a statute as vague and facially invalid, even if that statute is not impermissibly vague in all of its applications, if it infringes on a 'substantial amount of constitutionally protected conduct.'[110]

In *Humanitarian Law Project v. Gonzales (District Court–HLP III)*, the plaintiffs challenged the constitutionality of §2339B on vagueness grounds, affording the district court the opportunity to reconsider its earlier rulings in light of the 2004 IRTPA amendments.[111] The court ultimately concluded that the IRTPA amendments did not cure the problem with respect to the terms 'training,' 'expert advice or assistance,' and 'services.' However, with respect to the term 'personnel,' the court concluded that the IRTPA amendment sufficiently cured previous vagueness concerns.[112]

Training

In *District Court–HLP III*, the court held that the IRTPA amendment defining 'training' as 'instruction or teaching designed to impart a specific skill, as opposed to general knowledge' failed to cure the vagueness problem that the district court previously identified.[113] In *District Court–HLP I*, the court had concluded that 'training' was unconstitutionally vague because it punished protected activities, such as instructing members of a designated group on how to petition the United Nations to seek redress for human rights abuses.[114] The court agreed with plaintiffs that the new definition of 'training' actually exacerbated the vagueness problem, because plaintiffs must now guess whether teaching international law or lobbying constitutes a 'specific skill' or merely 'general knowledge.'[115] The court stated that, even as amended, 'the term "training" is not sufficiently clear so that persons of ordinary intelligence can reasonably understand what conduct the statute prohibits.'[116]

Expert advice or assistance

In *District Court–HLP III*, the court also found 'expert advice or assistance' to be impermissibly vague because the term could be construed to include activities protected by the First Amendment. The IRTPA amendments defined 'expert advice or assistance' as 'scientific, technical, *or other specialized knowledge*.'[117] As in the discussion of 'training,' the court reasoned that 'expert advice or assistance' remains impermissibly vague 'because "specialized knowledge" includes the same protected activities that "training" covers, such as teaching international law for peacemaking resolutions or how to petition the United Nations to seek redress for human rights violations.'[118] Accordingly, the court held that the term 'expert advice or assistance' is impermissibly vague.[119]

Service

In *District Court–HLP III*, the court also held that the term 'service' was impermissibly vague, because it would force plaintiffs to guess whether their human rights and political advocacy was prohibited under the statute.[120] The court concluded that '[a]s with "training" and "expert advice or assistance," the term "service" fails to meet the enhanced requirement of clarity for statutes affecting protected expressive activities and imposing criminal sanctions.'[121]

Personnel

The district court reversed its prior decision on 'personnel,' finding that the newly defined term cured the vagueness problem. The IRTPA defined 'personnel' to mean providing 'one or more individuals' to a foreign terrorist organization 'to work under that terrorist organization's direction or control or to organize, manage, supervise, or otherwise direct the operation of that organization.'[122] The amendment further provides that '[i]ndividuals who act entirely independently of the foreign terrorist organization to advance its goals or objectives shall not be considered to be working under the foreign terrorist organization's direction and control.'[123] The court held that '[l]imiting the provision of personnel to those working under the "direction or control" of a foreign terrorist organization or actually managing or supervising a foreign terrorist organization . . . sufficiently identifies the prohibited conduct such that persons of ordinary intelligence can reasonably understand and avoid such conduct.'[124]

Currency

As noted above, the term 'material support' is specifically defined as a number of enumerated actions. While the courts have ruled that three components of the material support definition – 'training,' 'expert advice or assistance,' and 'service'– are impermissibly vague, the vagueness of these prongs of the 'material support' definition does not affect individuals charged with providing material support in the form of 'currency.' The courts have consistently held that there is nothing vague about the term 'currency.' In *United States v. Hammoud*, the *en banc* Fourth Circuit affirmed defendant's conviction for violating §2339B for making a monetary donation to Hizballah, rejecting defendant's vagueness challenge.[125] Consequently, the courts have not hampered the Government's ability to prosecute individuals for providing money and other financial support or assistance to terrorist organizations under the 'material support' statute.

First Amendment Freedom of Association

The First Amendment 'restricts the ability of the State to impose liability on an individual solely because of his association with another.'[126] It is well established that a statute that punishes people merely for membership in a group or for espousing its views is unconstitutional. Further, the Supreme Court has held that liability may not be 'imposed by reason of association alone' unless it is 'establish[ed] that the group itself possessed unlawful goals and that the individual held a specific intent to further those illegal aims.'[127]

Defendants charged under the statute argue that §2339B runs afoul of the prohibition of 'guilt by association' because it does not demand a showing of specific intent to further the illegal aims of the FTO.[128] Defendants contend that the statute prohibits them from providing support to solely aid the legitimate humanitarian activities of certain organizations designated as FTOs. The statute punishes mere association by imposing criminal liability without regard for whether the donor intends to further the unlawful goals of the FTO.[129]

The courts have emphatically rejected the claim that §2339B punishes mere association with an FTO. In *Humanitarian Law Project*, the Ninth Circuit stated:

> The statute does not prohibit being a member of one of the designated groups or vigorously promoting and supporting the political goals of the group. Plaintiffs are even free to praise the groups for using terrorism as a means of achieving their ends. What AEDPA prohibits is the act of giving material support, and there is no constitutional right to facilitate terrorism by giving terrorists the weapons and explosives with which to carry out their grisly missions.[130]

In *United States v. Hammoud*, the *en banc* Fourth Circuit agreed.[131] The *Hammoud* Court explained that the defendant's First Amendment challenge 'fails because §2339B does not prohibit mere association; it prohibits the *conduct* of providing material support to a designated FTO.'[132]

Because §2339B is not aimed at interfering with the expressive component of defendant's conduct, but at stopping aid to terrorist groups, the statute does not warrant strict scrutiny.[133] Instead, intermediate scrutiny applies where, as here, a 'regulation . . . serves purposes unrelated to the content of expression.'[134] The intermediate scrutiny standard, as articulated by the Supreme Court in *United States v. O'Brien*, involves a four-part inquiry. The Supreme Court provides that a statute is valid if: (1) the regulation is within the power of the government; (2) it furthers an important or substantial government interest; (3) the government interest is unrelated to suppressing free expression; and (4) the incidental restriction on First Amendment freedoms is no greater than necessary to further that interest.[135]

The First Amendment freedom of association challenge to §2339B has been rejected by the Ninth Circuit in *Humanitarian Law Project v. Reno* and a number of other appellate courts.[136] Applying the four-pronged standard set forth in *O'Brien*, the Ninth Circuit found that the statute did not impermissibly infringe upon the First Amendment freedoms of expression and association.[137] First, the court concluded that the federal government clearly has the power to enact laws restricting U.S. citizens from dealing with foreign entities, including terrorist organizations.[138] Second, the court stated that the government has a legitimate interest in suppressing terrorism and such interest is substantial.[139] Third, 'this interest is unrelated to suppressing free expression because it restricts the actions of those who wish to give material support to the groups, not the expression of those who advocate or believe the ideas that the groups support.'[140] The court further found that the statute was sufficiently tailored to avoid unnecessary abridgement of associational freedoms. The court stated that all material support given to terrorist organizations aids their unlawful goals. '[M]oney is fungible; giving support intended to aid an organization's peaceful activities frees up resources that can be used for terrorist acts.'[141] Finally, in *United States v. Assi*, the district court also dismissed defendant's First Amendment challenge.[142] The court asserted that defendant's argument would invalidate any attempt to criminalize contributions of military hardware or weaponry to any organization, so long as the donor could identify some political purpose he sought to advance through his provision of material support. The district court declared: 'The First Amendment does not sweep so broadly in restricting the Government's efforts to fight terrorism.'[143]

The courts have also rejected the contention that §2339B is unconstitutionally overbroad because it 'indiscriminately' criminalizes both protected

First Amendment activity and unprotected conduct.[144] A statute is overbroad if it 'punishes a substantial amount of protected free speech, judged in relation to the statute's plainly legitimate sweep.'[145] The Supreme Court has 'insisted that a law's application to protected speech be "substantial," not only in an absolute sense, but also relative to the scope of the law's plainly legitimate application, before applying the strong medicine of overbreadth invalidation.'[146] At the same time, when a statute is addressed to conduct rather than speech, an overbreadth challenge is less likely to succeed. In *United States v. Hammoud*, the Fourth Circuit rejected the defendant's overbreadth challenge, finding that §2339B does not reach a substantial amount of protected First Amendment activity.[147] The court posited that the statute does not punish merely associating with members of an FTO, becoming a member of the organization or espousing the organization's views.[148] Instead, the statute criminalizes the affirmative conduct of providing 'material support or resources' to a designated FTO. Further, the court found that the statute advances the legitimate governmental aim of depriving terrorists of weapons, explosives and other forms of material support with which to carry out their grisly missions.[149] Because there is no constitutionally protected right to provide material support to members of an FTO, the statute does not infringe on constitutionally protected conduct.[150]

Collateral Attack of the FTO Designation

Defendants argue that §2339B deprives them of their constitutional rights because it prohibits them from collaterally attacking the designation of an organization as an FTO. Section 1189(a)(8), Title 8, United States Code, prevents defendants from contending, in defense of charges under 18 U.S.C. §2339B, that the designated group is not really a terrorist organization.[151] Every court that has considered the issue has denied the constitutional challenge. In *United States v. Hammoud*, the defendant argued that §1189(a)(8) deprived him of his constitutional right to a jury determination of every element of the charged offense.[152] Specifically, he maintained that Hizballah's designation as an FTO is an element of §2339B, and §1189(a)(8) prevented him from challenging the validity of the organization's designation at trial. The court disagreed, stating that 'Congress has provided that the *fact* of an organization's designation as an FTO is an element of §2339B, but the *validity* of the designation is not.'[153] The Fourth Circuit held that, since the validity of the designation was not an element of the crime, Hammoud's inability to challenge the designation was not a violation of his constitutional rights.

In *United States v. Afshari*, the Ninth Circuit reached the same conclusion, reasoning that 'the element of the crime that the prosecutor must prove in a §2339B case is the predicate fact that a particular organization *was* designated at the time the material support was given, not whether the government made a correct designation.'[154] The Ninth Circuit further reasoned:

> The defendants are right that §1189(a)(8) prevents them from contending, in defense of the charges against them under 18 U.S.C. §2339B, that the designated terrorist organization is not really terrorist at all. No doubt Congress was well aware that some might claim that 'one man's terrorist is another man's freedom fighter.' Congress clearly chose to delegate policymaking authority to the President and Department of State with respect to designation of terrorist organizations, and to keep such policymaking authority out of the hands of United States Attorneys and juries. Under §2339B, if defendants provide material support for an organization that has been designated under §1189, they commit the crime, and it does not matter whether the designation is correct or not.[155]

Finally, the court stated that due process principles were not violated because the predicate designation was against the Mujahedin-e-Klaq (MEK), not the defendants. Section 1189 provides for the organization to seek review of the predicate designation; which the MEK did each time it was designated. The court concluded that due process does not require another review of the predicate designation by the court adjudicating the instant §2339B criminal proceeding.[156]

TERRORIST FINANCING STATUTE, 18 U.S.C. §2339C

Section 2339C, Title 18, United States Code, makes it a crime to 'unlawfully and willfully' 'provide or collect' funds with the intention or knowledge that the funds are to be used to carry out (1) a crime which constitutes an offense within the scope of any of nine anti-terrorism treaties specified in the statute, or (2) another act intended to cause death or serious bodily injury to a civilian, when the purpose of the deadly act was 'to intimidate a population, or to compel a government or an international organization to do or to abstain from doing any act.'[157] An individual is also criminally liable if he attempts or conspires to commit an offense under the statute.[158] However, the statute does not require that the funds be traced to a particular terrorist act. The provision unequivocally states that '[f]or an act to constitute an offense . . . it shall *not* be necessary that the funds were actually used to carry out a predicate act.'[159]

Subsection (c) makes it a separate offense and punishes whoever 'knowingly conceals or disguises the nature, location, source, ownership, or control of any material support, or resources, or any funds or proceeds of such funds,' if such acts were done knowing or intending that the material support, resources, or funds were provided in violation of either 18 U.S.C.

§2339B or §2339C.[160] A violation of §2339C(c) is punishable by fine, imprisonment of up to ten years, or both.[161]

Section 2339C punishes providing or collecting funds for terror. The statute defines 'providing' to include 'giving, donating and transmitting' and 'collecting' to include both 'raising and receiving.'[162] The broader 'transmit' and 'receive' language indicates a congressional intent to create far-reaching liability. In other words, the statute is not limited to the donors and fund-raisers of terror money; persons who knowingly *transfer* money to aid terrorists are criminally liable as well. In *Linde v. Arab Bank*, which involved a civil cause of action, the court held that 'the banking activities of receiving deposits and transmitting funds between accounts' where 'the accounts (and funds) belong to groups engaged in terrorist activity' or are 'charity fronts that operate as agents of HAMAS' creates liability under §2339C.[163]

Unlike §2339B, §2339C requires proof that the defendant provided or collected funds with the specific intent or knowledge that the funds were to be used to carry out one of the specified offenses or acts.[164] Because the statute allows for liability where a defendant provides or collects funds 'with the intention that such funds be used, or with the knowledge that such funds are to be used' for terrorist purposes, it is not necessary for the Government to prove that the defendant intended to transmit or receive the funds for terrorist purposes.[165] That is, section '2339C only require[s] knowledge or intent that the resources given to terrorists are to be used in the commission of terrorist acts,' not the specific intent to aid or encourage a particular attack.[166]

Section 2339C is limited to providing or collecting funds for certain predicate acts specified under the statute, including offenses within the scope of a statutorily enumerated counter-terrorism 'treaty.' For purposes of §2339C, the term 'treaty' refers to any of the following international conventions implemented by the United States:

> (A) Convention for the Suppression of Unlawful Seizure of Aircraft, done at The Hague on December 16, 1970;
> (B) Convention for the Suppression of Unlawful Acts against the Safety of Civil Aviation, done at Montreal on September 23, 1971;
> (C) Convention on the Prevention and Punishment of Crimes against Internationally Protected Persons, including Diplomatic Agents, adopted by the General Assembly of the United Nations on December 14, 1973;
> (D) International Convention against the Taking of Hostages, adopted by the General Assembly of the United Nations on December 17, 1979;
> (E) Convention on the Physical Protection of Nuclear Material, adopted at Vienna on March 3, 1980;
> (F) Protocol for the Suppression of Unlawful Acts of Violence at Airports Serving International Civil Aviation, supplementary to the Convention for the

> Suppression of Unlawful Acts against the Safety of Civil Aviation, done at Montreal on February 24, 1988;
> (G) Convention for the Suppression of Unlawful Acts against the Safety of Maritime Navigation, done at Rome on March 10, 1988;
> (H) Protocol for the Suppression of Unlawful Acts against the Safety of Fixed Platforms located on the Continental Shelf, done at Rome on March 10, 1988; or
> (I) International Convention for the Suppression of Terrorist Bombings, adopted by the General Assembly of the United Nations on December 15, 1997.[167]

Thus, a person violates §2339C if he provides or collects funds with the intent or knowledge that the funds are to be used to commit an offense prohibited by any of these nine anti-terrorism conventions.

While §2339C was enacted by Congress in 2002, the statute seldom has been used to prosecute terrorist financing cases.[168] Perhaps the dual *mens rea* requirement that the defendant both knowingly provided or collected funds and did so with intent or knowledge that the funds be used for terrorist activities has caused prosecutors to favor filing terrorism financing charges under 18 U.S.C. §2339B. Under §2339B, the Government only has to prove that the defendant knowingly provided material support or resources, knowing that the organization was designated an FTO or knowing that the group participates or has participated in terrorist activities. To convict under §2339B, the Government is not required to prove that the defendant had knowledge or intended that the funds would be used to commit acts of terrorism. Further, even if the provision of financial support was not for the benefit of a designated FTO, excluding §2339B as a viable criminal charge, the prosecutor might still favor filing charges under §2339A, rather than §2339C. Under §2339C, where the funds were intended to be used to commit an act intended to cause death or serious bodily injury to a civilian, the Government must further prove that the violent act was committed with the purpose 'to intimidate a population, or to compel a government or an international organization to do or to abstain from doing any act.'[169] Section 2339A does not contain this additional requirement. However, §2339C is not rendered totally obsolete by §§2339A and 2339B. Section 2339C authorizes extraterritorial jurisdiction, which means that the court's jurisdiction extends to cases of the offense committed outside of the United States. Section 2339A does not explicitly provide for extraterritorial jurisdiction. Therefore, for example, if the provision or collection of funds occurred in a foreign country with the intent to carry out a terrorist attack in the United States, and the funds were not for the benefit of an FTO, the court would have jurisdiction under §2339C, but not §2339A. Furthermore, §2339B would not apply, because the FTO nexus requirement could not be satisfied.

UNLICENSED MONEY TRANSMITTING BUSINESS, 18 U.S.C. §1960

Congress has enacted important legislation to prevent money transmitting businesses or hawalas from being used to funnel money to terrorists. In 1992, Congress amended 18 U.S.C. §1960 seeking 'to combat the growing use of money transmitting businesses to transfer large amounts of the monetary proceeds of unlawful enterprises.'[170] Prior to 2001, the statute punished '[w]hoever conducts, controls, manages, supervises, directs, or owns all or part of a business, knowing the business is an illegal money transmitting business.'[171]

The term 'illegal money transmitting business' was defined by statute as a money transmitting business which affects interstate or foreign commerce in any manner or degree and

> (A) is *intentionally operated without an appropriate money transmitting license* in a State where such operation is punishable as a misdemeanor or a felony under State law; or
> (B) fails to comply with the money transmitting business registration requirements under section 5330 of title 31, United States Code, or regulations prescribed under such section . . . . [172]

In 2001, Congress passed the PATRIOT Act, which, among other things, amended 18 U.S.C. §1960(a). Congress was concerned that money transmitting businesses, including hawalas, were being used not only to transfer illicit proceeds to criminal enterprises but also to transfer both dirty and clean money to foreign countries to finance terrorist operations. In fact, DOJ investigations established that some of these hawalas 'funneled extensive amounts of money to terrorist groups abroad.'[173] Prior to the PATRIOT Act, individuals who operated *unlicensed* money transmitting businesses were able to 'rely on the affirmative defense that they had no knowledge of applicable state licensing requirements.'[174] Section 373 of the PATRIOT Act eliminated the requirement that the defendant have knowledge of the applicable state licensing provision.[175] As amended, section 1960 provides:

> (a) Whoever knowingly conducts, controls, manages, supervises, directs, or owns all or part of an *unlicensed* money transmitting business, shall be fined in accordance with this title or imprisoned not more than 5 years, or both.[176]

The term 'money transmitting' includes 'transferring funds on behalf of the public by any and all means including but not limited to transfers within this country or to locations abroad by wire, check, draft, facsimile, or courier.'[177]

Subsection (b)(1) of section 1960 was amended to provide three alternative definitions of 'unlicensed money transmitting business.' As amended, the term 'unlicensed money transmitting business' means a money transmitting business which affects interstate or foreign commerce in any manner or degree and

> (A) is operated without an appropriate money transmitting license in a State where such an operation is punishable as a misdemeanor or a felony under State law, whether or not the defendant knew that the operation was required to be licensed or that the operation was so punishable;
> (B) fails to comply with the money transmitting business registration requirements under Section 5330 of Title 31, United States Code, or regulation prescribed under such section;[178] or
> (C) otherwise involves the transportation or transmission of funds that are known to the defendant to have been derived from a criminal offense or are intended to be used to promote or support unlawful activity.[179]

A defendant is guilty of operating an 'unlicensed' money transmitting business within the meaning of §1960 if (1) the business was required to be licensed under state law, and was not, a violation of §1960(b)(1)(A); (2) the business was required to be registered with the Secretary of the Treasury pursuant to 31 U.S.C. §5330, and was not, a violation of §1960(b)(1)(B); or (3) the operator of the business was involved in transferring funds known to have been derived from criminal activity (dirty money) or intended to be used to carry out unlawful activity (dirty or clean money), a violation of §1960(b)(1)(C).

In order to convict for violating §1960(b)(1)(A), the state licensing provision, the Government must prove that the defendant '(1) operate[d] a money transmitting business, (2) that affect[ed] interstate commerce, and (3) that is unlicensed under state law, when (4) state law requires a license and (5) state law punishes lack of a license as a felony or misdemeanor.'[180] Section 1960(b)(1)(A) expressly states that a defendant is criminally liable for operating an unlicensed money transmitting business 'whether or not the defendant knew that the operation was required to be licensed' by applicable state law.[181] In *United States v. Talebnejad*, the Fourth Circuit reversed the district court's decision that Congress violated defendant's due process rights when it declared that ignorance of state licensing requirements is not a defense to liability under §1960(b)(1)(A). The Fourth Circuit held that §1960(b)(1)(A) is a general intent crime and 'passes constitutional muster because "it requires . . . defendants to know the facts that make their conduct illegal."'[182] Accordingly, the Due Process Clause does not require a *mens rea* as to the legal elements of the crime.

The courts have further consistently rejected defendants constitutional challenge to §1960(b)(1)(B), which bases criminal liability on the failure of the money transmitting business to be registered with the Treasury Department as required by 31 U.S.C. §5330. Defendants contend that §1960(b)(1)(B) is a specific intent crime requiring proof that the defendant knew he was required to register his money transmitting business with the Treasury Department and that he intentionally failed to do so. The argument is based on 'Congress's failure to amend 18 U.S.C. §1960(b)(1)(B) when it amended §(b)(1)(A) [and] the conventional understanding [that] *mens rea* is a fundamental component of every criminal act.'[183] In *United States v. Uddin*, the district court rejected this argument, stating:

> [T]here was no need to amend the federal registration subsection; the only 'loophole' that existed in the prior version of the statute was in subsection (A) which, before the Patriot Act amendments, required the government to show that the defendant knew that state law required a license to operate a money transmitting business and intentionally operated the business without an appropriate state license. The prior version of subsection (B) contained no such 'loophole,' and therefore, no amendment to subsection (B) was needed.[184]

The legislative history of the PATRIOT Act amendment to §1960 further supports the conclusion that §1960 is a general intent crime that does not require proof of the defendant's knowledge and intent to violate the federal registration requirement:

> The proposal makes clear that an offense under 1960 is a general intent crime for which a defendant is liable if he knowingly operates an unlicensed money transmitting business. For purposes of a criminal prosecution, the Government would not have to show that the defendant knew that a State license was required or that the Federal registration requirements promulgated pursuant to 31 U.S.C. §5330 applied to the business.[185]

In sum, the prosecution must prove the defendant's *knowledge* as to all of the *factual* elements of §1960: (1) that he was conducting a money transmitting business that affected interstate or foreign commerce and (2) the business was unregistered. Proof of the defendant's knowledge of either state licensing or federal registration requirements and the intent to violate these requirements is not required to sustain a conviction for a violation of §1960.[186] Although this section was amended to aid in the fight against terrorism, there are no reported court decisions interpreting §1960(b)(1)(C).

BULK CASH SMUGGLING

Bulk cash smuggling is an important method of transferring money globally to finance terrorist operations.[187] The PATRIOT Act makes it a crime to smuggle currency or other monetary instruments into or out of the United States. Specifically, 31 U.S.C. §5332(a)(1) punishes whoever, with the intent to evade a reporting requirement under section 5316, conceals more than $10,000 in currency or other monetary instruments, and transports or transfers, or attempts to transport or transfer, such currency or monetary instruments into or outside of the United States.[188] Section 5316 requires a person to file a currency and monetary instrument report or 'CMIR' with the Treasury Department when he transports more than $10,000 into or outside of the United States.[189] Thus, a person violates §5332(a)(1) if he (1) conceals (2) more than $10,000 in currency or other monetary instruments, and (3) transports or transfers those funds into or outside of the United States with (4) the intent to evade filing a CMIR with the Treasury Department. The currency smuggling statute is rarely charged by prosecutors in international terrorist financing cases. There are no reported court decisions involving convictions under the bulk cash smuggling statute.

INTERNATIONAL EMERGENCY ECONOMIC POWERS ACT (IEEPA)

The IEEPA grants the President the authority 'to deal with any unusual and extraordinary threat . . . to the national security, foreign policy, or economy of the United States, if the President declares a national emergency with respect to such threat.'[190] The President's authorities include the power to 'investigate, regulate, or prohibit' and 'block during the pendency of an investigation' certain financial transactions.[191] Section 1705(c) makes it unlawful to 'willfully' violate or attempt to violate any license, order or regulation issued pursuant to IEEPA and provides for imprisonment of up to 20 years for such a violation.[192]

In 1995, pursuant to IEEPA, President Clinton issued Executive Order (E.O. or Order) 12947, finding that 'grave acts of violence committed by foreign terrorists that disrupt the Middle East peace process' constitute an 'unusual and extraordinary threat to the national security, foreign policy, and economy of the United States.'[193] The E.O. specially designated 12 terrorist organizations as targeted entities due to their goal of disrupting the Middle East peace process.[194] E.O. 12947 blocks all property and interests in property of the entities designated in the Order, known as 'Specially Designated Terrorists' or 'SDTs.' The Order also delegated to the Secretary of State the ability to designate foreign persons as SDTs.[195] The Treasury Secretary was further authorized to promulgate regulations. The Secretary of the Treasury promulgated regulations that are contained in Title 31

C.F.R. part 595. Section 595.204 makes it unlawful to 'deal in property or interests in property of [an SDT], including the making or receiving of any contribution of funds, goods, or services to or for the benefit of an [SDT].'[196] The prohibition against financial transactions further extends to conspiracies and attempts.[197] In 1998, President Clinton amended E.O. 12947 to include Osama bin Laden, the al Qaeda organization, and two other individuals.[198] The next year, the Clinton Administration, upon a finding that the Taliban government provided a safe haven to bin Laden and al Qaeda, authorized the Treasury Department to block any transactions involving property belonging to the Taliban.[199]

Following the 9/11 terrorist attacks, the Bush Administration took similar action, issuing Executive Order 13224 declaring a national emergency with respect to the 'grave acts of terrorism and threats of terrorism committed by foreign terrorists . . . and [the] immediate threat of further attacks on United States nationals or the United States.'[200] The E.O. specifically provided that, 'because of the pervasiveness and expansiveness of the financial foundation of foreign terrorists,' the Government may block the assets of individuals and entities that 'provide support, services, or assistance to, or otherwise associate with, terrorists and terrorist organizations designated under the Order.'[201] E.O. 13224 designated 12 individuals and 15 organizations, including three charities and one business entity, as 'Specially Designated Global Terrorists' or 'SDGTs.'[202] Accordingly, any assets in which these individuals and entities had an interest were seized and transactions with these terrorists were prohibited by the Order. The number of individuals and groups designated under E.O. 13224 has since increased from the original 27 designations to over 480 SDGTs.

In *United States v. Al-Arian*, former University of South Florida professor Sami Al-Arian and other Palestinian Islamic Jihad (PIJ) members were charged with conspiracy to violate IEEPA, 50 U.S.C. §1705(c).[203] The indictment alleged that the defendants knowingly and willfully violated an order issued under E.O. 12947 by making and receiving contributions of funds, goods, and services for the benefit of the PIJ.[204] Because the annex to E.O. 12947 designated PIJ as an SDT, the provision of financial support and services to the PIJ violated IEEPA.[205] Among other issues raised by the defendants, the district court examined the *mens rea* requirement to convict for a criminal violation of IEEPA.

Section 1705(c) criminalizes only 'willfully' committed violations of an order or regulation issued under IEEPA. The court held that to sustain a conviction for a criminal violation of IEEPA, the government must prove a defendant: '(a) knew either that an organization was a SDT or committed unlawful activities that caused it to be designated as a SDT; and (b) had a specific intent that the contribution be used to further the unlawful activities of the SDT.'[206] The court stated that it is not enough to prove that the defendant acted with knowledge that the individual or organization had been designated as an SDT or engaged in unlawful activities that caused such designation. The government must prove that the defendant acted with the specific intent to further the illegal activities of the SDT.[207] The court's conclusion was based on the plain language of §1705(c), which criminalizes 'willful' violations of the E.O. and the regulations interpreting the Order. The court argued that 'willfully' in criminal statutes means an act 'undertaken with a "bad purpose." '[208] The court posited:

> While knowledge of IEEPA, the Executive Order, or the regulations thereunder is not necessary to support a conviction, some 'bad purpose' must be demonstrated by the government. This Court concludes that a 'bad purpose' cannot be demonstrated by proof of knowledge of past unlawful activity alone. The government must show some additional intent to further future unlawful activity to support criminal liability.[209]

The court stated that the statute should not be interpreted as reaching purely innocent or unwitting conduct. Without such a *scienter* requirement, the court was concerned that the prohibitions in the E.O. may be unconstitutionally vague or violate the Fifth Amendment's requirement of personal guilt.[210]

Applying the statute to a case involving financial support to al Qaeda, the government would have to prove that the defendant provided support, services or assistance to the terror group with knowledge that it had been designated an SDT or SDGT, or committed criminal acts that caused it to be so designated. However, knowingly providing money to al Qaeda members would not be enough to support criminal liability, according to the court in *Al-Arian*. The government would also have to show that the defendant acted with the specific intent to support al Qaeda's terrorist activities.[211] In the absence of such proof, a conviction for a violation of §1705(c) could not be sustained.[212]

CRIMINAL PROSECUTION VICTORIES AND LEGAL DEFEATS

Since 9/11, the Justice Department has brought few prosecutions targeting deep-pocket donors and front groups responsible for raising, collecting and funneling large sums of money needed to sustain the organizational and operational activities of al Qaeda, HAMAS, Hizballah, and other Islamist terrorist groups. Moreover, the relatively few major terrorist financing cases filed by the Justice Department have brought mixed results. While there have been some important prosecution successes on the financial front, the Department of Justice has suffered several disappointing legal setbacks.

Mohammed Ali Hasan Al-Moayad

On the positive side, in 2005 the Justice Department won an important legal victory in curtailing the flow of funds to al Qaeda and the Islamic Resistance Movement, or HAMAS. After a five-week trial, a federal jury in Brooklyn, New York, convicted Mohammed Ali Hasan Al-Moayad, a Yemeni cleric and influential political leader, and his assistant, Mohammed Mohsen Yahya Zayed, of conspiring to provide material support to al Qaeda and attempting to provide material support to HAMAS. The defendants were charged in a six-count indictment with conspiring to funnel millions of dollars from a Brooklyn mosque to al Qaeda fighters in Afghanistan and Bosnia, and to Palestinian suicide bombers on behalf of HAMAS.[213] Al-Moayad was also convicted of providing material support to HAMAS and attempting to provide support to al Qaeda. Al-Moayad and Zayed were arrested as part of a U.S. government 'sting' operation involving an undercover FBI agent offering to donate $2.5 million to terrorism causes. Al-Moayad was caught on undercover tape recordings discussing the collection of monies from the al Farook mosque in Brooklyn and his intent to distribute millions of dollars to al Qaeda and HAMAS to finance violent jihad.[214] On one tape recording, Al-Moayad referred to himself as a spiritual adviser to Osama bin Laden. Al-Moayad and Zayed were sentenced to 75 years and 45 years in prison, respectively. The case was important because the criminal charges directly linked Al-Moayad and Zayed to providing millions of dollars to al Qaeda and HAMAS.

Mohammed Hammoud

The Justice Department also successfully prosecuted Mohammed Hammoud for his involvement in a major cigarette smuggling operation. The members of the conspiracy were charged with purchasing large quantities of cigarettes in North Carolina, smuggling them to Michigan and selling them without paying Michigan taxes.[215] It is estimated that the conspiracy involved a quantity of cigarettes valued at approximately $7.5 million and that the state of Michigan was deprived of over $3 million in tax revenues.[216] Hammoud was implicated in raising money for Hizballah, a foreign terrorist organization. Hizballah was founded by Lebanese Shi'a Muslims in response to the 1982 invasion of Lebanon by Israel. The organization was designated as a foreign terrorist organization by the State Department for sponsoring acts of terrorism in support of its strong opposition to the existence of Israel and the United States' presence in the Middle East. According to the criminal charges, Hammoud was acquainted with Hassan Nasserallah, the Secretary General of Hizballah, Sheikh Fadlallah, the group's spiritual leader, and Sheikh Abbas Harake, a senior military commander for Hizballah. Hammoud allegedly raised money in the U.S. for Hizballah and then forwarded the money to Harake.[217]

On the basis of these and other activities, Hammoud was convicted of multiple federal offenses, including the sale of contraband cigarettes, money laundering, mail fraud, racketeering, conspiracy to provide material support to a designated FTO and providing material support to a designated FTO.[218] The material support charge involved Hammoud's personal donation of $3,500 to Hizballah.[219] However, despite the small amount of money involved, the prosecution was important because of Hammoud's connections to the senior leadership of Hizballah and commitment to raising money in the U.S. for the terror group.

Sami Al-Arian

One of the most disappointing legal setbacks for the U.S. Department of Justice involves the case of Sami Al-Arian, a former engineering professor at the University of South Florida, who was charged, along with seven other defendants, in a multi-count indictment by a federal grand jury in Tampa, Florida.[220] The 2003 indictment alleged that Al-Arian and his co-defendants were members of the Palestinian Islamic Jihad-Shiqaqi Faction (PIJ), who operated and directed PIJ's fund-raising and other organizational activities in the United States for almost 20 years. The PIJ was designated as an SDT in 1995 and as an FTO in 1997 because of the threat it posed to the Middle East peace process, and its use of violence against Israeli citizens.[221] The Government contended that Al-Arian was the alleged leader of the PIJ in the United States and Secretary of the 'Shura Council,' or worldwide governing group of the PIJ.[222]

The DOJ's 53-count indictment included: conspiracy to commit racketeering, in violation of 18 U.S.C. §1962(d) (Count 1); conspiracy to murder, maim or injure persons outside the U.S., in violation of 18 U.S.C. §956(a)(1) (Count 2); conspiracy to provide material support to an FTO, in violation of 18 U.S.C. §2339B (Count 3); conspiracy to make and receive contributions of funds, goods, or services to or for the benefit of SDTs, in violation of 50 U.S.C. §1705 and 18 U.S.C. §371 (Count 4); violations of the Travel Act, in violation of 18 U.S.C. §1952(a)(2)–(3) and 18 U.S.C. §2 (Counts 5 to 21); providing material support to a foreign terrorist organization, in violation of 18 U.S.C. §2339B(a)(1)–(2) (Counts 22 to 32); money laundering, in violation of 18 U.S.C. §1956 (Counts 33 to 43); violation of the immigration laws, in violation of 18 U.S.C. §§1425(a) and 1546(a) (Counts 44 to 45); obstruction of justice, in violation of 18 U.S.C. §§1503 and 1505 (Counts 46 and 53); and perjury, in violation of 18 U.S.C. §1621 (Counts 47 to 52).[223]

The indictment alleged that the PIJ constituted a RICO enterprise, which engaged in multiple acts of murder and extortion in Israel and the Occupied Territories (Gaza Strip and West Bank). The racketeering conspiracy count detailed some 323 overt acts, ranging from soliciting and raising funds to providing management, organizational, and logistical support to the PIJ. The overt acts included allegations of numerous suicide bombings and attacks by PIJ members, which resulted in the murders of over 100 people in Israel and the Occupied Territories, including two U.S citizens, and injuries to hundreds of other civilians, including seven American citizens.[224] The indictment further alleged that the Tampa-based defendants established a PIJ cell using the structure and facilities of the University of South Florida and two other entities, the World and Islam Studies Enterprise and the Islamic Concern Project, as a cover to conceal their terrorist activities.[225]

Attorney General John Ashcroft issued a press release announcing the indictment and the arrest of Al-Arian and three other defendants, stating:

> The individuals named in this indictment play a substantial role in international terrorism – they are 'material supporters' of foreign terrorist organizations. They finance, extol and assist acts of terror. Our message to them is clear: We make no distinction between those who carry out terrorist attacks and those who knowingly finance, manage or supervise terrorist organizations. We will bring justice to the full network of terror.[226]

Al-Arian and three co-defendants were ultimately tried before a federal jury in Tampa, Florida. After a six-month jury trial, followed by 13 days of deliberation, the jury failed to convict the defendants on any of the 53 charges against them.[227] Al-Arian was acquitted on 8 of 17 counts, while the jury remained deadlocked on the other nine charges against him. The jury was unable to reach a verdict on three of the four most serious charges against Al-Arian and co-defendant Hatem Naji Fariz – the RICO conspiracy, conspiracy to provide material support, and conspiracy to violate IEEPA.[228] Al-Arian and Fariz were acquitted of the conspiracy to murder persons abroad, Travel Act, material support and money laundering charges. Defendants Sameeh Taha Hammoudeh and Ghassan Zayed Ballut were acquitted of all criminal charges.[229]

Rather than pursue a retrial, the government entered into a plea agreement with Al-Arian. Pursuant to the agreement, Al-Arian pleaded guilty to one count of conspiracy to make or receive contributions of funds, goods or services to or for the benefit of the PIJ, in violation of 50 U.S.C. §1705(b) and 18 U.S.C. §371.[230] In return, the government agreed to dismiss the remaining eight charges against him (hung jury counts), not charge him with any other crimes, and make a recommendation at the low end of the federal sentencing guidelines, 46–57 months.[231] As part of the plea arrangement, Al-Arian agreed to expedited deportation, where he will be free to continue raising money and providing other material support to the PIJ.

Holy Land Foundation Case

The U.S. government suffered another stunning legal setback in the criminal prosecution of the Holy Land Foundation for Relief and Development (HLF), a purported Muslim charity based in Richardson, Texas, and five former officials. The HLF case was the largest and most complex legal effort to shut down American financing for terrorist organizations in the Middle East.[232] The defendants were accused of illegally funneling more than $12 million to Palestinian zakat committees in the West Bank and Gaza that served as fronts for HAMAS.[233] The government further alleged that HLF funds were used to support schools that encouraged children to become suicide bombers and to support the families of suicide bombers.[234] As a result of its terrorist-related activities, in December 2001, the HLF was designated as a Specially Designated Global Terrorist and its assets were blocked by the Treasury Department.[235]

In 2004, the U.S. Department of Justice brought criminal charges against the HLF and its directors and officers. The defendants charged in the case included: Ghassan Elashi (35 counts), the original HLF Treasurer and former Chairman of the Board; Shukri Abu Baker (34 counts), the former HLF CEO; Mohammad El-Mezain (32 counts), the Foundation's original chairman, who became Director of Endowments; Mufid Abdulqader (32 counts), a top fund-raiser and a former city of Dallas public works supervisor; and Abdulrahman Odeh (32 counts), HLF's New Jersey representative.[236] Two other defendants charged in the case, Haitham Maghawri and Akram Mishal, remained fugitives.[237]

In a superseding indictment filed in November 2005, the Government charged the HLF and its co-defendants with 42 counts related to funding terrorism. The case involved a combination of 197 counts, including:

- Counts 1–12: Conspiracy to provide material support or resources to an FTO (18 U.S.C. §2339B(a)(1)) by raising funds in the U.S. and sending them to organizations and programs operated on behalf of or under the control of HAMAS;

- Counts 13–25: Conspiracy to provide funds, goods and services to a specially designated terrorist (50 U.S.C. §§1701–6) by making regular payments to zakat committees who were acting on behalf of, or under the control of, HAMAS;
- Counts 26–38: Conspiracy to commit money laundering (18 U.S.C. §1956(h));
- Count 39: Conspiracy to impede and impair the IRS and to file false tax returns for an organization exempt from income tax (18 U.S.C. §371);
- Counts 40–42: Filing false tax returns for an organization exempt from income tax (26 U.S.C. §7206(1)).[238]

In October 2007, after almost two months of testimony and 19 days of deliberation, a federal judge declared a mistrial on what was widely seen as the Government's flagship terrorism financing case. The jury failed to issue a single guilty verdict. The jury acquitted one defendant on all but one charge, on which it deadlocked, and failed to reach a unanimous verdict on any of the other criminal counts.[239]

Muhammad Salah and Abdelhaleem Ashqar

In 2007, the U.S. Department of Justice suffered another disappointing legal defeat. A federal jury in Chicago acquitted Muhammad Salah and Abdelhaleem Ashqar of being members of the Palestinian extremist group HAMAS, of recruiting and training new members, and of raising money for HAMAS in the United States.[240] The case was one of the first to allege that the U.S. was being used as a fund-raising base for a government-designated terrorist organization. The indictment alleged that the defendants Salah and Ashqar operated a racketeering enterprise that recruited and trained new HAMAS members and raised money for the terror group in the United States.[241] Specifically, the indictment charged Salah, Ashqar, and others with conspiring to violate RICO by agreeing to conduct and participate, directly and indirectly, in the conduct of the affairs of the enterprise through a pattern of racketeering activity that included multiple acts of murder, solicitation of first-degree murder, money laundering, providing material support or resources to an FTO, hostage taking, and travel in aid of racketeering.[242] Salah was further accused of receiving in his Chicago-based bank account a series of wire transfers totaling approximately $985,000 to be distributed to HAMAS members in the West Bank and Gaza Strip.[243] After a three-month jury trial, and 14 days of deliberation, both Salah and Ashqar were acquitted of the most serious charge alleged in the indictment, participating in a

RICO conspiracy to provide funding, recruiting, training and other aid to HAMAS.[244]

Enaam Arnaout

Another disappointing result involved the prosecution of Enaam Arnaout, the executive director of the Benevolence International Foundation (BIF), a purported Islamic charity. Arnaout was charged in a multi-count indictment in the Northern District of Illinois with conspiracy to engage in a RICO enterprise; conspiracy to provide material support to al Qaeda, Hezb e Islami, and others engaged in violence and armed confrontation; providing material support, namely 2,900 pairs of anti-mine boots, to fighters in Chechnya; conspiracy to launder money; money laundering; and mail and wire fraud.[245] Specifically, the indictment alleged that Arnaout used BIF, a Chicago-based charity, as a front to illicitly obtain funds from unsuspecting donors to covertly support Osama bin Laden, al Qaeda, other Islamic terrorist groups, and armed violence in Bosnia. The indictment charged that BIF was a RICO enterprise responsible for 'support[ing] the activities of mujahideen in various areas of the world by raising funds and providing support to mujahideen and others engaged in violence and armed confrontation, including al Qaeda, Hezb e Islami and the Sudanese Popular Defense Force.'[246]

In 2003, Arnaout was permitted to plead guilty to racketeering conspiracy, admitting that he fraudulently obtained charitable donations and diverted charity money to pay for boots, uniforms and other equipment to support fighters in Chechnya and Bosnia-Herzegovina.[247] In return, the government dropped all terrorist-financing-related charges that Arnaout provided financial aid to al Qaeda and other terrorist groups.[248] In fact, the press release by the Department of Justice announcing the guilty plea did not even mention Osama bin Laden, al Qaeda or the financing of terrorism. In the press release, the U.S. Attorney stated:

> We are gratified that today's plea vindicates the Government's claim that Arnaout and BIF were victimizing well-intentioned donors. The government's investigation has always sought to vindicate the donors who gave money in good faith in an effort to serve peaceful, humanitarian concerns when instead violence was being funded. Many of the victim donors were law-abiding Muslims who were obligated by Islamic principles to donate to charity. By today's turn of events, the defendant has publicly admitted that this *fraud* occurred.[249]

Arnaout ultimately pleaded guilty to fraudulently obtaining charitable donations and diverting some of the funds to support the conflict in the Balkans, not financing al Qaeda and acts of terrorism. Thus, what was once hailed by the Department of Justice as a major terrorist financing case was plea-bargained down to a major fraud case.

In addition to the failed prosecutions on the main terrorist financing charges, another disturbing issue is the steadily declining number of international terrorism prosecutions being brought by the Department of Justice, including a dramatic drop in terrorist-financing-related cases. According to one source, there has been a major decline in international terrorism cases since 2002. While in the 12 months immediately after 9/11 the prosecutions of terrorism-related cases surged sharply higher than in the previous year, six years later the number of these prosecutions has returned to roughly what they were before the 2001 World Trade Center terrorist attacks. In 2005, the Justice Department prosecuted 46 international terrorism cases, down from 355 cases in 2002.[250] In 2007, the estimated number of international terrorism-related prosecutions was 30, down 26.8 percent from the previous year.[251] When the estimate of 2007 international terrorism prosecutions is compared to those five years ago, where there were 355 cases, the number of prosecutions was down 91.5 percent.[252] The dramatic decline in the number of terrorist *financing* cases is equally disturbing. During the first eight months of fiscal year 2007 the government reported 19 new terrorism-related *financing* prosecutions.[253] If this activity continues at the same pace, it is reported that the annual total will be 29 cases for 2007.[254] This estimate would represent a decrease of 40.8 percent over 2006, where the number of prosecutions totaled 49.[255]

In 2006, the Department of Justice published the *Counterterrorism White Paper* (*DOJ White Paper*), outlining its accomplishments in the war on terror during the five-year period following 9/11.[256] While stating that '[t]errorist financing has been a particular focus of [the Justice Department's] investigative efforts,' the *DOJ White Paper* reported convictions in only seven terrorist financing cases over the five-year period following 9/11.[257] Two of the cases hailed as prosecution successes included the Sami Al-Arian and Enaam Arnaout cases. As previously discussed, the jury in the Al-Arian case failed to convict Al-Arian and three other defendants on any of the 53 counts brought by the Department of Justice.[258] In the Arnaout case, the defendant pleaded guilty to racketeering conspiracy, admitting that he defrauded donors of BIF. However, Arnaout was not convicted of raising money for Osama bin Laden and al Qaeda as originally charged in the indictment.[259] Finally, the *DOJ White Paper* highlighted the convictions of Dr Rafil Dhafir, who fraudulently obtained charitable donations from unwitting donors and transferred the funds abroad in violation of U.S. economic sanctions and money laundering statutes, and Monasser Mosad Omian, who was convicted of conspiring to operate an unlicensed money business and disbursing money to Yemen.[260]

However, neither indictment alleged that any of funds handled by Dhafir or Omian were transferred for the benefit of foreign terrorist organizations or suspected terrorists.[261] In short, the purported terrorist financing cases lacked a terrorism nexus.

Rather than highlighting the success of the Department of Justice in the war on terrorism, the *DOJ White Paper* raises serious concerns with respect to the low number of terrorist financing cases targeting the major donors, fund-raisers, and financial networks of al Qaeda, HAMAS, Hizballah, and affiliated terror groups.[262] Some of the terrorism-financing-related prosecutions discussed in the *DOJ White Paper* are low-impact cases that are unlikely to disrupt al Qaeda's, Hizballah's or HAMAS' ability to acquire millions of dollars needed annually to sustain their organizational and operational terrorist activities. For example, the *DOJ White Paper* highlighted the conviction of Hassan Makki for providing 'more than $2,000 to Hizballah for the orphans of martyrs program in Southern Lebanon to benefit the families of those killed in Hizballah operations.'[263] While the value of prosecuting low-level financiers should not entirely be dismissed, those criminal enforcement actions are unlikely to have a significant impact on curtailing the flow of funds to al Qaeda, Hizballah and other terrorist groups. Instead, the Justice Department should prioritize its resources and focus on prosecuting major donors and fund-raisers for al Qaeda and other militant Islamic entities.

There are many possible explanations for the limited progress on the financial front in the war on terror. According to a recent report prepared by the Department of Homeland Security (DHS), Office of the Inspector General (OIG), criminal enforcement efforts continue to be plagued by petty turf battles and lack of coordination between the FBI, Immigration and Customs Enforcement (ICE), and other federal law enforcement agencies.[264] The DHS-OIG report suggests that the interagency squabbling over 'who's in charge' of terrorist financing investigations has impeded the government's ability to aggressively investigate, disrupt and dismantle al Qaeda's financial network. Perhaps complacency has contributed to the lack of success and overtaken the sense of urgency that existed immediately following 9/11 to deprive the terrorists of funding. Another possible rationale is that going after terrorist money is no longer a top priority for the federal government.

Whatever the explanation, the declining number of terrorist financing cases, the paucity of major terrorist financing prosecutions, and the jury acquittals and hung juries in high-profile terrorist financing cases should cause Congress and the Department of Justice to re-examine the U.S. government's counter-terrorist-financing strategy. At the very least, Congress should revisit the definition of 'material support or resources' set forth in 18

U.S.C. §2339A(1)(B), with respect to the terms 'training,' 'expert advice or assistance,' and 'services,' and amend the statute to cure the unconstitutional vagueness problem.[265] Furthermore, Congress should amend the IEEPA statute, 50 U.S.C. §1705(c), by deleting the requirement that the violation be committed 'willfully,' and provide that a person commits a violation of IEEPA if he knowingly engages in a transaction, knowing that the person has been designated an SDT or SDGT by the Treasury Department, or engaged in conduct that caused him to be so designated. It simply does not make sense to permit a criminal conviction under 18 U.S.C. §2339B for knowingly providing material support or resources to an FTO, knowing of the organization's FTO status or knowing that the organization engages in terrorism, but require the government to prove a defendant engaged in a financial transaction with a SDT or SDGT with the specific intent to further the group's terrorist activities in order to sustain a criminal violation of IEEPA.

NOTES

1. Head of Charity Indicted for Terror Links, Transcript, CNN.com (Oct. 9, 2002), *available at* http://transcripts.cnn.com/TRANSCRIPTS/0210/09/se.08.html.
2. Pub. L. No. 104–132, §301(a)(7), 110 Stat. 1247 (1996).
3. 18 U.S.C.A §2339A (West 2008) and 18 U.S.C. §2339B (2000 & Supp. IV 2004).
4. Eric Lichtblau, *1996 Statute Becomes the Justice Department's Antiterror Weapon of Choice*, N.Y. Times, Apr. 6, 2003, at B15, *available at* http://query.nytimes.com/gst/fullpage.html?res=9B0CE1DD1238F935A35757C0A9659C8B63&n=Top/Reference/Times%20Topics/Organizations/A/Al%20Qaeda.
5. U.S. Dep't of Justice, Counterterrorism White Paper 3 (2006), *available at* http://abajournal.com/files/09-2007/DOJcounterterrorismWhitePaper.pdf [hereinafter DOJ White Paper].
6. *See* 18 U.S.C.A §2339A (West 2008) and 18 U.S.C. §2339B (2000 & Supp. IV 2004). The term 'material support or resources' is a term of art and proscribes various types of material support prohibited under the statutes. *See* discussion *infra*, at notes 42, 94–101.
7. 18 U.S.C. §2339A punishes

   > Whoever provides material support or resources or conceals or disguises the nature, location, source, or ownership of material support or resources, knowing or intending that they are to be used in preparation for, or in carrying out, a violation of section 32, 37, 81, 175, 229, 351, 831, 842(m) or (n), 844(f) or (i), 930(c), 956, 1114, 1116, 1203, 1361, 1362, 1363, 1366, 1751, 1992, 2155, 2156, 2280, 2281, 2332, 2332a, 2332b, 2332f, or 2340A of this title, section 236 of the Atomic Energy Act of 1954 (42 U.S.C. 2284), section 46502 or 60123(b) of title 49, or any offense listed in section 2332b(g)(5)(B) (except for sections 2339A and 2339B), or in preparation for, or in carrying out, the concealment of an escape from the commission of any such violation, or attempts or conspires to do such an act.

8. For example, §2339A criminalizes the provision of financial assistance 'knowing or intending' that the funds be used in preparation for, or in carrying out, a conspiracy to kill, kidnap, maim, or injure persons in a foreign country, in violation of 18 U.S.C. §956.
9. 18 U.S.C. §2339B (2000 & Supp. IV 2004). 8 U.S.C. §1189 (2000 & Supp. IV 2004) empowers the Secretary of State to designate an entity as a "Foreign Terrorist

Organization" (FTO). An FTO designation yields serious consequences, such as authorizing the Government to freeze any funds which the organization has on deposit with any financial institution in the United States, and barring representatives and members of the organization from entering the United States. 8 U.S.C.A. §1182(a)(3)(B)(i)(IV & V) (West 2008); 8 U.S.C. §1189(a)(2)(C) (2000 & Supp. IV 2004).

10. 18 U.S.C. §§2339A, 2339B. In addition, assets involved in violations of §§2339A and 2339B are subject to civil forfeiture under 18 U.S.C.A. §981 (West 2008).
11. Suppression of the Financing of Terrorism Convention Implementation Act of 2002, Pub. L. No. 107-197, tit. II, 116 Stat. 724 (2002) (codified at 18 U.S.C.A. §2339C (West 2008)). The Act also expanded the predicate offenses under RICO, and amended the wiretap and money laundering statutes. *Id.*
12. International Convention for the Suppression of the Financing of Terrorism, Dec. 9, 1999, 39 I.L.M 270, *available at* http://untreaty.un.org/ENGLISH/TreatyEvent2003/treaty_11.htm. The anti-terrorist financing treaty was ratified by the U.S. Senate on June 26, 2002. The treaty is aimed at stopping the flow of financial resources to terrorists and terrorist organizations, and obligates signatory states to criminalize conduct relating to raising money and other assets that support terrorist activities. The Preamble calls on States to 'take steps to prevent and counteract, through appropriate domestic measures, the financing of terrorists and terrorist organizations, whether such financing is direct or indirect through organizations which also have or claim to have charitable, social or cultural goals or which are also engaged in unlawful activities.' *Id.* at Preamble.
13. 18 U.S.C. §2339C punishes

    Whoever, in a circumstance described in subsection (b), by any means, directly or indirectly, unlawfully and willfully provides or collects funds with the intention that such funds be used, or with the knowledge that such funds are to be used, in full or in part, in order to carry out–
    (A) an act which constitutes an offense within the scope of a treaty specified in subsection (e)(7), as implemented by the United States, or
    (B) any other act intended to cause death or serious bodily injury to a civilian, or to any other person not taking an active part in the hostilities in a situation of armed conflict, when the purpose of such an act, by its nature or context, is to intimidate a population, or to compel a government or an international organization to do or to abstain from doing any act.

14. 18 U.S.C.A. §2339C(d)(1) (West 2008).
15. *See* 18 U.S.C.A. §981(a)(1)(H) (West 2008).
16. *See* 18 U.S.C. §2339B(d)(1), (2) (2000 & Supp. IV 2004) and 18 U.S.C.A. §2339C(b)(2) (West 2008). Section 2339A is silent on whether there is extraterritorial jurisdiction over an offense under the statute.
17. *See* 31 U.S.C. 5311 *et seq.*, and its implementing regulations at 31 C.F.R. Part 103.
18. Bank Secrecy Act, 31 U.S.C. §5311 *et seq.* and 31 C.F.R. Part 103.
19. Uniting and Strengthening America by Providing Appropriate Tools Required to Intercept and Obstruct Terrorism (USA PATRIOT) Act of 2001, Pub. L. No. 107-56, Title III, §371(c), 115 Stat. 272 (codified in scattered sections of the U.S.C.), and amended Pub. L. No. 108–458, Title IV, §6203(h), 118 Stat. 3747 (2004) (amending 31 U.S.C. §5332 (2000 & Supp. IV 2004)).
20. 31 U.S.C. §5332(b)(1) (2000 & Supp. IV 2004). In addition, the court shall order that the defendant forfeit to the United States any property, real or personal, involved in the offense, and property traceable to such property. *Id.* §5332(b)(2).
21. 'Hawala is the practice of informally transferring value across borders without sending money. . . . In these and other guises, informal value transfer creates a vast international unregulated and untaxed banking system.' WAYNE MCCORMACK, LEGAL RESPONSES TO TERRORISM 353–4 (2005). Because of the lack of a paper trail, reliable access to remote or under-developed regions, potential anonymity, and low cost, hawala is attractive for the transfer of criminal proceeds and terrorist-related

funds. *See* U.S. Dep't of Treasury, 2003 National Money Laundering Strategy, at 14 (2003), *available at* http://www.ustreas.gov/offices/enforcement/publications/ml2003.pdf. A more comprehensive description of hawala is provided by Interpol at http://www.interpol.int/Public/FinancialCrime/MoneyLaundering/hawala/default.asp.

22. *See* Pub. L. No. 107-56, Title III, §373(a), 115 Stat. 339 (2001) (amending 18 U.S.C. §1960(a) (2000 & Supp. IV 2004)).
23. 18 U.S.C. §1960(a), (b)(1)(A)–(B) (2000 & Supp. IV 2004).
24. 18 U.S.C. §1960(b)(1)(C) (2000 & Supp. IV 2004).
25. 50 U.S.C. §1705(b) (West 2008) provides: 'A civil penalty may be imposed on any person who commits an unlawful act described in subsection (a) of this section in an amount not to exceed the greater of –

    (1) $250,000; or
    (2) an amount that is twice the amount of the transaction that is the basis of the violation with respect to which the penalty is imposed.'

    Section 1705(c) provides: 'A person who willfully commits, willfully attempts to commit, or willfully conspires to commit, or aids or abets in the commission of, an unlawful act described in subsection (a) of this section shall, upon conviction, be fined not more than $1,000,000, or if a natural person, may be imprisoned for not more than 20 years, or both.'

26. The SDGT list is based on Executive Order 13224, which authorizes the Treasury Department to block assets and freeze accounts of these designated individuals and entities. *See* Blocking Property and Prohibiting Transactions with Persons Who Commit, Threaten to Commit, or Support Terrorism, Exec. Order No. 13,224, 3 C.F.R. 786–90 (2001), *reprinted as amended in* 50 U.S.C. §1701 note (Supp. IV 2004). The SDT list contains groups and individuals whose conduct threatens the Middle East peace process.
27. 50 U.S.C.A. §1705(b)–(c) (West 2008).
28. Research on terrorist financing prosecutions did not uncover any reported federal court opinions involving convictions under 18 U.S.C. §2339C. Further, the DOJ White Paper published on June 22, 2006, discussing the Department's progress since 9/11 in prosecuting international terrorism cases, did not even mention §2339C. Additionally, only one terrorist financing case discussed in the DOJ White Paper included criminal charges under the bulk cash smuggling statute, 31 U.S.C. §5332. *See* DOJ WHITE PAPER, *supra* note 5, at 21 (discussing United States v. Omian, Case No. 2:05-CR-80338-AJT-MKM, 2006 WL 3240555 (E.D. Mich. 2006)).
29. *See generally* DOJ WHITE PAPER, *supra* note 5 (discussing progress in prosecuting international terrorism cases since the 9/11 attacks and highlighting approximately six terrorist financing cases, some of which did not even allege that the funds were intended to aid foreign terrorist organizations).
30. *See* Syracuse University, *Terrorism-Related Financing Prosecutions for 2007,* TRAC REPORTS (2007), *available at* http://tracfed.syr.edu/results/9x7047025f7a.html (estimating 29 terrorism-related financing prosecutions in 2007, down from approximately 105 prosecutions in 2003).
31. *Id.*
32. *See* Matt O'Connor, *Acquittal Joins Other Courtroom Setbacks*, CHICAGO TRIB., Feb. 1, 2007 (the acquittal of two Palestinians on the main terrorism financing charge represented another legal setback for the Bush Administration's war on terror). In 2005, a federal jury in Tampa, Florida acquitted or deadlocked on all 17 counts alleging Sami Al-Arian, a former University of South Florida professor, provided material financial support to the Palestinian Islamic Jihad, a designated FTO. *See* DOJ WHITE PAPER, *supra* note 5, at 21–2.
33. *The Terrorist Threat to the U.S. Homeland*, National Intelligence Estimate (July 2007), *available at* http://www.dni.gov/press_releases/20070717_release.pdf.

34. 18 U.S.C. §§2339A, 2339B. *See* DOJ WHITE PAPER, *supra* note 5, at 3 ('The material support statutes have been a cornerstone of our success in terrorism financing cases as well as in a wide range of other cases addressing all types of support to terrorism.').
35. AEDPA, *supra* note 2, at §301(a)(6), 110 Stat. 1214, 1247.
36. *See* Violent Crime Control and Law Enforcement Act of 1994, Pub. L. No. 103–322, §120005(a), 108 Stat. 1796, 2022–3 (1994) (codified at 18 U.S.C. §2339A).
37. 18 U.S.C.A. §2339A(a) (West 2008).
38. *See* AEDPA, *supra* note 2, §303(a), 110 Stat. 1250; Intelligence Reform and Terrorism Prevention Act of 2004, Pub L. No. 108–458, §6603(c)–(f), 118 Stat. 3638, 3762 (2004) (codified as amended at 18 U.S.C. §2339B).
39. Humanitarian Law Project v. Gonzales, 380 F. Supp. 2d 1134, 1146 (C.D. Cal. 2005).
40. *Id.* at 1137.
41. Intelligence Reform and Terrorism Prevention Act of 2004, Pub. L. No. 108–458, §6603, 118 Stat. 3638, 3762 (2004) (codified as amended at 18 U.S.C. §2339A, B).
42. 18 U.S.C.A. §2339A(b)(1) (West 2008) (defining 'material support or resources'). Sections 2339A and 2339B share in common the concept of 'material support or resources,' which is defined in §2339A(b) for purposes of §2339A, and incorporated by reference into §2339B. Section 2339B(g) provides: 'the term "material support or resources" has the same meaning given that term in section 2339A (including the definitions of "training" and "expert advice or assistance" in that section).' 18 U.S.C. §2339B(g)(4).
43. 18 U.S.C. §2339B(g)(6) (2000 & Supp. IV 2004).
44. 8 U.S.C. §1189(a)(1).
45. The U.S. Department of State has designated 44 foreign terrorist organizations: (1) Abu Nidal Organization (ANO); (2) Abu Sayyaf Group (ASG); (3) Al-Aqsa Martyrs Brigade; (4) Al-Shabaab; (5) Ansar al-Sunna (AS); (6) Armed Islamic Group (GIA); (7) Asbat al-Ansar; (8) Aum Shinrikyo (AUM); (9) Basque Fatherland and Liberty (ETA); (10) Communist Party of the Philippines/New People's Army (CPP/NPA); (11) Continuity Irish Republican Army (CIRA); (12) Gama'a al-Islamiyya (IG); (13) HAMAS; (14) Harakat ul-Jihad-i-Islami/Bangladesh (HUJI-B); (15) Harakat ul-Mujahidin (HUM); (16) Hizballah; (17) Islamic Jihad Group (IJG); (18) Islamic Movement of Uzbekistan (IMU); (19) Jaish-e-Mohammed (JEM); (20) Jemaah Islamiya Organization (JI); (21) al-Jihad (AJ); (22) Kahane Chai (Kach); (23) Kongra-Gel (KGK); (24) Lashkar-e Tayyiba (LT); (25) Lashkar i Jhangvi (LJ); (26) Liberation Tigers of Tamil Eelam (LTTE); (27) Libyan Islamic Fighting Group (LIFG); (28) Moroccan Islamic Combatant Group (GICM); (29) Mujahedin-e Khalq Organization (MEK); (30) National Liberation Army (ELN); (31) Palestine Liberation Front (PLF); (32) Palestinian Islamic Jihad (PIJ); (33) Popular Front for the Liberation of Palestine (PFLP); (34) Popular Front for the Liberation of Palestine–General Command (PFLP–GC); (35) al Qaeda in Iraq (AQI); (36) al Qaeda (AQ); (37) al Qaeda in the Islamic Maghreb (formerly GSPC); (38) Real IRA (RIRA); (39) Revolutionary Armed Forces of Colombia (FARC); (40) Revolutionary Nuclei (RN); (41) Revolutionary Organization 17 November; (42) Revolutionary People's Liberation Party/Front (DHKP/C); (43) Shining Path (SP); and (44) United Self-Defense Forces of Colombia (AUC). *See* U.S. Dep't of State, Office of the Coordinator for Counterterrorism, Foreign Terrorist Organizations (Apr. 8, 2008), *available at* http://www.state.gov/s/ct/rls/fs/08/103392.htm, last visited April 9, 2008.
46. 18 U.S.C. §2339B(a)(1) (2000 & Supp. IV 2004). To sustain a conviction for violating §2339B, 'a person must have knowledge that the organization is a designated terrorist organization (as defined in subsection (g)(6)), that the organization has engaged or engages in terrorist activity (as defined in section 212(a)(3)(B) of the Immigration and Nationality Act), or that the organization has engaged or engages in terrorism (as defined in section 140(d)(2) of the Foreign Relations Authorization Act, Fiscal Years 1988 and 1989).' *Id.* Satisfying the knowledge requirement may be difficult when the donor gives money to a charity or other front group acting on behalf of the FTO, because the Government must prove that the defendant knew the group was an FTO front.

47. *See* discussion of the §2339B *scienter* requirement, *infra* at notes 49–66 and accompanying text.
48. Jeff Breinholt, *Terrorist Financing*, 51 U.S. ATTORNEYS BULLETIN, at 30, July 2003.
49. Intelligence Reform and Terrorism Prevention Act of 2004, Pub. L. No. 108-458, §6603(c)–(f), 118 Stat. 3762, 3763 (2004) (codified at 18 U.S.C. §2339B(a)(1)).
50. 18 U.S.C. §2339B(a)(1) (2000 & Supp. IV 2004). Congress amended the statute to incorporate the *mens rea* requirement imposed by the Ninth Circuit in *Humanitarian Law Project v. U.S. Dep't of Justice*, 352 F.3d 382, 405 (9th Cir. 2003). Prior to the Ninth Circuit's decision in *Humanitarian Law Project* and the IRTPA amendments, §2339B punished whoever 'knowingly provides material support or resources to a foreign terrorist organization, or attempts or conspires to do so.' AEDPA, *supra* note 2, §303(a).
51. *See* United States v. Assi, 414 F. Supp. 2d 707, 719–20 (E.D. Mich. 2006); Humanitarian Law Project v. Gonzales, 380 F. Supp. 2d 1134, 1142 (C.D. Cal. 2005).
52. United States v. X-Citement Video, Inc., 513 U.S. 64, 72 (1994).
53. *See Assi*, 414 F. Supp. 2d at 720.
54. In *United States v. Al-Arian*, 308 F. Supp. 2d 1322, *reconsideration denied,* 329 F. Supp. 2d 1294 (M.D. Fla. 2004), the district court held that §2339B raised constitutional concerns that could only be avoided by construing the statute to require 'that the defendant knew (had a specific intent) that the support would further the illegal activities of a FTO.' *Id.* at 1337–8. However, several other courts have rejected this view. *See, e.g.*, United States v. Hammoud, 381 F.3d 316, 328 (4th Cir. 2004); *Assi*, 414 F. Supp. 2d at 723–4; United States v. Paracha, Case No. 03 CR. 1197(SHS), 2006 WL 12768, at *25 (S.D.N.Y. Jan. 3, 2006); Linde v. Arab Bank, 384 F. Supp. 2d 571, 587 & n. 11 (E.D.N.Y. 2005); United States v. Marzook, 383 F. Supp. 2d 1056, 1070 (N.D. Ill. 2005); Humanitarian Law Project v. Gonzales, 380 F. Supp. 2d 1134, 1147 & n. 15 (C.D. Cal. 2005).
55. Scales v. United States, 367 U.S. 203 (1961).
56. *Id.* at 206 & n.1.
57. *Id.* at 224–5.
58. *Id.* at 226 n.18, 228; *see also* Humanitarian Law Project v. U.S. Dep't of Justice, 352 F.3d 382, 395 (9th Cir. 2003).
59. *Humanitarian Law Project*, 380 F. Supp. 2d at 1143.
60. *Id.* at 1144; *see also* United States v. Marzook, 383 F. Supp. 2d 1056, 1067–8 (N.D. Ill. 2005); Linde v. Arab Bank, 384 F. Supp. 2d 571, 587 (E.D.N.Y. 2005).
61. *Humanitarian Law Project*, 380 F. Supp. 2d at 1146; *see also* United States v. Assi, 414 F. Supp. 2d 707, 722 (E.D. Mich. 2006) (citing *Humanitarian Law Project* with approval); *Marzook*, 383 F. Supp. 2d at 1070 (imposing a requirement under §2339B of specific intent to further the FTO's illegal activities would 'clash[ ] with Congress's intent' and 'thus would contravene the fundamental concepts of statutory construction').
62. *Humanitarian Law Project*, 380 F. Supp. 2d at 1146.
63. AEDPA, *supra* note 2, at §301(a)(7), 110 Stat. 1214, 1247.
64. Humanitarian Law Project v. Reno, 205 F.3d 1130, 1136 (9th Cir. 2000) (HLP 1).
65. Humanitarian Law Project v. Gonzales, 380 F. Supp. 2d 1134, 1146 (C.D. Cal. 2005); *see also Assi,* 414 F. Supp. 2d at 723 (advancing the same argument).
66. *See Assi*, 414 F. Supp. 2d at 723–4; United States v. Paracha, Case No. 03 CR. 1197(SHS), 2006 WL 12768, at *29 (S.D.N.Y. Jan. 3, 2006) ('The statutory definition of "material support or resources" limits what constitutes assistance sufficiently blameworthy to attach criminal liability.'); *Humanitarian Law Project*, 380 F. Supp. 2d at 1148.
67. 8 U.S.C. §1189(c)(1) (2000 & Supp. IV 2004) establishes a procedure for judicial review of the Secretary of State's decision to designate an organization as an FTO. Section 1189(b)(1) provides:

    (1) In general
    Not later than 30 days after publication in the Federal Register of a designation, an amended designation, or a determination in response to a petition for revocation, the designated organization may seek judicial review in the United States Court of Appeals for the District of Columbia.

(2) Basis of Review
Review under this subsection shall be based solely upon the administrative record, except that the Government may submit, for ex parte and in camera review, classified information used in making the designation, amended designation, or determination in response to a petition for revocation.
(3) Scope of Review
The Court shall hold unlawful and set aside a designation, amended designation, or determination in response to a petition for revocation the court finds to be –
(A) arbitrary, capricious, an abuse of discretion, or otherwise not in accordance with law;
(B) contrary to constitutional right, power, privilege, or immunity;
(C) in excess of statutory jurisdiction, authority, or limitation, or short of statutory right;
(D) lacking substantial support in the administrative record taken as a whole or in classified information submitted to the court under paragraph (2), or
(E) not in accord with the procedures required by law.

The term 'national security' means the 'national defense, foreign relations, or economic interests of the United States.' *Id.* §1189(d)(2).

68. Upon notification that the Secretary plans to designate an organization, the Secretary of the Treasury may require U.S. financial institutions that possess or control assets of that organization to block all financial transactions involving those assets. *Id.* at §1189(a)(2)(C).
69. Nat'l Council of Resistance of Iran v. Dep't of State, 251 F.3d 192 (D.C. Cir. 2001).
70. *Id.* at 196–7.
71. *Id.* at 209.
72. United States v. Verdugo-Urquidez, 494 U.S. 259, 271 (1990).
73. *See* 32 County Sovereignty Comm. v. Dep't of State, 292 F.3d 797, 799 (D.C. Cir. 2002) (finding that the organization had not demonstrated a property interest or a presence within the United States and therefore the Secretary did not have to provide the organization with any particular process before designating it as an FTO).
74. *See* People's Mojahedin Org. of Iran v. U.S. Dep't of State, 182 F.3d 17, 22 (D.C. Cir. 1999) (holding that '[a] foreign entity without property or presence in this country has no constitutional rights, under the due process clause or otherwise').
75. *Nat'l Council of Resistance of Iran,* 251 F.3d at 201. *But see 32 County Sovereignty Comm.*, 292 F.3d at 799 (evidence that some of the organization's American members rented post office boxes and utilized a bank account to transmit funds and information to the organization, but did not possess any controlling interest in property located in the United States and did not establish sufficient connections with the U.S. to trigger due process protection).
76. *Nat'l Council of Resistance of Iran*, 251 F.3d at 204.
77. *Id.* at 205.
78. *Id.* at 205–6.
79. *See* Mathews v. Eldridge, 424 U.S. 319, 334–5 (1976).
80. *Nat'l Council of Resistance of Iran,* 251 F.3d at 205 (quoting Morrissey v. Brewer, 408 U.S. 471, 481 (1972)).
81. *Id.* at 206 (citing Mathews v. Eldridge, 424 U.S. 319, 335 (1976)).
82. *Id.* at 206.
83. *Id.* at 207.
84. *Id.* at 206; *see also* 8 U.S. C. §1189(c)(4) (2000 & Supp. IV 2004).
85. *Id.* at 207.
86. *Id.* (quoting Haig v. Agee, 453 U.S. 280, 307 (1981)).
87. *Nat'l Council of Resistance of Iran*, 251 F.3d at 207–8.
88. *Id.* at 208.
89. *Id.*
90. *Id.*

91. *Id.* at 209.
92. *Id.*
93. *Id.*
94. Intelligence Reform and Terrorism Prevention Act of 2004, Pub. L. No. 108–458, §6603(b), 118 Stat. 3638, 3762 (2004) (codified as amended at 18 U.S.C. §2339A(b)).
95. *See* 18 U.S.C. §2339A(b)(1) (defining 'material support or resources' for both 18 U.S.C. §§2339A and 2339B).
96. The USA PATRIOT Act of 2001 amended the AEDPA to add 'expert advice or assistance' to the definition of 'material support or resources' to designated terrorist organizations. *See* 18 U.S.C. §§2339A(b)(1), 2339B(g)(4).
97. 18 U.S.C. §2339B(h) (2000 & Supp. IV 2004).
98. 18 U.S.C.A. §2339A(b)(2) (West 2008).
99. *Id.* §2339A(b)(3).
100. *Id.* §2339A(b)(1).
101. *See* Humanitarian Law Project v. Reno, 205 F.3d 1130, 1137–8 (9th Cir. 2000) (holding the terms 'personnel' and 'training' unconstitutionally vague); Humanitarian Law Project v. Ashcroft, 309 F. Supp. 2d 1185, 1198–1201 (C.D. Cal. 2004) (finding the term 'expert advice or assistance' impermissibly vague); United States v. Sattar, 272 F. Supp. 2d 348, 359–60 (S.D.N.Y. 2003) (finding the term 'personnel' unconstitutionally vague).
102. Humanitarian Law Project v. Reno, 9 F. Supp. 2d 1176 (C.D. Cal. 1998), *aff'd*, 205 F.3d 1130 (9th Cir. 2000) (HLP I). *But see* United States v. Lindh, 212 F. Supp. 2d 541, 574 (E.D. Va. 2002) (rejecting claim that term 'personnel' was unconstitutionally vague in the context of defendant Lindh, who joined the Taliban in combat against American forces).
103. Humanitarian Law Project v. Ashcroft, 309 F. Supp. 2d 1185, 1201 (C.D. Cal. 2004).
104. Kolender v. Lawson, 461 U.S. 352, 357 (1983).
105. Columbia Natural Res., Inc. v. Tatum, 58 F.3d 1101, 1104–5 (6th Cir. 1995).
106. *Id.*
107. Connally v. Gen. Constr. Co., 269 U.S. 385, 391 (1926); *see also* Giaccio v. Pennsylvania, 382 U.S. 399, 402–3 (1966) ('It is established that a law fails to meet the requirements of the Due Process Clause if it is so vague and standardless that it leaves the public uncertain as to the conduct it prohibits.'); Chicago v. Morales, 527 U.S. 41, 56 (1999) (same); Grayned v. City of Rockford, 408 U.S. 104, 108–9 (1972) (same).
108. Parker v. Levy, 417 U.S. 733, 756 (1974).
109. Village of Hoffman Estates v. Flipside, Hoffman Estates, Inc., 455 U.S. 489, 494–5 (1982).
110. *Id.* at 497.
111. Humanitarian Law Project v. Gonzales, 380 F. Supp. 2d 1134 (C.D. Cal. 2005).
112. *Id.* at 1149–50.
113. *Id.* at 1150.
114. Humanitarian Law Project v. Reno, 9 F. Supp. 2d 1176, 1204 (C.D. Cal. 1998), *aff'd*, 205 F.3d 1130 (9th Cir. 2000) (HLP I).
115. *Humanitarian Law Project,* 380 F. Supp. 2d at 1150.
116. *Id.*
117. 18 U.S.C.A. §2339A(b)(3) (West 2008) (emphasis added).
118. *Humanitarian Law Project*, 380 F. Supp. 2d at 1151.
119. *Id.*
120. *Id.* at 1152.
121. *Id.*
122. 18 U.S.C. §2339B(h) (2000 & Supp. IV 2004).
123. *Humanitarian Law Project*, 380 F. Supp. 2d at 1152. 18 U.S.C. §2339B(h), defines the term 'provision of personnel'.
124. *Id.* at 1152–3.
125. United States v. Hammoud, 381 F.3d 316, 330–1 (4th Cir. 2004) (*en banc*), *vacated on other grounds*, 543 U.S. 1097 (2005), *reinstated in relevant part*, 405 F.3d 1034 (4th Cir. 2005).
126. NAACP v. Claiborne Hardware Co., 458 U.S. 886, 908, 918–9 (1982).
127. *Id.* at 920 (footnote omitted).

128. *See Hammoud*, 381 F.3d at 328; Humanitarian Law Project v. Reno, 205 F.3d 1130, 1133 (9th Cir. 2000); United States v. Assi, 414 F. Supp. 2d 707, 713–4 (E.D. Mich. 2006).
129. *See Humanitarian Law Project*, 205 F.3d at 1133; *Assi*, 414 F. Supp. 2d at 713; Boim v. Quranic Literacy Inst. & Holy Land Found. for Relief & Dev., 291 F.3d 1000, 1026 (7th Cir. 2002).
130. *Humanitarian Law Project*, 205 F.3d at 1133.
131. *Hammoud*, 381 F.3d at 329.
132. *Id.*
133. *See id.*; *Humanitarian Law Project*, 205 F.3d at 1135.
134. Ward v. Rock Against Racism, 491 U.S. 781, 791 (1989).
135. *See* United States v. O'Brien, 391 U.S. 367, 377 (1968) (applying intermediate scrutiny to a regulation prohibiting burning a draft card).
136. *Humanitarian Law Project*, 205 F.3d at 1135–6 (9th Cir. 2000); *see also* United States v. Afshari, 426 F.3d 1150, 1160 (9th Cir. 2005); *Hammoud*, 381 F.3d at 328–9 (4th Cir. 2004); People's Mojahedin Org. of Iran v. Dep't of State, 327 F.3d 1238, 1244–5 (D.C. Cir. 2003) (quoting *Humanitarian Law Project* with approval in rejecting First Amendment challenge to §2339B); Boim v. Quranic Literacy Inst. & Holy Land Found. for Relief & Dev., 291 F.3d 1000, 1026 (7th Cir. 2002) (same).
137. *Humanitarian Law Project*, 205 F.3d at 1135; *see also Hammoud*, 381 F.3d at 329.
138. *Humanitarian Law Project*, 205 F.3d at 1135.
139. *Id.*
140. *Id.* In *Boim*, 291 F.3d at 1027, the Seventh Circuit 'conclude[d] that the government's interest in preventing terrorism is not only important but paramount,' and that this 'interest is unrelated to suppressing free expression,' but instead 'is aimed at prohibiting the funding of violent acts that these organizations wish to carry out.'
141. *Humanitarian Law Project,* 205 F.3d at 1136. '[T]errorist organizations do not maintain open books. Therefore, when someone makes a donation to them, there is no way to tell how the donation is used. [E]ven contributions earmarked for peaceful purposes can be used to give aid to the families of those killed while carrying out terrorist acts, thus making the decision to engage in terrorism more attractive.' *Id.*
142. United States v. Assi, 414 F. Supp. 2d 707, 715 (E.D. Mich. 2006).
143. *Id.*
144. *See, e.g.,* United States v. Awan, 459 F. Supp. 2d 167, 180–81 (E.D.N.Y 2006); United States v. Assi, 414 F. Supp. 2d 707, 716 (E.D. Mich. 2006); Humanitarian Law Project v. Gonzales, 380 F. Supp. 2d 1134, 1153 (C.D. Cal. 2005); United States v. Sattar, 314 F. Supp. 2d 279, 305 (S.D.N.Y. 2004)
145. Virginia v. Hicks, 539 U.S. 113, 118–19 (2003) (internal quotation marks and citation omitted).
146. *Id.* at 119–20 (internal quotation marks and citations omitted). *see also* Broadrick v. Oklahoma, 413 U.S. 601, 615 (1973) ('[T]he overbreadth of a statute must not only be real, but substantial as well, judged in relation to the statute's plainly legitimate sweep.').
147. United States v. Hammoud, 381 F.3d 316, 330 (4th Cir. 2004) (en banc), *vacated on other grounds*, 543 U.S. 1097 (2005), *reinstated in relevant part,* 405 F.3d 1034 (4th Cir. 2005); *see also* United States v. Assi, 414 F. Supp. 2d 707, 716–17 (E.D. Mich. 2006).
148. *Assi*, 414 F. Supp. 2d at 716.
149. *Id.* at 717; *see also* United States v. Sattar, 314 F. Supp. 2d 279, 305 (S.D.N.Y. 2004) (punishing the financing of terrorism is a legitimate exercise of Congress's power to criminalize 'harmful, constitutionally unprotected conduct'); United States v. Awan, 459 F. Supp. 2d 167, 180 (E.D.N.Y. 2006) (citing *Sattar* with approval).
150. *Assi*, 414 F. Supp. 2d at 717.
151. *See* 8 U.S.C. §1189(a)(8) (2000 & Supp. IV 2004).
152. *Hammoud*, 381 F.3d at 331.
153. *Id.*
154. United States v. Afshari, 426 F.3d 1150, 1159 (9th Cir. 2005).
155. *Id.* at 1155–6.
156. *Id.* at 1158–9.

157. 18 U.S.C.A. §2339C (West 2008). Section 2339C was intended to implement the International Convention for the Suppression of the Financing of Terrorism, which requires signatories to prosecute or extradite individuals who contribute to, or collect money for, terrorist groups. H.R. Rep. No. 107–307, at 6–7 (2001), 147 Cong Rec. E2397 (daily edn, Dec. 19, 2001).
158. *See* 18 U.S.C.A. §2339C(a)(2) (West 2008).
159. *Id.* §2339C(a)(3) (emphasis added). The predicate act of §2339C(a)(1)(A) encompasses offenses within listed treaties specified in subsection (e)(7) of the statute.
160. *Id.* §2339C(c).
161. *Id.* §2339C(d)(2).
162. 18 U.S.C.A. §2339C(e)(4), (5) (West 2008).
163. Linde v. Arab Bank, 384 F. Supp. 2d 571, 588 (E.D.N.Y. 2005); *see also* Strauss v. Credit Lyonnais, Case No. CV-06-0702 (CPS), 2006 WL 2862704, at *17 (E.D.N.Y. Oct. 5, 2006) (quoting *Linde*, 384 F. Supp. 2d at 588).
164. 18 U.S.C.A. §2339C(a) (West 2008).
165. *Id.*
166. *Linde,* 384 F. Supp. 2d at 586 n.9. *But see* Boim v. Quranic Literacy Inst. & Holy Land Found. for Relief & Dev., 291 F.3d 1000, 1023–4 (7th Cir. 2002).
167. 18 U.S.C.A. §2339C(e)(7) (West 2008).
168. *See* Nina J. Crimm, *High Alert: The Government's War of the Financing of Terrorism and Its Implications for Donors, Domestic Charitable Organizations, and Global Philanthropy*, 45 WM. & MARY L. REV. 1341, 1422 (2004) ('To date, no indictments have been brought under 18 U.S.C. §2339C against either individuals or organizations.').
169. 18 U.S.C.A. §2339C(a)(1)(B) (West 2008).
170. United States v. Velastegui, 199 F.3d 590, 593 (2d Cir. 1999), *quoted in* United States v. Telebnejad, 460 F.3d 563, 565 (4th Cir. 2006).
171. 18 U.S.C.A. §1960, historical and statutory notes (West Supp. 2006) (internal quotation marks omitted).
172. *Id.* (emphasis added; internal quotation marks omitted).
173. U.S. Department of Justice, *Report From The Field: The USA PATRIOT Act at Work*, at 10 (July 2004), *available at* http://www.usdoj.gov/olp/pdf/patriot_report_from_the_field0704.pdf. Defendants have been convicted for operating unlicensed money transmitting businesses that sent money from the U.S. to Iraq, Yemen, India, and other countries identified as a high risk for terrorism. To deal with these concerns, subsection (b)(1)(C) broadened the statute to make it a crime for the owner or operator of a money transmitting business to move funds that he knows are either the proceeds of a crime or are intended to be used to promote or support unlawful activity, including acts of terrorism. *Id.* at 11.
174. *Id.* at 10.
175. *See* H.R. REP. NO. 107–250, pt. I, at 54 (2001) (explaining that the amendment 'clarifies the scienter requirement in §1960 to avoid the problems that occurred when the Supreme Court interpreted the currency transaction reporting statutes to require proof that the defendant knew that structuring a cash transaction to avoid the reporting requirements had been made a criminal offense. *See* Ratzlaf v. United States, [510 U.S. 135 (1994)]. The proposal makes clear that an offense under 1960 is a general intent crime for which a defendant is liable if he knowingly operates an unlicensed money transmitting business.').
176. 18 U.S.C.A. §1960(a) (emphasis added) (West 2008).
177. *Id.* at §1960(b)(2).
178. 31 U.S.C. §5330 provides, in pertinent part:

    (a) Registration with Secretary of the Treasury required –
    (1) In general – Any person who owns or controls a money transmitting business shall register the business (whether or not the business is licensed as a money transmitting business in any State) with the Secretary of the Treasury not later than the end of the 180-day period beginning on the later of –

(A) the date of enactment of the Money Laundering Suppression Act of 1994; or
(B) the date on which the business is established.

(b) Contents of registration — The registration of a money transmitting business under subsection (a) shall include the following information:

(1) The name and location of the business.
(2) The name and address of each person who –
(A) owns or controls the business;
(B) is a director or officer of the business; or
(C) otherwise participates in the conduct of the affairs of the business.
(3) The name and address of any depository institution at which the business maintains a transaction account (as defined in section 19(b)(1)(C) of the Federal Reserve Act).
(4) An estimate of the volume of business in the coming year (which shall be reported annually to the Secretary).
(5) Such other information as the Secretary of the Treasury may require.

31 U.S.C. §5330(a), (b).

179. 18 U.S.C.A. §1960(b)(1) (West 2008).
180. United States v. Talebnejad, 460 F.3d 563, 568 (4th Cir. 2006).
181. 18 U.S.C.A. §1960(b)(1)(A) (West 2008).
182. *Talebnejad*, 460 F.3d at 569.
183. United States v. Talebnejad, 342 F. Supp. 2d 346, 356 (D. Md. 2004), *rev'd in* United States v. Talebnejad, 460 F.3d 563 (4th Cir. 2006).
184. United States v. Uddin, 365 F. Supp. 2d 825, 829 (E.D. Mich. 2005).
185. *See* H.R. Rep. NO. 107-250, pt. I, at 54 (2001).
186. *See* United States v. Talebnejad, 460 F.3d 563, 572 (4th Cir. 2006) ('Nothing in the statutory language–such as the use of the word "willful"–suggests that the Government must additionally prove knowledge of the law.'); United States v. Keleta, 441 F. Supp. 2d 1, 3 (D.D.C. 2006) (section 1960 'does not require that the Defendant either knew or willfully violated (or both) federal money transmitting registration requirements in order to have violated the statute'); United States v. Uddin, 365 F. Supp. 2d 825, 829–30 (E.D. Mich. 2005) ('Had Congress intended that the statute required proof of the defendant's knowledge of the federal registration or state licensing requirements, it would have used the word "willful." ').
187. *See 2003 National Money Laundering Strategy*, *supra* note 21, at 15 ('In the United States alone, the Border and Immigration Customs Enforcement executed 650 bulk cash seizures, totaling $28 million, including more than $19 million with a Middle East connection.').
188. 31 U.S.C. §5332(a)(1) (2000 & Supp. IV 2004).
189. 31 U.S.C. §5316(a)(1) (2000).
190. 50 U.S.C. §1701(a) (2000).
191. 50 U.S.C. §1702(a)(1)(A)–(B) (2000 & Supp. IV 2004).
192. 50 U.S.C.A. §1705(c) (West 2008).
193. *See* Prohibiting Transactions with Terrorists Who Threaten to Disrupt the Middle East Peace Process, Exec. Order No. 12,947, 60 Fed. Reg. 5079, *codified at* 3 C.F.R. 319–20 (1995), *reprinted as amended in* 50 U.S.C. §1701 note (2000 & Supp. IV 2004).
194. The 1995 E.O. designated the following twelve groups: Abu Nidal Organization (ANO), Democratic Front for the Liberation of Palestine (DFLP), Hizballah, Islamic Gama'at (IG), Islamic Resistance Movement (HAMAS), Islamic Jihad, Kach, Kahane Chai, Palestinian Islamic Jihad-Shiqaqi faction (PIJ), Palestine Liberation Front-Abu Abbas faction (PLF-Abu Abbas), Popular Front for the Liberation of Palestine (PFLP), Popular Front for the Liberation of Palestine–General Command (PFLP–GC). *Id.* at 5081.
195. *See id.* at 5079–80. The regulations are contained in Title 31 C.F.R. part 595. Section 595.204 makes it unlawful to 'deal in property or interests in property of a . . . [SDT], including the making or receiving of any contribution of funds, goods, or services to or for the benefit of an [SDT].' 31 C.F.R. §595.204.

196. 31 C.F.R. §595.204.
197. *See id.* §595.205.
198. Prohibiting Transactions With Terrorists Who Threaten To Disrupt the Middle East Peace Process, Exec. Order No. 13,099, 63 Fed. Reg. 45,167 (Aug. 20, 1998).
199. Blocking Property and Prohibiting Transactions With the Taliban, Exec. Order No. 13,129, 64 Fed. Reg. 36,759 (July 4, 1999).
200. Blocking Property and Prohibiting Transactions with Persons Who Commit, Threaten to Commit, or Support Terrorism, Exec. Order No. 13,224, 66 Fed. Reg. 49,079, 3 C.F.R. 786–90 (Sept. 23, 2001), *reprinted as amended in* 50 U.S.C. §1701 note (Supp. IV 2004).
201. *Id.*
202. *Id.*
203. United States v. Al-Arian, 308 F. Supp. 2d 1322, 1331 (M.D. Fla. 2004). In the case, defendants were charged with violation 50 U.S.C. §1705(b). However, this section is now 50 U.S.C. §1705(c) due to an amendment by Congress.
204. *Id.* at 1328.
205. *Id.* at 1331, 1339–40; *see also* E.O. 12,947, *supra* note 193.
206. *Al-Arian,* 308 F. Supp. 2d at 1339–40.
207. *Id.*
208. *Id.* at 1340 (*quoting* Bryan v. United States, 524 U.S. 184, 191 (1998)).
209. *United States v. Al-Arian,* 308 F. Supp. 2d at 1340.
210. *Id.* at 1341.
211. *Id.*
212. Apparently, the government was unable to meet this heightened specific intent *mens rea* standard. A federal jury was unable to convict Al-Arian and his co-defendants on the IEEPA counts. *See* United States v. Al-Arian, Verdict, Case No. 8:03-CR-77-T30 TBM (M.D. Fla., Dec. 6, 2005). However, pursuant to a subsequent plea agreement, Al-Arian pleaded guilty to conspiracy to make or receive contributions of funds, goods, or services to or for the benefit of PIJ, an SDT, in violation of 18 U.S.C. §371. *See* United States v. Al-Arian, Plea Agreement, Case No. 8:03-CR-77-T30 TBM (M.D. Fla., Feb. 28, 2006).
213. *See* United States v. Al-Moayad, et al., Superseding Indictment, Case No. 03-1322 (S-1) (SJ) (E.D.N.Y. 2004).
214. Statement of Daniel Meron, Principal Deputy Assistant Attorney General, Civil Division, and Barry Sabin, Chief, Counterterrorism Section, Criminal Division, U.S. Department of Justice, Testimony before the Senate Judiciary Subcomm. on Terrorism, Technology and Homeland Security (Apr. 20, 2005); *see also Terrorist Financing*, 51 U.S. Attorneys Bulletin, No. 4, at 20 (July 2003).
215. *See* United States v. Hammoud, 381 F.3d 316 (4th Cir. 2004).
216. *Id.* at 325–6.
217. *Id.* at 326.
218. *Id.*
219. *Id.*
220. *See* United States v. Al-Arian, No. 8:03-CR-77-T-30TBM (M.D. Fla.); *see also* Press Release, U.S. Dep't of Justice, Members of the Palestinian Islamic Jihad Arrested, Charged with Racketeering and Conspiracy to Provide Material Support to Terrorists (Feb. 20, 2003), *available at* http://www.usdoj.gov/opa/pr/2003/February/03_crm_099.htm. Eight defendants were charged in the indictment, but only four were arrested and detained. The other four defendants charged in the indictment remained overseas. *Id.* The original indictment filed on February 12, 2003, included 50 counts. Further charges for money laundering and material support to an FTO were subsequently added. *See* DOJ White Paper, *supra* note 5, at 21.
221. *See* Exec. Order No. 12,947, *supra note* 193, at 5080; *see also* Designation of Foreign Terrorist Organizations, 62 Fed. Reg. 52,650 (1997). The Secretary's designation of PIJ as an FTO was renewed in 1999, 2001, and 2003. *See* Designation of Foreign Terrorist Organizations, 64 Fed. Reg. 55,112 (1999); Redesignation of Foreign Terrorist

Organization, 66 Fed. Reg. 51,088 (2001); and Redesignation of Foreign Terrorist Organization, 68 Fed. Reg. 56,860 (2003).

222. *See* Press Release, U.S. Dep't of Justice, Members of the Palestinian Islamic Jihad Arrested, Charged with Racketeering and Conspiracy to Provide Material Support to Terrorists, (Feb. 20, 2003), *available at* http://www.usdoj.gov/opa/pr/2003/February/03_crm_099.htm.
223. Superseding Indictment, United States v. Al-Arian, et al., No. 8:03-Cr-77-T-30 TBM (M.D. Fla. Nov. 15, 2005).
224. *Id.*
225. *See* Press Release, U.S. Dep't of Justice, Members of the Palestinian Islamic Jihad Arrested, supra note 222.
226. *Id.*
227. *See* United States v. Al-Arian, Verdict, Case No. 8:03-CR-77-T30 TBM (M.D. Fla., Dec. 6, 2005).
228. *See id.*
229. *See id.*
230. *See* United States v. Al-Arian, Plea Agreement, Case No. 8:03-CR-77-T-30 TBM (2006); *see also* DOJ WHITE PAPER, *supra* note 5, at 22.
231. *Id.*
232. *See* Press Release, U.S. Dep't of Treasury, Shutting Down the Terrorist Financial Network (Dec. 4, 2001), *available at* http://www.treas.gov/press/releases/po841.htm.
233. *See id.*
234. *Id.*
235. *Id.* In December 2004, the parents of a young teen killed by HAMAS gunmen in the West Bank won a $156 million civil judgment against the HLF and other entities acting on behalf of HAMAS. *See* Judgment in Civil Case, Boim v. Quranic Literacy & Holy Land Found. for Relief & Dev., Case No: 00-C-2905 (N.D. Ill. 2004).
236. *See* Holy Land Foundation: About the Trial, THE DALLAS MORNING NEWS, Oct. 18, 2007, *available at* http://www.dallasnews.com/sharedcontent/dws/news/longterm/stories/092707dnmethlfabout.1127940bf.html; *see also* Leslie Eaton, *No Convictions in Trial Against Muslim Charity*, N.Y. TIMES, Oct. 22, 2007, *available at* http://www.nytimes.com/2007/10/22/us/22cnd-holyland.html.
237. *Id.*
238. United States v. Holy Land Found. for Relief & Dev., Superseding Indictment, No. 3:04-CR-240G (N.D. Tex. 2005).
239. United States v. Holy Land Found. for Relief & Dev., Mistrial Order, Case No. 3:04-CR-00240, Doc. 872 (Oct. 22, 2007).
240. Both Salah and Ashqar were convicted of less serious charges, affording some consolation to the Department of Justice. Salah was found guilty of obstruction of justice for lying under oath when questioned in a civil suit filed by the surviving family members of an American student killed in a HAMAS shooting in Israel. Ashqar was convicted of obstruction of justice and criminal contempt for refusing to testify before a grand jury. *See* Rudolph Bush and Jeff Coen, *Two Found Not Guilty of Supporting Hamas*, CHICAGO TRIBUNE, Feb. 2, 2007.
241. *See* United States v. Marzook, et al., Second Superseding Indictment, Case No. 1:03-CR-00978, (N.D. Ill. 2004).
242. *Id.*
243. *Id.*
244. *See* Bush & Coen, *supra* note 240.
245. Prepared Remarks of Attorney General John Ashcroft, Press Conference Announcing Enaam Arnaout Indictment (Oct. 9, 2002), *available at* http://www.usdoj.gov/archive/ag/speeches/2002/100902agremarksbifindictment.htm; *see also* United States v. Enaam M. Arnaout, Second Superseding Indictment, Case No. 1:02-Cr-00892 (N.D. Ill. 2003).
246. United States v. Enaam M. Arnaout, Second Superseding Indictment, Case No. 1:02-Cr-00892 (N.D. Ill. 2003).

247. Press Release, U.S. Dep't of Justice, Benevolence Director Pleads Guilty to Racketeering Conspiracy and Agrees to Cooperate with the Government (Feb. 10, 2003), *available at* http://www.usdoj.gov/usao/iln/pr/chicago/2003/pr 021003_01.pdf.
248. Eric Lichtblau, *February 9–15: International; Plea in Terror Case*, N.Y. TIMES, Feb. 16, 2003, at 2; *see also* Edward Alden, *Charity Guilty of Backing Muslim Fighters: Chicago Fraud Case Justice Department Fails to Secure Al-Qaeda Funding Conviction, Lesser Charges Brought After*, FINANCIAL TIMES, Feb. 12, 2003, at 12.
249. Press Release, U.S. Dep't of Justice, Benevolence Director, *supra* note 247 (emphasis added).
250. Syracuse University, *Criminal Terrorism Enforcement in the United States During the Five Years Since the 9/11/01 Attacks*, TRAC REPORTS (2006), *available at* http://trac.syr.edu/tracreports/terrorism/169/.
251. Syracuse University, *Terrorism-International Prosecutions for 2007*, TRAC REPORTS (2007), *available at* http://tracfed.syr.edu/results/9x6d46e84267.html.
252. *Id.*
253. Syracuse University, *Terrorism-Related Financing Prosecutions for 2007,* TRAC REPORTS *(2007), available at* http://tracfed.syr.edu/results/9x7047025f7a.html.
254. *Id.*
255. *Id.*
256. DOJ WHITE PAPER, *supra* note 5, at 3 ('This paper outlines the impressive success of the Department of Justice in the war on terrorism.').
257. *Id.* at 18.
258. *See* discussion *supra,* at notes 223–30 and accompanying text.
259. *See* discussion *supra,* at notes 48–9 and accompanying text.
260. *See* DOJ WHITE PAPER, *supra* note 5, at 20–21; *see also* United States v. Rafil Dhafir, et al., Indictment, No. 5:03-CR-64 (NAM), (N.D.N.Y. 2003); United States v. Monasser Omian, Plea Agreement, Cr. No. 05-80338 (E.D. Mich. 2006) (defendant pleaded guilty to conspiracy to operate an unlicensed money transmitting business and structuring to evade a reporting requirement).
261. *Id.*
262. The sentence imposed by the court is one relevant indicator of the nature and seriousness of the offense. The 2006 TRAC Report reveals that 213 individuals were convicted on terrorism-related charges in the five years following 9/11. From that group, 123 defendants were sentenced to prison. Only 14 defendants received a sentence of five years or more. Six defendants received a sentence of 20 years or more. Syracuse University, *Criminal Terrorism Enforcement in the United States During the Five Years Since the 9/11/01 Attacks*, TRAC REPORTS (2006), *available at* http://trac.syr.edu/tracreports/terrorism/169/.
263. DOJ WHITE PAPER, *supra* note 5, at 20.
264. *See* DEPARTMENT OF HOMELAND SECURITY, OFFICE OF INSPECTOR GENERAL, COORDINATION BETWEEN FBI AND ICE ON INVESTIGATIONS OF TERRORIST FINANCING (July 2007) [hereinafter OIG REPORT]. Following the 9/11 attacks, coordination issues quickly arose between the FBI and the Treasury Department. In October 2001, the Treasury Department established 'Operation Green Quest,' a multi-agency terrorist financing task force, formed to identify systems used by terrorist organizations to raise and transfer money to fund terrorist operations. *See* Press Release, U.S. Customs Service, Fact Sheet on Expansion of Operation Green Quest (Jan. 9, 2003), *available at* http://www.cbp.gov/xp/cgov/newsroom/news_releases/archives/cbp_press_releases/012003/01092003.xml; Press Release, U.S. Customs Service, Operation Green Quest Overview (Feb. 26, 2002), *available at* http://www.cbp.gov/xp/cgov/newsroom/news_releases/archives/legacy/2002/22002/02262002.xml. Operation Green Quest was led by the U.S. Customs Service, and included agents from the U.S. Secret Service, Internal Revenue Service, Bureau of Alcohol, Tobacco and Firearms, FBI, Office of Foreign Assets Control, the Financial Crimes Enforcement Network, the U.S. Postal Inspection Service, and the Naval Criminal Investigation Service. *Id.* By many accounts, Operation Green Quest was quite successful. In its first year and a half, the task force opened 2,000

cases, resulting in 79 arrests, 70 indictments, and seizures of $33 million. *See* OIG REPORT, *supra* at 5. The FBI strongly objected to the Treasury Department taking the lead in terrorist financing investigations. As a result, Operation Green Quest was eventually shut down pursuant to a Memorandum of Agreement (MOA), between the Department of Justice and the Department of Homeland Security (DHS), signed on May 13, 2003. *Id.* The MOA affirmed the FBI as the lead on terrorist financing cases and transferred terrorist financing investigations initiated by the Operation Green Quest task force to the FBI-led Joint Terrorism Task Forces (JTTFs). *Id.*

The Treasury Department was not a signatory to the MOA because, after the Homeland Security Act of 2002 created the DHS, agents from the U.S. Customs Service were consolidated with agents from the Immigration and Naturalization Service into a new organization called the Bureau of Immigration and Customs Enforcement (ICE). The ICE organization was transferred to the newly created DHS in March 2003.

265. *See* discussion of constitutional vagueness concerns implicated by the material support statutes, 18 U.S.C. §2339A and §2339B, *supra*, at notes 94–125 and accompanying text.

11. Private causes of action: using the civil justice system to hold terrorist financiers accountable

> The only way to imperil the flow of money and discourage the financing of terrorist acts is to impose liability on those who knowingly and intentionally supply the funds to the persons who commit the violent acts.[1]
>
> *Boim v. Quranic Literacy Institute* (7th Cir. 2002)

INTRODUCTION

Since the September 11, 2001 terror attacks, one of the U.S. Government's top goals in the Global War on Terror has been to deprive the terrorists of funding and dismantle their financial networks.[2] To accomplish these objectives, the Administration has emphasized criminal enforcement actions and freezing the assets of suspected terrorists and their financial supporters.[3] However, civil tort actions that seek large monetary damages provide an invaluable supplement to the criminal justice process and administrative blocking orders. Private lawsuits brought by the victims of terrorism can have a deterrent effect against the donors, corrupt charities, front organizations, financial institutions, and foreign states that provide financial support and services to terrorist organizations.[4] While the prospect of large civil monetary judgments may have little or no deterrent value for radical jihadists, the same may not be true of individual donors, charitable organizations and financial institutions that lend financial support or direction to foreign terrorist organizations (FTOs).[5] Such individuals and organizations are more likely to have substantial assets in the United States.[6] Attachment of those assets pursuant to a civil judgment could make it unprofitable to provide financial assistance to terrorist groups. Less ardent donors may be deterred from wittingly financing terrorist organizations for fear of having their assets attached to enforce a civil monetary judgment. In the case of corrupt Islamic charities, a civil judgment for aiding and abetting international terrorism could result in the attachment of the charities' assets to fulfill the judgment, bankrupting them and effectively putting them out of business.[7]

'Such civil actions could further deter terrorist groups from maintaining assets in the United States, from benefiting from investments in the United States and from soliciting funds from within the United States.'[8] A civil judgment for knowingly providing banking and administrative services to a terrorist organization could also expose financial institutions to significant operational and legal risks.[9] Merely being linked to a terrorist group could cause irreparable damage to the reputation of the particular financial institution, discouraging investors from doing business with the bank.[10] Additionally, successful civil lawsuits brought by terrorism victims against a foreign state sponsor of terrorism could further damage its reputation in the international community. Moreover, civil judgments 'condemn the terrorists or their sponsors as outlaws, and they may make it much more difficult for terrorists to finance their activities by exposing their assets to attachment.'[11] Finally, and more important yet, civil actions, which proceed against the assets of the financial sponsors of terrorism, can reduce the ability of terrorists to carry out their deadly attacks.[12]

There are numerous advantages in bringing civil actions for acts of terrorism. Because civil litigation requires a lower burden of proof, civil suits may be superior to pursuing criminal prosecution. In a civil action, plaintiffs are required to prove liability by a preponderance of the evidence, rather than the heightened criminal justice standard of guilt beyond a reasonable doubt. A criminal jury verdict also requires the jurors to unanimously agree on the defendant's guilt. A civil judgment may be based on less than a unanimous verdict. Additionally, plaintiffs benefit from more liberal discovery rules in civil causes of action. Finally, the government will likely prioritize its resources, focusing on the actual perpetrators of terrorist acts. As a result, the government's resources will limit its ability to pursue all individuals and organizations engaged in secondary conduct, such as providing financial support and services to a foreign terrorist organization.[13] The resources of 'private attorneys general' may be needed to regulate such secondary conduct. As one commentator observed: '[T]he time has come for private citizens to enter the battle on civil grounds through lawsuits aimed at crippling terrorist organizations at their [financial] foundation.'[14]

Unfortunately, enforcement of civil judgments against the state sponsors of terrorism is often hampered and obstructed by the U.S. government. In numerous anti-terrorism civil lawsuits, the government has intervened to quash writs of attachment to prevent prevailing plaintiffs from attaching assets to enforce their civil judgments against foreign state sponsors of terrorism.[15] Thus, for example, in order to enforce civil judgments against Iraq and Iran the plaintiffs victims of terrorism must succeed on two legal fronts. First, the plaintiffs must prevail on the merits of their tort claims against the foreign state defendants for aiding and abetting acts of terrorism. Second, after winning a judgment against these foreign governments, the plaintiffs must overcome the U.S. government's efforts to prevent them from satisfying their judgments. The difficulty in satisfying these legal judgments has serious deleterious effects. The legal expenses required to litigate these matters against the vast legal resources of the U.S. government, with no assurance that the plaintiffs will prevail, may discourage victims of terrorism from filing similar causes of action in future cases. Further, U.S. government intervention in such cases undermines the deterrent value of such lawsuits against the state sponsors of terrorism. Regrettably, the legal judgments in these civil tort actions often are reduced to no more than a pyrrhic moral victory. Finally, U.S. intervention in such lawsuits deprives the victims of terrorism of just compensation for their injuries. The victims of terrorism should not have to battle both the foreign state sponsors of terrorism and the U.S. government to recover damages awarded for the loss of loved ones and the suffering endured from acts of terrorism. In the absence of compelling reasons for doing so, the U.S. government should not be permitted to intervene in such cases and deny plaintiffs reasonable compensation.

SUING NON-STATE SPONSORS OF TERRORISM

Civil damages for acts of terrorism are authorized by the Antiterrorism Act of 1991 (ATA).[16] Plaintiffs may file suit pursuant to 18 U.S.C. §2333(a), enacted as part of the ATA, which provides:

> Any national of the United States injured in his or her person, property, or business by reason of an act of international terrorism, or his or her estate, survivors, or heirs, may sue therefor in any appropriate district court of the United States and shall recover threefold the damages he or she sustains and the cost of the suit, including attorney's fees.[17]

In order to state a claim for civil damages under §2333(a), plaintiffs must allege that they were injured 'by reason of' a crime that constitutes an act of 'international terrorism.' Section 2331(1) defines 'international terrorism' as activities that

> (A) involve violent acts or acts dangerous to human life that are a violation of the criminal laws of the United States or of any State, or that would be a criminal violation if committed within the jurisdiction of the United States or of any State;
> (B) appear to be intended–
> (i) to intimidate or coerce a civilian population;
> (ii) to influence the policy of a government by intimidation or coercion; or
> (iii) to affect the conduct of a government by mass destruction, assassination or kidnapping; and

(C) occur primarily outside the territorial jurisdiction of the United States, or transcend national boundaries in terms of the means by which they are accomplished, the persons they appear intended to intimidate or coerce, or the locale in which their perpetrators operate or seek asylum.[18]

The legislative history of the ATA reveals an intent 'to fill a gap in the law by establishing a civil counterpart to the existing criminal statutes.'[19] The statute was intended to deter and punish acts of international terrorism by holding terrorists and their facilitators accountable 'where it hurts them most: at their lifeline, their funds.'[20] The statute 'would allow victims to pursue renegade terrorist organizations, their leaders, and the resources that keep them in business, their money.'[21] Additionally, Congress intended to 'remove[ ] the jurisdictional hurdles in the courts confronting victims [of terrorism] and [to] empower[ ] victims with all the weapons available in civil litigation.'[22] The ATA was intended 'to codify general common law tort principles and to extend civil liability for acts of international terrorism to the full reaches of traditional tort law.'[23] One of the most significant features of the statute is the provision of treble damages, court costs, and reasonable attorney's fees.[24] That is, a successful plaintiff is entitled to triple his actual compensatory damages, and the losing party must pay his legal fees and court costs. Finally, the ATA is not limited to the actual perpetrators of international terrorism.[25] Instead, liability may be imposed 'at any point along the causal chain of terrorism.'[26] Thus, the financial supporters of terrorism may be held civilly liable for the harm caused by the terrorist attacks.

At the same time, the ATA imposes certain limitations. First, civil actions under section 2333(a) are limited to U.S. nationals.[27] Foreign nationals may not sue under the ATA. Second, a 1992 amendment to the ATA bars any actions under its provisions against a 'foreign state, an agency of a foreign state, or an officer or employee of a foreign state or an agency thereof acting within his or her official capacity or under color of legal authority.'[28] The ATA also excludes lawsuits for injury or loss by reason of an act of war, which could raise legal problems regarding causes of action arising from the armed conflict in Iraq and Afghanistan and the broader global war on terrorism.[29] Finally, the U.S. Attorney General may seek to stay any civil action brought under section 2333, or limit or stay discovery if the court finds that the civil action would substantially interfere with a criminal prosecution or national security operations.[30]

Suing Corrupt Islamic Charities and Terrorist Front Organizations

In *Boim v. Quranic Literacy Institute and Holy Land Foundation for Relief and Development*, [31] the seminal case on the application of the ATA, the court held that Muslim charities and front organizations that provide financial support to terrorist groups may be held civilly liable under 18 U.S.C. §§2331 and 2333.[32] In *Boim*, the parents of David Boim, a 17-year-old American citizen studying in Israel, brought a claim under 18 U.S.C. §2333 for the death of their son. In 1996, the Boims were living in Israel, where David was studying at a yeshiva. On the fatal day, David and several of his classmates were waiting at a bus stop near Beit El, a small West Bank village north of Jerusalem, when a car pulled off the road and stopped approximately ten feet away from the students.[33] One or more of the occupants of the vehicle opened fire at the crowd, striking David in the head. David's two assailants were later identified as members of HAMAS, a Palestinian terrorist organization committed to the destruction of Israel and the establishment of a fundamentalist Palestinian state.[34] Both men were apprehended by the Palestinian Authority in 1997, and then released pending trial.[35] One of the individuals killed himself in a suicide bombing at a shopping mall in Jerusalem later that same year. The other person was tried by a Palestinian Authority Tribunal and convicted of participating in the Boim killing.[36]

Pursuant to section 2333, the Boims sued a variety of individuals and organizations for their son's death, including Muhammad Abdul Hamid Khalil Salah (Salah), the American Muslim Society (AMS), the Quranic Literacy Institute (QLI), and the Holy Land Foundation for Relief and Development (HLF).[37] Salah was allegedly an active member of HAMAS and served as the leader of HAMAS's military wing in the U.S.[38] AMS is a now defunct organization, incorporated in the U.S., that allegedly provided financial support to HAMAS through HLF. QLI is an Illinois not-for-profit corporation that purportedly translated and published sacred Islamic texts.[39] The HLF, a not-for-profit California corporation with offices in Texas, Illinois and Jerusalem, is a charity whose alleged mission is to provide humanitarian relief and aid to Palestinians affected by the Second Intifada.[40] The Boims maintained that QLI, HLF, and AMS were financial fronts for HAMAS.[41] More specifically, they claimed that the defendants raised millions of dollars in the U.S. and channeled the funds to finance HAMAS's terrorist activities in the Middle East.[42] The money raised by HLF and QLI was allegedly laundered and transferred to HAMAS using complex financial transactions, fictitious front companies, and Swiss bank accounts in order to finance terrorist activities.[43] The essential theory of the *Boim* case was that, while two HAMAS terrorists actually murdered David Boim, the assailants were financially aided and abetted by HLF, QLI, AMS, and other entities and individuals.[44] The Boims sought $100 million in compensatory damages and $100 million in punitive damages, plus court costs and attorney's fees, and requested treble damages under the statute.[45]

The Boims alleged liability on three independent theories. First, the plaintiffs argued that mere provision of funds to HAMAS, without more, constitutes an act of international terrorism under 18 U.S.C. §2331.[46] Second, plaintiffs asserted that providing material support and resources to a designated foreign terrorist organization, in violation of 18 U.S.C. §§2339A and 2339B, falls within the definition of 'international terrorism' for purposes of 18 U.S.C. §2331.[47] Finally, plaintiffs claimed that defendants may be held civilly liable under §2331 for aiding and abetting international terrorism.[48]

Funding *simpliciter*

The first issue centered on whether the simple provision of funds to HAMAS by QLI and HLF constitutes an act of 'international terrorism' because it 'involve[s] violent acts or acts dangerous to human life.'[49] The Boims likened payments to HAMAS to murder for hire, reasoning that the payment 'involves' violent acts by bringing about the killing and providing an incentive for someone else to commit it.[50] While the court agreed that Congress intended sections 2331 and 2333 to 'reach beyond those persons who themselves commit the violent act that directly causes the injury,' it held that merely giving money to a terrorist organization without knowledge and intent to further its criminal actions does not constitute an act of 'international terrorism' under 18 U.S.C. §2331.[51] The court stated that '[t]o hold the defendants liable for donating money without knowledge of the donee's intended criminal use of the funds would impose strict liability.'[52] The court could find nothing in the language of the ATA statute or history to support that construction. In addition to proving knowledge and intent, the court stated that plaintiffs must show that murder was a reasonably foreseeable result of making a donation.[53]

Providing material support to terrorists and terrorist organizations

In their second theory of liability, the Boims argued that the provision of material support to an FTO constitutes an act of 'international terrorism' under §2333.[54] Section 2339A makes it a crime to provide material support or resources knowing or intending that they be used in the commission of specified violent acts.[55] Section 2339B criminalizes knowingly providing material support or resources to an organization that the United States has designated a foreign terrorist organization pursuant to 8 U.S.C. §1189(a).[56] Thus, if the provision of financial support meets the requirements for criminal liability under 18 U.S.C. §2339A or §2339B, plaintiffs contended that funding a terrorist organization may support a civil claim under §2333.

The court agreed, observing that, when Congress passed §§2339A and 2339B, it intended that persons who provide material support to the primary perpetrators of terrorism should also be held criminally liable for those violent acts. '[I]t would be counterintuitive,' the court stated, 'to conclude that Congress imposed criminal liability in sections 2339A and 2339B on those who financed terrorism, but did not intend to impose civil liability on those same persons through section 2333.'[57] The court held that, because Congress intended to hold individuals criminally accountable for funding terrorism by enacting 18 U.S.C. §§2339A and 2339B, it also intended through §§2333 and 2331 to impose civil liability for funding such violent activities.[58] However, the court added that, sponsoring acts of terrorism would give rise to civil liability under §2333 so long as 'knowledge and intent' are also shown. Thus, in order to establish liability under §2333, the court would require proof that the defendants knowingly provided financial support to a terrorist organization, intending that the funds be used to commit or facilitate terrorist activities.[59]

Terrorist financing

The court addressed the Boims' third theory of liability: that aiding and abetting terrorism is conduct that 'involves violent acts' as that term is used in §2331(1)(a). The defendants argued that §2333 does not provide for aiding and abetting liability, and such liability is available only when the statute expressly provides for it.[60] The court disagreed, reasoning that '[t]he statute would have little effect if liability were limited to those who pull the trigger or plant the bomb because such persons are unlikely to have assets, much less assets in the United States, and would not be deterred by the statute.'[61] Thus, persons who knowingly and intentionally supply funds to terrorist organizations are civilly liable under §2333 for aiding and abetting acts of terrorism.[62]

The district court found defendants Salah, HLF, and AMS liable to the Boims on summary judgment.[63] At the conclusion of a civil jury trial, QLI was also found liable. Ultimately, the jury awarded damages of $52 million, which the district court trebled to $156 million.[64]

Proximate cause

In *Boim v. Holy Land Foundation*, the Seventh Circuit reversed the entry of judgments against HLF, AMS, Salah, and QLI, and remanded the case back to the district court for further proceedings.[65] The Seventh Circuit held that the district court erred in failing to expressly find the existence of a causal link between the assistance the defendants gave to HAMAS and the murder of David Boim. The court ruled that proof that the defendants knew of HAMAS's illegal activities, desired to help those activities succeed, and engaged in some act of assisting HAMAS, without proof of some causal link between defendants' conduct and the death of Boim, was insufficient to render defendants liable under §2333.[66] Moreover, the court stated that the plaintiffs must prove that the injuries were both factually caused by defendants' conduct and were the type of injuries that were reasonably foreseeable by their conduct.[67] In other words, the defendants could not be held liable for any injury that was reasonably foreseeable without there also being proof that their conduct caused that injury.[68]

Despite the Seventh Circuit's ruling, the Boims should not have too much difficulty proving the necessary causal link between the defendants' actions and their son's death. In *Boim*, the court articulated several important guiding principles for establishing causation. First, the court stated that plaintiffs are not required to establish a direct link between defendants' donations and David Boim's murder. The plaintiffs are not required to trace the defendants' donations to the terrorists who killed Boim. Instead, the court stated that

> A factfinder reasonably could conclude those who provide money and other general support to a terrorist organization are as essential in bringing about the organization's terrorist acts as those who plan and carry out those acts. . . . For example . . . if an individual or organization established a funding network in the United States designed to provide ongoing financial support for Hamas's terrorist activities, a factfinder might reasonably infer that the act of establishing that network was a cause of ensuing acts of Hamas terrorism, even if no line could be drawn linking a particular dollar raised to a particular terrorist act.[69]

In order to establish liability the Boims are therefore not required to trace the funds supplied by the defendants to the purchase of the specific weapons used or finance the training of the assailants who killed their son.[70]

The relatively low threshold of proof required to demonstrate a causal link between the defendants' conduct and acts of terrorism was further underscored by the court's following statement:

> [I]f the plaintiffs were able to show that by providing funding to Hamas's other activities, including the hospitals, schools, and other charitable missions that it sponsors, a donor frees up Hamas resources for, or otherwise makes possible, Hamas's terrorist activities, then proof that the defendants provided support to Hamas ostensibly for its humanitarian activities, but with the knowledge and intent that Hamas be able to conduct terrorism also, might support the inference that the defendants were a cause of terrorist activity of the kind that resulted in David Boim's death.[71]

The court further noted that the defendants' conduct need not be the sole cause of the terrorist act in order to qualify as a cause in fact.[72] In other words, there may be multiple contributing causes for injuries suffered from the commission of terrorist acts. The *Boim* court stated that 'but-for causation does not demand a showing that the defendant's conduct was the sole cause of the plaintiff's injury; the conduct need only be one of the causes.'[73] Finally, the court emphasized that liability under §2333 does not require proof that the defendant's conduct was the predominant or primary cause of the injury. For example, 'a careful showing that many small donations collectively resulted in a cache of funds that in turn enabled a series of terrorist acts would permit a factfinder reasonably to infer a causal connection between the contribution made by a single donor and one of the terrorist acts made possible by that donor and others like him, even if a single donation would not by itself have been enough to cause that terrorist act.'[74] Thus, minor acts of support could be sufficient to render the donor liable for the injuries subsequently inflicted by the terrorists.[75]

Suing Banks that Provide Financial Services to Terrorist Organizations

Bank case studies

Arab Bank The ATA has been used to support civil causes of action against three foreign banks that allegedly provided financial and administrative services to agents of terrorist organizations. In *Linde v. Arab Bank, PLC (Arab Bank I)*,[76] American victims of terrorist attacks in Israel brought a complaint seeking more than $1 billion in damages against Arab Bank for knowingly providing banking and administrative services to Palestinian terrorist organizations that sponsored suicide bombings and other murderous attacks on innocent civilians in Israel.[77] Arab Bank is a Jordanian bank headquartered in Amman, Jordan, with a federally licensed branch office in the state of New York.[78] The Bank is a major international financial institution with over $32 billion in assets.[79] It has been characterized as a 'pillar of the Middle East economy' and the 'de facto treasurer for the Palestinian Authority.'[80]

The civil complaint alleged that Arab Bank administered accounts for various Islamic charities that operated as fund-raising front organizations for Palestinian terrorist groups. Specifically, plaintiffs alleged that, following the collapse of the peace negotiations between the State of Israel and the Palestinian Authority, Palestinian terrorist groups – including HAMAS, the Palestinian Islamic Jihad (PIJ), and the Al Aqsa Martyrs Brigade (AAMB) – launched the Al Aqsa Intifada, also known as the 'Second Intifada.'[81] The objectives of the Second Intifada were to intimidate and coerce the civilian population of Israel and to influence the policy of the Israeli government to withdraw from the Occupied Territories, meaning the West Bank and the Gaza Strip.[82] The terrorists utilized suicide bombers to launch thousands of attacks, which claimed more than 8,000 casualties, including over 1,000 civilian deaths, to accomplish their political goals.[83]

The complaint further identified several Islamic charities operating as front organizations for HAMAS, raising and channeling funds to support its terrorist activities. These Muslim charities included: the Al-Ansar Charity, Ramalla Charitable Committee, Tulkarem Charitable Committee, the Islamic Association, Al Mujama Al-Islami, Nablus Charitable Committee, Jenin Charitable Committee, and Islamic Charity Society of Hebron.[84] Although these charities hold themselves out as legitimate charitable organizations and collect money in the name of humanitarian causes, plaintiffs maintained that they in fact raised and channeled large sums of money to support the terrorist activities of HAMAS and other terrorist organizations.[85] The complaint further alleged that several of the charities held bank accounts at Arab Bank through which the Bank provided them with financial services, including receiving deposits and processing wire transfers.[86]

The most damning allegations involved Arab Bank's involvement with the Saudi Committee for the Support of the Al Quds Intifada (Saudi Committee). Shortly after the commencement of the Second Intifada, the Saudi Committee was established as a private charity registered in Saudi Arabia.[87] According to the plaintiffs, the Saudi Committee was established for the purpose of raising money for the families of the suicide bombers participating in the Palestinian terror campaign.[88] The Saudi Committee furnished a 'comprehensive insurance death benefit' and 'universal death and dismemberment plan,' consisting of a payment of $5,316.06 to the families of the 'martyrs' killed. or wounded in or imprisoned for perpetrating terrorist attacks.[89] Plaintiffs alleged that the death benefits plan operated, in effect, as a reward for perpetrators of suicide attacks. The Saudi Committee set up accounts at various financial institutions in the Middle East, primarily among them Arab Bank, to raise funds for the families of so-called martyrs of HAMAS and other Palestinian terrorist groups.[90] Public and private donations were deposited into these accounts.

Plaintiffs further claimed that Arab Bank administered the financial infrastructure by which the Saudi Committee distributed the death benefit payments to the families of the Palestinian terrorists.[91] Once the Saudi Committee prepared the list of eligible martyrs and prisoners, the names were provided to Arab Bank.[92] In consultation with the Saudi Committee and representatives of HAMAS, Arab Bank finalized the list and maintained a database of persons eligible to receive death benefits.[93] The Saudi Committee opened an account at Arab Bank in the beneficiary's name and then deposited a certain amount of U.S. dollars or Saudi riyals into the account.[94] Because Saudi riyals cannot be conveniently converted to Israeli currency, Arab Bank facilitated that conversion by routing those funds through its New York branch, where they were converted to U.S. dollars and then to Israeli currency.[95] After the funds were transferred to designated accounts in Arab Bank branches in the West Bank and Gaza, the Bank distributed the money to families of the suicide bombers.[96] In order to claim the reward, a suicide bomber's relatives were required to obtain an official certification of their deceased relative's status as a martyr, which included an individualized martyr identification number.[97] Families choosing to collect the reward would present certification cards to Arab Bank personnel to receive remittances. Finally, plaintiffs alleged that the death benefits plan 'facilitated and provided an incentive for the suicide bombings and other murderous attacks in that the individual attackers knew that, if they committed an attack, their families would be supported by the funds held in their names by Arab Bank.'[98]

National Westminster Bank In *Weiss v. National Westminster Bank (NatWest Bank)*,[99] plaintiffs brought action claiming that NatWest Bank was civilly liable for acts of terrorism pursuant to 18 U.S.C. §2333(a).[100] NatWest Bank is a British financial institution with its principal place of business in London.[101] The Bank conducts business in the United States through its branch offices in New York and Connecticut.[102] The plaintiffs included 12 individuals who were injured in ten different terrorist attacks that occurred in Israel between March 2002 and August 2003.[103] Eight plaintiffs were representatives of individuals killed in those attacks. The remaining plaintiffs were family members of the victims and experienced non-physical injuries including anxiety, extreme emotional distress, and severe mental anguish as a result of their relatives' injuries or death.[104]

Plaintiffs alleged that HAMAS received most of its financing through donations coordinated by a global network of charities known as the Union of Good, operated by the Muslim Brotherhood.[105] The Union of Good is headed by Dr Yussaf al-Qaradawi, an extremist Muslim scholar who publicly described the activities of Islamic charities as a 'new type of jihad, financial jihad, through which financial support is guaranteed to the martyrs families, Palestinian prisoners and detainees, and every Palestinian whose property is damaged during conflict.'[106]

The Union of Good is alleged to have used Interpal, a front organization for HAMAS, as its principal clearing house for funds raised in Europe and the Middle East.[107] According to the plaintiffs, for more than nine years NatWest Bank knowingly maintained numerous accounts for Interpal and received and transferred money between these accounts and accounts belonging to other HAMAS front entities.[108] More specifically, plaintiffs maintained that NatWest Bank accepted a deposit of $66,000 for Interpal from the Holy Land Foundation for Relief and Development (HLF).[109] Because of its relationship with HAMAS, HLF was designated a HAMAS front organization by the government of Israel in 1997, and designated a specially designated global terrorist (SDGT) by the U.S. Treasury Department in 2001.[110]

NatWest Bank also accepted deposits on two different occasions, one for $70,000 and the other totaling 295,000 euros, from the Yemen and Dutch branches of the Al-Aqsa Foundation, respectively.[111] In 2003, Dutch authorities blocked Al-Aqsa Foundation assets in the Netherlands on the basis of information that the funds were being provided to terrorist organizations in the Middle East.[112] In 2003, the U.S. government designated Al-Aqsa as an SDGT, accusing the organization of funneling money, including charitable donations, to HAMAS.[113]

Additionally, the Union of Good directed its prospective donors to make its donations via Interpal's NatWest Bank account.[114] Finally, the complaint alleged that NatWest Bank transferred funds to various HAMAS front organizations including the Jenin Committee and the Tulkarem Committee, organizations that allegedly raised money for families of HAMAS martyrs.[115]

In 1996, the Charity Commission, the regulator and registrar for charities in England and Wales, froze Interpal's accounts at NatWest Bank on the basis of evidence that the accounts had been used to transfer money to HAMAS.[116] In 1997, the government of Israel declared Interpal an 'unlawful organization' because of its support of HAMAS.[117] In 1998, the Israeli government designated Interpal a terrorist organization.[118] Finally, in 2003, Interpal was designated as an SDGT by the U.S. Treasury Department because it allegedly served as a 'conduit through which money flows to HAMAS from other charities.'[119]

Credit Lyonnais In *Strauss v. Credit Lyonnais*, 22 plaintiffs who were injured in 13 different terrorist attacks in Israel filed claims against Credit Lyonnais under the ATA.[120] Plaintiffs included the representatives of individuals killed in those attacks and also family members of the victims who have experienced non-physical injuries such as extreme emotional distress and loss of companionship as a result of their relatives' death or injuries.[121] Defendant Credit Lyonnais is a retail bank, headquartered in Paris, France.[122] The Bank conducts business in the United States and maintains an office in Miami, Florida.[123]

The plaintiffs alleged that, between 2000 and 2003, Credit Lyonnais knowingly transferred funds from Comité de Bienfaisance et de Secours aux Palestiniens (CBSP), a non-profit corporation with headquarters in France, to Islamic charities controlled by HAMAS, including: the Orphan Care Society, Al-Islah, Ramallah Al-Bireh Charitable Society, Jenin Charity Committee, Hebron Islamic Association, Tulkarem Charity

Committee, Al-Mujama al-Islami, Islamic Charitable Society in the Gaza Strip, Al-Salah Society, and Muslim Youth Association of Hebron.[124] According to the plaintiffs, CBSP is a member of the Union of Good and is part of HAMAS's fund-raising infrastructure.[125] In 2003, CBSP was placed on the Treasury Department list of SDGTs for providing financial support to HAMAS.[126] Pursuant to the designation, the Treasury Department issued a 'Blocking Notice' freezing all of CBSP's funds, accounts and real property located within the jurisdiction of the United States, and prohibiting all transactions involving property in which CBSP had any interest.[127]

ATA claims

Aiding and abetting murder In each of the three causes of actions, plaintiffs advanced three theories of liability under the ATA. First, plaintiffs claimed that the defendant banks aided and abetted the murder or serious bodily injury of U.S. nationals in violation of 18 U.S.C. §2332 by their provision of financial services to the various front organizations acting on behalf of HAMAS.[128] In *Arab Bank I*, the court held that 'the financial services provided by Arab Bank, and the administration of the death and dismemberment benefit plan, provided substantial assistance to international terrorism.'[129] The Bank was therefore liable under a theory of aiding and abetting murder, attempted murder, and serious bodily injury of U.S. nationals, in violation of §2332(a), (b), and (c). Further, plaintiffs alleged that the payments by Arab Bank to the surviving family members of the suicide bombers facilitated and provided an incentive for terrorist bombings because the terrorists knew that, if they committed an attack, their families would be financially supported by the funds held in their names by Arab Bank.[130] The court agreed, stating that by creating an incentive for the commission of terrorist attacks the Bank substantially assisted their commission.[131]

The courts in *Nat West* and *Credit Lyonnais* reached a different result on the aiding and abetting theory. These courts held that '[t]he maintenance of a bank account and the receipt or transfer of funds does not constitute [the] substantial assistance' necessary to sustain a claim for aiding and abetting liability.[132] In short, to support a claim of aiding and abetting, the plaintiffs must allege facts that the defendant provided 'substantial assistance' to the actual perpetrator of the terrorist acts. The mere receipt and transfer of funds to a terrorist front organization, without more, does not rise to the level of 'substantial assistance.'

The facts in *Nat West* and *Credit Lyonnais* are easily distinguishable from those in *Arab Bank*. In *Arab Bank I*, the defendant Bank played a central role in administering the plan to reward terrorists killed and injured in suicide attacks in Israel.[133] Arab Bank was involved in finalizing the list and maintaining a database of persons eligible to receive death benefits. Arab Bank also facilitated the conversion of Saudi riyals to Israeli currency by routing those funds through its New York branch, where they were converted to U.S. dollars and then to Israeli currency. Finally, after the funds were transferred to designated accounts in Arab Bank branches in the West Bank and Gaza, Arab Bank distributed the money to families of the suicide bombers.

The *Arab Bank I* court also sustained liability under the ATA on a theory of civil conspiracy, an issue not addressed in *Nat West* or *Credit Lyonnais*.[134] The court stated that plaintiffs' allegations sufficiently supported an inference that

> Arab Bank and the terrorist organizations were participants in a common plan under which Arab Bank would supply necessary financial services to the organizations which would themselves perform the violent acts. Administering the death and dismemberment benefit plan further supports not only the existence of an agreement but Arab Bank's knowing and intentional participation in the agreement's illegal goals.[135]

Finally, the court in *Arab Bank I* rejected defendant's argument that liability could not be established without a finding that the suicide bomber would not, or could not, have acted 'but for' the assistance of Arab Bank. The court stated that plaintiffs are not required to prove that Arab Bank was the 'but for' cause of the terrorist attacks. Instead, in order to prevail on their claims, the plaintiffs must prove that each of the victims was in fact killed by terrorists, and that each of the killers was within the coverage of the death and dismemberment benefit plan, to hold the Bank secondarily liable.[136]

Providing material support or resources All three courts agreed on the second theory of liability: that violations of the material support statutes, 18 U.S.C. §§2339A and 2339B, may properly serve as predicate crimes giving rise to liability under §2333(a).[137] The courts held that neither the material support nor the terrorist financing statutes require proof that defendants provided financial services with the intent to carry out terrorist attacks. The *Arab Bank I* court held that the material support provisions only require knowledge *or* intent that the resources given to terrorists are to be used to commit terrorist attacks. 'Neither requires the specific intent to aid or encourage the particular attacks that injured plaintiffs.'[138] The courts further refused to impute a specific intent requirement into §2339B, finding that '[s]ection 2339B is violated if the Bank provides material support in the form of financial services to a designated foreign terrorist organization and the Bank either knows of the designation [as an FTO] or knows that the designated organization has engaged or engages in terrorist activities.'[139] The *Arab Bank I* court further expressly rejected the ruling in *Boim*, stating: 'Insofar as *Boim* is read as requiring more than knowledge that the organization to which material support is provided is designated or is engaged in terrorist activity . . . it is not consistent with the language of Section 2339B.'[140]

The courts rejected the banking defendants' argument that the term 'financial services' as used in the material support statutes, 18 U.S.C. §§ 2339A and 2339B, does not encompass 'routine banking services.' In support of their position, defendants relied on *In re Terrorist Attacks on September 11, 2001*,[141] where the court found that allegations that the banking defendants maintained accounts for and received and transferred funds to terrorist organizations did not qualify as 'material support.'[142] The courts dismissed defendants' argument, stating that *In re Terrorist Attacks on September 11, 2001* stands for the proposition that providing routine banking services with *no knowledge* of client's terrorist activities cannot sustain a claim of providing material support. By contrast, where 'the Bank knows that the groups to which it provides services are engaged in terrorist activities' even the 'provision of basic services may qualify as material support.'[143]

Terrorist financing The plaintiffs' third claim alleged violations of 18 U.S.C. §2339C, the terrorist financing statute. The plaintiffs claimed that defendants 'unlawfully and willfully provide[d] or collecte[d] funds with the intention that such funds be used, or with the knowledge that such funds are to be used, in full or in part' to carry out terrorist acts, in violation of §2339C.[144] Defendants argued that the statutory terms 'provide' and 'collect' do not encompass the maintenance of bank accounts, and processing of deposits and withdrawals, but require active donations to terrorist organizations or active fund-raising on behalf of a terrorist organization.[145] Defendants' arguments did not persuade the courts. As used in §2339C, the term '"provides" includes giving, donating, and transmitting,' and ' "collects" includes raising and receiving.'[146] The courts held that '"the banking activities of receiving deposits and transmitting funds between accounts" where the "accounts (and funds) belong to groups engaged in terrorist activity" or are "charity fronts that operate as agents of HAMAS" ' constitute conduct prohibited by §2339C.[147] The courts found that plaintiffs' allegations that defendant banks knew that the funds were received as deposits and transmitted to various terrorist front organizations to finance terrorist activities were sufficient to state a claim under §2339C.[148] Thus, plaintiffs were not required to allege that defendants engaged in active fund raising for HAMAS.[149]

The courts' decisions in *Boim*, *Arab Bank*, *NatWest* and *Credit Lyonnais* demonstrate that the ATA affords U.S. citizens victimized by acts of terrorism an important civil cause of action. The ATA allows citizens to hold corrupt Islamic charities and front companies who raise and distribute funds for terrorist organizations responsible for the commission of terrorist acts. Likewise, the ATA statute has been consistently construed to support civil liability against banks that support terrorism. Such banks must knowingly provide material support to foreign terrorist organizations through the provision of financial and administrative services; alternatively, they must collect and provide funds for such criminal entities knowing that the funds have been or will be used to facilitate terrorist attacks. Further, depending on the nature of the financial and administrative services provided to the terrorist groups, banks may be held civilly liable as aiders and abettors to murder and other violent acts of terrorism. Finally, assuming the corrupt Islamic charities, front companies, and foreign banks have offices and assets in the United States, the prevailing plaintiffs may be able to attach those assets to enforce the courts' civil judgments. Thus, charities, front companies, and foreign banks can be held accountable for knowingly providing financial services and collecting and transferring funds to support foreign terrorist organizations.

Foreign Victims of Terrorism – Suing Under the Alien Tort Statute

The Alien Tort Claims Act, also referred to as the Alien Tort Statute (ATS), 28 U.S.C. §1350, affords *foreign* terrorism victims a civil cause of action for injuries suffered as the result of a 'violation of the law of nations or a treaty of the United States.'[150] The ATS authorizes subject matter jurisdiction for foreign nationals to sue in federal court for a tort only committed in violation of international law. Therefore, to sustain a claim of action under §1350, plaintiffs must '(1) be aliens, (2) claiming damages for a tort only, (3) resulting from a violation of the law of nations or a treaty of the United States.'[151]

The federal tort statute was passed by the nation's founders during the First Congress in 1789.[152] The statute was originally intended to afford a tort claim for acts of piracy on the high seas, violations of safe conduct, and assaults against ambassadors.[153] Interestingly, however, once passed the ATS lay virtually dormant until 1980, when it was invoked in *Filartiga v. Pena-Irala* (*Filartiga*) by a Paraguayan national whose 17-year-old son was tortured to death by Paraguayan police officials.[154] *Filartiga* is generally recognized as the 'starting point' for the modern re-emergence of the ATS.[155] Since the terrorist attacks of 9/11, foreign victims of terrorism have brought lawsuits under the ATS to hold terrorists, terrorist organizations, and their financial sponsors civilly liable.

In *Sosa v. Alvarez-Machain*, the Supreme Court held that the ATS is more than a jurisdictional statute.[156] The Court held that, while the ATS is jurisdictional, 'the jurisdiction was originally understood to be available to enforce a small number of international norms that a federal court could properly recognize as within the common law enforceable without further statutory authority.'[157] The Court further commented that 'although the ATS is a jurisdictional statute creating no new causes of action . . . [t]he jurisdictional grant is best read as having been enacted on the understanding that the common law would provide a cause of action for the modest number of international law violations with a potential for personal liability at the time.'[158] However, the Court concluded that the ATS does not limit jurisdiction to violations of the law of nations considered judicially enforceable in 1789, but extends to a narrow class of international norms recognized today.[159]

In determining whether a tort claim arises from a violation of the laws of nations, the Court articulated the following legal standard to be applied:

> [F]ederal courts should not recognize private claims under federal common law for violations of any international law norm with less definite content and acceptance among civilized nations than the historical paradigms familiar when §1350 was enacted.[160]

The Court's legal standard is essentially a two-part test. First, the international legal norm serving as the basis for the tort claim must be as sufficiently definite as those recognized when §1350 was enacted (that is, piracy on the high seas, violations of safe conduct, and assaults against ambassadors). Second, the international norm must have achieved general 'acceptance among civilized nations.'[161] The Court further stated that a plaintiff's claims must be 'gauged against the current state of international law.'[162] The sources of law from which a court should discern whether a particular norm has risen to the level of the law of nations include:

> [W]here there is no treaty, and no controlling executive or legislative act or judicial decision, resort must be had to the customs and usages of civilized nations; and, as evidence of these, to the works of jurists and commentators, who by years of labor, research, and experience, have made themselves particularly well acquainted with the subjects of which they treat. Such works are resorted to by judicial tribunals, not for the speculations of their authors concerning what the law ought to be, but for trustworthy evidence of what the law really is.[163]

Additionally, international conventions are highly relevant in discerning the current state of the law of nations.[164] The *Sosa* Court ultimately concluded that arbitrary detention of Alvarez-Machain by agents of the Drug Enforcement Administration did not violate the law of nations. The Court held that a 'single illegal detention of less than a day, followed by the transfer of custody to lawful authorities and a prompt arraignment, violates no norm of customary international law so well defined as to support the creation of a federal remedy.'[165]

In *Almog v. Arab Bank* (*Arab Bank II*),[166] more than 1,600 plaintiffs, consisting of United States and foreign nationals, brought claims under the ATS and the ATA against Arab Bank for knowingly providing banking and administrative services to various foreign terrorist organizations that sponsored suicide attacks on innocent civilians in Israel.[167] The U.S. nationals asserted claims under the ATA essentially identical to those brought in *Arab Bank I*.[168] However, because foreign nationals cannot sue under the ATA, the foreign plaintiffs asserted violations under the ATS.[169] The foreign nationals alleged that Arab Bank violated the law of nations by providing financial and administrative services to organizations that facilitated the commission of suicide bombings and other deadly attacks directed at civilians committed by the Islamic Resistance Movement (HAMAS), the Palestinian Islamic Jihad (PIJ), the Al Aqsa Martyrs' Brigade (AAMB), and the Popular Front for the Liberation of Palestine (PFLP).[170] The foreign nationals further alleged that Arab Bank aided and abetted, intentionally facilitated, and participated in a joint venture to engage in acts of genocide and commit crimes against humanity in violation of the law of nations by providing financial and other assistance to HAMAS and affiliated terrorist organizations.[171]

The court found that the foreign plaintiffs had properly alleged that Arab Bank aided and abetted violations of three international law norms: (1) genocide, (2) crimes against humanity, and (3) suicide bombings and other murderous attacks on innocent civilians intended to intimidate or coerce a civilian population (acts of terrorism). In concluding that plaintiffs had sufficiently pled a claim against Arab Bank for genocide, the court relied on the Convention on the Prevention and Punishment of the Crime of Genocide (Genocide Convention).[172] The Genocide Convention defines 'genocide' as

> any of the following acts committed with the intent to destroy, in whole or in part, a national, ethnical, racial or religious group, as such:
>
> (a) Killing members of the group;
> (b) Causing serious bodily or mental harm to members of the group;
> (c) Deliberately inflicting on the group conditions of life calculated to bring about its physical destruction in whole or in part;
> (d) Imposing measures intended to prevent births within the group;
> (e) Forcibly transferring children of the group to another group.[173]

The court further relied on *Kadic v. Karadzic*, where the Second Circuit found that genocide by private actors violates international law.[174]

In holding that plaintiffs sufficiently alleged that Arab Bank aided and abetted crimes against humanity, the court relied on Article 7 of the Rome Statute of the International Criminal Court (Rome Statute). The Statute defines crimes against humanity to include murder, extermination, or persecution against any identifiable group on political, racial, national, ethnic, cultural, religious, gender or other grounds that are universally recognized as impermissible under international law, and other inhumane acts of similar character. Such crimes must be 'committed as part of a *widespread or systematic attack directed against any civilian population*, with knowledge of the attack.'[175]

Applying the standards provided in the Genocide Convention and Article 7 of the Rome Statute, the court found that the suicide bombings and other murderous acts perpetrated by members of HAMAS, PIJ, AAMB, and the PFLP were allegedly committed for the purpose of eradicating the State of Israel, murdering Jews, and liberating the area by replacing it with an Islamic or Palestinian State.[176] These violent acts demonstrated an intent to target people based on criteria prohibited by both the Genocide Convention and the Rome Statute.[177] The terrorist attacks further satisfied the 'widespread' or 'systematic' action element necessary for claims of crimes against humanity.[178] The complaint alleged that the foreign terrorist organizations planned and perpetrated suicide bombings that resulted in the systematic and continuous killing and injury of thousands of unarmed civilians in Israel and the Occupied Territories. The court posited that '[t]hese are precisely the sorts of acts proscribed in both the Genocide Convention and the Rome statute.'[179] The plaintiffs therefore properly alleged violations of the law of nations under the ATS, to wit: genocide and crimes against humanity.

The third international norm allegedly violated by Arab Bank involved the financing of suicide bombings and other murderous attacks on innocent civilians which were intended to intimidate or coerce a civilian population. The court observed that the prohibition against attacks on innocent civilians is reflected in the International Convention for the Suppression of Terrorist Bombings (Terrorist Bombing Convention),[180] as well as the International Convention for the Suppression of the Financing of Terrorism (Terrorist Financing Convention).[181] The United States has ratified and enacted domestic legislation to implement both Conventions.[182] Further, the court stated that the condemnation of murdering and attacking innocent civilians is reflected in Common Article 3 of the Geneva Convention of 1949, principles of customary international humanitarian law, and United Nations Security Council Resolution 1566.[183] Resolution 1566 specifically condemns attacks against civilians intended to intimidate a civilian population, expressly acknowledging that such attacks are under no circumstances justifiable by political, philosophical, ideological, racial, ethnic, or religious considerations.[184] After examining these authoritative sources, the *Arab Bank II* court held: '[I]n light of the universal condemnation of organized and systematic suicide bombings and other murderous attacks intended to intimidate or coerce a civilian population . . . such conduct violates an established norm of international Law.'[185] The court further found that the conduct alleged by plaintiffs was sufficiently specific and well-defined to be recognized as a claim under the ATS.[186]

Next, the court considered whether aiding and abetting genocide, crimes against humanity, and terrorism-related crimes violates principles of international law. In support of its ruling that violations of international law are not limited to the actual perpetrators of the prohibited conduct, the court cited the Genocide, Terrorist Bombing, and Terrorist Financing Conventions, as well as the Statutes of the International Criminal Tribunal for the former Yugoslavia and Rwanda, which punish genocide and crimes against humanity and explicitly condemn acts of aiding and abetting by non-primary actors.[187] Moreover, the court stated that Arab Bank's alleged conduct established primary violations of the Terrorist Financing Convention (knowingly collecting and transferring funds for a terrorist organization, knowing or intending that the money will be used to finance terrorist acts).[188]

The court concluded that Arab Bank's mental state and conduct satisfied the legal standard for aiding and abetting liability. According to plaintiffs, Arab Bank knew that accounts of the various terrorist organizations were being used to fund suicide bombings.[189] Further, plaintiffs alleged that Arab Bank knowingly administered the program by which the Saudi Committee distributed death benefits to the families of homicide bombers. Plaintiffs maintained that Arab Bank knew that the Saudi Committee was soliciting and paying funds to the families of the 'martyrs.' The court concluded that, under international law, liability does not require that Arab Bank had specific intent to cause the specific acts which injured plaintiffs; 'it is sufficient that Arab Bank acted intentionally and with knowledge that its conduct would . . . facilitate the underlying violations when it engaged in the acts alleged.'[190]

Finally, the court held that plaintiffs' allegations satisfied the requirement that Arab Bank's conduct have a substantial effect in bringing about the underlying violations of international law norms. Under principles of international law, a person may be held liable for aiding and abetting if the defendant provided 'practical assistance, encouragement, or moral support which has a *substantial* effect on the perpetration of the crime.'[191] In other words, to establish liability under a theory of complicity, the defendant must have provided substantial assistance in facilitating the criminal conduct. The court held that plaintiffs' allegations that Arab Bank played an integral role in administering the death benefits program and distributing funds to the families of suicide bombers constituted substantial assistance to the terrorists.[192] Further, Arab Bank's alleged conduct provided an incentive for suicide bombings and other murderous attacks. The court held that '[t]he Bank's active participation in creating such an incentive is a sufficient basis for liability under the standards of aiding and abetting liability . . . which imposes secondary liability on those who substantially assist violations of the law of nations.'[193]

In sum, the ATS provides foreign nationals who are victims of terrorism an effective legal remedy to hold banks and front companies that provide financial support and services to terrorist organizations secondarily liable and accountable for the losses, harm and suffering caused by the commission of terrorist acts. While *Arab Bank II* focused on violations of international law involving acts of genocide, crimes against humanity, and suicide bombings intended to coerce a civilian population, the violation of other international norms related to terrorism could give rise to violations of the ATS, including torture,[194] aircraft sabotage and aircraft hijacking,[195] as well as hostage-taking.[196] Of course, like the ATA, the ultimate effectiveness of the ATS largely depends on the enforceability of the civil judgments obtained thereunder.

SUING STATE SPONSORS OF TERRORISM: THE TERRORIST EXCEPTION TO THE FOREIGN SOVEREIGN IMMUNITY ACT

The Foreign Sovereign Immunity Act (FSIA), as adopted in 1976, reflects a restrictive approach theory of sovereign immunity. This restrictive theory granted foreign states immunity except in cases arising out of commercial transactions.[197] Under the FSIA, foreign states are immune from civil lawsuits in U.S. courts unless Congress waives immunity under an enumerated exception.[198] The inability of plaintiffs to recover against states for the commission of crimes abroad led to efforts to amend the FSIA to permit recovery in limited cases. In 1996, as part of the Antiterrorism and Effective Death Penalty Act (AEDPA), Congress enacted the 'terrorism exception' to the FSIA, codified in 28 U.S.C. § 1605(a)(7), waiving the immunity of foreign states and their agents in any case

> in which money damages are sought against a foreign state for personal injury or death that was caused by an act of torture, extrajudicial killing, aircraft sab-

> otage, hostage taking, or the provision of material support or resources (as defined in section 2339A of title 18) for such an act if such act or provision of material support is engaged in by an official, employee, or agent of such foreign state while acting within the scope of his or her office, employment, or agency.[199]

The FSIA terrorism exception is limited in scope, negating sovereign immunity for foreign nations for actions arising from the commission of five different crimes: (1) torture, (2) extrajudicial killing, (3) aircraft sabotage, (4) hostage taking and (5) providing material support or resources to terrorists.[200] Additionally, the terrorism exception only waives immunity of a foreign state defendant that has been specifically designated by the State Department as a 'state sponsor of terrorism' (SST).[201] At present, the State Department has designated five countries as SSTs: Cuba, Iran, North Korea, Sudan and Syria.[202] The terrorism exception lifts sovereign immunity only against those states. All other states, such as Egypt, Saudi Arabia, Somalia, and Yemen, retain foreign sovereign immunity from prosecution under the FSIA.[203]

At the same time, the immunity exception does not apply if

> (i) the act occurred in the foreign state against which the claim has been brought and the claimant has not afforded the foreign state a reasonable opportunity to arbitrate the claim in accordance with accepted international rules of arbitration; or
> (ii) neither the claimant nor the victim was a national of the United States (as that term is defined in section 101(a)(22) of the Immigration and Nationality Act) when the act upon which the claim is based occurred.[204]

Thus, to fall within the terrorism exception to foreign sovereign immunity for suits based on torture or other terrorist acts permitted by §1605(a)(7), the following elements must be satisfied: (1) the plaintiff is seeking monetary damages against a foreign state designated as an SST at the time the act occurred, unless later so designated as a result of such acts,[205] (2) for personal injury or death 'caused by' an act of torture, extrajudicial killing, aircraft sabotage, hostage taking, or the provision of material support or resources (as defined in 18 U.S.C. §2339A),[206] (3) engaged in by an official, employee, or agent of such foreign state, (4) while acting within the scope of his or her office, employment, or agency; (5) the claimant or victim was a U.S. national;[207] and (6) if the act occurred within the designated foreign state against which the claim was brought, the claimant afforded the foreign state a reasonable opportunity to arbitrate the claim.[208]

The AEDPA also amended the FSIA to permit the attachment or execution of a judgment against the property of a foreign state located in the

U.S. that is used for 'commercial activity.'[209] The AEDPA further provides that the commercial assets of a foreign state sponsor of terrorism located in the U.S. may be attached even if those assets were not involved in the terrorist act that gave rise to the judgment.[210]

Shortly after the passage of the AEDPA, Congress enacted a separate provision, titled Civil Liability for Acts of State Sponsored Terrorism, which created a private cause of action against officials, employees, and agents of foreign states for the conduct described in §1605(a)(7).[211] This provision is known as the 'Flatow Amendment,' in recognition of the family of Alisa Flatow, a Brandeis University junior studying abroad who was killed as a result of a terrorist bombing in Israel.[212] The Flatow Amendment provides:

> (a) An official, employee, or agent of a foreign state designated as a state sponsor of terrorism designated under section 6(j) of the Export Administration Act of 1979 [section 2405(j) of the Appendix to Title 50, War and National Defense] while acting within the scope of his or her office, employment, or agency shall be liable to a United States national or the national's legal representative for personal injury or death caused by acts of that official, employee, or agent for which the courts of the United States may maintain jurisdiction under section 1605(a)(7) of title 28, United States Code [subsec. (a)(7) of this section] for money damages which may include economic damages, solatium, pain, and suffering, and punitive damages if the acts were among those described in section 1605(a)(7).[213]

In *Cicippio-Puleo v. Islamic Republic of Iran (Cicippio)*,[214] the D.C. Circuit Court of Appeals ruled that the Flatow Amendment does not permit a private cause of action by United States nationals against foreign state sponsors of terrorism.[215] In *Cicippio*, the court held that 'neither 28 U.S.C. §1605(a)(7) nor the Flatow Amendment, nor the two considered in tandem, creates a private right of action against a foreign government.'[216] The court reasoned that there is a distinction between statutory provisions that waive sovereign immunity and those that create a cause of action. It cannot be assumed that a claimant has a cause of action for damages merely because there has been a waiver of sovereign immunity, the Court stated.[217]

The Court found that the Flatow Amendment imposes liability and creates a cause of action, but the liability imposed by the provision is limited to 'an official, employee, or agent of a foreign state designated as a state sponsor of terrorism.'[218] 'Foreign states' are not within the scope of the cause of action created by the Flatow Amendment. The D.C. Circuit further restricted the scope of any private cause of action stating that 'insofar as the Flatow Amendment creates a private right of action against officials, employees, and agents of foreign states, the cause of action is limited to claims against those officials in their *individual*, as opposed to their official, capacities.'[219] According to the Court, a claim against an individual acting in his official capacity is 'in substance a claim against the government itself.'[220] Thus, the plaintiffs' only recourse is against foreign officials acting *ultra vires*.[221] The Court further refused to imply a cause of action against foreign states when Congress had not expressly recognized one in the language of §1605(a)(7) or the Flatow Amendment. The Court stated that 'it is for Congress, not the courts, to decide whether a cause of action should lie against foreign states.'[222]

In direct response to the ruling in *Cicippio*, Congress enacted section 1083, the terrorism exception to the jurisdictional immunity of a foreign state, as part of the National Defense Authorization Act of 2008, which authorizes a private cause of action against a 'state sponsor of terrorism.'[223] The new legislation, codified at 28 U.S.C. §1605A, eliminates sovereign immunity for foreign states designated as 'state sponsors of terror' (SSTs).[224] There are currently four states that have been designated by the Secretary of State as SSTs: Cuba, Iran, Sudan, and Syria.[225] Under the statute, which became effective January 28, 2008, these states lose their sovereign immunity in cases in which plaintiffs are seeking money damages against a foreign state for personal injury or death that was caused by an 'act of torture, extrajudicial killing, aircraft sabotage, hostage taking, or the provision of material support or resources' if the provision of material support or resources is engaged in by 'an official, employee, or agent of such foreign state while acting within the scope of his . . . office, employment or agency.'[226] The statute holds foreign states vicariously liable for the acts of their officials, employees, and agents.[227] A private cause of action is permitted against a foreign state designated an SST by the Secretary of State at the time the death or injury occurred, or was so designated as a result of such act, and remains so designated when the claim is filed.[228]

Section 1605A creates a private cause of action for '(1) a national of the United States, (2) a member of the armed forces, (3) an employee of the Government of the United States, or of an individual performing a contract awarded by the United States Government, acting within the scope of the employee's employment, or (4) the legal representative of a person described in paragraph (1), (2), or (3)' for personal injury or death caused by the commission of enumerated acts of terrorism of that foreign state or its officials, employees, or agents.[229] While §1605A is intended to afford United States nationals a private cause of action against foreign state sponsors of terrorism, foreign nationals may bring a claim if they are employees of the United States, or individuals performing a private contract awarded by the U.S. government, and were killed or injured while acting within the scope of their work or employment.[230] Additionally, a foreign national who is a legal representative of a United States national, member of the armed forces, or employee or contractor working for the U.S. government, killed or injured while acting within the scope of his employment, may bring suit under §1605A. In such action, plaintiffs may sue for damages, including economic damages, solatium, pain and suffering, punitive damages, and reasonably foreseeable property loss.[231]

Section 1605A extends to pending cases filed under 28 U.S.C. §1605(a)(7) that were adversely affected on the grounds that §1607(a)(7) did not create a private cause of action against a foreign state, and on the date of the enactment of the new legislation such case is pending before the court in any form, including on appeal.[232] The statute authorizes refiling such cases under §1605A.[233] Moreover, the statute eliminates the defenses of *res judicata*, collateral estoppel, and statute of limitations for cases refiled under § 1605A.[234] Finally, an action may be refiled under §1605A only if 'the original action was commenced not later than the latter of 10 years after April 24, 1996, or 10 years after the cause of action arose, and within the 60-day period beginning on the date of the enactment of this Act.'[235]

The property of a foreign state is subject to attachment to enforce a judgment whether or not the foreign state directly controls the property. The property of a foreign state against which a judgment is entered under section 1605A, and the property of an agency or instrumentality of such a state, is subject to attachment in aid of execution upon that judgment regardless of

(A) the level of economic control over the property by the government of the foreign state;
(B) whether the profits of the property go to that government;
(C) the degree to which officials of that government manage the property or otherwise control its daily affairs;
(D) whether that government is the sole beneficiary in interest of the property; or
(E) whether establishing the property as a separate entity would entitle the foreign state to benefits in United States courts while avoiding its obligations.[236]

One of the most important provisions for victims of foreign state-sponsored acts of terrorism is §1803(b), codified at 28 U.S.C. §1610(g)(2), which expressly waives United States sovereign immunity in certain situations.[237] Section 1610(g)(2) provides that property of a foreign state shall not be immune from attachment for execution of a judgment entered under §1605A, because the property is regulated by the U.S. government by reason of action taken against the foreign state under the Trading With the Enemy Act (TWEA) or the International Emergency Economic Powers Act (IEEPA).[238] Thus, for example, the statute would waive sovereign immunity for Iranian assets frozen pursuant to Executive Order (E.O.)

13382, which the President signed, in July 2005. This is aimed at freezing the assets of proliferators of weapons of mass destruction.[239] The authority to freeze such assets is conferred by IEEPA.[240] Using this authority, the Treasury Department has designated Iranian government entities, banks and other related entities and individuals, including the Islamic Revolutionary Guard Corps, Ministry of Defense and Armed Forces Logistics, Bank Sepah, Bank Melli, Bank Mellat, and various Iranian business entities.[241]

In May 2004, the U.S. government imposed economic sanctions against Syrian government officials and their associates for supporting Hizballah, HAMAS, and other Palestinian terrorist groups.[242] The Syrian economic sanctions were expanded in 2006 and 2008 to include additional persons subject to such sanctions.[243] If plaintiffs filed a writ of attachment against any frozen Iranian or Syrian assets to enforce a judgment under §1605A, the United States would be prohibited by 28 U.S.C. 1610(g)(2) from claiming sovereign immunity as a legal defense to attachment of the frozen foreign assets.[244] Subsection (g)(2) waives U.S. sovereign immunity with respect to property 'regulated' by the U.S. government by reason of action against a foreign state under TWEA or IEEPA. If the frozen assets had been confiscated and vested in or belonging to the United States, sovereign immunity would be available as a defense to prevent attachment of the confiscated assets.[245] Thus, whether subsection (g)(2) has waived U.S. sovereign immunity will depend on whether the frozen property is being 'regulated' by or vested in and belonging to the United States.[246]

Section 1605A authorizes the President to waive any provision of this section with respect to Iraq, if the President determines that (1) waiver is in the national security interest of the United States, (2) waiver will promote the reconstruction of, consolidation of democracy in, and relations of the United States with Iraq, and (3) Iraq continues to be a reliable ally of the United States and partner in the global war on terrorism.[247] While the Presidential waiver authorized under §1605A is limited to Iraq, when this is combined with §201(b)(1) of the TRIA, which authorizes the President to waive attachment of blocked assets belonging to currently designated state sponsors of terror, Cuba, Iran, North Korea, Sudan, and Syria, the President wields enormous power to block any civil action against an SST.[248]

Finally, as previously noted, foreign nationals may bring a cause of action against foreign states under the ATS.[249] Construing the ATS and FSIA in tandem could support a civil cause of action against state sponsors of terrorism for foreign victims. Moreover, in *Sosa v. Alvarez-Machain*, the U.S. Supreme Court held that the ATS creates a private cause of action for a narrow set of common law actions derived from the law of nations.[250]

The offenses for which foreign sovereign immunity has been waived under the FSIA terrorism exception are offenses condemned by the Torture,[251] Terrorist Bombing,[252] Aircraft Sabotage,[253] Hostage Taking,[254] and Terrorist Financing[255] Conventions. The offenses proscribed by these international conventions constitute offenses against the law of nations. Thus, because foreign sovereign immunity has been lifted by the FSIA terrorism exception, civil causes of action could be brought against designated state sponsors of terrorism for harm caused by the commission of those specified international crimes.[256] Further according to the reasoning articulated in *Arab Bank II*, state sponsors of terror could be held secondarily liable for aiding and abetting enumerated acts of terrorism.[257]

OBSTACLES TO ENFORCEMENT OF CIVIL JUDGMENTS

Attaching 'Blocked Assets'

The Terrorism Risk Insurance Act of 2002 (TRIA)[258] was enacted by Congress 'to deal comprehensively with the problem of enforcement of judgments rendered on behalf of victims of terrorism in any court of competent jurisdiction by enabling them to satisfy such judgments through the attachment of blocked assets of terrorist parties.'[259] The purpose of the TRIA was 'to provide justice to terrorist victims, to hold terrorist states accountable for their crimes and to deter them from perpetrating acts of terrorism against American citizens in the future.'[260] The TRIA authorizes the attachment of 'blocked assets' to enforce a civil judgment against a terrorist party found liable for the commission of acts of terrorism. Section 201(a) of the TRIA states:

> [I]n every case in which a person has obtained a judgment against a terrorist party on a claim based upon an act of terrorism, or for which a terrorist party is not immune under section 1605(a)(7) of title 28, United States Code, the blocked assets of that terrorist party (including the blocked assets of any agency or instrumentality of that terrorist party) shall be subject to execution or attachment in aid of execution in order to satisfy such judgment to the extent of any compensatory damages for which such terrorist party has been adjudged liable.[261]

The TRIA allows for execution of the blocked assets of a foreign state designated as a state sponsor of terrorism to satisfy an award of compensatory damages based on an act of terrorism if certain elements are met. First, a person must obtain a judgment against a terrorist party.[262] Second, the judgment must be for a claim based on a terrorist act or a claim for which a terrorist party is not immune under §1605(a)(7), the terrorist exception to FSIA.[263] Third, the assets sought to be attached must be 'blocked assets' within the meaning of the TRIA.[264] The TRIA allows the attachment of the blocked assets of any agency or instrumentality of a terrorist party even if the judgment is only against the terrorist party.[265] Finally, the assets sought to be attached can be sought only for compensatory damages, not punitive damages.

The TRIA defines 'blocked assets' as 'any asset seized or frozen by the United States under section 5(b) of the Trading With the Enemy Act (50 U.S.C.App. 5(b)) or under sections 202 and 203 of the International Emergency Economic Powers Act (50 U.S.C. 1701; 1702).'[266]

However, the term 'blocked assets' does not include property that

> (i) is subject to a license issued by the United States Government for final payment, transfer, or disposition by or to a person subject to the jurisdiction of the United States in connection with a transaction for which the issuance of such license has been specifically required by statute other than the International Emergency Economic Powers Act (50 U.S.C 1701 et seq.) or the United Nations Participation Act of 1945 (22 U.S.C. 287 et seq.); or
> (ii) in the case of property subject to the Vienna Convention on Diplomatic Relations or the Vienna Convention on Consular Relations, or that enjoys equivalent privileges and immunities under the law of the United States, is being used exclusively for diplomatic or consular purposes.[267]

Thus, the term 'blocked assets' excludes (1) property involved in certain transactions authorized by a license issued by the U.S. government pursuant to the International Emergency Powers Act (50 U.S.C. §§1701 et seq.) or the United Nations Participation Act (22 U.S.C. §§287 et seq.), and (2) diplomatic and consular property subject to protection under the Vienna Conventions that is 'being used exclusively for diplomatic or consular purposes.'[268]

Under the Vienna Convention on Diplomatic Relations, the United States is only obliged to protect 'the premises of the mission,' which is defined under Article 1 of the Convention as 'the building or parts of buildings and the land ancillary thereto, irrespective of ownership, used for the purposes of the mission including the residence of the head of mission.' Article 1 of the Vienna Convention on Consular Relations imposes a similar duty with respect to 'consular premises.' Therefore, the only property that the United States is required to 'respect and protect' under the conventions is the buildings, parts of buildings, and the land ancillary thereto, used exclusively for diplomatic and consular purposes.

Section 201(b)(1) authorizes the President to waive attachment of blocked assets upon determining on an asset-by-asset basis that waiver is necessary in the interests of national security.[269] Prior to the TRIA, legislation permitted the President to exercise a blanket waiver to protect blocked property. Now, the President is required to make an 'asset-by-asset' determination that waiver is necessary to protect national security. Finally, under §201(b)(2), a waiver under the statute shall not apply to 'property subject to the Vienna Convention on Diplomatic Relations or the Vienna Convention on Consular Relations that has been used by the United States for any nondiplomatic purpose (including use as rental property), or the proceeds of such use.'[270]

Property 'Being Used Exclusively for Diplomatic and Consular Purposes'

The U.S. government has regularly intervened in civil terrorism-related cases to quash writs of attachment to satisfy the recovery of damages awarded by the court in favor of the victims of terrorism against persons, entities, and foreign governments found liable for aiding and abetting acts of terrorism. In *Weinstein v. Islamic Republic of Iran*, the plaintiff, an American citizen, was injured in a suicide bombing perpetrated by members of HAMAS in Jerusalem.[271] Plaintiff initiated a suit against the Islamic Republic of Iran under the FSIA. The court entered a default against the defendant and awarded plaintiff $33.2 million in compensatory damages and $150 million in punitive damages.[272] Plaintiff subsequently filed writs of attachment upon the U.S. Departments of State, Defense and Treasury, seeking to attach funds in four Bank of America accounts and the Iran Foreign Military Sales Program account.[273] The United States intervened, asserting that the writs should be quashed because the doctrine of sovereignty bars the attachment of the assets sought in the writs.[274]

The court addressed two important issues in *Weinstein.* First, the court held that the TRIA did not function as an 'express waiver' of sovereign immunity allowing plaintiffs to attach the funds vested in or belonging to the United States.[275] With respect to funds held in an account by the U.S. representing payments from Iran for the sale of military equipment and services provided by the United States, the court held that the doctrine of federal sovereign immunity barred attachment of the account or any portion of the funds therein.[276]

The second issue involved whether funds in accounts designated to be used to pay for maintenance and repair expenses of the former Iranian diplomatic properties constituted property 'used exclusively for diplomatic and consular purposes' under the TRIA.[277] With respect to the funds in the four bank accounts, two of the accounts related to property in the U.S. that formerly served as sites of embassies or consular offices of the nation of Iran.[278] These former diplomatic properties were being leased by the United

States to third parties and the monies generated by these leases were deposited into these accounts.[279] Monies in the first account, and a portion of funds in the second account, were designated to be used to pay maintenance and repair expenses. The court agreed with the government's argument that the funds in these accounts constituted property 'being used exclusively for diplomatic and consular purposes.'[280] Thus, the court held that the funds are not subject to attachment because they do not constitute 'blocked assets' under the TRIA.[281] However, Iranian accounts not used for any diplomatic or consular purpose (the funds in the third and fourth accounts) could be attached pursuant to §201(a), the TRIA.[282]

In *Hegna v. Islamic Republic of Iran* (*Hegna*),[283] the court took a different view on both the express waiver of immunity and diplomatic/consular property issues. In *Hegna*, plaintiffs sought to satisfy a $375 million default judgment against the Islamic Republic of Iran and the Iranian Ministry of Information and Security for their sponsorship of Hizballah, which was responsible for the murder of Charles Hegna.[284] The plaintiffs issued writs of attachment upon two parcels of Chicago real estate owned by Iran to satisfy the award of damages. The United States intervened to quash the writs of attachment and argued that the specific properties identified in the plaintiffs' writs of attachment are Iranian consular property and not subject to attachment.[285] The court disagreed, holding that the TRIA overrides any immunity from execution under the Vienna Convention, FSIA, or the Foreign Missions Act (FMA). The court opined that

> [B]y including the phrase 'seized by the United States' in section 201(d)(2)(A), it was Congress' intent to include within the definition of 'blocked asset' any asset of a terrorist party that is held by the United States. This is intended as an *explicit waiver* of any principle of law under which the United States might not be subject to service and enforcement of any judicial order or process relating to execution of judgments, or attachments in aid of such execution, in connection with terrorist party assets that happen to be held by the United States.[286]

On the remaining issue, the government conceded that the condominiums were being rented as a means of preservation. The court held that use for rental purposes did not constitute use exclusively for diplomatic purposes.[287] Thus, the property constituted 'blocked assets' within the meaning of the TRIA and could be attached to satisfy plaintiffs' judgment against the Republic of Iran.[288]

'Notwithstanding Any Other Provision of Law'

The TRIA provides that 'notwithstanding any other provision of law' blocked assets of a terrorist party shall be subject to execution or attachment in order to satisfy a judgment for compensatory damages for which such terrorist party has been held liable.[289] In *Smith v. Federal Reserve Bank of New York*,[290] plaintiffs brought suit against several parties, including the Republic of Iraq, pursuant to §1605 of the FSIA on behalf of the estate of George Eric Smith, who was killed in the World Trade Center on September 11, 2001.[291] Following Iraq's invasion of Kuwait in 1990, the U.S. blocked certain Iraqi accounts located in the United States pursuant to the International Emergency Economic Powers Act (IEEPA).[292] However, on March 20, 2003, on the eve of the launch of Operation Iraqi Freedom, the President issued an executive order that confiscated and vested in the United States the blocked assets of the Republic of Iraq.[293] As a consequence, the government contended that funds in the previously blocked Iraqi accounts ceased to be the 'blocked assets' of Iraq.[294] The plaintiffs countered that the phrase 'notwithstanding any other provision of law' in the TRIA trumps the IEEPA, as amended by the USA PATRIOT Act, authorizing the President to take title of assets blocked pursuant to IEEPA.[295] The court rejected plaintiffs' argument, holding that 'the powers granted to the president by the IEEPA were not extinguished by the TRIA's "notwithstanding" phrase.'[296] The blocked assets of the former Republic of Iraq became assets of the United States after execution of the President's Executive Order. Thus, according to *Smith,* blocked assets that are subsequently vested in the United States are no longer 'blocked assets' within the meaning of the TRIA. Those assets become the property of the United States and therefore are shielded by sovereign immunity.[297]

ENHANCING PRIVATE CIVIL CAUSES OF ACTIONS FOR VICTIMS OF TERRORISM

Recently enacted section 1605A will greatly aid plaintiffs in civil lawsuits against state sponsors of terrorism, particularly in light of the D.C. Circuit Court ruling in *Cicippio*. Because the statute authorizes a private cause of action in federal courts against state sponsors of terrorism, plaintiffs need not file causes of action in state courts. The statute will provide uniformity and consistency, and facilitate suits by victims of terrorism. Further, the statute may allow more property to be subject to attachment or execution, enabling plaintiffs to achieve more than a moral victory.

However, Congress should consider measures to limit the ability of the U.S. government to intervene to quash writs of attachment filed by the victims of terrorism intended to enforce a civil judgment. At present, when private plaintiffs have been permitted to bring a cause of action against a foreign state sponsor of terrorism, the U.S. government often intervenes to quash writs of attachment filed upon government agencies to enforce the civil judgment. The U.S. government should be restrained from intervening in such causes of action in the absence of compelling interests. While the TRIA removes barriers to the attachment of blocked assets by requiring the President to make an 'asset-by-asset' determination that 'a waiver is necessary in the national security interest,' government attorneys often circumvent this authority by intervening to quash writs of attachment on various legal grounds.[298]

Pursuant to Rule 24 of the Federal Rules of Civil Procedure, a party may be 'permitted to intervene as of right if the applicant claims an interest relating to the subject matter of the case, if the disposition of the case stands to impair that interest, and if the applicant's interest is not adequately represented by the existing parties.'[299] However, victims of terrorism should not be required to do legal battle against both the foreign state sponsors of terrorism and the U.S. government to obtain compensation for the loss of loved ones killed during a terrorist attack. Rule 24 should take into account the unique role of civil lawsuits against terrorism. Government intervention should be prohibited in the absence of a 'compelling government interest.' Such a compelling interest might exist, for example, in the case of on-going sensitive diplomatic negotiations between the U.S. and a foreign country named in a civil tort action, where collapse of the negotiations would threaten national security or foreign policy. If the President is restrained from intervening to protect blocked assets from being attached to satisfy a civil judgment by having to make an 'asset-by-asset' showing that waiver is necessary in the interests of national security, Department of Justice lawyers should have to demonstrate a similar exigency prior to being permitted to intervene to quash writs of attachment or otherwise prevent victims of terrorism from enforcing a civil judgment against a defendant foreign state sponsor of terrorism.

NOTES

1. 291 F.3d 1000, 1021 (7th Cir. 2002).
2. *See generally* JOHN ROTH, ET AL., NATIONAL COMMISSION ON TERRORIST ATTACKS UPON THE UNITED STATES, MONOGRAPH ON TERRORIST FINANCING: STAFF REPORT TO THE COMMISSION 106 (Wash., D.C.: Gov't Printing Office 2004), *available at* http://govinfo.library.unt.edu/911/staff_statements/911_TerrFin_Monograph.pdf; *see also* Blocking Property and Prohibiting Transactions with Persons Who Commit, Threaten to Commit, or Support Terrorism, Exec. Order No. 13,224, 3 C.F.R. 786–90 (2001), *reprinted as amended in* 50 U.S.C. §1701 note (Supp. IV 2004).
3. *See* discussion of blocking actions and criminal prosecutions *supra*, at Chapters 8 and 10.
4. Debra M. Strauss, *Enlisting the U.S. Courts in a New Front: Dismantling the International Business Holdings of Terrorist Groups Through Federal Statutory and Common-Law Suits,* 38 VAND. J. TRANSNAT'L L. 679, 738–9 (May 2005).

5. CIVIL LITIGATION AGAINST TERRORISM 7 (John Norton Moore ed., Carolina Academic Press 2004) ('It is unrealistic to suppose that a person dedicated to jihad is going to be affected by financial calculations, but it is conceivable that actors who are on the periphery of the scheme may be given pause.').
6. *See* Marc Perelman, *Hamas's Banking Handmaidens,* NAT'L JOURNAL (Mar. 18, 2006), *available at* http://gage.cc/pdf/website%20-%20cochran.pdf ('Although financing of terrorist operations has largely gone underground, cash from support networks is still flowing through the banking system, especially for groups like Hamas that sometimes use money collected as charitable donations to finance terrorist activities.').
7. In December 2004, the jury returned a verdict in favor of plaintiffs in a civil case against the Holy Land Foundation for Relief and Development and several other charitable organizations in the amount of $52 million. The court tripled the amount of the jury verdict to $156 million. *See* Boim v. Quranic Literacy, et al., Judgment in a Civil Case, Case No. 00-C-2905 (Dec. 10, 2004). In *Saperstein v. Palestinian Authority and Palestinian Liberation Organization*, Case No. 04-20225-CIV-Seitz/Turnoff (S.D. Fla. 2007), the jury awarded the plaintiff terrorism victim a $16 million civil judgment.
8. Alan J. Kreczko, *Antiterrorism Act of 1990: Hearing on S. 2465,* Testimony before the Senate Subcomm. on Courts and Admin. Practice of the Senate Comm. on the Judiciary, 101st Cong. 12 (1990).
9. In addition to being the subject of several civil lawsuits, Arab Bank, a Jordanian bank with a New York branch, was assessed a $24 million civil penalty by the U.S. Department of the Treasury for failing to implement an effective anti-money laundering program in violation of 31 U.S.C. §5318(h)(1) (2000 & Supp. IV 2004) and 31 C.F.R. §103.120 (2006). *See* U.S. Dep't of Treasury, In the Matter of the Fed. Branch of Arab Bank PLC, New York, New York, No. 2005-2 (Aug. 17, 2005), *available at* http://www.fincen.gov/arab081705.pdf. The violations involved claims that Arab Bank provided financial services to HAMAS, a designated foreign terrorist organization. The civil suits triggered a probe by U.S. bank regulators and a U.S. Dep't of Justice criminal investigation. *See* Glenn R. Simpson, *Compound Interests: Arab Bank's Link to Terrorism Poses Dilemma for U.S. Policy*, WALL STREET JOURNAL, Apr. 20, 2005.
10. The Riggs Bank, based in Washington, D.C, was sued by its shareholders for allegedly mismanaging the bank by allowing it to become a haven for money laundering. Riggs agreed to pay $2.7 million to the shareholders and as much as $1.1 million in plaintiffs' legal fees to resolve the suits. Ultimately, PNC Financial Services Group agreed to buy Riggs in a deal valued at $652 million. *See Riggs Settles Suits Filed by Shareholders,* N.Y. TIMES, Mar. 4, 2005, *available at* http://query.nytimes.com/gst/fullpage.html?res=9B07E4D6103DF937A35750C0A9639C8B63&sec=&spon=&partner=permalink&exprod=permalink; *see also* MONEY LAUNDERING AND FOREIGN CORRUPTION: ENFORCEMENT AND EFFECTIVENESS OF THE PATRIOT ACT: CASE STUDY INVOLVING RIGGS BANK, REPORT PREPARED BY THE MINORITY STAFF OF THE PERMANENT SUBCOMMITTEE ON INVESTIGATIONS, UNITED STATES SENATE COMMITTEE ON GOVERNMENT AFFAIRS (July 15, 2004), *available at* http://www.senate.gov/~govt-aff/_files/ACF5F8.pdf. The U.S. Treasury Department also ordered Riggs Bank to pay a $25 million civil monetary penalty for willfully violating the suspicious activity and currency transaction reporting requirements of the Bank Secrecy Act (BSA), 31 U.S.C. §§5311 *et seq.* and 31 C.F.R. Part 103, and willfully violating the anti-money laundering program requirements of the BSA and its implementing regulations. *See* U.S. Dep't of Treasury, In the Matter of Riggs Bank, N.A., No. 2004-01, Assessment of Civil Money Penalty (May 13, 2004), *available at* http://www.fincen.gov/riggs assessment3.pdf.
11. STEPHEN DYCUS, WILLIAM C. BANKS, & PETER RAVEN-HANSEN, COUNTERTERRORISM LAW 733 (Aspen Press 2007).
12. CIVIL LITIGATION AGAINST TERRORISM, *supra* note 5, at 7.
13. Several counter-arguments have been advanced against civil actions directed at state sponsors of terrorism. Those arguments include: (1) such actions will encourage civil suits against Americans; (2) damages imposed by judges are often too high; (3) blocked

assets should be available to the State Department in obtaining concessions from foreign governments; (4) payment of terrorism judgments from blocked assets would be unfair to new democratic governments; (5) rush to the courthouse (fairness and priorities among claimants for a pool of blocked assets) will ensue; and (6) suits may undermine the conduct of U.S. foreign policy and result in retaliation against the U.S. *See* Civil Litigation Against Terrorism, *supra* note 5, at 13–26.

14. Strauss, *supra* note 4, at 682.
15. *See, e.g.*, Hegna v. Islamic Republic of Iran, 2003 U.S. Dist. LEXIS 14039 (N.D. Ill. 2003); Smith v. Fed. Reserve Bank of N.Y., 280 F. Supp. 2d 314 (S.D.N.Y. 2003); Weinstein v. Islamic Republic of Iran, 274 F. Supp. 2d 53, 55 (D.D.C. 2003); *see also* Acree v. Republic of Iraq, 370 F.3d 41, 42–3 (D.C. Cir. 2004) (government intervened to contest the district court's subject matter jurisdiction in civil action brought by 17 American soldiers seeking compensatory damages for the horrific acts of torture suffered during their captivity in the first Gulf War).
16. 18 U.S.C. §2333 (2000). For a brief background and review of the legislative history of the ATA, see *Almog v. Arab Bank*, 471 F. Supp. 2d 257, 265–6 (E.D.N.Y. 2007); *Ungar ex rel. Strachman v. Palestinian Authority*, 304 F. Supp. 2d 232, 238–9 (D.R.I. 2004) ('The legislative history of 18 U.S.C. §2333 evinces a clear congressional intent to deter and punish acts of international terrorism.').
17. 18 U.S.C. §2333(a) (2000).
18. 18 U.S.C. §2331(1)(A)–(C) (2000 & Supp. IV 2004). *See* Smith v. Islamic Emirate of Afghanistan, 262 F. Supp. 2d 217, 221–2 (S.D.N.Y. 2003) (holding that the 9/11 terrorist attacks fall within the definition of 'international terrorism' under section 2331(1)).
19. *Ungar*, 304 F. Supp. 2d at 238.
20. *Id.* (quoting 136 Cong. Rec. S14279-01 (1990) (statement of Sen. Grassley)).
21. *Id.* at 238 (quoting 138 Cong. Rec. S17,252 (1992) (statement of Sen. Grassley)).
22. 137 Cong. Rec. S4511-04 (1991) (statement of Sen. Grassley).
23. Boim v. Quranic Literacy Inst. & Holy Land Found., 291 F.3d 1000, 1010 (7th Cir. 2002), *aff'g* 127 F. Supp. 2d 1001 (N.D. Ill. 2001) (Boim II); *see also* 137 Cong. Rec. S4511-04(1991) ('The ATA accords victims of terrorism the remedies of American tort law, including treble damages and attorney's fees.').
24. 18 U.S.C. §2333(a) (2000).
25. *See Boim,* 291 F.3d at 1011 ('The statute clearly is meant to reach beyond those persons who themselves commit the violent act that directly causes the injury.').
26. S. Rep. No. 102-342, at 22 (Jul. 25, 1990); *see also* Boim v. Holy Land Found., 511 F.3d 707, 743 (7th Cir. 2007) ('Congress meant for liability to extend the full length of the causal chain of terrorism.'); Ungar ex rel. Strachman v. Palestinian Auth., 304 F. Supp. 2d 232, 239 (D.R.I. 2004) (same).
27. 18 U.S.C. §2333(a) (2000).
28. *Id.* §2337(2) (2000).
29. *Id.* §2336(a) (2000).
30. *Id.* §2336(c).
31. 127 F. Supp. 2d 1002.
32. *Id.*
33. *Id.* at 1004
34. *Id.* HAMAS is an acronym for 'Harakat al-Muqawama al-Islamiyya,' also known as the 'Islamic Resistance Movement.' HAMAS was formally named a Specially Designated Terrorist (SDT) by President Clinton in 1995 and a Foreign Terrorist Organization by the State Department in 1997. *See* Prohibiting Transactions with Terrorists Who Threaten to Disrupt the Middle East Peace Process, Exec. Order No. 12,947, 3 C.F.R. 319–20 (1995), *reprinted as amended in* 50 U.S.C. §1701 note (2000 & Supp. IV 2004) (designating HAMAS an SDT); OFAC list of SDGTs available at U.S. Dep't of the Treasury Office of Foreign Assets Control, Terrorism: What You Need to Know About U.S. Sanctions (Updated 2007), *available at* http://www.Treasury.gov/offices/enforcement/ofac/programs/terror/terror.pdf (designating HAMAS as a Specially Designated Global Terrorist). On October 8, 1997, the U.S. Secretary of State

designated HAMAS as a 'foreign terrorist organization,' pursuant to section 219 of the Immigration and Nationality Act, codified at 8 U.S.C. §1189. Section 1189 provides a procedure by which the Secretary of State, in consultation with the Secretary of the Treasury and the Attorney General, may designate a certain organization as an FTO. The designation of HAMAS as an FTO has been renewed every two years since 1997. *See* 2005 Country Reports on Terrorism, U.S. Dep't of State, Office of the Coordinator for Counterterrorism (Apr. 30, 2006)*, available at* http://www.state.gov/documents/organization/65462.pdf.

35. *See* Boim v. Holy Land Found., 511 F.3d 707, 711 (7th Cir. 2007).
36. *Id.*
37. *See id.* at 710–13.
38. Ultimately, Salah pleaded guilty to terrorism-related offenses and was incarcerated in Israel. In 2004, a grand jury in the Northern District of Illinois indicted Salah and others on RICO, material support and obstruction of justice charges. However, the Government dropped the material support charges before trial. In February 2007, a federal jury acquitted Salah of the RICO charge and convicted him of the obstruction charge. *Id.* at 713.
39. Boim v. Quranic Literacy Inst. & Holy Land Found., 291 F.3d 1000, 1003 (7th Cir. 2002).
40. *Id.* On September 29, 2000, following the collapse of peace negotiations between Israel and the Palestinian Authority, HAMAS and other Palestinian terrorist groups launched the Al Aqsa Intifada or Intifada Al Quds – known in the West as the 'Second Intifada' – that was marked by multiple killings of civilians by these terrorist organizations. 'The objectives of the Second Intifada include intimidating and coercing the civilian population of Israel and attempting to influence the policy of the Israeli government to withdraw from territory it presently controls.' Linde v. Arab Bank, 384 F. Supp. 2d 571, 576 (E.D.N.Y. 2005). In 1992, HLF moved its headquarters to Richardson, Texas. *See The Holy Land Story: A Timeline*, DALLAS MORNING NEWS, Sept. 26, 2007, *available at* http://www.dallasnews.com/sharedcontent/dws/news/longterm/stories/092707dnmethlftimeline.1125ab6c1.html.
41. *Boim*, 291 F.3d at 1003. Also named as defendants in the lawsuit were individuals Mohammed Abdul Hamid Khalil Salah, the admitted U.S.-based leader of the military branch of HAMAS, and Mousa Mohammed Abu Marzook, who served for many years as the leader of the political wing of HAMAS. *See id.* at 1003–4 & n.4. Both Salah and Marzook allegedly coordinated HAMAS fund-raising and money laundering operations in the United States. *Id.* at 1003 n.3, 1006.
42. *Id.* at 1003, 1006–07. In December 2001, HLF was designated a Specially Designated Global Terrorist and its assets were blocked under E.O. 13224. *See* Press Release, U.S. Dep't of Treasury, Shutting Down the Terrorist Financial Network (Dec. 4, 2001), *available at* http://www.treas.gov/press/releases/po841.htm.
43. *Boim,* 291 F.3d, at 1004, 1006–07.
44. *Id.*
45. *Id* at 1004. A civil jury returned a verdict in favor of the Boims and awarded them $156 million in damages. *See* Boim v. Holy Land Found., 511 F.3d 707, 710 (7th Cir. 2007).
46. *Boim*, 291 F.3d. at 1009.
47. *Id.* at 1005.
48. *Id.*
49. *Id* at 1009.
50. *Id.*
51. Boim v. Quranic Literacy Inst. & Holy Land Found., 291 F.3d 1000, 1011–12 (7th Cir. 2002).
52. *Id.* at 1012.
53. *Id.* Thus, the Seventh Circuit affirmed the district court's ruling, stating:

> To say that funding *simpliciter* constitutes an act of terrorism is to give the statute an almost unlimited reach. Any act which turns out to facilitate terrorism, however

remote that act may be from actual violence and regardless of the actor's intent, could be construed to 'involve' terrorism. Without also requiring the plaintiffs to show knowledge of and intent to further the payee's violent criminal acts, such a broad definition might also lead to constitutional infirmities by punishing mere association with groups that engage in terrorism. *Id.* at 1011.

54. *Id.* at 1012.
55. 18 U.S.C.A. §2339A (West 2008)
56. 18 U.S.C. §2339B (2000 & Supp. IV 2004).
57. *Boim,* 291 F.3d. at 1014.
58. *Id.* at 1015.
59. *Id.* The court disagreed with the district court that the term 'material' in the context of §§2339A and 2339B means 'substantial or considerable.' The Seventh Circuit posited that the term relates to the type of aid provided rather than whether it is substantial or considerable. *Id.* The court stated that 'even small donations made knowingly and intentionally in support of terrorism may meet the standard for civil in section 2333.' *Id.*
60. *Id.* at 1016 (citing Central Bank of Denver v. First Interstate Bank of Denver, 511 U.S. 164 (1994)).
61. *Id.* at 1021.
62. *Id.*
63. *See* Boim v. Quranic Literacy Inst., 340 F. Supp. 2d 885, 931 (N.D. Ill. 2004).
64. *See* Boim v. Holy Land Found., 511 F.3d 707, 710 (7th Cir. 2007).
65. *Id.* at 710.
66. *Id.* at 709–10.
67. *Id.* at 740.
68. *Id.*
69. *Id.* at 741.
70. *See also* Weiss v. Nat'l Westminster Bank, 453 F. Supp. 2d 609, 631 (E.D.N.Y. 2006) (rejecting defendant's argument that the plaintiff must trace the funds given to a particular terrorist act); Strauss v. Credit Lyonnais, Case No. CV-06-0702 (CPS), 2006 WL 2862704, at *17–*18 (E.D.N.Y. Oct. 5, 2006) (same).
71. Boim v. Holy Land Found., 511 F.3d 707, 742 (7th Cir. 2007).
72. *Id.* at 745.
73. *Id.* at 742.
74. *Id.* at 743.
75. This view appears to conflict with the standard for causation articulated by the district court in *Weiss v. National Westminster Bank*, 453 F. Supp. 2d 609, 631 (E.D.N.Y. 2006) ('A showing of proximate cause requires plaintiffs to show that defendant's actions were a "substantial factor in the sequence of responsible causation," and that the injury was "reasonably foreseeable or anticipated as a natural consequence."'). *Accord* Strauss v. Credit Lyonnais, Case No. CV-06-0702 (CPS), 2006 WL 2862704, at *17 (E.D.N.Y. Oct. 5, 2006).
76. Linde v. Arab Bank, PLC, 384 F. Supp. 2d 571 (E.D.N.Y. 2005) [hereinafter *Arab Bank I*].
77. *Id.* at 584; *see also* Simpson, *supra* note 9. *Arab Bank I* involved essentially identical claims under the ATA brought in two other separate complaints: Litle v. Arab Bank, 04-CV-05449 (NG) (VVP), and Coulter v. Arab Bank, 05-CV-00365 (NG) (VVP). *See Arab Bank I,* 384 F. Supp. 2d at 575 n. 1. Arab Bank is the sole defendant in five other related cases: Bennett v. Arab Bank, 05-CV-03183 (July 1, 2005), Roth v. Arab Bank, 05-CV-03738 (Aug. 5, 2005); Miller v. Arab Bank, 05-CV-05518 (Nov. 28, 2005); Weiss v. Arab Bank, 06-CV-01623 (Apr. 7, 2006); and Jesner v. Arab Bank, 06-CV-03869 (Aug. 9, 2006).
78. *Arab Bank I,* 384 F. Supp. 2d at 575.
79. *See* Simpson, *supra* note 9.
80. *Id*
81. *Arab Bank I,* 384 F. Supp. 2d at 576.
82. *Id.*
83. *See* Coulter v. Arab Bank, 05-CV-00365 (NG) (VVP).

84. *Arab Bank I,* 384 F. Supp. 2d at 576.
85. *Id.*
86. *Id.*
87. *Id.*
88. *Id.* at 576–7.
89. *Id.* at 577.
90. *Id.*
91. *Id.*
92. *Id.*
93. *Id.*
94. Almog v. Arab Bank, PLC, 471 F. Supp. 2d 257, 263 (E.D.N.Y. 2007) [hereinafter *Arab Bank II*].
95. *Id.*
96. *Id.*
97. *Id.* at 263. To obtain the martyr certification, 'families must provide the Saudi Committee with the martyr's name, personal information, and details concerning the date and manner of death.' *See Arab Bank I,* 384 F. Supp. 2d at 577.
98. *Arab Bank II,* 471 F. Supp. 2d at 263.
99. 453 F. Supp. 2d 609 (E.D.N.Y. 2006).
100. *Id.* at 612.
101. *Id.* at 615.
102. *Id.*; *see also* Weiss v. National Westminster Bank PLC, Civil Complaint, No. 05-CV-04622-CPS-KAM (Apr. 18, 2007).
103. Weiss v. Nat'l Westminster Bank, 453 F. Supp. 2d 609, 614 (E.D.N.Y. 2006).
104. *Id.*
105. *Id.* at 615.
106. *Id.* at 617 (quoting al-Qaradawi).
107. *Id.* at 616.
108. Weiss v. Nat'l Westminster Bank, 453 F. Supp. 2d 609, 618 (E.D.N.Y. 2006).
109. *Id.*
110. *Id.* at 617.
111. *Id.* at 618.
112. *Id.*
113. Weiss v. Nat'l Westminster Bank, 453 F. Supp. 2d 609, 617 (E.D.N.Y. 2006).
114. *Id.*
115. *Id.* at 618–19.
116. *Id.* at 617. However, the Charity Commission ultimately distinguished between the military wing of HAMAS and its social and charitable wing, and, finding no 'pro-terrorist' bias in Interpal's distribution of funds, unfroze Interpal's accounts at NatWest. *Id.* at 616.
117. *Id.* at 616.
118. *Id.*
119. *Id.* at 617; *see also* Press Release, U.S. Dep't of Treasury, U.S. Designates Five Charities Funding Hamas and Six Senior Hamas Leaders as Terrorist Entities (Aug. 22, 2003), *available at* http://www.treasury.gov/press/releases/js 672.htm.
120. Strauss v. Credit Lyonnais, Case No. CV-06-0702 (CPS), 2006 WL 2862704, at * 2 (E.D.N.Y. 2006).
121. *Id.*
122. *Id.* at *3.
123. *Id.*
124. *Id.* at *6.
125. *Id.* at *4.
126. *Id.* at *5; *see also* Press Release, U.S. Dep't of Treasury, U.S. Designates Five Charities, *supra* note 119.
127. Strauss v. Credit Lyonnais, Case No. CV-06-0702 (CPS), 2006 WL 2862704, at *5 (E.D.N.Y. 2006).

128. *See* Weiss v. Nat'l Westminster Bank, 453 F. Supp. 2d 609, 621 (E.D.N.Y. 2006); *Credit Lyonnais*, 2006 WL 2862704, at *9; Linde v. Arab Bank, 384 F. Supp. 2d 571, 578 (E.D.N.Y. 2005) (*Arab Bank I*).
129. *Arab Bank I*, 384 F. Supp. 2d at 584.
130. *Id.* at 582.
131. *Id.* at 584.
132. *Credit Lyonnais*, 2006 WL 2862704, at *9; *see also* Weiss v. Nat'l Westminster Bank, 453 F. Supp. 2d 609, 622 (E.D.N.Y. 2006).
133. *Arab Bank I*, 384 F. Supp. 2d at 588.
134. *Id.*
135. *Id.* at 584. The court also rejected defendant's argument that plaintiffs must prove the death benefit plan motivated the terrorist attacks. *Id.*
136. *Id.* at 585.
137. *See Arab Bank I*, 384 F. Supp. 2d at 581; *Nat'l Westminster Bank*, 453 F. Supp. 2d at 623–7; *Credit Lyonnais,* 2006 WL 2862704, at *10–*15.
138. *Arab Bank I*, 384 F. Supp. 2d at 586 n. 9; *see also Nat'l Westminster Bank*, 453 F. Supp. 2d at 625–6; *Credit Lyonnais*, 2006 WL 2862704, at *13.
139. *Arab Bank I*, 384 F. Supp. 2d at 587; *see also Credit Lyonnais,* 2006 WL 2862704, at *17 ('[I]t is not necessary for plaintiffs to allege that defendant intended to transmit or receive the funds for terrorist purposes.'); *Nat'l Westminster Bank,* 453 F. Supp. 2d at 629–30 (same).
140. *Arab Bank I*, 384 F. Supp. 2d at 587 n. 11. Only one other court has sided with *Boim* on this issue. *See* United States v. Al-Arian, 308 F. Supp. 2d 1322, 1339, *reconsideration denied,* 329 F. Supp. 2d 1294 (M.D. Fla. 2004).
141. 349 F. Supp. 2d 765 (S.D.N.Y. 2005).
142. *Id.* at 833.
143. *Arab Bank I,* 384 F. Supp. 2d at 588. *Accord Nat'l Westminster Bank,* 453 F. Supp. 2d at 625; *Credit Lyonnais*, 2006 WL 2862704, at *12.
144. 18 U.S.C. §2339C.
145. *Nat'l Westminster Bank*, 453 F. Supp. 2d at 628; *see also Credit Lyonnais,* 2006 WL 2862704, at *15; *Arab Bank I,* at 384 F. Supp. 2d at 588.
146. 18 U.S.C. § 2339C(e)(4) & (5).
147. *Nat'l Westminster Bank*, 453 F. Supp. 2d at 629 (quoting *Arab Bank I*, 384 F. Supp. 2d at 588). *Accord Credit Lyonnais,* 2006 WL 2862704, at *17 (E.D.N.Y.).
148. *Id.*
149. *Arab Bank I,* 384 F. Supp. 2d at 589. The court dismissed counts based on claims that Arab Bank's failure to comply with the reporting requirements of §2339B(a)(2) provided material support to a terrorist organization, in violation of §2339B(a)(2). *Id.* at 590. The court also denied plaintiffs' claim for intentional infliction of emotional distress against the Bank. *Id.* at 591. Finally, in *Arab Bank I,* the court held that the scope of §2333 was not limited to *physical* injuries to U.S. nationals. Instead, §2333 extends to claims of U.S. nationals and their families suing on the basis of their non-physical injuries, such as emotional distress and loss of consortium, after their family members, including those who were not U.S. nationals, became victims of acts of terrorism. *Id.* at 589.
150. 28 U.S.C. §1350.
151. Almog v. Arab Bank, 471 F. Supp. 2d 257, 269 (E.D.N.Y 2007) (*Arab Bank II*).
152. *See* Sosa v. Alvarez-Machain, 542 U.S. 692, 712 (2004).
153. *Id.* at 720; *see also* Filartiga v. Pena-Irala, 630 F.2d 876, 880 (2d Cir. 1980).
154. In *Filartiga*, Dr Joel Filartiga, a Paraguayan physician who was an outspoken critic of Paraguayan President Alfredo Stroessner's government, alleged that his 17-year-old son was kidnapped and tortured to death in Asuncion, Paraguay, by the government's Inspector General of Police, Americo Norberto Pena-Irala. *Id.* at 878. After fleeing the United States and filing for political asylum, Filartiga filed an action under the ATS alleging that Pena had wrongly caused his son's death by torture. *Id.* at 879. The district court dismissed the action for lack of subject matter jurisdiction. *Id.* at 880. The case

was later reversed by the Second Circuit Court of Appeals on the grounds that the complaint properly alleged torture perpetrated under color of official authority, which violates universally accepted norms of international human rights. *Id.* at 878. The court held that 'wherever an alleged torturer is found and served with process by an alien within our borders, [the ATS] provides federal jurisdiction.' *Id.*

155. *See* Anne-Marie Slaughter & David L. Bosco, *Alternative Justice,* GLOBAL POLICY FORUM (last visited Jan. 28, 2007), *available at* http://www.globalpolicy.org/intljustice/atca/2001/altjust.htm.
156. In *Sosa,* plaintiff-respondent Humberto Alvarez-Machain was seeking civil damages in response to an allegedly improper arrest and detention by Mexican police officials acting as agents of the DEA. Alvarez-Machain was arrested at his office in Guadalajara, Jalisco, Mexico, and forcibly transported to El Paso, Texas, where he was arrested on federal charges for his role in the kidnapping and murder of DEA Agent Enrique Camarena-Salazar. Sosa v. Alvarez-Machain, 542 U.S. 692, 697 (2004). The Court ultimately rejected Alvarez-Machain's claims under the ATS. *See id.* at 738.
157. *Id.* at 729.
158. *Id.* at 724.
159. *Id.* at 729.
160. Sosa v. Alvarez-Machain, 542 U.S. 692, 732 (2004).
161. *Id.*
162. *Id.* at 733.
163. *Id.* at 734 (quoting The Paquete Habana, 175 U.S. 677, 700 (1900)); *see also* Filartiga v. Pena-Irala, 630 F.2d 876, 880 (2d Cir. 1980) (same).
164. *See Filartiga,* 630 F.2d at 881 n.8; *see also* Almog v. Arab Bank, 471 F. Supp. 2d 257, 272 (E.D.N.Y. 2007); Article 38 of the Statute of the International Court of Justice.
165. *Sosa,* 542 U.S., at 738.
166. 471 F. Supp. 2d 257 (E.D.N.Y, 2007).
167. *Id.* at 259–60.
168. *Id.* at 260. The court dismissed allegations in Count One alleging violations of 18 U.S.C. §2339B(a)(2) (2000) (failure to retain funds and report the existence of certain funds). Defendant's motion to dismiss was denied as to all other ATA claims in Counts One and Two pursuant to the reasoning in *Arab Bank I. Id.* at 268–9. The amended complaint further alleged various tort claims said to arise under federal common law, which were dismissed by the court. Specifically, Count Six alleged that Arab Bank assisted in the intentional injury of others by allowing its facilities to be used by HAMAS and other Palestinian terrorist groups; Count Seven alleged that Arab Bank recklessly disregarded injury to others; Count Eight alleged wrongful death; Count Nine alleged survival claims; and Count Ten alleged negligent and intentional infliction of emotional distress. *Id.* at 265.
169. *Id.* at 260. The foreign nationals consist mostly of Israeli citizens, but also include victims from Afghanistan, Australia, Belarus, Canada, France, Iran, Iraq, Peru, South Africa, Turkmenistan, Ukraine, and Uzbekistan. *Id.* at 260 n. 3.
170. *Id.* at 265.
171. *Id.*
172. *Id.* at 274; *see* Genocide Convention, art. 2, Dec. 9, 1948, 78 U.N.T.S. 227, *implemented in* Genocide Convention Implementation Act of 1987, 18 U.S.C. §1091 (2000). More than 135 states have ratified the Genocide Convention.
173. *Id.*
174. Kadic v. Karadzic, 70 F.3d 232, 239–41 (2d Cir. 1995).
175. Art. 7, Rome Statute of the International Criminal Court, July 17, 1998, 37 I.L.M. 999, 1004–5 (emphasis added).
176. *Almog*, 471 F. Supp. 2d at 275.
177. *Id.* at 275–6.
178. *Id.* at 276.
179. *Id.*

180. *Id.* at 276. International Convention for the Suppression of Terrorist Bombings, Jan. 12, 1998, G.A. Res. 52/164, 1, U.N. Doc. A/RES/52/164. The Terrorist Bombing Convention has been ratified by over 145 States, including the United States (June 26, 2002). Article 2 defines the prohibited conduct:

> Any person commits an offense within the meaning of this Convention if that person unlawfully and intentionally delivers, places, discharges or detonates an explosive or other lethal device in, into or against a place of public use, a State or government facility, a public transportation system or an infrastructure facility:
> (a) With the intent to cause death or serious bodily injury; or
> (b) With the intent to cause extensive destruction of such a place, facility or system, where such destruction results in or is likely to result in major economic loss.

181. *Almog*, 471 F. Supp. 2d at 277–8. International Convention for the Suppression of the Financing of Terrorism, Dec. 9, 1999, S. Treaty Doc. No. 106-49, 2178 U.N.T.S. 229, *available at* http://untreaty.un.org/ENGLISH/bible/englishinternetbible/partI/chapterXVIII/treaty12.asp. The Terrorist Financing Convention has been ratified by 150 countries, including the United States (June 26, 2002). The Convention makes it an offense to finance certain acts, including those proscribed in the Terrorist Bombing Convention. Article 2 provides:

> Any person commits an offence within the meaning of this Convention if that person by any means, directly or indirectly, unlawfully and willfully provides or collects funds with the intention that they should be used or in the knowledge that they are to be used, in full or in part, in order to carry out:
> (a) An act which constitutes an offence within the scope of and as defined in [the Terrorist Bombing Convention]; or
> (b) Any other act intended to cause death or serious bodily injury to a civilian . . . when the purpose of such act, by its nature and context, is to intimidate a population, or to compel a government or an international organization to do or to abstain from doing any act.

182. *See* Terrorist Bombings Convention Implementation Act of 2002, Pub. L. No. 107-197, 116 Stat. 721 (2002), *enacting* 18 U.S.C. §2332f, and Suppression of the Financing of Terrorism Convention Implementation Act of 2002, *enacting* 18 U.S.C. §2339C.
183. *Almog,* 471 F. Supp. 2d at 278–9.
184. S.C. Res. 1566, ¶3, U.N. Doc. S/RES/1566 (Oct. 8, 2004).
185. *Almog,* 471 F. Supp. 2d at 284. The court rejected defendant's argument that the underlying suicide bombings alleged in Count Three of the amended complaint cannot be a violation of the law of nations because there is no consensus on the definition of 'terrorism.' The court stated it was unnecessary to resolve any definitional dispute regarding the meaning of 'terrorism.' The pertinent issue is whether the conduct alleged by plaintiffs violates a norm of international law, however labeled. *Id.* at 280. The court concluded that the acts alleged by plaintiffs, including suicide bombings and other murderous attacks on innocent civilians, are universally condemned. *Id.* at 281. *But see* Saperstein v. Palestinian Auth., Case No. 1:04-cv-20225-PAS, 2006 WL 3804718, at *7 (S.D. Fla. Dec. 22, 2006) (stating that because the international community has been unable to agree on a definition of 'terrorism,' 'if the conduct of the Defendants is construed as terrorism, then Plaintiffs have not alleged a violation of the law of nations').
186. *Almog,* 471 F. Supp. 2d at 284.
187. *Id.* at 286.
188. *Id.*
189. *Id.* at 290.
190. *Id.* at 291.
191. Presbyterian Church of Sudan v. Talisman Energy, Inc., 244 F. Supp. 2d 289, 323 (emphasis added), *quoted in Almog*, 471 F. Supp. 2d at 286.

192. *Almog*, 471 F. Supp. 2d at 268, 292.
193. *Id.*
194. *See* Filartiga v. Pena-Irala, 630 F.2d 876, 878 (2d Cir. 1980) ('[D]eliberate torture perpetrated under color of official authority violates universally accepted norms of the international law of human rights.'); *see also* Convention Against Torture and Other Cruel, Inhuman or Degrading Treatment or Punishment, Dec. 10, 1984, 1465 U.N.T.S. 85.
195. United States v. Yunis, 681 F. Supp. 896, 900–01 (D.D.C. 1988), *aff'd* 924 F.2d 1086 (D.C. Cir. 1991) (aircraft piracy and hostage taking are universally condemned and fit within the category of heinous international crimes for purposes of asserting universal jurisdiction); Hague Convention on the Suppression of Unlawful Seizure of Aircraft, Dec. 16, 1970, 860 U.N.T.S. 105, 22 U.S.T. 1641, T.I.A.S. 7192; Montreal Convention for the Suppression of Unlawful Acts Against the Safety of Civil Aviation, Sept. 23, 1971, 974 U.N.T.S. 177, 24 U.S.T. 564, T.I.A.S. No. 7570. The Hague and Montreal Conventions have been ratified by 181 and 183 states respectively.
196. *See* International Convention Against the Taking of Hostages, Dec. 17, 1979, 1316 U.N.T.S. 205. The Hostage Taking Convention has been ratified by 153 states.
197. 28 U.S.C. §1604 (2000). The FSIA provides that '[s]ubject to existing international agreements to which the United States is a party at the time of enactment of this Act a foreign state shall be immune from the jurisdiction of the courts of the United States and of the States except as provided in sections 1605 to 1607 of this chapter.' *Id.*
198. In *Argentine Republic v. Amerada Hess Shipping Corp.*, 488 U.S. 428, 434 (1989), the U.S. Supreme Court ruled unanimously that the FSIA provides the sole basis for obtaining jurisdiction over a foreign state in U.S. courts.
199. 28 U.S.C.A §1605(a)(7) (West 2008).
200. *Id.*
201. 28 U.S.C.A §1605(a)(7)(A) (West 2008).
202. The State Department list of state sponsors of terror (SSTs), as of February 26, 2007, includes: Syria, Cuba, Iran, North Korea and Sudan. U.S. Dep't of State, State Sponsors of Terrorism, 2007, *available at* http://www.state.gov/s/ct/c14151.htm.
203. In order to sustain a cause of action against foreign states that are not designated as state sponsors of terrorism, plaintiffs have relied on two other exceptions to jurisdictional immunity of foreign states. Section 1605(a)(2) provides that a foreign state shall not be immune from the jurisdiction of the courts of the United States for actions based upon a 'commercial activity' carried on in the United States by a foreign state. 28 U.S.C. §1605(a)(2) (2000). Additionally, section 1605(a)(5) provides a noncommercial torts exception. Section 1605(a)(5) provides that a foreign state shall not be immune from the jurisdiction of courts in the U.S. in any case

> (5) [i]n which money damages are sought against a foreign state for personal injury or death, or damage to or loss of property, occurring in the United States and caused by the tortious act or omission of that foreign state or of any official or employee of that foreign state while acting within the scope of his office or employment. 28 U.S.C. §1650(a)(5).
>
> Subsection A then provides an exception to this exception:
>
> [Section (a)(5) shall not apply to] any claim based upon the exercise or performance or the failure to exercise or perform a discretionary function regardless of whether the discretion be abused. 28 U.S.C. §1650(a)(5)(A).

However, courts have consistently denied terrorism-related claims based on the 'commercial activity' and 'noncommercial tort' exceptions, holding either that the foreign state was not engaged in 'commercial activity' in the United States or the 'discretionary function' exception to the foreign sovereign immunity exception applied. *See* Burnett v. Al Baraka Inv. & Dev. Corp., 292 F. Supp. 2d 9, 17–21 (D.D.C. 2003); *In re* Terrorist Attacks on Sept. 11, 2001, 03 MDL 1570 (RCC) (S.D.N.Y.).

204. 28 U.S.C.A §1605(a)(7)(B) (West 2008).
205. Pursuant to §1605(a)(7)(A), the foreign state must be designated as a 'state sponsor of terrorism' 'under section 6(j) of the Export Administration Act of 1979 (50 U.S.C. App. 2405(j)) or section 620A of the Foreign Assistance Act of 1961 (22 U.S.C. 2371), at the time the act occurred, unless later so designated as a result of such act.'
206. The courts have held that jurisdictional causation under §1605(a)(7) is different from the substantive causation element of a claim. The 'caused by' language of §1605(a)(7) has been interpreted to require only a showing of proximate cause. 'Plaintiffs must establish jurisdictional causation by alleging facts sufficient to establish a reasonable connection between a country's provision of material support to a terrorist organization and the damage arising out of a terrorist attack.' Rux v. Republic of Sudan, 461 F.3d 461, 473 (4th Cir. 2006); *see also* Kilburn v. Socialist People's Libyan Arab Jamahiriya, 376 F.3d 1123, 1128 (D.C. Cir. 2004); Owens v. Republic of Sudan, 412 F. Supp. 2d 99, 111 (D.D.C. 2006).
207. *See* Abur v. Republic of Sudan, 437 F. Supp. 2d 166, 176–7 (D.D.C. 2006) (dismissing claims by 112 Kenyan-citizen plaintiffs for lack of subject matter jurisdiction; in order to be a 'national' of the United States, within the meaning of §1605(a)(7), one must be either a citizen of the U.S. or a person who has completed the naturalization process; marriage alone does not confer 'national' status on a non-U.S. citizen).
208. *See* Roeder v. Islamic Republic of Iran, 195 F. Supp. 2d 140, 149 (D.D.C. 2002), *aff'd by* 333 F.3d 228 (D.C. Cir. 2003).
209. 28 U.S.C.A §1610(a) (West 2008).
210. *See* 28 U.S.C.A §1610(b)(2) (West 2008).
211. *See* Omnibus Consolidated Appropriations Act, Pub. L. No. 104-208, §589, 110 Stat. 3009-172 (1997), *reprinted in* 28 U.S.C. §1605 note (2000);
212. *See* Flatow v. Islamic Republic of Iran, 999 F.Supp. 1, 12 (D.D.C. 1998).
213. 28 U.S.C. §1605 note.
214. 353 F.3d 1024 (D.C. Cir. 2004).
215. *Id.* at 1031.
216. *Id.* at 1033.
217. *Id.* at 1033 (citing FDIC v. Meyer, 510 U.S. 471, 484 (1994)). As the Supreme Court has stated: The first inquiry is whether there has been a waiver of sovereign immunity. If there has been such a waiver . . . the second inquiry comes into play – that is, whether the source of substantive law upon which the claimant relies provides an avenue for relief. *Meyer*, 510 U.S. at 484.
218. *Cicippio-Puleo*, 353 F.3d at 1033 (quoting 28 U.S.C. §1605 note).
219. *Id.* at 1034.
220. *Id.*
221. Prior to the court's decision in *Cicippio*, numerous district courts in the D.C Circuit had ruled that the Flatow Amendment provided a cause of action against a foreign state. *See* Price v. Socialist People's Libyan Arab Jamahiriya, 274 F. Supp. 2d 20, 32 (D.D.C. 2003) (holding that FSIA affords victims of state-sponsored acts of terrorism a cause of action); Smith v. Islamic Emirate of Afghanistan, 262 F. Supp. 2d 217, 228 (S.D.N.Y. 2003) ('While not free from doubt, the better view . . . is that the Flatow Amendment likely provides a cause of action against a foreign state.'); Cronin v. Islamic Republic of Iran, 238 F. Supp. 2d 222, 231 (D.D.C. 2002) (holding that the Flatow Amendment provides a cause of action against a foreign state). *Cicippio* overrules those earlier decisions.
222. *Cicippio-Puleo*, 353 F.3d at 1036. *Accord* Acree v. Republic of Iraq, 370 F.3d 41, 58–9 (D.C. Cir. 2004), *cert. denied,* 544 U.S. 1010 (2005). *Cicippio*, however, did not completely foreclose the possibility of suits against state sponsors of terrorism. In *Dammarell v. Islamic Republic of Iran*, the district court held that 'the causes of action that may be brought against the foreign state . . . include any claims that could be brought against a private individual in like circumstances. Those claims can include, in appropriate cases, state common and statutory law, federal statutory law, and even the law of a foreign state.' *See* Case No. Civ.A. 01-2224(JDB), 2005 WL 756090, at *8, *14 (D.D.C. 2005) (reasoning that 28 U.S.C. §1606, which directed courts as to admissible

causes of action under 28 U.S.C. §1605 exceptions, provided that a foreign state could be liable in the same manner as private individuals). After amending their complaints, the court awarded plaintiffs damages in the amount of $316,919,657. *Dammarell v. Islamic Republic of Iran*, Case No. CIV.A.01-2224(JDB), 2006 WL 2583043, at *1 (D.D.C. Sep. 7, 2006). Several other district court decisions in the District of Columbia had applied *Dammarell*'s reasoning when faced with civil suits against states sponsors of terrorism. *See, e.g.*, Beaty v. Republic of Iraq, 480 F. Supp. 2d 60, 93 (D.D.C. 2007) (finding that plaintiffs sufficiently stated a claim for relief for intentional infliction of emotional distress); Oveissi v. Islamic Republic of Iran, 498 F. Supp. 2d 268, 277–8 (D.D.C. 2007) (following *Dammarell*'s choice of law analysis); Vine v. Republic of Iraq, 459 F. Supp. 2d 10, 28 (D.D.C. 2006) (denying Iraq's motion to dismiss state common law and foreign law claims, but dismissing the Flatow Amendment as a cause of action); Holland v. Islamic Republic of Iran, 496 F. Supp. 2d 1, 35 (D.D.C. 2005) (granting plaintiffs leave to amend their complaint to explicitly incorporate Kentucky state law causes of action); Salazar v. Islamic Republic of Iran, 370 F. Supp. 2d 105, 114, 117 (D.D.C. 2005) (allowing plaintiffs to proceed with claims under Illinois state law and awarding plaintiffs compensatory damages in the amount of $18,297,000).

223. 28 U.S.C.A §1605A (West 2008) (effective Jan. 28, 2008).
224. *Id.* at §1605A(a)(2).
225. *See* U.S. Dep't of State, State Sponsors of Terrorism, *available at* http://www.state.gov/s/ct/c14151.htm (last visited Feb. 11, 2008).
226. 28 U.S.C.A §1605A(a)(1) (West 2008).
227. *Id.* at §1605(c).
228. Section 1605A(h)(6) defines the term 'state sponsor of terrorism' to mean a State which the Secretary of State has determined, for purposes of section 6(j) of the Export Administration Act of 1979 (50 U.S.C. App. 2405(j)), section 620A of the Foreign Assistance Act of 1961 (22 U.S.C. 2371), section 40 of the Arms Export Control Act (22 U.S.C. 2780), or any other provision of law, is a government that has repeatedly provided support for acts of international terrorism.
229. 28 U.S.C.A §1605A(c).
230. *Id.*
231. *Id.* and 28 U.S.C. §1605A(d).
232. The Act provides that the amendments made by this section shall apply to any claim arising under §1605A with respect to any action brought under 28 U.S.C. §1607(a)(7), or section 589 of the Foreign Operations, Export Financing, and Related Programs Appropriations Act (1997), before the date of the enactment of this Act, where plaintiffs relied upon either provision as creating a cause of action and were adversely affected on the grounds that these provisions failed to create a cause of action against a foreign state, and as of the date of enactment the action is before the court in any form, including on appeal. *See* Pub. L. No. 110-181, Div A, Title X, Subtitle F, §1083(c)(2)(A), 122 Stat. 342; *see also* 28 U.S.C. §1605A note.
233. *Id.*
234. Pub. L. No. 110-181, Div A, Title X, Subtitle F, §1083(c)(2)(B), 122 Stat. 342; *see also* 28 U.S.C.A §1605A note.
235. Pub. L. No. 110-181, Div A, Title X, Subtitle F, §1083(c)(2)(C), 122 Stat. 342; *see also* 28 U.S.C.A §1605A note.
236. 28 U.S.C.A §1610(g)(1) (West 2008).
237. Prior to the enactment of section 1083, the courts were divided on whether the Terrorism Risk Insurance Act of 2002 waived U.S. sovereign immunity with respect to attachment of blocked assets. *See, e.g.*, Weinstein v. Islamic Republic of Iran, 274 F. Supp. 2d 53, 58 (D.D.C. 2003) (holding no explicit waiver of sovereign immunity); Hegna v. Islamic Republic of Iran, 2003 U.S. Dist. LEXIS 14039, * 25 (N.D. Ill.) (holding that the TRIA waives U.S. sovereign immunity).
238. 28 U.S.C.A §1610(g)(2) (West 2008).
239. Executive Order 13382 authorized the Treasury Department to freeze the assets of proliferators of weapons of mass destruction. *See* Exec. Order No. 13,382, 3 C.F.R. 170 (2005).

240. *Id.*
241. *See* Press Release, U.S. Dep't of Treasury, Iran's Bank Sepah Designated by Treasury, Sepah Facilitating Iran's Weapons Program (Jan. 9, 2007), *available at* http://www.treasury.gov/press/releases/hp219.htm; *see also* Press Release, U.S. Dep't of Treasury, Fact Sheet: Designation of Iranian Entities and Individuals for Proliferation Activities and Support for Terrorism (Oct. 25, 2007), *available at* http://www.treasury.gov/press/releases/hp644.htm.
242. *See* Exec. Order No. 13,338: Blocking Property of Certain Persons and Prohibiting the Export of Certain Goods to Syria (May 11, 2004), 69 Fed. Reg. 26,751, *available at* http://www.treasury.gov/offices/enforcement/ofac/legal/eo/13338.pdf.
243. *See* Exec. Order No. 13,399: Executive Order Blocking Property of Additional Persons in Connection with the National Emergency with Respect to Syria (Apr. 26, 2006), 71 Fed. Reg. 25059, *available at* http://www.treasury.gov/offices/enforcement/ofac/legal/eo/13399.pdf; *see also* Executive Order 13,460: Blocking Property of Additional Persons in Connection with National Emergency with Respect to Syria (Feb. 13, 2008), 73 Fed. Reg. 9001, *available at* http://www.treasury.gov/offices/enforcement/ofac/legal/eo/13460.pdf.
244. 28 U.S.C.A §1610(g)(2) (2008).
245. *See* 50 U.S.C. §§1701–7. The IEEPA was enacted by Congress in 1977, and amended by the USA PATRIOT Act, Pub. L. No. 105-56, Title I, §106, 115 Stat. 272 (Oct. 26, 2001). Among other things, the Act amended the IEEPA to authorize the confiscation of blocked assets.
246. *See* Weinstein v. Islamic Republic of Iran, 274 F. Supp. 2d 53, 57–8 (D.D.C. 2003) (holding that the Terrorism Risk Insurance Act, §201(a) did not constitute an explicit waiver of sovereign immunity).
247. Pub. L. No. 110-181, Div A, Title X, Subtitle F, §1083(d)(1), 122 Stat. 343.
248. Pub. L. No. 107-297, §201(b)(1), 116 Stat. 2322 (2002) (codified as amended at 28 U.S.C. §1610 note.
249. Section 2337, Title 18 of the United States Code, expressly prohibits U.S. nationals from suing states under the ATA. Section 2337 under the ATA provides that '[n]o action shall be maintained under section 2333 of this title against . . . a foreign state, an agency of a foreign state, or an officer or employee of a foreign state or an agency thereof acting within his or her official capacity or under color of legal authority.' 18 U.S.C. §2337(2). The courts have held that '[s]ection 2337 could not be clearer: it prevents suits under §2333 [the ATA] against foreign states and officers wherein a plaintiff who prevails would be entitled to treble damages.' Smith v. Islamic Emirate of Afghan., 262 F. Supp. 2d 217, 225 (S.D.N.Y. 2003); *see also* Cronin v. Islamic Republic of Iran, 238 F. Supp. 2d 224, 231 n. 2 (D.D.C. 2002) (same).
250. Sosa v. Alvarez-Machain, 542 U.S. 692, 721 (2004).
251. Convention Against Torture and Other Cruel, Inhuman or Degrading Treatment or Punishment, Dec. 10, 1984, 1465 U.N.T.S. 85.
252. International Convention for the Suppression of Terrorist Bombings, Jan. 12, 1998, G.A. Res. 52/164, 1, U.N. Doc. A/RES/52/164.
253. Montreal Convention for the Suppression of Unlawful Acts Against the Safety of Civil Aviation, Sept. 23, 1971, 974 U.N.T.S. 177, 24 U.S.T. 564, T.I.A.S. No. 7570.
254. International Convention Against the Taking of Hostages, Dec. 17, 1979, 1316 U.N.T.S. 205.
255. International Convention for the Suppression of the Financing of Terrorism, Dec. 9, 1999, G.A. Res. 54/109, 1, U.N. Doc. A/RES/54/109.
256. *See* Acree v. Republic of Iraq, 370 F.3d 41, 51 (D.C. Cir. 2004) (holding that the Emergency Wartime Supplemental Appropriations Act (EWSAA), §1503 was not intended to alter the jurisdiction of the federal courts under FSIA; §1503 of EWSAA does not trump 28 U.S.C. § 1605(a)(7)).
257. *See* Almog v. Arab Bank, 471 F. Supp. 2d 257, 291–2 (E.D.N.Y. 2007); *see also* Burnett v. Al Baraka Inv. & Dev. Corp., 274 F. Supp. 2d 86, 100 (D.D.C. 2003) ('[P]roof that [defendants] were accomplices, aiders and abettors, or co-conspirators would support

a finding of liability under ATCA.'); Presbyterian Church of Sudan v. Talisman Energy, Inc., 244 F. Supp. 2d 289, 321 (S.D.N.Y. 2003) (same); Mehinovic v. Vuckovic, 198 F. Supp. 2d 1322, 1355 (N.D. Ga. 2002) (same).

258. Pub. L. No. 107-297, §201, 116 Stat. 2322 (2002) (codified as amended at 28 U.S.C. §1610 note.
259. H.R. Conf. Rep. No. 107-779, at 27 (2002), *as reprinted in* 2002 U.S.C.C.A.N. 1430, 1434–5; *see also* Weininger v. Castro, 462 F. Supp. 2d 457, 483 (S.D.N.Y. 2006) (discussing intention of TRIA drafters).
260. Hill v. Republic of Iraq, Case No. Civ.A. 1:99CV03346TP, 2003 WL 21057173, at *2 (D.D.C. 2003); *see also* 148 Cong. Rec. S11527 (remarks of Sen. Harkin); 148 Cong. Rec. S5510 (June 13, 2002) (remarks of Sen. Allen); 148 Cong. Rec. H6134 (Sept. 10, 2002) (remarks of Rep. Fosella and Rep. Cannon).
261. TRIA, §201(a), 116 Stat. at 2337. Section 1605(a)(7) provides, in pertinent part, that a foreign state shall not be entitled to immunity in any case in which 'money damages are sought against a foreign state for personal injury or death that was caused by an act of . . . hostage taking . . . if such act . . . is engaged in by an official, employee, or agent of such foreign state while acting within the scope of his or her office, employment, or agency.' 28 U.S.C. §1605(a)(7).
262. The term 'terrorist party' means a 'terrorist, a terrorist organization (as defined in section 212(a)(3)(B)(vi) of the Immigration and Nationality Act (8 U.S.C. §1182(a)(3)(B)(vi)), or a foreign state designated as a state sponsor of terrorism under section 6(j) of the Export Administration Act of 1979 (50 U.S.C. App. 2405(j)) or section 620A of the Foreign Assistance Act of 1961 (22 U.S.C. §2371).' TRIA, §201(d)(4), 116 Stat. at 2340; *see also* Weininger v. Castro, 462 F. Supp. 2d 457, 479 (S.D.N.Y. 2006).
263. *Weininger*, 462 F. Supp. 2d at 479.
264. *Id. See* Ungar ex rel. v. Palestinian Auth., 304 F. Supp. 2d 232, 241–2 (D.R.I. 2004) (ordering the attachment of 'blocked assets' of the Holy Land Foundation for Relief and Development (HLF), blocked by the Treasury Department pursuant to Executive Orders 12947 and 13224, because HLF operates as a fund-raiser for HAMAS).
265. *Id.*
266. TRIA, §201(d)(2)(A), 116 Stat. at 2339.
267. *Id.* §201(d)(2)(i)–(ii), 116 Stat. at 2339–40. In turn, 'property subject to the Vienna Convention on Diplomatic Relations or the Vienna Convention on Consular Relations' is defined as 'any property . . . the attachment in aid of execution or execution of which would result in a violation of an obligation of the United States under the Vienna Convention on Diplomatic Relations or the Vienna Convention on Consular Relations.' Weinstein v. Islamic Republic of Iran, 274 F. Supp. 2d 53, 60 (D.D.C. 2003). Article 45 of the Vienna Convention on Diplomatic Relations provides that '[i]f diplomatic relations are broken off between two States, or if a mission is permanently or temporarily recalled . . . [t]he receiving State must, even in case of armed conflict, respect and protect the premises of the mission, together with its property and archives.' Vienna Convention on Diplomatic Relations, Apr. 18, 1961, 23 U.S.T. 3227, T.I.A.S. No. 7502, *available at* http://untreaty.un.org/ilc/texts/instruments/english/conventions/9_1_1961.pdf. Article 27 of the Vienna Convention on Consular Relations imposes a similar obligation with respect to the consular premises, property and archives. Vienna Convention on Consular Relations, Apr. 24, 1963, 21 U.S.T. 77, T.I.A.S. No. 6820, *available at* http://untreaty.un.org/ilc/texts/instruments/english/conventions/9_2_1963.pdf.
268. TRIA, §201(d)(2).
269. *See* Hegna v. Islamic Republic of Iran, Case No. 02 C 8643, 2003 U.S. Dist. LEXIS 14039, at *19 (N.D. Ill. 2003) ('The TRIA removes barriers to the attachment of blocked assets by severely limiting the availability of the presidential waiver to protect blocked assets.'). Section 201(b)(1) provides:

(b) Presidential Waiver–
(1) In General. – Subject to paragraph (2), upon determining on an asset-by-asset basis that a waiver is necessary in the national security interest, the President may waive the requirements of subsection (a) in connection with (and prior to the enforcement of) any judicial order directing attachment in aid of execution or execution against any property subject to the Vienna Convention on Diplomatic Relations or the Vienna Convention on Consular Relations.

270. TRIA, §201(b)(2)(A).
271. Weinstein v. Islamic Republic of Iran, 274 F. Supp. 2d 53, 55 (D.D.C. 2003).
272. *Id.*
273. *Id.* at 55–6.
274. *Id.* at 55.
275. Weinstein v. Islamic Republic of Iran, 274 F. Supp. 2d 53, 58, 62 (D.D.C. 2003).
276. *Id.* at 58.
277. *Id.* at 60.
278. *Id.* at 59.
279. *Id.*
280. Weinstein v. Islamic Republic of Iran, 274 F. Supp. 2d 53, 60 (D.D.C. 2003).
281. *Id.* at 61.
282. *Id.* at 61–2. A portion of the funds in the second account had been designated by Congress to satisfy judgments pursuant to the Victims of Trafficking and Violence Protection Act. *Id.* at 59. The court held that those funds were unavailable for attachment by plaintiffs. *Id.*
283. Case No. 02 C 8643, 2003 U.S. Dist. LEXIS 14039 (N.D. Ill. 2003).
284. *Id.* at *1.
285. *Id.* at *2.
286. *Id.* at *25 (quoting 148 Cong. Rec. S11524, S11528–9 (Nov. 19, 2002)) (emphasis added). The court, however, did not expressly address whether the TRIA functions as an express waiver of sovereign immunity. *See also* Hill v. Republic of Iraq, Case No. Civ.A. 1:99CV03346TP, 2003 WL 21057173, at *2 (D.D.C. Mar. 11, 2003) (holding that the 'notwithstanding' phrase of the TRIA 'by its plain terms . . . overrides any immunity from execution that blocked Iraqi property might otherwise enjoy under the Vienna Convention or the FSIA').
287. *Id.* at *32.
288. *Id.*
289. Pub. L. No. 102-297, §201(a), 116 Stat. 2322, 2337 (Nov. 26, 2002).
290. 280 F. Supp. 2d 314 (S.D.N.Y. 2003).
291. *Id.* at 315.
292. *See* Exec. Order No. 12,722, 55 Fed. Reg. 31,803 (Aug. 2, 1990).
293. *Smith,* 280 F. Supp. 2d at 318 (citing Exec. Order No. 13, 290, 68 Fed. Reg. 14, 307 (Mar. 20, 2003)).
294. *Id.* at 319.
295. *Id.*
296. *Id.* at 321.
297. *Id.* at 321–2.
298. *See, e.g.*, Weinstein v. Islamic Republic of Iran, 274 F. Supp. 2d 53, 55 (D.D.C. 2003); Hegna v. Islamic Republic of Iran, 2003 U.S. Dist. LEXIS 14039, at *1 (N.D. Ill.); Smith v. Fed. Reserve Bank of New York, 280 F. Supp. 2d 314, 315 n. 1 (S.D.N.Y. 2003).
299. Acree v. Republic of Iraq, 370 F.3d 41, 49 (D.C. Cir. 2004).

PART V

Has the legal response to the financing of terrorism been effective?

12. Accomplishments, failures, and recommendations for enhancing the Anti-Terrorist Financing Legal Regime

> Vigorous efforts to track terrorist financing must remain front and center in U.S. counterterrorism efforts. [1]
>
> The 9/11 Commission Report: Final Report of the National Commission on Terrorist Attacks upon the United States

> 'Al Qaeda, the Taliban, and other terrorist groups continue to have access to the funds they need for active and expanded indoctrination, recruitment, maintenance, armament and operations.'[2]
>
> Statement of Senator E. Charles Grassley, Hearing of the Senate Finance Committee on Anti-Terrorism Financing: Progress Made and Challenges Ahead (April 1, 2008)

GENERAL ASSESSMENT

If the success of the legal regime constructed post-9/11 to curtail the financing of terrorism is measured by whether al Qaeda and the Taliban have been deprived of funding and no longer constitute a serious threat to international peace and security, the legal response has been a dismal failure. According to the 2008 *Annual Threat Assessment of the Director of National Intelligence* (*DNI National Threat Assessment*), al Qaeda and its affiliates from north Africa to Southeast Asia continue to pose significant terrorist threats to the United States and the international community.[3] Al Qaeda has retained a safe haven in Pakistan's Federally Administered Tribal Areas (FATA), where a core group of senior al Qaeda leaders has been able to direct the organization's terrorist operations around the world.[4] Further, the 2008 *DNI National Threat Assessment* ominously warns that al Qaeda is 'improving the last key aspect of its ability to attack the US: the identification, training, and positioning of operatives for an attack on the Homeland.'[5] Al Qaeda has been strengthened by its recent merger with the Salafist Group for Call and Combat (GSPC). In 2006, coinciding with the fifth anniversary of the 9/11 terror attacks, GSPC merged with al Qaeda, forming a new terrorist organization called Al Qaeda in the Islamic Maghreb (AQIM).[6] The terror group's aim is to overthrow the Algerian government and replace it with a fundamentalist Islamic state. AQIM is a formidable threat to the region. In 2007, it claimed responsibility for launching multiple terrorist attacks in Algiers, killing hundreds of innocent civilians and injuring hundreds more.[7]

Despite the U.S. government's counter-terrorism efforts, the Taliban has experienced a resurgence over the past two years. A report prepared by the United Nations Al-Qaida and Taliban Analytical Support and Sanctions Monitoring Team ('U.N. Sanctions Monitoring Team') in November 2007 concluded that the Taliban has no shortage of money to hire foot soldiers and purchase weapons, including the components for sophisticated improvised explosive devices.[8] More disturbing yet, the Taliban has turned to the illicit opium drug trade to help finance its military operations in Afghanistan. A recent study by the United Nations Office on Drugs and Crime (UNODC) found that illicit drug trafficking is providing the Taliban an important source of income.[9] Afghanistan now accounts for 93 percent of the world's opium supply.[10] In 2007, the total export value of opium and heroin in Afghanistan was $4 billion, an increase of 29 percent over 2006.[11] Approximately 50 percent of the Afghan opium crop comes from the Helmand province, an area controlled by the Taliban.[12] Thus, the Taliban is flush with funding to finance its military operations in Afghanistan.

While the picture remains bleak on the financial front, the anti-terrorist financing legal regime has made it more difficult and costly for jihadist sympathizers to raise and transfer funds globally to support acts of terrorism. Two significant accomplishments are particularly worth highlighting. First, enhanced anti-money laundering and counter-terrorist financing regulations have reduced the risk of banks and money transmitting businesses being used to facilitate terrorist financing. Second, the economic sanctions regime developed by the United States and the international community for designating and freezing the assets of suspected terrorists and their associates has disrupted the ability of corrupt Islamic charitable organizations to raise millions of dollars to finance terrorist activities.

However, while some progress has been made in stemming the flow of money to terrorists, substantial challenges remain. For example, criminal prosecutions have been extremely disappointing. Approximately seven years after 9/11, the United States Department of Justice has failed to successfully prosecute a major terrorist financing case. Justice Department attorneys have suffered several legal setbacks, with few blockbuster convictions and several high-profile hung juries or acquittals.[13] Equally disturbing, the number of designations of suspected terrorists for asset freeze has substantially diminished since September 2001.[14] Many countries are non-compliant with U.N. Security Council resolutions requiring States to submit the names of suspected terrorists for inclusion on the U.N. Consolidated List and to freeze their assets.[15] Further, the United States Treasury Department has contributed to the demise of the international asset freeze program. In 2007, only 11 individuals and entities were designated as Specially Designated Global Terrorists and submitted to the U.N. Sanctions Committee for inclusion on the Consolidated List.[16] The number of Treasury Department designations linked to al Qaeda represents an all time record low, continuing a long-term downward trend.[17] Finally, the United States and the international community have failed to adjust to new sources of terrorism financing, including the use of the Afghan opium drug trade to finance the Taliban, and new methods to transfer terror money globally such as through trade-based financing and the use of stored value cards.

ACCOMPLISHMENTS

Enhancing the Financial Regulatory Regime

Prior to September 11, 2001, financial institutions were not monitoring transactions or accounts for possible connections to terrorists and terrorist organizations. While bank employees were monitoring financial transactions for possible money laundering, terrorist financing was not on their radar screen. As a result, banks and other financial institutions were being used as conduits to finance terrorist activities. In the aftermath of the 9/11 terrorist attacks, Congress enacted the USA PATRIOT Act of 2001 (PATRIOT Act), which amended the Bank Secrecy Act (BSA).[18] Title III of the PATRIOT Act, known as the International Money Laundering Abatement and Anti-Terrorist Financing Act of 2001 (IMLAA), strengthened the financial regulatory regime to prevent international money laundering and terrorist financing.[19]

Among other amendments to the BSA, the IMLAA enhanced the 'know your customer' principle by imposing minimum requirements for the identification and verification of customers opening an account. Specifically, pursuant to 31 U.S.C. §5318(l)(2), financial institutions, including foreign banks with U.S. branches, are required to implement procedures for 'consulting lists of known or suspected terrorists or terrorist organizations provided to the financial institution by any government agency to determine whether a person seeking to open an account appears on any such list.'[20] For example, the U.S. Treasury Department's Office of Foreign Assets Control (OFAC) maintains a list of individuals and entities designated as 'Specially Designated Global Terrorists' (SDGTs). Approximately 500 names have been placed on the OFAC terror list. Pursuant to section 5318(l)(2), prior to opening a customer account, banks are required to check the list of SDGTs to ensure that the customer's name does not appear on the list. Thus, for the first time, financial institutions began to implement reasonable measures to ensure that they are not providing financial services to known or suspected terrorists.

Additionally, prior to September 11, 2001, banks were required to file suspicious activity reports (SARs) with the Financial Crimes Enforcement Network (FinCEN), a U.S. Treasury Department agency responsible for enforcing BSA regulations.[21] However, few banks, if any, were monitoring and reporting transactions suspected of being linked to terrorist financing. Furthermore, filing suspicious transactions related to terrorist financing was not a priority for FinCEN. The Treasury agency did not even record or report the number of SARs submitted by financial institutions related to terrorist financing.[22] It was not until after the 9/11 terrorist attacks that FinCEN began to stress the importance of filing terrorist-financing-related SARs.[23] By 2003, financial institutions were regularly reporting such suspicious transactions. Between April 1, 2003, and June 30, 2004, approximately 2,175 SARs were submitted to FinCEN by depository institutions, casinos, money services businesses, and securities broker-dealers, concerning possible terrorist financing.[24] According to FinCEN, approximately 4 percent of the 2,175 SAR filings involved charities suspected of terrorist financing.[25] Further, a total of 334 money services businesses in 42 states filed 1,116 SARs that identified terrorist financing as the category of suspicious activity.[26] Finally, approximately 8 percent of the SARs filed by money services business involved Middle Eastern countries.[27] Since 9/11, a significant shift has taken place in banks and other financial institutions with respect to monitoring financial transactions. Banks are now scrutinizing accounts and transactions for possible links to terrorists and terrorist organizations, making it more difficult for terrorists to move money through the financial sector.

The PATRIOT Act also sought to prevent terrorists from using non-depository institutions to transfer money abroad. The Act expanded the definition of 'financial institutions' covered by the BSA to include persons involved in real estate closings and settlements, insurance companies, dealers in precious metals, stones, or jewels, money services businesses, and other business entities believed to be vulnerable to money laundering and terrorist financing.[28] These financial institutions are required to develop an anti-money laundering program 'to prevent, detect, and prosecute international money laundering and the financing of terrorism.'[29] For example, money services businesses are required to establish an anti-money laundering/counter-terrorist financing program that includes, at a minimum, (i) the development of internal policies, procedures, and controls; (ii) the designation of a compliance officer; (iii) an ongoing employee training program; and (iv) an independent audit function to test the program.[30] Money services businesses are required to file currency transaction reports of transactions in currency of more than $10,000,[31] and to file SARs with respect to any transaction of $2,000 or more that the business knows, suspects, or has reason to suspect involves funds from illegal activity or is designed to conceal their origin, is designed to evade BSA obligations, or has no apparent business or lawful purpose or involves the use of the MSB to facilitate criminal activity, such as terrorism.[32]

The BSA was further amended to require any person who owns or controls a money transmitting business to register the business with the Treasury Department.[33] Failure to register with FinCEN, or submitting false or incomplete information in the registration statement, could result in a civil penalty of $5,000 per day while the violation continues.[34] Congress further enacted 18 U.S.C. §1960, which criminalizes operating a money services business in violation of FinCEN's registration requirement.[35] A violation of section 1960 is punishable by a maximum sentence of five years' imprisonment.[36] As a result of the new registration provision, approximately 39,000 money transmitting businesses have registered with FinCEN.[37] These provisions and other regulations promulgated by Title III of the PATRIOT Act have created a comprehensive regulatory regime to prevent banks and non-depository financial institutions from being abused by terrorists to facilitate the financing of terrorism. The anti-terrorist financing regulatory regime that exists today represents a major improvement over the system that operated before September 11, 2001.

Freezing the Assets of Corrupt Islamic Charities

Following the 9/11 terrorist attacks, the United States and the U.N. Security Council devised a legal framework to freeze the assets of terrorists, terrorist organizations, and individuals and groups associated with them.[38] The legal regime has been particularly effective at preventing corrupt Islamic charities from being used to raise and transfer money to finance terrorist activities. Pursuant to Executive Order 13224, the United States Treasury Department has designated 44 Islamic charities as SDGTs, and the property and interests in property of these charities have been ordered to be frozen.[39] Moreover, U.S. persons are prohibited from doing business with any SDGTs. Approximately 30 of these charitable organizations are suspected of raising money for al Qaeda.[40] Several of these charities were designated as SDGTs for conducting terrorist fund-raising activities in the United States.[41] The names of the al Qaeda-related charities have been submitted to the U.N. Al-Qaida and Taliban Sanctions Committee for inclusion on the U.N. Consolidated List, and countries are required to freeze their assets pursuant to Security Council Resolutions 1267 and 1333.[42] Eight other charities designated by the Treasury Department are believed to be raising money for HAMAS.[43] The remaining five charities included on the Treasury list have been linked to fund-raising for Hizballah, the Palestinian Islamic Jihad, or the Liberation Tigers of Tamil Eelam, entities listed by the U.S. State Department as 'foreign terrorist organizations.'[44] The freeze orders issued by the Treasury Department and the U.N. Al-Qaida and Taliban Sanctions Committee have shut down major pipelines of funding for al Qaeda terrorists. Since September 11, 2001, approximately 500 individuals and entities have been designated by the Treasury Department and the U.N. Sanctions Committee, and roughly $85 million dollars have been frozen under the international sanctions regime.[45]

FAILURES

The Diminishing Relevance of the U.N. Asset Freeze Program

While freezing the assets of suspected terrorists has been a central component of the global counter-terrorism strategy since 9/11, each year fewer and fewer names are being submitted by States for inclusion on the U.N. Consolidated List.[46] In 2007, only eight names were added to the Consolidated List, the lowest annual rate ever, continuing a downward trend.[47] In 2001 there were 278 listings; 2002 – 54; 2003 – 77; 2004 – 44; 2005 – 32; 2006 – 24; and 2007 – 8.[48] The Treasury Department has contributed to the decline of the asset freeze program. In 2001, Treasury designated 164 individuals and entities as SDGTs; 2002 – 87; 2003 – 94; 2004 – 51; 2005 – 30; 2006 – 42; and 2007 – 20.[49] Of the 20 names placed on the OFAC list in 2007, only 11 were submitted for inclusion on the U.N. Consolidated List.[50]

Further, several prominent leaders of al Qaeda and the Taliban have not been listed.[51] For example, neither Baitullah Mehsud, the militant leader of the Taliban in Pakistan, nor Hamza al-Dayan or Nasir al-Wahayshi, senior al Qaeda leaders in Yemen, has been included on the Consolidated List.[52] Hamza al-Dayan is allegedly responsible for a terrorist attack against the U.S. embassy in Yemen, and the resurgence of al Qaeda in Yemen is attributed to al-Wahayshi.[53] Further, Mohammed Hamid ('Osama bin London'), an al Qaeda sympathizer who recruited and trained terrorists in

London, and Abu Hamza al-Masri, a radical Islamic cleric who preached violent jihad at the Finsbury Park Mosque in North London, have been convicted on terrorism charges, but neither individual appears on the Consolidated List.[54] Moreover, in March 2008, the State Department designated the military wing of a Somali Islamic militant group, al-Shabab ('the Youth'), and a Bangladeshi Islamist group, Harkat-ul-Jihad al Islami, as foreign terrorist organizations (FTOs).[55] The designations require U.S. financial institutions to freeze any assets held by the groups in the United States and make it illegal for people subject to U.S. jurisdiction to provide material support or resources to them.[56] However, al-Shabab's leader, Aden Hashi Ayro, and Harkat-ul-Jihad al Islami's senior leaders, Mufti Hannan and Mufti Abu Zandal, have not been added to either the Treasury Department or the U.N. terror lists.

The U.N. sanctions program suffers from another serious deficiency. Even when names are submitted for designation, States are not freezing terrorist-related assets. In fact, the cumulative amount of frozen assets has been declining over the last few years. In 2007, approximately $85 million remained frozen under the U.N. sanctions regime, down from a previous high of $91.4 million in 2006.[57] Thus, according to every objective measurement, the international economic sanctions program is failing. Unless significant measures are undertaken to improve compliance with U.N. Security Council resolutions requiring States to freeze terrorist-related funds 'without delay,' the U.N. economic sanctions program will cease to be relevant in the global struggle against terrorism.

Criminal Prosecution Failures

The U.S. Department of Justice has failed to successfully prosecute networks of deep-pocket donors and financial facilitators responsible for financing al Qaeda, HAMAS, and affiliated terrorist organizations. One of the most disappointing legal setbacks involves the criminal prosecution of the Holy Land Foundation for Relief and Development (HLF), a purported Muslim charity based in Richardson, Texas, and five former HLF officials. In November 2005, HLF and five other defendants were charged in a 42-count superseding indictment, accusing them of fund-raising for HAMAS.[58] A superseding indictment alleged multiple criminal violations, including: conspiracy to provide material support or resources to HAMAS, a designated foreign terrorist organization (18 U.S.C. §2339B(a)(1)); conspiracy to provide funds, goods and services to a specially designated terrorist (50 U.S.C. §§1701–6); conspiracy to commit money laundering (18 U.S.C. §1956(h)); conspiracy to impede and impair the IRS and to file false tax returns for a tax-exempt organization (18 U.S.C. §371); and filing false tax returns for a tax-exempt organization (26 U.S.C. §7206(1)).[59] However, in October 2007, after a two-month jury trial, the jury failed to return a guilty verdict on a single criminal count. The jury acquitted one defendant on all but one charge, on which it deadlocked, and failed to reach a unanimous verdict on any of the remaining criminal counts, resulting in a hung jury.[60] Ultimately, the judge declared a mistrial on what was widely hailed as the government's flagship terrorism financing case.[61]

The Department of Justice suffered another embarrassing legal defeat in the Sami Al-Arian case. In 2003, Al-Arian, a former engineering professor at the University of South Florida, and seven other defendants were charged by a federal grand jury with operating and directing the fund-raising activities of the Palestinian Islamic Jihad-Shiqaqi Faction (PIJ) in the United States.[62] Al-Arian was accused of heading a cell of the PIJ, and serving as the Secretary of the Shura Council, the worldwide governing body of the PIJ.[63] The indictment included 53 counts, alleging racketeering conspiracy, detailing 323 overt acts; conspiracy to provide material support to the PIJ; money laundering; conspiracy to murder persons abroad; and other related offenses.[64]

After a six-month trial, the jury failed to convict the defendants on any of the 53 counts. Al-Arian was acquitted on 8 of 17 counts, while the jury deadlocked on the other nine charges against him.[65] The jury failed to reach a verdict on three of the four most serious charges against Al-Arian and co-defendant Hatem Naji Fariz – the RICO conspiracy, conspiracy to provide material support, and conspiracy to violate IEEPA counts. Al-Arian and Fariz were acquitted of the conspiracy to murder persons abroad, Travel Act, material support and money laundering charges.[66] The remaining two defendants were acquitted on all criminal charges.

The Government also failed to convict Muhammad Salah on charges that he was a major conduit for raising and transferring money for HAMAS.[67] Salah was accused of receiving in a Chicago bank account a series of wire transfers totalling approximately $985,000 to be distributed to members of HAMAS in the West Bank and the Gaza Strip.[68] The federal indictment alleged that Salah and co-defendant Ashqar conspired to violate RICO by conducting the affairs of an enterprise through a pattern of racketeering activity that included multiple acts of murder, solicitation of murder, money laundering, providing material support to HAMAS, hostage taking, and travel in aid of racketeering.[69] After a three-month jury trial, both Salah and Ashqar were acquitted of the most serious charge of participating in a RICO conspiracy to provide funding, recruiting and training to HAMAS.[70]

Finally, the Justice Department failed to convict Enaam Arnaout, the executive director of the Benevolence International Foundation (BIF), for providing financial support and other assistance to Osama bin Laden and al Qaeda.[71] The indictment alleged that Arnaout used BIF, a Chicago-based charity, as a front to raise funds from unsuspecting donors to covertly support Osama bin Laden, al Qaeda, and other Islamic terror groups. Specifically, the indictment charged a RICO conspiracy, conspiracy to provide material support to al Qaeda, conspiracy to launder money, money laundering, and mail and wire fraud.[72] However, on the first day of trial the government permitted Arnaout to plead guilty to racketeering conspiracy, admitting that he fraudulently obtained charitable donations and diverted the funds to pay for boots to be used by fighters in Chechnya, and boots, tents, uniforms and other equipment for fighters in Bosnia-Herzegovina.[73] In return, the government dismissed all terrorist financing-related charges that Arnaout provided financial aid to al Qaeda and other terrorist groups.[74] In fact, the plea agreement omitted any reference to Osama bin Laden, al Qaeda or providing material support to terrorists.[75] The government's highly publicized terrorist financing case was reduced to defrauding a charity.

RECOMMENDATIONS

1. Strengthening the U.N. Sanctions Regime

The U.N. Security Council sanctions program suffers from two major problems. First, Member States are reluctant or unwilling to submit names for inclusion on the Consolidated List. Second, countries are not freezing the assets of persons and entities whose names appear on the List. The U.N. Sanctions Monitoring Team correctly notes that the 'inconsistent relevance' of the Consolidated List to the current terrorist threat is undermining the effectiveness of the sanctions regime.[76] Various reasons are given for not submitting names for listing, including:

> political, for example, when the people concerned are non-nationals whose listing may seem an intrusion into the affairs of another State; domestic, when listing may appear to stigmatize a particular segment of the community or could be interpreted as a political act against an opposition figure; practical, when the publicity attracted by a listing might jeopardize an investigation; or legal, when a State might fear the consequences of a legal challenge to its application of the measures. States may also hesitate to suggest the listing of their own nationals for fear that this would suggest a particular problem with terrorism.[77]

Whatever the actual reasons, if Member States are unwilling to submit names for inclusion on the Consolidated List, the U.N. economic sanctions regime is guaranteed to fail. In order to salvage the international asset freeze program, the following recommendations are proposed. First, while countries should be encouraged to submit names for listing, the U.N. Sanctions Committee should not rely exclusively on State submissions. The Sanctions Committee must play a more prominent role in the listing process. The Monitoring Team should submit names it believes merit consideration for listing to the Sanctions Committee.[78] The names submitted by the Monitoring Team should be accompanied by a statement of the case, justifying the designation. Additionally, detailed identifier information should be included to assist States in properly identifying the person or entity for asset freeze. Finally, any decision by the U.N. Sanctions Committee to add a name to the List should be by consensus.

Second, the Sanctions Committee should make it a priority to ensure that the names of senior members of al Qaeda, the Taliban, and affiliated terrorist groups are placed on the Consolidated List. For example, the State Department has designated 44 international entities as FTOs. More than 20 of those FTOs are affiliated with al Qaeda. The senior leaders of each of the al Qaeda-related FTOs should be included on the Consolidated List and States should be required to freeze their assets. Their identities are known to law enforcement, the intelligence communities, and counter-terrorism experts. There is simply no excuse for not designating the prominent leaders of al Qaeda, the Taliban and their affiliates. If States are unwilling to submit the names of these individuals for inclusion on the U.N. List, the Sanctions Committee should initiate designation. The credibility and value of the listing process are seriously jeopardized when prominent leaders of al Qaeda-affiliated terrorist organizations are omitted from the U.N. List.

At the same time, increasing the number of names for inclusion on the Consolidated List addresses only half of the problem. Once names are placed on the List, States have a legal duty to freeze 'without delay' the assets of those individuals and entities.[79] Unfortunately, States are not complying with their legal obligations. For example, the U.N. Sanctions Monitoring Team has reported that over 95 percent of the total value of assets frozen under the economic sanctions regime has resulted from the freezing actions of nine States.[80] Further, only 36 States have reported freezing any assets since 9/11.[81] While there were 29 new listings between January 2006 and November 2007, according to the Monitoring Team, freezing actions occurred in relation to only four of the designated individuals and entities.[82] These findings prove that a large majority of States are ignoring their legal obligations under U.N. Security resolutions 1267 and 1333 to freeze the assets of individuals and entities on the Consolidated List. Finally, this evidence highlights the growing lack of international cooperation to deprive al Qaeda and the Taliban of funding.

The international community should hold States accountable for failure to freeze terrorist-related assets. If the U.N. sanctions regime is going to retain any credibility, the Security Council should consider imposing sanctions on non-compliant States. At a minimum, States that wilfully fail to comply with relevant Security Council resolutions should be identified and included on a list of non-cooperative countries on terrorist financing (NCCTF). The Security Council should adopt a resolution directing the U.N. Sanctions Monitoring Team to identify States that have failed to comply with anti-terrorist financing measures. The names of non-compliant States should be submitted to the Security Council for further action. In identifying such countries, the Monitoring Team should consider whether States have enacted domestic legislation for the identification, detection, and freezing of terrorist-related assets. The Monitoring Team should further examine whether countries have legislation to bring proceedings against persons and financial institutions that violate the duty to freeze terrorist assets 'without delay.'[83] Other important considerations should include whether States have issued blocking orders against individuals and entities placed on the U.N. Consolidated List, and whether assets located within their jurisdiction have been frozen.

Because political considerations will likely prevent the Security Council from agreeing on which countries to include on the NCCTF list, an alternative approach should involve the Financial Action Task Force (FATF) on Money Laundering. FATF could revive the 'name and shame' process for identifying non-cooperative countries or territories (NCCTs) on money laundering.[84] A similar process should be used to monitor whether countries are in compliance with the Nine Special Recommendations on Terrorist Financing.[85] FATF special Recommendation III: Freezing and Confiscating Terrorist Assets requires jurisdictions to implement measures to freeze terrorist-related funds without delay in accordance with relevant Security Council resolutions.[86] Inclusion on the NCCTF list would establish that the listed States are not in compliance with international standards on terrorist financing. Such listing would further support a finding that the State has breached its obligations under relevant anti-terrorist financing Security Council resolutions. Additionally, if the target State is a signatory to the International Convention on the Suppression of the Financing of Terrorism, listing by FATF would be probative of whether the State has breached it duties under the Convention. Such listing could also damage the State's reputation in the international community reflecting negatively on that State's commitment to preventing terrorism. Ultimately, the threat of being listed by FATF as an NCCTF could motivate States to comply with their legal obligations under Resolutions 1267 and 1333.[87]

Finally, the Security Council should ensure that States are holding financial institutions accountable for freezing terrorist assets. Security Council Resolution 1333 calls upon States to bring proceedings and impose appropriate penalties against persons and entities within their jurisdiction that breach their obligation to freeze terrorist-related assets.[88] Ultimately, the effectiveness of the U.N. economic sanctions regime depends on actions taken by financial institutions to freeze terrorist assets. If financial institutions delay in implementing asset freeze orders, terrorist assets will be transferred to avoid sanctions. The Security Council should ensure that States enact and enforce domestic legislation to hold financial institutions accountable for failure to freeze 'without delay' the assets of Osama bin Laden, al Qaeda, the Taliban, and their associates. At present, few countries have imposed penalties against banks for failing to freeze terrorist funds. Since 2001, the U.S. Treasury Department has sanctioned only one financial institution for breaching its legal duties relating to terrorist financing.[89] In sum, for the U.N. economic sanctions regime to be effective, both States and financial institutions must be held accountable for failure to implement measures imposed by Security Council Resolutions 1267 and 1333.

2. Regulating Corrupt Islamic Charities

Corrupt Islamic charities are an important source of funding for militant jihadist groups. The FATF has noted that '[t]he sheer volume of funds and other assets held by the charitable sector means that the diversion of even a very small percentage of these funds to support terrorism constitutes a grave problem.'[90] Charitable organizations designated pursuant to E.O. 13224 and submitted for inclusion on the U.N. Consolidated List are suspected of raising tens of millions of dollars for terrorist organizations.[91] The problem is compounded by the fact that some of these charities have foreign offices in as many as 40 countries throughout the world. It becomes almost impossible to trace the funds after they are transferred abroad and disbursed. To prevent terrorists from abusing charities, States should enact laws and procedures to regulate charities and ensure that adequate controls are in place to audit and monitor the disbursement of charitable funds. Individuals managing charities operating in high-risk countries for terrorism should be held accountable for the disbursement of funds which they know, or should have known, were intended to support al Qaeda or affiliated terrorist organizations.

Further, adequate penalties should be imposed for violations of such practices or procedures. FATF Special Recommendation VIII on Non-Profit Organizations calls on countries to review the adequacy of laws and regulations to prevent charities from being abused for terrorist financing.[92] FATF has offered some general guidance that focuses on: '(1) outreach to the charitable sector; (2) supervision or monitoring of the sector; (3) information gathering and investigation of terrorists and their networks that abuse the charitable sector; and (4) international engagement to protect the sector globally.'[93]

However, a high risk of abuse arises from the lack of transparency and regulated audits, especially for charities that raise money domestically and transfer those funds to their foreign branch offices that operate in countries where there is a strong al Qaeda presence. Regulated audits are needed to account for the flow of funds (1) from donors to charities, (2) from charities to foreign-based humanitarian organizations, and (3) from those groups to the actual projects and persons they claim to fund. Charities that are granted tax-exempt status by the IRS and which transfer funds to support humanitarian projects overseas should be required to file detailed reports accounting for the receipt, transfer and disbursement of funds. At a minimum, the director of the charity should be required to answer the following questions: How much money was collected domestically? How much money was distributed abroad? Who is the foreign-based recipient? What was the purpose of the funding? Were the funds used for the intended purpose? Further, the director of the charity should be required to certify or swear under oath under penalty of perjury as to the accuracy and veracity of the information in reports filed with the government. Finally, any person who knowingly files a material false statement to the IRS in response to these questions should be subject to criminal prosecution.

3. Criminal Enforcement Actions

Despite public statements to the contrary, the lack of major terrorist financing prosecutions and convictions strongly suggests that prosecuting terrorist financing cases is not a priority for the U.S. government.[94] Criminal enforcement actions suffer from two major problems. First, there have been few criminal prosecutions directed at deep-pocket donors and major terrorist financial networks.[95] Second, the few major terrorist financing cases brought by the Department of Justice have resulted in hung juries or acquittals. One possible explanation is that federal prosecutors and criminal investigators may lack the requisite training and expertise to investigate and successfully prosecute the individuals, charities, and front entities bankrolling al Qaeda and the Taliban. Terrorist financing cases are complex and labor intensive, requiring knowledge of the international banking system, including bank regulations, and the use of Islamic charities, hawala, commercial trade, shell corporations, front companies, the

Internet, and bulk cash couriers to transfer funds to terrorist cells located throughout the world. Not every prosecutor or federal investigator possesses the requisite training and experience to follow the terrorist money trail. In response to the dearth of terrorist financing prosecutions, the Department of Justice should establish a Terrorist Financing Section (TFS) within the Criminal Division. Prosecuting terrorist financiers and their financial networks should be the top priority for prosecutors in the TFS. Dedicating a special unit to exclusively prosecuting terrorist financing cases would increase both the quantity and quality of such cases.

The TFS should consist of a core group of federal prosecutors with extensive training and expertise in conducting complex financial investigations and prosecuting financial crimes, such as money laundering, tax fraud, bank fraud, mail and wire fraud, and computer crimes.[96] These terrorist financing prosecutors should be trained on the methods and techniques used by jihadi terrorist organizations to raise, conceal, and transfer funds internationally to finance acts of terrorism. These terrorist financing experts should be knowledgeable on how terrorists use the formal financial sector, commercial trade, alternative remittance systems, including hawala, stored value cards, and cash couriers to transfer money globally for terrorist financing. They should further receive training on the al Qaeda terror network comprised of more than 20 international terror groups and how jihadists use Islamic charities, non-profit organizations, the Internet, and computer websites for terrorist fund-raising.[97] The prosecutors should also be trained in Arabic in order to translate documents written in Arabic and interview witnesses that are Arabic speakers. This group of elite terrorist financing experts could also serve as an important resource to assist federal prosecutors in conducting terrorist financing investigations and prosecutions in the 94 U.S. Attorneys Offices across the country. Finally, a core group of veteran investigators with the IRS Criminal Investigations Division (CID) should be assigned to the TFS. IRS-CID agents have extensive training and experience in following the money trail and conducting complex financial investigations.

Department of Justice attorneys must do a better job of prosecuting terrorist financing cases. Several recommendations are proffered to avoid jury acquittals and hung juries in future terrorist financing prosecutions. First, federal prosecutors must refrain from over-charging terrorist financing cases. For example, in the *Sami Al-Arian* case prosecutors returned a 53-count indictment charging violations of a dozen different federal statutes against multiple defendants.[98] The racketeering conspiracy count alone detailed some 323 overt acts.[99] As a result, the jury trial lasted six months. Additionally, the *Holy Land Foundation* (*HLF*) case involved over 40 counts against HLF and five other defendants. Defendant Ghassan Elashi was charged with 35 counts; Shukri Abu Baker with 34 counts; and Mohammad El-Mezain, Mufid Abdulqader, and Abdulraham Odeh with 32 counts each.[100] However, when prosecuting criminal cases, more is not necessarily better. Returning lengthy and complicated indictments can be counter-productive, running the risk of unduly lengthening the trial and confusing the jury.[101] The *Al-Arian* and *HLF* cases are good examples. Both trials resulted in either acquittals or hung juries on all counts in the indictment. Prosecutors should follow the golden rule – 'keep it simple.' There is no good reason for returning a 50-count indictment. Obtaining a conviction on half a dozen terrorism-related counts will expose the defendant to a lengthy prison term, often resulting in a *de facto* sentence of life imprisonment.

Next, Congress should amend the material support statute, 18 U.S.C. §2339B, to make it explicitly clear that the Government is *not* required to prove that the defendant intended to further the aims of a foreign terrorist organization by the provision of material support or resources. As amended in 2004, §2339B criminalizes the provision of material support or resources if the defendant had knowledge that the organization is a designated foreign terrorist organization or engages or has engaged in acts of terrorism.[102] However, the district court in the *Al-Arian* case interpreted the statute to require proof that the defendant acted with the specific intent to facilitate the terrorist organization's goal and objectives, making it more difficult for prosecutors to convict under the statute.[103] The district court's interpretation of §2339B is inconsistent with the actual text of the statute. Moreover, several other federal courts have addressed the issue, rejecting the argument that §2339B requires proof of specific intent.[104] Nonetheless, Congress should eliminate any confusion created by the district court in *Al-Arian* and expressly state that proof of specific intent to further the criminal objectives of a terrorist organization is not required to convict under §2339B.

Congress should also consolidate 18 U.S.C. §§2339A, B, and C and make it a criminal offense to knowingly provide material support or resources to *any* individual or organization that perpetrates acts of terrorism, not simply a 'foreign terrorist organization.' A person should be convicted of violating the material support statute if he provides financial assistance to any organization or individual with knowledge that such entity or person has engaged or engages in acts of terrorism. At present, §2339B only makes it a crime to provide material support to a designated 'foreign terrorist organization.'[105] If the organization has not been designated as such by the Secretary of State, the defendant must be prosecuted under either §2339A or §2339C. To sustain a conviction for violating §2339A, the government must prove that the defendant provided financial support 'knowing or intending' that the funds would be used to carry out a statutorily enumerated terrorist offense.[106] On the other hand, to support a violation of §2339C, the government must prove that the provision or collection of funds was with the intention or knowledge that such funds would be used to commit a terrorist-related offense specified in the statute. In either case, the government must establish that the defendant had the intent to finance a terrorist attack *or* acted with knowledge that the organization would use the funds to commit acts of terrorism. Providing financial support for some other purpose (not specified in the statute) would not violate either §2339A or §2339C. For example, neither §2339A nor §2339C would punish the provision of financial assistance to the surviving family members of a suicide bomber. In such a case, the defendant did not have the intention or knowledge that the funds were to be used to commit a terrorist offense enumerated in the statute. Moreover, the defendant would not be criminally liable under §2339B if the terrorist organization had not been designated a 'foreign terrorist organization.' However, the defendant's donation arguably aided recruitment of suicide bombers, knowing that their family members would be cared for after their death. In sum, it should be a criminal offense to give money to a terrorist organization, whether designated an FTO or not, with knowledge that the organization has engaged or engages in acts of terrorism.[107] At present, such conduct is not covered by section 2339A, 2339B, or 2339C.

The material support statute should further be amended to explicitly provide that 'willful blindness' is the legal equivalent of knowledge. A person acts with willful blindness when he asserts a lack of guilty knowledge but the evidence supports an inference of deliberate ignorance.[108] A person should not be able to avoid responsibility for providing financial support to a terrorist organization by deliberately ignoring what is obvious. A defendant acts with willful blindness or deliberate ignorance where '"the evidence shows (1) subjective awareness of a high probability of the existence of illegal conduct and (2) purposeful contrivance to avoid learning of the illegal conduct."'[109] For example, under a theory of willful blindness, a defendant could be convicted under the material support statute if he knowingly provides funds to a Muslim charity with awareness of a high probability that the charity's funds will be used to support the activities of a terrorist organization but deliberately closes his eyes to that fact.

The material support statute should also be amended to criminalize the provision of financial support when the defendant acts with a reckless state of mind. The Model Penal Code provides that '[a] person acts recklessly with respect to a material element of an offense when he consciously disregards a substantial and unjustifiable risk that the material element exists or will result from his conduct.'[110] A person would violate §2339B if he provided or collected funds and consciously disregarded a substantial and unjustifiable risk that such funds were to be used by an organization that has engaged or engages in acts of terrorism. Thus, for example, a defendant would be guilty of violating the material support statute if he provided money to a non-profit organization that publicly supports HAMAS and advocates the killing of innocent civilians in the Palestinian Territories. In such a case, the defendant acted recklessly by providing funds to a so-called charitable entity and disregarding a substantial and unjustifiable risk that the group would forward funds to HAMAS or an affiliated group that engages in terrorist killings.

Finally, the IEEPA statute, 50 U.S.C. §1705(c) should be amended to punish individuals who knowingly engage in financial transactions with persons and organizations determined by the President to be a threat to the national security, foreign policy, or economy of the United States.[111] At present, §1705(c) makes it unlawful to 'willfully' violate an order or regulation issued pursuant to IEEPA. Moreover, the statute has been interpreted to require proof that the defendant acted with knowledge of IEEPA, the Executive Order, or regulation issued thereunder, and *intended* to further the illegal activities of the person or entity subject to the IEEPA sanctions.[112] The statute should be amended, consistent with 18 U.S.C. §2339B, to make it a crime to engage in a financial transaction with a person or entity with knowledge that such person or entity is the subject of IEEPA sanctions or engages or has engaged in activities that threaten the national security, foreign policy, or economy of the United States.

4. Regulatory Measures to Prevent Terrorists from Abusing the International Financial System

The Treasury Department has failed to fully utilize its authorities under section 311 of the USA PATRIOT Act against a foreign jurisdiction, foreign financial institution, or type of account or transaction that poses a serious terrorist financing concern.[113] Section 311 enables the Department of the Treasury to impose any one or combination of a range of special measures that U.S. financial institutions must take to protect against money laundering risks associated with the designated target.[114] While section 311 has been used to designate Nauru, Ukraine, Burma, and numerous foreign banks, including Asia Wealth Bank, Banco Delta Asia, First Merchant Bank OSH Ltd., Info Bank, Multibanka, and Myanmar Mayflower Bank, as being a 'primary money laundering concern' (PMLC), the special measure provision has been used only once in a terrorist financing context.[115] In May 2004, the Treasury Department designated the Commercial Bank of Syria (CBS) a primary money laundering concern, finding that the CBS had been used to facilitate the financing of terrorism.[116] However, during the six and a-half years since the enactment of section 311, the U.S. government has been reluctant to use this extraordinarily powerful tool against problematic foreign jurisdictions and other financial institutions suspected of providing financial support and assistance to terrorist organizations.

One possible explanation is that the section 311, codified at 31 U.S.C. §5318A, is tilted towards preventing money laundering, rather than terrorist financing. For example, the seven jurisdictional factors to be considered in determining whether a foreign jurisdiction should be designated a 'primary money laundering concern' involve threats principally related to money laundering. Such factors include whether the jurisdiction offers bank secrecy advantages to nonresidents, the substance and quality of the anti-money laundering laws of the jurisdiction, whether the jurisdiction is characterized as an offshore banking or money laundering haven, and the extent to which the jurisdiction is characterized by high levels of government corruption.[117] These factors are more relevant to protecting against money laundering, than terrorist financing. Likewise, determining whether a foreign financial institution should be designated a PMLC requires considerations of three factors: (1) the extent to which the foreign financial institution is used to facilitate or promote money laundering; (2) the extent to which such institution is used for legitimate business purposes in the jurisdiction; and (3) the extent to which designation as a PMLC is sufficient to guard against international money laundering and other financial crimes. These statutorily enumerated factors also focus more on threats of money laundering than terrorist financing.

Congress should amend section 311 of the USA PATRIOT Act to authorize designation of a foreign jurisdiction, or foreign financial institution, account or type of transaction as a 'primary terrorist financing concern' (PTFC). In determining whether a foreign jurisdiction poses a PTFC, Treasury Department officials should consider the extent to which the foreign country is in compliance with the Nine Special Recommendations on Terrorist Financing adopted and promoted by FATF.[118] For example, does the foreign jurisdiction criminalize the financing of terrorism?[119] Does it punish bulk cash smuggling?[120] Has the foreign country enacted domestic legislation to freeze 'without delay' funds of suspected terrorists?[121] Is the foreign jurisdiction a party to the International Convention on the Suppression of the Financing of Terrorism?[122] Is the foreign jurisdiction in compliance with U.N. Security Council Resolutions 1267 and 1333?[123] A country that violates the international standards on terrorist financing poses a terrorist financing threat. For example, the Director of National Intelligence has stated that Saudi Arabia remains a major 'source of recruits and finances for Iraq and Levant-based militants and Saudi extremists.'[124] While the Saudis have taken some significant steps to reduce the flow of funds to jihadists, 'the Kingdom remains the single most important source for terror financing in general, and for the abuse of charities in particular.'[125] In sum, a compelling argument can be made that Saudi Arabia is a primary terrorist financing concern and should be subject to the types of sanctions authorized under section 311.

Finally, banks should be designated as PTFCs for failure to comply with BSA regulations and international standards intended to prevent the financing of terrorism. Factors relevant to whether a foreign financial institution constitutes a PTFC include whether such financial institution reports suspicious transactions related to terrorism, requires complete originator information (name, address, and account number) on wire funds transfers, and freezes 'without delay' the funds of individuals and entities included on the U.N. Consolidated List.[126]

The Treasury Department's duty to safeguard the financial system from abuse by terrorists has been undermined by its reluctance to hold financial institutions accountable for violations of the Bank Secrecy Act (BSA) related to terrorist financing. Since passage of the USA PATRIOT Act in 2001, the Financial Crimes Enforcement Network (FinCEN) has imposed a civil monetary penalty for violations of the BSA related to terrorist financing in only one instance. In 2004, FinCEN imposed a $24 million civil penalty against Arab Bank's New York branch for failure to report suspicious transactions linked to Palestinian terrorist groups.[127] FinCEN and the federal financial regulators need to be more active in holding banks accountable for non-compliance with BSA anti-terrorist financing regulations.

5. Designating a Director of Counter-Terrorist Financing

The President should designate a Director of Counter-Terrorist Financing (CTF) to be in charge of combating terrorist financing.[128] It is common knowledge that counter-terrorist financing efforts have been hampered by government agency turf battles and lack of coordination. The FBI and the Treasury Department engaged in a bitter dispute over the creation of the Treasury-led task force known as 'Operation Green Quest.'[129] In October 2001, the Treasury Department established an inter-agency task force dedicated to identifying and disrupting terrorist financing operations within the United States and abroad. Operation Green Quest was led by the U.S. Customs Service, but included other federal law enforcement agencies such as the FBI, Internal Revenue Service, U.S. Secret Service, Drug Enforcement Administration, Financial Crimes Enforcement Network, U.S. Postal Service, and Office of Foreign Assets Control.[130] In its first year and a half, the task force opened 2,000 terrorist financing cases, resulting in 79 arrests, 70 indictments, and seizures of $33 million.[131] Despite its success, the FBI maintained that it should be in charge of all terrorist financing investigations and the Treasury Department should pursue terrorist financing cases through participation in the FBI's joint terrorism task forces (JTTFs) or outside of the JTTFs with only the FBI's express approval.[132] In other words, Treasury Department law enforcement agencies should conduct terrorist financing investigations only when directed to do so by the FBI. Ultimately, the FBI prevailed on the matter and Operation Green Quest was dismantled.[133]

Lack of coordination and agency in-fighting have also plagued the Treasury's work with the State Department. A 2006 report by the General Accounting Office (GAO) found that '[t]he U.S. government lacks an integrated strategy to coordinate the delivery of counter-terrorism financing training and technical assistance to countries vulnerable to terrorist financing.'[134] The GAO concluded that lack of a strategic plan with accepted roles and responsibilities has contributed to inter-agency squabbling between the Treasury and State Departments over which agency should retain leadership for the delivery of training and technical assistance to countries abroad.[135]

Agency in-fighting and lack of coordination could be reduced by the appointment of a Director of CTF, designated by the President. The Director of CTF would report to the President through either the national security adviser or the Secretary of Homeland Security.[136] This new director would be responsible for developing, publishing and implementing a national terrorist financing strategy. No such strategy exists today. Additionally, the Director of CTF would be responsible for directing and coordinating the day-to-day activities of the 19 federal government agencies involved in preventing and suppressing the financing of terrorism.

Congress must also increase its oversight responsibilities with respect to preventing the financing of terrorism. At a minimum, the relevant congressional committees should designate a member of their staff to monitor terrorist financing criminal cases and OFAC designations for asset freeze, and propose legislative changes to enhance anti-terrorist financing efforts. Finally, the U.S. government must develop a comprehensive strategy to deal with the funding of the Taliban and al Qaeda with illicit proceeds derived from the lucrative Afghan opium trade.

In sum, despite declarations to the contrary, counter-terrorist financing is not a major U.S. government priority in the global war on terror. As a result, U.S. efforts to curtail the financing of terrorism have achieved mixed results. Moreover, while the United States and the international community have taken some important steps to combat terror financing, progress has stalled. Further, the commitment of the international community to stemming the flow of terrorist funds is receding. Regrettably, al Qaeda, the

Taliban, HAMAS, Hizballah, and affiliated terrorist groups retain the financial means to continue to wage a jihad against the United States, the West, and moderate Muslim governments perceived as the enemies of Islam. To effectively confront the global threat posed by the jihadists, the legal response to the financing of terror must be re-examined and enhanced. The current legal framework suffers from multiple deficiencies, including the lack of enforcement of existing legal tools against jurisdictions, financial institutions, other entities, and individuals that violate these legal norms and obligations. Although instituting a new legal framework, the U.S. and the international community must realize that terrorist financing presents a unique threat. As such, it requires resources and expertise to tailor the fight to this distinct threat. The battle against terrorist financing must be a top priority in order to prevail in the larger struggle against global terrorism. Unfortunately, preventing the financing of terrorism is not.

NOTES

1. The National Commission on Terrorist Attacks, The 9/11 Commission Report: Final Report of the National Commission on Terrorist Attacks Upon the United States 382 (W.W. Norton & Company 2004), *available at* http://www.9-11commission.gov/report/911Report.pdf.
2. Hearing of the Senate Finance Committee on *Anti-Terrorism Financing: Progress Made and Challenges Ahead* (statement of Senator Charles Grassley quoting Victor D. Comras, former State Department and United Nations terrorism finance official) (Apr. 1, 2008).
3. *See* Annual Threat Assessment of the Director of National Intelligence for the Senate Select Committee on Intelligence, at 7 (Feb. 5, 2008) [hereinafter *2008 DNI National Threat Assessment*].
4. *Id.* at 6.
5. *Id.*
6. *See* Andrew Black, *The Reconstructed Al-Qaeda Threat in the Maghreb*, 5 Terrorism Monitor (Feb. 1, 2007), *available at* http://www.jamestown.org/terrorism/news/article.php?articleid=2370242; *see also* Craig Whitlock, *Al-Qaeda's Far-Reaching New Partner*, Wash. Post, Oct. 5, 2006, *available at* http://www.washingtonpost.com/wp-dyn/content/article/2006/10/04/AR2006100402006_pf.html.
7. *See* Katrin Bennhold & Craig S. Smith, *Twin Bombs Kill Dozens in Algiers*, N.Y. Times (Dec. 12, 2007) *available at* http://www.nytimes.com/2007/12/12/world/africa/12algiers.html?; *see also Maghreb Al Qaeda Deputy Killed in Algeria*, Reuters, Oct. 9, 2007, *available at* http://www.nytimes.com/reuters/world/international-algeria-qaeda.htm; John Thorne, *Bombings May Signal New Algeria Violence*, Wash. Post, Feb. 15, 2007.
8. U.N. Security Council, Analytical Support and Sanctions Monitoring Team, Seventh Report of the Analytical Support and Sanctions Monitoring Team, ¶17, U.N. Doc. S/2007/677 (Nov. 29, 2007), *available at* http://www.un.org/sc/committees/1267/monitoringteam.shtml [hereinafter Seventh Report of the U.N. Sanctions Monitoring Team].
9. *See* Afghanistan Opium Survey 2007, U.N. Office on Drugs and Crime (Oct 2007), *available at* http://www.unodc.org/pdf/research/Afghanistan_Opium_Survey_2007.pdf [hereinafter *Afghan Opium Survey 2007*].

10. *Id.*
11. *Id.*
12. *Id.*; *see also 2008 DNI National Threat Assessment*, *supra* note 3, at 18; SEVENTH REPORT OF THE U.N. SANCTIONS MONITORING TEAM, *supra* note 8, at ¶21.
13. *See* Carrie Johnson & Walter Pincus, *Few Clear Wins in U.S. Anti-Terrorism Cases*, WASH. POST, A01, Apr. 21, 2008, *available at* http://www.washingtonpost.com/wp-dyn/content/article/2008/04/20/AR2008042002227.html.
14. *See* SEVENTH REPORT OF THE U.N. SANCTIONS MONITORING TEAM, *supra* note 8, at ¶25.
15. *Id.* at ¶58 ('[O]ver 95 per cent of the total value of assets reported frozen results from the freezing action of nine States').
16. *See* OFAC List of Specially Designated Global Terrorists, U.S. Dep't of Treasury Office of Foreign Assets Control, What You Need to Know About U.S. Sanctions, *available at* http://www.treas.gov/offices/enforcement/ofac/programs/terror/terror.pdf [hereinafter OFAC List]; *see also* The Al-Qaida and Taliban Sanctions Committee, The Consolidated List of the United Nations Security Council's Al-Qaida and Taliban Sanctions Committee, *available at* http://www.un.org/sc/committees/1267/consolist.shtml (last visited Apr. 15, 2008) [hereinafter Consolidated List].
17. *See* OFAC List, *supra* note 16.
18. Uniting and Strengthening America by Providing Appropriate Tools Required to Intercept and Obstruct Terrorism (USA PATRIOT) Act of 2001, Pub. L. No. 107-56, 115 Stat. 272 (codified in scattered sections of the U.S.C.).
19. Title III of the USA PATRIOT Act amends the anti-money laundering provisions of the BSA, codified at 12 U.S.C. §1829b, 12 U.S.C. §§1951–9, and 31 U.S.C. §§ 5311–14, 5316–32.
20. 31 U.S.C. §5318(l)(2) (2000 & Supp. IV 2004).
21. Pursuant to the BSA, financial institutions are required to file SARs if the financial institution knows, suspects, or has reason to suspect that the transaction: '(i) involves funds derived from illegal activities or is intended or conducted in order to hide or disguise funds or assets derived from illegal activities . . . ; (ii) [t]he transaction is designed to evade any . . . regulations promulgated under the Bank Secrecy Act . . .; or (iii) [t]he transaction has no business or apparent lawful purpose or is not the sort in which the particular customer would normally be expected to engage, and the [financial institution] knows of no reasonable explanation for the transaction after examining the available facts, including the background and possible purpose of the transaction.' 31 C.F.R. §103.18.
22. *See* FinCEN, 1st Review of the Suspicious Activity Reporting System (SARS) (Apr. 1998), *available at* http://www.fincen.gov/sarptfin.html.
23. *See* The SAR Activity Review, Issue 4, 17 (Aug. 2002), *available at* http://www.fincen.gov/sarreview082002.pdf; *see also* The SAR Activity Review, Issue 5, 19–21, *available at* http://www.fincen.gov/sarreviewissue5.pdf; The SAR Activity Review, Issue 6, 3, *available at* http://www.fincen.gov/sarreviewissue6.pdf.
24. *See* SAR Activity Review, Issue 8, at 5 (April 2005), *available at* http://www.fincen.gov/sarreviewissue8.pdf.
25. *Id.* at 6.
26. *Id.* at 8.
27. *Id.* at 11.
28. Section 352(a) of the PATRIOT Act, which became effective on April 24, 2002, amended 31 U.S.C.A. §5318(h) (West 2008) of the BSA. As amended, §5318(h)(1) requires every 'financial institution' to establish an anti-money laundering program. Section 5312(a)(1), as amended, defines 'financial institution' to include a broker or dealer in securities, an insurance company, dealer in precious metals, stones, or jewels, persons involved in real estate closings, and other non-depository financial institutions. *See* 31 U.S.C. §5312(a)(1) (2000 & Supp. IV 2004). Further, §5312(a)(1)(R) defines 'financial institution' to include 'a licensed sender of money or any other person who engages as a business . . . in an informal money transfer system or any network of people who engage as a business in facilitating the transfer of money domestically or

internationally outside of the conventional financial institutions system.' *See id.* §5312(a)(1)(R).

29. Financial Crimes Enforcement Network, Anti-Money Program Requirements for 'Persons Involved in Real Estate Closings and Settlements,' Advanced Notice of Proposed Rulemaking, 68 Fed. Reg. 17569 (Apr. 10, 2003).
30. 31 C.F.R. §103.125 (Apr. 24, 2002); *see also* Financial Crimes Enforcement Network, Interpretive Release 2004-1, Anti-Money Laundering Program Requirements for Money Services Businesses with Respect to Foreign Agents or Foreign Counterparties, 69 Fed. Reg. 74439 (Dec. 14, 2004).
31. 31 C.F.R. §103.22.
32. 31 C.F.R. §103.20(a) (requirement for MSBs, other than check cashiers and issuers, sellers or redeemers of stored value to file SARs).
33. 31 U.S.C. §5330(a)(1) (2000 & Supp. IV 2004).
34. *Id.* §5330(e).
35. 18 U.S.C.A. §1960 (West 2008).
36. *Id.*
37. *See* U.S. Dep't of Treasury, FinCEN, Money Service Business Registration List, *available at* http://www.msb.gov/pdf/msb_registration_list.pdf.
38. Blocking Property and Prohibiting Transactions with Persons Who Commit, Threaten to Commit, or Support Terrorism, Exec. Order No. 13,224, 3 C.F.R. 786–90 (2001), *reprinted as amended in* 50 U.S.C. §1701 note (Supp. IV 2004) [hereinafter E.O. 13224]; *see also* S.C. Res. 1267, U.N. Doc. S/RES/1267 (1999), S.C. Res. 1333, U.N. Doc. S/RES/1333 (2000).
39. *See* U.S. Dep't of Treasury, Protecting Charitable Organizations, Terrorism and Financial Intelligence, *available at* http://www.treas.gov/offices/enforcement/key-issues/protecting/fto.shtml (last visited Mar. 20, 2008). In June 2008, the Treasury Department designed the Al Haramain Islamic Foundation, including its headquarters in Saudi Arabia. *See* Press Release, U.S. Dep't of Treasury Designates Al Haramain Islamic Foundation (June 19, 2008), *available at* http://www.treasury.gov/press/release/hp1043.htm.
40. *Id.*
41. *Id.* (indicating primary jurisdictions of known operation).
42. *See* Consolidated List, *supra* note 16; *see also* S.C. Res. 1267, U.N. Doc. S/RES/1267 (1999), S.C. Res. 1333, U.N. Doc. S/RES/1333 (2000).
43. *Id.*
44. *Id.* The al Qaeda-related charities include: Makhtab al-Khidamat; Al Rashid Trust; WAFA Humanitarian Organization; Rabita Trust; Umman Tameer E-Nau; Revival of Islamic Heritage Society; Afghan Support Committee; Al Haramain Foundation (13 branches); Aid Organization of the Ulema; Global Relief Foundation; Benevolence International Foundation; Lajnat al Daawa al Islamiya; Al Akhtar Trust; Taibah International; Al Haramain & Al Masjed Al-Aqsa Charity Foundation; Al Furqan; Islamic African Relief Agency; and International Islamic Relief Organization. OFAC List, *supra* note 16.
45. Seventh Report of the U.N. Sanctions Monitoring Team, *supra* note 8, at Annex III; *see also* U.N. Consolidated List, *supra* note 16; OFAC List, *supra* note 16.
46. *See* Seventh Report of the U.N. Sanctions Monitoring Team, *supra* note 8, at ¶25.
47. *Id.*
48. *Id.* at ¶25 n. 37.
49. *See* OFAC List, *supra* note 16.
50. 'Specially Designated Global Terrorists' are not limited to members of al Qaeda and the Taliban, but include suspected members of other terrorist groups such as HAMAS, Hizballah, Palestinian Islamic Jihad, and non-Muslim terrorist organizations such as ETA, the Basque terrorist organization, and the FARC, a terror group operating in Colombia. *Id.*
51. *Id.*; *see also* Seventh Report of the U.N. Sanctions Monitoring Team, *supra* note 8, at ¶25; *see also* U.N. Sec. Council, Analytical Support and Sanctions

MONITORING TEAM, SIXTH REPORT OF THE ANALYTICAL SUPPORT AND SANCTIONS MONITORING TEAM (Mar. 8, 2007), U.N. Doc. S/2007/132, *available at* http://www.un.org/sc/committees/1267/monitoringteam.shtml [hereinafter SIXTH REPORT OF THE SANCTIONS MONITORING TEAM].

52. *See* Kathy Gannon, *New Taliban Chief Entering Limelight*, ASSOC. PRESS, Jan. 26, 2008, *available at* http://ap.google.com/article/ALeqM5i38Cj7htJXGfd40DmfC37DGw778AD8UDNOQO1; *Yemen: Al Qaeda's Resurgence*, STRATFOR (Apr. 22, 2008), *available at* http://www.stratfor.com/analysis/yemen_al_qaedas_resurgence; SIXTH REPORT OF THE U.N. SANCTIONS MONITORING TEAM, *supra* note 51, at ¶8; *see also* Consolidated List, *supra* note 16; Ahmed al-Haj, *Al Qaida Blamed in Failed US Site Attack*, ASSOC. PRESS, Mar. 22, 2008.
53. *See* al-Haj, *supra* note 52; *see also Yemen: Al Qaeda's Resurgence*, *supra* note 52.
54. *See* Don Van Natta, *British Jury Finds Muslim Cleric Guilty of Inciting Murder*, N.Y. TIMES, Feb. 7, 2006, *available at* http://www.nytimes.com/2006/02/07/international/europe/07cnd-cleric; Lucy Bannerman & Sean O'Neill, *Osama bin London, Trainer of 21/7 Plotters, is Convicted*, TIMESONLINE, Feb. 27, 2008, *available at* http://www.timesonline.co.uk/tol/news/uk/crime/article3441588.ece.
55. *See U.S. Designates Somali Group Terrorists*, ASSOC. PRESS, Mar. 18, 2008; *see also U.S. Brands Bangladeshi Islamist Group 'Terrorist,'* REUTERS, Mar. 7, 2008, *available at* http://www.reuters.com/article/latestCrisis/idUSN07285929.
56. *See* E.O. 13224, *supra* note 38, at ¶1(b); *see also* 18 U.S.C. §2339B (2000 & Supp. IV 2004) (criminalizing the provision of material support or resources to a foreign terrorist organization).
57. *See* SEVENTH REPORT OF THE U.N. SANCTIONS MONITORING TEAM, *supra* note 4, at ¶57.
58. United States v. Holy Land Found. for Relief & Dev., Superseding Indictment, No. 3:04-CR-240G (N.D. Tex. 2005).
59. *Id.*
60. United States v. Holy Land Found. for Relief & Dev., Mistrial Order, Case No. 3:04-CR-240, Doc. 872, Oct. 22, 2007. The jury could not reach a unanimous verdict on any count with respect to the defendants Holy Land Foundation for Relief and Development, Shukri Abu Baker, Ghassan Elashi, Mufid Abdulqader, and Abdulrahman Odeh. Additionally, the jury could not reach a unanimous verdict on Count I with respect to Mohammed El-Mezain. The court declared a mistrial with respect to those counts and defendants. *See* United States v. Holy Land Found. for Relief and Dev., No. 3:04-CR-240-G, Order Declaring a Mistrial (Oct. 18, 2007). El-Mezain was found not guilty on counts 2 through 32. *See* United States v. Mohammad El-Mezain, Judgment of Acquittal, No. 3:04-CR-240-G(03) (Oct. 22, 2007).
61. *see also* United States v. Holy Land Found. for Relief and Dev., No. 3:04-CR-240-G, Order Declaring a Mistrial (Oct. 18, 2007).
62. United States v. Al-Arian, et al., No. 8:03-CR-77-T-30TBM (M.D. Fla.); *see also* Press Release, U.S. Dep't of Justice, Members of the Palestinian Islamic Jihad Arrested, Charged with Racketeering and Conspiracy to Provide Support to Terrorists (Feb. 20, 2003), *available at* http://www.usdoj.gov/opa/pr/2003/February/03_crm_099.htm. Eight defendants were charged in the indictment, but only four were arrested and detained. The other four defendants remained fugitives. The original indictment filed on February 12, 2003, included 50 counts. However, additional counts for money laundering and providing material support to a foreign terrorist organization were subsequently added. *See* U.S. Dep't of Justice, *Counterterrorism White Paper*, at 3 (2006), *available at* http://abajournal.com/files/09-2007/DOJcounterterrorismWhitePaper.pdf.
63. *See* Press Release, U.S. Dep't of Justice, Members of the Palestinian Islamic Jihad Arrested, *supra* note 62
64. Superseding Indictment, United States v. Al-Arian, et al., No. 8:03-Cr-77-T-30TBM (M.D. Fla. Nov. 15, 2005).
65. United States v. Al-Arian, No. 8:03-cr-77-T-30TBM, Judgment in a Criminal Case (May 1, 2006) (Al-Arian acquitted on eight counts). *See also* Al-Arian Goes on Hunger Strike, ST PETERSBURG TIMES, March 7, 2008, at 5B.

66. Al-Arian pleaded guilty to one count of conspiring to provide material support for the PIJ, and agreed to deportation to avoid a retrial. He was sentenced to 57 months and given credit for time served. *See* United States v. Al-Arian, No. 8:03-cr-77-T-30TBM, Judgment in a Criminal Case (May 1, 2006).
67. United States v. Marzook, et al., Second Superseding Indictment, No. 1:03-CR-00978 (N.D. Ill. 2004).
68. *Id.*
69. *Id.*
70. *See* Rudolph Bush and Jeff Coen, *Two Found Not Guilty of Supporting Hamas*, CHICAGO TRIBUNE, Feb. 2, 2007. However, Salah and Ashqar were convicted of lesser charges. Salah was convicted of obstruction of justice for lying under oath in a civil lawsuit. Ashqar was found guilty of obstruction of justice and criminal contempt for refusing to testify before a grand jury. *Id.*
71. United States v. Enaam M. Arnaout, Second Superseding Indictment, Case No. 1:02-Cr-00892 (N.D. Ill. 2003).
72. *Id.*
73. Press Release, U.S. Dep't of Justice, Benevolence Director Pleads Guilty to Racketeering Conspiracy and Agrees to Cooperate with the Government (Feb. 10, 2003), *available at* http://www.usdoj.gov/usao/iln/pr/chicago/2003,pr021003_01.pdf; *see also* United States v. Enaam M. Arnaout, Plea Agreement, Case No. 02-CR-892 (N.D. Ill. Feb. 9, 2003).
74. *See* Eric Lichtblau, *February 9–15: International; Plea in Terror Case*, N.Y. TIMES, Feb. 16, 2003, at 2; *see also* Edward Alden, *Charity Guilty of Backing Muslim Fighters: Chicago Fraud Case Justice Department Fails to Secure Al-Qaeda Funding Conviction, Lesser Charges Brought After*, FINANCIAL TIMES, Feb. 12, 2003, at 12.
75. *See* United States v. Enaam M. Arnaout, Plea Agreement, Case No. 02-CR-892 (N.D. Ill. Feb. 9, 2003).
76. SEVENTH REPORT OF THE SANCTIONS MONITORING TEAM, *supra* note 8, ¶25.
77. *Id.* at ¶26.
78. *Id.* at ¶27 (recommending that the Monitoring Team submit names to the Sanctions Committee to update the Consolidated List).
79. S.C. Res. 1333, art. 8(c), U.N. Doc. S/RES/1333 (2000).
80. *See* SEVENTH REPORT OF THE U.N. SANCTIONS MONITORING TEAM, *supra* note 8, at ¶58.
81. *Id.* at ¶57.
82. *Id.* at ¶59.
83. S.C. Res. 1333, art. 8(c), 18, U.N. Doc. S/RES/1333 (2000); *see also* International Convention for the Suppression of the Financing of Terrorism, Dec. 9, 1999, S. Treaty Doc. No. 106-49, art. 8, 2178 U.N.T.S. 229, *available at* http://untreaty.un.org/ENGLISH/bible/englishinternetbible/partI/chapterXVIII/treaty12.asp [hereinafter Terrorist Financing Convention].
84. For an explanation of the process for identifying and evaluating non-cooperative countries or territories (NCCT), see Financial Action Task Force (FATF), Annual Review of Non-Cooperative Countries and Territories 2006–2007: Eighth NCCT Review (Oct. 12, 2007), *available at* http://www.oecd.org/dataoecd/14/11/39552632.pdf.
85. *See* Financial Action Task Force (FATF), 9 Special Recommendations (SR) on Terrorist Financing (TF) (last visited Apr. 14, 2008), *available at* http://www.fatf-gafi.org/pages/0,2987,en_32250379_32235720_1_1_1_1_1,00.html [hereinafter Nine Special Recommendations on Terrorist Financing].
86. *Id.*
87. *See* TERRORIST FINANCING, REPORT OF AN INDEPENDENT TASK FORCE SPONSORED BY THE COUNCIL ON FOREIGN RELATIONS 28 (2002) [hereinafter 2002 REPORT BY THE COUNCIL ON FOREIGN RELATIONS]. The Council on Foreign Relations has made a similar recommendation, proposing '[m]aking formal recommendations to the FATF concerning which countries should be included in its "naming and shaming" process on the basis of passive acquiescence to terrorist financing.' *Id.*
88. *See* S.C. Res. 1333, art. 8, 18, U.N. Doc. S/RES/1333 (2000).

89. *See* Assessment of Civil Money Penalty, In the Matter of The Federal Branch of Arab Bank PLC, New York, New York, No. 2005-2, U.S. Dep't of Treasury, Financial Crimes Enforcement Network (Aug. 17, 2005) (imposing a $24 million civil money penalty for violating provisions of the Bank Secrecy Act involving persons and entities acting on behalf of HAMAS).
90. FINANCIAL ACTION TASK FORCE (FATF), REPORT ON TERRORIST FINANCING 25 (Feb. 29, 2008), *available at* http://www.fatf-gafi.org/dataoecd/28/43/40285899.pdf [hereinafter FATF TERRORIST FINANCING REPORT].
91. *See* discussion *supra* at Chapter 6 on corrupt Islamic charities.
92. *See* Nine Special Recommendations on Terrorist Financing, *supra* note 85. *See also* Interpretative Notes to the Special Recommendations on Terrorist Financing, *available at* http://www.fatf-gafi.org/document/53/0,3343,en_32250379_32236947_34261877_1_1_1_1,00.html.
93. FATF TERRORIST FINANCING REPORT, *supra* note 90, at 28–9; *see also* Interpretative Note to Special Recommendation VIII, ¶6, *supra* note 92.
94. For example, on September 24, 2001, President George W. Bush stated:

> We will direct every resource at our command – every means of diplomacy, every tool of intelligence, every instrument of law enforcement, every financial influence, and every necessary weapon of war – to the disruption and to the defeat of the global terror network . . . We will starve terrorists of funding.

95. *See* discussion *supra* at Chapter 10 – 'The law enforcement response to terrorist financing.'
96. A minimum commitment of 40 to 50 federal prosecutors devoted exclusively to prosecuting terrorist financing cases is needed to direct investigations of the multiple sources of terrorist financing raising millions of dollars annually for al Qaeda and related terrorist organizations.
97. *See* FATF REPORT ON TERRORIST FINANCING, *supra* note 90, at 21–7 (discussing how terrorists move funds).
98. United States v. Al-Arian, et al., Superseding Indictment, No. 8:03-Cr-77-T-30TBM (M.D. Fla. Nov. 15, 2005).
99. *Id.*
100. United States v. Holy Land Found. for Relief & Dev., Superseding Indictment, No. 3:04-CR-240G (N.D. Tex. 2005).
101. *See* United States v. Casamento, 887 F.2d 1141 (2d Cir. 1989) (establishing specific guidelines for simplifying prosecution of complex criminal cases).
102. 18 U.S.C. §2339B.
103. United States v. Al-Arian, 308 F. Supp. 2d 1322, 1340 (M.D. Fla. 2004), *reconsideration denied*, 329 F. Supp. 2d 1294.
104. *See, e.g.*, United States v. Hammoud, 381 F.3d 316, 328 (4th Cir. 2004); United States v. Assi, 414 F. Supp. 2d 707, 723–4 (E.D. Mich. 2006); United States v. Paracha, Case No. 03 CR 1197 (SHS), 2006 WL 12768 at * 25 (S.D.N.Y Jan. 3, 2006); Linde v. Arab Bank, 384 F. Supp. 2d 571, 587 & n. 11 (E.D.N.Y. 2005); United States v. Marzook, 383 F. Supp. 2d 1056, 1070 (N.D. Ill. 2005); Humanitarian Law Project v. Gonzales, 380 F. Supp. 2d 1134, 1147 & n. 15 (C.D. Cal. 2005).
105. 18 U.S.C. §2339B (2000 & Supp. IV 2004).
106. 18 U.S.C.A. §2339A (West 2008).
107. *See* 18 U.S.C. §2331 defining 'international terrorism.'
108. United States v. Florez, 368 F.3d 1042, 1044–5 (8th Cir. 2004); *see also* JOSHUA DRESSLER, UNDERSTANDING CRIMINAL LAW 136–7 (LexisNexis 2006) (4th edn) (discussing the wilful blindness doctrine).
109. United States v. Saucedo-Munoz, 307 F.3d 344, 348 (5th Cir. 2002) (quoting United States v. Threadgill, 172 F.3d 357, 368 (5th Cir. 1999) (citation omitted)).
110. Model Penal Code §2.02(2)(c).
111. 50 U.S.C.A. §1705(c) (West 2008).

112. *See* United States v. Al-Arian, 308 F. Supp. 2d 1322, 1340 (M.D. Fla. 2004).
113. Uniting and Strengthening America by Providing Appropriate Tools Required to Intercept and Obstruct Terrorism (USA PATRIOT) Act of 2001, Pub. L. No. 107-56, Title III, §371(c), 115 Stat. 272 (codified in scattered sections of the U.S.C.). Section 311 is codified at 31 U.S.C.A. §5318A (West 2008).
114. 31 U.S.C.A. §5318A(b)(1)-(5) (West 2008).
115. *See* U.S. Dep't of Treasury, FinCEN, Section 311 – Special Measures, *available at* http://www.fincen.gov/reg_section311.html; *see also* UPDATE ON THE GLOBAL CAMPAIGN AGAINST TERRORIST FINANCING, SECOND REPORT OF AN INDEPENDENT TASK FORCE ON TERRORIST FINANCING SPONSORED BY THE COUNCIL ON FOREIGN RELATIONS 25 (June 15, 2004) [hereinafter SECOND REPORT BY THE COUNCIL ON FOREIGN RELATIONS].
116. Imposition of a Special Measure Against Commercial Bank of Syria, Including Its Subsidiary, Syrian Lebanese Commercial Bank, as a Financial Institution of Primary Money Laundering Concern, 69 Fed. Reg. 28098 (Proposed Rule) (May 18, 2004).
117. 31 U.S.C.A. §5318A(b)(1)–(5) (West 2008).
118. Nine Special Recommendations on Terrorist Financing, *supra* note 85.
119. *Id.* Special Recommendation II: Criminalising the Financing of Terrorism.
120. *Id.* Special Recommendation IX: Bulk Cash Smuggling.
121. *Id.* Special Recommendation III: Freezing and Confiscating Terrorist Assets.
122. *Id.* Special Recommendation I: Ratification and Implementation of UN Instruments.
123. *Id.*
124. *2008 DNI National Threat Assessment, supra* note 3, at 27; *see also* Steven Emerson, Testimony before the U.S. Senate Judiciary Committee, Saudi Arabia: Friend or Foe in the War on Terror? 3–5 (Nov. 8, 2005); Josh Meyer, *Saudi Arabia Is Prime Source of Terror Funds U.S. Says*, L.A. TIMES, April 2, 2008, *available at* http://www.latimes.com/news/nationworld/nation/la-na-terror 2apr 02,1,1851447.story; Susan Schmidt, *Spreading Saudi Fundamentalism in U.S.*, WASH. POST, Oct. 2, 2003, *available at* http://www.washingtonpost.com/ac2/wp-dyn/A31402-2003Oct1?language=printer.
125. Matthew Levitt, *Charitable Organizations and Terrorist Financing: A War on Terror Status-Check*, at 5, Washington Institute for Near East Policy (Mar. 19, 2004), *available at* http://www.washingtoninstitute.org/print.php?template=C07&CID=104.
126. *See* Nine Special Recommendations on Terrorist Financing, *supra* note 85, Special Recommendations IV: Reporting Suspicious Transactions Related to Terrorism and VII: Wire Transfers.
127. *See* In the Matter of the Federal Branch of Arab Bank PLC, New York, New York, No. 2005-2 (Aug. 17, 2005).
128. *See* 2002 REPORT BY THE COUNCIL ON FOREIGN RELATIONS, *supra* note 87, at 23 (recommending that the 'president should designate a special assistant to the president for combating terrorist financing [with the] specific mandate to lead U.S. efforts on terrorist financing issues.').
129. *See* Dep't of Homeland Security, Office of Inspector General, Coordination Between FBI and ICE on Investigations on Terrorist Financing, No. OIG-07-55 (July 2007).
130. *Id.* at 4.
131. *Id.* at 4–5.
132. *Id.* at 5.
133. *Id.* at 5–6.
134. *See* TERRORIST FINANCING: BETTER STRATEGIC PLANNING NEEDED TO COORDINATE U.S. EFFORTS TO DELIVER COUNTER-TERRORISM FINANCING TRAINING AND TECHNICAL ASSISTANCE ABROAD, U.S. GOV'T ACCOUNTABILITY OFFICE 14, GAO-06-19 (Oct. 2005).
135. *Id.*
136. *See* 2002 REPORT BY THE COUNCIL ON FOREIGN RELATIONS, *supra* note 87, at 23.

ANNEX: RECOMMENDATIONS TO STRENGTHEN THE LEGAL REGIME TO PREVENT THE FINANCING OF TERRORISM

I. U.N. Economic Sanctions

- Hold Member States accountable for failure to comply with measures imposed by U.N. Security Council Resolutions 1267 and 1333, including the failure to freeze the assets of suspected terrorists and their sympathizers.
- Establish a list of non-cooperative countries on terrorist financing (NCCTF). The names of States failing to comply with measures adopted by the Security Council to prevent terrorist financing should be included on the NCCTF list, which would be administered by the Financial Action Task Force (FATF) on Money Laundering and Terrorist Financing, in close coordination with the U.N. Sanctions Monitoring Team.
- The U.N. Security Council should authorize the Sanctions Monitoring Team to submit names for inclusion on the Consolidated List.
- The names of senior members of al Qaeda, the Taliban and affiliated terrorist groups should be included on the Consolidated List.
- The Security Council should ensure that States are holding financial institutions accountable for freezing terrorist assets 'without delay.'

II. Regulating Corrupt Charities

- States should enact laws to regulate charities and ensure that adequate controls are in place to monitor the disbursement of charitable funds.
- Charities that are granted tax-exempt status should be required to file an annual report with the IRS accounting for the receipt, transfer and disbursement of funds. In such annual reports, charities should disclose how much money was collected during the reporting time period, how much money was distributed abroad, the identity of the foreign-based recipients, the purpose of the funding, and whether the funds were used for the intended purpose. Further, the executive director of the charity should be required to declare under penalty of perjury that the annual report does not contain any material false statements or omissions.

III. Criminal Prosecutions

- Establish a Terrorist Financing Prosecution Section (TFPS) within the Department of Justice, Criminal Division, devoted exclusively to prosecuting terrorist financing cases. The TFPS would target major terrorist financial networks and be responsible for increasing both the number and quality of terrorist financing prosecutions.

- Federal prosecutors should refrain from over-charging terrorist financing cases. Charging 40 or 50 criminal counts under multiple federal criminal statutes runs the risk of confusing the jury, resulting in an acquittal or a hung jury. Prosecutors should follow the golden rule: 'Keep it simple.'
- Congress should amend the material support statutes, 18 U.S.C. §§2339A, 2339B, and 2339C, to punish the provision of material support where the defendant acted with 'willful blindness' or 'deliberate ignorance' that the funds were to be used to finance terrorist activities. Congress should make explicitly clear that proof that the defendant acted with the specific intent to finance a terrorist act is *not* required.
- The material support statutes should further be amended to criminalize the provision of financial support where the defendant acted with a reckless state of mind. A person should be criminally punished for providing or collecting funds and consciously disregarding a substantial and unjustifiable risk that such funds were to be used to finance terrorist activities.
- The IEEPA statute, 50 U.S.C. §1705(c), should be amended to punish individuals who knowingly (not merely, 'willfully') engage in a financial transaction with persons and entities determined by the President to pose a threat to the national security, foreign policy, or economy of the United States.
- Hold the Department of Justice accountable for its failure to successfully prosecute major terrorist financing cases. Congress should increase its oversight role by holding hearings on why the Department of Justice has filed so few terrorist financing cases and why many of the major terrorist cases it has prosecuted have resulted in an acquittal or a hung jury.
- Congressional committees with Department of Justice and Treasury oversight responsibilities should designate a member of their staff to monitor terrorist financing cases and OFAC designations for asset freeze and propose legislative changes to enhance anti-terrorist financing efforts.

IV. Protecting Financial Institutions from Being Used to Facilitate Terrorist Financing

- Section 311 of the USA PATRIOT Act, codified at 31 U.S.C. §5318A, should be amended to authorize the designation of a foreign jurisdiction, foreign financial institution, foreign entity, account or type of transaction as a 'primary terrorist financing concern' (PTFC). The amended statute should provide for the imposition of a wide range of special measures against such PTFCs.
- The Financial Crimes Enforcement Network (FinCEN) and federal regulators should be more vigilant in holding banks accountable for non-compliance with the Bank Secrecy Act regulations intended to prevent terrorist financing.
- Congress should increase its oversight of the Treasury Department's enforcement of Bank Secrecy Act money laundering and terrorist financing regulations.
- Congress should increase its oversight of the Treasury Department's efforts to ensure that banks 'freeze without delay' the assets of individuals and entities designated under E.O. 13224 and placed on the OFAC list. The amount of assets frozen by U.S. banks has continued to decline over the last several years.

V. Civil Causes of Action

- Congress should enact legislation restricting the U.S. government's ability to intervene in civil cases where the government seeks to prevent the enforcement of civil judgments awarded in favor of the victims of terrorism. The government should only be permitted to intervene to prevent the execution of such judgments upon a showing of an extraordinary threat or compelling interest related to U.S. national security, foreign policy or economy.

VI. The Afghan Opium Trade Funding the Taliban

- Develop a comprehensive strategy to combat funding the Taliban with proceeds derived from the Afghan opium trade. Such strategy should include an emphasis on drug enforcement (increased deployment of DEA resources), training the Afghan police in narcotics enforcement and anti-money laundering, and eradication of the opium fields and crop substitution.

VII. Director of Counter-Terrorist Financing

- The President should designate a Director of Counter-Terrorist Financing (DCTF) to be in charge of all activities related to preventing the financing of terrorism. The DCTF should report to the President and be responsible for developing and implementing a national counter-terrorist financing strategy. The DCTF would also be responsible for coordinating U.S. government activities, reducing federal agency turf battles, and ensuring that counter-terrorist financing is a top government priority in the global struggle against terrorism.

Bibliography

BOOKS

KAREN ARMSTRONG, HOLY WAR (Macmillan 1988).
ABDEL BARI ATWAN, THE SECRET HISTORY OF AL QAEDA (University of California Press 2006).
DANIEL BENJAMIN & STEVEN SIMON, THE AGE OF SACRED TERROR (Random House 2002).
PETER L. BERGEN, HOLY WAR, INC.: INSIDE THE SECRET WORLD OF OSAMA BIN LADEN (Simon & Schuster 2002).
PETER L. BERGEN, THE OSAMA BIN LADEN I KNOW (Free Press 2006).
DAVID BUKAY, FROM MUHAMMAD TO BIN LADEN (Transaction Publishers 2007).
JASON BURKE, AL-QAEDA: CASTING A SHADOW OF TERROR (I.B. Tauris 2003).
MICHAEL CHANDLER & ROHAN GUNARATNA, COUNTERING TERRORISM (Reaktion Books Ltd. 2007).
STEVE COLL, GHOST WARS: THE SECRET HISTORY OF THE CIA, AFGHANISTAN, AND BIN LADEN, FROM THE SOVIET INVASION TO SEPTEMBER 10, 2001 (Penguin Books 2004).
STEPHEN DYCUS, WILLIAM C. BANKS & PETER RAVEN-HANSEN, COUNTERTERRORISM LAW (Aspen Press 2007).
STEVEN EMERSON, JIHAD INCORPORATED (Prometheus Books 2006).
JOHN ESPOSITO, UNHOLY WAR (Oxford University Press 2002).
REUVEN FIRESTONE, JIHAD: THE ORIGIN OF HOLY WAR IN ISLAM (Oxford University Press 1999).
WILLIAM C. GILMORE, DIRTY MONEY: THE EVOLUTION OF MONEY LAUNDERING COUNTERMEASURES (Council of Europe Press 1995).
ROHAN GUNARATNA, INSIDE AL QAEDA: GLOBAL NETWORK OF TERROR (Columbia University Press 2002).
JIMMY GURULÉ, COMPLEX CRIMINAL LITIGATION: PROSECUTING DRUG ENTERPRISES AND ORGANIZED CRIME (Lexis Law Publ. 2nd ed. 2000).
SAMUEL P. HUNTINGTON, THE CLASH OF CIVILIZATIONS AND THE REMAKING OF THE WORLD ORDER (Simon & Schuster 1996).
MAJID KHADDURI, WAR AND PEACE IN THE LAW OF ISLAM (Johns Hopkins Press 1955).

BRUCE LAWRENCE (ED.), OSAMA BIN LADEN, MESSAGES TO THE WORLD: THE STATEMENTS OF OSAMA BIN LADEN (James Howarth trans., Verso 2005).

MATTHEW LEVITT, HAMAS: POLITICS, CHARITY, AND TERRORISM IN THE SERVICE OF JIHAD (Yale University Press 2006).

WAYNE MCCORMACK, LEGAL RESPONSES TO TERRORISM (LexisNexis 2005).

ALISTAIR MILLAR & ERIC ROSAND, ALLIED AGAINST TERRORISM (Century Foundation Press 2006).

LORETTA NAPOLEONI, MODERN JIHAD: TRACING THE DOLLARS BEHIND THE TERROR NETWORKS (Pluto Press 2003).

THE NATIONAL COMMISSION ON TERRORIST ATTACKS, THE 9/11 COMMISSION REPORT: FINAL REPORT OF THE NATIONAL COMMISSION ON TERRORIST ATTACKS UPON THE UNITED STATES (W.W. Norton & Company 2004), *available at* http://www.9-11commission.gov/report/911Report.pdf.

JOHN NORTON MOORE (ED.) CIVIL LITIGATION AGAINST TERRORISM (Carolina Academic Press 2004).

RANDALL B. HAMUD (ED.), OSAMA BIN LADEN: AMERICA'S ENEMY IN HIS OWN WORDS (Nadeem Pub. 2005).

WALID PHARES, FUTURE JIHAD: TERRORIST STRATEGIES AGAINST AMERICA (Palgrave MacMillan/St. Martin's Press 2005).

SAYYID QUTB, MILESTONES, *available at* http://majalla.org/books/2005/qutb-milestone.pdf.

ANGEL RABASA, ET AL., BEYOND AL QAEDA: THE GLOBAL JIHADIST MOVEMENT (Rand Corp. 2006).

ANGEL RABASA, ET AL., MONEY IN THE BANK: LESSONS LEARNED FROM PAST COUNTERINSURGENCY (Rand Corp. 2007).

MICHAEL SCHEUER, THROUGH OUR ENEMIES' EYES: OSAMA BIN LADEN, RADICAL ISLAM, AND THE FUTURE OF AMERICA (Brassey's 2002).

MICHAEL SCHEUER, IMPERIAL HUBRIS: WHY THE WEST IS LOSING THE WAR ON TERROR (Potomac Books 2004).

STEPHEN SCHWARTZ, THE TWO FACES OF ISLAM: THE HOUSE OF SA'UD FROM TRADITION TO TERROR (Doubleday 2002).

LAWRENCE WRIGHT, THE LOOMING TOWER: AL-QAEDA AND THE ROAD TO 9/11 (Kopf 2006).

LAW REVIEW AND JOURNAL ARTICLES

Saima Akbar Ahmed, *Global Need for a New Economic Concept: Islamic Economics*, 1 INT'L J. ISLAMIC FIN. SERV. (2000).

Ilias Bantekas, *The International Law of Terrorist Financing*, 97 AM. J. INTL L. (Apr. 2003).

Clinton Bennett & Geros Kunkel, *The Concept of Violence, War, and Jihad in Islam*, 18 DIALOGUE & ALLIANCE (2004).

Jonathan Benthall, *Financial Worship: The Quranic Injunction to Almsgiving*, J. ROYAL ANTHROPOLOGICAL INST. (1999).

Daniel L. Byman, *Al-Qaeda as an Adversary: Do We Understand Our Enemy?*, 56 WORLD POLITICS (2003).

John Calvert, *The World is an Undutiful Boy!: Sayyid Qutb's American Experience*, 11 ISLAM AND CHRISTIAN MUSLIM RELATIONS (2000).

Nina J. Crimm, *High Alert: The Government's War of the Financing of Terrorism and Its Implications for Donors, Domestic Charitable Organizations, and Global Philanthropy*, 45 WM. & MARY L. REV. (2004).

Hartley Dean & Zafar Khan, *Muslim Perspectives on Welfare*, 26 J. SOC. POL'Y (1997).

Matthew Levitt, *Charitable Organizations and Terrorist Financing: A War on Terror Status-Check*, THE WASHINGTON INSTITUTE FOR NEAR EAST POLICY (Mar. 19, 2004), *available at* http://www.washingtoninstitute.org/print.php?template=C07&CID=104.

M.M. Metwally, *Economic Consequences of Applying Islamic Principles in Muslim Societies*, 24 INT'L J. SOC. ECON. (1997).

Ross Q. Panko, *Banking on the USA PATRIOT Act: An Endorsement of the Act's Use of Banks to Combat Terrorist Financing and a Response to Critics*, 122 BANKING L. J. (2005).

Marc Perelman, *Hamas's Banking Handmaidens*, NAT'L J. (March 18, 2006).

James Phillips, *The Evolving Al-Qaeda Threat*, HERITAGE FOUND. (March 17, 2006), *available at* http://www.heritage.org/Research/Homeland Security/hl928.cfm.

Bruce Riedel, *Al Qaeda Strikes Back*, FOREIGN AFFAIRS (May/June 2007), *available at* http://www.foreignaffairs.org/20070501faessay86304/bruce-riedel/al-qaeda-strikes-back.html.

Bruce Riedel & Bilal Y. Saab, *Al Qaeda's Third Front: Saudi Arabia*, 33 WASH. Q. (Spring 2008).

Anne-Marie Slaughter & David L. Bosco, *Alternative Justice*, GLOBAL POLICY FORUM (last visited Jan. 28, 2007) *available at* http://www.globalpolicy.org/intljustice/atca/2001/altjust.htm.

Debra M. Strauss, *Enlisting the U.S. Courts in a New Front: Dismantling the International Business Holdings of Terrorist Groups Though Federal Statutory and Common-Law Suits*, 38 VAND. J. TRANSNAT'L L. (May 2005).

Jean-François Thony, *Money Laundering and Terrorism Financing: An Overview*, *available at* http://www.imf.org/external/np/leg/sem/2002/cdmfl/eng/thony.pdf.

John D.G. Waszak, *The Obstacles to Suppressing Radical Islamic Terrorist Financing*, 36 CASE W. RES. J. INT'L L. (2004).

Quintan Wiktorowicz & Suha Taji Farouki, *Islamic NGOs and Muslim Politics: a Case from Jordan*, 21 THIRD WORLD QUARTERLY (2000).

REPORTS

THE 1267 (AL QAIDA/TALIBAN) COMMITTEE AND THE 1540 (WMD) SANCTIONS COMMITTEE, UPDATE REPORT NO. 5 (Jan. 16, 2006).

CHRISTOPHER M. BLANCHARD, AL QAEDA: STATEMENTS AND EVOLVING IDEOLOGY, CRS REPORT FOR CONGRESS (July 9, 2007).

JEFF BREINHOLT, TERRORIST FINANCING, 51 U.S. ATTORNEYS BULLETIN (July 2003).

BUREAU FOR INTERNATIONAL NARCOTICS AND LAW ENFORCEMENT AFFAIRS, INTERNATIONAL NARCOTICS CONTROL STRATEGY REPORT (Mar. 2006), *available at* http://www.state.gov/p/inl/rls/nrcrpt/2006/vol2/html/62144.htm.

COMMITTEE ON LEGAL AFFAIRS AND HUMAN RIGHTS, COUNCIL OF EUROPE, UNITED NATIONS SECURITY COUNCIL AND EUROPEAN UNION BLACKLISTS (Nov. 16, 2007).

COUNCIL ON FOREIGN RELATIONS, TERRORIST FINANCING: REPORT OF AN INDEPENDENT TASK FORCE SPONSORED BY THE COUNCIL ON FOREIGN RELATIONS (Oct. 2002), *available at* http://www.cfr.org/pdf/Terrorist_Financing_TF.pdf.

COUNCIL ON FOREIGN RELATIONS, UPDATE ON THE GLOBAL CAMPAIGN AGAINST TERRORIST FINANCING, SECOND REPORT OF AN INDEPENDENT TASK FORCE ON TERRORIST FINANCING SPONSORED BY THE COUNCIL ON FOREIGN RELATIONS (June 15, 2004).

FINANCIAL ACTION TASK FORCE, ABOUT THE NON-COOPERATIVE COUNTRIES AND TERRITORIES (NCCT) INITIATIVE (Updated 2008).

FINANCIAL ACTION TASK FORCE, ANNUAL REVIEW OF NON-COOPERATIVE COUNTRIES AND TERRITORIES 2006–2007: EIGHTH NCCT REVIEW (Oct. 12, 2007).

FINANCIAL ACTION TASK FORCE, COMBATING THE ABUSE OF ALTERNATIVE REMITTANCE SYSTEMS: INTERNATIONAL BEST PRACTICES (June 20, 2003), *available at* http://www.fatf-gafi.org/dataoecd/32/15/34255005.pdf.

FINANCIAL ACTION TASK FORCE, DETECTING AND PREVENTING THE CROSS-BORDER TRANSPORTATION OF CASH BY TERRORISTS AND OTHER CRIMINALS, INTERNATIONAL BEST PRACTICES (Feb. 12, 2005), *available at* http://www.fatf-gafi.org/dataoecd/50/63/34424128.pdf.

FINANCIAL ACTION TASK FORCE, FATF MEMBERS AND OBSERVERS (Updated 2008), *available at* http://www.fatf-gafi.org/document/52/0,3343,en_32250379_32237295_34027188_1_1_1_1,00.html.

FINANCIAL ACTION TASK FORCE, THE INTERPRETATIVE NOTES TO THE SPECIAL RECOMMENDATIONS (SR) ON TERRORIST FINANCING (TF) (Oct. 3, 2003).

FINANCIAL ACTION TASK FORCE, NINE SPECIAL RECOMMENDATIONS (SR) ON TERRORIST FINANCING (TF) (Oct. 22, 2004), *available at* http://www.fatf-gafi.org/document/9/0,3343,en_32250379_32234920_34032073_1_1_1_1,00.html.

FINANCIAL ACTION TASK FORCE, NON-COOPERATIVE COUNTRIES AND TERRITORIES TIMELINE (Last updated Oct. 13, 2006).

FINANCIAL ACTION TASK FORCE, REPORT ON TERRORIST FINANCING (Feb. 29, 2008).

FINANCIAL ACTION TASK FORCE, TRADE BASED MONEY LAUNDERING (June 23, 2006).

FINANCIAL ACTION TASK FORCE ON MONEY LAUNDERING, COMBATING THE ABUSE OF NON-PROFIT ORGANISATIONS – INTERNATIONAL BEST PRACTICES (Oct. 11, 2002), *available at* http://www.oecd.org/dataoecd/39/19/34033761.pdf

FINANCIAL ACTION TASK FORCE ON MONEY LAUNDERING, FREEZING OF TERRORIST ASSETS: INTERNATIONAL BEST PRACTICES (2003).

FINANCIAL ACTION TASK FORCE ON MONEY LAUNDERING, THE FORTY RECOMMENDATIONS (June 20, 2003), *available at* http://www.fatf-gafi.org/dataoecd/7/40/34849567.pdf.

INTERNATIONAL CONVENTION FOR THE SUPPRESSION OF THE FINANCING OF TERRORISM, 9 G.A. RES. 109, U.N. GAOR 54TH SESS., 76TH MTG., U.N. DOC A/RES/54/109 (Dec. 9, 1999), *available at* http://untreaty.un.org/English/Terrorism/Conv12.pdf.

THE INVESTIGATIVE PROJECT ON TERRORISM, AL QAEDA IN IRAQ (Apr. 30, 2006), *available at* http://www.investigativeproject.org/profile/124.

KENNETH KATZMAN, AL QAEDA: PROFILE AND THREAT ASSESSMENT, CRS REPORT FOR CONGRESS (Aug. 17, 2005).

NATIONAL STRATEGY FOR COMBATING TERRORISM (2003), *available at* http://www.whitehouse.gov/news/releases/2003/02/counter_terrorism/counter_terrorism_strategy.pdf.

ALFRED B. PRADOS & CHRISTOPHER M. BLANCHARD, SAUDI ARABIA: TERRORIST FINANCING ISSUES, CONGRESSIONAL RESEARCH SERVICE REPORT FOR CONGRESS (Sept. 15, 2007).

PRESIDENT'S COMMISSION ON ORGANIZED CRIME, THE CASH CONNECTION: ORGANIZED CRIME, FINANCIAL INSTITUTIONS, AND MONEY LAUNDERING (1984).

JOHN ROTH, ET AL., NATIONAL COMMISSION ON TERRORIST ATTACKS UPON THE UNITED STATES, MONOGRAPH ON TERRORIST FINANCING: STAFF REPORT TO THE COMMISSION (Wash., D.C.: Gov't Printing Office 2004), *available at* http://govinfor.library.unt.edu/911/staff_statements/911_TerrFin_Monograph.pdf.

SYRACUSE UNIVERSITY, CRIMINAL TERRORISM ENFORCEMENT IN THE UNITED STATES DURING THE FIVE YEARS SINCE THE 9/11/01 ATTACKS, TRAC REPORTS (2006).

SYRACUSE UNIVERSITY, TERRORISM-INTERNATIONAL PROSECUTIONS FOR 2007, TRAC REPORTS (2007).

SYRACUSE UNIVERSITY, TERRORISM-RELATED FINANCING PROSECUTIONS FOR 2007, TRAC REPORTS (2007).

THE TERRORIST THREAT TO THE U.S. HOMELAND, NATIONAL INTELLIGENCE ESTIMATE (July 2007), *available at* http://www.dni.gov/press_releases/20070717_release.pdf.

U.N. OFFICE ON DRUGS AND CRIME, AFGHANISTAN OPIUM SURVEY 2007 (Oct. 2007), *available at* http://www.unodc.org/pdf/research/Afghanistan_Opium_Survey_2007.pdf.

U.N. SECURITY COUNCIL, THE AL-QAIDA AND TALIBAN SANCTIONS COMMITTEE, THE CONSOLIDATED LIST OF THE UNITED NATIONS SECURITY COUNCIL'S AL-QAIDA AND TALIBAN SANCTIONS COMMITTEE (Last updated Oct. 27, 2008), *available at* http://www.un.org/sc/committees/1267/consolist.shtml.

U.N. SECURITY COUNCIL, THE AL-QAIDA AND TALIBAN SANCTIONS COMMITTEE, FACT SHEET ON DE-LISTING (Updated 2008), *available at* http://www.un.org/sc/committees/1267/fact_sheet_delisting.shtml.

U.N. SECURITY COUNCIL, THE AL-QAIDA AND TALIBAN SANCTIONS COMMITTEE, FACT SHEET ON LISTING (Updated 2008), *available at* http://www.un.org/sc/committees/1267/fact_sheet_listing.shtml.

U.N. SECURITY COUNCIL, THE AL-QAIDA AND TALIBAN SANCTIONS COMMITTEE, GUIDELINES OF THE COMMITTEE FOR THE CONDUCT OF ITS WORK (Feb. 12, 2007), *available at* http://www.un.org/sc/committees/1267/pdf/1267_guidelines.pdf.

U.N. SECURITY COUNCIL, ANALYTICAL SUPPORT AND SANCTIONS MONITORING TEAM, THIRD REPORT OF THE ANALYTICAL SUPPORT AND SANCTIONS MONITORING TEAM, U.N. DOC. S/2005/572 (Sept. 9, 2005).

U.N. SECURITY COUNCIL, ANALYTICAL SUPPORT AND SANCTIONS MONITORING TEAM, FOURTH REPORT OF THE ANALYTICAL SUPPORT AND SANCTIONS MONITORING TEAM, U.N. DOC. S/2006/154 (Mar. 10, 2006).

U.N. SECURITY COUNCIL, ANALYTICAL SUPPORT AND SANCTIONS MONITORING TEAM, FIFTH REPORT OF THE ANALYTICAL SUPPORT AND

SANCTIONS MONITORING TEAM, U.N. DOC. S/2006/750 (Sept. 20, 2006), *available at* http://www.un.org/sc/committees/1267/1267mg.htm.

U.N. SECURITY COUNCIL, ANALYTICAL SUPPORT AND SANCTIONS MONITORING TEAM, SIXTH REPORT OF THE ANALYTICAL SUPPORT AND SANCTIONS MONITORING TEAM, U.N. DOC. S/2007/132 (March 8, 2007), *available at* http://www.un.org/sc/committees/1267/monitoring team.shtml.

U.N. SECURITY COUNCIL, ANALYTICAL SUPPORT AND SANCTIONS MONITORING TEAM, SEVENTH REPORT OF THE ANALYTICAL SUPPORT AND SANCTIONS MONITORING TEAM, U.N. DOC. S/2007/677 (Nov. 29, 2007), *available at* http://www.un.org/sc/committees/1267/monitor ingteam.shtml.

U.N. SECURITY COUNCIL, ANALYTICAL SUPPORT AND SANCTIONS MONITORING TEAM, EIGHTH REPORT OF THE ANALYTICAL SUPPORT AND SANCTIONS MONITORING TEAM, U.N. DOC. S/2008/324 (May 13, 2008), *available at* http://www.un.org/sc/committees/1267/monitoringteam.shtml.

U.N. SECURITY COUNCIL, COUNTER-TERRORISM COMMITTEE, REPORT OF THE COUNTER-TERRORISM COMMITTEE TO THE SECURITY COUNCIL, U.N. DOC. S/2007/675 (Nov. 20, 2007).

U.N. SECURITY COUNCIL, ORGANIZATIONAL PLAN FOR THE COUNTER-TERRORISM COMMITTEE EXECUTIVE DIRECTORATE, U.N. DOC. S/2004/642 (Aug. 12, 2004), *available at* http://www.un.org/sc/ctc/cted.shtml.

U.N. SECURITY COUNCIL, REPORT OF THE SECURITY COUNCIL WORKING GROUP ESTABLISHED PURSUANT TO RESOLUTION 1566, U.N. DOC. S/2005/789 (2004), *available at* http://seagrass.goatchurch.org.uk/~undemocracy/undata/pdf/S-2005-789.pdf.

U.S. DEP'T OF HOMELAND SECURITY, OFFICE OF INSPECTOR GENERAL, COORDINATION BETWEEN FBI AND ICE ON INVESTIGATIONS OF TERRORIST FINANCING (July 2007).

U.S. DEP'T OF JUSTICE, COUNTERTERRORISM WHITE PAPER (2006).

U.S. DEP'T OF JUSTICE, REPORT FOR THE FIELD: THE USA PATRIOT ACT AT WORK (July 2004).

U.S. DEP'T OF STATE, FACT SHEET: EXECUTIVE ORDER 13224 (Dec. 20, 2002), *available at* http://www.state.gov.s/ct/rls/fs/2002/16181.htm.

U.S. DEP'T OF STATE, OFFICE OF THE COORDINATOR FOR COUNTERTERRORISM, 2005 COUNTRY REPORTS ON TERRORISM (Apr. 28, 2006), *available at* http://www.state.gov/s/ct/rls/crt/2005/64337.htm.

U.S. DEP'T OF STATE, OFFICE OF THE COORDINATOR FOR COUNTERTERRORISM, 2006 COUNTRY REPORTS ON TERRORISM (Apr. 30, 2007), *available at* http://www.state.gov/s/ct/rls/crt/2006/82738.htm.

U.S. DEP'T OF STATE, OFFICE OF THE COORDINATOR FOR COUNTERTERRORISM, FACT SHEET (Apr. 8, 2008).

U.S. DEP'T OF STATE, OFFICE OF THE COORDINATOR FOR COUNTERTERRORISM, FOREIGN TERRORIST ORGANIZATIONS (Apr. 8, 2008).

U.S. DEP'T OF STATE, OFFICE OF THE COORDINATOR FOR COUNTERTERRORISM, FOREIGN TERRORIST ORGANIZATIONS FACT SHEET (2005), *available at* http://www.state.gov/s/ct/rls/fs/37191.htm.

U.S. DEP'T OF STATE, PATTERNS OF GLOBAL TERRORISM (2003), *available at* http://www.state.gov.s.ct.rls.crt.2003/c12108.htm.

U.S. DEP'T OF STATE, STATE SPONSORS OF TERRORISM (2007), *available at* http://www.state.gov/s/ct/c14151.htm.

U.S. DEP'T OF TREASURY, ANTI-TERRORIST FINANCING GUIDELINES: VOLUNTARY BEST PRACTICES FOR U.S.-BASED CHARITIES (revised Dec. 2005), *available at* http://www.treas.gov/offices/enforcement/key-issues/protecting/charities-intro.shtml.

U.S. DEP'T OF TREASURY, CONTRIBUTIONS BY THE DEPARTMENT OF THE TREASURY TO THE FINANCIAL WAR ON TERRORISM: FACT SHEET (Sept. 2002), *available at* http://www.treasury.gov/press/releases/reports/2002910184556291211.pdf.

U.S. DEP'T OF TREASURY, FINANCIAL CRIMES ENFORCEMENT NETWORK, FIRST REVIEW OF THE SUSPICIOUS ACTIVITY REPORTING SYSTEM (SARS) (Apr. 1998).

U.S. DEP'T OF TREASURY, FINANCIAL CRIMES ENFORCEMENT NETWORK, FREQUENTLY ASKED QUESTIONS, CONDUCTING INDEPENDENT REVIEW OF MONEY SERVICES BUSINESS ANTI-MONEY LAUNDERING PROGRAMS (Sept. 22, 2006), *available at* http://www.fincen.gov/Guidance_MSB_Independent_Audits 9-21.pdf.

U.S. DEP'T OF TREASURY, FINANCIAL CRIMES ENFORCEMENT NETWORK, MONEY SERVICE BUSINESS REGISTRATION LIST (Last updated Oct. 11, 2008), *available at* http://www.msb.gov/pdf/msb_registration_list.pdf.

U.S. DEP'T OF TREASURY, FINANCIAL CRIMES ENFORCEMENT NETWORK, THE ROLE OF DOMESTIC SHELL COMPANIES IN FINANCIAL CRIME AND MONEY LAUNDERING (Nov. 2006), *available at* http://www.fincen.gov/LLCAssessment_FINAL.pdf.

U.S. DEP'T OF TREASURY, FINANCIAL CRIMES ENFORCEMENT NETWORK, THE SAR ACTIVITY REVIEW, ISSUE 8 (Apr. 2005).

U.S. DEP'T OF TREASURY, FINANCIAL CRIMES ENFORCEMENT NETWORK, THE SAR ACTIVITY REVIEW – BY THE NUMBERS, ISSUE 9 (Jan. 2008).

U.S. DEP'T OF TREASURY, HAWALA & ALTERNATIVE REMITTANCE SYSTEMS, TERRORISM AND FINANCIAL INTELLIGENCE (NOV. 30, 2006), *available at* http://www.treasury.gov/offices/enforcement/key-issues/hawala.

U.S. DEP'T OF TREASURY, LIST OF TERRORIST FINANCIERS (Last updated Oct. 30, 2008), *available at* http://www.treasury.gov/offices/enforcement/ofac/programs/terror/terror.pdf.

U.S. DEP'T OF TREASURY, NATIONAL MONEY LAUNDERING STRATEGY (2003), *available at* http://www.treasury.gov/offices/enforcement/publications/ml2003.pdf.

U.S. DEP'T OF TREASURY, OFFICE OF FOREIGN ASSETS CONTROL, TERRORISM: WHAT YOU NEED TO KNOW ABOUT U.S. SANCTIONS (Updated 2007), *available at* http://www.treasury.gov/offices/enforcement/ofac/programs/terror/terror.pdf.

U.S. DEP'T OF TREASURY, OFFICE OF TERRORISM AND FINANCIAL INTELLIGENCE, PROTECTING CHARITABLE ORGANIZATIONS: DESIGNATED CHARITIES AND POTENTIAL FUNDRAISING FRONT ORGANIZATIONS FOR FTOS (Updated 2008), *available at* http://www.treas.gov/offices/enforcement/key-issues/protecting/fto.shtml

U.S. DEP'T OF TREASURY, OFFICE OF TERRORIST FINANCING AND FINANCIAL CRIMES, U.S. MONEY LAUNDERING THREAT ASSESSMENT (Dec. 2005), *available at* http://www.treasury.gov/offices/enforcement/pdf/mlta.pdf.

U.S. DEP'T OF TREASURY, PROGRESS IN THE WAR ON TERRORIST FINANCING (Sept. 11, 2003), *available at* http://www.ustreas.gov/press/releases/reports/js 721.pdf.

U.S. DEP'T OF TREASURY, REPORT TO CONGRESS IN ACCORDANCE WITH SECTION 359 OF THE UNITING AND STRENGTHENING AMERICA BY PROVIDING APPROPRIATE TOOLS REQUIRED TO INTERCEPT AND OBSTRUCT TERRORISM ACT OF 2001 (Nov. 2002), *available at* http://www.fincen.gov/hawalarptfinal11222002.pdf.

U.S. DEP'T OF TREASURY, TERRORIST ASSETS REPORT, CALENDAR YEAR 2001, ANNUAL REPORT TO THE CONGRESS ON ASSETS IN THE UNITED STATES OF TERRORIST COUNTRIES AND INTERNATIONAL TERRORISM PROGRAM DESIGNEES (2001).

U.S. DEP'T OF TREASURY, TERRORIST ASSETS REPORT, CALENDAR YEAR 2002, ANNUAL REPORT TO THE CONGRESS ON ASSETS IN THE UNITED STATES OF TERRORIST COUNTRIES AND INTERNATIONAL TERRORISM PROGRAM DESIGNEES (2002).

U.S. DEP'T OF TREASURY, TERRORIST ASSETS REPORT, CALENDAR YEAR 2003, ANNUAL REPORT TO THE CONGRESS ON ASSETS IN THE UNITED STATES OF TERRORIST COUNTRIES AND INTERNATIONAL TERRORISM PROGRAM DESIGNEES (2003).

U.S. DEP'T OF TREASURY, TERRORIST ASSETS REPORT, CALENDAR YEAR 2004, THIRTEENTH ANNUAL REPORT TO THE CONGRESS ON ASSETS IN THE UNITED STATES OF TERRORIST COUNTRIES AND INTERNATIONAL TERRORISM PROGRAM DESIGNEES (2004).

U.S. Dep't of Treasury, Terrorist Assets Report, Calendar year 2005, Fourteenth Annual Report to the Congress on Assets in the United States of Terrorist Countries and International Terrorism Program Designees (2005).

U.S. Gov't Accountability Office, Better Strategic Planning Needed to Coordinate U.S. Efforts to Deliver Counter-Terrorism Financing Training and Technical Assistance Abroad (Oct. 2005), available at http://www.gao.gov/new.items/d0619.pdf.

U.S. Government Accountability Office, Treasury's Roles and Responsibilities Relating to Selected Provisions of the USA PATRIOT Act, Report to the Chairman, House Judiciary Committee (May 2006).

Watson Institute for International Studies, Strengthening Targeted Sanctions Through Fair and Clear Procedures (2006).

CONGRESSIONAL TESTIMONY

Zahid H. Bukhari, *Starving Terrorists of Money: The Role of Middle Eastern Financial Institutions*, Hearing before the Subcommittee on Oversight and Investigations and the Subcommittee on International Terrorism and Nonproliferation of the House Committee on Financial Services (109th Cong. 31).

Steven Emerson, *Fund-Raising Methods and Procedures for International Terrorist Organizations*, Testimony before the House Financial Services Subcommittee on Oversight and Investigations (Feb. 12, 2002), *available at* http://www.investigativeproject.org/documents/testimony/14.pdf.

Steven Emerson, *Money Laundering and Terror Financing Issues in the Middle East*, Testimony before the U.S. Senate Committee on Banking, Housing, and Urban Affairs (July 13, 2005), *available at* http://www.investigativeproject.org/documents/testimony/19.pdf.

Steven Emerson, *Saudi Arabia: Friend or Foe in the War on Terror*, Testimony before the Senate Committee on the Judiciary (Nov. 8, 2005), *available at* http://judiciary.senate.gov/testimony.cfm?id=1669&wit_id=4791.

Daniel Glaser, Deputy Assistant Secretary for Terrorist Financing and Financial Crimes & Adam J. Szubin, Director of the Office of Foreign Assets Control, U.S. Dep't of Treasury, *Isolating Proliferators and Sponsors of Terror: The Use of Sanctions and the International Financial System to Change Regime Behavior*, Joint Testimony before the House Foreign Affairs Subcommittee on Terrorism, Nonproliferation and Trade and the Financial Services Subcommittee on Domestic and International Monetary Policy, Trade, and Technology (Apr. 18, 2007).

Daniel Glaser, Deputy Assistant Secretary for Terrorist Financing and Financial Crimes, *The Iranian Threat*, Testimony before the House Foreign Affairs Subcommittee on the Middle East and South Asia and the Subcommittee on Terrorism, Nonproliferation and Trade (Apr. 17, 2008).

Jimmy Gurulé, *Contributions by the Department of the Treasury to the Financial War on Terrorism*, Testimony before the U.S. Senate Finance Committee (Oct. 9. 2002), *available at* http://www.treasury.gov/press/releases/po3518.htm.

Bruce Hoffman, *Challenges for the U.S. Special Operations Command Posed by the Global Terrorist Threat: Al Qaeda on the Run or on the March?*, Written Testimony before the House Armed Services Subcommittee on Terrorism, Unconventional Threats & Capabilities (Feb. 14, 2007), *available at* http://www.investigativeproject.org/documents/testimony/267.pdf.

Alan J. Kreczko, *Antiterrorism Act of 1990: Hearing on S. 2456*, Testimony before the Senate Subcommittee on Courts and Admin. Practice of the Senate Comm. on the Judiciary, 101st Cong. 12 (1990).

Stuart A. Levey, Under Secretary, Office of Terrorism and Financial Intelligence, U.S. Dep't of Treasury, *Combating Terrorist Financing in the Middle East*, Testimony before the House Financial Services Subcommittee on Oversight and Investigations and House International Relations Subcommittee on International Terrorism and Non-proliferation (May 4, 2005).

Stuart A. Levey, Under Secretary, Office of Terrorism and Financial Intelligence, U.S. Dep't of Treasury, *Terrorist Financing and Money Laundering in the Middle East*, Testimony before the Senate Committee on Banking, Housing, and Urban Affairs (July 13, 2005), *available at* http://www.treas.gov/press/releases/js 2629.htm.

Stuart A. Levey, Under Secretary, Office of Terrorism and Financial Intelligence, U.S. Dep't of Treasury, *Anti-Terrorism Financing: Progress Made and the Challenges Ahead*, Testimony before the Senate Financing Committee (Apr. 1, 2008).

Matthew Levitt, *Hezbollah: Financing Terror Through Criminal Enterprise*, Testimony before the U.S. Senate Committee on Homeland Security and Governmental Affairs (May 25, 2005).

J. Michael McConnell, Director of National Intelligence, *Annual Threat Assessment of the Director of National Intelligence* (*DNI National Threat Assessment*), Senate Select Committee on Intelligence (Feb. 5, 2008).

Daniel Meron, Principal Deputy Assistant Attorney General, Civil Division, & Barry Sabin, Chief, Counterterrorism Section, Criminal Division, U.S. Dep't of Justice, *Concerning the Federal Material Support Statutes*, Testimony before the Senate Judiciary Subcommittee on Terrorism, Technology, and Homeland Security (Apr. 20, 2005), *available at* http://www.lifeandliberty.gov/subs/testimony/042005-civ-meroncrm-sabin.pdf.

George Tenet, Director of the CIA, *Threats to National Security*, Testimony before the Senate Armed Services Comm. (Feb. 12, 2003).

OTHER SOURCES

18 U.S.C. §§2339A, B & C (West 2008).

Blocking Property and Prohibiting Transactions with Persons Who Commit, Threaten to Commit, or Support Terrorism, Exec. Order No. 13,224, 3 C.F.R. 786-90 (2001).

Board of Governors of the Federal Reserve System, Bank Secrecy Act Anti-Money Laundering Examination Manual (1997), *available at* http://www.federalreserve.gov/boarddocs/supmanual/bsa/7-00bsaman.pdf.

Convention Against Torture and Other Cruel, Inhuman, or Degrading Treatment or Punishment, 1465 U.N.T.S. 85 (Dec. 10, 1984).

Egmont Group, Statement of Purpose of the Egmont Group of Financial Intelligence Units, *available at* http://www.egmontgroup.org.

Intelligence Reform and Terrorism Prevention Act of 2004, Pub L. No. 108-458, §6603©-(f), 118 Stat. 3638, 3762 (2004).

International Convention Against the Taking of Hostages, 1316 U.N.T.S. 205 (Dec. 17, 1979).

International Convention for the Suppression of the Financing of Terrorism, S. Treaty Doc. No. 106-49, 2178 U.N.T.S. 229 (Dec. 9, 1999).

International Convention for the Suppression of Terrorist Bombings, G.A. Res. 52/164, 1, U.N. Doc A/RES/52/164 (Jan. 12, 1998).

The International Money Laundering Abatement and Anti-Terrorism Financing Act of 2001, Pub L. No. 107-56, tit. III, Oct. 26, 2001, 115 Stat. 296.

Montreal Convention for the Suppression of Unlawful Acts Against the Safety of Civil Aviation, 974 U.N.T.S. 177, 24 U.S.T. 564, T.I.A.S. No. 7570 (Sept. 23, 1971).

Prohibiting Transactions with Terrorists Who Threaten to Disrupt the Middle East Peace Process, Exec. Order No. 12,947, 60 Fed. Reg. 5079, *codified at* 3 C.F.R. 319-20 (1995).

Suppression of the Financing of Terrorism Convention Implementation Act of 2002, Pub. L. No. 107-197, tit. II, 116 Stat. 724 (2002) (codified at 18 U.S.C.A. §2339C (West 2008)).

Uniting and Strengthening America by Providing Appropriate Tools Required to Intercept and Obstruct Terrorism (USA PATRIOT) Act of 2001, Pub. L. No. 107-56, 115 Stat. 272 (codified in scattered sections of the U.S.C.).

Violent Crime Control and Law Enforcement Act of 1994, Pub. L. No. 103-322, §120005(a), 108 Stat. 1796, 2022-3 (1994) (codified at 18 U.S.C. §2339A).

Index